Foundation Game Design with HTML5 and JavaScript

Rex van der Spuy

friendsof

DESIGNER TO DESIGNER™

an Apress® company

FOUNDATION GAME DESIGN WITH HTML5 AND JAVASCRIPT

ISBN 978-1-4302-4716-6

ISBN 978-1-4302-4717-3 (eBook)

Trademarked names, logos, and images may appear in this book. Rather than use a trademark symbol with every occurrence of a trademarked name, logos, or image, we use the names, logos, or images only in an editorial fashion and to the benefit of the trademark owner, with no intention of infringement of the trademark.

The use in this publication of trade names, service marks, and similar terms, even if they are not identified as such, is not to be taken as an expression of opinion as to whether or not they are subject to proprietary rights.

Distributed to the book trade worldwide by Springer Science+Business Media LLC., 233 Spring Street, 6th Floor, New York, NY 10013. Phone 1-800-SPRINGER, fax (201) 348-4505, e-mail orders-ny@springer-sbm.com, or visit www.springeronline.com.

For information on translations, please e-mail rights@apress.com or visit www.apress.com.

Apress and friends of ED books may be purchased in bulk for academic, corporate, or promotional use. eBook versions and licenses are also available for most titles. For more information, reference our Special Bulk Sales–eBook Licensing web page at www.apress.com/bulk-sales.

The information in this book is distributed on an "as is" basis, without warranty. Although every precaution has been taken in the preparation of this work, neither the author(s) nor Apress shall have any liability to any person or entity with respect to any loss or damage caused or alleged to be caused directly or indirectly by the information contained in this work.

The source code for this book is freely available to readers at http://www.apress.com/9781430247166 in the Downloads section.

Credits

President and Publisher: Paul Manning	**Copy Editor:** Christine Dahlin
Lead Editor: Ben Renow-Clarke	**Compositor:** SPi Global
Technical Reviewers: Gaëtan Renaudeau	**Indexer:** SPi Global
Editorial Board: Steve Anglin, Mark Beckner, Ewan Buckingham, Gary Cornell, Louise Corrigan, Jonathan Gennick, Jonathan Hassell, Michelle Lowman, Matthew Moodie, Jeff Olson, Jeffrey Pepper, Frank Pohlmann, Douglas Pundick, Ben Renow-Clarke, Dominic Shakeshaft, Gwenan Spearing Matt Wade, Tom Welsh	**Artist:** SPi Global **Cover Image Artist:** Corné van Dooren **Cover Designer:** Anna Ishchenko
Coordinating Editor: Christine Ricketts	

For Soren and Mats, so you can learn to how to make video games.

Contents at a Glance

Contents

Contents

About the Author

Rex van der Spuy is a video-game designer and writer. He's written *Foundation Game Design with Flash*, *Advanced Game Design with Flash*, and *Foundation Game Design with AS3.0*. Rex has designed games and done interactive interface programming with Agency Interactive (Dallas), Scottish Power (Edinburgh), DC Interact (London), Draught Associates (London), and the Bank of Montreal (Canada). He also builds game engines and interactive interfaces for museum installations for PixelProject (Cape Town). In addition, he created and taught advanced courses in game design for the Canadian School of India (Bangalore, India). When not writing about, making, or playing games, he amuses himself by building "experimental, autonomous, self-aware, multicellular parallel universes" out of "shoe boxes, scotch tape, spare milk bottle caps, and bits of string." However, he claims, this is "a lot less entertaining than you might think."

About the Technical Reviewer

Gaëtan Renaudeau (aka @greweb) is a web enthusiast studying toward a master's degree in computer science in France. Since 2009, he has worked as a web architect for a web startup company called Zenexity, based in Paris, where he builds web applications, web services, and mobile applications. He enjoys being involved both in front-end (JavaScript, HTML5, CSS3) and server-side (Play framework mainly) development.

For fun you'll find him trying to push the limits of the Web forward, making web experiments, libraries, applications, and games, such as "Drone Tank Arena," his recent WebGL (3D) game made in seven days for the 7DFPS contest. His work is frequently published on `http://greweb.fr/`.

Gaëtan's current hobbies are practicing archery and learning Chinese.

About the Cover Image Artist

Corné van Dooren designed the front cover image for this book. After taking a brief hiatus from friends of ED to create a new design for the Foundation series, he worked at combining technological and organic forms, the results of which now appear on this and other book covers.

Corné spent his childhood drawing on everything at hand and then began exploring the infinite world of multimedia—and his journey of discovery hasn't stopped since. His mantra has always been "the only limit to multimedia is the imagination"—a saying that keeps him constantly moving forward.

Corné works for many international clients, writes features for multimedia magazines, reviews and tests software, authors multimedia studies, and works on many other friends of ED books. You can see more of his work at and contact him through his website at www.cornevandooren.com.

Acknowledgments

A huge thank you to the incredibly hard-working team at Apress and friends of ED—you guys rock!

A particular note of thanks to the technical reviewer, Gaëtan Renaudeau, whose deep insights and excellent suggestions made this an undoubtedly richer and better book.

Introduction

In 1980, when I was 10 years old, my parents sat me down and formally announced that they were going to buy me a computer for Christmas. Somewhere, somehow, they had heard that a computer could, they told me, "help you with your homework."

I was astonished.

"Of course it will help me with my homework. Computers are really good for math!" I exclaimed. "And science too!"

I was going to let them believe whatever they wanted to believe. As long as they got me that computer, fast, before whatever spell they were under wore off. Because the only thing I wanted a computer for was to play video games, but no way was I going to let that out of the bag.

All I lived for was video games. My friends and I had spent that whole summer biking around town, looking for lost change on the sidewalk that we could use to play arcade games with. The closest arcade machine that didn't have "bad kids" hanging around it was Ms. Pac Man, which was a 20-minute bike ride away in the corner of a dingy old diner. But it was worth it, because we had memorized the solutions to all the level maps in our Ms. Pac Man strategy book and could play for an amazingly long time, to the wonder of the littler kids who gathered around to watch. When we couldn't find any quarters we made our own arcade games out of boxes, crayons, thumbtacks, and plastic coat buttons. And at the end of that summer, we made the most blissful discovery: a malfunctioning Space Invaders machine that could be played using pennies if you flicked them in at just the right angle. I came back from the bank with a roll of 100 pennies, and I spent the last 2 weeks of that August in an ecstatic, bleary-eyed, space-invading dreamworld.

So that Christmas morning, in a giddy fever, I ripped open the red-and-white candy-cane wrapping paper. It was everything I had hoped for: a state-of-the-art Commodore Vic-20. It had a whopping 5K of memory, the latest cassette-tape storage drive, and a display of 16 colors. The computer at school could just display two colors: green and black. I was in heaven! I fumbled with the instructions and, with trembling hands, carefully plugged my gleaming new Vic-20 into the family TV set and switched it on.

Nothing happened. The TV was completely blank, except for a small, calmly blinking blue square at the top left corner of the screen.

"Where are the games?" I thought, "Where's Ms. Pac Man? Where are the aliens?"

I jiggled the power cable and fiddled with the wires at the back of the TV. But, no, there was just that steady blue, blinking square, silently mocking me. This blue square, I discovered, was called the "cursor." I hated it and felt sick.

The games, it turned out, came on audio cassettes that you could load into the computer by hooking up the cassette player and pressing the play button. But you had to buy them. They cost $20 each. The nearest shop that sold them was a 45-minute drive, in a car, over a mountain. It was impossible—there was just no way. And, anyway, I was supposed to be using this thing to "do my homework."

But in the computer's box I found a book about BASIC programming. I had no idea what that meant and couldn't understand anything in that book at all. It was full of all kinds of bits of scrambled English words and numbers written in big capital letters that were supposed to make the computer do things. "Programming code," it was called. Maybe this was just stuff for grown-ups? "No," I thought, "computers are for children, and grown-ups are scared of them." And so I persisted. At the very back of the book, I found a section called "Programs to try." My eye fell across the words "Killer Comet." It was a video game! Beneath it was a long list of inscrutable codes. But I finally figured out that if I could type these codes into my Vic-20, I could play a game.

That was it!

If "programming" means "you can play video games for free," I was going to figure out programming. I spent the next two days in a frenzy, reading through the book and typing in all those codes, trying to get Killer Comet to work. I had barely any idea what I was doing and my computer kept displaying "Syntax Error! Syntax Error! Syntax Error!" over and over again whenever I tried to run the program. I was pulling my hair out and wanted to scream! But then, late on the second day, something miraculous happened—it worked:

A small white square moved from the top of the screen to the bottom of the screen.

If you pressed the right number of keys in the right way, the square disappeared.

That was all.

It was the most beautiful thing I'd ever seen in my life.

And that's when I discovered that making video games is way, way, way more fun than playing them. And so, here, Dear Reader, you have that book that I truly believe should come in the box with every new computer. Hope you have as much fun reading it as I did writing it!

Chapter 1

Learning HTML and CSS

What's more fun than playing video games? Making them! And this book will show you how. You don't need to know anything about programming or any other complicated technical computer-y things. You don't even need to know much math. This book will show you everything you need to make great games that you can play on the Web, on desktop computers, or as apps on mobile phones and tablets.

There are lots and lots of ways to make video games. But you don't need to know all of them—you only need to know the best way. By "best," I mean the easiest and most fun way, and that's the way that you're going to learn from this book. It's also the way that will give your games the widest audience, give you the most solid set of game-design skills, and give you the best chance of making a bit of money from it too.

To make games, you have to learn a **computer-programming language**, which you can use to communicate with the computer to tell it what to do. A computer-programming language can look a lot like English, and such languages are easy to learn. People might argue with you that technically HTML and CSS are markup languages, not programming languages, but I'm going to call them all programming languages here and be done with it.

This book is about making games using a technology suite called HTML5. HTML5 is based on three separate computer-programming languages that work together:

- **HTML** (HyperText Markup Language): A programming language that describes how games and applications are structured. Games and most websites are built using HTML.

- **CSS** (Cascading Style Sheets): A programming language that describes how HTML code should be visually presented.

- **JavaScript**: A programming language that lets you control how your games behave.

You're going to learn all three languages in this book. In this chapter you'll learn about HTML and CSS. They're extremely easy to use, and what we cover in this chapter will be enough to get you started making games. You can also use the skills you learn in this chapter to use HTML and CSS to start building websites if that is something you'd like to do. To make games, you'll need to learn JavaScript, and that's what much of the rest of the book is all about.

These programming languages let you access and control many specialized technologies that are all part of the HTML5 standard. The most important of these for games is **canvas**. Canvas is a display technology that's great for animation and action games. You'll learn all about how to use canvas to make games starting with Chapster 6.

> Note: If you already know HTML and CSS, you can jump ahead to Chapter 2 to learn JavaScript. If you already know JavaScript and just want to start making games, jump ahead to Chapter 3. If you already know JavaScript and how to program in general, but you just want to start making games with canvas, Chapters 6, 7, and 8 are all yours!

What you need

Surprisingly, video-game design can be a relatively low-tech affair. Here's the basic equipment you'll need to make use of this book.

A computer

You need a reasonably up-to-date computer, either running Windows or the latest version of Mac OS X, or even Linux. You should have basic computer literacy skills, which includes understanding how to make new files and how to organize them in folders.

Programming software

Luckily, this costs nothing and you probably already have all the programming software you need already installed on your computer. Here's what you'll need:

- **A text editor**: If you're using Windows, Notepad works well. If you're using Mac OS X, you may use TextEdit.

- **Safari, Chrome, Firefox,** or **Opera**: These web browsers include some great features for building and testing HTML5 games. This book will explain how to use them to help you make games. Safari, Chrome, Firefox, and Opera are available for Windows and Mac. Chrome is available for Linux. If you're using a Mac, Safari is already installed on your computer. If you're using Windows, you can download Chrome or Safari here: www.google.com/chrome, and www.apple.com/safari/download

This book describes how to use these software programs and tools to program games—you won't need anything else.

However, there is some more specialized, but optional, software that you might want to try if you're doing a lot of programming and want to make things a little easier for yourself.

- **Komodo Edit** or **jEdit**: These are free text editors for Windows, Mac OS X, and Linux. They're specialized for writing programming code. They number each line of code and highlight important programming words in different colors (*syntax highlighting*). Both these features make writing code easier because you can find and change sections of your code more easily. Once you start to get the hang of programming, and you want to try a slightly more sophisticated text editor than Notepad or TextEdit, Komodo Edit or jEdit is a good next step.

- **Aptana Studio**: This is a free IDE (integrated development environment) based on Eclipse, for Windows and Mac OS X. It includes syntax highlighting and numbered lines of code, and you can install a plug-in that helps you debug JavaScript.

- **Dreamweaver**: This was, for a long time, the most widely used software for building web pages. It's not free and is perhaps overly complex for the simpler needs of a game designer, but it's specialized for writing HTML, CSS, and JavaScript code. Dreamweaver is available for Windows and Mac from Adobe: www.adobe.com.

- If you're using Mac OS X, you have two further options. **Coda** is an efficient code editor with a built-in JavaScript debugger and a live preview window of what your game looks like as you're programming it. **Textmate** is another excellent OS X-only code editor that also provides a live preview window of your game, as well as integrated JavaScript debugging. Neither Coda nor Textmate is free, but if you do a lot of programming they're probably worth the cost for the time they'll save you. Both Coda and Textmate are available through the Mac OS X app store.

HTML5 is a very new and quickly changing technology, and it's likely that by the time you are reading this there will be many more, and possibly better, tools for creating HTML5 games than those I've listed above. Keep a lookout for new software, and try everything!

If you already have some experience programming, you probably enjoy just using one of these editors. But if you're just starting, they'll only confuse you. Remember, all you'll ever really need is a simple text editor and a good web browser. Keep it simple and you can't go wrong.

> Note: If you decide to use TextEdit with the latest version of Mac OS X, you'll need to set it up so that it lets you write in **plain text**, which is important for programming. Here's how:
>
> Select **Preferences** from TextEdit's main menu.
>
> Select **Plain Text** in the **Format** section.
>
> In the **Open and Save** section, uncheck "add 'txt' extension to plain text files".
>
> Select **"ignore rich text commands in HTML files."**

Graphic design software (optional)

This book is just about programming games. I won't show you how to make graphics or illustrations for your games, so if this is something you're interested in, you'll need to learn how. In fact, if you don't have any experience creating computer graphics, you might want to learn a little bit about it before starting with this book.

The two most widely used applications for making game graphics are Photoshop and Illustrator (both available from Adobe). Other options are GIMP and Inkscape, both of which are free. Here's what you should learn about computer graphic design to make the best use of this book:

■ Making PNG images with alpha transparency

■ Changing the sizes of images and knowing how to crop them

■ Mastering basic illustration skills, such as how to draw characters and game objects

You'll find many online tutorials and books about how to do these tasks using any of the software already mentioned.

What kinds of games can I make?

This book is mostly about how to make two-dimensional action, adventure, and arcade games; it also touches on puzzle, logic, and strategy games. HTML5 is a fantastic medium for creating these types of games. Each chapter guides you through every step of the design process, but the projects are very open-ended. I encourage you to come up with your own original ways of using the techniques in your own games. This book starts with all the basics of computer programming, and we will gradually build on those techniques until you're making very sophisticated games from scratch. You're going to learn the simplest possible way of making games so that you can easily understand how they work and can then develop them into more complex games on your own.

The games you'll make you'll be able to upload for anyone to play on the Web. Or you can package them for mobile phones and tablet computers, and then sell them through app stores. Everything you'll need to know to get started on a professional career as a game designer, from start to finish, is right here in this book.

How hard is it?

It's about as easy to learn to make games as it is to learn basic conversation in a foreign language or to understand how to read and write music. So if you've done one of those tasks before, you'll know that it's not hard at all. You just have to take things slowly, step by step and methodically. Practice the skills you learn as much as you can, and don't move on to a new topic until you thoroughly understand the current one. You won't get any benefit if you rush through this book. You might spend a few days, a few weeks, or even a few months on any chapter. Take as much time as you need, because this book isn't going anywhere! But if you make the effort, you'll be a great game designer when you're finished.

Learning HTML

There are three related programming languages you need to know to make games: HTML, CSS, and JavaScript. We'll start with the easiest: HTML.

HTML is a kind of computer-programming language known as a markup language. Markup languages can describe information. This is different from JavaScript, which is a logical programming language. Logical programming languages are used to analyze and make decisions about information. HTML is used for making websites, and it is the foundation for making games. It's currently in version number 5, which is why it's known as HTML5.

Tags

HTML is used to describe information. It uses **tags** to tell computers the kind of information a document contains. A tag is just a word surrounded by left- and right-pointing arrow characters (sometimes called carets). Here's an example of a tag:

```
<thisIsATag>
```

Here's a tag that identifies the heading of a web page.

```
<h1>The main heading</h1>
```

`<h1>` means "Heading 1." Tags usually come in pairs of an opening tag and a closing tag. The opening tag looks like this:

```
<h1>
```

The closing tag adds a forward slash, /, to show that the tag is now finished describing the information:

```
</h1>
```

In this example anything that's between the opening and closing tags will be identified as a heading, like this:

```
<h1>Anything between the opening and closing tags is part of the heading</h1>
```

It's a really simple system, and you can use it to identify any kind of information in any way you like.

Note: HTML also lets you use stand-alone tags that don't need to be closed, like this:

```
<br>
```

This tag stands for "break," and it creates a line space in the text. It isn't used to describe any containing information.

If you've used earlier versions of HTML, you were probably required to write stand-alone tags with a forward slash at the end of the tag name, to indicate that the tag is self-closing, like this:

```
<br />
```

You don't have to do this in HTML5.

Tags and the information they contain are called **elements**. Remember this! When I mention HTML elements in this book, I'm talking about the tag and whatever is inside it.

Structuring HTML documents

To make a game or website with HTML tags, you have to structure the tags as a document. HTML5 is extremely flexible and lenient about how to structure HTML documents. However, most games, applications, and websites that are made with HTML follow some standard conventions about how documents are structured and how to use the tags they're built with. The reason for this is so that computers reading those documents can easily interpret the information they contain and display it correctly on any screen. In this section I'm going to show you how to build a very basic website with the most commonly used HTML tags.

Here's the classic structure for building a website with HTML:

```
<!doctype html>
<html>
  <head>
    <title>The title of the web page</title>
  </head>
  <body>
    <p>Anything you want to appear on the screen goes inside the body section.</p>
  </body>
</html>
```

You can see that everything is surrounded by a pair of <html></html> tags. Inside those tags are another pair called <head></head> followed by another pair called <body></body>.

In between the <head> tags you provide any information that you want to tell computers reading your document what they need to know to display the information correctly. None of the information in the <head> section is actually visible in the browser window. In this example the <head> section contains an element called <title>.

```
<head>
```

`<title>The title of the web page</title>`

```
</head>
```

The <title> element describes the page's title.

Anything that appears between the <body> tags is visible in the web browser—it's what you see as a web page. This is where most of the information of your HTML document will go. In this example, the <body> section contains a sentence that's inside a <p> tag.

```
<body>
```

`<p>Anything you want to appear as a paragraph of text on the screen goes inside the body section.</p>`

```
</body>
```

The <p> tag stands for **paragraph**. You use it to display sentences or paragraphs.

At the very top of the document is a special stand-alone tag that looks like this:

```
<!doctype html>
```

This needs to be the first tag in an HTML5 document. It just means, "Hey, computer, this is an HTML5 document!" That's all.

Building an HTML5 game or website generally means adding tags and information into the <head> and <body> sections. Lastly, you'll notice that the tags that are nested inside other tags are indented by two spaces from the left margin.

```
<html>
  <head>
    <title></title>
  </head>
  <body>
    <p></p>
  </body>
</html>
```

The indentation makes it easier to see that the inner tags are being contained inside an outer tag.

> Note: It's a common convention to indent HTML code that is inside enclosing tags. However, indenting it in this way can sometimes actually make big HTML documents with long lines of text more difficult to read. As you'll see in the next example, I've chosen not to indent most of the tags that are inside other tags, except for the short list items and the page title. You'll need to decide how you want to indent your HTML code, depending on what style you find more readable. It doesn't matter to the web browser how you indent it; it just makes it easier to read if needed.

Let's see how we can use this structure to make a very basic web page.

A basic web page

Let's use what you know about HTML to build a real web page. We'll look at a web page that's built using some of the most common HTML tags.

In the chapter's source file, you'll find a file called simpleWebpage.html. Double-click on it, and it will automatically open in a web browser. Figure 1-1 shows you what you'll see.

A simple web page

Everything you see on this page was made using basic HTML tags.

This is a sub-heading

You use HTML tags to *structure information*. This is a paragraph of text structured with a p tag.

Making lists

You can also use tags to **make a list** of things.

- First item
- Second item
- Third item

Adding links

Its easy to create hyperlinks to other web pages, or to create a link to generate an email. Here's how:

- Here's a good resource for learning HTML.
- If you want to say Hi, Send me an email.

Add a photo with an img tag, like this:

Figure 1-1. A very basic web page

This HTML web page is made with the most basic and useful tags. A web page is just a plain text file with an HTML file extension. Here's how to view the HTML code that creates this page:

1. Open your text editor, which is either Notepad (Windows) or TextEdit (Mac OS X)

2. Select File ➤ Open and open the simpleWebpage.html file.

3. It will load the HTML file, with all the tags visible. This is what you'll see:

```
<!doctype html>
<html lang="en">

<head>
<title>A web page</title>
</head>

<body>

<h1>A simple web page</h1>
<p>Everything you see on this page was made using basic HTML tags.</p>

<h2>This is a sub-heading</h2>
<p>You use HTML tags to <em>structure information</em>.
This is a paragraph of text structured with a p tag.</p>

<h2>Making lists</h2>
<p>You can also use tags to <strong>make a list</strong> of things.</p>
<ul>
   <li>First item</li>
   <li>Second item</li>
   <li>Third item</li>
</ul>

<!-- This is a comment in the document. It won't appear in the web browser-->

<h2>Adding links</h2>
<p>Its easy to create hyperlinks to other web pages, or to create a link
to generate an email. Here's how:</p>
<ul>
   <li><a href="http://www.w3schools.com" target="_blank">Here's a good resource</a>
for learning HTML</li>
   <li>If you want to say Hi, <a href="mailto:hello@kittykatattack.com?Subject=Hello%20
there!">Send me an email.</a></li>
</ul>

<p>Add a photo with an img tag, like this:</p>
<img src="ocean.jpg" alt="A photo of the ocean">

</body>
</html>
```

(Alternatively, you can also select View > View Source from your web browser to view this HTML code.)

Don't let this scare you! Notice that all the web-page text is surrounded by tags, and each of the tags changes the way that the text is displayed in the web browser. Figure 1-2 is a side-by-side illustration that shows the effect that the HTML text has on the text in the web browser. I've added some blank lines in the HTML document so that it's a little easier to see where each section begins and ends. However, the web browser ignores those blank lines and uses its own rules for spacing the text.

```
<!doctype html>
<html lang="en">

<head>
<title>A web page</title>
</head>

<body>

<h1>A simple web page</h1>
<p>Everything you see on this page was made using basic
HTML tags.</p>

<h2>This is a sub-heading</h2>
<p>You use HTML tags to <em>structure information</em>.
This is a paragraph of text structured with a p tag.</p>

<h2>Making lists</h2>
<p>You can also use tags to <strong>make a list</strong>
of things.</p>
<ul>
  <li>First item</li>
  <li>Second item</li>
  <li>Third item</li>
</ul>

<h2>Adding links</h2>
<p>Its easy to create hyperlinks to other web pages, or
to create a link to generate an email. Here's how:</p>
<ul>
  <li><a href="http://www.w3schools.com"
target="_blank">Here's a good resource</a> for learning
HTML.</li>
  <li>If you want to say Hi, <a
href="mailto:hello@kittykatattack.com?Subject=Hello
%20there!">Send me an email</a>.</li>
</ul>

<p>Add a photo with an img tag, like this:</p>
<img src="ocean.jpg" alt="A photo of the ocean">

</body>
</html>
```

A simple web page

Everything you see on this page was made using basic HTML tags.

This is a sub-heading

You use HTML tags to *structure information*. This is a paragraph of text structured with a p tag.

Making lists

You can also use tags to **make a list** of things.

- First item
- Second item
- Third item

Adding links

Its easy to create hyperlinks to other web pages, or to create a link to generate an email. Here's how:

- Here's a good resource for learning HTML.
- If you want to say Hi, Send me an email.

Add a photo with an img tag, like this:

Figure 1-2. The HTML code is interpreted by the web browser to create the page layout

Let's see how each of these new HTML tags changes the way the text is displayed.

Using an attribute to set the document language

HTML tags can include extra information called **attributes**. Attributes are added inside the tag, after the tag name. The following attribute in the <html> tag sets the web page's language to English.

```
<html lang="en">
```

The name of the attribute is lang (for language). "en" stands for English, and it's assigned to the attribute using an equal sign lang="en" means that the web-page content is written in English.

Although it's optional to do this, it's often a good idea to set the language for web pages because the browser may change the way it displays text based on which language it thinks you're using.

You'll see how attributes can be used to create links to other web pages and to load images in the examples ahead.

Adding a page title

The first bit of code adds a title to the web page using the `<title>` tag.

```
<head>
<title>A web page</title>
</head>
```

This title doesn't appear inside the actual web page. It appears in the title bar of the web browser. Look at your web browser carefully, and you'll see the words "A web page" at the very top of the browser window.

Cool, huh? You might also see it displayed in a browser tab. The `<title>` tag should always be used inside the `<head>` section.

Page headings

The first tag inside the `<body>` tag is `<h1>`. That stands for "heading 1," which is the main web-page heading.

```
<h1>A simple web page</h1>
```

The browser interprets this as the main heading of the page, and it displays the heading text in large, bold letters. Look a little further down the page and you'll notice that the other page headings are created with `<h2>` tags.

```
<h2>This is a sub-heading</h2>
<h2>Making lists</h2>
<h2>Adding links</h2>
```

The browser displays these in a smaller font size. You can use the `<h1>` to `<h6>` tags to create different levels of headings and subheadings in your web page.

Paragraph text

Most of the text on the page is surrounded by `<p>` tags, which show that the text is part of a paragraph.

```
<p>Everything you see on this page was made using basic HTML tags.</p>
```

The web browser will set paragraphs in a smaller font than the headings. Most of your website's text will be inside `<p>` tags.

> *Note: If you ever need to force a line break inside a paragraph of text, use a single <br> tag.
 stands for "break" and will cause whatever text that follows it to appear on a new line.*

Italic and bold text

If you want to emphasize any text, surround it with <em> or <strong> tags. Web browsers usually interpret the <em> tag as italic text.

```
<em>This text will be italicized</em>
```

The <strong> tag is usually interpreted as bold text.

```
<strong>This text will be bold</strong>
```

You usually use the <em> and <strong> tags inside a <p> tag, like this:

```
<p>Here is some text which is <em>italic</em> and <strong>bold</strong></p>
```

Making lists

Use the <ul> and <li> tags together to create a list of items. <ul> stands for unordered list, which just means that the list items don't have numbers. You create an unordered list by first adding a pair of <ul> tags, like this:

```
<ul>
</ul>
```

You then insert the <li> tags inside the <ul> tags, like this:

```
<ul>
  <li>First item</li>
  <li>Second item</li>
  <li>Third item</li>
</ul>
```

The web browser will automatically add bullets (little round circles) before each of the list items.

> *Note: If you want your list items to be numbered, use <ol> instead of <ul>. <ol> stands for ordered list, and the web browser will automatically add a number before each of the <li> list items.*

Adding links

You can easily create a link to another web page by using the <a> tag. <a> stands for anchor. It uses an attribute called href that lets you add the website address you want to link to. Whenever anyone clicks whatever is between the <a> and </a> tags, the web browser will open the page you specified with the href attribute.

You use the <a> tag like this:

```
<a href="http://anyLinkToAnyWebsite">Click to go to the link</a>
```

If you now click **Click to go to the link**, a new web page will open the address you specified with the href attribute. (href stand for *hypertext reference*, in case you're wondering.)

You can create a link to any web page on the Internet.

```
<a href="http://www.apress.com">Visit Apress</a>
```

> *Note: The fancy name for* website address *is URL. That stands for Uniform Resource Locator. It's important to know this because you'll see the term URL used a lot. Now you know!*

You can also link to another web page that's on your computer, like this:

```
<a href="anotherWebPage.html">The next page</a>
```

This last example will open an HTML file called anotherWebPage.html that's in the same folder as the current one. Use this technique to build a website by linking together many individual HTML files.

When you click a link, the browser will either open the new page by replacing what's currently in the browser window, or it will open a completely new browser window that floats on top of the old one. You can control this behavior with an additional attribute called target.

Use target="_blank" to force the browser to open the link in a new browser window. Here's how:

```
<a href="http://www.apress.com" target="_blank">Visit Apress</a>
```

If you want the page to open in the same window as the current page, use target="_self", like this:

```
<a href="http://www.apress.com" target="_self">Visit Apress</a>
```

> *Note: Web browsers will usually load a new page into the current one automatically, however, so there's usually no need to specify this with "_self." Just leave the whole target attribute out completely if that's the behavior you want.*

You can also create a link that generates an e-mail to any address with the special mailto: command. Here's the format you use to specify the e-mail address and the e-mail subject.

```
<a href="mailto:anyone@email.com?Subject=Hello%20from%20me!">Send an email.</a>
```

This will automatically open an e-mail client and create a new blank e-mail that will be addressed to anyone@email.com. It will also add the subject line "Hello from me!"

You'll notice that between each word in the subject are these characters:

%20

This is code for a blank space. You can't use blank spaces in any links you provide in an `href` attribute. So, if you need spaces, you have to replace them with %20. The web browser will correctly reinterpret this as a blank space when it generates the e-mail.

Linking to something on the same page

You can also use an `<a>` tag to link to a section on the same page. First, create the section you want to link to inside an `<a>` tag. Use a name attribute to give the section a name. The name can be any word you want to use.

```
<a name="information">Any kind of information</a>
```

The name for this section is now "information". You can create a link to it like this

```
<a href="#information">Click to find more information</a>
```

Now if you click this link, the page will jump to the information section.

Prefetching pages

Usually when you click on a link to another page, you have to wait a few seconds before it loads. You can set your web page up so that it loads certain pages in advance, while you're still on the current page. That means when you click the link, the new page opens instantly. This is called **prefetching** a page. To do this, use the `<link>` tag inside the `<head>` element. Here's a link tag that prefetches `www.apress.com`.

```
<head>
<link rel="prefetch" href="http://www.apress.com">
</head>
```

It will load the main page of `www.apress.com` in the background while you're still reading the current page. You can use the `<link>` tag to prefetch as many pages as you like, from either your own website or anywhere else on the Internet.

Adding images

The `<img>` tag lets you add an image to your web page. It has an `src` attribute that lets you specify where the browser should look to find the image.

```
<img src="anyImage.jpg">
```

As long as you have an image with that exact same name in the same folder as the HTML document, the image will load.

But the image doesn't just have to be on your computer, it can be anywhere on the Internet. Just use a website address that points to an image, like this:

```
<img src="http://www.anywebsite.com/ocean.jpg">
```

You can also use an image as a link by adding the <img> tag inside an <a> tag, like this:

```
<a href="newPage.html"><img src="anyImage.jpg"></a>
```

Now if you click on the image, the browser will open an HTML file called newPage.html. The <a> tag can be used to create a link for any HTML element in this same way.

> *Note: Image files can have the extensions JPG, GIF, or PNG. These are all types of compressed image file formats that are used on the Web. Compressed image formats have small file sizes but still look good. The smaller the file size, the faster the image will load over the Internet.*
>
> *The most common format for photographs is JPG, because it can display millions of colors. That's important for accurately displaying subtle shades and gradients in photographs. JPG files can't contain areas of transparency, however.*
>
> *Simpler graphics usually use the GIF format. GIF images aren't used for photographs because they can't contain as much color information as JPG images. However, GIF images can contain some basic transparency and can be compressed into very small file sizes.*
>
> *A good compromise format is PNG, which allows for transparency and can display millions of colors. It tends to have a slightly larger file size than JPG or GIF.*

The <img> tag also has an attribute called alt, which is text that will be displayed if the image doesn't load. Use the alt attribute inside the <img> tag like this:

```
<img src="www.anywebsite.com/ocean.jpg" alt="A description of the image">
```

If the web browser can't find the image or the network connection is too slow to load it, the text from the alt attribute will be displayed instead. The text also helps search engines identify what your image is, so that it will be easier to find if anyone searches for it.

Making comments

Sometimes when you're creating an HTML document you might need to make a note to yourself about a certain section. HTML lets you add a comment using this format:

```
<!-- This is a comment in the document. It won't be displayed in the web browser -->
```

Any text between the opening <!-- comment tag and closing --> comment tag won't be displayed in the web browser.

Character encoding

A final thing that you should consider adding to your page is **character encoding**. This is optional, but it tells the web browser how the characters (letters and numbers) in your document should be interpreted. If you open a web page and the words are scrambled in strange characters it could mean that the web browser isn't interpreting the character encoding properly. You set the character encoding with a `<meta>` tag inside the `<head>` tag, like this:

```
<head>
  <meta charset="utf-8">
  <title>Your page title</title>
</head>
```

The `<meta>` tag sets the character encoding to `utf-8`, which is the most common standard. It should be the first tag inside the `<head>` element, before the `<title>`. It's a good habit to get into adding character encoding to your HTML documents, just to make sure your pages are displayed the way you expect them to be.

More about HTML

Amazingly enough, this is most of the HTML you'll ever need to know. You'll learn more specific tips through the course of this book. See how easy it is? HTML is just a simple way of describing to a computer how to interpret information.

The best thing that you can do now is take a short break from this book for an hour or so, and try making your own HTML web page. Add a title, some headings, some paragraph text, a list or two, a few links, and try to add some images. To start, follow these steps:

1. Open your text editor, which should be either Notepad (Windows) or TextEdit (Mac OS X).

2. Select File ➤ New and start creating your page with HTML tags and text.

When you're finished, save your work:

3. Select File ➤ Save As… (Windows) or File ➤ Save As… (Mac OS X)

4. Give your HTML document the name test.html.

5. Save it somewhere on your computer.

To see how your HTML document looks in a web browser, follow these steps:

6. Open a web browser. Select File ➤ Open File…

7. Choose the test.html file that you've just created and open it.

8. You'll see your HTML document displayed as a web page in the browser window.

If this is the first time you've created a web page, there's a very good chance that you've made some small mistakes somewhere that prevent it from displaying properly. Here are some things to check:

- Make sure that you've closed all the tags. This is an extremely common mistake to make.

- Make sure that everything you want to display in the browser is enclosed in the opening and closing <body> tags.

- Check that you've spelled the tag names correctly. This is also a very common error.

- If an image isn't displaying, make sure that the image is in the same folder as the HTML page, and that you've used the correct image file extension for the file name: **.jpg**, **.gif**, or **.png**.

In the next section we'll learn about how you can change the appearance of HTML tags by using CSS.

Note: In HTML5, the <html>, <head>, and <body> tags are optional. Here's the most basic valid HTML document:

<!doctype.html>

<title></title>

That's it! Enjoy the simplicity. You'll see this format employed by most of the examples in this book.

Make it prettier with CSS

As you just saw in the previous section, the web browser interprets all the HTML elements in its own way. It automatically makes headings big and bold; chooses the fonts, colors, and sizes for you; and decides on the spacing between all the HTML elements. You can't control these things with HTML.

To change the visual style of HTML documents, you need to use the descriptive programming language CSS. CSS programming code is usually just referred to as a **style sheet**. You can use a style sheet to control the colors, fonts, sizes, and positions of all the HTML elements. You'll see that CSS is as easy and straightforward to learn and use as HTML is. In fact, it helps if you think of them as part of the same technology, because HTML and CSS are almost always used together.

Style sheets are often created as separate CSS files and are then loaded into an HTML document. This is useful because it means that you can completely change the way an HTML document looks just by loading a different style sheet. You can also change the way multiple HTML documents look by using just one style sheet. However, for simple HTML documents, and especially while you're learning, it's better to keep the style sheet and HTML code together in the same document.

It's very easy to use CSS to change the way that tags are displayed. First, type the name of the element you want to modify. Then change the style property you want to change inside a pair of curly braces. Like this:

```
elementName
{
  change the tag's style here;
}
```

Any change you make inside those curly braces will affect the way the element is displayed in the browser.

Let's look at an example of CSS in action. In the chapter's source files you'll find an HTML document called styledWebpage.html. Open it in a web browser. Figure 1-3 shows what you'll see.

A simple web page

Everything you see on this page was made using basic HTML tags.

This is a sub-heading

You use HTML tags to *structure information*. This is a paragraph of text structured with a p tag.

Making lists

You can also use tags to make a list of things.

- First item
- Second item
- Third item

Adding links

Its easy to create hyperlinks to other web pages, or to create a link to generate an email. Here's how:

- Here's a good resource for learning HTML.
- If you want to say Hi, Send me an email.

Add a photo with an img tag, like this:

Figure 1-3. The HTML document is now styled with CSS

The font types, sizes, and colors have been changed. The image is a little smaller and has a border around it. If you move the mouse over either of the links, you'll also see that they are highlighted.

The text and the HTML code have not changed at all. Instead, the document now includes some CSS code that changes the way the tags are displayed.

CSS code is added between special <style> tags inside the <head> section of the HTML document.

```
<head>
  <style>
  ... The CSS code goes here
  </style>
</style>
```

The <style> tag tells the browser that you're adding CSS code.

> *Note: Earlier versions of HTML required that you add a type attribute to the <style> tag that looks like this:*
>
> **<style type= "text/css">**
>
> *HTML5 no longer requires this. However, you might still want to use it because many programming language editors use this attribute as a cue to switch on syntax highlighting, which you'll find useful for writing programs.*

Here's the complete CSS code that had been added to the HTML document. I'll explain how it all works in the pages ahead.

```
<!doctype html>
<html lang="en">
<head>
<title>A web page</title>
<style>

h1
{
   font-family: Georgia, "Times New Roman", serif;
   font-size: 30px;
   color: #7924ff;
   font-style: italic;
   font-weight: bold;
}

h2
{
   font-family: "Lucida Console", Monaco, monospace;
   font-size: 20px;
   color: teal;
}

p, li
{
   font-family: Arial, Helvetica, sans-serif;
   font-size: 16px;
}

em
{
   text-decoration: underline;
   font-style: normal;
}
```

```css
strong
{
  font-weight: bold;
  color: red;
}

li
{
  list-style-type: square;
}

a
{
  color: green;
  text-decoration: none;
}

a:hover
{
  background-color: black;
  color: white;
}

img
{
  width: 250px;
  height: auto;
  border-style: dashed;
  border-width: 2px;
  border-color: navy;
  padding: 10px;
}

</style>
</head>
... the rest of the HTML document is the same
```

You'll recognize all the tags that we've used in the HTML document: h1, h2, p, li, a, img, and a few others. The CSS code has changed the properties of those tags in order to modify the way that those tags appear in the browser. Let's see exactly how this works.

If you choose to omit the optional <head> tag, the browser will understand that it's implied.

Font styles

CSS lets you easily choose the font style you want to use, its size, and its color. The first bit of CSS code in our web page changes the way text inside the <h1> tag appears. It changes five **properties.** You can probably guess what they do just by looking at them. They set the main heading text to Georgia font, set its size to 30 pixels, change its color to violet, and make it both bold and italic.

```
h1
{
    font-family: Georgia, "Times New Roman", serif;
    font-size: 30px;
    color: #7924ff;
    font-style: italic;
    font-weight: bold;
}
```

A property is something about the style of that tag that you want to change. Each of these five properties is on its own line inside the curly braces. Each line is indented from the left margin so that you can clearly see that it's contained inside the braces. Each property name is followed by a colon, and then a value that changes the property. It is very important to include a semicolon at the end of each line:

```
;
```

This means "I'm finished changing this property." It's like a period at the end of the sentence. You have to add a semicolon at the end of each line of CSS code. If you forget this, any new code you add after that point won't work.

Let's look at what these properties do.

Font family

The `font-family` property lets you set the font you want to use.

```
font-family: Georgia, "Times New Roman", serif;
```

There are three fonts listed on the above line: Georgia, "Times New Roman," and serif. The first font is Georgia, and the web browser will use that font if it can. If Georgia isn't installed on the computer viewing this web page, then the browser will try to load the second font, "Times New Roman." If that one also can't be found, it just loads a general font style called serif. It's always important to provide second or third fall-back fonts just in case the first font can't be loaded for some reason.

The names of the fonts are separated by commas. If the name of your font is more than one word, it needs to be surrounded by quotation marks, like "Times New Roman" or "Lucida Console."

There are three general font families that most fonts fall into: serif, sans-serif, and monospace.

Serif fonts use letters with decorative details on their edges. Times New Roman, Georgia, and Baskerville are common serif fonts. You often find serif fonts used in books and newspapers.

Sans-serif fonts don't use any details on the edges of letters. Common sans-serif fonts are Arial, Helvetica, and Futura. They're the kinds of fonts you'll tend to see on highway signs, in airports, and super modern art galleries and magazines. Here's how to use the font-family property to assign a sans-serif font:

```
font-family: Helvetica, Arial, sans-serif;
```

The browser will first try to load Helvetica. If it can't find Helvetica, it will try to load Arial instead. If that fails, it falls back on any general sans-serif font it can find. In our example web page, the `<p>` tags are displayed using sans-serif fonts.

The third main font family is called monospace (sometimes called fixed-width). These fonts have a fixed spacing between letters and are designed to be extremely easy to read. Common monospace fonts are Courier, Lucida Console, and Monaco. They're used on old-school computer console displays and typewriters. Programmers like them because indentations and spaces line up nicely, which makes them very easy to read on a computer screen. Here's how you can assign a monospace font family with CSS:

```
font-family: "Lucida Console", Monaco, monospace;
```

In our simple example web page, the p and li elements are displayed using a san-serif font, and the h2 elements are displayed in a monospace font, like this:

```
h2
{
    font-family: "Lucida Console", Monaco, monospace;
    font-size: 20px;
    color: teal;
}

p, li
{
    font-family: Helvetica, Arial, sans-serif;
    font-size: 16px;
}
```

In the example above, notice that the p and li elements share the same CSS code. You can assign styles to more than one element by listing elements with a comma separating them, like this:

```
p, li
{
}
```

This saves you from having to write the same code twice. As many elements as you like can share the same styles.

Embedding custom fonts

If you want to use a font that isn't commonly installed on most people's computers you need to **embed** it with @font-face. Here's how to embed and use a custom font in an HTML document.

1. Find the font file for the type of font you want to use. The two most common font formats are True Type Fonts (which have a TTF file extension) and Open Type Fonts (which have an OTF extension). Copy the font file into the same folder that contains your HTML and CSS files.

Use @font-face in your style sheet to load the font and create a new font family for it. Here's some CSS code that embeds a font called Londrina Solid-Regular.

```
@font-face
{
  font-family: LondrinaSolid-Regular;
  src: url("LondrinaSolid-Regular.otf");
}
```

Now you can assign this new font family to any element you wish. Here's how to assign it to an h1 element.

```
h1
{
  font-family: LondrinaSolid-Regular, "Courier New", monospace;
  font-size: 40px;
}
```

You can assign any other font properties you wish, such as the size and color. As with any font, it's also important to assign one or two fall-back fonts, just in case your embedded font doesn't load for some reason.

Font sizes

The font-size property lets you change the size of the font. px stands for **pixels**. Pixels are the tiny dots that make up text and graphics on computer screens. This code sets the size of the font to 40 pixels.

```
font-size: 40px;
```

> Note: CSS lets you use different units for specifying the size of fonts. If you need your font sizes to change dynamically depending on different screen resolutions, consider using em instead of px. Here's how:
>
> font-size: 1em;
>
> 1em will be whatever the default font size is of the browser displaying the page. In most browsers, this is equal to about 16 pixels. If you want a font size that's double that, use 2em. That will display the font at about 32 pixels. A value of 0.75em will give you a font size of about 12 pixels.

Font colors

You can change the color of a font with the color property.

```
color: #7924ff;
```

The color I've used in this example is a **hexadecimal color** value. They're also called **hex colors**. Hex colors are a standard way of describing colors using a string of numbers and letters, preceded by a hash symbol (number sign).

Here are the hexadecimal codes for a few common colors:

```
Black: #000000
White: #FFFFFF
Red: #FF0000
Blue: #0000FF
Green: #00FF00
Yellow: #FFFF00
Orange: #FF9900
Violet: #CC33FF
```

> *Note: You can shorten black to #000 and white to #FFF. If all six characters in the hexadecimal code are the same, you only need to use the first three characters.*
>
> *A web search for "hexadecimal color chart" will bring up a comprehensive list of colors and their matching hexadecimal codes. You can also find hex color codes in the color palettes of graphic design software, like Photoshop or Illustrator.*

However, you don't just need to use hex colors. CSS also lets you assign basic colors using many common color names, like this:

```
color: blue;
```

Here are the color names that CSS understands: aqua, black, blue, fuchsia, gray, green, lime, maroon, navy, olive, purple, red, silver, teal, white, and yellow.

More about colors

Hex colors are not the only color system you can use. You can optionally use the RGB/RGBA or HSL/HSLA color systems. They all produce the same colors, but they describe them in different ways.

The RGB system uses three numbers that describe the relative amounts of red, green, and blue that are mixed together to produce any color. The numbers can be from 0 to 255. Here's the RGB color code for a dark violet: rgb(204, 51, 255)

You could apply this to a CSS property, like a font color, like this:

```
color: rgb(205, 51, 255);
```

The RGBA system adds one more number that describes how transparent a color is. 0 means that the color is completely transparent, and 1 means that it's completely opaque (solid). A value of 0.5 makes the color semitransparent. Here's a semitransparent RGBA version of dark violet.

```
rgba(204, 51, 255, 0.5)
```

You can see that the color values for red, green, and blue are the same as the RGB system. The fourth number, 0.5, is the transparency amount.

The "A" in RGBA stands for **alpha,** which is a graphic design term that means transparency.

RGBA colors are nice to use because if you make them semitransparent they'll allow objects under them to still be visible, which is a lovely effect. This is especially useful for drop-shadow effects, which you'll learn about in Chapter 3.

The HSL system describes a color based on hue, saturation, and lightness. Here's the same dark violet color described by HSL:

```
hsl(285, 100%, 60%)
```

The first number, hue, is a degree from 0 to 360 that locates the position of a color on a color wheel. The second number, saturation, is a percentage from 0 to 100 that describes how saturated (vivid) the color is. The third number, lightness, is also a percentage from 1 to 100 that describes how light or dark the color is.

The HSLA system, like RGBA, adds a fourth number from 0 to 1 that describes how transparent the color is. Here's the HSLA dark violet color with a 0.5 semitransparency.

```
hsla(285, 100%, 60%, 0.5)
```

It's entirely up to you which color system you prefer to use. You can use color palettes in graphic design software like Photoshop or Illustrator to find these color codes, as well as many online tools that help you do this.

Bold, italic, and underline font styles

To make a font italic, use the **font-style** property, like this:

```
font-style: italic;
```

If a font is displaying in italics and you want to turn it off, assign the **font-style** property a value of **normal**.

Use the **font-weight** property to make the text bold:

```
font-weight: bold;
```

To underline text, use the **text-decoration** property, like this:

```
text-decoration: underline;
```

Other optional values for the text-decoration property are: **line-through** and **over-line**. If you want to remove all text decoration from a font, use **none**.

You can see all these styles in use in the CSS code that modifies the <em> and <strong> tags.

Any text inside the <em> (*emphasis*) tag is underlined.

```
em
{
  text-decoration: underline;
  font-style: normal;
}
```

(The font-style is set to **normal** to turn off the automatic italicization that most browsers assign to <em> tags.)

Any text inside the <strong> tag is bold and colored red:

```
strong
{
  font-weight: bold;
  color: red;
}
```

These are all the basics you need to know for styling fonts. Let's look at a few more features of our CSS code.

List styles

In our web-page example you'll notice that each of the three list items is preceded by a square bullet (a small black square). Figure 1-4 illustrates this.

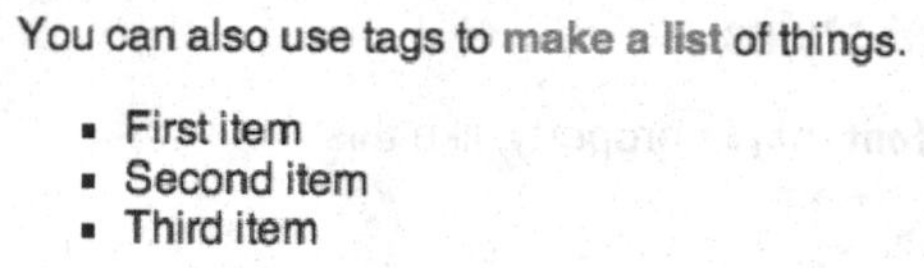

You can also use tags to **make a list** of things.

- First item
- Second item
- Third item

Figure 1-4. Square bullets mark each list item

The **list-style-type** property is responsible for this effect:

```
li
{
  list-style-type: square;
}
```

There are many optional values you can use, but the most useful are **square** and **circle**. Use **none** if you don't want any bullets on your list.

Highlighting links

If you move the mouse over any of the links (the <a> tags) in our example, you'll see that the text turns white and the whole tag is highlighted by a black background. Figure 1-5 illustrates this.

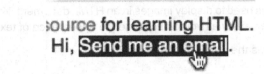

Figure 1-5. Change the element's background color when the mouse moves over it

Here's how this is accomplished.

First, the <a> tag element is styled to make links appear green and to switch off the automatic underline style that most web browsers add to links.

```
a
{
   color: green;
   text-decoration: none;
}
```

a:hover is a special style selector that describes what the <a> tag element should look like when the mouse "hovers over it."

```
a:hover
{
   background-color: black;
   color: white;
}
```

It sets the <a> tag's background color to black and the font color to white. This is what creates the highlighting effect. It only happens when the mouse is over the link. When the mouse leaves the area of the <a> tag, the link's colors return to normal.

All elements have a **background-color** property, and it can be used to change the background color of any element.

a:hover is a feature of CSS called a **pseudo-class**. Pseudo-classes let you achieve special effects like this. You can always recognize a pseudo-class because the element name is separated by the effect name with a colon.

There are a few more useful pseudo-classes you can use with the <a> tag:

- **a:visited**: The color the link should be if it's been clicked before.

- **a:active**: The currently active link.

- **a:link**: The link before it's been clicked.

Make sure to assign a style to `a:hover` before `a:link` and `a:visited` in order for those pseudo-classes to work.

Borders, padding, height, and width

Remember that the `<img>` tag is used to display images in an HTML document. You can change the way images are displayed with CSS, just as easily as you can change the appearance of text.

Here's the CSS code that styles the image in our example.

```
img
{
  width: 250px;
  height: auto;
  border-style: dashed;
  border-width: 2px;
  border-color: navy;
  padding: 10px;
}
```

The code makes the image a little smaller by changing its width. The height matches the change in width automatically to maintain the image's proportion. The image is surrounded with a two-pixel-wide, navy border with a dashed line style. It also adds 10 pixels of padding between the image and the border. Figure 1-6 illustrates the effect of this code on the image.

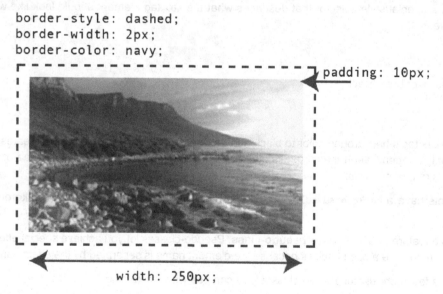

Figure 1-6. Change the size and add a border to the image

The width and height properties determine how big in pixels the image should be.

```
width: 250px;
height: auto;
```

auto means that the height should adjust automatically to keep the image in proportion if the width changes.

The **padding** property adds 10 pixels of empty space between the image and the border evenly on all four sides.

```
padding: 10px;
```

If you want to give different padding values for each of the four sides, you can use some CSS code that looks like this:

```
padding: 10px 30px 20px 5px;
```

This changes the padding on four sides, in this order: top, right, bottom, and left. (You can remember this because the order is clockwise, from the top.)

> Note: There are a few more shortcuts to assign padding:
>
> padding: 20px 30px 50px;
>
> The top padding is 20 pixels, the right and left padding is 30 pixels, and the bottom padding is 50pixels.
>
> padding: 20px 50px;
>
> The top and bottom padding is 20 pixels, and the right and left padding is 50 pixels.

You can also assign padding individually for each side, like this:

```
padding-top: 10px;
padding-bottom: 20px;
padding-right: 30px;
padding-left: 5px;
```

> Note: The padding value is added to the element's height and width. That means that if the element is 250 pixels wide, and you add 10 pixels of padding on its right and left sides, the element's actual width will become 270 pixels. This is very important to remember if you're doing complex layouts: padding values add to width and height values.

The border properties determine the border's style, width, and color.

You can change the border style with the **border-style** property:

```
border-style: dashed;
```

This creates a dashed line around the element. Values you can use are **dashed**, **double**, **dotted**, **groove**, **ridge**, **hidden**, **inset**, and **outset**. To remove a border, set this value to **none**. Figure 1-7 illustrates these border styles.

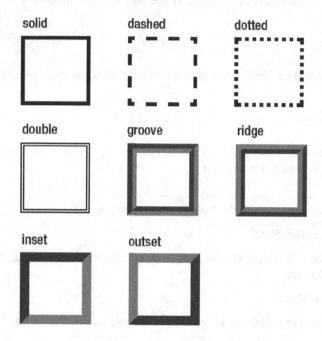

Figure 1-7. Border styles

You can set the width of the border with the **border-width** property:

```
border-width: 2px;
```

You'll usually set the width in pixels, but you can also use one of the three predefined values: **thin**, **medium**, or **thick**. Just like adding padding, the border width adds to the element's total width and height.

The **border-color** property changes the color of the border:

```
border-color: navy;
```

It accepts the same color values as the text **color** property.

You can use a shortcut to define all these border properties in one line of code, like this:

```
border: 2px dashed navy;
```

If you use this shortcut style, make sure you list the properties in this order: line thickness, style, and color.

Cascading styles

You may be wondering what the "cascading" part of Cascading Style Sheets means. It means that if you assign a style to an element at the beginning of the CSS code, you can add to or change that style later in the code. Here's an example of how this works in our style sheet.

The p and li elements both share the same initial style.

```
p, li
{
   font-family: Helvetica, Arial, sans-serif;
   font-size: 16px;
}
```

But later in the style sheet, the li element is assigned a new style:

```
li
{
   list-style-type: square;
}
```

This style is *added to* the style that was first defined. This is a useful feature, because it means that many elements can share the same styles, but you can then customize individual elements.

If you wanted to, however, you could completely overwrite the original style, by adding this new style after the first one:

```
li
{
   list-style-type: square;
   font-family: "Lucida Console", Monaco, monospace;
   font-size: 10px;
}
```

Whichever styles are set last are the ones that are applied to the HTML element.

Using <DIV> elements

In the previous examples we used some standard HTML tags to display page elements, like <h1>, <h2>, <p>, <ul>, and <img>. Sometimes, however, you'll want to add something to a page that doesn't fit into any of the neat categories defined by the standard tags. This is especially true if you use HTML to create games and applications, which use elements that are very different from those found on ordinary web pages. For these cases, HTML has a generic tag called <div>, which can be used for anything.

> *Note: The <div> tag was originally intended to be used for indicating web-page divisions (different sections of a web page), but it's long since transcended its original use.*

31

When you create a `<div>` element, you usually also give it a name so that you can easily style it with CSS. This name can be either an `id` or `class` attribute. Let's see how this works.

Using an id

If you have only one element of a certain kind, give it a name with an `id` attribute.

```
<div id="elementName"></div>
```

The `id` is a unique name that only a single element can have. You can use the `id` to style the element using CSS, like this:

```
#elementName
{
  Change any style properties here
}
```

A hash character, #, must be in front of the element's id name.

> Note: You can use any name you like for the id, but don't use names that contain blank spaces. Try and keep the id name to one word, and use lowercase letters.
>
> If you want to use an id name that's more than one word, consider using camelCaseNotation. It's a style of writing multiple words together without spaces, which is very common in computer programming. In camelCaseNotation, the first word is written in lowercase, and each subsequent word is capitalized, like this:
>
> firstSecondThird
>
> Can you figure out why it's called camelCaseNotation? You'll see it used in most of the examples in this book.

In the chapter's source files you'll find a file called id.html that demonstrates a simple example. Open it in a web browser and you'll see that it displays a simple rectangle with a dashed border, as shown in Figure 1-8.

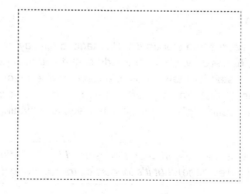

Figure 1-8. Use a `<div>` tag with an id to display a simple rectangle

Here's the HTML and CSS coding that makes this work:

```
<!doctype html>
<title>Using an id</title>

<style>

#stage
{
  width: 400px;
  height: 300px;
  border: 1px dashed black;
}

</style>

<div id="stage"></div>
```

The `<div>` element has the `id` attribute `"stage"`. The CSS code gives it a height, width, and border. You can see that this is very similar to styling other HTML elements, except that, instead of using the tag name, the CSS code uses the tag's `id` attribute.

In this book I use the name `"stage"` for the rectangular space that contains the action in our games.

Using a class

If more than one element shares the same properties, then you should assign it to a `class`. Here's how:

```
<div class="theClassName">
```

A class works in exactly the same way as an id, except that more than one element can belong to the same class. Open the class.html file in the chapter's source files for a simple example. You'll see the names of three animals, all styled in the same way.

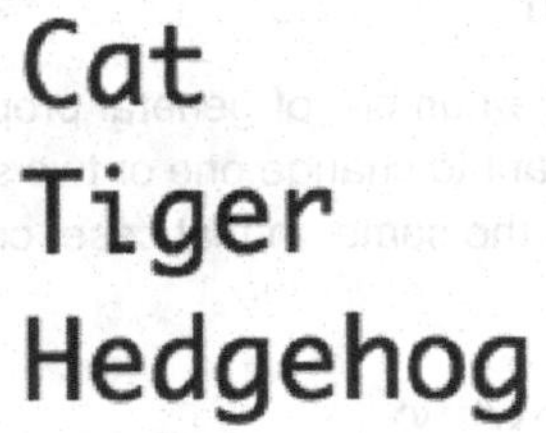

Cat
Tiger
Hedgehog

Figure 1-9. Use a class to style many elements in the same way

Here's the code that makes this work:

```
<!doctype html>
<title>Using a class</title>

<style>

.animal
{
  font-family: Monaco, "Courier New", monospace;
  font-size: 30px;
}

</style>

<div class="animal">Cat</div>
<div class="animal">Tiger</div>
<div class="animal">Hedgehog</div>
```

You can see that the three `<div>` elements all share the same class name: `"animal"`.

The CSS code has a style called `.animal` that sets the font to `Monaco` and the size to `30px`. Any elements that belong to the animal class will share these properties.

To style a class with CSS, always precede the class name with a dot, like this:

```
.className
{
  Set the class's style properties here
}
```

In these examples, I've shown you how to use the `id` and `class` attributes with `<div>` tags, but you can also use them with any HTML tags. Elements can also have an id and belong to a class at the same time. Let's see how that can be useful.

Using an id and class together

If you have elements that share a large number of general properties, it makes sense to assign them all to the same class. However, you might want to change one or two single properties in individual elements, while keeping most of the general properties the same. In that case, create an element with both a class and an id, as in this example:

```
<div class="general" id="specific"></div>
```

You could then assign all the general styles to the class, and the specific styles to the id.

Let's look at a concrete example. Open the classAndId.html file in the chapter's source files. You'll see three animal names, each sharing the same font and size, but each is styled differently. Figure 1-10 shows what you'll see when you open the file in a web browser.

Cat
Tiger
<u>Hedgehog</u>

Figure 1-10. Use a class and id together to customize elements that share related properties

The cat is italicized, the tiger is bold, and the hedgehog is underlined. Here's the HTML and CSS code that produces this effect:

```
<!doctype html>
<title>Using a class and id together</title>

<style>

.animal
{
  font-family: Monaco, "Courier New", monospace;
  font-size: 30px;
}

#cat
{
  font-style: italic;
}

#tiger
{
  font-weight: bold;
}

#hedgehog
{
  text-decoration: underline;
}

</style>

<div class="animal" id="cat">Cat</div>
<div class="animal" id="tiger">Tiger</div>
<div class="animal" id="hedgehog">Hedgehog</div>
```

All the elements share the same animal class. That means that they share the same basic font and font size. But notice that they've also been assigned unique ids:

```
<div class="animal" id="cat">Cat</div>
<div class="animal" id="tiger">Tiger</div>
<div class="animal" id="hedgehog">Hedgehog</div>
```

The CSS code can use those ids to customize each element:

```
#cat
{
   font-style: italic;
}

#tiger
{
   font-weight: bold;
}

#hedgehog
{
   text-decoration: underline;
}
```

These styles are applied to each element *in addition to* the styles they all share as part of the animal class. Combining classes and ids like this is a very simple but powerful way to create complex styles that are easy to manage.

Elements can also belong to more than one class.

Loading background images into HTML elements

You saw in the webpage example how you can use the `<img>` tag to display images in a browser window. But there's another way that you can load images, which is often better for games and interactive applications. You can load an image into an element's **background-image** property. Here's the format to use:

```
background-image: url("imageName.png");
```

The image file name is enclosed in quotation marks, and it must include the file-type extension. You can use JPG, GIF, or PNG images. The image will load as long as it's in the same folder as the CSS code. (The element also needs to be a *block element*. You'll learn all about block elements later.)

Here's how to use the **background-image** property to load an image into an element.

Start with an HTML element that represents the image you want to display.

```
<div id="cat"></div>
```

Then create a style for the cat id. Give it a height and width that exactly matches the height and width of the image you want to display. Then load the image into the **background-image** property.

```
#cat
{
  height: 100px;
  width: 100px;
  background-image: url("cat.png");
}
```

The **cat.png** image will be loaded into the <div> element and appear in the browser window.

You can find a working example of this in the backgroundImages folder in this chapter's source files. Open the backgroundImages.html file in a text editor and you'll find some simple code that displays a picture of a cat. Here's the code:

```
<!doctype html>
<title>Background images</title>

<style>

#cat
{
  width: 100px;
  height: 100px;
  background-image: url("cat.png");
}

</style>
<div id="cat"></div>
```

Figure 1-11 shows how the HTML code loads the image file and displays it in a web browser.

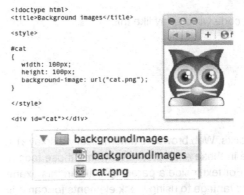

Figure 1-11. Load an image into an element with the background-image property

Now that you know how to load one image, let's load two more and learn how to position them in the browser.

Positioning elements with CSS

CSS can be used to position elements in precise locations. The style sheet gives you complete control over where in the browser window elements appear. Positioning elements is as important for games as it is for websites, and we'll take a look at some concrete examples that show you how to do this.

First, you need to understand the difference between inline elements and block elements.

Inline and block elements

Inline elements all share space on the same horizontal line. A good example of this are the `<em>` and `<strong>` elements. You can use them inside `<p>` tags and all the text will stay on the same line. Here's an example of some simple HTML using `<em>` and `<strong>` tags.

```
<p>This is some text with <em>italic</em> and <strong>bold</strong> letters.</p>
```

This HTML code will display like this:

This is some text with *italic* and **bold** letters.

Because the `<em>` and `<strong>` tags are inline elements, they all stay "in line."

Block elements behave in the opposite way: they stack on top of each other like blocks. You can turn any element into a block element with the `display` property, like this:

```
display: block;
```

You could use this property to turn the `<em>` and `<strong>` elements into blocks, like this:

```
em, strong
{
  display: block;
}
```

Now that same line of HTML code will display like this:

This is some text with
italic
and
bold
letters.

They form a tower, like toy blocks. Web browsers automatically display `<h1>`, `<h2>`, `<p>`, and `<div>` tags as block elements, which you can see in these examples. Every time those tags are used, the elements are displayed below other block elements. For text inside a paragraph, like in this example, this is pretty useless, but it's not so for images in games. An advantage to using block elements for game images is that you can precisely position them anywhere in the browser window. Let's see how you can use CSS to do this.

> Note: If you need to make any block elements inline, you can set the display property for those elements to inline, like this:
>
> display: inline;

Floating elements

CSS gives you lots of options for positioning block elements. Instead of stacking vertically, you can make blocks float so that they line up horizontally. This makes them look like inline elements but with the advantage that they have solid dimensions that can hold images and have styled borders.

In the chapter's source files you'll find a folder called floatingElements.html. Double-click on it to open it in a web browser. You'll see three animals stacked vertically, surrounded by a rectangle. Figure 1-12 shows what you'll see.

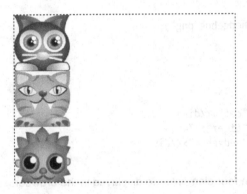

Figure 1-12. Three animals aligned vertically inside a rectangle

Open the floatingElements.html file in a text editor, and you will see this HTML code:

```
<!doctype html>
<title>Floating elements</title>

<style>

#stage
{
  display: block;
  width: 400px;
  height: 300px;
  border: 1px dashed black;
}
```

```
.animal
{
  display: block;
  width: 100px;
  height: 100px;
}

#cat
{
  background-image: url("cat.png");
}

#tiger
{
  background-image: url("tiger.png");
}

#hedgehog
{
  background-image: url("hedgehog.png");
}

</style>

<div id="stage">
  <div class="animal" id="cat"></div>
  <div class="animal" id="tiger"></div>
  <div class="animal" id="hedgehog"></div>
</div>
```

Figure 1-13 shows how these four elements are displayed in the browser.

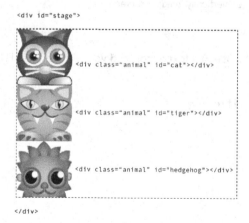

Figure 1-13. The animals are contained inside the rectangular stage

The `<div id="stage">` element is a 400-by-300-pixel rectangle with a dashed border. Here's the CSS code that styles it:

```css
#stage
{
  display: block;
  width: 400px;
  height: 300px;
  border: 1px dashed black;
}
```

The animals are also rectangles. They're each 100 by 100 pixels.

```css
.animal
{
  display: block;
  width: 100px;
  height: 100px;
}
```

All the animals share these same properties. However, each animal also has a unique image. The code uses **id** attributes to give each animal a unique name, as you can see in the HTML code.

```html
<div class="animal" id="cat"></div>
<div class="animal" id="tiger"></div>
<div class="animal" id="hedgehog"></div>
```

The ids allow us to refer to each animal individually as **cat**, **tiger**, and **hedgehog**. The CSS code does exactly this to load each element with a unique background image.

```css
#cat
{
  background-image: url("cat.png");
}

#tiger
{
  background-image: url("tiger.png");
}

#hedgehog
{
  background-image: url("hedgehog.png");
}
```

This is another useful example of how you can customize each element by targeting its unique id and changing specific things about it.

Because the animals are block elements, they're stacked vertically. We can make the animals float to the left of each other in a neat horizontal row with this bit of CSS code:

```
float: left;
```

Try adding that line to the animal style definition in the floatingElements.html file:

```
.animal
{
  display: block;
  width: 100px;
  height: 100px;

  float: left;
}
```

Save the file and refresh the browser window. Figure 1-14 shows that the animals now line up horizontally.

Figure 1-14. Block elements float to form a horizontal row

Using the float property is like filling up each animal with helium and making it float to the top. The left value means that each animal will take up any available space to the left. This makes the elements left-aligned. Use float: right to make the elements align to the right.

Adding margins to space the elements

You can center the animals within the upper half of the stage by adding some left and top margins. You can set the top margin to 50 pixels and the left margin to 25 pixels with this code:

```
margin-top: 50px;
margin-left: 25px;
```

Add these two lines to the **animal** style definition:

```
animal
{
  display: block;
  width: 100px;
  height: 100px;
  float: left;
  margin-top: 50px;
  margin-left: 25px;
}
```

Save the file and refresh the browser. You'll see that the margins have been added to the top and left of each of the animals, as shown in Figure 1-15. They're now evenly spaced.

Figure 1-15. Add margins to space the animals evenly

Clearing floating elements

If you want to add a new element below some floating elements, you need to set the new element's clear property. Here's how to clear elements that are floating to the left:

```
clear: left;
```

This will cause the new element to appear under left-floating elements. The clear property also accepts the values **right** and **both**.

Let's see how you can use the clear property to center some text below our three floating animals.

Add an <h1> element inside the <div id="stage"> element:

```
<div id="stage">
<div class="animal" id="cat"></div>
```

```
<div class="animal" id="tiger"></div>
<div class="animal" id="hedgehog"></div>
<h1>Dangerous Animals!</h1>
</div>
```

To make the text appear below the animals, set the h1 element's clear property to left:

```
h1
{
  clear: left;
}
```

Use the text-align property to center the text within the stage element:

```
h1
{
  clear: left;
  text-align: center;
}
```

The text-align property can also take the values left, right, and justify.

Figure 1-16 shows the effect of the clear code in the browser window.

Figure 1-16. Use the clear property to make the text appear below the floating elements

Use @font-face to embed a custom font, and add some padding to space the text more evenly within the stage:

```
@font-face
{
  font-family: LondrinaSolid-Regular;
  src: url("LondrinaSolid-Regular.otf");
}
```

```
h1
{
    clear: left;
    display: block;
    text-align: center;
    padding-top: 50px;
    font-family: LondrinaSolid-Regular;
    font-size: 40px;
}
```

Note: Most browsers automatically style <h1> and <div> elements as blocks, so using display: block is optional for these elements.

Figure 1-17 shows this effect on the browser window.

Figure 1-17. Customize the heading

You can find all this working code in the floatingElementsFinished.html file in the chapter's source files.

More about centering elements

You now know that you can center text inside an element with the text-align property like this:

text-align: center;

You can also give it the values left, right, justify, and inherit. justify spaces the text so that it's stretched across an element. inherit means that it should follow whatever text-align rule that its containing element is using.

You can use text-align to center text, but it won't work for block elements. If you want to center a block element inside another element, use the margin property and give it these values:

margin: 0px auto;

This gives the element equal, automatic left and right margins, which centers it. You can use this bit of code to center any block element inside another block element. You can also use it to center an element inside the browser window. Use it with the body element to center a whole web page, like this:

```
body
{
  margin: 0px auto;
}
```

Using margins, padding, float, and clear like this is usually the most flexible way of positioning elements, because the elements will automatically adjust themselves to the available space. Elements will re-space and re-position themselves if you add or remove them. However, you can also position elements using precise pixel positions, which I'll show you how to do next.

Absolute positioning

Figure 1-18 shows a black square that's precisely positioned inside a rectangle.

Figure 1-18. Use absolute positioning to give elements precise pixel positions

The square's top left corner is 120 pixels below the enclosing rectangle's top border, and 200 pixels from the rectangle's left border. You'll find this working code in the absolutePositioning.html file in the chapter's source files.

```
<!doctype html>
<title>Absolute positioning</title>

<style>

#stage
{
  position: relative;
  display: block;
  width: 400px;
  height: 300px;
  border: 1px dashed black;
}
```

```
#square
{
  position: absolute;
  top: 120px;
  left: 200px;
  display: block;
  width: 100px;
  height: 100px;
  background-color: black;
}

</style>

<div id="stage">
  <div id="square"></div>
</div>
```

For this to work, you first need to enclose the element you want to position inside another element. In this example the square is enclosed inside the rectangular stage, with this HTML code:

```
<div id="stage">
  <div id="square"></div>
</div>
```

Next, you need to set the position property of the containing element to relative:

```
#stage
{
  position: relative;
}
```

You then need to set the position property of the inner element to absolute:

```
#square
{
  position: absolute;
}
```

This makes the square part of the stage's coordinate system. You can now position the square by telling it how far it should position itself from the stage's top and left border, like this:

```
#square
{
  position: absolute;
  top: 120px;
  left: 200px;
}
```

This positions the square 120 pixels from the stage's top border, and it will also be 200 pixels from its left border. The square is positioned from its top left corner. Figure 1-19 demonstrates this.

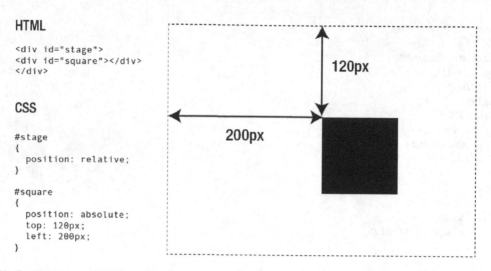

Figure 1-19. Position the square relative to the stage by assigning how many pixels it should be from the stage's top and left borders

You could optionally position the square relative to the stage's bottom and right borders, like this:

```css
#square
{
  position: absolute;
  bottom: 120px;
  right: 200px;
}
```

This produces the effect shown in Figure 1-20. The square's bottom right corner is offset from the stage's bottom and right borders.

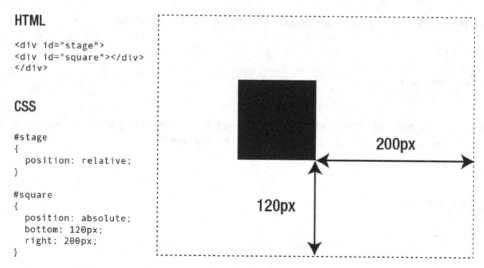

Figure 1-20. Optionally offset the square from the bottom and right borders

Positioning elements with CSS can become quite complex, but it doesn't need to be. Stick to the models I've used in these simple examples, and you can't go wrong.

> Note: If you need to, you can also use position: fixed to lock the position of an HTML element relative to the browser window. The left and top values will be calculated from the left and top edges of the browser. It means the HTML element will remain fixed in place even if you change the size of the browser window or scroll the page. This is useful if you want to make elements that float above the page and aren't affected by the normal document flow.

More about block sizes: The box model

Block elements have width and height properties that you can change. However, they *only* refer to the width and height of the *content inside the block*. The total height and width of the entire block is actually determined by combining the content's width and height with the block's margin, borders, and padding. This system is called the **box model**. It can be confusing because if you don't understand how the box model calculates a block's final size, the block may not have the final width and height that you expect it to. But luckily it's easy to predict how the box model calculates the block's size after you set its padding, borders, and margins.

How is the block's final width and height determined? Imagine that you've got a block element with these properties.

```
width: 100px;
height 100px;
padding: 10px;
border: 10px;
margin: 10px;
```

Here's how you find the total width:

totalWidth = width + leftPadding + rightPadding + leftBorder + rightBorder + leftMargin + rightMargin

If you translate that into real numbers, you end up with this:

totalWidth = 100 + 10 + 10 + 10 + 10 + 10 + 10

That means the total width of the block is 160 pixels.

totalWidth = 160

You calculate the block's total height in the same way. Figure 1-21 illustrates how this works.

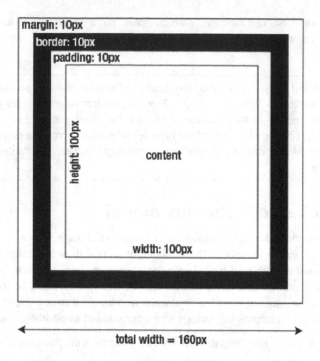

Figure 1-21. The box model calculates the block's final width and height by combining the size of the content with the padding, borders, and margins

If you're ever confused about why your block elements don't appear to be spacing or positioning themselves correctly, come back to this section of the chapter and check whether you've determined their sizes correctly based on the box model.

Organizing your files

In the examples in this chapter the HTML and CSS code were together in the same file. This is very convenient for small projects, but if you're designing a complex website or game with lots of code to manage, it can quickly become unwieldy. It's usually better to separate the HTML and CSS code into separate files. Let's look at a few examples of how to do this.

Separating HTML and CSS code

Here's a very simple HTML document that displays a page heading and some paragraph text that's styled with CSS.

```
<!doctype html>
<title>A simple document</title>

<style>
```

```
h1
{
   font-size: 40px;
}

p
{
   font-family: Helvetica, Verdana, Arial, sans-serif;
}

</style>

<h1>Page Heading</h1>
<p>A bit of text.</p>
```

Let's split this document into two separate HTML and CSS files:

1.   In your text editor, create a new file.

2.   Copy all the CSS code into the new file.

```
h1
{
    font-size: 40px;
}

p
{
    font-family: Helvetica, Verdana, Arial, sans-serif;
}
```

3.   Save this file as newStyle.css. Make sure that you save it in the same folder as the HTML file.

4.   In the HTML file, delete the **<style>** tags and all the CSS code that's inside them.

5.   Add the following just below the **<title>** tag:

```
<link rel="stylesheet" href="newStyle.css">
```

This <link> tag loads the **newStyle.css** file into the HTML document using the href attribute. The rel attribute tells the HTML document that the file that's being loaded is a style sheet. Here's how the complete HTML document should now look:

```
<!doctype html>
<title>A simple document</title>
<link rel="stylesheet" href="newStyle.css">

<h1>Page Heading</h1>
<p>A bit of text.</p>
```

This will display exactly the same way in the web browser, using the styles from the loaded style sheet. You'll find a working example of this in the organizingFiles folder in the chapter's source files. You'll see that the folder contains two files: simpleDocument.html and newStyle.css.

There are two big advantages to splitting the HTML and CSS code into two separate files:

- If you ever want to completely change the style of your HTML document, just create a new CSS file, and link the HTML file to it. That means that you can test out new styles without changing the original ones and without having to change anything in the HTML file, except the link to the style sheet.

- Your code becomes much less cluttered. This is very important for complex games, applications, and websites where you could be writing hundreds of lines of CSS and HTML code. Keeping the CSS and HTML separate means you only have half as much code to look at at any one time, and that's much more manageable.

For games and websites you'll also need to organize images and probably audio files and videos as well. Let's look at how to keep different types of media in different folders and load them into the main HTML file.

Organizing code and media

Figure 1-22 illustrates an efficient way to organize an HTML5 project. There's a project folder, with four sub-folders: src (which stands for **source code**), images, videos, and sounds. The HTML and CSS files are in the src folder. "Source code" is another name for a computer program. It's a very common convention to keep programming code in a folder called src. It's also very common to give the main project file the name main. The main.html file loads the images, videos, and audio files from the other folders.

Figure 1-22. Organizing project files and folders

Here's the main.html file that loads an image, a video, and a sound.

```
<!doctype html>
<title>Organizing project folders</title>
<link rel="stylesheet" href="style.css">

<h1>Organizing project folders</h1>
```

```
<h2>Images</h2>
<img src="../images/photo.jpg">

<h2>Video</h2>
<video controls>
<source src="../videos/movie.mp4">
</video>

<h2>Audio</h2>
<audio controls>
<source src="../sounds/song.mp3">
</audio>
```

You can see that the `<img>`, `<video>`, and `<audio>` tags are used to load the photo, movie, and song. But take a close look at the path to the files:

`../images/photo.jpg`

You can see that `photo.jpg` is the image file that's being loaded. But what does the rest of it mean?

`../images/`

Let's break this down into smaller pieces.

Whenever you see a forward slash after a word in a file pathname, it means "this is a folder."

`images/`

So we know that the `photo.jpg` file is in a folder called **images**:

`images/photo.jpg`

But we also need to know where the images folder is. That's what these characters tell us:

`../`

Two dots and a forward slash tell the program to look for the images folder in the directory just outside the current directory. Figure 1-23 illustrates how this works.

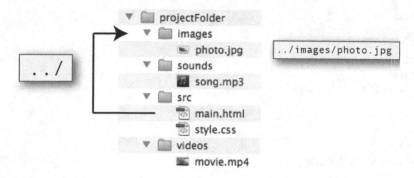

Figure 1-23. Look for the images folder outside the folder that the HTML file is in

If you don't add ../, the HTML file will look for the images folder inside the src folder.

The audio and video files load the song and movie in the same way.

In later chapters in this book you'll see this structure used to organize the code and media in more complex game projects.

More about the video and audio elements

Use the <video> tag to load a video into an HTML document, like this:

```
<video>
<source src="movieName.mp4">
</video>
```

HTML5 currently lets you load any movies that have MP4, OGG, or WEBM formats. More formats may be added in the future.

The optional control attribute displays controls to play and pause the video.

```
<video control>
```

Every web browser will display a different set of controls.

Use the <audio> tag to load sounds into an HTML document in the same way:

```
<audio>
<source src="soundName.mp3">
</audio>
```

You can currently load any sounds that have MP3, OGG, and WAV formats, although, as with the video, HTML5 may support more formats in the future.

The audio element also has an optional `control` attribute that displays controls for playing and pausing sounds.

```
<audio control>
```

There are some other optional attributes that you can use with the video and audio elements:

Attribute	What it does	Values you can assign to it
autoplay	Automatically plays the media as soon it begins to load.	None.
loop	Plays the media again after it reaches the end.	None.
preload	Determines whether or not the media should be loaded when the page loads.	It can take the values auto, none, or metadata.
		`preload="auto"`: The media will begin to load before it starts playing. This buffers the playback so that it's less likely to be interrupted by a slow or uneven network connection.
		`preload="none"`: The media starts playing immediately without buffering.
		`preload="metadata"`: Only information about the media is loaded, such as its title and duration.
		Note that the autoplay attribute will usually override these options.
Video-only attributes:		
height	Sets the height of the video.	A value in pixels, like this: `height="720"`
width	Sets the width of the video.	A value in pixels, like this: `width="400"`
poster	Displays an image before the video starts playing.	The path to any image file, like this: `poster="photo.jpg"`

At the time of writing, audio and video in HTML5 sometimes behave in quirky ways, depending on which web browser you're using or how the video or audio file was encoded.

If you want to be absolutely sure your video will load, provide versions of your video in MP4, OGG, and WEBM formats. If a browser doesn't support one format, it will load the other. You can implement this by using three source elements inside the `<video>` tag, linking each to a different version of the file, like this:

```
<video>
<source src="movieName.mp4">
<source src="movieName.ogg">
<source src="movieName.webm">
</video>
```

Do the same for the audio:

```
<audio>
<source src="soundName.mp3">
<source src="soundName.wav">
<source src="soundName.ogg">
</audio>
```

This will make sure that your video and audio plays in all modern web browsers.

If you're certain that you only need to use one video or audio format, you don't need to use the `<source>` tag. You can add the video or audio `src` attribute directly in the `<video>` and `<audio>` tags, like this.

```
<video src="movie.mp4"></video>
```

```
<audio src="song.mp3"></audio>
```

Also, consider using the optional `type` attribute, which specifies which format the audio or video is in.

```
<video src="movie.mp4" type="video/mp4"></video>
```

```
<audio src="song.mp3" type="audio/mp3"></audio>
```

This helps the browser to decide whether or not it should attempt to load the file.

Learning more about HTML and CSS

This is most of the CSS and HTML you'll need to know for creating games. There are a few more tricks you'll learn before you reach the end of this book, but all the basics are right here in this chapter.

But if you want to use HTML and CSS to design websites, you'll need to learn a little more. You'll need to learn about organizing page content and dealing with complex layouts that can adapt to different screen resolutions and orientations. Here are few topics you'll want to research further.

- **HTML tags**: We've covered all the basic HTML5 elements in this chapter, but there are many more that can be used to define areas of a web page more specifically. You'll find the entire list of HTML5 elements, with examples of how they should be used, at the World Wide Web consortium's website: www.w3.org/community/webed/wiki/HTML/Elements.

- **Flexible Box Model**: Web pages usually need to dynamically change the layout of the content they display if the size of the web browser changes. The Flexible Box Model is CSS code that you can use to make elements that proportionately resize, depending on the space they have available on the page. You can also use the Flexible Box Model to easily make multicolumn layouts.

- **CSS selectors and pseudo-classes**: In this chapter you learned how to use CSS to select HTML tags, ids, and classes that you could style in specific ways. You also learned how to use a:hover to create a highlighting effect when the mouse moves over a link. CSS has many more very specific ways in which you can style elements, and you can find the complete list at the World Wide Web Consortium's website: http://www.w3.org/TR/selectors.

A web search for any of these topics will turn up many useful articles and tutorials that are too numerous to mention here.

> Note: A good introduction to HTML and CSS is Beginning HTML5 and CSS3 by Christopher Murphy, Richard Clark, Oliver Studholme, and Divya Manian. It builds on all the topics covered in this chapter.

Summary

You now know all the HTML and CSS you need to start building websites and, more importantly, games.

We've covered all the basic HTML tags. You've learned how to style and position them with CSS, and you learned how to write programming code using a text editor. Yes, there's lots more you can learn about HTML and CSS, and you should learn as much more as you can. They're extremely important technologies to know. But you'll be happy to know that although HTML and CSS can become quite complex, the basic concepts are no more difficult than what we've covered in this chapter.

There's one more important HTML tag that we haven't discussed in this chapter: `<canvas>`. It gives you access to the canvas display technology, which is great for animation and fast-paced video games. You'll learn all about how to use it starting in Chapter 6.

Now that you know HTML and CSS, you need to learn one more programming technology to start making games: JavaScript. That's what the rest of this book is about, and JavaScript is what makes the real game magic happen. It's the fun part. In the next chapter I'm going to take you through a gentle introduction to JavaScript and cover all its basic functionality in a series of simple and focused examples. If you've never done any computer programming before now, you'll soon discover that programming is one of the most fun things you can ever do with a computer.

Chapter 2

Learning JavaScript

JavaScript is a computer-programming language that's at the heart of an HTML5 game. Almost everything that's important in your game is going to be controlled by JavaScript in some way. JavaScript is one of the easiest programming languages to learn. You can learn everything that's important to know about JavaScript in a few hours or days, and, with a bit of practice, you'll be writing it fluently in no time.

In this chapter you're going to learn everything that's important in JavaScript that you need to know to start making games. In the chapters that follow I'll show you how to apply these skills to real game projects.

Take your time with this chapter. Its all about learning how to think like a programmer. Spend as much time as you need to with each example so that you fully understand any new concepts and create your own test programs to play around with these techniques.

Setting up

To start programming with JavaScript, you need a text editor and a web browser. You'll need to configure your web browser to display a **JavaScript console.** The console is used to display messages from your programs, and it will also help you find mistakes. You'll see how it's used very soon.

Here's how to display the JavaScript console in Safari, Chrome, and Firefox. Each browser has a different name for the console, but they all do the same thing:

Safari:

- Select Develop ➤ Show Error Console from Safari's main menu. This will open a new window called the Web Inspector. Optionally, click the window icon on the Web Inspector's bottom left corner to dock it to Safari's main window.

Chrome:

- Select View ➤ Developer ➤ JavaScript Console.

Firefox:

- Select Tools ➤ Web Developer ➤ Web Console.

You can arrange your text editor, the web browser, and the console on your computer desktop so that they're all visible at the same time. Figure 2-1 shows how I've arranged them on my computer.

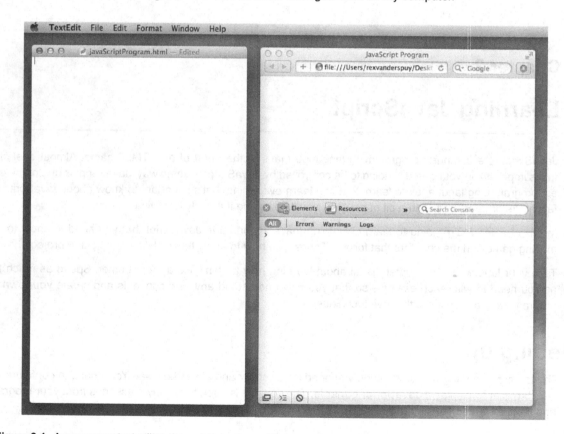

Figure 2-1. Arrange your text editor, the web browser, and the console

Note: If you're using Mac OS X, you can assign this layout to its own desktop by using Mission Control. That will make any file easier to work on without the clutter of other open windows on your desktop.

Displaying messages in the console

Let's now write a simple JavaScript program that will display the words "Hello World!" in the JavaScript console.

1. Enter the following into your text editor.

    ```
    <!doctype html>
    <title>Display console output</title>

    <script>

    console.log("Hello World!");

    </script>
    ```

2. Save this with the file name displayConsoleOutput.html.

3. Open this file in the web browser. You should see nothing but a blank page. Don't worry: that's what you should see!

4. Display the console if it isn't already open. You'll see that it displays the words "Hello World!" Figure 2-2 shows what you'll see.

Figure 2-2. Display the words "Hello World!" in the console

Congratulations, you've just written your first JavaScript program! Let's see how it works.

You write JavaScript in an HTML document inside the `<script>` tags:

```
<script>
... add JavaScript here
</script>
```

> Note: Earlier versions of HTML required that you add a type attribute to the `<script>` tag that looks like this:
>
> `<script type="text/javascript">`
>
> HTML5 no longer requires this. However, you might still want to use it because many JavaScript text editors use this attribute as a cue to switch on syntax highlighting, which can help you read your program more easily.

This is the JavaScript code that displays the words in the console:

```
console.log("Hello World!");
```

This line of code is called a **directive**. A directive is an action that you want to perform. You can always spot a directive because it ends with a semicolon. The semicolon tells the program, "Do this now!"

The words are displayed in the console using a **method** called `console.log()`:

```
console.log();
```

Methods are special phrases that let you perform a task. The `console.log` method lets you display words in the Web Inspector's console. Any words you put inside its parentheses will be displayed like this:

```
console.log("You can write any words here.");
```

The words must be surrounded by quotation marks.

Try it yourself and see if you can make new words appear in the console. Change the HTML file in your text editor so that the `console.log` method displays different words. Here's an example:

```
<!doctype html>
<title>Display console output</title>

<script>

console.log("Can you really write anything?");

</script>
```

Save the file and click your web browser's refresh button. You should now see the new words you wrote appear in the console.

And that's it! See how easy JavaScript can be? If you've got everything set up properly, and you're getting the results I've just described, you're all set to work through the rest of the examples in this chapter.

> Note: Loading a JavaScript program into a web browser is called **running** it. Whenever you see the phrase "run the program" in this book, I mean open it in a web browser and watch what happens.

What should you do if your program doesn't work?

If you're new to programming, there's a very good chance that you may have made a small mistake somewhere that prevented the program from running. Here are some things that could have gone wrong:

- If the web browser displays a jumbled list of strange characters, it probably means that your text editor didn't save the file as plain text. Check your text editor's preferences and make sure it's not saving your work in rich text format. Rich text format adds extra formatting codes to the file and prevents the web browser from reading plain JavaScript code.

- The console gave you an error message. If you made a mistake in entering the JavaScript code, it won't work and the console will try and tell you what it thinks is wrong. Carefully check the code you wrote and compare it to the code in this book. Are they the exactly the same? Figure 2-3 shows the error message you'll get if you forget to add the dot between "console" and "log". It will display as **ReferenceError: Can't find variable: consolelog**

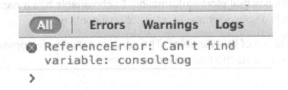

Figure 2-3. A typical error message

As you can see, this error message doesn't actually tell you that you forgot the dot. But it is telling you that it thinks the problem is related to "console.log" so that at least gives you an idea of where you should look in your program for any mistakes.

There are dozens of small mistakes like this that you could make. Each mistake can trigger dozens of different error messages, most of which will be totally incomprehensible to you. It's going to take you a lot of practice, making lots of mistakes, to learn exactly what those error messages are trying to tell you.

For now, just regard an error message as the computer's way of telling you there's a mistake somewhere. It could be anything, anywhere in your program. Go back to your program and triple-check it for small errors. You'll find working examples of all the code in this chapter in the book's source files, so compare those against your own programs if you have any doubts.

At the end of this chapter you'll find a section called "A quick guide to debugging code," which lists many common mistakes you're likely to make and the error messages that they generate. Use that for help if you get badly stuck.

Enough of that, let's learn about programming!

Note: For the sake of simplicity, the examples that follow are pure JavaScript, without the HTML code that surrounds them. To run these examples inside an HTML document, insert the code between the `<script>` *tags using this format:*

`<!doctype html>`

`<title>Example name</title>`

`<script>`

`Add the JavaScript code here`

`</script>`

You'll find all working examples, with the HTML code, in the chapter's source files.

Variables

A variable is like a little box that stores information. Each variable has a name. Whenever you use that name in a program, the variable displays whatever information it contains.

Figure 2-4 is an illustration of two variables. The variable called `name` contains the name of a game player. The variable called `score` contains the player's current score.

Figure 2-4. Variables are boxes that store information

Whenever the words `name` or `score` are used in a program, they'll be replaced by whatever is in those boxes.

You can put a number into a variable like this:

```
score = 1288;
```

The equal sign copies `1288` into a variable called `score`. Now whenever the program sees the word `score`, it will replace it with `1288`.

Variables can also store words, like this:

```
name = "Rex";
```

Just surround the word with quotation marks. If the program now sees the word `name`, it will replace it with `"Rex"`:

If you're using a variable for the first time, you need to create it using a **keyword** called var. Here's how:

```
var score;
```

Keywords are special words that JavaScript understands. `var` tells the program to make a variable called score. It creates the variable. But in the example above, the variable is empty. It doesn't contain a value. If you need to put some information into it, you can now do it like this:

```
score = 128;
```

If you want to create a variable and put information into it at the same time, you can do it like this:

```
var score = 1288;
```

Let's look at some practical examples of how variables work.

Working with numbers

Here's a JavaScript program that displays the value of a variable in the console.

```
var number = 12;
console.log(number);
```

Run this program (open it in a web browser) and you'll see this displayed in the console:

```
12
```

The program first creates a variable called number. It puts 12 into it:

```
var number = 12;
```

You can then use `console.log` to display the value of the variable by inserting the variable between the parentheses:

```
console.log(number);
```

What's important to notice is that it doesn't display the variable's name, which is `number`. It only displays what the variable *contains*. You can put any other value into the variable, like this:

```
var number = 2900;
console.log(number);
```

The console will now display **2900**.

The variable's name can be anything you like. If you change its name to `alarmingStatistic`, it will still display the number **2900**.

```
var alarmingStatistic = 2900;
console.log(alarmingStatistic);
```

The name of the variable is entirely up to you. And now you know how many hippo attacks there are each year too. Be careful on your next trip to the zoo.

A variable can also contain a mathematical calculation, like this:

```
var number = 4 + 6;
console.log(number);
```

The value of `number` will now be displayed as **10**. JavaScript does the math for you.

You can also add variables together. This next example shows how you can assign values to variables, add those variables together, and then display the total in a third variable.

```
var firstNumber = 4;
var secondNumber = 3;
var total = firstNumber + secondNumber;

//Display the total
console.log(total);
```

This displays 7 in the console.

It's easy to see how it works. First, two numbers are assigned to some variables:

```
var firstNumber = 4;
var secondNumber = 3;
```

Those numbers are then added together in a third variable called `total`.

```
var total = firstNumber + secondNumber;
```

This means that the total now has the value of 7.

There's something new in this example that I'm sure you're wondering about. What is this line of code?

```
//Display the total
```

This is a **comment**. Any time you see two forward-slash characters, it means that whatever words come after them on that line shouldn't be run as JavaScript code. Comments are notes that programmers write to themselves to remind themselves what a section of a program does.

If you want to write a longer comment on more than one line, you can surround it with a set of characters that look like this:

```
/*
Whatever is between
this set of characters is a comment
and won't be run as JavaScript code
*/
```

> Note: Because anything inside a comment won't be run as programming code, comments are sometimes used to temporarily disable lines or sections of code for testing how a program runs without them.

You can do more with numbers than just add them together. You can also subtract, multiply, and divide them by using these symbols.

+	add
-	subtract
*	multiply
/	divide
%	Modulus
	Returns the remainder of a division problem. For example:
	5 % 2 = 1
	5 divided by 2 is 4, with 1 remainder. The modulus represents the remainder.

> Note: Don't worry too much about the modulus operator for now, but it will turn out to become surprisingly useful for games, as you'll see later in the book.

These symbols are called **mathematical operators**. Here's an example of a program that shows how each of these operators is used.

```
var firstNumber = 4;
var secondNumber = 3;

//Mathematical operations
var total = firstNumber + secondNumber;
var product = firstNumber * secondNumber;
var quotient = firstNumber / secondNumber;
var difference = firstNumber - secondNumber;

//Display the total
console.log(total);

//Display the product
console.log(product);

//Display the quotient
console.log(quotient);

//Display the difference
console.log(difference);
```

Here's what this program displays in the console:

```
7
12
1.3333333333333333
1
1
```

Notice that decimal places are automatically added to the result of the division operation. You'll learn how to round numbers up or down to the nearest whole number in the next chapter.

Try changing the values of `firstNumber` and `secondNumber` and watch how the results change when you save and run the program again. You're not that far away from building your own calculator.

Working with number variables is easy, and you'll see that it's just as easy to store words in variables as well.

Working with strings

In programming terminology, a "word" is called a "string." This name came about because words are made up of "strings of letters." This is an important term to remember, because computer programmers always use the term "string" when they're talking about words or letters. It's just how they roll. So I'll do the same from now on. String!

A variable can store a string, just as easily as it can store a number. This JavaScript program displays the string "Hungry hippo" in the console.

```
var message = "Hungry hippo";
console.log(message);
```

Strings always have to be surrounded by quotation marks.

You can combine strings into new phrases or sentences by using a plus sign, like this:

```
firstWord + secondWord
```

Here's an example of a program that shows you how this works:

```
var firstWord = "Hungry";
var secondWord = "hippo";
var combinedWords = firstWord + secondWord;

console.log(combinedWords);
```

This displays:

```
Hungryhippo
```

Do you see how the plus sign is used to combine the two strings together, and then copy the result into a new variable?

> Note: Programmers use the term **concatenation** for joining strings together like this.

But you can also see that there's a problem with it. There should be a space between "Hungry" and "hippo". You can solve this by inserting a blank space between the two words, like this:

```
var combinedWords = firstWord + " " + secondWord;
```

The blank space is represented by empty quotation marks that surround one blank space:

```
" "
```

If you make this change to the program it will display the combined words as you would expect:

```
Hungry hippo
```

In JavaScript, a blank space is just an invisible character. You now know almost everything there is to know about numbers, strings, and variables. But there's one more variable type you'll need to know to start making games.

Working with true or false variables

You can also set a variable to be either just true or false. Imagine that you're making a space adventure game where the player has to save the universe from being eaten by a giant, multidimensional wombat. At the beginning of the game, the universe hasn't yet been eaten, obviously. So you could inform the game of this by creating a variable called universeEaten and set it to false.

```
var universeEaten = false;
```

If the player fails to save the universe, you then set the variable to true.

```
universeEaten = true;
```

And the game would end. (Or, if you were a really clever postmodern game designer, continue the game within the wombat's stomach.)

Let's see if this actually works. Here's a program that initializes universeEaten to false, and then sets it to true and displays the result.

```
//Initialize the variable to false when the game starts
var universeEaten = false;

//Change it to true later in the game
universeEaten = true;

//Display its value
console.log(universeEaten);
```

This will display **true** in the console, which is the last value that is set. (Notice also that var is only used once, when the variable is first created.)

True and false values are called **Boolean** values. This name comes from George Boole whose ideas on logic using true and false values formed the basis of modern computer science.

Now that you know how to use variables, let's see how you can use some logic to start making more interesting programs.

Decision making

Most of your games and programs will have to make decisions between things. You'll need a way to figure out if certain numbers are higher or lower than other numbers, as well as whether certain objects are the same or different than other objects.

For example, let's consider a common decision-making problem you encounter in everyday life. You're driving your car off the edge of a cliff to escape a stampeding herd of hippos. If your car has more than 5 liters of rocket fuel, it will be enough fuel for the rocket strapped to the roof to get you to the other side over the plunging canyon. If it has less than 5 liters of rocket fuel, you'll fall short and spiral to your doom in the wombat-infested raging river far below. You can phrase the problem like this:

```
If I have more than 5 liters of fuel,
I'll live.
Otherwise,
I won't live.
```

That's simple enough, isn't it? Here's how that exact same logic looks like in JavaScript code.

```
if(fuel > 5)
{
  live = true;
}
else
{
  live = false;
}
```

This is called an **if statement**. The keyword if checks to see if whatever is in the parentheses is true. If it is true, then the code that's inside the curly braces that follows it runs.

```
if(this thing is true)
{
  then do this;
}
```

You can leave the if statement just like this, or you can add an optional **else statement**. An else statement lets you run some code if whatever the if statement was checking for is false. Here's how:

```
if(this thing is true)
{
  then do this;
}
else
{
  do this;
}
```

If the thing is not true, then the else statement runs the code that's inside its curly braces. It's a simple choice between one thing or another. Let's look at some practical examples.

*Note: Any sections of programming code that are contained within a pair of curly braces is called a **block**. Like this:*

```
{

    All the stuff in here is part of the block

}
```

The code that's inside a block is usually separate from the code from another block, although blocks can share information. You'll see how soon.

Here's a program that checks whether two numbers are the same or different.

```
var firstNumber = 10;
var secondNumber = 12;

if(firstNumber === secondNumber)
{
  console.log("The numbers are the same");
}
else
{
  console.log("The numbers are different");
}
```

This will display "The numbers are different" in the console. If you change `firstNumber` to `12` and run the program again, the console will display "The numbers are the same".

The if statement uses a triple equal sign to check whether the numbers are the same.

```
if(firstNumber === secondNumber)
```

If this is true, then the code that directly follows it inside the braces is run. If it's false, the code inside the else section's braces is run.

You can also use an if statement to check whether a value is greater or lesser than another value. Here's an example:

```
var firstNumber = 10;
var secondNumber = 12;

if(firstNumber > secondNumber)
{
  console.log("The first number is greater");
}
```

```
else
{
  console.log("The second number is greater");
}
```

In this example the console will display "The second number is greater". The if statement uses a greater than symbol, >, to check if the first number is greater than the second one.

```
if(firstNumber > secondNumber)
```

If you change the value of firstNumber to 13 and run the program again, the console will display "The first number is greater".

These symbols, === and >, are called **conditional operators**. Here are the important conditional operators you need to know.

===	Is equal to
!==	Is not equal to
>	Greater than
<	Less than
>=	Greater than or equal to
<=	Less than or equal to

Using only these conditional operators and an if statement, you can create some extremely complex logic for games. This book is full of examples. Let's take a look at another one.

You can use if statements to check whether two strings (words) are the same or different. Here's a simple program that checks whether a cat is the same as a hippo.

```
var firstAnimal = "cat";
var secondAnimal = "hippo";

if(firstAnimal === secondAnimal)
{
  console.log("The animals are the same");
}
else
{
  console.log("The animals are different");
}
```

This will display "The animals are different" in the console.

Checking more conditions

In the previous examples the if statements checked two different things to see if one of them was true. If you want to check more than two things, here's how.

This is an if statement that tries to figure out what kind of animal a "cat" is.

```
var animal = "cat";

if(animal === "horse")
{
   console.log("It's a horse");
}
else if(animal === "mouse")
{
   console.log("It's a mouse");
}
else if(animal === "cat")
{
   console.log("It's a cat");
}
else
{
   console.log("I don't know what it is");
}
```

Notice the extra else if statements in there that check for more conditions. This program will display "It's a cat" when you run it. If you change the value of the animal variable to "mouse", it will display "It's a mouse". If you change the animal variable to something the program doesn't understand, like "giraffe", it will display "I don't know what it is".

Let's break this down so that you can clearly see how it's working. Start with a simple if statement like this:

```
var animal = "cat";

if(animal === "cat")
{
   console.log("It's a cat");
}
else
{
   console.log("I don't know what it is");
}
```

This is easy. The console will display "It's a cat". If you change the value of animal to anything else, it will display "I don't know what it is".

Now imagine that you also want to check whether the animal might be a mouse. You can do this by inserting an **else if statement** to check for this. Here's what the else if statement would look like, highlighted in bold:

```
var animal = "cat";

if(animal === "cat")
{
  console.log("It's a cat");
}
else if(animal === "mouse")
{
  console.log("It's a mouse");
}
else
{
  console.log("I don't know what it is");
}
```

You can see that the middle else if statement checks for another specific condition, just as the first if statement does. If the value of animal is "mouse", this program will display "It's a mouse" in the console.

You can squeeze in as many else if statements as you like, to check for as many conditions as you need to. The final else statement in the chain will run if none of the other conditions are true. That's called the **default condition**. It's optional. You could leave that final else statement out entirely if you wanted to, like this:

```
var animal = "cat";

if(animal === "cat")
{
  console.log("It's a cat");
}
else if(animal === "mouse")
{
  console.log("It's a mouse");
}
```

In this example, if the value of animal isn't "cat" or "mouse," nothing will happen. That's just fine.

This is where logic starts to get complex and interesting. But you can see the rules are really quite simple. Keep it simple like this, and you'll be a happy programmer.

Using a switch statement

Complex if statements like the one in the example above are very common, and you'll be using them all the time in your game projects. They're so common that JavaScript gives you an alternative way to write them, which can be slightly easier to read. It's called a **switch statement**.

Here's a switch statement that does exactly the same thing as the if statement we just looked at:

```
var animal = "cat";

switch(animal)
{
  case "horse":
    console.log("It's a horse");
    break;

  case "mouse":
    console.log("It's a mouse");
    break;

  case "cat":
    console.log("It's a cat");
    break;

  default:
    console.log("I don't know what it is");
}
```

The result is the same as the previous if statement: the console will display "It's a cat". Here's how the switch statement works.

Use the switch keyword and follow it with the thing that you want to check for in parentheses.

```
switch(animal)
```

The body of the switch statement is inside a pair of curly braces.

```
switch(animal)
{
    ...the body of the switch statement goes here
}
```

Inside the curly braces you then check each case that you want to test for, like this:

```
case "horse":
  console.log("It's a horse");
  break;
```

If "horse" matches the value of animal, then the console will display "It's a horse". It will also run a break directive:

```
break;
```

This stops the program for checking any other cases, and the switch statement quits. You can add as many cases as you like, and each case can contain as many directives as you like. But you must remember that each case needs to end with a break directive:

```
case "horse":
  console.log("It's a horse");
  break;

case "mouse":
  console.log("It's a mouse");
  break;

case "cat":
  console.log("It's a cat");
  break;
```

> Note: Don't forget that break statement! It's a very common mistake to leave it out, and, if you do, your program won't run the way you expect it to. If any of your programs are behaving strangely and you can't figure out why, double-check that you haven't left out a break somewhere.

Notice that all the directives inside each case are indented by two spaces and that a blank line separates each case. These are visual cues to show you how each case is separated.

Switch statements also use an optional default case, which runs if there are no matches.

```
default:
  console.log("I don't know what it is");
```

> Note: The computer-y word **default** just means "the thing that will happen if nothing else happens." It's like when you order pizza and watch a video if all your friends are busy on Saturday night.

It's up to you to decide whether you want to use a chain of if statements or a switch statement. Figure 2-5 is a side-by-side comparison. They do exactly the same thing if the condition they're checking for is the same for all cases. There's no technical reason for using one over the other: the only difference is the way they look. Which do you prefer?

if

```
var animal = "cat";

if(animal === "horse")
{
  console.log("It's a horse");
}
else if(animal === "mouse")
{
  console.log("It's a mouse");
}
else if(animal === "cat")
{
  console.log("It's a cat");
}
else
{
  console.log("I don't know what it is");
}
```

switch

```
var animal = "cat";

switch(animal)
{
  case "horse":
    console.log("It's a horse");
    break;

  case "mouse":
    console.log("It's a mouse");
    break;

  case "cat":
    console.log("It's a cat");
    break;

  default:
    console.log("I don't know what it is");
}
```

Figure 2-5. The if statement and the switch statement do the same thing. Use whichever you like

In this book I use switch statements because they're easier to read in the context of a complex program.

Using && and ||

Sometimes you'll want something to happen only if more than one condition is true. You can use the **and operator** to check two or more conditions at the same time, and it will perform an action if they're both true. The and operator is a double ampersand sign:

&&

You use it with an if statement like this:

```
if(thisIsTrue && thisIsAlsoTrue)
{
  ... do these things
}
```

Imagine that you're creating an adventure game that will end only if both the spell is broken *and* the witch is dead. You could check whether the game is over like this:

```
var spellIsBroken = true;
var witchIsDead = true;

if(spellIsBroken && witchIsDead)
{
  console.log("Game Over!");
}
```

```
else
{
    console.log("Keep playing...");
}
```

If *both* the variables `spellIsBroken` and `witchIsDead` are `true`, then the console will display "Game Over!" But if either one of them is set to `false`, the console will display "Keep playing ..." Both variables need to be `true` for the game to finish.

Sometimes you'll want to perform an action if one thing *or* another is true. In that case you use the or operator, which looks like this:

```
||
```

It's a double *pipe symbol*. You'll find the pipe symbol (a straight vertical line) on your keyboard somewhere if you look closely enough. It's often on the same key as the backslash character, which in a lot of cases is under your Backspace or Delete key.

You use the or operator like this:

```
if(thisIsTrue || thisIsTrue)
{
    ... do these things
}
```

Only one of those things needs to be true, not both.

Let's imagine that you've changed the rules of your adventure game to make it a bit easier. Players can win if the spell is broken *or* the witch is dead. They don't have to complete both tasks. You could use an or operator to check for this condition:

```
var spellIsBroken = true;
var witchIsDead = false;

if(spellIsBroken || witchIsDead)
{
    console.log("Game Over!");
}
else
{
    console.log("Keep playing...");
}
```

If either `spellIsBroken` or `witchIsDead` is true, the console will display "Game Over!" Either of them can be true, it doesn't matter which. But if they are *both* `false`, the console will display "Keep playing ..."

You can see that using && and || can give you a lot of fine control over game logic.

Using functions

If your program has some specialized work to do, it's often a good idea to create a **function**. You can put that work into a function to keep it separated from the rest of your program. Whenever you need that work done, you just have to call the function.

Creating and using a function is a two-step process. You first have to **define** it. Defining a function is like setting it up for the first time. Once it's defined, you have to **call** it. This is like telling your program to do the things you set up in the function.

You define a function like this:

```
function theFunctionName()
{
    ... any work your want the function to do
}
```

Use the keyword `function`, then write the function's name. Its name can be anything you like, but you have to follow it with empty parentheses. Inside the curly braces, enter in all the work that you want the function to do. This is called a **function definition**.

Whenever you want the function to do its work, you **call** it. Just write the name of the function, followed by parentheses, and a semicolon.

```
theFunctionName();
```

That will tell the function to start working. Whatever programming code you inserted between the function definition's curly braces will then run.

It's easier to understand this with a practical example. Here's a program that uses a function to add two numbers.

```
var firstNumber = 4;
var secondNumber = 3;

add();

function add()
{
    var total = firstNumber + secondNumber;
    console.log(total);
}
```

This displays 7 in the console.

Let's break this down into smaller pieces. First, take a look at the function definition.

```
function add()
{
  var total = firstNumber + secondNumber;
  console.log(total);
}
```

It's adding the numbers together and copying the result into its own new variable called `total`. It then displays the value of `total` in the console. That's why 7 is displayed.

> Note: Because the variable called `total` is declared inside the function, it can be used in this function only. The rest of the program can't see it. Any variables that you create inside a function are invisible to the rest of the program. These are known as **local variables**.
>
> Also, because `firstNumber` and `secondNumber` are declared outside the function, the function can use them. They can also be used by any other function. They're called **global variables**, because they can be used anywhere in the program.

But the function will only do its work of adding and displaying the numbers if it's called. That's what this line does:

```
add();
```

It tells the `add` function to start working. If this line wasn't in our program, the function definition wouldn't run its code.

> Note: You'll also notice that it doesn't matter that the function is defined after it's called. The function definition just needs to be somewhere in the program. So where should you put it?
>
> You'll make your programs easier to read if you keep all the function definitions at the end of the program. That's because they tend to do a lot of repetitive work and you'll rarely need to look at them again after you've written them. This will keep all the important logic that uses these functions in one place near the top of your program. That's where you'll be doing most of your creative programming work.

By assigning specific jobs to functions, you make your programs easier to manage by modularizing them. If you know that a particular function does a specific job, you'll know where to look to make changes or fix things in your program.

Functions with extra information

You might be wondering why functions have empty parentheses after their names. This is so that you can give the function some extra information to do its work.

Here's a simple example of how to create a function with some extra information. This is a function that will display the word "Hello" in the console. The word "Hello" is sent to the function through the function's parentheses.

```
displayAnything("Hello");

function displayAnything(thingToDisplay)
{
  console.log(thingToDisplay);
}
```

When this program runs, "Hello" appears in the console.

Here's how this works. First, the word "Hello" is inserted into the function call's parentheses.

```
displayAnything("Hello");
```

You can think of the parentheses as a giant mouth or as a wormhole to another universe. It's swallowing "Hello" and sending it directly to the function definition's parentheses:

```
function displayAnything(thingToDisplay)
{...
```

The function automatically copies "Hello" into a variable called thingToDisplay. This variable is now automatically declared for you, and you can use it anywhere in the function. Now, whenever the function uses thingToDisplay, it will replace it with "Hello".

```
function displayAnything(thingToDisplay)
{
  console.log(thingToDisplay);
}
```

Do you see it?

As far as the function is concerned, the code it's running looks like this:

```
console.log("Hello");
```

That's why it's displaying "Hello".

If you are new to programming, you may find this confusing. Take a good look at Figure 2-6. It illustrates how "Hello" is being transferred to the function definition to be processed. Or, if you like the giant mouth analogy, it shows how it's being, um, digested.

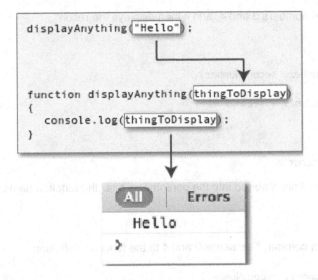

Figure 2-6. "Hello" is sent to the function, which displays it in the console

Why is this useful? Because you can replace the word "Hello" with any other information you like, and the function definition will display it. You don't need to make any changes to the code inside the function definition. Here's an example. Replace "Hello" with "You can send anything to the function":

```
displayAnything("You can send anything to the function");

function displayAnything(thingToDisplay)
{
  console.log(thingToDisplay);
}
```

This displays "You can send anything to the function". You'll see that this is much more useful if you have a more complex function.

Functions with multiple arguments

The extra information that you send to a function through its parentheses is called an **argument**. This is an important term to know, because all programmers use it, and you'll see it used in every book on computer programming and game design. In the previous example, we sent one argument to the function: "Hello". You can send more than one argument to a function. Just separate the arguments with commas. Let's look at a simple example of how this works.

This program adds the numbers 3 and 4, and it then displays the result:

```
add(3, 4);

function add(firstNumber, secondNumber)
{
  var total = firstNumber + secondNumber;
  console.log(total);
}
```

This displays 7 in the console.

You can see that 3 and 4 are inserted into the parenthesis after the function name:

```
add(3, 4);
```

They're separated by a comma. This sends 3 and 4 to the function definition:

```
function add(firstNumber, secondNumber)
{ ...
```

They're copied into variables called firstNumber and secondNumber. Now, whenever the function uses firstNumber, it will replace it with 3. Whenever it uses secondNumber, it will replace it with 4.

```
function add(firstNumber, secondNumber)
{
  var total = firstNumber + secondNumber;
  console.log(total);
}
```

As far as the function is concerned, the code it's running looks like this:

```
  var total = 3 + 4;
  console.log(total);
```

That's why its displaying 7.

Figure 2-7 illustrates how this works.

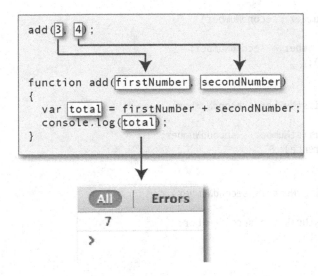

Figure 2-7. You can send more than one argument to a function

This is now something really useful. You've created your own little addition calculator. You can replace 3 and 4 with any two numbers, and the function will add them together and display the result. Put the numbers 10 and 32 into the function call's parentheses and run the program again:

```
add(10, 32);
```

The console will now display 42. You didn't need to change the function definition at all, only the information you gave it. Do you now see how useful this could be?

The calculator function

You now know enough about JavaScript to create your own little calculator. Try to create four functions that add, subtract, multiply, and divide two numbers. Your function calls should look like this:

```
add(12, 6);
subtract(67, 45);
multiply(34, 26);
divide(100, 5);
```

What will your four matching function definitions look like? Try and work this out for yourself; you'll learn a lot if you can figure this out on your own. But if you get stuck, here's a completed calculator program that does just this.

```
add(12, 6);
subtract(67, 45);
multiply(34, 26);
divide(100, 5);
```

```
function add(firstNumber, secondNumber)
{
  var total = firstNumber + secondNumber;
  console.log(total);
}

function subtract(firstNumber, secondNumber)
{
  var difference = firstNumber - secondNumber;
  console.log(difference);
}

function multiply(firstNumber, secondNumber)
{
  var product = firstNumber * secondNumber;
  console.log(product);
}

function divide(firstNumber, secondNumber)
{
  var quotient = firstNumber / secondNumber;
  console.log(quotient);
}
```

See, it really is as easy as you thought it was!

Functions that return values

There's one more important feature about functions that you should know about. You can make functions return a value directly back to the main program. Here's an example:

```
var total = add(4, 4);

console.log(total);

function add(firstNumber, secondNumber)
{
  var sum = firstNumber + secondNumber;
  return sum;
}
```

This displays 8 in the console. Can you figure out why?

Yes, this is a bit of a head-swirler! So let's break this down so you can see what's happening.

The program creates a variable called total:

```
var total
```

But total isn't just given an ordinary value, like a number or a string. The value of total is *the add function*:

```
var total = add(4, 4);
```

That means the *result* of the add function is going to be copied into total. The total variable actually gets the value "8".

```
var total = 8;
```

This works because of the keyword return in the function definition (highlighted below):

```
function add(firstNumber, secondNumber)
{
  var sum = firstNumber + secondNumber;
  return sum;
}
```

return tells the function to *return the value of a variable* back to the main program. In this case it's returning the value of its own variable, sum, which equals 4 plus 4.

It's a circular journey, which you can best see illustrated in Figure 2-8.

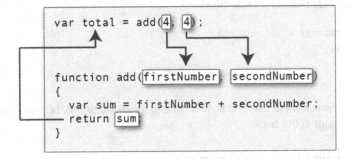

Figure 2-8. A function can return the value of a function back to the main program. In this example, it sends the number "8" back to the total

A good way to practice using return functions is to re-write the calculator you programmed in the previous section. Create functions that return the result of the calculations back to the main program, like this example does. If you get stuck, you'll find a working example of this in the chapter's source files called returnFunctionCalculator.html.

All three styles of functions we've just looked at can produce the same result, and often it won't be clear which is the best one to use. With a bit of practice and a little more experience, you'll begin to realize which style of writing functions is going to be useful for whatever program you're working on. You'll see all these styles used in lots of different contexts in this book.

Function expressions

You can create functions using an alternative syntax. It looks like this:

```
var functionName = function(arguments)
{
  //The code you want the function to run
};
```

You call the function in the same way, like this:

```
functionName(arguments);
```

This style of writing functions is called a **function expression**. It assigns the function to a variable. It works in the same way as a normal function, except now you can use the function like a variable as well. Apart from this, there are two important differences:

- You have to define a function expression before you call it.
- There's a semicolon after the last brace.

Here's a function expression that adds two numbers:

```
var add = function(firstNumber, secondNumber)
{
  var total = firstNumber + secondNumber;
  console.log(total);
};
add(4, 4);
```

It's up to you whether you want to use this style of writing functions or not, but we'll see some specific uses for function expressions later in the book.

Controlling HTML and CSS

JavaScript can control all the elements in an HTML document. It can also change CSS styles or create new styles. You can also use JavaScript to program buttons that read user input from a textfield. You can then use that input in your program. If you know how to do this, it's the first and most important step to starting to build games and applications. Let's find out how.

Creating new text in an HTML element

In the previous examples I used `console.log` to display the results of our test programs in the JavaScript console. This is great for testing how your programs are working, but wouldn't it be better if you could display the result directly in the web browser? That's easy to do.

All HTML elements have a property called `innerHTML`. The `innerHTML` property represents the text that's between a pair of opening and closing tags.

```
<p>All this stuff between the tags is the innerHTML</p>
```

You can access the innerHTML of any element by using JavaScript. Here's how it works.

Imagine that you've got an empty HTML element with an id called output.

```
<p id="output"></p>
```

JavaScript first needs to know that output is referring to the element's id. You use a built-in JavaScript method called document.querySelector to do this:

```
document.querySelector("#output");
```

It searches through the HTML document until it finds an element with the id output.

The next step is to store this information in a variable. You can give the variable any name you like, but it's simplest just to give it the same name as the id of the element you're looking for. Here's how to assign the element to a variable called output.

```
var output = document.querySelector("#output");
```

This new output variable now directly refers to the `<p id="output">` tag in the HTML document. It's what connects the HTML code to the JavaScript code.

> Note: This shows you that variables can store more than just a numbers, strings, or true/false values. You can store almost anything in a variable, as you'll see in many more examples in this book.

You can now use this variable to change what the element is displaying with innerHTML like this:

```
output.innerHTML = "Hello World!";
```

Now the element will display "Hello World!" directly in the web browser. The HTML code has actually been changed by JavaScript so that it looks like this:

```
<p id="output">Hello World!</p>
```

It's a neat trick. You won't see this change in your code, but it's happening invisibly behind the scenes in the web browser. Let's look at a real live HTML document that shows exactly how this works.

```
<!doctype html>
<title>Display HTML text</title>

<p id="output"></p>

<script>

var output = document.querySelector("#output");
output.innerHTML = "Hello World!";

</script>
```

As you would expect, this HTML document displays "Hello World!" The text has been added to the empty <p> tag just using JavaScript.

In this example I used document.querySelector to find an element with a specific id. You can also use it to find a specific class. Just replace the hash symbol, #, with a dot. Here's how you would find a class called button:

```
document.querySelector(".button");
```

This is the same as in CSS: A hash refers to an id, and a dot refers to a class. You can refer to HTML tags directly by just using the tag name, without a hash or a dot. Here's how you could find the <body> tag:

```
document.querySelector("body");
```

> Note: If you have more than one tag with the same name in your HTML document, such as lots of <p> tags, document.querySelector will just find the first one. To find all of the tags with the same name, you can use document.querySelectorAll. It will give you a list of all the tags in the HTML document with the same name. The list will be in a format called an **array**. You'll find out how to use arrays in Chapter 4 if this is ever something you'll need to do, but don't worry about this now.

Changing CSS with JavaScript

You can use JavaScript to change any element's CSS styles. Here's a simple example. The JavaScript code in this HTML document changes the style of the words "Hello World!" It makes them red, 50 pixels in height, and underlined. Can you see how?

```
<!doctype html>
<title>Change CSS</title>

<p class="example">Hello World!</p>

<script>

var example = document.querySelector(".example");
example.style.color = "red";
example.style.fontSize = "50px";
example.style.textDecoration = "underline";

</script>
```

This works in very much the same way as the previous examples. First, document.querySelector is used to find an element with the class name example.

```
var example = document.querySelector(".example");
```

It's copied into a variable also called example.

Next, the CSS styles are changed by using this format:

```
example.style.anyCSSproperty = "value";
```

This is code that changes the element's style:

```
example.style.color = "red";
example.style.fontSize = "50px";
example.style.textDecoration = "underline";
```

Notice that all the style values are surrounded by quotation marks. These values are the same as any values you would give to style properties in CSS code.

The names of the CSS properties are also the same as any ordinary CSS properties. If you want to change a font color, just use the CSS color property, like this:

```
example.style.color = "red";
```

The only difference in property names is with properties that are composed of more than one word. In CSS, this is the property that affects font size:

```
font-size
```

In JavaScript, that same property is written like this:

```
fontSize
```

The dash between the words is removed and the second word is capitalized. All CSS properties that use a dash to separate words are written like this in JavaScript.

Just keep this simple format in mind and you can change any element's CSS properties with JavaScript.

Being able to change CSS with JavaScript is really useful for games because it means you can change the styles of HTML elements interactively, depending on how a player is playing the game. You'll soon see how.

Creating and removing HTML elements

You can use JavaScript to create and remove HTML elements. Here's an example of how to add a `<p>` element into the body of a document and then add some text to it.

```
<!doctype html>
<title>Creating HTML elements</title>

<body></body>

<script>
```

```
var p = document.createElement("p");
document.body.appendChild(p);
p.innerHTML = "Hello World!";

</script>
```

This creates a <p> tag containing the words "Hello World!" If you could see the HTML code that it produces, it would look like this:

```
<body>
  <p>Hello World!</p>
</body>
```

When the HTML document first loads, it's blank. It just contains an empty <body> tag.

```
<body></body>
```

The JavaScript code uses a method called document.createElement to create a new <p> tag, like this:

```
document.createElement("p");
```

Assign it to a variable called p:

```
var p = document.createElement("p");
```

The next step is to place this newly created <p> tag into the document somewhere. A method called appendChild lets you add this new tag into an already existing element. In this case you want to add the <p> tag into the existing <body> tag. Here's how to use appendChild to do this:

```
document.body.appendChild(p);
```

This is what the new HTML document will now look like:

```
<body><p></p></body>
```

The last step is to add some text into the <p> tag. This is easy to do with the innerHTML property:

```
p.innerHTML = "Hello World!";
```

The HTML document will now look like this:

```
<body><p>Hello World!</p></body>
```

If you need to give your new element an id or class name, you can use the setAttribute method. Here's how to give the <p> element the id name example:

```
p.setAttribute("id", "example");
```

Your new HTML document will now look like this:

```
<body><p id="example">Hello World!</p></body>
```

You can create a new class for an element just as easily. Here's how to use `setAttribute` to create a new class for the `<p>` element:

```
p.setAttribute("class", "anyClassName");
```

Use this same format to add any attribute you might need.

Removing HTML elements

In a game you might have a situation where you have to remove an element. For example, if a missile hits a spaceship, you'll want to remove the spaceship from the game. To remove any HTML element, use the `parentNode.removeChild` method. Here's how to use it to remove the `<p>` tag we just created:

```
p.parentNode.removeChild(p);
```

The `parentNode` is the element that's enclosing the `<p>` tag. In this case, the `parentNode` is the `<body>` element. So this code is actually telling the `<body>` element to remove the `<p>` tag. The reason for this is that elements aren't allowed to remove themselves; instead, only the elements that enclose them can remove them.

Yes, this is very confusing, roundabout logic, but don't let that worry you. Just follow this format to remove elements, and everything will be A-OK. It works!

Clicking on buttons

You can create a button with HTML and then use JavaScript to make something happen when the button is clicked. This is the first step in building interactive games and applications.

To make this work, you need to use a special function called an **event listener**. An event listener will "listen" for something happening in your program. You can attach an event listener to a button so that something happens when you click on it.

The easiest way to understand how this works is with a practical example. In the chapter's source file you'll find an HTML file called `eventListener.html`. Open it in a web browser, and make sure that the JavaScript console is open so that you can read `console.log` messages. You'll see a button with the label "click me". Click on the button and the words "Button clicked" will be displayed in the console.

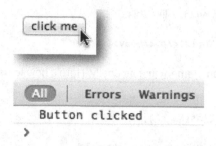

Figure 2-9. Click the button to display a message in the console

Here's the HTML code that makes this work. I'll explain how all of it works in detail:

```html
<!doctype html>
<title>Event listener</title>

<button>click me</button>

<script>

var button = document.querySelector("button");
button.addEventListener("click", clickHandler, false);

function clickHandler()
{
  console.log("Button clicked");
}

</script>
```

The HTML code is very simple: it just creates a `<button>` element, which is what you see as the button in the browser.

```html
<button>click me</button>
```

We need to know when the button is clicked. So the JavaScript code adds something called an **event listener** to the button. When the button is clicked, the event listener runs a function called `clickHandler` that displays the message in the console.

```javascript
var button = document.querySelector("button");
button.addEventListener("click", clickHandler, false);

function clickHandler()
{
  console.log("Button clicked");
}
```

Can you see how it works? Let's break this down into smaller steps.

The first thing the JavaScript code does is to use `document.querySelector` to find the button element and copy it into a variable, also called `button`.

```
var button = document.querySelector("button");
```

We now have a variable that references the HTML button. We can use this variable to start controlling the button with JavaScript code. We can attach an event listener to it to listen for mouse clicks.

This is done with a special method called `addEventListener`. The event listener will listen for a "click" on the button.

```
button.addEventListener("click", clickHandler, false);
```

You can see that the `addEventListener` method is attached to the button variable with a dot. In the parentheses are three arguments.

```
("click", clickHandler, false)
```

What do they do?

`"click"` tells the event listener that it should be listening for button clicks. `clickHandler` is the name of a function that should run when the button is clicked:

```
function clickHandler()
{
  console.log("Button clicked");
}
```

Now whenever the button is clicked, this function will run. That's why the words "Button clicked" appear in the console. A neat trick, isn't it?

> *Note: The last argument is "false".*
>
> *("click", clickHandler, **false**)*
>
> *What does it mean? The short answer is that you don't need to worry about why it's there, but you should always remember to add "false" as the last argument. But if you must know, here's the long answer: it determines whether the event is dispatched in the **capture phase** (true) or the **bubble phase** (false). These phases are part of the process that creates and listens for events in programs. This is a technical detail that you won't need to worry about for any of the projects in this book. And you will possibly never need to worry about it ever. You may only want to do some further research into this if you're trying to listen for events on elements that are inside other elements and you're getting some unexpected results.*

Functions that do the work for an event listener are called **event handlers**. They "handle" the event. That's why the name of this function is clickHandler. "click" is the event, and by adding the word "Handler" you know that this is a function that deals with button clicks. You can give these functions any name you like, but by following this simple naming convention you'll always know what the function is supposed to do. You'll see that all the functions that handle events in this book are named using the word "Handler."

You can see that there's a very close relationship between addEventListener and the function that runs when the button is clicked. Figure 2-10 illustrates this in greater detail.

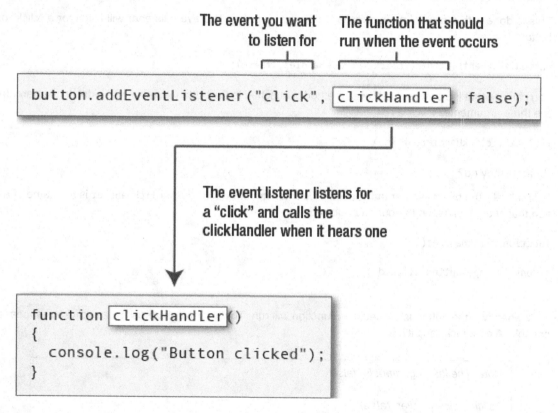

Figure 2-10. An event listener runs a special function called an event handler when the button is clicked

In this example, the event listener is waiting for a "click" event. That happens when the left mouse button is released. But there are many other mouse events that elements can listen for, and they are shown in this chart.

Mouse event	When does it happen?
mousedown	When the left mouse button is pressed down over an element.
mouseup	When the left mouse button is released over an element.
click	When the left mouse button is both pressed down and then released over the same element.

(continued)

Mouse event	When does it happen?
dblclick	When the mouse double-clicks an element.
mousemove	When the mouse is being moved.
mouseover	When the mouse is moved onto an element.
mouseout	When the mouse moves off of an element.

You can replace "click" with any of these events in the example code to observe the effect it has. For example, if you want a button to react when the mouse button is pressed down (but not released), use the "mousedown" event.

```
button.addEventListener("mousedown", clickHandler, false);
```

These mouse events in the table will work with any HTML elements, not just buttons. All these events are built into JavaScript. Make sure you spell them correctly if you use them, because if you make a small typo, they won't work, but you won't get an error message telling you that you've made a typo.

Note: JavaScript also makes it possible to combine the event listener and handler in a single block of code, like this:

```
button.addEventListener("click", function()

{

    console.log("Button clicked");

}, false);
```

Look carefully and you'll notice that after "click" is a function. This function contains the code that should run when the button is clicked. The whole function is actually the event listener's second argument. That means you still have to add the third argument, false, after the function. Consider using this format if the function doesn't need to be used by other listeners, and you know your program won't ever need to remove it.

Removing an event listener

If you want to stop listening for an event, you can remove it with a method called removeEventListener. Here's code you can use to remove the "click" event listener from the button in the example we just looked at.

```
button.removeEventListener("click", clickHandler, false);
```

How could this be useful? Let's imagine that you have a game where you only want the player to be able to press a button once, and never again. You could disable the button by removing the listener after the first click. Here's how you could do this in our example program. Add this new line of code to the click handler:

```
function clickHandler()
{
  console.log("Button clicked");
  button.removeEventListener("click", clickHandler, false);
}
```

If you now run the program, you'll see that the words "Button clicked" will only be displayed once. If you click the button again, the words won't be displayed.

If you want to make the button disappear completely, use JavaScript to set its CSS display property to none, like this:

```
button.style.display = "none";
```

Here's how you could use this code in the clickHandler:

```
function clickHandler()
{
  console.log("Button clicked");
  button.removeEventListener("click", clickHandler, false);
  button.style.display = "none";
}
```

The button will now disappear from the browser window after it's been clicked.

Setting an element's CSS display property to none is often a better alternative to using removeChild to get rid of it, which is what we used in the previous section. That's because, even if its display property is none, the element will still exist. So if you want to make it visible again you just need to set its display property to block, rather than having to recreate it from scratch.

Now that you know how to make a button, let's use one to demonstrate another very important programming technique.

Counting

Something you'll want to do in your games is incrementally change the values of variables. For example, you might want to add 1 to a score each time a player does something right. If the score was 7, you might want to update it to 8. Here's a simple example that shows how you can do this. Each time the button is clicked, 1 is added to the value of score.

```
//Access the button
var button = document.querySelector("button");
button.addEventListener("click", clickHandler, false);
```

```
//Create a score variable and initialize it to zero

var score = 0;
console.log(score);

function clickHandler()
{
  score = score + 1;
  console.log(score);
}
```

The first thing the program does is create a `score` variable and set its initial value to zero.

```
var score = 0;
```

Giving a variable its first value when a program loads is called **initializing** it. Initializing variables is usually the first thing your programs will do.

When the button is clicked, the `clickHandler` runs. It adds 1 to the current value of the score:

```
score = score + 1;
```

This directive runs every time the button is clicked. On the second click, `score` becomes 2, and on the third click, it becomes 3. Why is that? If you're new to programming, this can be very confusing, so let's break it down into smaller steps.

This is what the directive is saying:

The score's new value is the value of whatever the score currently is, plus one.

Remember that the score is initialized to 0 when the program first loads. That means that the first time the program runs, you can interpret this directive like this:

```
score = 0 + 1;
```

0 + 1 is 1, so 1 is *copied back into* the score variable. That means the score will now be 1.

What happens the second time the button is clicked? Because the score has been changed to 1, you can now interpret the directive like this:

```
score = 1 + 1;
```

`score` will now have a new value of 2.

On the third guess, the score will still be 2. So the directive is interpreted like this:

```
score = 2 + 1;
```

`score` will now be 3. Do you see the pattern? It's a very simple way of adding values to a variable to keep count.

Using variables to count like this is so common that JavaScript has a shorthand way of doing it by using the special **increment** and **decrement** operators:

```
+=
-=
```

Here's how you can use an increment operator to add 1 to the score:

```
score += 1;
```

This is the same as writing `score = score + 1`. One is being added to the current value of the score. You can subtract 1 from `score` with the decrement operator, like this:

```
score -= 1;
```

Try changing the example program so that the click operator uses the += operator to add 1 to the `score`, like this:

```
function clickHandler()
{
  score += 1;
  console.log(score);
}
```

You can see that the result is the same.

You can add or subtract any number from a variable like this. Here's how to use a += operator to increase `score` by 5 each time the button is clicked.

```
function clickHandler()
{
  score += 5;
  console.log(score);
}
```

If you save and run the program again, you'll see that the console displays: 0, 5, 10, 15, and so on. This produces the same result as if you wrote:

```
score = score + 5;
```

But if you just want to add or subtract 1 from a variable, JavaScript has an even simpler way of doing it. You can use the special **postfix operators**:

```
++
--
```

To add 1 to the score, you can use the double plus sign, like this:

```
score++
```

To subtract one from it, use the double minus sign:

```
score--
```

Try using the double plus sign to add 1 to the score in the `clickHandler`:

```
function clickHandler()
{
  score++;
  console.log(score);
}
```

Incrementally changing the values of variables like this is something all your games will do, and you'll see many more examples of this throughout the book.

Detecting keyboard key presses

There are also some hidden things that you can control with JavaScript that aren't HTML elements. We've seen one of these hidden things already: the **document object**. It contains the method called `querySelector` that we used to help us find an element we were looking for.

```
document.querySelector()
```

JavaScript also lets you access a **window object**. You can use the window object to access or change properties of the browser window. You can also attach an event listener to the window object so that you can detect when certain keys are being pressed. This is very useful for entering text into a program by pressing the Enter key or for moving game objects with the keyboard's arrow keys.

Let's look at an example of how you can use the window object to detect whether someone is pressing the Enter key. In the chapter's source files you'll find a file called **enterKey.html**. Open it in a web browser with the console open. Press the Enter key. You'll see the message "Enter key pressed" displayed in the console. Here's the code that makes this work:

```
window.addEventListener("keydown", keydownHandler, false);

function keydownHandler(event)
{
  if(event.keyCode === 13)
  {
    console.log("Enter key pressed");
  }
}
```

You can see from the first line that the event listener is attached to the `window` object with a dot (showing that it's a **method** of the `window` object—more on that later):

```
window.addEventListener("keydown", keydownHandler, false);
```

The event that it's listening for is called keydown, which detects when any keys are being pressed. If it detects a key press, it calls the keydownHandler.

```
function keydownHandler(event)
{
  if(event.keyCode === 13)
  {
    console.log("Enter key pressed");
  }
}
```

All keys have key code numbers attached to them. The Enter key's key code is 13. An if statement checks whether the key code matches 13.

```
if(event.keyCode === 13)
{
  console.log("Enter key pressed");
}
```

If it does, it means the Enter key was pressed, and so the message is displayed in the console.

There's one slightly odd thing about this function that you haven't seen before. It includes the word "event" in the parentheses:

```
function keydownHandler(event)
{ ...
```

This is because the keydown event sends the function some extra information about the key that's being pressed. The function needs somewhere to store that information, so it uses a variable called event to store it. The information that it stores is the key code that represents the key being pressed. You can access the key code like this:

```
event.keyCode
```

In this example event.keyCode equals 13, which indicates the Enter key.

Don't worry too much if you find this slightly confusing right now. You'll see many more examples of how event handlers use extra information about the event like this throughout the rest of the book. For now, just remember that this is what your JavaScript code should look like if you want your program to react to a key press.

> Note: The key code numbers are all based on ASCII (American Standard Code for Information Interchange). A web search for ASCII character codes will bring up a complete list of the codes for all the keys on the keyboard.

You now know how to use the window object's keydown event to listen for when a key is pressed down. If you want to detect when a key is released, you can use the keyup event.

Let's now take what we've learned in this chapter and put it all together to make a simple user interface that you're going to find a lot of use for in the first part of this book.

Entering and displaying text

Games are all about interactivity. They're about the interactivity between the player and the evil genius that is your game. The player needs to do something, and your game needs to react to it. This means that you need some way of getting information into the game from the player. HTML provides a very simple way to do this with the `<input>` element. In this section I'll show you how to use it to let players enter information into a game or program.

In the chapter's source files you'll find a program called **enteringText.html**. It lets you enter some text into a textfield. When you click the button, the text you entered is displayed below the textfield. Figure 2-11 shows what you'll see. It's a simple interface, but as you'll see it's the first step to making an interactive game.

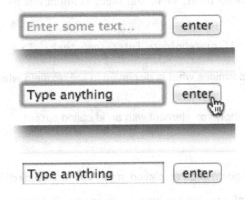

Figure 2-11. Enter some text, click the button, and the text is displayed

Here's the HTML and JavaScript code that makes this work:

```
<!doctype html>
<title>Entering and displaying text</title>

<input id="input" type="text" placeholder="Enter some text...">
<button>enter</button>
<p id="output"></p>

<script>

var button = document.querySelector("button");
button.addEventListener("click", clickHandler, false);
button.style.cursor = "pointer";
```

```
function clickHandler()
{
  var input = document.querySelector("#input");
  var output = document.querySelector("#output");
  output.innerHTML = input.value;
}

</script>
```

The HTML creates the textfield, the button, and an empty `<p>` element.

```
<input id="input" type="text" placeholder="Enter some text...">
<button>enter</button>
<p id="output"></p>
```

The textfield is an element called `input`. When the `input` element has its type attribute set to "text", you can type something into it.

```
<input id="input" type="text" placeholder="Enter some text...">
```

The `placeholder` attribute determines what is displayed in the textfield when it's first created, as you can see in Figure 2-11.

The HTML also contains an empty `<p>` element with an id called `output`.

```
<p id="output"></p>
```

The output of this program is going to be displayed in this `<p>` tag's `innerHTML`.

The JavaScript code gets a reference to the button with `querySelector`, and it then adds a click event listener to it.

```
var button = document.querySelector("button");
button.addEventListener("click", clickHandler, false);
```

But it also makes a change to the button's CSS. It changes its `cursor` property to `pointer`.

```
button.style.cursor = "pointer";
```

This makes the button appear as a pointing hand when the mouse is over it, as you can see in Figure 2-11.

When the button is clicked, the `clickHandler` is called.

```
function clickHandler()
{
  var input = document.querySelector("#input");
  var output = document.querySelector("#output");
  output.innerHTML = input.value;
}
```

It gets a reference to the input textfield and also the empty `<p>` element, which is called output. It then copies the value of the input textfield into the output, like this:

```
output.innerHTML = input.value;
```

Each textfield has a property called value that tells you what's been typed into it. This line of code copies that value into the `<p>` tag's innerHTML property. The result is that whatever you type in the textfield is displayed in the `<p>` tag.

You now have a simple way of getting information from the player into the game. What will your game do with that information? That's the big question, and that's what the rest of this book is all about.

Other cursor properties

In the previous example you saw that you could change the mouse arrow into a pointing hand by changing the button's CSS cursor property to pointer. Here are some other values you could give the cursor property to change the way the mouse looks when it hovers over an element:

- move: Changes the mouse into an arrow pointing in four directions.

- wait: Changes the cursor into a spinning circle, which implies that the program is loading or processing something.

- help: Changes the cursor into a question mark, to show that by clicking the element you'll see some information about how the program works.

- crosshair: Changes the cursor into a crosshair, which is for aiming or fine positioning.

- text: The standard cursor for entering text.

- auto or default: The browser sets the cursor style automatically.

- n-resize: This turns the cursor into an arrow pointing north (up). The "n" stands for north. If you want an arrow that points in another direction, you can replace the "n" with any of these values: ne, e, se, s, sw, w, nw. For example, if you want an arrow pointing southwest, use this property: sw-resize.

You may find many of these useful for games.

Organizing your JavaScript code

For small programs and games, the best place to put JavaScript code is between the `<script>` tags in the main HTML document. This is what I've done in this chapter, and for most of the small example games in this book. It's neat, simple, and efficient.

For bigger projects you'll want to keep your JavaScript code in its own file or in multiple files. This is important because many complex games rely on common functions and other programming components that might need to be shared by more than one game. If your JavaScript code is independent from the main HTML document, you can easily link it to any other project you like. It also means you can break long programs into a series of smaller files that are easier to work with. Let's find out how with this next example.

1. Create a new document with your text editor called **program.js**. Carefully enter the following JavaScript code.

```
(function(){

window.alert("The JavaScript program has loaded!");

}());
```

The window.alert method will display a box in the browser window containing the words inside the parentheses.

2. Save the program.js file.

3. Create a new HTML file called main.html. It should be in the same folder as the program.js file. Enter the following HTML code:

```
<!doctype html>
<title>Organizing files</title>
<script src="program.js"></script>
```

4. Save the main.html file and open it in a web browser. You'll see an **alert window** open with the words "The JavaScript program has loaded!", shown in Figure 2-12.

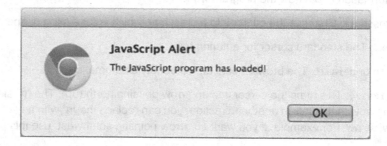

Figure 2-12. Link a JavaScript file to the main HTML document

Linking the JavaScript program to the HTML document

You can see that the main.html file loaded the program.js file by using the <script> tag's src attribute.

```
<script src="program.js"></script>
```

If you have a complex HTML document that uses a <body> element, add the <script> tag just before the closing </body> tag, like this:

```
<!doctype html>
<title>Organizing files</title>
```

```
<body>
<p>Any other HTML code</p>
<script src="program.js"></script>
</body>
```

This ensures that the JavaScript will load after the HTML elements have loaded. That's important if the program depends on any of the HTML code to work.

Using the program.js file

The program.js file contains just one important line of JavaScript code.

```
window.alert("The JavaScript program has loaded!");
```

That's what displays the alert box in the browser window.

But notice that this line of code is surrounded by a chaotic-looking jumble of characters above and below it.

```
(function(){
```

```
window.alert("The JavaScript program has loaded!");
```

```
}());
```

What is that stuff? It's something called an **immediate function**. It usually looks like this:

```
(function(){ }());
```

An immediate function is a function that runs automatically. You don't have to call it. Anything that's inside its inner curly braces will run right away. Here's an immediate function that displays "Hello World!" in the console.

```
(function(){console.log("Hello World!");}());
```

I know: it looks like a rat's nest! It's easier to read if you format it like this:

```
(function(){

  console.log("Hello World!");

}());
```

There's usually never any need to use an immediate function in a game project. Its only use is to enclose an independent JavaScript program. That means when you create a JavaScript file, you should write your entire program inside the function's curly braces, like this:

```
(function(){

//Write your entire JavaScript program
//inside the immediate function's curly braces

}());
```

Why do you need to do this? There are two very good reasons.

First, it means your program will run immediately as soon as the HTML file loads it.

Second, it protects all the variables you're using in your program from conflicting with variables that might have the same names in other programs. It's very likely that in a big game project you'll need to link many JavaScript files together, each of which performs a specialized task in the game. If those different files happen to use variables with the same names, your program might be confused about which variable you're referring to. Wrapping your program inside a function protects those variables from conflicting with variables in other programs that are being used at the same time.

> Note: There's a technical reason for this that's important to understand. When you create a variable inside a function, it's local to that function. It's called a **local variable**. That means that it can't be used or understood by any other part of your program outside of that function's curly braces. When you create a variable outside of a function, it's global to your entire program. It's called a **global variable**. That means it can be used anywhere in your program by any function or even by other linked JavaScript programs running at the same time. Global variables sound like they are very convenient, and they are. But you have to use them with extreme caution, otherwise you risk naming conflicts with other variables from other programs. As a best practice, don't use global variables at all. Wrap your whole program inside an immediate function so that the program's variables are local only to that program. That protects them from global naming conflicts.
>
> Whether variables are local or global is a topic in computer programming called **scope**.

You'll find a working example of how to link an external JavaScript file to an HTML file in the `organizingFiles` folder in the chapter's source files. In later chapters you'll learn how to build complex games using this system with multiple linked JavaScript files.

A quick guide to debugging code

On September 9, 1947, the Mark II computer at Harvard University was experiencing problems. The Mark II was a monster of a computer: it was composed of thousands of wires, switches, knobs, buttons, and glowing vacuum tubes, all packed into rows of steel cabinets occupying the area of a small house. It also attracted bugs. An operator investigated, and from behind one of the Mark II's panels he pulled out a moth. Problem solved! The Mark II was successfully "debugged." Since that day, programmers have referred to the process of looking for and fixing problems with code as **debugging**.

Fortunately, you don't need to go looking for nesting insects in your computer when something goes wrong with your programs (although sometimes you may wish the solutions were that easy!). Usually the mistakes you'll make will be one of these very common ones. Ask yourself these questions:

- Did you spell everything correctly and use the correct case?
- Did you accidentally use a single equal sign, =, instead of a triple equal sign, ===, in an if statement?
- Have you closed all your curly braces and parentheses?

The JavaScript debugger that's part of your browser's console will also try and tell you what it thinks is wrong with your program. But, as I'm sure you've noticed by now, the error messages are extremely cryptic and, even if you manage to decipher them, they may not actually tell you what's wrong.

However, if you know how to interpret the error messages, they can actually be extremely useful. Here are some common error messages and what they might actually be trying to tell you. (The debugger will also tell you the line number of your program where it thinks the error is.)

`Reference error: Can't find variable`

You probably misspelled the name of a variable or function.

`SyntaxError: Unexpected token ")"`

You may have forgotten to close a pair of parentheses.

`SyntaxError: Unexpected EOF`

You might have forgotten to close a pair of quotation marks surrounding a string. (In case you're wondering, EOF stands for end of file. This implies that the debugger got confused, can't make sense of your program, and can't figure out where your program is supposed to end.)

`SyntaxError: Expected an identifier but found "somethingElse" instead`

You probably misspelled a JavaScript keyword like function or var.

`SyntaxError: Unexpected token "}"`

You may have forgotten to close a pair of curly braces.

`TypeError: "undefined" is not a function`

You may have misspelled a function name. For example, maybe you spelt console.log as console.lg.

And here are some more general pointers that you should always keep in mind while debugging your programs:

■ If you receive more than one error message, always try and fix the first one first. Subsequent errors are usually the result of bits of code that depend on the earlier bits of code working correctly. Fix the first one, and the correction will cascade through the code and often magically correct the rest.

■ Check the line of code that's just above the line that the debugger thinks is the problem. Often, small mistakes in the line above, which might not be big enough in themselves to generate an error, could be enough to trip up the code in the next line down.

■ *Always save the file you're working on before you run it again.* I can't stress enough how common an oversight this is. A programmer will find an error and fix it but will then get exactly the same error message when the program is run again. This is because the file wasn't saved after the fix was made, so the earlier incorrect version of the file is the one that the debugger is actually running.

■ Make only one single change before you save and test the program again. If your program worked and then suddenly stopped working after you made that change, you know exactly what is causing the problem. If you run it only after making five changes and it doesn't work, you won't know which of those five things is tripping you up.

■ Finally, observe the programmer's universal mantra: test early; test often. Do lots of testing and solve lots of tiny manageable problems early on to avoid having to deal with hulking intractable problems that can grind your project to a halt later.

It takes a lot of practice to debug code properly, but don't let the debugger frustrate you. Take your time with the problem, and carefully compare the code you're using to similar examples in this book. Small mistakes are very easy to make but are just as easy to fix.

Summary

In this chapter you learned all the nuts and bolts of JavaScript programming. These techniques are common to all programming languages. Variables, if statements, functions, and input/output systems are what programming is all about.

How much more is there to learn about programming? A little bit, but believe it or not, you now know all the core JavaScript programming techniques that you need to know to start making games. You've opened the box, but the pieces are still all lying around on the floor, and you don't yet know how to put them together to make something useful. That's what we're going to do in the next chapter. We're going to build our first games using all the bits and pieces of programming code that you learned in this chapter.

Chapter 3

Your First Games

This chapter will be your first real look at how to design complete games. They're short, simple games, but they contain all the elements of game design that you'll be returning to again and again. Assigning input and output, decision making, keeping score, figuring out whether the player has won or lost, using random numbers, and knowing whether two objects are touching—they're all here. You'll also be taking a much closer look at variables and if statements and how to use functions to simplify a big program by breaking it into smaller chunks. By the end of the chapter, you'll have all the skills necessary to build complex logic and turn-based games based on this simple model. If the previous chapter taught you to think like a programmer, this chapter teaches you to think like a game designer.

The first game we'll build is a simple number-guessing game. The game asks you to guess a number between 0 and 99. If you guess too high or too low, the game tells you until you'll be able to figure out what the mystery number is by deduction. Figure 3-1 shows you what the game will look like when it's done.

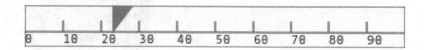

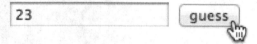

That's too low. Guess: 4, Remaining: 6

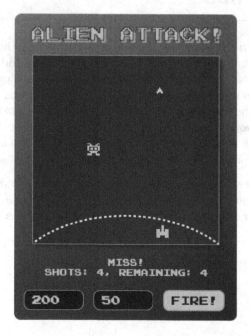

Figure 3-1. The number-guessing game

We'll actually build this game in a few phases. You'll start with the most basic version of the game, and then you'll gradually add more features such as limiting the number of guesses, giving the player more detailed information about the status of the game, and randomizing the mystery number. We're also going to look at how to make custom game buttons that change the way they look, depending on how you interact with them. Finally, we'll add some graphics that display the game information visually.

But that's not all. I'm also going to show you how to modify the basic game concept into an entirely different game: Alien Attack!, shown in Figure 3-2. You'll learn how to change images that are displayed depending on game events, and you will learn how to figure out if two objects are touching.

Figure 3-2. Save the world from an alien attack

Sound like a lot? Don't worry, we'll take it slowly, and you'll be surprised at how easy this all is when you put all the pieces together.

A basic number-guessing game

Our first game is a number-guessing game. The simplest form of this game is something you could certainly write yourself, without any further help from me. In fact, if you've worked through the previous chapter, you can! So, before reading on, why don't you try? Here's what your game should do:

- Ask the player to guess a mystery number between 0 and 99.

- Allow the player to enter a guess in a textfield by clicking a button.

- Use an if statement to figure out if the number entered is greater than, less than, or the same as the mystery number.

- Display a message that tells the player if they guessed too low, too high, or are correct.

Figure 3-3 shows how the game should work when it runs.

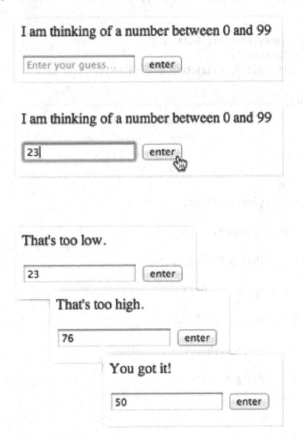

Figure 3-3. The finished number-guessing game

Here's my version of the game, which you'll find in the chapter's source files. It uses all the techniques from the previous chapter. Do you see how the if statement analyzes the input and displays the result?

```html
<!doctype html>
<title>Number guessing game</title>

<p id="output">I am thinking of a number between 0 and 99.</p>
<input id="input" type="text" placeholder="Enter your guess...">
<button>guess</button>

<script type="text/javascript">

//Game variables
var mysteryNumber = 50;
var playersGuess = 0;

//The input and output fields
var input = document.querySelector("#input");
var output = document.querySelector("#output");

//The button
var button = document.querySelector("button");
button.style.cursor = "pointer";
button.addEventListener("click", clickHandler, false);

function clickHandler()
{
    playGame();
}

function playGame()
{
    playersGuess = parseInt(input.value);

    if(playersGuess > mysteryNumber)
    {
        output.innerHTML = "That's too high.";
    }
    else if(playersGuess < mysteryNumber)
    {
        output.innerHTML = "That's too low.";
    }
    else if(playersGuess === mysteryNumber)
    {
        output.innerHTML = "You got it!";
    }
}

</script>
```

There are a few new things here that you may find a bit puzzling, so let's discuss why I wrote the program in this way.

Initializing variables

After setting up the HTML user interface, the JavaScript code creates two variables. I call them "game variables" because they'll help the game figure out if the player is winning or losing.

```
var mysteryNumber = 50;
var playersGuess = 0;
```

The game works by comparing the mysteryNumber to the playersGuess. You can see that they're both given initial values. mysteryNumber is set to 50, and playersGuess is set to zero. The player hasn't made any guesses when the game first loads, so setting playersGuess to zero shows that it's empty. In this first phase of the game, the mystery number will always be 50, but we'll randomize it later.

Using functions to modularize the program

The program uses functions to help organize main sections of the program. Here's how the program is structured:

1. The first part of the program initializes the game variables; creates input, output, and button variables; and adds a click event listener to the button.

2. When the button is clicked, the playGame function is called. The playGame function contains the if statement that analyzes the player's guess by comparing it to the mystery number. It displays the result by updating the output's innerHTML.

The playGame function is run when the player clicks the button. But that doesn't happen right away. The button first calls the clickHandler, and the clickHandler then calls the playGame function. Figure 3-4 illustrates this.

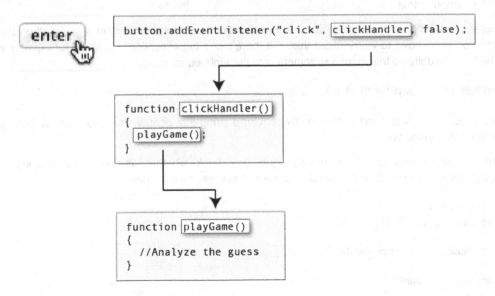

Figure 3-4. How the button calls the *playGame* function

The only thing the clickHandler does is call the playGame function. This seems to be a useless intermediary step. Why isn't the if statement not running directly in the clickHandler?

The reason is because this increases the flexibility of the game for the future. For example, you might also want the playGame function to run when the player presses the Enter key. By separating the button action from the actual code that runs when the button is pressed, you give your program a lot more flexibility to expand later. It means that if you decide to add an event listener for the Enter key, it could also run the same playGame function. You wouldn't have to make any changes to the program except adding an event listener for the Enter key that calls the playGame function. In later steps I'll show you how to do this, and you'll see how useful adding this intermediary step really is.

Using functions to divide specific tasks into useful chunks is called **modularization**. If you modularize your program like this carefully, it will be easy for you to add new things to the game without having to change other things that are already working. You'll soon see how as we develop this game in the pages ahead.

Forcing strings to become numbers

There's a line of code in the playGame function that is completely new to you:

```
playersGuess = parseInt(input.value);
```

This forces the player's input to be interpreted as a number, and it copies the result into the playersGuess variable. This is a little technical detail you have to deal with when your program reads number values from an HTML input field, so let's find out why it's important.

Whatever you type into an HTML input field is a string. That means if you type the numbers "1234" they're interpreted like words, such as "bicycle" or "guitar" and not as numbers. Numbers in a string can't be manipulated mathematically or compared against other numbers. They're just a meaningless set of characters, like any other string of text.

However, JavaScript is pretty good about automatically interpreting numbers in a string when it needs to, so usually you don't have to worry about this. But there's one big exception: checking for equality with another number. You usually do this in an if statement with the triple equal sign:

```
if(anyNumber === anyOtherNumber)
```

In this case, JavaScript won't automatically convert a string that contains numbers into actual numbers. You need to do this manually.

A simple example illustrates this. Here's a program that checks whether two numbers are the same or different. Notice that secondNumber is surrounded by quotes: that means it's a string.

```
var firstNumber = 12;
var secondNumber = "12";

if(firstNumber === secondNumber)
{
    console.log("same");
}
```

```
else
{
    console.log("different");
}
```

This displays "different" in the console. The reason is because secondNumber isn't a number: it's being interpreted as a word, like "bicycle" or "guitar". The string "12" is not the same as the number 12.

If you remove the quotes around "12" JavaScript will interpret secondNumber as a normal number:

```
var secondNumber = 12;
```

If you run the program again, the console will display "same", just as you'd expect.

Sometimes you need to force a string to become a number. You can do this with the parseInt method. Here's how you could use parseInt in this example program to force the string to be interpreted as a number:

```
var firstNumber = 12;
var secondNumber = "12";

if(firstNumber === parseInt(secondNumber))
{
    console.log("same");
}
else
{
    console.log("different");
}
```

This now displays "same".

parseInt works by forcing whatever is between its parentheses to become a number.

```
parseInt(secondNumber)
```

You can use it just like that, or you can assign the converted value back to a new variable, like this:

```
var anyNumber = parseInt("1234");
```

The variable anyNumber will now contain the number 1234.

That's the strategy that I took in the number-guessing game. The playGame function copies the string from the input textfield into a new variable called playersGuess. It simultaneously converts it into a number using parseInt. The new playersGuess variable is then used in the if statement to compare it against the mystery number:

```
function playGame()
{
    playersGuess = parseInt(input.value);
```

```
   if(playersGuess > mysteryNumber)
   {
      output.innerHTML = "That's too high.";
   }
   else if(playersGuess < mysteryNumber)
   {
      output.innerHTML = "That's too low.";
   }
   else if(playersGuess === mysteryNumber)
   {
      output.innerHTML = "You got it!";
   }
}
```

You should always remember to use parseInt to convert a string from an input field into a number, if your program needs to interpret that value as a number.

---

*Note: You can let JavaScript automatically convert a string to a number by using a **double equal** sign in the comparison statement, like this:*

```
if(12 == "12")

{

    console.log("same");

}

else

{

    console.log("different");

}
```

This will produce "same". Using a double equal sign like this can be convenient. However, the number 12 and the string "12" are definitely not the same type of thing. If this were an important distinction, your if statement could produce unexpected results if you haven't planned for this. For this reason, using the triple equal sign is safer, which is why I've used it for the projects in this book.

A little more about parseInt

parseInt stands for "parse integer." The word *parse* means to make logical sense of information. An *integer* is a whole number, or a number without a decimal point. That means that the number parseInt creates from a string won't include any fractional information like decimals. If there are decimal values, it will drop them. Here's an example:

```
parseInt("12.8");
```

This will produce 12. The decimal value will be dropped.

If you need to retain decimal places, you can use a related method called parseFloat.

```
parseFloat("12.8");
```

This produces 12.8.

> Note: The word "float" refers to "floating point," which is another way of saying numbers with decimal or fractional values.

Displaying the game state

Let's start making some improvements to the number-guessing game. In its current version, the game gives you an endless number of guesses and even after you guess the mystery number correctly; you can keep playing forever if you want to. To limit the number of guesses, the program needs to know a little more about the state of the game and then what to do when the conditions for winning or losing have been reached. We'll solve this in two parts, beginning with displaying the game state.

To know whether the player has won or lost, the game needs to know a few more things:

- How many guesses the player has remaining before the game finishes. We need a new variable called guessesRemaining to store this information.

- How many guesses the player has made. We need another new variable called guessesMade to keep track of this.

- What the status of the game is. We need a third variable called gameStatus that will display this information in the `<p id="output">` tag.

Let's add these features to the game:

1. Add the following three new variables to the program, just below the other variables (in all these examples, the bold text represents the new code):

```
//Game variables
var mysteryNumber = 50;
var playersGuess = 0;
var guessesRemaining = 10;
var guessesMade = 0;
var gameState = "";
```

2.   Add this new code to the playGame function:

```
function playGame()
{
    guessesRemaining = guessesRemaining - 1;
    guessesMade = guessesMade + 1;
    gameState = " Guess: " + guessesMade + ", Remaining: " + guessesRemaining;

    playersGuess = parseInt(input.value);

    if(playersGuess > mysteryNumber)
    {
        output.innerHTML = "That's too high." + gameState;
    }
    else if(playersGuess < mysteryNumber)
    {
        output.innerHTML = "That's too low." + gameState;
    }
    else if(playersGuess === mysteryNumber)
    {
        output.innerHTML = "You got it!";
    }
}
```

Save and run the game, and you'll now get a message telling you how many guesses you've made, as well as how many are still remaining. Figure 3-5 shows what you'll see.

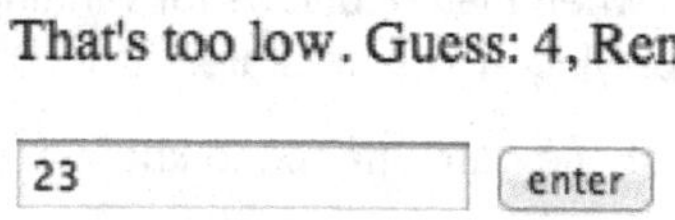

That's too low. Guess: 4, Remaining: 6

> 23   enter

Figure 3-5. The game tells you how many guesses you've made and how many you still have left

The new code creates three new variables and gives them initial values:

```
var guessesRemaining = 10;
var guessesMade = 0;
var gameState = "";
```

The total number of guesses the player gets before the game ends is stored in the guessesRemaining variable. You gave it an initial value of 10, but you can, of course, change this to make the game easier or harder to play. You also want to count the number of guesses the player makes, so a guessesMade variable is created to store that information. When the game first starts, the player has obviously not made any guesses, so the guessesMade variable is set to 0. The gameState variable is a string that will be used to display this new information, and you'll see how it does this in a moment. It contains no text initially (it's just assigned a pair of empty quotation marks).

Counting guesses

Here are the three new directives in the playGame function that change these variables:

```
function playGame()
{
   guessesRemaining = guessesRemaining - 1;
   guessesMade = guessesMade + 1;
   gameState
     = " Guess: " + guessesMade + ", Remaining: " + guessesRemaining;
```

> Note: The last line is very long, so to allow it to print easily in this book, I've split it up over two lines by breaking it at the equal sign. In your program, you can probably keep it all together as a single unbroken line of code, as you can see in Figure 3-6. I'll be breaking all long lines of code in this book by following this same rule. Remember, if you're in doubt you can always spot the end of a line of code by looking for the semicolon. How you space or break your lines doesn't make any difference to how it runs.

```
function playGame()
{
   guessesRemaining = guessesRemaining - 1;
   guessesMade = guessesMade + 1;
   gameState = " Guess: " + guessesMade + ", Remaining: " + guessesRemaining;
```

Figure 3-6. Keep long bits of code together on a single line.

The first line subtracts 1 from the current value of guessesRemaining:

```
guessesRemaining = guessesRemaining - 1;
```

If guessesRemaining has a value of 10 when the game first starts, it will now have a value of 9. You learned about how this works in the "Counting" section of Chapter 2.

The program uses the same technique to add 1 to guessesMade:

```
guessesMade = guessesMade + 1;
```

Each time the button is clicked, guessesMade is increased by 1.

You could optionally use the postfix operators, ++ and --. To subtract 1 from the guessesRemaining variable, you could use this directive:

```
guessesRemaining--;
```

You could add 1 to guessesMade like this:

```
guessesMade++;
```

This is an efficient way to add or subtract 1 from a variable, and you'll see it in use later in the chapter.

Tying up strings

The game uses another new variable called gameState. Each time the playGame function runs, it tells the player how many guesses have been made and how many are remaining:

```
gameState = " Guess: " + guessesMade + ", Remaining: " + guessesRemaining;
```

It's a string that combines the variables with words. The first time you make a guess in the game, gameState will produce this:

```
Guess: 1, Remaining: 9
```

The if statement that follows then uses the gameState variable to display the complete message in the output element:

```
if(playersGuess > mysteryNumber)
{
    output.innerHTML = "That's too high." + gameState;
}
else if(playersGuess < mysteryNumber)
{
    output.innerHTML = "That's too low." + gameState;
}
else if(playersGuess === mysteryNumber)
{
    output.innerHTML = "You got it!";
}
```

The plus signs add the contents of the gameState variable to the output textfield. This shows how you can mix game variables with text to tell the player what's happening in the game.

Winning and losing

The game now has enough information about what the player is doing to figure out whether the game has been won or lost. All you need to do now is to find a way to say, "Hey, the game is over!" and tell players how well they did.

To do this, add the following to the program:

- A Boolean (true/false) variable called gameWon that is set to true if the game has been won and false if it hasn't.

- If statements to check whether the game is over.

- A method called endGame that tells players whether they've won or lost.

Let's make these changes to the program and see what happens.

Add the new gameWon variable to the beginning of the program. Its initial value is false.

```
//Game variables
var mysteryNumber = 50;
var playersGuess = 0;
var guessesRemaining = 10;
var guessesMade = 0;
var gameState = "";
var gameWon = false;
```

Add the following new code in bold to the playGame function:

```
function playGame()
{
    guessesRemaining = guessesRemaining - 1;
    guessesMade = guessesMade + 1;
    gameState = " Guess: " + guessesMade + ", Remaining: " + guessesRemaining;

    playersGuess = parseInt(input.value);

    if(playersGuess > mysteryNumber)
    {
        output.innerHTML = "That's too high." + gameState;

    //Check for the end of the game
    if (guessesRemaining < 1)
    {
        endGame();
    }
    }
    else if(playersGuess < mysteryNumber)
    {
        output.innerHTML = "That's too low." + gameState;

    //Check for the end of the game
    if (guessesRemaining < 1)
    {
        endGame();
    }
    }
    else if(playersGuess === mysteryNumber)
    {
        gameWon = true;
        endGame();
    }
}
```

Add this new endGame function just below the playGame function:

```
function endGame()
{
  if (gameWon)
  {
    output.innerHTML
      = "Yes, it's " + mysteryNumber + "!" + "<br>"
      + "It only took you " + guessesMade + " guesses.";
  }
  else
  {
    output.innerHTML
      = "No more guesses left!" + "<br>"
      + "The number was: " + mysteryNumber + ".";
  }
}
```

Optionally, delete the following directive from the if statement in the playGame method. This text will be replaced by the new text from the endGame method. There's actually no harm in leaving it in, but it's redundant.

```
output.innerHTML = "You got it!"
```

Save the program and play the game. It now prevents you from guessing more than 10 times and tells you whether you've won or lost. Figure 3-7 shows what your game might now look like if you guess correctly.

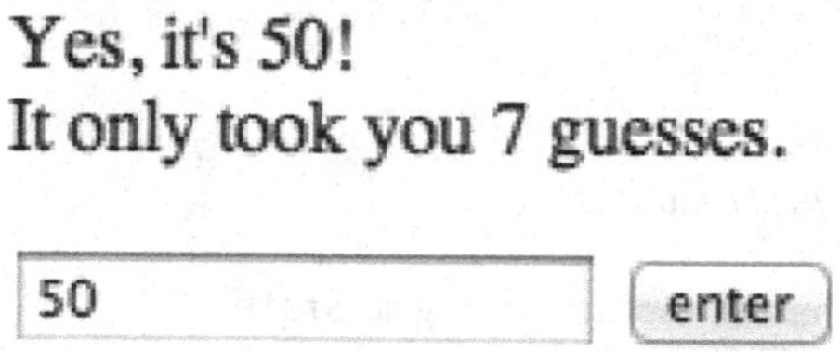

Yes, it's 50!
It only took you 7 guesses.

```
50                          enter
```

Figure 3-7. The game can now be won or lost

Before you added the new code, the game could count the guesses, but it didn't know what to do with that information. The new code adds a place for that information so that it can be relayed back to the user.

The first two blocks of the if statement now also check whether guessesRemaining is less than 1. If it is, they call the new endGame function.

```
if(playersGuess > mysteryNumber)
{
  output.innerHTML = "That's too high." + gameState;

  //Check for the end of the game
  if(guessesRemaining < 1)
  {
    endGame();
  }
}
```

```
else if(playersGuess < mysteryNumber)
{
    output.innerHTML = "That's too low." + gameState;

    //Check for the end of the game
    if(guessesRemaining < 1)
    {
        endGame();
    }
}
```

An if statement inside another if statement is called a **nested if statement**. This is the first time you've seen one. Nested if statements are always useful for adding one extra layer of logic to your decision making.

The if statement's last block checks whether the player's guess matches the mystery number. If it does, the player has won the game, so it calls the new endGame function. And also, very importantly, it sets the gameWon variable to true.

```
else if(playersGuess === mysteryNumber)
{
    gameWon = true;
    endGame();
}
```

So what does that endGame function do? It checks whether the player has won the game. If the gameWon variable is true, then the player has won and the appropriate message is displayed. But if gameWon is false, the function tells the player that he or she has lost.

```
function endGame()
{
    if(gameWon)
    {
        output.innerHTML
            = "Yes, it's " + mysteryNumber + "!" + "<br>"
            + "It only took you " + guessesMade + " guesses.";
    }
    else
    {
        output.innerHTML
            = "No more guesses left!" + "<br>"
            + "The number was: " + mysteryNumber + ".";
    }
}
```

The message that the player sees will be different depending on whether gameWon is true or false. gameWon is only set to true if the player guesses the correct number. Otherwise, it will remain false, which is what it was set to when it was initialized.

If statements and Boolean variables

You may recall from the previous chapter that variables that contain only true or false values are called Boolean. Enjoy using that delightful word because computer programming is the only area where you'll have the chance to use it. gameWon is a Boolean variable because it can only be set to `true` or `false`.

Look at how the if statement checks the gameWon variable:

```
if(gameWon)
{...
```

This means "If the gameWon variable is true, do this." But it's very different from how the other if statements have been written. Why is that?

If statements work by running their directives *if the condition in the parentheses is true*. As you know, you can use an equality operator (a triple equal sign) to compare any Boolean value with a true or false value, like this:

```
if(gameWon === true)
```

If gameWon is `false`, this statement is read overall as being false, and the directives don't run. If gameWon is `true`, the statement is read overall as being true, and the directives run. You know all this already from the previous chapter, but here's something new. If you just need to check whether a Boolean variable is true or false, it's much more convenient and often makes your code easier to read when you use this shorthand:

```
if(gameWon)
```

Because the value of gameWon can be *only* true or false, it provides exactly the same information as the first example.

We'll be using this as the preferred way for checking the value of Boolean variables in if statements throughout the book. `if(gameWon)` is very close to the English phrase "If the game is won." Choose the names of your variables carefully and you'll soon see that this style of writing if statements can make your programs easy to read.

HTML code within strings

Another new feature of this code is that the final messages include an HTML `<br>` tag. This breaks the message onto two lines. Here's what the winning message looks like:

```
output.innerHTML
    = "Yes, it's " + mysteryNumber + "!" + "<br>"
    + "It only took you " + guessesMade + " guesses.";
```

You can see that the `<br>` tag creates a line-break after mysteryNumber as shown in Figure 3-8. This is a complex example of how you can combine strings, variables, and HTML tags into interactive game messages. Can you see how the code produces the output you see in the game? Think carefully about how you want your messages to display and how they should look and you'll soon find it's easy to write code like this with a bit of practice.

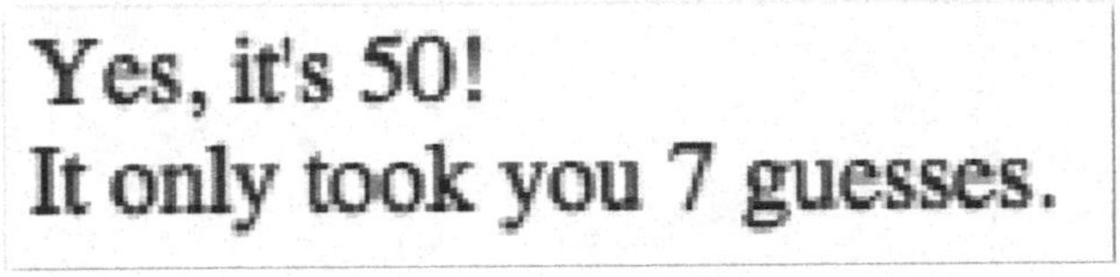

Yes, it's 50!
It only took you 7 guesses.

```
output.innerHTML
    = "Yes, it's " + mysteryNumber + "!" + "<br>"
    + "It only took you " + guessesMade + " guesses.";
```

Figure 3-8. Combine strings, variables, and HTML tags to create complex game messages

Modular programming with functions

You should be able to see how the playGame and endGame functions are used to help modularize the code. In truth, you could have written this program without them by adding all the conditions they check for in one extremely long if statement. But if you'd done so, you'd have to repeat a lot of the code, and it would all start to become very difficult to read and debug.

Modularizing specific tasks inside self-contained functions allows you to modify or debug those bits of code in isolation without having to change (and possibly mess up) other parts of the program that are working. It also means that whenever you want to perform a certain task, you don't need to duplicate any of the code you've already written; you just have to call the function you need to do the job.

Using functions to modularize your code might take you a bit of practice, and you might find it a bit of a brain-twister until you've seen a few more examples and experimented with using them in your own projects. Look at how the game is working so far and see if you can figure out how the interrelationships between function definitions and function calls are working. Figure 3-9 is a map of how it all fits together. You can think of each function as a "module" in the program.

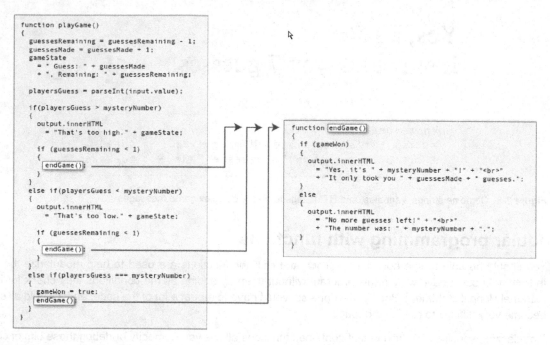

```
function playGame()
{
  guessesRemaining = guessesRemaining - 1;
  guessesMade = guessesMade + 1;
  gameState
    = " Guess: " + guessesMade
    + ", Remaining: " + guessesRemaining;

  playersGuess = parseInt(input.value);

  if(playersGuess > mysteryNumber)
  {
    output.innerHTML
      = "That's too high." + gameState;

    if (guessesRemaining < 1)
    {
      endGame();
    }
  }
  else if(playersGuess < mysteryNumber)
  {
    output.innerHTML
      = "That's too low." + gameState;

    if (guessesRemaining < 1)
    {
      endGame();
    }
  }
  else if(playersGuess === mysteryNumber)
  {
    gameWon = true;
    endGame();
  }
}
```

```
function endGame()
{
  if (gameWon)
  {
    output.innerHTML
      = "Yes, it's " + mysteryNumber + "!" + "<br>"
      + "It only took you " + guessesMade + " guesses.";
  }
  else
  {
    output.innerHTML
      = "No more guesses left!" + "<br>"
      + "The number was: " + mysteryNumber + ".";
  }
}
```

Figure 3-9. Use methods to modularize specific tasks

Using functions like this is not the only way to modularize your code. In Chapter 6 you'll see how to create and use **objects** to help you do this as well.

Polishing up

About 30% of the time that it takes to program a piece of software goes into making it work, and the other 70% goes into making it work well. There's no better example of this principle at work than the number-guessing game. It's playable, but there's a lot lacking that most players would complain about.

Here are some things we can improve:

- We should make sure that the player can only enter numbers, not words, into the input field.

- The player should be able to enter a guess with the Enter key, as well as with the mouse.

- The game should prevent the player from continuing to play after the game is finished.

- We should randomize the mystery number.

Let's roll up our sleeves and see if we can fix these problems. You'll find a working example of the game with all these modifications in the **numberGame_4.html** file in the chapter's source files.

Allowing only numbers to be entered

In the current version of the game the player can enter anything into the input field, not just numbers. Let's make a refinement to the game so that if you enter words, the game displays a message asking you to enter numbers.

To do this, the program first needs a way to tell the difference between numbers and strings. JavaScript has a method called isNaN that tells you this. isNaN stands for "is not a number". You use it like this:

```
isNaN("anyValue");
```

If you put a string inside the parentheses, isNaN will produce the following:

```
true
```

This means "It's a string." If you put an actual number into the parentheses, like this,

```
isNaN(2600)
```

it will produce

```
false
```

This means "It's not a string." You can use this in the game by testing the player's input like this:

```
isNaN(playersGuess)
```

If this produces true, then you know that the player has entered a string.

We're going to use this in the game by creating a completely new function called validateInput that checks this for us. When the player clicks the button, the clickHandler will first call validateInput. If the input is a number, validateInput will then call the playGame function, and the game will play as normal. But if the input is a string, validateInput will display a message asking the player to enter a number.

The new validateInput function will act as a filter between the clickHandler and playGame. Here are the changes you need to make to the game:

1. Change the clickHandler so that it looks like this:

   ```
   function clickHandler()
   {
     validateInput();
   }
   ```

2. Add the new validateInput function just below the clickHandler:

   ```
   function validateInput()
   {
     playersGuess = parseInt(input.value);
   ```

```
         if(isNaN(playersGuess))
         {
            output.innerHTML = "Please enter a number.";
         }
         else
         {
            playGame();
         }
      }
```

3. Notice that this following line of code has been moved from the playGame function into this new validateInput function:

    ```
    playersGuess = parseInt(input.value);
    ```

You should remove it from the playGame function.

You can see that the isNaN method is directly inside the if statement's parentheses:

```
if(isNaN(playersGuess))
{...
```

If it produces a result of true, the if statement will display "Please enter a number." If it's false, it will call the playGame function and let the game play as usual. Figure 3-10 illustrates how validateInput acts as a filter between the clickHandler and the playGame function.

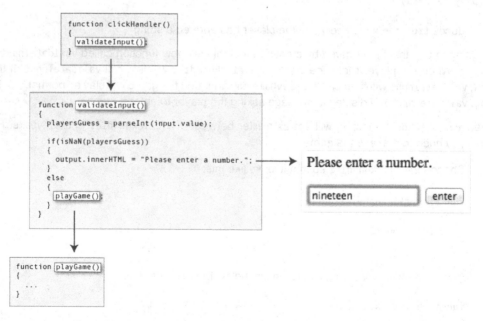

Figure 3-10. Filter the input to make sure that the player enters a number

You can see that, because you've modularized your program, it's now easy to add new features like this without having to change code you've already written. You'll see another good example of this in the next section.

> Note: JavaScript has some special built-in methods for validating input that will help you if have lots of input fields, like you might for forms on websites. Research the "HTML5 Forms API" to find out more about this.

Using the Enter key to input numbers

In the previous chapter you learned how to use the Enter key to provide information for a program. You can use the same technique here with the number-guessing game. The one new thing here, however, is that both the mouse or Enter key can be used to input the same information. This will work because if you click the mouse or press the Enter key, both actions will call the validateInput function.

Add this new code just above the clickHandler:

```
window.addEventListener("keydown", keydownHandler, false);

function keydownHandler(event)
{
  if(event.keyCode === 13)
  {
    validateInput();
  }
}
```

Remember that 13 is the ASCII code for the Enter key. If event.keyCode matches the number 13, the if statement will call the validateInput function.

Save and run the game again, and you'll now be able to enter numbers by either clicking the button or pressing the Enter key. Figure 3-11 shows how either the button or Enter key can now call the validateInput function.

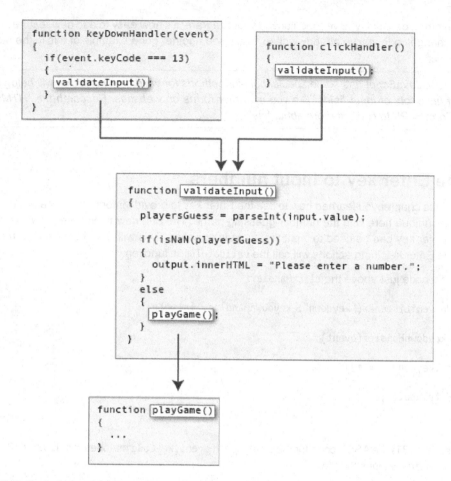

Figure 3-11. Both the button and the Enter key can call the same function

Improving the user interface

The **user interface** refers to all buttons, textfields, and other interactive elements that the player needs to use to play your game. You'll often see this referred to as **UI** or sometimes **GUI** (graphical user interface). How well your UI responds to the way players expect it to will play a big part in how much they'll enjoy playing your game. Let's make the UI for our game a little more user-friendly.

Adding focus to the input field

In the current version of the game you need to click in the input field with the mouse before you can enter any numbers. You can make a small change to the HTML code so that the blinking input cursor appears in the field automatically when the game first starts. The player can then enter numbers immediately without having to click the field first. This is called giving the field **focus**.

All you need to do is add an autofocus attribute to the input element:

```
<input id="input" type="text" placeholder="Enter your guess..." autofocus>
```

Save the game and play it again. You'll now see that a blinking cursor appears immediately in the input field, so you can start entering numbers right away. Figure 3-12 illustrates this.

Figure 3-12. Add focus to the input field

You can add autofocus to any UI element, including buttons.

Disabling the input field, button, and the Enter key

After the game is finished, the player can actually still continue entering guesses and clicking the button. You can prevent this by disabling the input field, button, and Enter key when the game ends. Add the following new code in bold, at the end of the endGame function.

```
function endGame()
{
  if(gameWon)
  {
    output.innerHTML
      = "Yes, it's " + mysteryNumber + "!" + "<br>"
      + "It only took you " + guessesMade + " guesses.";
  }
  else
  {
    output.innerHTML
      = "No more guesses left!" + "<br>"
      + "The number was: " + mysteryNumber + ".";
  }

  //Disable the button
  button.removeEventListener("click", clickHandler, false);
  button.disabled = true;

  //Disable the enter key
  window.removeEventListener("keydown", keydownHandler, false);

  //Disable the input field
  input.disabled = true;
}
```

You can see that removeEventListener is used so that the button and Enter key no longer call the event handlers. This makes them stop working.

But the code also disables the button and Enter key by setting their `disabled` properties to `true`, like this:

```
button.disabled = true;
input.disabled = true;
```

When the button is disabled, it's dimmed in the browser window and you can't click on it. When the input field is disabled, you can't click on it to enter text.

`disabled` is a property of all HTML input elements, like buttons and textfields. Set to it `true` whenever you want to prevent them from working. Set `disabled` to `false` to make them start working again.

Creating random numbers

You'll almost certainly find yourself needing to use random numbers in most of your game projects. JavaScript has many built-in methods that are useful for manipulating numbers. One of these is the `Math.random` method, which generates a random number between 0 and 1. Here's what it looks like:

```
Math.random()
```

You can assign this random number to a variable just as you assign other values to variables, as in this example:

```
var randomVariable = Math.random();
```

`randomVariable` is now assigned a random number between 0 and 1, with up to 16 decimal places. So it could be anything; for example, 0.3669164208535294 or 0.5185672459021346.

What use is a random number between 0 and 1 with 16 decimal places, you ask? As you've guessed, practically none whatsoever! Fortunately, you can do a bit of tweaking to get something more useful.

First, random numbers for games usually need to be integers—whole numbers. All those decimal places have got to go. Can you imagine what a nightmare the guessing game would be to play if the mystery number were something like 33.6093155708325684? If you chop off all those decimals, you'll have something useful, such as 33, which is within the realms of most human lifetimes to be able to guess.

JavaScript fortunately has a few built-in methods that can help us round decimals up or down:

- `Math.round`: Can be used to round numbers either up or down. For example, `Math.round(3.4)` returns a value of 3. `Math.round(3.8)` returns 4. `Math.round(3.5)` also returns 4.

- `Math.floor`: Always rounds numbers down. `Math.floor(3.2)` returns 3. `Math.floor(3.9)` also returns 3.

- `Math.ceil`: Always rounds numbers up. `Math.ceil(3.2)` returns 4, and `Math.ceil(3.9)` also returns 4. (ceil is short for *ceiling*. Ceilings are up; floors are down. Make sense?)

To use any of these methods along with the `Math.random` method, you need to use a format that looks like this:

```
Math.round(Math.random())
```

Think about what this is doing. Math.random() generates a random number between 0 and 1 with loads of decimals. So imagine that it came up with a deliciously useless number such as 0.6781340985784098. You could pretend that the preceding line of code now looks like this:

```
Math.round(0.6781340985784098)
```

How would you round that number? You'd round it up, and the result would be the following:

```
1
```

But what would happen if the random number were lower, like this?

```
Math.round(0.2459678308703125)
```

It would be rounded down to this:

```
0
```

This means that you can use the line of code `Math.round(Math.random())` to generate a random number that has a 50% chance of being either 0 or 1. This is not yet quite what you're looking for in the game, but it's not entirely useless either. There will be many instances where calculating a 50% chance of something happening will be really useful in your games, and you can use this little snippet of code to do exactly that.

> Note: In fact, you can use this bit of code to generate random Boolean (true/false) values. Let's pretend that you have a Boolean variable called rainToday. You could initialize it with a value of false:
>
> ```
> rainToday = false;
> ```
>
> Oh, if only that were true! So to make it a little more realistic, you can give it a 50% chance of being either true or false. All you need to do is use the Math.round(Math. random()) code snippet in an if/else statement and compare it against a value of 1. Here's what the code might look like:
>
> ```
> if(Math.round(Math.random()) === 1)
>
> {
>
>     rainToday = true;
>
> }
>
> else
>
> {
> ```

```
    rainToday = false;

}
```

Math.round(Math.random()) *has an exactly 50% chance of generating either the number*
1 or 0. If it happens to be 1, the first directive runs and rainToday becomes true. If it's 0,
no rain today!

So a random number between 0 and 1 is slightly more useful but not exactly what you're looking for in the game. How can you get a number between 0 and 99? Here's how:

```
Math.floor(Math.random() * 100)
```

This line of code multiplies the random number by 100 and then uses `Math.floor` to round it down. That means the lowest number it can possibly be is 0, and the highest is 99. That gives us a perfect random whole number that falls within the range of 0 to 99.

Here's another way of looking at it. Let's say that the random number is 0.3378208608542148. That would mean the code will look like this:

```
Math.floor(0.3378208608542148 * 100)
```

Multiplied by 100, the random number will then look like this:

```
Math.floor(33.78208608542148)
```

The decimal point is just moved two spaces to the right, giving a nice big number to work with. But you still have the problem of those infuriating decimals to deal with! Not to worry: `Math.floor` comes to the rescue by rounding the whole thing down. So the result is very satisfying:

```
33
```

Perfect for the number-guessing game! Figure 3-13 shows an example of this process in action.

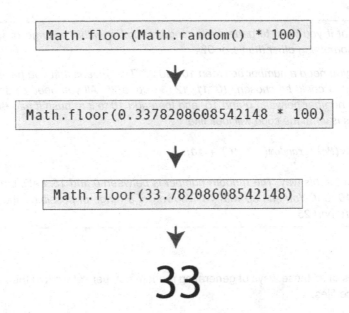

Figure 3-13. From useless to useful: `Math.random` and `Math.floor` help to generate random whole numbers within a specific range

If you need a random number between 1 and 100, you can create it by using code that looks like this:

```
Math.ceil(Math.random() * 100);
```

`Math.ceil` rounds the random number up, so the lowest it can be is 1, and the highest it can be is 100.

You can use this same format for any range of numbers simply by changing the number that you multiply the random number by. Here are some examples:

- `Math.ceil(Math.random() * 10)` generates a random number between 1 and 10.

- `Math.ceil(Math.random() * 27)` generates a random number between 1 and 27.

- `Math.ceil(Math.random() * 5)` generates a random number between 1 and 5.

The reason why using `Math.ceil` starts the range of random numbers with 1 is that any number less than 1, such as 0.23, will be rounded up to 1. That saves you from having to deal with values of 0, which are often not useful for the ranges of numbers you'll be looking for in your games. If you do want 0 to be part of the range, however, use `Math.floor` and multiply the random number by 101.

```
Math.floor(Math.random() * 101)
```

This will give you a random number between 0 and 100. Why do you need to multiply the random number by 101? Because if the random number is over 100, `Math.floor` will push it back down to 100. It can never reach 101.

> *Note: What if you want to generate a random number within a range of numbers that starts at something other than 1 or 0?*
>
> *Let's say you need a number between 10 and 25. That means that you have 15 possible numbers that could be chosen: 10, 11, 12 . . . up to 25. All you need to do is generate a random number between 0 and 15, and then add 10 to it to push it into the range you need. This is what the code will look like:*
>
> *Math.floor(Math.random() * 16) + 10;*
>
> *Think about it this way. The random number is between 0 and 15. Let's say it's 8. Then you add 10 to it. You end up with 18. You've got a range of possible random numbers between 10 and 25.*

You'll find examples of all these ways of generating random numbers at work in the randomNumbers.html file in the chapter's source files.

Now let's use what we've learned about random numbers and apply it to the game. We need a random number between 0 and 99, so change the line that initializes the mysteryNumber so that it looks like this.

```
var mysteryNumber = Math.floor(Math.random() * 100);
console.log(mysteryNumber);
var playersGuess = 0;
var guessesRemaining = 10;
var guessesMade = 0;
var gameState = "";
var gameWon = false;
```

You can add the optional line console.log(mysteryNumber) so that the number is displayed in the console, which is useful while you're testing the game.

Save the program and run the game again. You'll now have a different number each time you play!

Adding character encoding

A small technical detail is that you should always make sure that your finished game includes the <meta> tag that describes the document's character encoding.

```
<!doctype html>
<meta charset="utf-8">
<title>Number guessing game</title>
```

This is important because even the latest modern web browsers don't always interpret characters correctly, particularly in textfields. If you see some scrambled words or numbers somewhere in your games, it's likely that you haven't included the character encoding.

Finishing the game

We've made a lot of changes to the number-guessing game in this section, so here's a complete code listing of the game for you to refer to if you have any questions about how it all fits together.

```html
<!doctype html>
<meta charset="utf-8">
<title>Number guessing game</title>

<p id="output">I am thinking of a number between 0 and 99.</p>
<input id="input" type="text" placeholder="Enter your guess..." autofocus>
<button>guess</button>

<script>

//Game variables
var mysteryNumber = Math.floor(Math.random() * 100);
console.log(mysteryNumber);
var playersGuess = 0;

var guessesRemaining = 10;
var guessesMade = 0;
var gameState = "";
var gameWon = false;

//The input and output fields
var input = document.querySelector("#input");
var output = document.querySelector("#output");

//The button
var button = document.querySelector("button");
button.addEventListener("click", clickHandler, false);
button.style.cursor = "pointer";

//Listen for enter key presses
window.addEventListener("keydown", keydownHandler, false);

function keydownHandler(event)
{
  if(event.keyCode === 13)
  {
    validateInput();
  }
}

function clickHandler()
{
  validateInput();
}
```

```
function validateInput()
{
  playersGuess = parseInt(input.value);

  if(isNaN(playersGuess))
  {
    output.innerHTML = "Please enter a number.";
  }
  else
  {
    playGame();
  }
}

function playGame()
{
  guessesRemaining = guessesRemaining - 1;
  guessesMade = guessesMade + 1;
  gameState
    = " Guess: " + guessesMade
    + ", Remaining: " + guessesRemaining;

  playersGuess = parseInt(input.value);

  if(playersGuess > mysteryNumber)
  {
    output.innerHTML = "That's too high." + gameState;

    //Check for the end of the game
    if (guessesRemaining < 1)
    {
      endGame();
    }
  }
  else if(playersGuess < mysteryNumber)
  {
    output.innerHTML = "That's too low." + gameState;

    //Check for the end of the game
    if (guessesRemaining < 1)
    {
      endGame();
    }
  }
  else if(playersGuess === mysteryNumber)
  {
    gameWon = true;
    endGame();
  }
}
```

```
function endGame()
{
  if (gameWon)
  {
    output.innerHTML
      = "Yes, it's " + mysteryNumber + "!" + "<br>"
      + "It only took you " + guessesMade + " guesses.";
  }
  else
  {
    output.innerHTML
      = "No more guesses left!" + "<br>"
      + "The number was: " + mysteryNumber + ".";
  }

  //Disable the button
  button.removeEventListener("click", clickHandler, false);
  button.disabled = true;

  //Disable the enter key
  window.removeEventListener("keydown", keydownHandler, false);

  //Disable the input field
  input.disabled = true;
}

</script>
```

So far this game has just used text, but you can use all your HTML and CSS skills to add color and graphics. In the next few sections you'll learn how to make a custom input button and then how to add a visual display.

Making really nice buttons

When you interact with a button in most games or software, you'll notice that it behaves in three important ways:

- When your mouse moves over it, there's a highlighting effect.

- When you click or hold the mouse button down, the button often changes color. Sometimes it will change position slightly to appear as though it's being pressed down.

- The button returns to normal when the mouse leaves it.

These three basic button states are called **up**, **hover**, and **active**. There are many different ways you could represent these states, and if you look closely at how buttons behave within websites, games, and applications, you'll see countless variations and styles. Figure 3-14 illustrates a simple example of how these states could look on the button I'll show you how to make.

up
black background

hover
green background

active
yellow background

Figure 3-14. A button's *up*, *hover*, and *active* states

To create your own custom buttons, you need some way of representing these three separate states. You could use three images, each representing one state. Then you would change the background image depending on which state you want to display. Or you could style a button with CSS and switch its state just by changing its style. That's the most flexible approach, and this is what you'll learn next.

You'll find a working example of this button in the customButton.html file in the chapter's source files. Here's the entire file. It's just HTML and CSS, so there's no JavaScript.

```
<!doctype html>
<title>Custom button</title>

<style>

button
{
  font-family: Arial, Helvetica, sans-serif;
  font-size: 14px;
  color: #fff;
  padding: 10px 20px;
  border: 2px solid #000;
  cursor: pointer;

  -webkit-border-radius: 10px;
  -moz-border-radius: 10px;
  border-radius: 10px;
```

```
background:-webkit-linear-gradient(top, #a3a3a3, #000);
background:-moz-linear-gradient(top, #a3a3a3, #000);
background: linear-gradient(top, #a3a3a3, #000);

-webkit-box-shadow: 5px 5px 3px rgba(0,0,0,0.5);
-moz-box-shadow: 5px 5px 3px rgba(0,0,0,0.5);
box-shadow: 5px 5px 3px rgba(0,0,0,0.5);

-webkit-user-select: none;
-moz-user-select: none;
user-select: none;
}

button:hover
{
  background: -webkit-linear-gradient(top, #acc7a3, #506651);
  background: -moz-linear-gradient(top, #acc7a3, #506651);
  background: linear-gradient(top, #acc7a3, #506651);
}

button:active
{
  background: -webkit-linear-gradient(top, #858565, #c5c9a9);
  background: -moz-linear-gradient(top, #858565, #c5c9a9);
  background: linear-gradient(top, #858565, #c5c9a9);
}

</style>

<button>guess</button>
```

This is a big chunk of code, so let's break it down into understandable bits. First, take a look at the CSS that styles the button. The first part sets things like the border style, font color, padding, and the cursor style, which are all the properties you learned in Chapters 1 and 2.

```
font-family: Arial, Helvetica, sans-serif;
font-size: 14px;
color: #fff;
padding: 10px 20px;
border: 2px solid #000;
cursor: pointer;
```

You should be able to see how the code is affecting the button styles.

But after these styles are three new properties you haven't seen before: border-radius, linear-gradient, and box-shadow. At the time of writing these are new "experimental" styles, which means that they're not yet an official part of the CSS standard. To get them working reliably on different browsers, you need to use at least three different versions of them. The ones with the preface -webkit- will work on Safari and Chrome. Those with the preface -moz- will work on Firefox. The final one doesn't have any preface and is the pure version of the property. One day soon, when these properties become part of the official standard, that last one should be the only one you'll need to use.

> Note: To simplify these examples, I won't continue to include the -webkit- and -moz- versions of the properties, but just know that you should add them to all your final code until you're certain you don't need them. Use the code listing above as a model of how to do this. These prefixes to the CSS properties are called **vendor prefixes**.
>
> Here are the vendor prefixes for other popular browsers in case you need them:
>
> Internet Explorer: -ms-
>
> Konqueror: -khtml-
>
> Opera: -o-

Round corners

Here's the border-radius property. It determines how rounded the corners of the button should be.

```
border-radius: 10px;
```

Imagine that the corners are part of a circle with a radius of 10 pixels. That's what's determining the roundness. Figure 3-15 shows how different values like 20px and 5px affect the border radius.

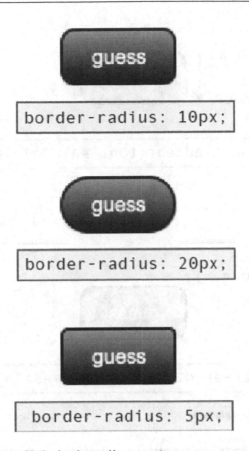

Figure 3-15. Create rounded corners with the *border-radius* property

Gradients

The `linear-gradient` background property creates a gradual change in the button's color from light to dark. The top of the button is light gray, and it gradually darkens to black at the bottom. This is an effect called a **gradient**, and here's the code that achieves this:

```
background: linear-gradient(top, #a3a3a3, #000);
```

The first hex color, #a3a3a3, is the gradient's start color, which is light gray. The second hex color, #000, is its end color, which is black.

`top` is the start position. This can optionally be `bottom`, `left`, or `right`, depending on which direction you want the gradient to start from. If you want the gradient to display on an angle, such as from the top left corner to the bottom right corner, you can use code that looks like this:

```
background: linear-gradient(300deg, #a3a3a3, #000);
```

Just add the degrees of an angle that you want the gradient to follow. Figure 3-16 illustrates how the `linear-gradient` background property achieves these effects.

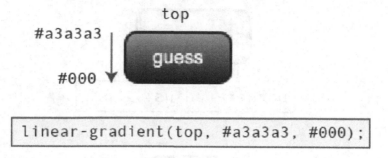

```
linear-gradient(top, #a3a3a3, #000);
```

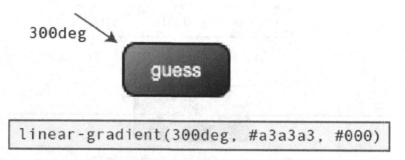

```
linear-gradient(300deg, #a3a3a3, #000)
```

Figure 3-16. Create a background gradient

For more complex gradient effects, you can assign a percentage to each color that determines how much of the area the gradient should cover. This bit of code assigns the first color to the top 20% of the element.

```
linear-gradient(top, #a3a3a3 20%, #000);
```

You can also have a gradient with more than two colors. Here's a gradient that transitions from gray to blue and from yellow to black.

```
linear-gradient(top, #a3a3a3, #0000FF, #FFFF00, #000);
```

> *Note: For round gradients, use the **radial-gradient** property.*
>
> *radial-gradient(startPosition, shape, firstColor, second Color)*
>
> *The start position can be a number in pixels, a percentage, or any combination of these words: "top", "left," "bottom", "right," or "center". Shape can be either "circle" or "ellipse". The color values follow the same rules as linear gradients.*

You can use RGB/RGBA or HSL/HSLA color values for any gradients instead of hex values if you prefer. Refer back to Chapter 1 for more information about these alternative color systems.

Gradients can get pretty complex! Don't let this worry you. You don't have to use all or even any of these options, but you should know they exist, just in case.

Drop shadows

The button can also have a drop-shadow effect, which is made with the box-shadow property.

```
box-shadow: 5px 5px 3px rgba(0,0,0,0.5);
```

The values determine the horizontal and vertical offset of the shadow as well as how blurry it is, its size in pixels, and its color.

```
box-shadow: horizontalOffset verticalOffset blurriness color;
```

This shadow is offset by 5 pixels to the right and below the button and is blurred by 3 pixels. The RGBA color is black with a 0.5% transparency. It's usually a good idea to use RGBA or HSLA values with drop shadows because transparencies will allow anything under the shadow to still be visible, like a real shadow.

Preventing the player from selecting the button text

Any text in an HTML document can be selected with the mouse. This is useful for copying and pasting information from a website to another document. However, you can also select the text inside the <button> tag.

```
<button>All this text can be selected with the mouse</button>
```

This is a problem because the mouse will become confused about whether you want to click the button or select the text inside it. You can prevent it from trying to select text by setting the user-select property to none, like this:

```
user-select: none;
```

You can set this back to auto or text if you want to restore the ability to select text later.

You now know how the button's up state was created. Let's find out how the button changes to its hover and active states.

Understanding the :hover and :active states

All three buttons states are set by using CSS. The hover state determines what the button looks like when the mouse is "hovering" over it. The active state determines how the button looks when it's being pressed.

```
button:hover
{
    ... when the mouse hovers over the button.
}
```

```
button:active
{
    ... when the button is pressed.
}
```

Let's see how they work.

> Note: One quirk in CSS is that you have to define the active state after the hover state for it to work. In CSS terminology, these states are called **pseudo-classes** (fake classes). You can always recognize a CSS pseudo-class because there will be a colon in front of it.

When the mouse is over the button, the hover state creates a highlighting effect by making the background green.

```
button:hover
{
    background: linear-gradient(top, #acc7a3, #506651);
}
```

When the left mouse button is pressed down over the button, the active state changes the background to yellow. It also reverses the direction of the gradient, so that it goes from light to dark. This creates an illusion that the button is being pushed in.

```
button:active
{
    background: linear-gradient(top, #858565, #c5c9a9);
}
```

The button resets to the hover state when the mouse is released. It resets to its normal state when the mouse is no longer over the button. And there you have all three button states that control the display of the button!

> Note: To save you the work of having to write your own CSS code for buttons from scratch, do a web search for "CSS3 button generator." You'll find many websites that let you design buttons with a visual interface and generate the CSS code for you automatically.
>
> If you need more control over your button states than CSS gives you, consider using JavaScript mouse events to change a button's appearance.

The next step is to add this button to the number-guessing game. You should now have enough programming skills to do this yourself, so I'll leave that job up to you. But in case you get stuck, you'll find a working example in the `numberGameWithButton.html` file. Figure 3-17 shows what this looks like.

Figure 3-17. Add a custom button to the number-guessing game

Seeing the game

Here's something really important that you need to know: *All games are just information*. In the number-guessing game, that information is the `mysteryNumber`, the `playersGuess`, the `guessesMade`, and `guessesRemaining`. How you choose to display that information is entirely up to you. In the previous examples, the information was displayed as text. But there's no reason why you can't display that same information visually. In this next section I'll show you two examples of how to add a visual display to the number-guessing game.

Adding a visual display to the number-guessing game

In the chapter's source files you'll find a folder called `numberGameWithGraphics.html`. Open the file in a web browser and play the game. It's a slightly simplified version of the number-guessing game. You'll see that an arrow moves smoothly to a number on a scale that matches the player's guess. Figure 3-18 shows what you'll see.

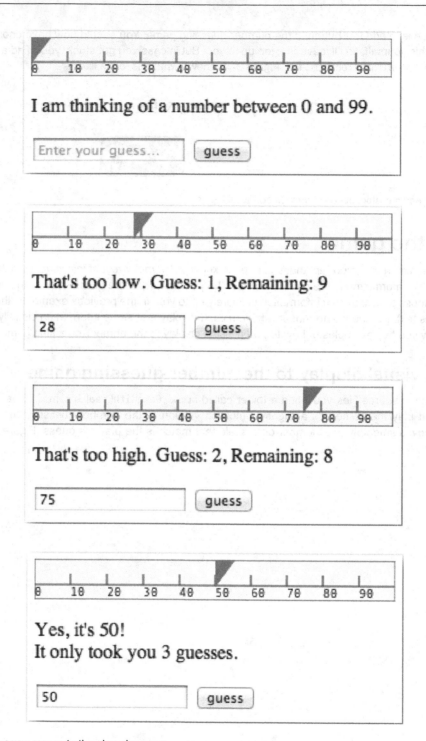

Figure 3-18. An arrow moves to the player's guess

This was done by using JavaScript to move an image of an arrow to the position on the scale that matches the player's guess. It also uses a CSS **transition** to make the arrow move smoothly. It's a very simple example, but if you understand how it works you'll find it easy to understand how more complicated games work that use the same technique. Let's take a close look at how this is done.

The scale and the arrow are just images. They're two separate PNG files. Open the project folder and you'll see that they're in the images folder. This project uses the format for organizing your files that I suggest you use in Chapter 1. Figure 3-19 illustrates this.

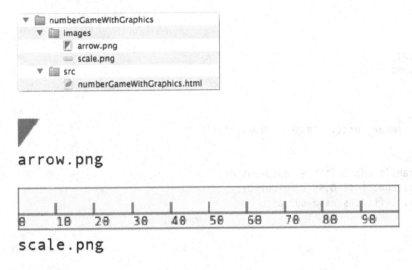

Figure 3-19. The files and folders

The HTML file displays the images. It uses CSS positioning to plot them in the correct positions inside a <div> tag with an id called stage. The JavaScript code then uses a new render function to change the arrow's CSS position to match the player's guess. These new features have only been added to the game; no changes were made to the game logic. Here's the complete HTML file that does all this. I'll explain it all in the pages ahead.

```
<!doctype html>
<meta charset="utf-8">
<title>Number guessing game with graphics</title>

<style type="text/css">

#stage
{
  width: 300px;
  height: 33px;
  position: relative;
}
```

```css
#scale
{
  width: 300px;
  height: 33px;
  position: absolute;
  top: 0px;
  left: 0px;
  background-image: url(../images/scale.png);
}

#arrow
{
  width: 17px;
  height: 22px;
  position: absolute;
  top: 0px;
  left: 0px;
  background-image: url(../images/arrow.png);

  /*Transition*/
  -webkit-transition: left 0.5s ease-out 0s;
  -moz-transition: left 0.5s ease-out 0s;
  transition: left 0.5s ease-out 0s;
}

</style>
```

```html
<div id="stage">
  <div id="scale"></div>
  <div id="arrow"></div>
</div>

<p id="output">I am thinking of a number between 0 and 99.</p>
<input id="input" type="text" placeholder="Enter your guess...">
<button>guess</button>

<script type="text/javascript">
```

```javascript
//Game variables
var mysteryNumber = 50;
var playersGuess = 0;
var guessesRemaining = 10;
var guessesMade = 0;
var gameState = "";
var gameWon = false;

//The input and output fields
var input = document.querySelector("#input");
var output = document.querySelector("#output");
```

```
//The button
var button = document.querySelector("button");
button.style.cursor = "pointer";
button.addEventListener("click", clickHandler, false);

//The arrow
var arrow = document.querySelector("#arrow");

function render()
{
  //Position the arrow
  //Multipy the players guess by 3 to get the
  //correct pixel position on the scale
  arrow.style.left = playersGuess * 3 + "px";
}

function clickHandler()
{
  playGame();
}

function playGame()
{
  guessesRemaining = guessesRemaining - 1;
  guessesMade = guessesMade + 1;
  gameState = " Guess: " + guessesMade + ", Remaining: " + guessesRemaining;

  playersGuess = parseInt(input.value);

  if(playersGuess > mysteryNumber)
  {
    output.innerHTML = "That's too high." + gameState;

  //Check for the end of the game
    if (guessesRemaining < 1)
    {
      endGame();
    }
  }
  else if(playersGuess < mysteryNumber)
  {
    output.innerHTML = "That's too low." + gameState;

  //Check for the end of the game
    if (guessesRemaining < 1)
    {
      endGame();
    }
  }
```

```
  else if(playersGuess === mysteryNumber)
  {
    gameWon = true;
    endGame();
  }

  //Update the graphic display
  render();
}

function endGame()
{
  if (gameWon)
  {
    output.innerHTML
      = "Yes, it's " + mysteryNumber + "!" + "<br>"
      + "It only took you " + guessesMade + " guesses.";
  }
  else
  {
    output.innerHTML
      = "No more guesses left!" + "<br>"
      + "The number was: " + mysteryNumber + ".";
  }
}
```

```
</script>
```

The images of the scale and the arrow are positioned with CSS by using absolute positioning. It follows the same model that you learned in Chapter 1. The CSS code positions the images relative to the stage <div> tag. The scale and arrow will be aligned to the stage's top left corner.

```
<style type="text/css">

#stage
{
  width: 300px;
  height: 33px;
  position: relative;
}

#scale
{
  width: 300px;
  height: 33px;
  position: absolute;
  top: 0px;
  left: 0px;
  background-image: url(../images/scale.png);
}
```

```
#arrow
{
  width: 17px;
  height: 22px;
  position: absolute;
  top: 0px;
  left: 0px;
  background-image: url(../images/arrow.png);

  /*Transition*/
  -webkit-transition: left 0.5s ease-out 0s;
  -moz-transition: left 0.5s ease-out 0s;
  transition: left 0.5s ease-out 0s;
}

</style>
```

The scale and arrow have heights and widths that match the sizes of the images they contain. The stage is the same size as the largest element it contains, which in this case is the scale. (The arrow also contains the transition property, which makes it move smoothly. I'll explain how it works later.)

The JavaScript then does the usual job of initializing the game variables and interface elements. But it now also needs a variable to reference to the arrow:

```
var arrow = document.querySelector("#arrow");
```

It needs this reference so that the code can change the arrow's position with CSS.

The rest of the code will be very familiar to you. When the player clicks the button, the clickHandler runs and calls the playGame function. The code is exactly the same as the code in previous examples, but with one small addition. Right at the end is a call to the render function:

```
function playGame()
{
  ... same code as usual...
  render();
}
```

This is the render function that it's calling:

```
function render()
{
  arrow.style.left = playersGuess * 3 + "px";
}
```

It's changing the arrow's left position so that it matches the player's guess. The number scale is 300 pixels wide, but the range of possible numbers that the player can guess is only between 0 and 99. That means we have to multiply the player's guess by 3 so that the arrow appears on the correct position on the scale.

Also, notice that the code is adding "px" at the end.

```
arrow.style.left = playersGuess * 3 + "px";
```

It has to do that because you'll remember that CSS position values need to end in px. If the player guesses 36, the line of code would be interpreted in CSS like this:

```
arrow.style.left = "108px";
```

(This indicates that 36 times 3 is 108, plus "px".)

The CSS code that it produces would look like this:

```
#arrow
{
  left: 108px;
}
```

Remember that this represents the distance between the arrow's left edge and the left edge of the containing stage element.

Every time the player clicks a button, this render function is called and it then updates the CSS position of the arrow to match the player's guess.

Animation with CSS transitions

The arrow's transition property is what makes it move smoothly from one position to the next. Whenever the arrow's left property is changed, the arrow takes 0.5 seconds to move to the next position, as shown in Figure 3-20.

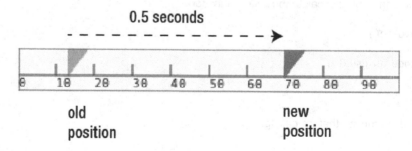

Figure 3-20. The arrow gradually eases into its new position

Here's the CSS code that does this:

```
transition: left 0.5s ease-out 0s;
```

It's a bit confusing, but look closely and you'll see that it has four different parameters. Each is separated by a space.

- `left`: This tells the transition that it should happen if the arrow's `left` property changes. You can change this to any CSS property. For example, if you want to the transition to occur when the top property changes, just change this to `top`. It will work for most CSS properties, including `height`, `width`, and `color`. If you want the transition to happen when more than one property changes, separate the properties by commas. Use `all` if you want the transition to happen when any of the element's properties change.

- `0.5s`: This is the duration of the transition, in seconds: 0.5s is half a second; 1s would be one second; 0.3s would be 300 milliseconds. You can use any time you like.

- `ease-out`: This is the animation effect that the transition should use. `ease-out` means that the animation should gradually slow to a stop. You can use any of these other effects: `ease`, `linear`, `ease-out`, or `ease-in-out`. Try them and see which ones you like.

- `0s`: This is the delay, in seconds. It's an optional parameter. It means that there should be no delay before the transition starts. Usually you'll just keep this at 0s. If you want a delay of, for example, half a second, you could set this to 0.5s.

The `transition` property is extremely easy to use once you get used to it. With just one simple line of code, you can beautifully animate any of your HTML elements. This is great for animating titles, game screens, and other user interface elements.

Separating the game information from the display

Remember that a game is just information. The `render` function that we used in this example is like a lens that lets us see that information more clearly. What's important to realize is that this game works perfectly well, and in exactly the same way, with or without the visual display. Adding the graphics doesn't change how the game works. And the code that controls the position of the arrow isn't changing the game information in any way. The visual display is separated from the information.

You'll soon see how important separating the game information from the display is. If you can solve your game as pure information, it becomes very easy to display it visually. Learning to do this is the key to becoming a good game designer.

Let's look at a more exciting example that illustrates the benefits of this approach much more clearly.

Alien Attack!

The number-guessing game was a very clear example of how to build a simple game. But, let's face it, it reminds us of math class! We're game designers, *we make fun games*; math class is not what we signed up for! So how can we use what we know so far to make a really fun game? All we need is a little imagination.

Imagine that instead of guessing a mystery number, you're trying to guess the position of an invading space alien so that you can shoot it down with nuclear missiles. That sounds like a lot of fun to me! You'll see a working example of this in the **alienAttack.html** file. Figure 3-21 shows what you'll see.

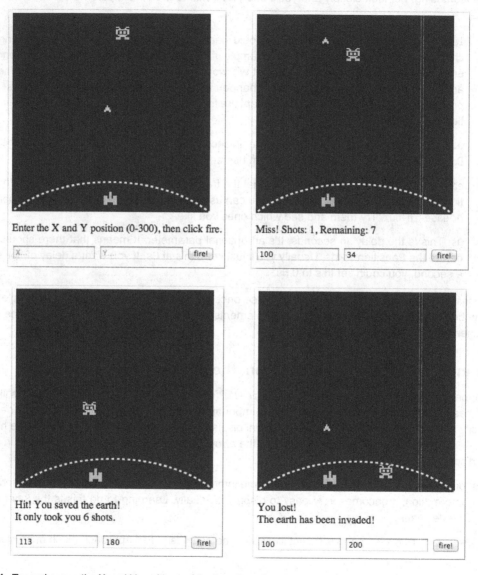

Figure 3-21. Try and guess the X and Y positions of the invading alien

Try and guess the alien's position to shoot it down. Enter X and Y positions between 0 and 300 and click the Fire! button. The X position is the horizontal distance in pixels, from the left side. The Y position is the vertical distance in pixels, from the top of the screen. If you miss, the alien moves closer to Earth and chooses a new random X position. If it reaches Earth within eight turns, you lose. But if you hit it, you save Earth! Each time you make a guess, your cannon moves to the X position you entered, and your missile moves to the X and Y positions that you guessed.

Does it seem like this would be complicated to make? Don't be fooled, it's nothing more than our plain-old number-guessing game, all dolled up for a night out on the town. But instead of guessing just one number, you're now guessing two: the alien's X and Y positions. And the technique used to display the game graphics is exactly the same as those we used to display and change the arrow in the number-guessing game. But this time around you're repositioning three images, not just one.

Here's the entire code listing, and I'll take you through a step-by-step tour of how it works. You'll soon see that it's much simpler than you might think at first glance.

```
<!doctype html>
<meta charset="utf-8">
<title>Alien attack</title>

<style>

#stage
{
  width: 300px;
  height: 300px;
  position: relative;
}

#background
{
  width: 300px;
  height: 300px;
  position: absolute;
  top: 0px;
  left: 0px;
  background-image: url(../images/background.png);
}

#cannon
{
  width: 20px;
  height: 20px;
  position: absolute;
  top: 270px;
  left: 140px;
  background-image: url(../images/cannon.png);
}
```

```css
#alien
{
  width: 20px;
  height: 20px;
  position: absolute;
  top: 20px;
  left: 80px;
  background-image: url(../images/alien.png);
}

#missile
{
  width: 10px;
  height: 10px;
  position: absolute;
  top: 240px;
  left: 145px;
  background-image: url(../images/missile.png);
}

</style>
```

```html
<div id="stage">
  <div id="background"></div>
  <div id="cannon"></div>
  <div id="missile"></div>
  <div id="alien"></div>
</div>

<p id="output">Enter the X and Y position (0-300), then click fire.</p>
<input id="inputX" type="text" placeholder="X...">
<input id="inputY" type="text" placeholder="Y...">
<button>fire!</button>

<script>
```

```javascript
//Game variables
var alienX = 80;
var alienY = 20;
var guessX = 0;
var guessY = 0;
var shotsRemaining = 8;
var shotsMade = 0;
var gameState = "";
var gameWon = false;

//The game objects
var cannon = document.querySelector("#cannon");
var alien = document.querySelector("#alien");
var missile = document.querySelector("#missile");
```

```
//The input and output fields
var inputX = document.querySelector("#inputX");
var inputY = document.querySelector("#inputY");
var output = document.querySelector("#output");

//The button
var button = document.querySelector("button");
button.style.cursor = "pointer";
button.addEventListener("click", clickHandler, false);

function render()
{
  //Position the alien
  alien.style.left = alienX + "px";
  alien.style.top = alienY + "px";

  //Position the cannon
  cannon.style.left = guessX + "px";

  //Position the missile
  missile.style.left = guessX + "px";
  missile.style.top = guessY + "px";
}

function clickHandler()
{
  playGame();
}

function playGame()
{
  shotsRemaining = shotsRemaining - 1;
  shotsMade = shotsMade + 1;
  gameState = " Shots: " + shotsMade + ", Remaining: " + shotsRemaining;

  guessX = parseInt(inputX.value);
  guessY = parseInt(inputY.value);

//Find out whether the player's x and y guesses are inside
//The alien's area

  if(guessX >= alienX && guessX <= alienX + 20)
  {
  //Yes, it's within the X range, so now let's
  //check the Y range

    if(guessY >= alienY && guessY <= alienY + 20)
    {
      //It's in both the X and Y range, so it's a hit!
```

```
            gameWon = true;
            endGame();
        }
    }
    else
    {
        output.innerHTML = "Miss!" + gameState;

        //Check for the end of the game
        if (shotsRemaining < 1)
        {
            endGame();
        }
    }

    //Update the alien's position if the
    //game hasn't yet been won

    if(!gameWon)
    {
        //Update the alien's X position
        alienX = Math.floor(Math.random() * 280);

        //Add 30 to the new Y position so that
        //the alien moves down toward earth
        alienY += 30;
    }

    //Render the new game state
    render();
    console.log("X: " + alienX);
    console.log("Y: " + alienY);
}

function endGame()
{
    if(gameWon)
    {
        output.innerHTML
            = "Hit! You saved the earth!" + "<br>"
            + "It only took you " + shotsMade + " shots.";
    }
    else
    {
        output.innerHTML
            = "You lost!" + "<br>"
            + "The earth has been invaded!";
    }
}
</script>
```

Setting up the game

The project folder uses the same format as in the previous example. The HTML file is in the src folder. The game uses images that are in an images folder. Figure 3-22 illustrates this.

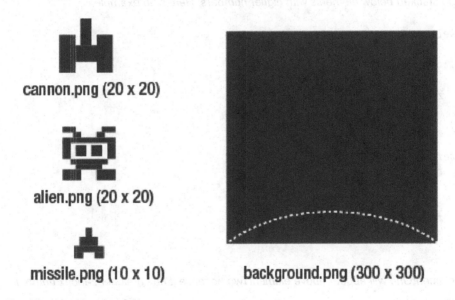

Figure 3-22. The Alien Attack! project folder

The alien and cannon are each 20 x 20 pixels. The missile is 10 x 10 pixels. The background is 300 x 300 pixels. These are all PNG images that I've designed to make them look like they are from a retro video game. But you can use any images of any sizes that you like.

You'll see that the format for this program follows exactly the format of the previous example. The HMTL code creates the visual game elements inside the stage:

```
<div id="stage">
  <div id="background"></div>
  <div id="cannon"></div>
  <div id="missile"></div>
  <div id="alien"></div>
</div>
```

The order in which you add these is important. The first image you add will be behind the images you add next. That means you have to add the background first if you want it to appear behind the other images. If the background is added last, it will cover up the other images. The images are stacked in **layers**, just as they are with graphic design software like Photoshop or Illustrator.

Note: You can use the CSS z-index property to change the stacking order of elements. Give elements z-index numbers such as 1, 2, 3, or 4. Elements with lower numbers will be stacked below elements with higher numbers. Here's an example:

```
#elementOne

{

    z-index: 2;

}

#elementTwo

{

    z-index: 1;

}
```

elementOne will appear above elementTwo because it has a higher z-index number.

The z-index properly only works with elements that have been positioned with CSS property.

The game has two input fields. inputX lets you enter the X position of the missile, and inputY lets you enter the Y position.

```
<p id="output">Enter the X and Y position (0-300), then click fire.</p>
<input id="inputX" type="text" placeholder="X...">
<input id="inputY" type="text" placeholder="Y...">
<button>fire!</button>
```

The CSS code loads the images and gives all the objects absolute positions relative to the stage's top left corner. The dimensions of the stage are as large as the largest thing it contains, which in this case is the background.

```
<style>

#stage
{
   width: 300px;
   height: 300px;
   position: relative;
}

#background
{
   width: 300px;
   height: 300px;
   position: absolute;
   top: 0px;
   left: 0px;
   background-image: url(../images/background.png);
}

#cannon
{
   width: 20px;
   height: 20px;
   position: absolute;
   top: 270px;
   left: 140px;
   background-image: url(../images/cannon.png);
}

#alien
{
   width: 20px;
   height: 20px;
   position: absolute;
   top: 20px;
   left: 80px;
   background-image: url(../images/alien.png);
}
```

```
#missile
{
  width: 10px;
  height: 10px;
  position: absolute;
  top: 240px;
  left: 145px;
  background-image: url(../images/missile.png);
}

</style>
```

These are the positions of the objects when the game first loads.

The code then initializes all the variables it needs so that it can access and modify these objects. This should all be pretty familiar to you by now.

```
//Game variables
var alienX = 80;
var alienY = 20;
var guessX = 0;
var guessY = 0;
var shotsRemaining = 8;
var shotsMade = 0;
var gameState = "";
var gameWon = false;

//The game objects
var cannon = document.querySelector("#cannon");
var alien = document.querySelector("#alien");
var missile = document.querySelector("#missile");

//The input and output fields
var inputX = document.querySelector("#inputX");
var inputY = document.querySelector("#inputY");
var output = document.querySelector("#output");

//The button
var button = document.querySelector("button");
button.style.cursor = "pointer";
button.addEventListener("click", clickHandler, false);
```

There are two variables that will store the player's X and Y position guesses:

```
var guessX = 0;
var guessY = 0;
```

The guessesRemaining and guessesMade variables from the number-guessing game have been changed to match our new space-war theme.

```
var shotsRemaining = 8;
var shotsMade = 0;
```

Their jobs are the same.

The `alienX` and `alienY` variables store the position of the alien on the stage. Together they describe its starting position. `alienX` is initialized to 80, which is 80 pixels left of the stage. `alienY` is initialized to 20, which is 20 pixels below the top of the stage.

```
var alienX = 80;
var alienY = 20;
```

These two variables have been set to the same left and top values that the alien was assigned in the CSS code. It's the CSS code that sets the alien's initial position, not these variables. However, when the game plays we're going to use these variables to change the CSS values. That's what will make the alien move. Giving these variables the same values as the CSS values is a good starting point.

Figuring out if the alien has been hit

When the player clicks the button, the `playGame` function is called. It first calculates the `shotsRemaining` and `shotsMade`, and it updates the `gameState`. It also copies the `inputX` and `inputY` values from the textfields into the `guessX` and `guessY` variables.

```
function playGame()
{
  shotsRemaining = shotsRemaining - 1;
  shotsMade = shotsMade + 1;
  gameState = " Shots: " + shotsMade + ", Remaining: " + shotsRemaining;

  guessX = parseInt(inputX.value);
  guessY = parseInt(inputY.value);
  //...
```

All of this is similar to what happened in the number-guessing game.

What's new is that now that the game has to figure out whether the player's guesses are correct. How does it do this? Here's the code in the `playGame` function that figures out if the alien has been hit. It uses a nested if statement to do this:

```
if(guessX >= alienX && guessX <= alienX + 20)
{
  //Yes, it's within the X range, so now let's
  //check the Y range

  if(guessY >= alienY && guessY <= alienY + 20)
  {
    //It's in both the X and Y range, so it's a hit!
```

```
    gameWon = true;
    endGame();
  }
}
```

This code is checking whether the guesses are within an X and Y range occupied by the alien. It first checks guessX. If guessX is a number that's greater or equal to the alien's X position *and* less than its width (alienX + 20), then the guess is correct. That means there might be a hit on the horizontal axis. But it's only a hit if guessY is also correct, which is what the second if statement checks. It checks whether guessY is a number that's greater or equal to the alien's Y position *and* less than its height (alienY + 20). If both of these are true, then the guesses are in a range occupied by the alien, and the player wins.

This logic is pretty condensed, but if you walk though it carefully you'll see that it really makes a lot of sense. Let's break it down into more bite-size chunks.

Imagine that the alien is at an X position of 50 and a Y position of 30. The player guesses that the X position is 55. Remember that these positions refer to the alien's *top left corner*. Figure 3-23 illustrates this.

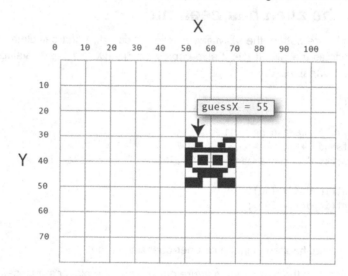

Figure 3-23. Did the player guess an X position that's within the range occupied by the alien?

We need to figure out if the player's guess, 55, is within the range occupied by the alien on the X axis. We know that the alien's top left corner is at position 50. And the alien is 20 pixels wide, which means it occupies a space between 50 and 70. Is 55 between 50 and 70? It sure is! That's what the first if statement tells us. Here's what the if statement looks like with these actual numbers:

```
if(55 >= 50 && 55 <= 70)
{
  //Yes, it's within the X range
```

So we know that the player is at least half-right. The alien might have been hit. But we'll only know for sure if we also check the player's Y position guess.

Let's imagine the player guesses 45. Is this within the range occupied by the alien? Figure 3-24 shows that it is.

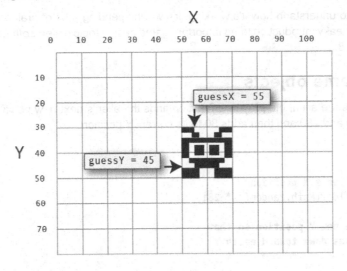

Figure 3-24. Is *guessY* withn the alien's range?

```
if(45 >= 30 && 45 <= 50)
{
    //It's within both the X and Y range, so it's a hit!
    gameWon = true;
    endGame();
}
```

You can see in Figure 3-25 that guessX and guessY are actually pointing to X and Y positions inside the alien.

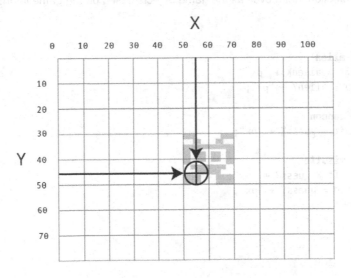

Figure 3-25. It's a hit!

So math is actually useful for shooting down aliens, and that's cool with us!

Take a bit of time to understand how it's working; it's worth spending a bit of brainpower on this until it clicks. This is actually a sneaky introduction to an important game design topic called **collision detection**. You'll learn about it in Chapter 8.

Moving the game objects

If the player misses the alien, the playGame function finds the alien's next new position. It gives it a random X position between 0 and 280 and then adds 30 to its current Y position.

```
if(!gameWon)
{
  //Update the alien's X position
  alienX = Math.floor(Math.random() * 281);

  //Add 30 to the new Y position so that
  //the alien moves down toward earth
  alienY += 30;
}
```

The alien is 20 pixels wide, so giving it a random range of between 0 and 280 means that its right side will never cross the right side of the background. This keeps it within the playing field.

Remember, this code doesn't move the alien yet. It's just the game information. It just figures out where the alien should go when it's rendered. The job of moving the image of the alien to this position is done by calling the render function:

```
render();
```

Here's the render function that moves all the game objects based on the game information:

```
function render()
{
  //Position the alien
  alien.style.left = alienX + "px";
  alien.style.top = alienY + "px";

  //Position the cannon
  cannon.style.left = guessX + "px";

  //Position the missile
  missile.style.left = guessX + "px";
  missile.style.top = guessY + "px";
}
```

The alien is moved to a new position based on the new `alienX` and `alienY` values that the game just figured out:

```
alien.style.left = alienX + "px";
alien.style.top = alienY + "px";
```

This code is changing the alien's CSS position values to actually move it to a real new position in the browser.

The cannon is moved to the `guessX` position:

```
cannon.style.left = guessX + "px";
```

And the missile is moved to the precise X and Y positions that the player guessed:

```
missile.style.left = guessX + "px";
missile.style.top = guessY + "px";
```

It's important to remember that these points represent the top left corners of the objects. For now, that will do, but often you'll want to move objects relative to their center points. That involves a little more simple math, and you'll find out how to do this in Chapter 8.

Making the game better

I've kept this game as simple as possible so that you can see how the underlying programming logic works. There's nothing stopping you from making it better by using some of the many other techniques you've learned in this chapter and adding some of your own ideas. Here are some suggestions of improvements you could make.

Adding an explosion

Create an explosion when the alien is hit. Figure 3-26 shows what this could look like.

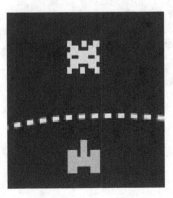

Figure 3-26. Add an explosion when the alien is hit

The explosion should appear in the same place as the alien. The alien and the missile should disappear.

You're smart enough to do this on your own, but here are some hints:

- Add a new <div> element with the id explosion.

- In the CSS code, set the explosion's display property to none so that it's not visible when the game first starts.

- Create a variable that references the explosion using document.querySelector.

- In the render function, add an if statement that checks whether the game has been won. If it has, your code should do these things:

  - Make the explosion visible by setting its CSS display property to block.

  - Give the explosion the same X and Y positions as the alien.

  - Make the alien and missile invisible by setting their display properties to none.

If you get stuck, take a look at the alienExplosion.html file in the chapter's source files for a working example.

Validating the new input numbers

Prevent the player from entering anything except numbers. Also, prevent players from entering numbers greater than 300. You'll need to do this in the validateInput function, which might look like this:

```
function validateInput()
{
  guessX = parseInt(inputX.value);
  guessY = parseInt(inputY.value);

  if(isNaN(guessX) || isNaN(guessY))
  {
    output.innerHTML = "Please enter a number.";
  }
  else if(guessX > 300 || guessY > 300)
  {
    output.innerHTML = "Please enter a number less than 300.";
  }
  else
  {
    playGame();
  }
}
```

Adding some more HTML and CSS styling

Use what you've learned so far to improve how the game looks and plays. Here are some obvious things:

- Create a custom Fire button.

- Apply all the polishing-up techniques you learned from the final number-guessing game: let the player use the Enter key; add focus to the first input field; disable input fields and buttons at the end of the game.

- Finally, try and use what you know about HTML and CSS to make the game look much better. You could add a heading with an embedded font, enclose the whole game in its own box, and use some gradient or drop-shadow effects.

Figure 3-27 shows what your finished game might look like, and you'll find a working example with all these modifications in the alienAttackFinished folder in the chapter's source files.

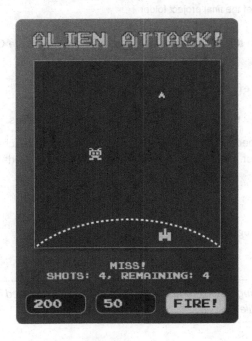

Figure 3-27. Add some finishing touches to your game

Let's take a quick look at how this finished game was put together, and I'll show you a few new HTML and CSS tricks you might want to use.

Figure 3-28 illustrates how the project files and folders have been organized.

Figure 3-28. The organization of the final project folder

There's a lot of CSS code in this project, so I've put it in its own separate CSS file and linked it to the HTML with the <link> element.

```
<link rel="stylesheet" href="alienAttack.css">
```

Look back to Chapter 1 if you need a review how to link external CSS files.

The game also uses an embedded font called emulogic.ttf for that old-school video-game vibe. It's in a fonts folder inside the project folder. Here's the CSS code that loads and embeds it.

```
@font-face
{
  font-family: emulogic;
  src: url("../fonts/emulogic.ttf");
}
```

> Note: If you are using Firefox, embedded fonts can only be loaded if they are in the same folder as the CSS file.

I want all the elements to use this font, including the button and input fields, so I've used the **universal selector**, an asterisk, to force all the elements to use it.

```
*
{
  font-family: emulogic;
  padding: 0px;
  margin: 0px;
}
```

Any properties you set with the universal selector will apply to *all* your CSS elements.

I've also used the universal selector to give all the elements a padding and margin of zero. This overrides the automatic padding and margins that the web browser gives some elements. Building up your paddings and margins up from zero will usually be the easiest and clearest way for you to start laying out elements.

You can see in Figure 3-27 that the whole stage and the user interface are surrounded by a box. I did this by creating a special `<section id="game">` element that surrounds all the other HTML code.

Do you see where the `<section>` begins and ends? That's the box that encloses the game.

```html
<!doctype html>
<meta charset="utf-8">
<title>Alien explosion</title>
<link rel="stylesheet" href="alienAttack.css">

<section id="game">

<h1>Alien Attack!</h1>

<div id="stage">
  <div id="background"></div>
  <div id="cannon"></div>
  <div id="missile"></div>
  <div id="alien"></div>
  <div id="explosion"></div>
</div>

<p id="output">Enter the X and Y position (0-300), then click fire.</p>
<input id="inputX" type="text" placeholder="X..." autofocus>
<input id="inputY" type="text" placeholder="Y...">
<button>fire!</button>

</section>
```

You can use a `<section>` element to enclose any group of HTML code that you want to keep together for some reason. The `<section id="game">` element has rounded corners, a background gradient, a drop shadow, and some padding, and it is large enough to comfortably contain all the other elements.

```css
#game
{
  margin: 0px auto;
  width: 330px;
  height: auto;
  padding: 15px;
  border: black;
  background: linear-gradient(top, #588063, #000);
  box-shadow: 5px 5px 5px rgba(0, 0, 0, 0.5);
  border-radius: 10px;
}
```

You'll also notice that it is centered in the browser window, which, as you learned in Chapter 1, is thanks to the `margin` property:

```
margin: 0px auto;
```

This gives the element equal, automatic left and right margins, which centers it in the browser. The stage element, which contains the game images, is also centered inside the game element with the same line of code:

```
#stage
{
  margin: 0px auto;
  ...
}
```

This works for block elements but not for text. Remember that if you want to center text inside another element, use the CSS `text-align` property and give it the value `center`:

```
text-align: center;
```

Using a text outline and shadows

The game title, Alien Attack!, has a black outline and a lime green drop shadow. To outline text, use the CSS `text-stroke` property. It needs two values: the thickness of the line in pixels, and the color:

```
-webkit-text-stroke: 1px #000;
-moz-text-stroke: 1px #000;
text-stroke: 1px #000;
```

This outlines the text with a 1-pixel-wide black line.

> Note: At the time of writing, the text-stroke property only works on Webkit-based browsers like Chrome and Safari.

Use the `text-shadow` property to create a drop shadow for the text. It needs three values: the x offset, the y offset, and the color. This is the code that creates a green drop shadow in the example:

```
text-shadow: 3px 3px lime;
```

The green shadow is offset by 3 pixels down and to the right. The color can be a preset color, like lime, or any hex, RGB/RGBA, or HSL/HSLA color.

You can also add an additional optional value, which is the blur amount. And you can also use an RGBA color value for the shadow, which will make it semitransparent. This bit of code creates a semitransparent shadow, offset by 5 pixels, with a 3 pixel blur:

```
text-shadow: 5px 5px 3px rgba(0, 0, 0, 0.5);
```

This is a nice effect because the semitransparency allows any images under it to be visible.

With these new techniques, and everything you learned about CSS in the previous chapters, you should be able to make a really nice-looking game.

Summary

And now you know how to start making games! Even though you can and will build more complex, larger-scale games, these little games are a model for the kinds of problems your games need to solve. If you understand the problems of game design and the solutions you found for them here, you'll be in a very strong position when you attempt something a bit more ambitious.

In this chapter, you learned all the basics for making a turn-based game. Before you continue in this book, take a short break and try to create your own game. You know how to move objects around, find out if objects are touching, analyze game information, and use random numbers to keep things unpredictable. There's no better way to learn than to try things out in your own way, and it will give you a greater appreciation for some of the more advanced techniques we'll be looking at in the chapters ahead.

You also now understand how game information will create and interact with game rules. Next, I'm going to show you how to use information to make an entire, immersive game world.

Chapter 4

Creating a Game World

One of the reasons games are fun to play is that they're simplified simulations of the real world. The real world is often not much fun at all, because it's far too complicated and has too many rules. In the real world we have to deal with things like food, rain, deadlines, traffic, mosquitoes, and gravity, sometimes all at the same time. It can be tiresome! But game worlds have much simpler, clearer rules. We can solve game problems much more easily, understandably, and quickly than real-world problems, and this gives us a great feeling of success and achievement. And because games are interactive, players can change the game world and watch how their changes interact with the world's rules. This creates a wonderful sense of immediate immersion.

In this chapter you'll learn how to use information to build a game world and how to apply rules to that information to create an interactive game. In the first part of this chapter you're going to learn two very important new programming techniques: arrays and loops. And in the second part of this chapter I'll show you how to use them to build a fantasy adventure game, "The Forest of Lyrica," shown in Figure 4-1.

Figure 4-1. A fantasy adventure game

You could use this game as a model for creating a very complex, immersive adventure game of your own. But as you'll see in the chapters ahead, the core techniques that are used to make it are at the heart of making *any* type of game, including action and arcade games.

Loops

Loops are used to repeat a section of code for a certain number of times. There are quite a few different kinds of loops you can create in JavaScript but the most common is the **for loop**. It lets you repeat a section of code "**for** any number of times," from just once to hundreds or thousands of times.

Here's how a loop could be useful. Imagine that you want to display the words "Hello world!" five times. Here's what your code would look like without a loop:

```
console.log("Hello world!");
console.log("Hello world!");
console.log("Hello world!");
console.log("Hello world!");
console.log("Hello world!");
```

That's a bit tedious to type out. Wouldn't it be easier just to write one line of code and tell it to repeat five times? That's what a for loop lets you do. Here's a for loop that displays the words "Hello world!" five times:

```
for(var i = 0; i < 5; i++)
{
    console.log("Hello world!");
}
```

Here's what it displays in the console:

```
Hello world!
Hello world!
Hello world!
Hello world!
Hello world!
```

The structure of the for loop might look weird and confusing at first because its arguments actually contain three separate statements. Each statement is separated by a semicolon.

```
for(firstStatement; secondStatement; thirdStatement)
{
    ...things you want to repeat;
}
```

But it's easy to understand how it works if you break down what it does into smaller parts. The first thing it does is declare the variable that will be used to count the number of loops. This variable is called the **index variable** (highlighted in bold below):

```
for(var i = 0; i < 5; i++)
{
    ...things you want to repeat;
}
```

This creates a variable called i, which is initialized to 0.

```
var i = 0;
```

Although you can use any variable name you like, everyone uses "i" by convention because "i" stands for "index."

The next statement tells the loop how many times it should repeat:

```
for(var i = 0; i < 5; i++)
{
   ...things you want to repeat;
}
```

This is a conditional statement. It tells the loop to repeat "while the index variable is less than 5."

```
i < 5;
```

In this example, the index variable is initialized to 0, so the loop will repeat until it reaches 4. It makes the loop run from 0 to 4, which is five times if you start at 0: 0, 1, 2, 3, and 4. You can use any kind of conditional statement you want here.

The last statement increases the index variable by 1 each time the loop runs: i++:

```
for(var i = 0; i < 5; i++)
{
   ...things you want to repeat;
}
```

The first time the loop runs, i starts at 0. The next time it repeats, the ++ operator adds 1.

```
i++
```

That means that i then equals 1 (because 0 plus 1 equals 1, of course). The next time the loop repeats, 1 is added to i again, which results in a value of 2. This repeats while i is less than 5. As soon as it gets a value of 5, the loop stops dead in its tracks.

Although i++ is the most common way to increase the value of the index variable, you can use any statement you like to increase or decrease it. For example, i += 2 will increase the index variable by 2 each time the loop repeats. i-- will decrease it by 1 if you want your loop to count backward.

Here's an example of a for loop that displays the numbers from 0 to 4.

```
for(var i = 0; i < 5; i++)
{
   console.log(i);
}
```

Here's how it displays in the console:

```
0
1
2
3
4
```

It's just displaying the value of i, the loop index variable, each time the loop runs. You can now clearly see how the loop runs 5 times. It starts at 0 and quits before it gets to 5.

You can initialize i to any number you like, and you can use any condition to quit the loop. Here's another example: i is initialized to 1, and the loop repeats until it becomes 5:

```
for(var i = 1; i <= 5; i++)
{
  console.log(i);
}
```

This displays the following:

```
1
2
3
4
5
```

In this example the loop displays the final number 5. The loop runs while i is less than or equal to 5.

```
i <= 5;
```

The loop will only quit if i becomes greater than 5.

Initializing the index variable to 1 and quitting the loop on 5 is particularly useful because it makes it very clear where the loop starts and ends.

We'll look at a few different ways to use for loops in this chapter. Figure 4-2 is a quick-reference diagram of how for loops work.

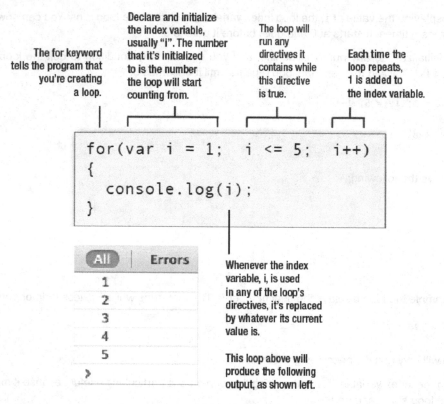

The for keyword tells the program that you're creating a loop.

Declare and initialize the index variable, usually "i". The number that it's initialized to is the number the loop will start counting from.

The loop will run any directives it contains while this directive is true.

Each time the loop repeats, 1 is added to the index variable.

```
for(var i = 1;  i <= 5;  i++)
{
    console.log(i);
}
```

All | Errors

1
2
3
4
5
>

Whenever the index variable, i, is used in any of the loop's directives, it's replaced by whatever its current value is.

This loop above will produce the following output, as shown left.

Figure 4-2. How for loops work

Note: Although the for loop is a perennial favorite, JavaScript allows you to create loops in a few other ways as well. You can also create a **while loop** or a **do-while loop**. They all do the same things as the for loop, although they have nuances that might be useful in certain situations.

The while loop can be particularly useful for games. It looks like this:

```
while(a certain condition is true)

{

    //...the code you want to run

}
```

While loops don't run for a set number of times: they run as many times as they need to until the condition in the parentheses becomes false. When you use while loops in your programs, you have to make sure that the condition eventually will become false. If it doesn't, the loop will run "forever" and the program might hang.

While loops will only run the directives they contain if the condition they're checking for is true. That means the loop might never run if the condition never becomes true. However, in some cases you might need a loop that runs at least once. In that case you can use a do-while loop.

The do-while loop uses this format:

```
do

{

    //... the code you want to repeat

}

while (this condition is true);
```

You can see that the while statement is checking the condition only after the directives inside the braces have run. That means those directives will have a chance to run at least once before the while statement checks whether the loop condition is true.

Using arrays for storing lots of information

Variables are used to store information. But one variable can only store one piece of information at a time. If you want to store lots of information using variables, you need to use lots of variables.

But there's a better way to store lots of information. You can use an **array**. An array is like a storage closet that you can keep any number of things in. When you have lots of information you want to keep track of, it's often better to store all the information inside one array, rather than in lots of variables.

To create an empty array, choose a name for your array and assign it a pair of empty square brackets, like this:

```
var closet = [];
```

The name of this array is closet, but you can use any name you like. The empty brackets show that it doesn't contain anything yet. It's empty. Sometimes you'll want to start with an empty array like this at the start of your program and add things to it as the game progresses.

Your arrays don't have to start empty; you can create them already filled with things. Here's an array called closet that stores three things:

```
var closet = ["hat", "umbrella", "katana"];
```

It stores "hat", "umbrella", and "katana" (a katana is an extremely dangerous Japanese sword)—everything you need for a fun night out on the town. All the things in the arrays are surrounded by square brackets and they're each separated by commas. "hat", "umbrella", and "katana" are strings, but you can store anything you like in arrays: strings, variables, numbers, or even other arrays. The things that an array stores are called **elements**. The closet array has three elements.

Array basics

Let's look at some simple examples that demonstrate how to use arrays to store and find information.

All the elements in an array are numbered sequentially, starting with 0. These numbers are called **index numbers**. In the preceding example, "hat" has an index number of 0, "umbrella" has an index number of 1, and "katana" has an index number of 2.

You can find out which element is at which index number like this:

```
closet[1]
```

This has the value of "umbrella" because "umbrella" has an index number of 1.

It's really very simple. An array is just a numbered list of elements. Figure 4-3 illustrates an empty array compared with an array with three elements.

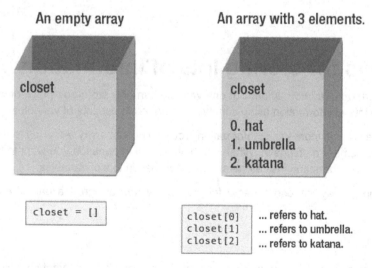

Figure 4-3. Arrays and array elements

There are several ways to put elements into arrays. In the previous example, the three elements were added to the array when it was initialized. But you can also assign elements directly to a position in the array's index at any time:

```
closet[2] = "katana";
```

Then whenever your code sees `closet[2]` it interprets it as `"katana"`.

Let's look at a slightly more concrete example. Here's a program called **basicArray.html** that you'll find in the chapter's source files.

```
//Create an empty array
var closet = [];

//Add three things
closet[0] = "hat";
closet[1] = "umbrella";
closet[2] = "katana";

//View the entire array contents
console.log("Entire array: " + closet);

//View individual elements
console.log("Element 0: " + closet[0]);
console.log("Element 1: " + closet[1]);
console.log("Element 2: " + closet[2]);
```

Here's what it displays in the console:

```
Entire Array: hat,umbrella,katana
Element 0: hat
Element 1: umbrella
Element 2: katana
```

Here's how the entire array contents is displayed:

```
console.log("Entire array: " + closet);
```

This is how it appears in the console:

```
Entire Array: hat,umbrella,katana
```

When an array is combined with a string like this, all the array's elements are automatically converted into a single string:

```
"hat,umbrella,katana"
```

The individual array elements are displayed like this:

```
console.log("Element 0: " + closet[0]);
console.log("Element 1: " + closet[1]);
console.log("Element 2: " + closet[2]);
```

The array elements, closet[0], closet[1], and closet[2], are also interpreted as ordinary strings. That's why the lines above produce the following output:

```
Element 0: hat
Element 1: umbrella
Element 2: katana
```

It's easy to see from this example that arrays are just storage containers.

Pushing elements into an array

Another very common way to put elements into an array is to use an array's push method. You can use push to literally "push" an element into an array by using this format:

```
arrayName.push(elementName);
```

When you push an element into an array, you add it to the end of the array. The element gets an index number that's one higher than the last element that's already in the array. This means that if the last element has an index number of [2], the new element that you push into it will have an index number of [3].

Using push is really helpful because you don't need to worry about which index number to add the element to. The array figures this out for you. It's just like shoving stuff into a big bag, and you don't have to worry about the order. The ones at the top are the last ones you shoved in.

Here's a simple program that uses push to add elements to an array:

```
//Create an empty array
var closet = [];

//Add three things
closet.push("hat");
closet.push("umbrella");
closet.push("katana");

//View the entire array contents
console.log("Entire array: " + closet);

//View individual elements
console.log("Element 0: " + closet[0]);
console.log("Element 1: " + closet[1]);
console.log("Element 2: " + closet[2]);
```

The output is exactly the same as the first example. The fact that you don't need to worry about the index numbers is really convenient.

You'll find the working code for this example in the usingPush.html file in this chapter's source files.

Removing elements from an array

To remove an element from an array, you can use the array's pop method. The following code uses pop to remove the last element from an array:

```
closet.pop();
```

If the array had three elements, it would now have only two, with the last one missing. You can think of it like this: if you squeeze the array, the last one "pops" out.

The element that's removed can be copied directly into a new variable. Here's how:

```
var removedElement = closet.pop();
```

If the last element was "katana", removedElement now has the value of "katana". It also means that the closet array now contains only two elements: "hat" and "umbrella".

Here's a working example:

```
//Create an empty array
var closet = ["hat", "umbrella", "katana"];

//Pop the last element
var lastElement = closet.pop();

//View the value of lastElement
console.log("The popped element: " + lastElement);

//View the new closet array
console.log("The closet array: " + closet);
```

Here's what it displays in the console:

```
The popped element: katana
The closet array: hat,umbrella
```

You can also add and remove elements in an array by using the splice method. This lets you remove an element at an exact index number position. Here's an array with three elements:

```
var closet = ["hat", "umbrella", "katana"];
```

If you want to cut out umbrella, at index number 1, you can use splice to do it like this:

```
closet.splice(1, 1);
```

There are two numbers in the parentheses. The first is the index position number of the element you want to cut out. The second is the number of elements from that point onward that you want to remove. In this case we're removing the element with an index number 1, and just removing one element at that point.

You could remove both umbrella and katana like this:

```
closet.splice(1, 2);
```

In this case two elements are being removed starting from index number 1.

Just as with pop, you can assign the element you remove with splice into a new variable, like this:

```
var removedElement = closet.splice(1, 1);
```

removedElement would now have the value "umbrella". The closet array will now contain only "hat" and "katana".

> Note: removedElement is not an ordinary variable; it's actually an array itself. In this example, it only contains one value: "umbrella". However, if you splice more than one element from the closet array, removedElement would contain all of them. You could then treat removedElement like any ordinary array.

Here's a working example of the splice method:

```
//Create an empty array
var closet = ["hat", "umbrella", "katana"];

//Splice out the middle element
var middleElement = closet.splice(1, 1);

//View the value of middleElement
console.log("The spliced element: " + middleElement);

//View the new closet array
console.log("The closet array: " + closet);
```

This is what you'll see in the console:

```
The spliced element: umbrella
The closet array: hat,katana
```

You'll find the **usingPop.html** and **usingSplice.html** files in the chapter's source files with all the working code for these examples.

These are all the important techniques you need to know for working with arrays for all the games in the rest of this book.

It's alive!

If you store information in arrays, you have much more control over that information than you would if you were using simple variables. That's because using an index number to access the information lets you use simple math tricks, formulas, and loops to find and organize that information in interesting ways. The rest of this chapter will be about how to do this. But let's start with a fun and useful example.

Is it possible that we could ever create a living, conscious computer? And if we did, how would we know for sure that it were really conscious? It turns out this is a particularly knotty problem, because no one has yet been able to identify or define what consciousness itself is. We have no idea know how to pinpoint consciousness in things we usually think of as alive, like plants and animals. However, Alan Turing, the father of the modern computer, proposed that this uncertainly actually makes the problem much easier to solve. We don't need to ask, "Is a computer conscious?"; we just need to ask, "Does it behave like other things that we think of as conscious?" He proposed a simple test: If a real person chats with a computer, and that computer tricks the person into thinking that it's also a real person, then we have to assume that the computer is conscious.

Oh, really? Let's find out.

In the chapter's source files you'll find a program called artificialLife.html. It will ask you some questions. Chat with it a bit and see how it responds. Is it really alive? Figure 4-4 shows you one of the conversations you might have.

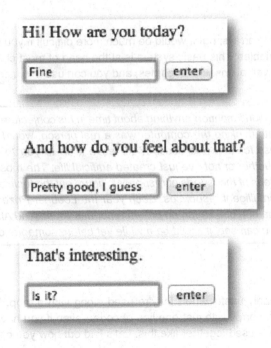

Figure 4-4. Use random numbers to make a chatbot

As you might guess, the program randomly chooses a response from a prewritten list. The computer can reply in five different ways. Each reply is an element in an array called replies.

```
var replies = [];
replies[0] = "Oh really??";
replies[1] = "That's interesting.";
replies[2] = "Now I'm not so sure. Can you explain?";
replies[3] = "And how do you feel about that?";
replies[4] = "Is that usual for you?";
```

Each time you click the button, a random number is chosen, from 0 to 4. The program uses that number to choose a response.

```
function clickHandler()
{
  var randomNumber = Math.floor(Math.random() * 5);
  output.innerHTML = replies[randomNumber];
}
```

You can see that the array's index number is just replaced with the randomly chosen number:

```
replies[randomNumber]
```

This is very easy to do using arrays, but it would be much more difficult if you were just storing the computer's replies in five separate variables. This basic system is at the heart of most chatbots and nonplayer characters (NPC) you might have conversations with in games, and you can use this trick in your own games.

> Note: Alan Turing didn't mention anything about time in his conjecture. If you were tricked for one second into thinking the computer was a real person, would the computer have had consciousness for that one second? I'll leave it up to you to write your doctoral dissertation on whether or not I've just created artificial life. The most advanced chatbot systems contain tens of thousands of responses, figure out the topic of conversation, and give remarkably intelligent responses. Each year the Loebner Prize runs a competition to find the best chatbot, but, so far, no programmer has yet passed Alan Turing's original, simple test. As you can see, it might be a while yet before someone does.

Looping arrays

Arrays become extraordinarily useful when they're used along with a loop. You can use a for loop to loop through every element in an array with just one line of code—even if you have hundreds of elements. Arrays and loops are almost always used together like this. Let's find out how you can use a loop to read all the elements in an array.

Each array has a built-in property called `length`, which tells you how many elements it has. You can access an array's `length` property like this:

`arrayName.length`

The numbering of the length property starts at 1. That means if you have an array with 10 elements, the `length` property will be 10. This seems obvious, but it can become a bit confusing because arrays start their numbering at 0. That means an array with 10 elements will have index numbers like this: 0, 1, 2, 3, 4, 5, 6, 7, 8, 9. The "10th element" has the index number "9". So you need to remember that the array `length` property will always be a number that's one more than the array's last index number.

> Note: To find the index number of the last element in an array, you could use code that looks like this: arrayName.length – 1.

You can use an array's `length` property to control the number of times a loop repeats. This is really useful because you don't need to know how many elements are in the array in advance.

Here's a basic example of the format you can use:

```
for(var i = 0; i < arrayName.length; i++)
{
    console.log(arrayName[i]);
}
```

This code displays all the elements in the array, starting with element 0 and running through all the way to the end of the array, however long it happens to be.

Here's the **arrayLoop.html** program that contains an example of how to use a for loop to list the contents of an array:

```
var closet = [];

closet[0] = "hat";
closet[1] = "umbrella";
closet[2] = "katana";

//View the entire array
for(var i = 0; i < closet.length; i++)
{
    console.log("Element " + i + ": " + closet[i]);
}
```

Here's what it displays:

```
Element 0: hat
Element 1: umbrella
Element 2: katana
```

This little bit of code is one of the most common and useful for game design, and you'll see it in most of the projects in this book.

Searching arrays

You can use loops to search arrays for information. Just throw an if statement into the mix. It's really simple. Check to see whether an array element in the loop matches a certain search term. If you have a match, the element you're looking for has been found.

Here's the basic format for searching an array:

```
for(var i = 0; i < arrayName.length; i++)
{
  if(arrayName[i] === "searchTerm")
  {
    console.log("Search term found.");
    break;
  }
}
```

One new thing here is the keyword break, which is used to stop a loop immediately without waiting for it to finish. When you use loops to search through arrays, you're often looking for only one item. Once that item has been found, it doesn't make sense to continue the loop, so you can use break to stop it early. Because your program doesn't have to do any unnecessary checking, your game will run more efficiently.

You'll find arraySearch.html in the chapter's source files. It uses an if statement inside a loop to check whether the array contains an element called "umbrella". Once the if statement finds the correct element, a break directive stops the loop from continuing:

```
var closet = [];

closet[0] = "hat";
closet[1] = "umbrella";
closet[2] = "katana";

//Search for umbrella

for(var i = 0; i < closet.length; i++)
{
  if(closet[i] === "umbrella")
  {
    console.log("Umbrella found at position: " + i);
    break;
  }
}
```

Here's what the program displays:

```
Umbrella found at position: 1
```

Because you included a break directive, the loop stops at that point. It never checks element [2], which is a good thing. The loop has found what it's looking for, so it doesn't need to check any further.

Imprint this bit of code into your brain cells with a hot iron brand. Whenever you see it, you should think, "This is an array search!" It's one of the most important bits of programming code you need to know.

A simple database

Things start to get really interesting if you have more than one array. Imagine that you want to plan your summer holiday to a nearby planet. The planet should be close to Earth and should have good weather in August. Create three arrays to store the names, distances, and weather conditions of planets you're considering. (The distances are in astronomical units, centered on each planet's orbit around the sun.)

```
var planetNames = ["Jupiter", "Venus", "Saturn", "Mars"];
var distancesFromEarth = [5.2, 0.72, 9.5, 1.5];
var sunnyInAugust = [false, true, false, true];
```

The key here is that all the planet information must have the same array index numbers. If Saturn is in position 2, then its distance and weather information should also be in position 2. You can then loop through these arrays and display the information for each planet. Here's how:

```
for(var i = 0; i < planetNames.length; i++)
{
    console.log(planetNames[i]);
    console.log(distancesFromEarth[i]);
    console.log(sunnyInAugust[i]);
    console.log("----------");
}
```

This displays as follows:

```
Jupiter
5.2
false
----------
Venus
0.72
true
----------
Saturn
9.5
false
----------
```

```
Mars
1.5
true
----------
```

This works because the index position numbers for each planet's information is the same in all the arrays.

You can find out which planets are sunny in August by adding an if statement to the loop. Loop through the planetNames array and check whether each planet's matching sunnyInAugust information is true or false. Then just display the names of the sunny planets. Here's how:

```
console.log("These planets are sunny in August:");

for(var i = 0; i < planetNames.length; i++)
{
  if(sunnyInAugust[i])
  {
    console.log(planetNames[i]);
  }
}
```

Here's how this displays:

```
These planets are sunny in August:
Venus
Mars
```

(However, at that time of year I hear that Venus occasionally suffers from toxic, sulfuric acid gas-cloud storms and poisonous carbon dioxide crystal rain.) Now you know how to find the sunny planets, but how can you find the closest one?

Compare the distance of each planet with the distance of another planet in the array. Find out which distance is less, and then save that planet's name and distance. Then compare that planet with the next one in the array. If you do this for all the array elements, you'll end up with the name and distance of the closest planet.

For this to work you need to create two new temporary variables: shortestDistance and closestPlanet. Each time the loop repeats, the distance and the name of the closest planet will be copied into these variables. They'll then be used to test the next element in the array. When the loop is finished, shortestDistance and closestPlanet will end up with the best information you're looking for. Here's the code that finds the closest planet:

```
var closestPlanet = "";
var shortestDistance = 10;

for(var i = 0; i < planetNames.length; i++)
{
  if(distancesFromEarth[i] < shortestDistance)
```

```
    {
      shortestDistance = distancesFromEarth[i];
      closestPlanet = planetNames[i];
    }
}
console.log("Closest planet: " + closestPlanet);
console.log("Shortest distance: " + shortestDistance);
```

Here's what this code displays:

```
Closest planet: Venus
Shortest distance: 0.72
```

The two new variables help us track the current closest planet:

```
var closestPlanet = "";
var shortestDistance = 10;
```

shortestDistance is initialized to 10 so that it's a number that's larger than the largest number in the distancesFromEarth array. That's a good place to start.

Each time the loop repeats, it checks whether the current distancesFromEarth number is less than the shortestDistance.

```
if(distancesFromEarth[i] < shortestDistance)
{...
```

If it is, that number is copied into the shortestDistance variable, and the name of that planet is copied into the closestPlanet variable.

```
shortestDistance = distancesFromEarth[i];
closestPlanet = planetNames[i];
```

The first time the loop repeats this will be Jupiter, which has a distance of 5.2. That's less than 10, so 5.2 is copied into shortestDistance.

The next time the loop repeats, shortestDistance will still have that new value of 5.2. The next planet, Venus, has a distance of 0.72, which is even less. So 0.72 is now copied into shortestDistance and the planet name "Venus" is copied into closestPlanet.

The loop then checks Saturn and Mars. But because neither has a distance less than 0.72, shortestDistance and closestPlanet won't be changed. That's why Venus comes out the winner at the end of the loop. Have fun, but don't forget the sunblock and the gas mask.

You'll find working examples of all this code in the **database.html** file in the chapter's source folders.

Making an adventure game

Now that you know how to store information in arrays and can find that information by using loops, you can start using those techniques to make games. We're going to create an adventure game called "The Forest of Lyrica." The game lets you explore a mysterious forest, solve a puzzle, and slay a dragon. We're going to start with something simple, add features as we go, and finally add images and a user interface. This game uses the classic adventure-game programming techniques that have fueled thousands of commercial games, and you'll be able to use these techniques for a wide variety of different game genres.

> Note: The best-known classic adventure game is Infocom's Zork, from 1977. Download and play it if you haven't already; it's a blast and is the great-grandfather of all modern role-playing and open-world games. It was created in the days when home computers were not powerful enough to render 3D graphics, so it depended on the human imagination to do the rendering for it. Adventure games were the most popular genre of computer games at the time, and they represented the cutting edge of game-design and artificial intelligence techniques. The tradition of text-only adventure games has evolved since then into a thriving genre called **interactive fiction**. But these techniques are at the heart of adventure and fantasy games of all kinds, from Monkey Island, to Zelda to Myst and Skyrim. Adventure games are a very rich genre that is still ripe for experimentation and innovation, and there's still plenty of room for a game of your own creation.

Here's how I suggest you read the rest of this chapter. For each new phase of the game that I describe, try building your own version from scratch. Instead of a fantasy game, maybe set it in a science fiction universe, or even in the real world, like your neighborhood. The final game is complex, as most game projects are. But, by breaking it down into small bite-sized pieces and building it slowly, step by step, you'll understand and solve each small problem as you go.

Drawing the map

The first step is to draw the map of your world. "The Forest of Lyrica," which is the game world we're creating, is very small. There are only nine locations to explore. You can describe the whole game world in a 3-by-3 grid, shown in Figure 4-5. Each grid square represents a location in the forest.

0 stone keep	1 well	2 sunny glade
3 sleeping dragon	4 path	5 ancient gate
6 river's edge	7 wooden bench	8 cottage

Figure 4-5. Map your game world on a grid

The grid squares are numbered from 0 to 8, from left to right. The map represents an array and each location on the map is an element in that array. The numbers tell you which location belongs in which array element.

The next step is to create an array that matches the map you've drawn. Here's what it could look like:

```
var map = [];

map[0] = "An old stone keep.";
map[1] = "A deep well.";
map[2] = "A sunny glade.";
map[3] = "A sleeping dragon.";
map[4] = "A narrow pathway.";
map[5] = "An ancient gate.";
map[6] = "The edge of a river.";
map[7] = "A lonely wooden bench.";
map[8] = "An isolated cottage. Faint music comes from inside.";
```

You then need to decide where the player should start the game. The narrow pathway, right at the center of the map, is as good a place as any. Create a variable called `mapLocation`, and give it the value 4, to match the index number of the pathway on the map.

```
var mapLocation = 4;
```

All you need to do now is display this to the player. You'll find the lyrica1.html file in the chapter's source files that does this. It uses a simple `<p>` output tag for the player to know his or her bearings. Here's the complete HTML file:

```
<!doctype html>
<title>The Forest of Lyrica - 1</title>

<p id="output"></p>

<script>
```

```
//Create the map
var map = [];

map[0] = "An old stone keep.";
map[1] = "A deep well.";
map[2] = "A sunny glade.";
map[3] = "A sleeping dragon.";
map[4] = "A narrow pathway.";
map[5] = "An ancient gate.";
map[6] = "The edge of a river.";
map[7] = "A lonely wooden bench.";
map[8] = "An isolated cottage. Faint music comes from inside.";

//Set the player's start location
var mapLocation = 4;

//The output element
var output = document.querySelector("#output");

//Display the player's location
output.innerHTML = map[mapLocation];

</script>
```

When you run this, it will display the player's start location:

```
A narrow pathway.
```

Try changing the value of mapLocation to another number, such as 3 or 7, and you'll see that a different start location is displayed. It's just referencing a different element in the map array.

Congratulations, you've just created your first game world! The next steps are to make it interactive. We'll start by letting the player move around and explore the map.

Moving around the world

In the chapter's source files you'll find **lyrica2.html**. This version of the game has an input field and a button. Enter any of these four actions: "north," "east," "south," or "west." Then click the button. The game correctly displays your new map location based on the direction you chose. If you enter a word it doesn't understand, it displays *"I don't understand that."* Figure 4-6 illustrates how the game correctly moves you through the world based on our map.

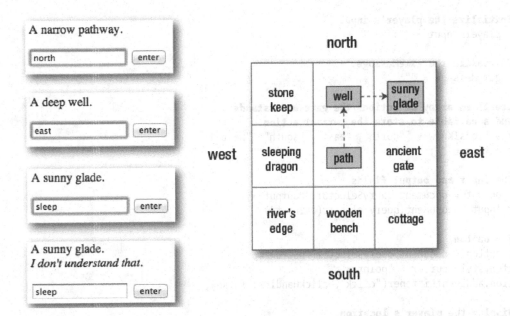

Figure 4-6. Enter a direction to move through the game world

Here's the complete code listing, and I'll walk you through how it works in detail:

```
<!doctype html>
<title>The Forest of Lyrica - 2</title>

<p id="output"></p>
<input id="input" type="text" placeholder="Enter your action...">
<button>enter</button>

<script>

//Create the map
var map = [];

map[0] = "An old stone keep.";
map[1] = "A deep well.";
map[2] = "A sunny glade.";
map[3] = "A sleeping dragon.";
map[4] = "A narrow pathway.";
map[5] = "An ancient gate.";
map[6] = "The edge of a river.";
map[7] = "A lonely wooden bench.";
map[8] = "An isolated cottage. Faint music comes from inside.";

//Set the player's start location
var mapLocation = 4;
```

```javascript
//Initialize the player's input
var playersInput = "";

//Initialize the gameMessage
var gameMessage = "";

//Create an array of actions the game understands
//and a variable to store the current action
var actionsIKnow = ["north", "east", "south", "west"];
var action = "";

//The input and output fields
var output = document.querySelector("#output");
var input = document.querySelector("#input");

//The button
var button = document.querySelector("button");
button.style.cursor = "pointer";
button.addEventListener("click", clickHandler, false);

//Display the player's location
render();

function clickHandler()
{
  playGame();
}

function playGame()
{
    //Get the player's input and convert it to lowercase
    playersInput = input.value;
    playersInput = playersInput.toLowerCase();

    //Reset these variables from the previous turn
    gameMessage = "";
    action = "";

    //Figure out the player's action
    for(i = 0; i < actionsIKnow.length; i++)
    {
      if(playersInput.indexOf(actionsIKnow[i]) !== -1)
      {
        action = actionsIKnow[i];
        console.log("player's action: " + action);
        break;
      }
    }
```

```
//Choose the correct action
switch(action)
{
    case "north":
        mapLocation -= 3;
        break;

    case "east":
        mapLocation += 1;
        break;

    case "south":
        mapLocation += 3;
        break;

    case "west":
        mapLocation -= 1;
        break;

    default:
        gameMessage = "I don't understand that.";
}

//Render the game
render();
}

function render()
{
    //Render the location
    output.innerHTML = map[mapLocation];

    //Display the game message
    output.innerHTML += "<br><em>" + gameMessage + "</em>";
}

</script>
```

This new version of the game follows the exact same model as the number-guessing game from Chapter 3, so you should recognize this format. The playGame function analyzes the player's input and figures out what to do with it. If the action makes sense, it calls the render function, which displays the result in the browser.

What's new here is how the game finds the player's correct action and also how it figures out the correct location.

Finding the player's action

An interesting feature of the game is that you can type anything you like into the input field. As long as it contains a word the game understands, the input will work. So far, the game understands the words "north," "east," "south," and "west." If you use any of these words in a sentence, the game will correctly notice that you're using a word it understands. For example, if you want to go north, you can type any of these sentences:

```
north
I want to go north
move to the north
```

All that matters is that you've used the word "north" somewhere. The game recognizes "north" as an action it knows and it then uses a switch statement to perform the correct action in the game.

This works because of a method called indexOf. The indexOf method can tell you if a string that you're looking for is inside a longer string. Here's the basic format for using it.

```
var longStringOfText = "This string contains the word north.";
longStringOfText.indexOf("north");
```

If longStringOfText *doesn't* contain "north," indexOf will produce "-1". This is not as useless as it might first seem. It means that you can tell whether a longer string contains the word you're looking for by testing whether or not indexOf is coming up with "-1". Use an if statement to do this, which is how indexOf is almost always used.

```
var longStringOfText = "This string contains the word north.";

if(longStringOfText.indexOf("north") !== -1)
{
  console.log("word found");
}
else
{
    console.log("word not found");
}
```

The if statement checks whether indexOf *doesn't* produce "-1". If it doesn't, the word you're looking for has been found.

This is how you check for one word. But in games you'll often need to check for a whole list of possible words. The way to do this is to put all the words you want to look for in an array. Then loop through all those words, and test them one by one by using indexOf each time the loop repeats. That's the system I've used in "The Forest of Lyrica," so let's look at how this works.

First the game creates an array called actionsIKnow that contains all the possible game actions.

```
var actionsIKnow = ["north", "east", "south", "west"];
```

It also initializes a variable called `action`, which will be used to store the player's current action for each turn of the game.

```
var action = "";
```

When the player enters some text and clicks the button, the `playGame` function is called. Here's the first section of the `playGame` function that reads the player's input and finds the correct action.

```
function playGame()
{
    //Get the player's input and convert it to lowercase
    playersInput = input.value;
    playersInput = playersInput.toLowerCase();

    //Reset these variables from the previous turn
    gameMessage = "";
    action = "";

    //Figure out the player's action
    for(i = 0; i < actionsIKnow.length; i++)
    {
      if(playersInput.indexOf(actionsIKnow[i]) !== -1)
      {
        action = actionsIKnow[i];
        console.log("player's action: " + action);
        break;
      }
    }
}
```

...

The first thing it does is copy the text from the HTML input field into a variable called `playersInput`:

```
playersInput = input.value;
```

It then converts the player's input to lowercase characters by using the `toLowerCase` method:

```
playersInput = playersInput.toLowerCase();
```

This is important because the player might type words that contain both uppercase and lowercase characters. JavaScript is case-sensitive, so to avoid having to test for uppercase versions of words like "North" or "South" it's simpler just to force them all to be lowercase.

The program then loops through all four words in the `actionsIKnow` array (north, east, south, west). It uses `indexOf` to check each word against the `playersInput` every time it loops. If one of the words *doesn't* produce −1, then the program knows the player entered a word it understands.

```
for(i = 0; i < actionsIKnow.length; i++)
{
  if(playersInput.indexOf(actionsIKnow[i]) !== -1)
  {
    action = actionsIKnow[i];
    console.log("player's action: " + action);
    break;
  }
}
```

Don't let this bit of code confuse you! It looks complex, but walk yourself through it slowly. This is the same basic search code that I asked you to brand into your brain cells—do you remember it?

When the word is found, the program copies that word from the actionsIKnow array into the action variable.

```
action = actionsIKnow[i];
```

We can now use this action variable in the game to choose the correct action.

The last thing the if statement does is break the loop when a word is found:

```
break;
```

This prevents the loop from checking for more words after it successfully finds the first.

> Note: An imaginative player might type something into the game like "I don't want to go north, only south." That's a case where both "north" and "south" are used in the same sentence, and both are legitimate actions. Which one will the game choose? The first one. That's because the break directive stops the loop after finding the first action. You'll need to decide whether or not this could be a problem in your game, and, if it is, how your game could deal with it.

Finding the player's location

The player's action is now captured in the action variable. The next step is to use a switch statement to change the map location based on the action.

```
switch(action)
{
  case "north":
    mapLocation -= 3;
    break;

  case "east":
    mapLocation += 1;
    break;
```

```
case "south":
  mapLocation += 3;
  break;

case "west":
  mapLocation -= 1;
  break;

default:
  gameMessage = "I don't understand that.";
}
```

You can see that this code is adding or subtracting 1 or 3 to mapLocation, depending on the direction. If you look at your original map, with each location assigned an array index number, you'll see why this works.

If the action is "west," the game subtracts 1 from mapLocation. If mapLocation was 4, it becomes 3. Have a look at the map and you'll see that the location with the index value of 3 is directly to the west of location 4.

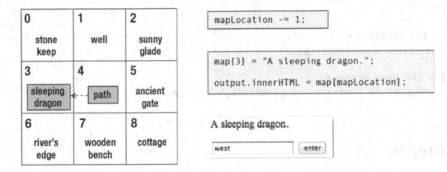

Figure 4-7. Add or subtract to find the correct location

If the player types "east," 1 will be *added* to mapLocation. You can see that the new variable matches an array element that corresponds to a map location going toward the east. The game adds or subtracts 3 for "south" or "north," and that matches the correct locations for those directions as well. You can see that this will be true no matter where on the map the player is. There's no trickery here: it's just first-grade math!

> Note: Adding or subtracting 3 to move north and south works because we're using a 3-by-3 grid. If you were using a 9-by-9 grid, for example, you would have to add or subtract 9.

One problem with our game world at the moment is that there are no limits to the map edges. The player can jump from location 3, the sleeping dragon in the west, to location 2, the sunny glade in the east, with just one move westward. The game shouldn't allow this, but it's easy to fix, as you'll soon see.

Displaying messages and rendering the output

The game uses a variable called gameMessage, which tells the player what's happening. It's initialized to an empty string when the game starts.

```
var gameMessage = "";
```

You're going to use gameMessage a lot, but the first place it's used is with the switch statement. If the player enters an action that the game doesn't understand, the switch statement's default case runs. It sets gameMessage to "I don't understand that."

```
default:
  gameMessage = "I don't understand that.";
```

This will happen if the player inputs something that doesn't include any words the game understands.

The last thing the playGame function does is call the render function. It displays the new map location and the gameMessage.

```
function render()
{
    //Render the location
    output.innerHTML = map[mapLocation];

    //Display the game message
    output.innerHTML += "<br><em>" + gameMessage + "</em>";
}
```

Adding images

It's just as easy to display images for each location as it is to display text. The technique is identical, except that instead of changing an innerHTML property for text, you're changing an <img> tag's src property. You'll find a working example of the game with images in the lyrica3.html file. Move around the world, and you'll now see an image that matches each location, as shown in Figure 4-8.

Figure 4-8. Add some images to the world

This is much easier to do than you might think, and it requires only a few small additions to the existing program. The key to making this work is that the name of each image file is stored in an array that exactly matches the order of locations in the `map` array. That means that if `mapLocation` is 3, you can use that same number to reference the correct description and the correct image file. Let's find out how this all works.

First, there are nine PNG images in the project's images folder, as you can see in Figure 4-9.

Figure 4-9. PNG files in the images folder

lyrica3.html has a new `<img>` tag with an empty `src` element when the game first loads.

```
<img src="" width="300" height="267">
<p id="output"></p>
<input id="input" type="text" placeholder="Enter your action...">
<button>enter</button>
```

The game then initializes an array called `images`. Each element in the array has the same name as a PNG file name.

```
var images = [];
images[0] = "keep.png";
images[1] = "well.png";
images[2] = "glade.png";
images[3] = "dragon.png";
images[4] = "path.png";
images[5] = "gate.png";
images[6] = "river.png";
images[7] = "bench.png";
images[8] = "cottage.png";
```

The array index numbers of the images exactly match the map locations they depict. This means that we can find the correct image for the current location like this:

```
images[mapLocation]
```

The game also needs a reference to the `<img>` tag so that it can access it.

```
var image = document.querySelector("img");
```

The last change is in the render function. The `<img>` tag's src property is changed so that the correct image file is loaded into it.

```
function render()
{
    //Render the location
    output.innerHTML = map[mapLocation];
    image.src = "../images/" + images[mapLocation];

    //Display the game message
    output.innerHTML += "<br><em>" + gameMessage + "</em>";
}
```

You can see that the file path `"../images/"` is combined with the file name from the images array that matches the map location.

```
image.src = "../images/" + images[mapLocation];
```

If mapLocation were 7, this line of code would be interpreted like this:

```
image.src = "../images/bench.png";
```

Because mapLocation keeps track of where in the world you are, and the image file names are in array index positions that exactly match the map locations, the correct image will be loaded every time.

> Note: In Chapters 2 and 3 you learned how to load images into a `<div>` element's background-image property. In this example I've just used a plain `<img>` tag and changed its src property. It's entirely up to you which system you prefer to use. Because `<img>` tags are stand-alone (they don't have closing tags), they can't contain other elements. That might be a factor in your decision.

And that's it! There are no other changes to make. See how efficient and easy it is to use arrays to organize complex information?

Checking game-world boundaries

In the next version of the game we'll prevent the player from crossing the edges of the game world. When the player is at the extreme north, east, south, and west edges, the game should prevent the player from moving further in those directions. You can find a working example of this in the **lyrica4.html** file. If you try to move beyond the edge of the map, you're stopped and will receive a unique message for each part of the world you're in. Figure 4-10 illustrates this.

Figure 4-10. Add some boundaries to the game world

The first step is to create an array for all the blocked-path messages you want to display for each location. I've called my array blockedPathMessages, and it looks like this:

```
var blockedPathMessages = [];
blockedPathMessages[0] = "It's too dangerous to move that way.";
blockedPathMessages[1] = "A mysterious force holds you back.";
blockedPathMessages[2] = "A tangle of thorns blocks your way.";
blockedPathMessages[3] = "You can't step over the dragon.";
blockedPathMessages[4] = "";
blockedPathMessages[5] = "The gate locks shut.";
blockedPathMessages[6] = "The river is too deep to cross.";
blockedPathMessages[7] = "The trees are too thick to pass.";
blockedPathMessages[8] = "You're too scared to go that way.";
```

You can see that each message has an index number that matches its location in the world. This is the same trick we used for displaying location descriptions and images. (The center of the map, location 4, doesn't have any blocked directions, so it's just been assigned an empty string.)

The next step is to add extra conditions to the switch statement that chooses "north", "east", "south", or "west". These conditions check where the player is. If the player is at a location that should prevent movement in a certain direction, it doesn't update mapLocation. It also displays the blocked-path message for that location to tell the player he or she can't go further for some reason.

The "west" and "east" directions make some clever use of the mysterious modulus operator, %, that I introduced in Chapter 2. I'll explain how in the pages ahead.

```
switch(action)
{
  case "north":
    if(mapLocation >= 3)
    {
      mapLocation -= 3;
    }
    else
    {
      gameMessage = blockedPathMessages[mapLocation];
    }
    break;

  case "east":
    if(mapLocation % 3 != 2)
    {
      mapLocation += 1;
    }
    else
    {
      gameMessage = blockedPathMessages[mapLocation];
    }
    break;

  case "south":
    if(mapLocation < 6)
    {
      mapLocation += 3;
    }
    else
    {
      gameMessage = blockedPathMessages[mapLocation];
    }
    break;

  case "west":
    if(mapLocation % 3 != 0)
    {
      mapLocation -= 1;
    }
    else
    {
      gameMessage = blockedPathMessages[mapLocation];
    }
    break;
```

```
      default:
        gameMessage = "I don't understand that.";
  }
```

Let's find out how this code prevents the player from moving off the map.

Imagine that the player is standing at the well, at the very north of the map. That's location 1. The player types "I want to go north." The if statement checks whether the player is in a location that should prevent movement to the north.

```
case "north":
  if(mapLocation >= 3)
  {
    mapLocation -= 3;
  }
  else
  {
    gameMessage = blockedPathMessages[mapLocation];
  }
  break;
```

The top row of the map contains location numbers 0, 1, and 2. That means that the player should be allowed to move north only if the current mapLocation is greater than those numbers. If it is, it means that the player is on a row that's below the top row. An if statement checks to see if this is true. If it is, the player can move north.

```
if(mapLocation >= 3)
{
  mapLocation -= 3;
}
```

However, if the player is currently on the top row, such as the well in location 1, the mapLocation won't change. Instead the else statement displays the blocked-path message.

```
gameMessage = blockedPathMessages[mapLocation];
```

It finds the correct blocked-path message by using mapLocation. The message is copied into the gameMessage. The gameMessage will be displayed by the render function, and the result is as you see it in the game.

If the player wants to go south, the same logic is used to make sure that the player isn't already on the most southerly row. In this case, it checks whether mapLocation is greater than 6, which means that the player will be on either the middle or top tow.

```
case "south":
  if(mapLocation < 6)
  {
    mapLocation += 3;
  }
```

```
    else
    {
      gameMessage = blockedPathMessages[mapLocation];
    }
```

Now what happens if the player is on the very left side of the map and types "west"?

Take a look at the map you drew at the beginning. Notice that the location numbers are 0, 3, and 6. What do they have in common? If you divide any of those numbers by 3, they won't have any remainders. This seemingly useless fact actually means that we can tell if the player is on the west side of the map. Why? Because if we divide the mapLocation by 3 and there's no remainder, then the player must be on the very western edge of the map. If that's the case, we want to stop the player from moving farther west.

Here's where the special modulus operator, % , comes to the rescue. Its job is to tell you what the remainder of a division problem is. We can use it to divide the mapLocation by 3.

```
mapLocation % 3
```

If it doesn't produce a remainder of 0, then the player should be allowed to move west. But if it does produce 0, the game should display a blocked-path message. Here's how the switch statement does just this.

```
case "west":
  if(mapLocation % 3 != 0)
  {
    mapLocation -= 1;
  }
  else
  {
    gameMessage = blockedPathMessages[mapLocation];
  }
  break;
```

The switch statement checks whether the player is to the eastern side of the map in the same way. The location numbers on the map's eastern edge are 2, 5, and 8. If you divide any of those numbers by 3, you'll get a remainder of 2. So all you need to do is use the modulus operator to check for this, and you can tell whether or not the player is on the very eastern edge of the map.

```
case "east":
  if(mapLocation % 3 != 2)
  {
    mapLocation += 1;
  }
  else
  {
  gameMessage = blockedPathMessages[mapLocation];
  }
  break;
```

Sneaky, huh? The modulus operator has plenty more tricks up its sleeve, as you'll see in other examples throughout the rest of this book.

Again, we've used arrays to achieve a remarkably complex behavior with very little code or brainpower. Because all the arrays are synchronized to the `mapLocation` value, the whole system is self-organizing. If you need more detail in your world, just keep adding more arrays with more information and follow this same system.

You now have a complete game world that you can move around in with defined boundaries. The next step is to add items that you can interact with.

Game items

We're going to add three items to the game: a sword, a flute, and a stone. These items can be picked up, moved to a different location, and dropped. You can also use them, and how they behave might be different depending on the location. Try it by running the **lyrica5.html** file. Wander around, and when you find an item, try commands like "take the sword," "drop the sword," and "use the sword." You can't use an item unless you're carrying it, but the game also tells you what you're carrying. Figure 4-11 shows some of the ways you can interact with these items. You can move items to other areas of the map, and the game automatically figures out what you're carrying. As you can see, this creates some very complex and sometimes surprising interactions. But you'll be happy to know that it's all just the result of a few simple rules using the same basic techniques we've already used. Let's find out how.

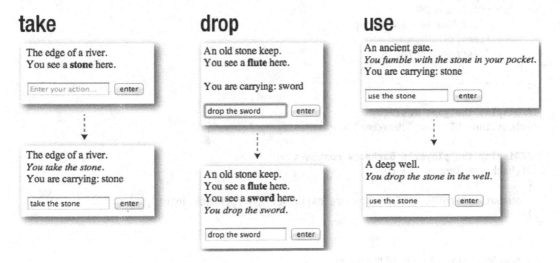

Figure 4-11. Take, drop, and use the game items

Adding and displaying items

Because they're mobile, the game items can't be fixed to a single location. Instead, we'll use two arrays for each object: one to store the object name, and another to store its current location on the map.

```
var items = ["flute", "stone", "sword"];
var itemLocations = [1, 6, 8];
```

itemLocations stores the map location for each of the three items. The order of the items doesn't matter, but their positions in the items array has to match the same array positions as their itemLocations order. That means the first item, flute, will be at location 1. Stone will be at location 6, and sword will be at location 8. You'll soon see that the game keeps these arrays synchronized quite effortlessly.

The render function displays the items by looping through the items array. If the mapLocation matches a number in the itemLocations array, it displays the item.

```
function render()
{
    //Render the location
    output.innerHTML = map[mapLocation];
    image.src = "../images/" + images[mapLocation];

    //Display an item if there's one in this location
    //1. Loop through all the game items
    for(var i = 0; i < items.length; i++)
    {
        //Find out if there's an item at this location
        if(mapLocation === itemLocations[i])
        {
            //Display it
            output.innerHTML
            += "<br>You see a <strong>"
            + items[i]
            + "</strong> here.";
        }
    }

    //Display the game message
    output.innerHTML += "<br><em>" + gameMessage + "</em>";

    //Display the player's backpack contents
    if(backpack.length !== 0)
    {
        output.innerHTML += "<br>You are carrying: " + backpack.join(", ") ;
    }
}
```

A for loop first loops through all the items.

```
for(var i = 0; i < items.length; i++)
{...
```

The game starts with three items in the world, but this can change. The player can remove items from the items array by taking them, and the game could create new items if the player solves puzzles. So you'll never know exactly how many items there'll be in the items array. By looping through the array for as many times as there are items, the game automatically adjusts for the number of items it contains.

With every loop, an if statement checks whether the current `mapLocation` matches an item location.

```
if(mapLocation === itemLocations[i])
{...
```

If it finds a match, it displays the item.

```
output.innerHTML
  += "<br>You see a <strong>"
  + items[i]
  + "</strong> here.";
```

This version of the game doesn't use images for items, but you could easily add them by creating a third array with image file names and then display them in this loop.

Interacting with items

When you take an item, the item is moved from the `items` array into an array called `backpack`. When you drop an item, it will be moved from `backpack` into the `items` array at the current location. The `backpack` array is initialized as empty when the game starts, because the player isn't carrying anything.

```
var backpack = [];
```

The game also needs to understand what the player means if he or she types "take the flute." It needs to understand that "take" is an action and "flute" is an item. The game already knows that "north," "east," "south," and "west" are actions, so add any more game actions to the same `actionsIKnow` array that we've already been using.

```
var actionsIKnow = ["north", "east", "south", "west", "take", "use", "drop"];
var action = "";
```

The game also needs to know about items, so create another array called `itemsIKnow` and fill it with the names of the game items. You also need a variable called `item` that will track the current item the player chooses.

```
var itemsIKnow = ["flute", "stone", "sword"];
var item = "";
```

> Note: Rather than creating the `itemsIKnow` array, you could just use the existing `items` array, because it contains the same item names. However, all the game items won't always be in the items array; they could be in the backpack or some other array you devise. It simplifies our code a bit if we don't need to search through multiple arrays to find item names, although you may want to implement this later when you're a more accomplished programmer.

When the player enters some text and clicks the button, the playGame function now has to find both the action and the item that the player wants to interact with. The code used to find the item in the playersInput is identical to the code used to find the action. It loops through all the words in itemsIKnow and tries to match them with a string in playersInput. If it finds a match, it copies the words into the item variable.

```
for(i = 0; i < itemsIKnow.length; i++)
{
  if(playersInput.indexOf(itemsIKnow[i]) !== -1)
  {
    item = itemsIKnow[i];
    console.log("player's item: " + item);
  }
}
```

We end up with a variable called item that contains the name of the item the player wants to interact with. As you know from previous steps, we already have a variable called action that matches the action name.

The next step is to use the switch statement to choose the correct action. All you need to do is add a new case for each new action. We already have cases for "north", "east", "south", and "west", so you just need to add "take", "drop", and "use". Here's what the new switch statement looks like (I've abridged the direction cases to simplify the code):

```
switch(action)
{
  case "north":
    ...
    break;

  case "east":
    ...
    break;

  case "south":
    ...
    break;

  case "west":
    ...
    break;

  case "take":
    takeItem()
    break;

  case "drop":
    dropItem();
    break;
```

```
  case "use":
    useItem();
    break;

  default:
    gameMessage = "I don't understand that.";
}
```

You can see that each action calls a function: takeItem, dropItem, and useItem. Let's find out how these work.

Taking items

The following code displays the takeItem function:

```
function takeItem()
{
    //Find the index number of the item in the items array
    var itemIndexNumber = items.indexOf(item);

    //Does the item exist in the game world and is it at the player's current location?
    if(itemIndexNumber !== -1
    && itemLocations[itemIndexNumber] === mapLocation)
    {
        gameMessage = "You take the " + item + ".";

        //Add the item to the player's backpack
        backpack.push(item);

        //Remove the item from the game world
        items.splice(itemIndexNumber, 1);
        itemLocations.splice(itemIndexNumber, 1);
    }
    else
    {
        //Message if the player tries to take an item that isn't in the current location
        gameMessage = "You can't do that.";
    }
}
```

The code first finds out if the item the player wants to take is actually in the items array. It does this with the help of the indexOf method that we looked at earlier.

```
items.indexOf(item)
```

indexOf will tell you the index position number of any known array element that you insert into its parentheses. If it can find the item that the player wants to take in the items array, it will tell you what its array index number is. If it can't find the item, it will return −1. In the code above, the number it returns is stored in a variable called itemIndexNumber.

```
var itemIndexNumber = items.indexOf(item);
```

If `itemIndexNumber` is −1, it means that the item the player wants to use wasn't found in the `items` array. But if it's not −1, it means the item does exist in the world.

But is the item also in the player's current map location? If it is, it means the player can take the item. An if statement checks for these two conditions:

```
if(itemIndexNumber !== -1
&& itemLocations[itemIndexNumber] === mapLocation)
{...
```

If both conditions are true, the code lets the player take the item. It first updates the game message to tell the player the item is taken.

```
gameMessage = "You take the " + item + ".";
```

If the item was the flute, this game message will display: "You take the flute."

Next, the code pushes the item to the player's backpack.

```
backpack.push(item);
```

Remember that the backpack is an array that stores the items the player is carrying.

We then need to remove the item from the game world. To do this, we need to splice the item from the `items` array, and then splice its map location number from the `itemLocations` array.

```
items.splice(itemIndexNumber, 1);
itemLocations.splice(itemIndexNumber, 1);
```

Remember that `itemIndexNumber` is the array position number of the item in the `items` array. That's why we can use it in the above code to splice the item from the arrays at the correct position. Because you're splicing both arrays at exactly the same index numbers, the other elements in those arrays will stay synchronized. (If you had a third array for item image names, you'd have to splice it like this as well.)

The game has now moved the item from the game world into the player's backpack. If there had been three items in the `items` array, there would be two remaining in the array. If the `backpack` had been empty, it would now contain one item.

If the player tries to take an item that isn't in the `items` array or isn't at the current map location, the game displays a message to inform the player.

```
else
{
  gameMessage = "You can't do that.";
}
```

If the backpack contains items, the render function displays it. Here's an abridged version of the render function with the code that displays the things in the backpack:

```
function render()
{
  ...
  if(backpack.length !== 0)
  {
    output.innerHTML += "<br>You are carrying: " + backpack.join(", ");
  }
}
```

The items will be displayed only if the backpack contains something. The first thing the code does is use an if statement to find out if the length of the backpack array isn't 0.

```
if(backpack.length !== 0)
{...
```

If it's not 0, the backpack array must contain at least one element, and so it displays the items.

Here's the line of code that displays the backpack contents:

```
output.innerHTML += "<br>You are carrying: " + backpack.join(", ");
```

If the player is carrying a flute, it will display the following: "You are carrying: flute."

But there's something new here that you haven't seen before. What does this bit of code do?

```
backpack.join(", ")
```

This is the array's join method. It determines how array elements should be separated when they're displayed. Whatever characters you insert between the double quotes in the parentheses will be used to separate the array elements. In this example, the join method inserts a comma and space between them. That means if you have more than one element in the backpack array, a comma and space will separate each element. For example, imagine that the player is carrying the flute, stone, and sword. Here's how the backpack array will be displayed:

```
You are carrying: flute, stone, sword
```

Do you notice the comma and space between each item? That's thanks to the join method.

> Note: It would also be trivial to add an **inventory** action that the player could type to display everything in the backpack rather than keeping it on screen all the time. This is a very common feature of adventure games.

Dropping items

Dropping objects is almost the opposite of taking objects. The code checks whether the item is in the backpack, and, if it is, adds it to the items array. Here's the dropItem function that does this:

```
function dropItem()
{
    //Try to drop the item only if the backpack isn't empty
    if(backpack.length !== 0)
    {
        //Find the item's array index number in the backpack
        var backpackIndexNumber = backpack.indexOf(item);

        //The item is in the backpack if backpackIndex number isn't -1
        if(backpackIndexNumber !== -1)
        {

        //Tell the player that the item has been dropped
        gameMessage = "You drop the " + item + ".";

        //Add the item from the backpack to the game world
        items.push(backpack[backpackIndexNumber]);
        itemLocations.push(mapLocation);

            //Remove the item from the player's backpack
            backpack.splice(backpackIndexNumber, 1);
        }
        else
        {
        //Message if the player tries to drop something that's not in the backpack
        gameMessage = "You can't do that.";
        }
    }
    else
    {
        //Message if the backpack is empty
        gameMessage = "You're not carrying anything.";
    }
}
```

The code first makes sure that the backpack isn't empty.

```
if(backpack.length !== 0)
{...
```

If the backpack isn't empty, the program uses indexOf to find the array index number of the item in the backpack array.

```
var backpackIndexNumber = backpack.indexOf(item);
```

It stores the item's array index number in a variable called backpackIndexNumber. If it can't find the item the player wants to drop, this number will be −1. But if it's not −1, it means the item is in the backpack. An if statement checks for this.

```
if(backpackIndexNumber !== -1)
{...
```

If this is true, it lets the player drop the item. First, it updates the game message to tell the player the item has been dropped.

```
gameMessage = "You drop the " + item + ".";
```

If the player dropped the flute, this would be interpreted as "You drop the flute."

Next, the code needs to add the item to the game world. Remember that every element in the items array has to have a matching element at the same position in the itemLocations array. The code pushes the item into the items array from the backpack. It also pushes the mapLocation into the itemLocations array.

```
items.push(backpack[backpackIndexNumber]);
itemLocations.push(mapLocation);
```

Because both the item and the map location are pushed into the arrays together, they'll stay synchronized at the same index numbers. This adds the item to the same location in the world where the player is currently standing.

The item is then spliced out of the backpack array.

```
backpack.splice(backpackIndexNumber, 1);
```

If the backpack contains an item, but not the item that the player wants to drop, the following message is displayed:

```
else
{
  gameMessage = "You can't do that.";
}
```

If the backpack is empty, the player will see this message:

```
else
{
  gameMessage = "You're not carrying anything.";
}
```

Now that we know how to take and drop items, let's find out how to use them.

Using items

The useItem function is slightly more complex than the other two functions because it does two separate things. First, it checks whether the backpack contains the item the player wants to use. If it does, it finds out how that item should behave depending on game conditions, such as the map location. Breaking these related steps into two parts simplifies some of the logic. Here's the entire useItem function, and I'll walk you through how it works.

```
function useItem()
{
    //1. Find out if the item is in the backpack

    //Find the item's array index number in the backpack
    var backpackIndexNumber = backpack.indexOf(item);

    //If the index number is -1, then it isn't in the backpack.
    //Tell the player that he or she isn't carrying it.
    if(backpackIndexNumber === -1)
    {
        gameMessage = "You're not carrying it.";
    }

    //If there are no items in the backpack, then
    //tell the player the backpack is empty
    if(backpack.length === 0)
    {
        gameMessage += " Your backpack is empty";
    }

    //2. If the item is found in the backpack
    //figure out what to do with it
    if(backpackIndexNumber !== -1)
    {
        switch(item)
        {
            case "flute":
                gameMessage = "Beautiful music fills the air.";
                break;

            case "sword":
                if(mapLocation === 3)
                {
                    gameMessage
                        = "You swing the sword and slay the dragon!";
                }
                else
```

```
        {
          gameMessage
            = "You swing the sword listlessly.";
        }
        break;

    case "stone":
      if(mapLocation === 1)
      {
        gameMessage = "You drop the stone in the well.";

        //Remove the item from the player's backpack
        backpack.splice(backpackIndexNumber, 1);
      }
      else
      {
        gameMessage
          = "You fumble with the stone in your pocket.";
      }
      break;
    }
  }
}
```

The first thing the code does is use indexOf to find the item's array index number in the backpack. That index number is copied into a variable called backpackIndexNumber.

```
    var backpackIndexNumber = backpack.indexOf(item);
```

If backpackIndexNumber is −1, it means that the item the player wants to use wasn't found in the backpack. The game can use that information to tell the player that he or she isn't carrying it.

```
    if(backpackIndexNumber === -1)
    {
      gameMessage = "You're not carrying it.";
    }
```

If the backpack is empty, the game can also tell that to the player.

```
    if(backpack.length === 0)
    {
      gameMessage += " Your backpack is empty";
    }
```

If backpackIndexNumber isn't −1, then we know the item has been found in the backpack and the program will let the player use the item. A switch statement performs the item actions. There's a case for each item. Here's an abridged version of the switch statement, which shows you how simple the structure really is:

```
if(backpackIndexNumber !== -1)
{
  switch(item)
  {
    case "flute":
      ...
      break;

    case "sword":
      ...
      break;

    case "stone":
      ...
      break;
  }
}
```

If you have more items in the game, just create a new case for each new item. If the items have complex behaviors that use lots of code, create functions for them. In a big adventure game, you may have dozens of items and dozens of item functions.

Let's find what happens when you use each item. The flute is easy. It just makes some beautiful music, no matter where in the world you are.

```
case "flute":
  gameMessage = "Beautiful music fills the air.";
  break;
```

The sword is more complex. In most world locations, using it just displays "You swing the sword listlessly." But if you're in location 3, with the sleeping dragon, it displays "You swing the sword and slay the dragon!"

```
case "sword":
  if(mapLocation === 3)
  {
    gameMessage
      = "You swing the sword and slay the dragon!";
  }
  else
  {
    gameMessage
      = "You swing the sword listlessly.";
  }
  break;
```

In a finished game, you could set an endGame variable to true if the player kills the dragon, and then it would run whatever other actions you want to happen at the end of the game.

The stone has the most complex behavior. In most locations using it will just display "You fumble with the stone in your pocket." But at location 1, the well, the stone is dropped in the well.

```
case "stone":
  if(mapLocation === 1)
  {
    gameMessage = "You drop the stone in the well.";

    //Remove the item from the player's backpack
    backpack.splice(backpackIndexNumber, 1);
  }
  else
  {
    gameMessage
      = "You fumble with the stone in your pocket.";
  }
  break;
```

The stone is dropped by displaying a message and then removing the stone from the backpack.

```
backpack.splice(backpackIndexNumber, 1);
```

This is why it was important to record the backpackIndexNumber when the code first searched for the item in the player's backpack. You need it if you want to remove the item from the backpack.

These are simple examples of behaviors your items could have, but they really just scratch the surface. Using items could change any game variables, make items appear or disappear anywhere in the world, change location descriptions or images, load new world maps—anything at all. It's in these behaviors where you turn your interactive world into a game.

The complete code listing

What we've created up until now is a model for an interactive adventure world that can scale to a map of any rectangular size. All the hard work is done. You won't have to write any more code for a bigger game except to add information to arrays and cases for new actions. The takeItem and dropItem functions will work as-is whether you have 1 item or 1,000 items. For more item behaviors, just add more cases in the useItem function and use your imagination to decide what they should do.

```
<!doctype html>
<title>The Forest of Lyrica - 6</title>

<img src="" width="300" height="267">
<p id="output"></p>
<input id="input" type="text" placeholder="Enter your action...">
<button>enter</button>
```

```
<script>

    //Create the map
    var map = [];

    map[0] = "An old stone keep.";
    map[1] = "A deep well.";
    map[2] = "A sunny glade.";
    map[3] = "A sleeping dragon.";
    map[4] = "A narrow pathway.";
    map[5] = "An ancient gate.";
    map[6] = "The edge of a river.";
    map[7] = "A lonely wooden bench.";
    map[8] = "An isolated cottage. Faint music comes from inside.";

    //Set the player's start location
    var mapLocation = 4;

    //Set the images
    var images = [];
    images[0] = "keep.png";
    images[1] = "well.png";
    images[2] = "glade.png";
    images[3] = "dragon.png";
    images[4] = "path.png";
    images[5] = "gate.png";
    images[6] = "river.png";
    images[7] = "bench.png";
    images[8] = "cottage.png";

//Set the blocked-path messages
var blockedPathMessages = [];
blockedPathMessages[0] = "It's too dangerous to move that way.";
blockedPathMessages[1] = "A mysterious force holds you back.";
blockedPathMessages[2] = "A tangle of thorns blocks your way.";
blockedPathMessages[3] = "You can't step over the dragon.";
blockedPathMessages[4] = "";
blockedPathMessages[5] = "The gate locks shut.";
blockedPathMessages[6] = "The river is too deep to cross.";
blockedPathMessages[7] = "The trees are too thick to pass.";
blockedPathMessages[8] = "You're too scared to go that way.";

//Create the items and set their locations
var items = ["flute", "stone", "sword"];
var itemLocations = [1, 6, 8];

//An array to store what the player is carrying
var backpack = [];
```

```
//Initialize the player's input
var playersInput = "";

//Initialize the gameMessage
var gameMessage = "";

//Create an array of actions the game understands
//and a variable to store the current action
var actionsIKnow = ["north", "east", "south", "west", "take", "use", "drop"];
var action = "";

//An array of items the game understands
//and a variable to store the current item
var itemsIKnow = ["flute", "stone", "sword"];
var item = "";

//The img element
var image = document.querySelector("img");

//The input and output fields
var output = document.querySelector("#output");
var input = document.querySelector("#input");

//The button
var button = document.querySelector("button");
button.style.cursor = "pointer";
button.addEventListener("click", clickHandler, false);

//Display the player's location
render();

function clickHandler()
{
  playGame();
}

function playGame()
{
    //Get the player's input and convert it to lowercase
    playersInput = input.value;
    playersInput = playersInput.toLowerCase();

    //Reset these variables from the previous turn
    gameMessage = "";
    action = "";

    //Figure out the player's action
    for(i = 0; i < actionsIKnow.length; i++)
```

```
  {
    if(playersInput.indexOf(actionsIKnow[i]) !== -1)
    {
      action = actionsIKnow[i];
      console.log("player's action: " + action);
      break;
    }
  }

//Figure out the item the player wants
for(i = 0; i < itemsIKnow.length; i++)
{
  if(playersInput.indexOf(itemsIKnow[i]) !== -1)
  {
    item = itemsIKnow[i];
    console.log("player's item: " + item);
  }
}

//Choose the correct action
switch(action)
{
  case "north":
    if(mapLocation >= 3)
    {
      mapLocation -= 3;
    }
    else
    {
      gameMessage = blockedPathMessages[mapLocation];
    }
    break;

  case "east":
    if(mapLocation % 3 != 2)
    {
      mapLocation += 1;
    }
    else
    {
      gameMessage = blockedPathMessages[mapLocation];
    }
    break;

  case "south":
    if(mapLocation < 6)
    {
      mapLocation += 3;
    }
    else
```

```
      {
        gameMessage = blockedPathMessages[mapLocation];
      }
      break;

    case "west":
      if(mapLocation % 3 != 0)
      {
        mapLocation -= 1;
      }
      else
      {
        gameMessage = blockedPathMessages[mapLocation];
      }
      break;

    case "take":
      takeItem()
      break;

    case "drop":
      dropItem();
      break;

    case "use":
      useItem();
      break;
    default:
      gameMessage = "I don't understand that.";
  }

  //Render the game
  render();
}

function takeItem()
{
  //Find the index number of the item in the items array
  var itemIndexNumber = items.indexOf(item);

  //Does the item exist in the game world and is it at the player's current location?
  if(itemIndexNumber !== -1
  && itemLocations[itemIndexNumber] === mapLocation)
  {
    gameMessage = "You take the " + item + ".";

    //Add the item to the player's backpack
    backpack.push(item);
```

```
        //Remove the item from the game world
        items.splice(itemIndexNumber, 1);
        itemLocations.splice(itemIndexNumber, 1);

        //Display in the console for testing
        console.log("World items: " + items);
        console.log("backpack items: " + backpack);
    }
    else
    {
        //Message if the player tries to take an item that isn't in the current location
        gameMessage = "You can't do that.";
    }
}

function dropItem()
{
    //Try to drop the item only if the backpack isn't empty
    if(backpack.length !== 0)
    {
        //Find the item's array index number in the backpack
        var backpackIndexNumber = backpack.indexOf(item);

        //The item is in the backpack if the backpackIndexNumber isn't -1
        if(backpackIndexNumber !== -1)
        {

            //Tell the player that the item has been dropped
            gameMessage = "You drop the " + item + ".";

            //Add the item from the backpack to the game world
            items.push(backpack[backpackIndexNumber]);
            itemLocations.push(mapLocation);

            //Remove the item from the player's backpack
            backpack.splice(backpackIndexNumber, 1);
        }
        else
        {
            //Message if the player tries to drop something that's not in the backpack
            gameMessage = "You can't do that.";
        }
    }
    else
    {
        //Message if the backpack is empty
        gameMessage = "You're not carrying anything.";
    }
}
```

```
function useItem()
{
  //1. Find out if the item is in the backpack

  //Find the item's array index number in the backpack
  var backpackIndexNumber = backpack.indexOf(item);

  //If the index number is -1, then it isn't in the backpack.
  //Tell the player that he or she isn't carrying it.
  if(backpackIndexNumber === -1)
  {
    gameMessage = "You're not carrying it.";
  }

  //If there are no items in the backpack, then
  //tell the player the backpack is empty
  if(backpack.length === 0)
  {
    gameMessage += " Your backpack is empty";
  }

  //2. If the item is found in the backpack
  //figure out what to do with it
  if(backpackIndexNumber !== -1)
  {
    switch(item)
    {
      case "flute":
        gameMessage = "Beautiful music fills the air.";
        break;

      case "sword":
        if(mapLocation === 3)
        {
          gameMessage
            = "You swing the sword and slay the dragon!";
        }
        else
        {
          gameMessage
            = "You swing the sword listlessly.";
        }
        break;

      case "stone":
        if(mapLocation === 1)
        {
          gameMessage = "You drop the stone in the well.";
```

```
                //Remove the item from the player's backpack
                backpack.splice(backpackIndexNumber, 1);
            }
            else
            {
                gameMessage
                    = "You fumble with the stone in your pocket.";
            }
            break;
        }
    }
}

function render()
{
    //Render the location
    output.innerHTML = map[mapLocation];
    image.src = "../images/" + images[mapLocation];

    //Display an item if there's one in this location
    //1. Loop through all the game items
    for(var i = 0; i < items.length; i++)
    {
        //Find out if there's an item at this location
        if(mapLocation === itemLocations[i])
        {
            //Display it
            output.innerHTML
            += "<br>You see a <strong>"
            + items[i]
            + "</strong> here.";
        }
    }

    //Display the game message
    output.innerHTML += "<br><em>" + gameMessage + "</em>";

    //Display the player's backpack contents
    if(backpack.length !== 0)
    {
        output.innerHTML += "<br>You are carrying: " + backpack.join(", ");
    }
}

</script>
```

Creating quests and puzzles

We now have an interactive world, but we don't yet have a game. The trick to making a good fantasy adventure game is to change the world in interesting ways when players interact with it. They need puzzles to solve or quests to fulfill. This is more about imagination and creativity than programming, and the really fun part of making a game can start. Here are some simple ideas to help you build your game.

- Add useful new game items when players complete a task.

- Let players use the new game items to solve other game puzzles.

- Let players enter new areas of the world when they complete tasks.

- Change locations and item descriptions or images based on players' actions.

These will be easy to implement with your programming skills so far and the model we're using. To help you get started, run lyrica6.html. When the game begins, the only item in the world is the stone. Take the stone and drop it to the bottom of the well, and the flute will appear. Take the flute to the cottage. Play the flute outside the cottage and an old man will step outside and present you with a sword. Take the sword to the dragon and use it to slay the dragon and save the forest. Figure 4-12 illustrates the game walkthrough.

Figure 4-12. Add some puzzles to the game world

This was achieved by making only very small changes to the existing code.

When the game starts, the only object in the world is the stone.

```
var items = ["stone"];
var itemLocations = [6];
```

The rest of the changes are in the useItem function. If the player uses the stone at the well, mapLocation 1, the flute is added to the items array and a message informs the player.

```
case "stone":
  if(mapLocation === 1)
  {
    gameMessage = "You drop the stone in the well.";
    gameMessage += " A magical flute appears!";

    //Remove the stone from the player's backpack
    backpack.splice(backpackIndexNumber, 1);

    //Add the flute to the world
    items.push("flute");
    itemLocations.push(mapLocation);
  }
  else
  {
    gameMessage
      = "You fumble with the stone in your pocket.";
  }
  break;
}
```

The player can now take and use the flute, which lets him or her unlock other game secrets. If the player uses the flute at the cottage, mapLocation 8, a message appears to tell the player that an old man has provided a sword. The sword is then added to the game world by pushing it into the items array.

```
case "flute":
  if(mapLocation === 8)
  {
    gameMessage = "Beautiful music fills the air.";
    gameMessage += "A wizend old man steps outside ";
    gameMessage += "and hands you a sword!";

    //Add the sword to the world
    items.push("sword");
    itemLocations.push(mapLocation);
  }
```

```
    else
    {
      gameMessage = "You try and play the flute "
      gameMessage += "but it makes no sound here.";
    }
    break;
```

You can also see here that if the player uses the flute anywhere else in the world, it doesn't work properly. The player will see this message: "You try and play the flute but it makes no sound here." This is a clue to let the player know that the flute *might* work somewhere in the game if he or she can just figure out where to play it. The cottage description includes the sentence "Faint music comes from inside," and a perceptive player would think that maybe this could be a good place to try playing the flute.

The sword case is pretty much unchanged. Use it at mapLocation 8 to slay the dragon and save the forest.

```
case "sword":
  if(mapLocation === 3)
  {
    gameMessage
      = "You swing the sword and slay the dragon! ";
    gameMessage
      += "You've saved the forest of Lyrica!";
  }
  else
  {
    gameMessage
      = "You swing the sword listlessly.";
  }
  break;
```

You can see that we've created a reasonably complex little puzzle by just making small changes to the item behaviors. The rest of the game code is untouched and takes care of itself. Plan your game carefully and you'll be able to construct very complex and interesting quests and puzzles just by carefully considering how using items changes the world.

Making your own game

Now that you know how to make an adventure game, there's a lot that you can do to improve it. In the finished game I've added a bit of basic CSS to improve the style: see Figure 4-13 for an example.

Figure 4-13. Add some style

I also added a help system. If you type "help," the game will tell you which words it understands. It will also give you hints for solving puzzles if you're at the location with the well, the dragon, or the cottage. For example, if you're standing at the well and type "help," the game displays this:

```
I wonder if you could 'use' something to find out how deep the well is?
```

If a player solves a puzzle, the help message is cleared. This took only a few minutes to implement and uses exactly the same logic as the blockedPathMessages.

First, I created an array called helpMessages. Each element matches a map location.

```
var helpMessages = [];
helpMessages[0] = "";
helpMessages[1] = "I wonder if you could 'use' something to find out how deep the well is?";
helpMessages[2] = "";
helpMessages[3] = "Maybe if you had a sword, you could slay the dragon?";
helpMessages[4] = "";
helpMessages[5] = "";
helpMessages[6] = "";
helpMessages[7] = "";
helpMessages[8] = "This seems like a nice place for music.";
```

Locations without specific help messages are just empty quotation marks.

I then added a new help case in the switch statement of the playGame function. It displays a helpMessage if there is one at this location. If there isn't, it just displays a general list of the words the game understands.

```
case "help":
    //Display a hint if there is one for this location
    if(helpMessages[mapLocation] !== "")
    {
        gameMessage = helpMessages[mapLocation] + " ";
    }
    gameMessage += "Try any of these words: ";
    gameMessage += "north, east, south, west, take, drop, ";
    gameMessage += "use, stone, flute, sword.";
    break;
```

When the player solves a puzzle at any of the three locations, the helpMessage is cleared by assigning it empty quotes. I've highlighted how the helpMessage is cleared when the player takes the stone in this code below:

```
case "stone":
    if(mapLocation === 1)
    {
        gameMessage = "You drop the stone in the well.";
        gameMessage += " A magical flute appears!";

        //Remove the stone from the player's backpack
        backpack.splice(backpackIndexNumber, 1);

        //Add the flute to the world
        items.push("flute");
        itemLocations.push(mapLocation);

        //Reset the location's help message
        helpMessages[mapLocation] = "";
    }
    else
```

```
    {
        gameMessage = "You fumble with the stone in your pocket.";
    }
    break;
}
```

In a more complex game you could insert a new, updated help message for this location if the player needs to solve a new puzzle.

Game designers often think their games are much easier to play than they really are, so adding a generous help system like this will make the game more fun. Ask friends and family to test the game to find out which puzzles they find especially hard, and think about how to gently guide players into coming up with a solution with carefully worded hints.

This help system was one easy improvement to the game, but here are some other changes you might want to try:

- Instead of typing text, let players choose game actions from a point-and-click or touch interface. By Chapter 6 you'll have enough new skills to do this.

- Make a larger game world. A good size to start with is a 4-by-4 game world, which gives you 16 locations. This is ideal for a challenging but short game that won't take you too long to make. An 8-by-8 world with 64 locations is the classic size for an adventure game, but be prepared for a lot of work.

- You're not just limited to text and images: how about adding video and sound as well?

- Add characters that the player can talk to. Think of a character as an "item." Use a "talk" action to interact with it. Maybe your characters recognize certain words that could give the player hints about how to solve the game?

- Make characters or items that move between different locations by themselves. How will you do this? If you think about it for a few moments, you'll realize that you already know how. But if you get stuck, you'll find a good solution in the next chapter.

- Create a score variable and award the player points for completing tasks. If the player knows what the maximum points are in the game he or she will have an idea of how much of the game has already been completed.

- You could create a combat system. For example, to fight the dragon, create two new variables called playerHitPoints and dragonHitPoints. The player could then input "fight the dragon." The game would check the "fight" action and would discover that it should run a function that figures out how many hit points the player and dragon might lose each round, if the item is "dragon." This could be random, or it could be based on another variable that sets the player's skill. This will be fun and challenging to implement—try it!

■ Add a map with a marker that shows the player his or her location in the world. An easy way to do this would be to have nine different map images, one for each location, with each image showing where the player is. You could then just load new map images for each location, just as you did to load the other images. A better but more challenging way is to load a single image of a map and then to move a marker to the player's location on this map. You learned in the previous chapter how to position images, so you just need to figure out how to apply those skills to this new game. If you get stuck, you'll learn how to do this in the next chapter.

Design your game with thought and care, work with some good illustrations, package it as an app for phones and tablets, and you'll have a great little game that you can sell. Maybe your game will be the one to spark the long-overdue renaissance of the adventure-game genre?

Summary

I don't want to say that I tricked you but, well, I kind of did! What I've been calling an "adventure game" is really just a classic database management system. The techniques that you've learned are basic for the creation of any kind of database in which you can store, search, and retrieve information. In our adventure game we're storing and retrieving game information, but you can use exactly this same model for storing and retrieving *any* kind of information. If anyone ever asks you to make a "product catalogue," a "student database," or an "inventory management system," just think of these as boring versions of an adventure game and you can do it. Yes, you're a real programmer now!

But, trust me, you don't want to make product catalogues or inventory management systems! Life is too short for that. You want to make games, and these techniques are at the core of video-game design. Not only do you now have the skills to make many kinds of games using text, but you'll also soon see that they're just as essential for making all types of action and arcade-style games as well.

In this chapter you learned how to build an interactive game world. In Chapter 5, we'll take a closer look at game maps and how to use them to make a role-playing strategy game.

Chapter 5

Making Maps

In this chapter you'll learn how to start making role-playing games, strategy games, and board games. You're going to learn only one important new technique—how to use a two-dimensional (2D) array—but it's going to totally blow the lid off of the kinds of games you'll be able to make from now on. I'll show you how to make a basic hybrid strategy/role-playing game from scratch that you'll be able to use as a model for your own games.

Arrays inside arrays

In the previous chapter you saw how important arrays are for managing game information. In this chapter I'm going to show you how to make and use something called a 2D array. These types of arrays are arrays in which each element contains another array. You can use them to very easily create a game map or level. You'll love using them for your games once you learn how. You'll need to expend a little brainpower to understand how they work, but you'll see that 2D arrays can give you extremely simple solutions to very complex problems. Learning to use 2D arrays is possibly the single most important game-programming skill.

A single, empty array looks like this:

[ ]

It's just a pair of square brackets with nothing inside them. If you want to put three new arrays inside that first empty array, you can do it like this:

[[ ], [ ], [ ]]

The first array now contains three new empty arrays. But it's confusing to look at it like this, so here's an easier way to visualize this:

```
[
  [ ],
  [ ],
  [ ]
]
```

It's now very clear to see that the surrounding array contains three new arrays within it. This is the 2D array.

Imagine that you've got a big closet with three shelves in it. You've got one shelf for toys, another for books, and a third for musical instruments. You can create a 2D array for your closet that looks like this:

```
var closet =
[
  ["ball", "yoyo", "teddy"],
  ["Austen", "Bronte", "Swift"],
  ["guitar", "tabla", "flute"]
];
```

You now have one array called closet that contains three internal arrays. (Note that there's no comma after the last array and there's a semicolon after the final square bracket.)

Each internal array is just an element of the containing array. If you want to access the array that contains the instruments, you can do it like this:

```
closet[2]
```

This gives you "guitar", "tabla", and "flute".

If you want to find the second element of that array, you can do it like this:

```
closet[2][1]
```

This gives you "tabla".

Here's another example. If you want to find the third element of the second array, you could find it like this:

```
closet[1][2]
```

This gives you: "Swift".

In the chapter's source files you'll find twoDimensionalArrays.html, which has a working example of this.

```
var closet =
[
  ["ball", "yoyo", "teddy"],
  ["Austen", "Bronte", "Swift"],
  ["guitar", "tabla", "flute"]
];
```

```
//View the entire array.
//ball, yoyo, teddy, Austen, Bronte,
//Swift, guitar, tabla, flute

console.log("Entire 2D array: " + closet);

//View the first array.
//ball, yoyo, teddy

console.log("Array 0: " + closet[0]);

//View the second array.
//Austen, Bronte, Swift

console.log("Array 1: " + closet[1]);

//The first element in the second array.
//Austen

console.log("First element of second array: " + closet[1][0]);

//The third element in the third array.
//flute

console.log("Third element of third array: " + closet[2][2]);

//The second element in the first array.
//yoyo

console.log("Second element of first array: " + closet[0][1]);
```

Here's the output from the above code:

```
Entire 2D array: ball,yoyo,teddy,Austen,Bronte,Swift,guitar,tabla,flute
Array 0: ball,yoyo,teddy
Array 1: Austen, Bronte, Swift
First element of second array: Austen
Third element of third array: flute
Second element of first array: yoyo
```

Figure 5-1 illustrates how this 2D array works.

```
var closet =
[
  ["ball", "yoyo", "teddy"],
  ["Austen", "Bronte", "Swift"],
  ["guitar", "tabla", "flute"]
];
```

```
closet[0]          ... ball, yoyo, teddy
closet[1]          ... Austen, Bronte, Swift
closet[1][0]       ... Austen
closet[2][2]       ... flute
closet[0][1]       ... yoyo
closet              ... ball,yoyo,teddy,Austen,Bronte,
                       Swift,guitar,tabla,flute
```

Figure 5-1. Understanding 2D arrays

A 2D array is a very efficient way of organizing complex information, and it's very easy to find what you're looking for if you understand the system.

Looping through a 2D array

In the previous chapter you learned how to search for and find information in an array by looping through it with a for loop. You can do this with 2D arrays as well.

A 2D array is actually a grid of information, as you can see in Figure 5-2.

```
var closet =
[
  ["ball", "yoyo", "teddy"],
  ["Austen", "Bronte", "Swift"],
  ["guitar", "tabla", "flute"]
];
```

	columns	
ball	yoyo	teddy
Austen	Bronte	Swift
guitar	tabla	flute

rows

Figure 5-2. A 2D array is really just a grid

Here's some code that reads each element in the 2D array. It starts by reading the first of the three inner arrays, from left to right. When it's done reading the first, it jumps down to the next array and continues reading. It follows this pattern to read all the elements of all the arrays until the loop is finished.

The code uses two loops to do this. The first loop checks each row. A second inner loop checks each column of that row. All the elements in the 2D array are included this way. I'll explain how all this works ahead.

```
var closet =
[
  ["ball", "yoyo", "teddy"],
  ["Austen", "Bronte", "Swift"],
  ["guitar", "tabla", "flute"]
];

//Find the number of rows and columns
var ROWS = closet.length;
var COLUMNS = closet[0].length;

//Loop through each row
for(var row = 0; row < ROWS; row++)
{
  console.log("--- Array: " + row);

  //Loop through each element of each row
  for(var column = 0; column < COLUMNS; column++)
  {

    //Display the row
    console.log(closet[row][column]);
  }
}
```

Figure 5-3 shows how these loops work together to display the array contents.

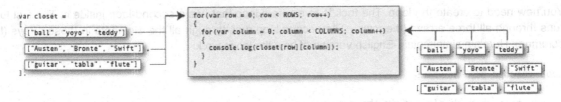

Figure 5-3. The outer loop reads the arrays. The inner loop reads each of the inner array elements

Let's look at this in detail.

You know that the closet array has three rows and three columns. The first step is to define the number of rows and columns with variables, like this:

```
var ROWS = closet.length;
var COLUMNS = closet[0].length;
```

I've capitalized ROWS and COLUMNS because, unlike normal variables, I don't ever want their values to change. A variable that contains information that shouldn't change is called a **constant**. It's a common programming convention to use all capital letters for constant names. This is just so that you won't forget that you shouldn't change these values after you first create them. It's purely optional, but in the pages ahead you'll see how useful all-capped constants can be to help you to better read and understand your programs.

> Note: Although it's not yet an official JavaScript standard, modern browsers let you declare constants using the const keyword, like this:
>
> const CONSTANT_NAME = "Any value";
>
> If you use the const keyword, the program won't let you change the constant's initial value after you first declare it.

ROWS gets the same value as the length of the closet array.

```
var ROWS = closet.length;
```

This will be three, because the closet array contains the three inner arrays.

COLUMNS is set to the length of the first array inside the closet.

```
var COLUMNS = closet[0].length;
```

This will also be three, because there are three elements in the first array. All the arrays in this example have the same number of elements because they represent a rectangular grid.

You now need to create the loop. The trick is to create a loop that has a second loop inside it. The first loop runs through all three arrays (the rows). The second loop runs through all the elements in those arrays (the columns). Here's a simple plain-English version of how the loops work:

```
loop through all the rows
{
  loop through each element in the current row
  {
    Do something with this element
  }
}
```

This will check each element of each row, one by one. With this in mind, here's the actual JavaScript code that does this for our 2D closet array. It displays each element in each array, row by row.

```
for(var row = 0; row < ROWS; row++)
{
  for(var column = 0; column < COLUMNS; column++)
  {
    console.log(closet[row][column]);
  }
}
```

You can see that the for loops don't use "i" as a loop counter. Instead, they use the variable names row and column. This makes it much easier to understand how the loop is working.

The outer loop runs for as many times as whatever we set ROW to. In this example, ROW equals 3.

```
for(var row = 0; row < ROWS; row++)
{ ...
```

This will loop through all three arrays inside the containing closet array.

The inner loop checks the individual elements of those arrays:

```
  for(var column = 0; column < COLUMNS; column++)
  { ...
```

You can then access each element with its row and column number, like this:

```
closet[row][column]
```

> Note: If you want to organize the information in the 2D array within columns instead of rows, just swap the row and column loop counters, like this: closet[column][row]. The elements will then be displayed from top to bottom, in their columns, like this: ball, Austen, guitar, yoyo, Bronte, tabla, teddy, Swift, flute.

In this example, the array elements are just displayed in the console. But, of course, in your game you can do anything to them that you need to. You can apply all the same techniques for searching and finding information in arrays that you learned in the previous chapter.

I've overexplained this a little because it's one of the most important bits of game-programming code you need to know. You're going to be using it all the time from now on, for all sorts of crazy things you've probably never thought of. It's not obvious from this example, but it will be in the next one.

Visualizing 2D arrays

You now know that a 2D array is a grid. You can use this grid to make patterns, such as a game board or a level map. All you need to do is display something interesting for each cell in the grid and then display it in the right place. In this next example I'll show you how.

Open the visualizing2DArrays.html file and you'll see a pattern of nine black and white squares, shown in Figure 5-4.

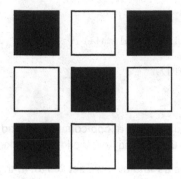

Figure 5-4. Use a 2D array to display a grid pattern

Figure 5-4 is a visualization of a 2D array that looks like this:

```
var pattern =
[
  [1, 0, 1],
  [0, 1, 0],
  [1, 0, 1]
];
```

Each "1" is a black square. You can actually *see* the pattern in the array. This is no longer some abstract programming code but something you can almost touch. If you change this array and run the program again, the display will change to match it. Try changing the array in the source code so that it looks like this:

```
var pattern =
[
  [1, 0, 0],
  [1, 0, 1],
  [1, 0, 1]
];
```

Run the program again, and Figure 5-5 shows you what you'll see.

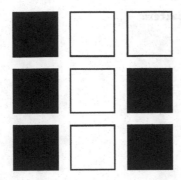

Figure 5-5. Change the array to change the pattern

The program makes this work by looping through the array and adding a new HTML element for each array element. The HTML element is positioned in the correct place. It's given a black background if the array element is a 1. If it's a 0 the HTML element remains white. Here's the complete code, and I'll explain it all in the pages ahead.

```
<!doctype html>
<title>Visualizing 2D arrays</title>

<style>
#stage
{
  position: relative;
}

.cell
{
  position: absolute;
  width: 30px;
  height: 30px;
  border: 1px solid black;
  background-color: white;
}

</style>

<div id="stage"></div>

<script>

//Get a reference to the stage
var stage = document.querySelector("#stage");
```

```
//The 2D array that defines the pattern
var pattern =
[
  [1, 0, 1],
  [0, 1, 0],
  [1, 0, 1]
];

//The size of each cell
var SIZE = 30;

//The space between each cell
var SPACE = 10;

//Display the array
var ROWS = pattern.length;
var COLUMNS = pattern[0].length;

for(var row = 0; row < ROWS; row++)
{
  for(var column = 0; column < COLUMNS; column++)
  {
    //Create a div HTML element called cell
    var cell = document.createElement("div");

    //Set its CSS class to "cell"
    cell.setAttribute("class", "cell");

    //Add the div HTML element to the stage
    stage.appendChild(cell);

    //Make it black if it's a "1"
    if(pattern[row][column] === 1)
    {
      cell.style.backgroundColor = "black";
    }

    //Position the cell in the correct place
    //with 10 pixels of space around it
    cell.style.top = row * (SIZE + SPACE) + "px";
    cell.style.left = column * (SIZE + SPACE) + "px";
  }
}

</script>
```

You can see that the CSS code defines a class called cell. This determines the size of the cell and its background color, which is white. Its position is set to absolute, which is relative to the stage <div> element. This means you can position cells precisely by using the top and left CSS properties.

```css
.cell
{
  position: absolute;
  width: 30px;
  height: 30px;
  border: 1px solid black;
  background-color: white;
}
```

The program then defines the pattern that we want to display as a 2D array.

```javascript
var pattern =
[
  [1, 0, 1],
  [0, 1, 0],
  [1, 0, 1]
];
```

After the pattern array is defined, two constants define the size of each cell, as well as the spacing between them.

```javascript
var SIZE = 30;
var SPACE = 10;
```

SIZE matches the height and width in the CSS cell class. SPACE is actually optional but still useful. Any number you assign to SPACE will determine the horizontal and vertical spacing between the cells.

The loop then runs through the 2D array's rows and columns, in exactly the same way you saw in the previous example.

```javascript
for(var row = 0; row < ROWS; row++)
{
  for(var column = 0; column < COLUMNS; column++)
  {
```

The inner loop reads each element of the 2D array. It creates a <div> tag, assigns the cell class to it, and adds the <div> to the stage.

```javascript
var cell = document.createElement("div");
cell.setAttribute("class", "cell");
stage.appendChild(cell);
```

It then checks whether the array element is 1. If it is, it changes its backgroundColor to black.

```javascript
if(pattern[row][column] === 1)
{
  cell.style.backgroundColor = "black";
}
```

The last thing the loop does is position the cell by using a simple formula. The `top` position is found by adding the cell's size and spacing together, then multiplying it by the value of `row`.

```
cell.style.top = row * (SIZE + SPACE) + "px";
```

The first time the outer loop runs, `row` is 0. So the formula is interpreted like this:

```
cell.style.top = 0 * (30 + 10) + "px";
```

Anything multiplied by 0 is 0, so the CSS `top` value now looks like this:

```
top: 0px;
```

This places the cell right at the top of the stage. The next time the outer loop runs, the row equals 1.

```
cell.style.top = 1 * (30 + 10) + "px";
```

This means `top` now has a value of 40.

```
top: 40px;
```

This places the second row of `<div>` elements 40 pixels below the top of the stage. Because each cell is 30 pixels high, there are 10 pixels of space between each cell.

On the last loop, `row` equals 2.

```
cell.style.top = 2 * (30 + 10) + "px";
```

This gives `top` a value of 80.

```
top: 80px;
```

This means that the last row is positioned 80 pixels below the top of the stage. The positioning of the columns follows exactly the same format.

You should know that this code is actually creating nine `<div>` tags. They're being appended to the containing stage `<div>` tag. This happens in the browser when the program runs, so you don't see this in your code. But if you could see the HTML code it was making, it would look like this:

```
<div id="stage">
  <div class="cell"></div>
  <div class="cell"></div>
  <div class="cell"></div>
  <div class="cell"></div>
  <div class="cell"></div>
  <div class="cell"></div>
  <div class="cell"></div>
  <div class="cell"></div>
  <div class="cell"></div>
</div>
```

Because these `cell` tags are inside the enclosing `stage` element, they're called the `stage` element's **children**. Yes, `stage` is like a mom with nine little `cell` children. Keep this concept in mind because it's going to be important to remember in the next part of the chapter.

This is a very widely used standard system for creating and displaying a grid layout, and you'll use it in many of this book's projects. You'll soon be very comfortable with it.

In this example, the numbers in the 2D array are interpreted as cell colors. But you can interpret the information in the arrays in any way you like. In the next section you'll see how you can use this information in a game to create a map that the player can interact with.

Case study: Island Adventure

Why are 2D arrays so important for games? Think of chess or checkers: they're just grids. When you move the playing pieces around the board, you're changing information on that grid. Strategy and role-playing video games are also just really big grids, although you usually can't see the grid lines. Take a close look at most action games as well, and you'll notice that the game objects fall neatly into an invisible grid pattern. If you know how to use 2D arrays, you can make these kinds of games.

I'm going to show you how by introducing a game called Island Adventure. Play the islandAdventureFinished. html file in the chapter's source files. Use the arrow keys to move a ship around the board. Visit islands to trade gold for coconuts. Fight pirates to win more gold. Try not to get eaten by the wandering sea monster. The goal is to reach home at the top right corner with as much gold and food as your ship can carry. You need a bit of strategy and a bit of luck. What's the highest score you can achieve? Figure 5-6 illustrates the game.

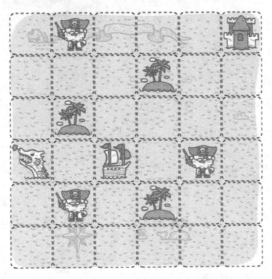

Figure 5-6. Island Adventure

Island Adventure is the simplest possible game that contains all the techniques you need to know to make your own role-playing, strategy, or board game. All these kinds of games share a common set of techniques, and they're all right here in Island Adventure. When you understand how to make a simple game like this, just add a little more detail and imagination, and you'll be able to build your own really great games in any of these genres.

The best way to read this chapter is to try and build your own version of the game as you go. I've broken it down into lots of small self-contained phases, and you'll find each phase in the chapter's source files. Carefully compare your code with mine, and when you understand it, move on to the next section. In many ways the code for this game is much simpler than the adventure game from the previous chapter. 2D arrays make things easy.

Drawing the map

The first step is to build the game map. Find the islandAdventure1.html file that does just that. It loops through a 2D array and displays a grid pattern of images that will match the array contents.

This is essentially the same code that you saw in the previous example where the program plotted a 3-by-3 pattern of squares. In this version the array contains four different numbers, and each number corresponds to a different image. Figure 5-7 shows the array, the image number codes, the actual images, and the final display. Can you see how the numbers in the array match the map images? You'll see how the code uses these numbers to display the correct images in the correct positions next. (The individual images are displayed over a larger image of the seafarer's map that's loaded into the containing `stage` element's `background-image` property.)

```
[
    [0, 2, 0, 0, 0, 3],
    [0, 0, 0, 1, 0, 0],
    [0, 1, 0, 0, 0, 0],
    [0, 0, 0, 0, 2, 0],
    [0, 2, 0, 1, 0, 0],
    [0, 0, 0, 0, 0, 0]
];
```

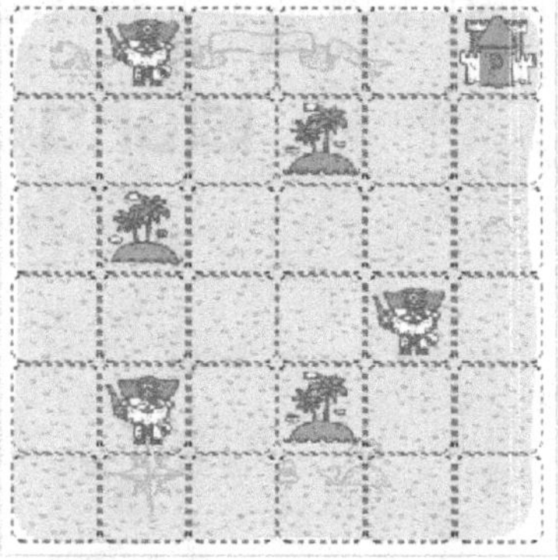

```
//Map code
var WATER = 0;
var ISLAND = 1;
var PIRATE = 2;
var HOME = 3;

//The size of each cell
var SIZE = 64;

//The number of rows and columns
var ROWS = map.length;
var COLUMNS = map[0].length;
```

water.png   island.png

pirate.png   home.png

Figure 5-7. The map components

Here's all the code that draws the map. I'll walk you through all the details of what's new and how it all works.

```
<!doctype html>
<title>Island Adventure 1</title>

<style>

#stage
{
  position: relative;
  width: 384px;
  height: 384px;
  background-image: url("../images/background.png");
}

.cell
{
  display: block;
  position: absolute;
  width: 64px;
  height: 64px;
}

p
{
  width: 400px;
}

</style>

<div id="stage"></div>
<p id="output"></p>

<script>

//Get a reference to the stage and output
var stage = document.querySelector("#stage");
var output = document.querySelector("#output");

//The game map
var map =
[
  [0, 2, 0, 0, 0, 3],
  [0, 0, 0, 1, 0, 0],
  [0, 1, 0, 0, 0, 0],
  [0, 0, 0, 0, 2, 0],
  [0, 2, 0, 1, 0, 0],
  [0, 0, 0, 0, 0, 0]
];
```

```
//Map code
var WATER = 0;
var ISLAND = 1;
var PIRATE = 2;
var HOME = 3;

//The size of each cell
var SIZE = 64;

//The number of rows and columns
var ROWS = map.length;
var COLUMNS = map[0].length;

render();

function render()
{
  //Clear the stage of img tag cells
  //from the previous turn

  if(stage.hasChildNodes())
  {
    for(var i = 0; i < ROWS * COLUMNS; i++)
    {
      stage.removeChild(stage.firstChild);
    }
  }

  //Render the game by looping through the map arrays
  for(var row = 0; row < ROWS; row++)
  {
    for(var column = 0; column < COLUMNS; column++)
    {
      //Create an img tag called cell
      var cell = document.createElement("img");

      //Set its CSS class to "cell"
      cell.setAttribute("class", "cell");

      //Add the img tag to the <div id="stage"> tag
      stage.appendChild(cell);

      //Find the correct image for this map cell
      switch(map[row][column])
      {
        case WATER:
          cell.src = "../images/water.png";
          break;
```

```
      case ISLAND:
        cell.src = "../images/island.png";
        break;

      case PIRATE:
        cell.src = "../images/pirate.png";
        break;

      case HOME:
        cell.src = "../images/home.png";
        break;
    }

    //Position the cell
    cell.style.top = row * SIZE + "px";
    cell.style.left = column * SIZE + "px";
    }
  }
}

</script>
```

The 2D array uses a really simple code for each element: 0 is water, 1 is an island, 2 is a pirate, and 3 is home. All these values are represented by constants.

```
var map =
[
  [0, 2, 0, 0, 0, 3],
  [0, 0, 0, 1, 0, 0],
  [0, 1, 0, 0, 0, 0],
  [0, 0, 0, 0, 2, 0],
  [0, 2, 0, 1, 0, 0],
  [0, 0, 0, 0, 0, 0]
];
```

```
//Map code
var WATER = 0;
var ISLAND = 1;
var PIRATE = 2;
var HOME = 3;
```

Representing each number with a constant like this will make your code very easy to read and understand.

The next bit of code defines the size of each cell in the grid.

```
var SIZE = 64;
```

This matches the size of the PNG images, which are each 64 by 64 pixels. The CSS cell class that the image will be loaded into is also this same size.

```
.cell
{
 display: block;
 position: absolute;
 width: 64px;
 height: 64px;
}
```

> Note: Computers display image sizes that are multiples of 2 very efficiently. These are sizes such as 2x2, 4x4, 8x8, 16x16, 32x32, 64x64, and so on. Computer memory is organized into grids that match these sizes, so they're able to read pixel information that shares these dimensions very quickly. If the pixel dimensions are a multiple of 2, the computer can read and store an image without having to do much processing. That's good for games that depend on displaying and changing images quickly. You'll see that most of the image sizes in this book will be in multiples of 2 from now on.

The program then defines the ROWS and COLUMNS constants that our loops will need to display the array:

```
var ROWS = map.length;
var COLUMNS = map[0].length;
```

They both have a value of 6.

Displaying the map

After the map is defined, the render function is called. It displays the array in HTML code. It does this by using the exact same format that our earlier example used to display the pattern of black and white squares. It displays a 6-by-6 grid of 36 <img> tags, each containing the correct image. However, there's one important addition. In the final game, every time the player presses an arrow key on the keyboard, the program will change the map array to update it with the ship's new position. This means the render function will have to be called again to show the changes to the array. If there are already 36 <img> tags from a previous turn, those should be removed before the new updated ones are displayed. That's the first thing our render function does—let's find out how.

Clearing the cells from any previous turns

You'll remember from the earlier example that the grid's <div> tags are all the *children* of the stage element. We have to get rid of those children if there are any. JavaScript has a method called hasChildNode that will be true if an HTML element has children. If it does, you can remove those children with another method called removeChild. Here's the code in the render function that does this:

```
if(stage.hasChildNodes())
{
  for(var i = 0; i < ROWS * COLUMNS; i++)
  {
    stage.removeChild(stage.firstChild);
  }
}
```

The if statement uses hasChildNodes to check whether the stage element has any children. This will be true for every turn of the game except when the game runs for the very first time. If the stage does have <img> tag children, there will be 36 of them, one for each grid cell. The for loop repeats 36 times (because ROWS and COLUMNS both equal 6, and 6 times 6 is 36). With each loop, it uses removeChild to get rid of one of the stage's children. That child is represented by the stage's firstChild property.

```
stage.removeChild(stage.firstChild);
```

With that done, the stage is free of <img> tag children from the previous turn and is ready for 36 more.

Creating new cells

The next bit of the render function creates the 36 new <img> tags. It loops through all 36 elements of the map array. It creates an <img> tag for each array element and loads the correct image into it depending on its map code. It then positions the <img> in the correct position in the browser window.

```
for(var row = 0; row < ROWS; row++)
{
  for(var column = 0; column < COLUMNS; column++)
  {
    //Create an img tag called cell
    var cell = document.createElement("img");

    //Set its CSS class to "cell"
    cell.setAttribute("class", "cell");

    //Add the img tag to the <div id="stage"> tag
    stage.appendChild(cell);

    //Find the correct image for this map cell
    switch(map[row][column])
    {
      case WATER:
        cell.src = "../images/water.png";
        break;

      case ISLAND:
        cell.src = "../images/island.png";
        break;

      case PIRATE:
        cell.src = "../images/pirate.png";
        break;

      case HOME:
        cell.src = "../images/home.png";
        break;
    }
```

```
    //Position the cell
    cell.style.top = row * SIZE + "px";
    cell.style.left = column * SIZE + "px";
  }
}
```

The loop first creates the <img> tag, and it then assigns it to a variable called cell. It also sets its CSS class to cell and then appends the <img> tag to the stage.

```
var cell = document.createElement("img");
cell.setAttribute("class", "cell");
stage.appendChild(cell);
```

The loop then uses a switch statement to find out the value of the current array element. You'll recall that you can find the value of the array element that's currently being checked in the loop like this:

```
map[row][column]
```

Remember that in our map this will be either be 0, 1, 2, or 3: 0 is WATER, 1 is ISLAND, 2 is PIRATE, and 3 is HOME. Depending on what it finds, it loads the correct image into the <img> tag's src property:

```
switch(map[row][column])
{
  case WATER:
    cell.src = "../images/water.png";
    break;

  case ISLAND:
    cell.src = "../images/island.png";
    break;

  case PIRATE:
    cell.src = "../images/pirate.png";
    break;

  case HOME:
    cell.src = "../images/home.png";
    break;
}
```

Pretty easy stuff, huh?

> *Note: I've used <img> tags for this game, but you could just as easily use <div> tags and change the cell image by changing the <div> tag's CSS background-image property. There's no technical reason for using <img> tags over <div> tags, but in this case using <img> tags results in simpler code.*

The last thing the loop does is position the new cell <img> tag by using the same formula I showed you earlier in the chapter.

```
cell.style.top = row * SIZE + "px";
cell.style.left = column * SIZE + "px";
```

This plots the grid of <img> cells so that it exactly matches the array.

And there you have it! A very complex result made with some fairly simple code.

> Note: In this game, all the <img> cell tags are removed and new ones added with each turn. This keeps the code simple and foolproof. You can change, add, and remove things from the map array, and the render function automatically displays it correctly. However, it might be more efficient to just create the <img> cells once when the game first loads and then only change the src property for cells that have to be changed. It will make your code a little more complicated, but you might want to try this when you fully understand how this system works and you're feeling adventurous.

Adding the ship

The ship is different than the other items in the game because it moves around. That means it will always be overlapping one of the other map cells, like the water, islands, or pirates. If the ship is over one of these cells, the map array will need to know that there are two things in one cell grid. It's possible for an array element to contain more than one value, if those values are stored in yet another array. This type of array is a 3D array. But a simpler and possibly better solution for this game is to make a new, separate array for the moving objects. This new array will have exactly the same number of rows and columns as the map array but it just contains the items in your game that move around. You can then layer this new array over the original map and the two arrays will synchronize perfectly.

In Island Adventure the gameObjects array will contain all the moving objects in the game. In this phase I just add the ship, but later I'll add the roaming sea monster as well. In the islandAdventure2.html file you'll see how this new array is used to add the ship.

Here are the original map array and the new gameObjects array. gameObjects contains the number 4 at the bottom left corner, which represents the ship.

```
var map =
[
  [0, 2, 0, 0, 0, 3],
  [0, 0, 0, 1, 0, 0],
  [0, 1, 0, 0, 0, 0],
  [0, 0, 0, 0, 2, 0],
  [0, 2, 0, 1, 0, 0],
  [0, 0, 0, 0, 0, 0]
];
```

```
var gameObjects =
[
  [0, 0, 0, 0, 0, 0],
  [0, 0, 0, 0, 0, 0],
  [0, 0, 0, 0, 0, 0],
  [0, 0, 0, 0, 0, 0],
  [0, 0, 0, 0, 0, 0],
  [4, 0, 0, 0, 0, 0]
];

var WATER = 0;
var ISLAND = 1;
var PIRATE = 2;
var HOME = 3;
var SHIP = 4;
```

The game now understands that the SHIP has the value 4.

Each time the player presses an arrow key, the program will move the ship by changing its row and column numbers. That means we need to keep track of the ship's row and column with variables. These are easy to add.

```
var shipRow;
var shipColumn;
```

They're created without any initial values. That's because the program uses a loop to figure out where the ship is in the gameObjects array. The loop assigns these values to the shipRow and shipColumn variables.

```
for(var row = 0; row < ROWS; row++)
{
  for(var column = 0; column < COLUMNS; column++)
  {
    if(gameObjects[row][column] === SHIP)
    {
      shipRow = row;
      shipColumn = column;
    }
  }
}
```

At the end of this loop shipRow has the value 5, and shipColumn has the value 0. You can see that this exactly matches the ship's position in the gameObjects array. The advantage of using a loop to find these values is that if you later decide to change the position of the ship in the array, this loop will automatically change these values to match. This makes the game very easy to change and maintain.

The last step is to render the gameObjects array. Here's the whole loop from the render function that creates the <img> tag cells. The code that adds the ship is a switch statement right near the end.

```
for(var row = 0; row < ROWS; row++)
{
  for(var column = 0; column < COLUMNS; column++)
  {
    //Create an img tag called cell
    var cell = document.createElement("img");

    //Set its CSS class to "cell"
    cell.setAttribute("class", "cell");

    //Add the img tag to the <div id="stage"> tag
    stage.appendChild(cell);

    //Find the correct image for this map cell
    switch(map[row][column])
    {
      case WATER:
        cell.src = "../images/water.png";
        break;

      case ISLAND:
        cell.src = "../images/island.png";
        break;

      case PIRATE:
        cell.src = "../images/pirate.png";
        break;

      case HOME:
        cell.src = "../images/home.png";
        break;
    }

    //Add the ship from the gameObjects array
    switch(gameObjects[row][column])
    {
      case SHIP:
      cell.src = "../images/ship.png";
      break;
    }

    //Position the cell
    cell.style.top = row * SIZE + "px";
    cell.style.left = column * SIZE + "px";
  }
}
```

You can see that it's rendered by using the same format for the other map objects. It loads the ship.png image into the cell's `src` property. The only difference is that it's not referring to the row and column from the map array. Instead, it is referring to our new gameObjects array.

```
switch(gameObjects[row][column])
{
  case SHIP:
    cell.src = "../images/ship.png";
    break;
}
```

In later steps we'll add the sea monster to this `switch` statement in order to display it in exactly the same way.

The result is that the gameObjects array is layered on top of the map array. Because it's rendered after the map, anything in the gameObjects array will be displayed *above* the map cells. That's perfect for this game because we want the ship to appear on top of the map, not under it. Figure 5-8 illustrates this.

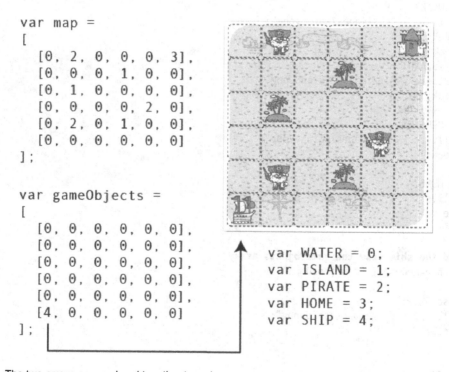

```
var map =
[
    [0, 2, 0, 0, 0, 3],
    [0, 0, 0, 1, 0, 0],
    [0, 1, 0, 0, 0, 0],
    [0, 0, 0, 0, 2, 0],
    [0, 2, 0, 1, 0, 0],
    [0, 0, 0, 0, 0, 0]
];


var gameObjects =
[
    [0, 0, 0, 0, 0, 0],
    [0, 0, 0, 0, 0, 0],
    [0, 0, 0, 0, 0, 0],
    [0, 0, 0, 0, 0, 0],
    [0, 0, 0, 0, 0, 0],
    [4, 0, 0, 0, 0, 0]
];
```

```
var WATER = 0;
var ISLAND = 1;
var PIRATE = 2;
var HOME = 3;
var SHIP = 4;
```

Figure 5-8. The two arrays are rendered together to make one game map

Moving the ship

Open islandAdventure3.html and you can now move the ship around the map by pressing the arrow keys. What's important to know is that the arrow keys do not directly reposition the ship. They just change the ship's row and column in the gameObjects array. The `render` function runs after each key press and reads the updated array and displays the ship's new position.

The first new addition is a keydown event listener.

```
window.addEventListener("keydown", keydownHandler, false);
```

It calls the keydownHandler. (To keep the code for this game as simple as possible, I've kept all the game logic in the keydownHandler rather than creating a special playGame function, like I did for the games in the previous chapters.)

You'll recall from Chapter 2 that each key on the keyboard has a special key code number. As you learned in a previous chapter, the Enter key has the value 13. The up, down, left, and right arrow keys also have their own numbers. To make our program easier to read, assign these numbers to constants:

```
var UP = 38;
var DOWN = 40;
var RIGHT = 39;
var LEFT = 37;
```

You can now use these constants to check which arrow key is being pressed. That's what the keydownHandler does. It uses a switch statement to figure out which key is pressed. It then changes the ship's row and column number in the gameObjects array to move the ship in the right direction. Here's how the keydownHandler is structured.

```
function keydownHandler(event)
{
  switch(event.keyCode)
  {
    case UP:
      //Move the ship up one row in the gameObjects array
      break;

    case DOWN:
      //Move the ship down one row in the gameObjects array
      break;

    case LEFT:
      //Move the ship left one column in the gameObjects array
      break;

    case RIGHT:
      //Move the ship right one column in the gameObjects array
      break;
  }

  //Render the game
  render();
}
```

The actual code is slightly more complex, but don't be fooled. You'll be stunned at how easy this is when you understand it.

```
function keydownHandler(event)
{
  switch(event.keyCode)
  {
    case UP:

      //Find out if the ship's move will be within the playing field
      if(shipRow > 0)
      {
        //If it is, clear the ship's current cell
        gameObjects[shipRow][shipColumn] = 0;

        //Subtract 1 from the ship's row to move it up one row on the map
        shipRow--;

        //Apply the ship's new updated position to the array
        gameObjects[shipRow][shipColumn] = SHIP;
      }
      break;

    case DOWN:
      if(shipRow < ROWS - 1)
      {
        gameObjects[shipRow][shipColumn] = 0;
        shipRow++;
        gameObjects[shipRow][shipColumn] = SHIP;
      }
      break;

    case LEFT:
      if(shipColumn > 0)
      {
        gameObjects[shipRow][shipColumn] = 0;
        shipColumn--;
        gameObjects[shipRow][shipColumn] = SHIP;
      }
      break;

    case RIGHT:
      if(shipColumn < COLUMNS - 1)
      {
        gameObjects[shipRow][shipColumn] = 0;
        shipColumn++;
        gameObjects[shipRow][shipColumn] = SHIP;
      }
      break;
  }
```

```
  //Render the game
  render();
}
```

The same logic is repeated four times, once for each direction. If you understand how it works for one direction, you'll understand the others. Let's find out what happens when the up arrow key is pressed.

```
case UP:
    //Find out if the ship's move will be within the playing field
    if(shipRow > 0)
    {
        //If it is, clear the ship's current cell
        gameObjects[shipRow][shipColumn] = 0;

        //Subtract 1 from the ship's row to move it up one row on the map
        shipRow--;

        //Apply the ship's new updated position to the array
        gameObjects[shipRow][shipColumn] = SHIP;
    }
    break;
```

This is a bit abstract so let's look at a practical example. Imagine that the ship is at the second row and in the third column. The gameObjects array will look like this.

```
gameObjects =
[
  [0, 0, 0, 0, 0, 0],
  [0, 0, 4, 0, 0, 0],
  [0, 0, 0, 0, 0, 0],
  [0, 0, 0, 0, 0, 0],
  [0, 0, 0, 0, 0, 0],
  [0, 0, 0, 0, 0, 0]
];
```

The shipRow and shipColumn variables will have these values:

```
shipRow = 1
shipColumn = 2
```

(Remember, arrays start numbering at 0. That means the top row is "row number 0" and the left column is "column number 0".) So you can refer to the ship's position like this:

```
gameObjects[shipRow][shipColumn]
```

This would be the same as if you accessed it like this:

```
gameObjects[1][2]
```

Not so hard, so far, is it? Figure 5-9 illustrates how all this corresponds to the ship's position on the map.

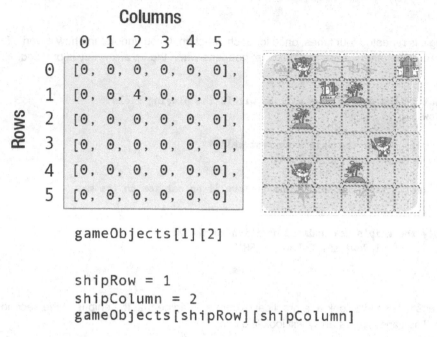

Columns

```
     0  1  2  3  4  5
  0 [0, 0, 0, 0, 0, 0],
  1 [0, 0, 4, 0, 0, 0],
  2 [0, 0, 0, 0, 0, 0],
  3 [0, 0, 0, 0, 0, 0],
  4 [0, 0, 0, 0, 0, 0],
  5 [0, 0, 0, 0, 0, 0]
```

Rows

```
gameObjects[1][2]


shipRow = 1
shipColumn = 2
gameObjects[shipRow][shipColumn]
```

Figure 5-9. Different ways to describe the ship's position on the map

If you want the ship to go up, you have to move the number 4 into the row above the current one. But you also want to remove the ship from the row that it's currently on. You want to end up with an array that looks like this:

```
gameObjects =
[
  [0, 0, 4, 0, 0, 0],
  [0, 0, 0, 0, 0, 0],
  [0, 0, 0, 0, 0, 0],
  [0, 0, 0, 0, 0, 0],
  [0, 0, 0, 0, 0, 0],
  [0, 0, 0, 0, 0, 0]
];
```

The first thing you need to do is to set the ship's current row to 0, so it no longer contains the number **4**.

```
gameObjects[shipRow][shipColumn] = 0;
```

This clears the ship from its current position. You now have a blank array that looks like this:

```
gameObjects =
[
  [0, 0, 0, 0, 0, 0],
  [0, 0, 0, 0, 0, 0],
  [0, 0, 0, 0, 0, 0],
  [0, 0, 0, 0, 0, 0],
  [0, 0, 0, 0, 0, 0],
  [0, 0, 0, 0, 0, 0]
];
```

The next step is to add the number 4 into the top row, which is row number 0. shipRow has a value of 1. So what's 1 minus 1? It's 0. That means you can describe the ship's new row like this:

```
shipRow - 1
```

All you need to do now is use this to tell the array to copy the number 4 into this new position.

```
gameObject[shipRow - 1][shipColumn] = 4;
```

The array now looks like this:

```
gameObjects =
[
  [0, 0, 4, 0, 0, 0],
  [0, 0, 0, 0, 0, 0],
  [0, 0, 0, 0, 0, 0],
  [0, 0, 0, 0, 0, 0],
  [0, 0, 0, 0, 0, 0],
  [0, 0, 0, 0, 0, 0]
];
```

The ship has been moved up one row. When the render function reads this new updated array, it displays the image of the ship to match its new array position. Figure 5-10 illustrates how this works.

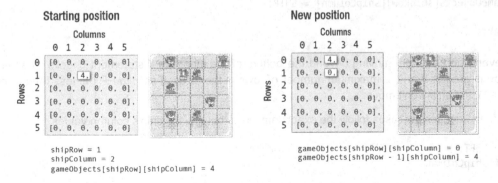

Figure 5-10. Subtract 1 from the ship's row to move it up one row in the map

Deviously simple! The up arrow key in Island Adventure does exactly the same thing to move the ship up one row in the array. That's what this code does:

```
case UP:
  if(shipRow > 0)
  {

    gameObjects[shipRow][shipColumn] = 0;
    shipRow--;
    gameObjects[shipRow][shipColumn] = SHIP;
  }
  break;
```

Keeping the ship inside the map

This code does one more thing. The if statement prevents the ship from moving up beyond the edge of the map. It does this by checking whether the row the ship wants to move into is greater or equal to 0.

```
if(shipRow > 0)
{ ...
```

Remember that 0 is the number of the array at the very top of the map. If shipRow is equal to 0, it means that the ship is already on the top row. If that's the case we shouldn't allow the ship to move further up. We should only allow that if shipRow is greater than 0, which means the ship isn't on the top row. The if statement checks for this. A player can press the up arrow key a hundred times, but the ship will not move off the map.

This is how the up arrow key works, but all the other directions work in the same way. If the player presses the down arrow key, the code adds 1 to shipRow.

```
case DOWN:
  if(shipRow < ROWS - 1)
  {

    gameObjects[shipRow][shipColumn] = 0;
    shipRow++;
    gameObjects[shipRow][shipColumn] = SHIP;
  }
  break;
```

To prevent the ship from moving beyond the bottom of the map, the if statement checks whether the new position is greater than the maximum number of rows in the array. If shipRow + 1 is less than or equal to 6 (ROWS -1), the ship won't move.

The left and right arrow cases follow the exact same logic but use the ship's column values.

```
  case LEFT:
    if(shipColumn > 0)
    {
      gameObjects[shipRow][shipColumn] = 0;
```

```
      shipColumn--;
      gameObjects[shipRow][shipColumn] = SHIP;
    }
    break;

  case RIGHT:
    if(shipColumn < COLUMNS - 1)
    {
      gameObjects[shipRow][shipColumn] = 0;
      shipColumn++;
      gameObjects[shipRow][shipColumn] = SHIP;
    }
    break;
```

And now you know how to move objects around on the map!

Figuring out where the ship is

The game needs to know where the ship is on the map. Is it over water, on an island, fighting pirates, or safely at home? The next phase of our game, shown in **islandAdventure4.hmtl**, displays a message in the console that tells you what kind of cell the ship is on. Move the ship around a bit, and you'll see the ship's journey displayed in the console. Figure 5-11 shows what you might see.

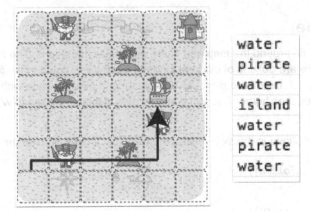

Figure 5-11. The program knows which kind of cell the ship is on

It seems like this might be complicated to figure out, but it's easy. The code that does this is a switch statement in the keydownHandler.

```
switch(map[shipRow][shipColumn])
{
  case WATER:
    console.log("water");
    break;
```

```
  case PIRATE:
    console.log("pirate");
    break;

  case ISLAND:
    console.log("island");
    break;

  case HOME:
    console.log("home");
    break;
}
```

Really, this is all there is. How does it work?

You know where the ship is in the array thanks to the `shipRow` and `shipColumn` variables. The program updates these variables with the ship's new position each time the ship moves. To find out where the ship is, just use the variables to figure out what's in exactly the same place on the map array.

```
map[shipRow][shipColumn]
```

This will be either 0 (WATER), 1 (ISLAND), 2 (PIRATE), or 3 (HOME).

You're just comparing a position in the `gameObjects` array against the same position in the `map` array. That's it!

Creating the game

We can now move the ship around the map and figure out where the ship is. The next step is to turn this into some kind of game. There are dozens of different kinds of games you could make from what we've got so far. My game is not complicated. I want the player to be able to fight pirates, trade with islands, and for the game to end when the player reaches home. The game should also display a message when the ship is sailing over open water.

The first step is to add functions to the `switch` statement we just looked at to let these things happen.

```
switch(map[shipRow][shipColumn])
{
  case WATER:
    gameMessage = "You sail the open seas."
    break;

  case PIRATE:
    fight();
    break;

  case ISLAND:
    trade();
    break;
```

```
case HOME:
    endGame();
    break;
}
```

I'll show you how these functions work soon, but first we need some game variables. I want the player to be able to win gold from pirates, buy food from islands, and gain some experience when a task is accomplished. I also want to give the player messages about what's happening in the game. I need some variables for all these things.

```
var food = 10;
var gold = 10;
var experience = 0;
var gameMessage = "Use the arrow keys to find your way home.";
```

These variables are all initialized at the beginning of the program.

The player starts the game with 10 food items (coconuts, I guess) and 10 gold pieces. I want the player to lose a bit of food each turn. The ship's crew gets hungry, after all. And if the player runs out of food or gold, the game should end. This bit of code at the bottom of the `keydownHandler` will do all these things.

```
//Subtract some food each turn
food--;
```

```
//Find out if the ship has run out of food or gold
if(food <= 0 || gold <= 0)
{
    endGame();
}
```

Now let's look at the heart of the game: the `fight`, `trade`, and `endGame` functions. I came up with these by just spending an hour or so playing around with the game variables to find a balance that seemed fair and fun. We need a bit of strategy and a bit of luck. Okay, I'll admit it, it's mostly luck! But there's enough variety that the player will be fooled into thinking there's more strategy than there really is. These are some ideas to get you started thinking about your own game, but you'll certainly be able to come up with your own recipes that will be much better than these.

Trading with islands

If the ship is on an island, the `trade` function runs. The amount of food on the island is calculated by adding the player's gold and experience together. The cost is random but is based on the amount of food the island has. If the player has enough gold to buy the food, the food variable is increased by the `islandsFood` variable. The player also gets two experience points for a successful trade. If the player doesn't have enough gold, the game displays a message. But the player also gets one experience point for trying.

```
function trade()
{
  //Figure out how much food the island has and how much it should cost
  var islandsFood = experience + gold;
  var cost = Math.ceil(Math.random() * islandsFood);

  //Let the player buy food if there's enough gold to afford it
  if(gold > cost)
  {
    food += islandsFood;
    gold -= cost;
    experience += 2;

    gameMessage
      = "You buy " + islandsFood + " coconuts"
      + " for " + cost + " gold pieces.";
  }
  else
  {
    //Tell the player if he or she does not have enough gold
    experience += 1;
    gameMessage = "You don't have enough gold to buy food.";
  }
}
```

Fighting pirates

The fight function is a little more complex. It first calculates the ship's strength by generating a random number based on half the player's food and gold. It then calculates the pirates' strength by generating a random number up to twice that amount. If the player loses, the gold is subtracted by half the pirates' strength. If the player wins, he or she gets all the pirates' gold.

```
function fight()
{
  //The ship's strength
  var shipStrength = Math.ceil((food + gold) / 2);

  //A random number between 1 and the ship's strength
  var pirateStrength = Math.ceil(Math.random() * shipStrength * 2);

  //Find out if the pirates are stronger than the player's ship
  if(pirateStrength > shipStrength)
  {
    //The pirates ransack the ship
    var stolenGold = Math.round(pirateStrength / 2);
    gold -= stolenGold;
```

```
    //Give the player some experience for trying
    experience += 1;

    //Update the game message
    gameMessage
       = "You fight and LOSE " + stolenGold + " gold pieces."
       + " Ship's strength: " + shipStrength
       + " Pirate's strength: " + pirateStrength;
  }
  else
  {
    //The player wins the pirates' gold
    var pirateGold = Math.round(pirateStrength / 2);
    gold += pirateGold;

    //Add some experience
    experience += 2;

    //Update the game message
    gameMessage
       = "You fight and WIN " + pirateGold + " gold pieces."
       + " Ship's strength: " + shipStrength
       + " Pirate's strength: " + pirateStrength;
  }
}
```

There's always just a 50/50 chance or winning or losing each fight. But because the food and gold variables are always changing, it creates a nice bit of variety. You could give the player an advantage by adding experience to shipStrength.

Ending the game

The endGame function is called if the player runs out of food or gold or if the ship reaches home. If the player reaches home safely, the score is calculated by adding together the food, gold, and experience. The keydown event listener is also removed to disable any more key presses.

```
function endGame()
{
  if(map[shipRow][shipColumn] === HOME)
  {
    //Calculate the score
    var score = food + gold + experience;

    //Display the game message
    gameMessage
       = "You made it home ALIVE! " + "Final Score: " + score;
  }
```

```
    else
    {
        //Display the game message if the player has run out of gold or food
        if(gold <= 0)
        {
            gameMessage += " You've run out of gold!";
        }
        else
        {
            gameMessage += " You've run out of food!";
        }
        gameMessage
            += " Your crew throws you overboard!";
    }

        //Remove the keyboard listener to end the game
        window.removeEventListener("keydown", keydownHandler, false);
}
```

Rendering the game output

Finally, the game needs to render the gameMessage and variables. These will be updated after each turn. This code appears just below the code that renders the arrays.

```
function render()
{
    //... the code that renders the arrays

    //Display the game message
    output.innerHTML = gameMessage;

    //Display the player's food, gold, and experience
    output.innerHTML
        += "<br>Gold: " + gold + ", Food: "
        + food + ", Experience: " + experience;
}
```

And that's it! We now have a complete working game.

The game code so far

Here's the entire code listing from the islandAdventure5.hmtl file. Compare it with your own game if you need to check how all the pieces fit together so far.

```
<!doctype html>
<title>Island Adventure 1</title>

<style>
```

```css
#stage
{
  position: relative;
  width: 384px;
  height: 384px;
  background-image: url("../images/background.png");
}

.cell
{
  display: block;
  position: absolute;
  width: 64px;
  height: 64px;
}

p
{
  width: 400px;
}
```

```html
</style>

<div id="stage"></div>
<p id="output"></p>

<script>
```

```javascript
//Get a reference to the stage and output
var stage = document.querySelector("#stage");
var output = document.querySelector("#output");

//Add a keyboard listener
window.addEventListener("keydown", keydownHandler, false);

//The game map
var map =
[
  [0, 2, 0, 0, 0, 3],
  [0, 0, 0, 1, 0, 0],
  [0, 1, 0, 0, 0, 0],
  [0, 0, 0, 0, 2, 0],
  [0, 2, 0, 1, 0, 0],
  [0, 0, 0, 0, 0, 0]
];
```

```
//The game objects map
var gameObjects =
[
  [0, 0, 0, 0, 0, 0],
  [0, 0, 0, 0, 0, 0],
  [0, 0, 0, 0, 0, 0],
  [0, 0, 0, 0, 0, 0],
  [0, 0, 0, 0, 0, 0],
  [4, 0, 0, 0, 0, 0]
];

//Map code
var WATER = 0;
var ISLAND = 1;
var PIRATE = 2;
var HOME = 3;
var SHIP = 4;

//The size of each cell
var SIZE = 64;

//The number of rows and columns
var ROWS = map.length;
var COLUMNS = map[0].length;

//Arrow key codes
var UP = 38;
var DOWN = 40;
var RIGHT = 39;
var LEFT = 37;

//Find the ship's start position
var shipRow;
var shipColumn;

for(var row = 0; row < ROWS; row++)
{
  for(var column = 0; column < COLUMNS; column++)
  {
    if(gameObjects[row][column] === SHIP)
    {
      shipRow = row;
      shipColumn = column;
    }
  }
}
```

```
//The game variables
var food = 10;
var gold = 10;
var experience = 0;
var gameMessage = "Use the arrow keys to find your way home.";

render();

function keydownHandler(event)
{
  switch(event.keyCode)
  {
    case UP:

      //Find out if the ship's move will be within the playing field
      if(shipRow > 0)
      {
        //If it is, clear the ship's current cell
        gameObjects[shipRow][shipColumn] = 0;

        //Subtract 1 from the ship's row to move it up one row on the map
        shipRow--;

        //Apply the ship's new updated position to the array
        gameObjects[shipRow][shipColumn] = SHIP;
      }
      break;

    case DOWN:
      if(shipRow < ROWS - 1)
      {
        gameObjects[shipRow][shipColumn] = 0;
        shipRow++;
        gameObjects[shipRow][shipColumn] = SHIP;
      }
      break;

    case LEFT:
      if(shipColumn > 0)
      {
        gameObjects[shipRow][shipColumn] = 0;
        shipColumn--;
        gameObjects[shipRow][shipColumn] = SHIP;
      }
      break;

    case RIGHT:
      if(shipColumn < COLUMNS - 1)
      {
        gameObjects[shipRow][shipColumn] = 0;
```

```
          shipColumn++;
          gameObjects[shipRow][shipColumn] = SHIP;
        }
        break;
    }

    //Find out what kind of cell the ship is on
    switch(map[shipRow][shipColumn])
    {
      case WATER:
        gameMessage = "You sail the open seas."
        break;

      case PIRATE:
        fight();
        break;

      case ISLAND:
        trade();
        break;

      case HOME:
        endGame();
        break;
    }

    //Subtract some food each turn
    food--;

    //Find out if the ship has run out of food or gold
    if(food <= 0 || gold <= 0)
    {
      endGame();
    }

    //Render the game
    render();
}

function trade()
{
    //Figure out how much food the island has and how much it should cost
    var islandsFood = experience + gold;
    var cost = Math.ceil(Math.random() * islandsFood);

    //Let the player buy food if there's enough gold to afford it
    if(gold > cost)
    {
      food += islandsFood;
      gold -= cost;
      experience += 2;
```

```
        gameMessage
          = "You buy " + islandsFood + " coconuts"
          + " for " + cost + " gold pieces."
    }
    else
    {
        //Tell the player if he or she does not have enough gold
        experience += 1;
        gameMessage = "You don't have enough gold to buy food."
    }
}

function fight()
{
    //The ship's strength
    var shipStrength = Math.ceil((food + gold) / 2);

    //A random number between 1 and the ship's strength
    var pirateStrength = Math.ceil(Math.random() * shipStrength * 2);

    //Find out if the pirates are stronger than the player's ship
    if(pirateStrength > shipStrength)
    {
        //The pirates ransack the ship
        var stolenGold = Math.round(pirateStrength / 2);
        gold -= stolenGold;

        //Give the player some experience for trying
        experience += 1;

        //Update the game message
        gameMessage
          = "You fight and LOSE " + stolenGold + " gold pieces."
          + " Ship's strength: " + shipStrength
          + " Pirate's strength: " + pirateStrength;
    }
    else
    {
        //The player wins the pirates' gold
        var pirateGold = Math.round(pirateStrength / 2);
        gold += pirateGold;

        //Add some experience
        experience += 2;
```

```
    //Update the game message
    gameMessage
      = "You fight and WIN " + pirateGold + " gold pieces."
      + " Ship's strength: " + shipStrength
      + " Pirate's strength: " + pirateStrength;
  }
}

function endGame()
{
  if(map[shipRow][shipColumn] === HOME)
  {
    //Calculate the score
    var score = food + gold + experience;

    //Display the game message
    gameMessage
      = "You made it home ALIVE! " + "Final Score: " + score;
  }
  else
  {
    //Display the game message if the player has run out of gold or food
    if(gold <= 0)
    {
      gameMessage += " You've run out of gold!";
    }
    else
    {
      gameMessage += " You've run out of food!";
    }

    gameMessage
      += " Your crew throws you overboard!";
  }

  //Remove the keyboard listener to end the game
  window.removeEventListener("keydown", keydownHandler, false);
}

function render()
{
  //Clear the stage of img cells from the previous turn

  if(stage.hasChildNodes())
  {
    for(var i = 0; i < ROWS * COLUMNS; i++)
    {
      stage.removeChild(stage.firstChild);
    }
  }
```

```
//Render the game by looping through the map arrays
for(var row = 0; row < ROWS; row++)
{
  for(var column = 0; column < COLUMNS; column++)
  {
    //Create an img tag called cell
    var cell = document.createElement("img");

    //Set its CSS class to "cell"
    cell.setAttribute("class", "cell");

    //Add the img tag to the <div id="stage"> tag
    stage.appendChild(cell);

    //Find the correct image for this map cell
    switch(map[row][column])
    {
      case WATER:
        cell.src = "../images/water.png";
        break;

      case ISLAND:
        cell.src = "../images/island.png";
        break;

      case PIRATE:
        cell.src = "../images/pirate.png";
        break;

      case HOME:
        cell.src = "../images/home.png";
        break;
    }

    //Add the ship from the gameObjects array
    switch(gameObjects[row][column])
    {
      case SHIP:
      cell.src = "../images/ship.png";
      break;
    }

    //Position the cell
    cell.style.top = row * SIZE + "px";
    cell.style.left = column * SIZE + "px";
  }
}
```

```
//Display the game message
output.innerHTML = gameMessage;

//Display the player's food, gold, and experience
output.innerHTML
  += "<br>Gold: " + gold + ", Food: "
  + food + ", Experience: " + experience;
}

</script>
```

Now let's find out how to add the most interesting part of the game: the wandering sea monster.

Adding the monster

The monster is added to the game in exactly the same way as the ship. First, it's added as 5 to the gameObjects array.

```
var gameObjects =
[
  [0, 0, 0, 0, 0, 0],
  [0, 0, 5, 0, 0, 0],
  [0, 0, 0, 0, 0, 0],
  [0, 0, 0, 0, 0, 0],
  [0, 0, 0, 0, 0, 0],
  [4, 0, 0, 0, 0, 0]
];

var WATER = 0;
var ISLAND = 1;
var PIRATE = 2;
var HOME = 3;
var SHIP = 4;
var MONSTER = 5;
```

The game then creates monsterRow and monsterColumn variables that will keep track of the monster's position. They're assigned values by the same loop that assigns the shipRow and shipColumn variables.

```
var shipRow;
var shipColumn;
var monsterRow;
var monsterColumn;

for(var row = 0; row < ROWS; row++)
{
  for(var column = 0; column < COLUMNS; column++)
```

```
  {
    if(gameObjects[row][column] === SHIP)
    {
      shipRow = row;
      shipColumn = column;
    }
    if(gameObjects[row][column] === MONSTER)
    {
      monsterRow = row;
      monsterColumn = column;
    }
  }
}
```

The monster is then rendered along with the ship in the render function:

```
function render()
{

    //... the code that renders the map

    //Add the ship and monster from the gameObjects array
    switch(gameObjects[row][column])
    {
      case SHIP:
        cell.src = "../images/ship.png";
        break;

      case MONSTER:
        cell.src = "../images/monster.png";
        break;
    }

    //...the code that positions the cell
}
```

All this code makes the monster visible at its starting position when the game first loads.

Moving the monster

Every time you press an arrow key, the monster moves into a new random cell, next to the cell it's already in. But the monster travels on only water. It never crosses the island, pirate, or home cells, as shown in Figure 5-12.

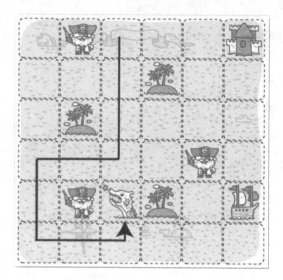

Figure 5-12. The monster moves around randomly, but on only water

The program moves the monster in a random direction but into only WATER cells. How is this done?

First, a new moveMonster function is called in the keydownHandler.

```
moveMonster();
```

It's called just after the switch statement that figures out where on the map the ship is. The moveMonster function is long, but, as you'll see in the explanation ahead, it won't be hard to understand when you break it down into smaller steps.

```
function moveMonster()
{
    //The 4 possible directions that the monster can move
    var UP = 1;
    var DOWN = 2;
    var LEFT = 3;
    var RIGHT = 4;

    //An array to store the valid direction that the monster is allowed to move in
    var validDirections = [];

    //The final direction that the monster will move in
    var direction = undefined;

    //Find out what kinds of things are in the cells
    //that surround the monster. If the cells contain WATER,
    //push the corresponding direction (UP, DOWN, LEFT, or RIGHT) into the validDirections array
    if(monsterRow > 0)
    {
     var thingAbove = map[monsterRow - 1][monsterColumn];
```

```
    if(thingAbove === WATER)
    {
      validDirections.push(UP)
    }
}
if(monsterRow < ROWS - 1)
{
  var thingBelow = map[monsterRow + 1][monsterColumn];
  if(thingBelow === WATER)
  {
    validDirections.push(DOWN)
  }
}
if(monsterColumn > 0)
{
  var thingToTheLeft = map[monsterRow][monsterColumn - 1];
  if(thingToTheLeft === WATER)
  {
    validDirections.push(LEFT)
  }
}
if(monsterColumn < COLUMNS - 1)
{
  var thingToTheRight = map[monsterRow][monsterColumn + 1];
  if(thingToTheRight === WATER)
  {
    validDirections.push(RIGHT)
  }
}


//The validDirections array now contains 0 to 4 directions that
//contain WATER cells. Which of those directions will the monster
//choose to move in?

//If a valid direction was found, randomly choose one of the
//possible directions and assign it to the direction variable
if(validDirections.length !== 0)
{
  var randomNumber = Math.floor(Math.random() * validDirections.length);
  direction = validDirections[randomNumber];
}

//Move the monster in the chosen random direction
switch(direction)
{
  case UP:
    //Clear the monster's current cell
    gameObjects[monsterRow][monsterColumn] = 0;
    //Subtract 1 from the monster's row
    monsterRow--;
```

```
//Apply the monster's new updated position to the array
gameObjects[monsterRow][monsterColumn] = MONSTER;
break;

case DOWN:
  gameObjects[monsterRow][monsterColumn] = 0;
  monsterRow++;
  gameObjects[monsterRow][monsterColumn] = MONSTER;
  break;

case LEFT:
  gameObjects[monsterRow][monsterColumn] = 0;
  monsterColumn--;
  gameObjects[monsterRow][monsterColumn] = MONSTER;
  break;

case RIGHT:
  gameObjects[monsterRow][monsterColumn] = 0;
  monsterColumn++;
  gameObjects[monsterRow][monsterColumn] = MONSTER;
  }
}
```

The function first creates four constants that represent possible directions the monster can move in.

```
var UP = 1;
var DOWN = 2;
var LEFT = 3;
var RIGHT = 4;
```

However, not all of those directions will be valid. The monster can travel on only water, so there might be islands or pirates blocking its way. As you will see, this function runs tests that will tell us what the monster's valid movement directions are. Those directions will be stored in an array called validDirections.

```
var validDirections = [];
```

It's initialized as empty when the function starts, but you'll soon see how we'll add valid directions to it. When the function is finished running, it will contain directions that contain only WATER cells.

We'll also use a variable called direction that will store the one, final direction that the monster chooses to move in. It's initialized with a value of undefined at the beginning of the function.

```
var direction = undefined;
```

undefined means that the variable has no value at all, not even 0. If you're unsure if a number variable will ever be assigned a value, it's a good idea to initialize it as undefined.

The monster needs to know what kinds of things are in the map cells surrounding it. Is there water above, a pirate below, or an island to the left? Four if statements can tell us this. If they find a cell containing WATER, they push the corresponding direction into the validDirections array. When these if statements finish their checks, validDirections will contain the directions that contain only WATER cells. I'll explain how all this works ahead.

```
if(monsterRow > 0)
{
  var thingAbove = map[monsterRow - 1][monsterColumn];
  if(thingAbove === WATER)
  {
    validDirections.push(UP)
  }
}
if(monsterRow < ROWS - 1)
{
  var thingBelow = map[monsterRow + 1][monsterColumn];
  if(thingBelow === WATER)
  {
    validDirections.push(DOWN)
  }
}
if(monsterColumn > 0)
{
  var thingToTheLeft = map[monsterRow][monsterColumn - 1];
  if(thingToTheLeft === WATER)
  {
    validDirections.push(LEFT)
  }
}
if(monsterColumn < COLUMNS - 1)
{
  var thingToTheRight = map[monsterRow][monsterColumn + 1];
  if(thingToTheRight === WATER)
  {
    validDirections.push(RIGHT)
  }
}
```

The first if statement checks the cell above the monster. However, it shouldn't check for a cell above if the monster is already at the very top of the map, because if the monster is on the top row, there won't be any cells above it. The if statement checks for this by using the same map boundary check that we used to keep the ship inside the map.

```
if(monsterRow > 0)
{ ...
```

If there is a row above the monster, the code then figures out what is in the cell directly above the monster.

```
var thingAbove = map[monsterRow - 1][monsterColumn];
```

For example, imagine that the monster is on row number 6. monsterRow - 1 will equal row number 5. Lower-numbered rows are above higher-numbered rows on the map, so row 5 is directly above row 6. This lets the monster see what's in the cell directly above it. The map array contains the numbers 0, 1, 2, and 4; 0 is WATER and the sea monster will travel on only WATER cells, so it checks for this:

```
if(thingAbove === WATER)
{ ...
```

If the above cell *is* WATER, the UP direction is pushed into the validDirections array.

```
validDirections.push(UP)
```

If the cell isn't WATER, the direction isn't added to validDirections and the next direction is tried. When all four if statements have finished, validDirections will contain those directions that contain only WATER cells. Figure 5-13 illustrates how the game knows which cells are above, below, to the right, and to the left of the monster.

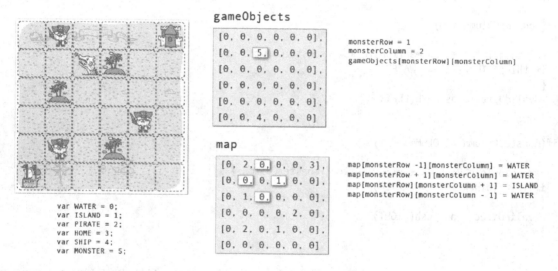

Figure 5-13. *The program finds out which cells are surrounding the monsters*

> *If you want to modify this game so that only the player's ship travels on water as well, use this same technique. This is the classic way to create a maze game that prevents the player from traveling through walls.*

The next step is to randomly choose one of the valid directions. Whatever final direction is chosen is copied into the direction variable.

```
if(validDirections.length !== 0)
{
  var randomNumber = Math.floor(Math.random() * validDirections.length);
  direction = validDirections[randomNumber];
}
```

This is a bit dense, so let's take a closer look at how this works.

First, we want to prevent a direction from being chosen if the validDirections array is empty. In some more complex game maps, the monster could be trapped on all four sides and can't move. In that case, no valid direction will have been found and we don't want the monster to try and move in any direction. You'll know whether validDirections is empty if its length property is 0.

```
if(validDirections.length !== 0)
{ ...
```

If it's not empty, it means that validDirections will contain up to four possible direction values. The next step is to generate a random number between 0 and the number of elements that validDirections contains. Here's the code that does this:

```
var randomNumber = Math.floor(Math.random() * validDirections.length);
```

For example, if validDirections contains three elements, randomNumber will be any number between 0 and 2 (0, 1, or 2). We can now use this number to choose one of the directions from the validDirections array. Just use randomNumber as the index number.

```
direction = validDirections[randomNumber];
```

direction will now have the value of either UP, DOWN, LEFT, or RIGHT. We won't know which this will be, but we do know that it can only be a direction that contains a WATER cell.

Lastly, all we have to do is use this direction with a switch statement to move the monster into its new position in the gameObjects array.

```
switch(direction)
{
  case UP:
    //Clear the monster's current cell
    gameObjects[monsterRow][monsterColumn] = 0;
    //Subtract 1 from the monster's row
    monsterRow--;
    //Apply the monster's new updated position to the array
    gameObjects[monsterRow][monsterColumn] = MONSTER;
    break;

  case DOWN:
    gameObjects[monsterRow][monsterColumn] = 0;
    monsterRow++;
    gameObjects[monsterRow][monsterColumn] = MONSTER;
    break;

  case LEFT:
    gameObjects[monsterRow][monsterColumn] = 0;
    monsterColumn--;
    gameObjects[monsterRow][monsterColumn] = MONSTER;
    break;
```

```
  case RIGHT:
    gameObjects[monsterRow][monsterColumn] = 0;
    monsterColumn++;
    gameObjects[monsterRow][monsterColumn] = MONSTER;
}
```

The code that moves the monster into the chosen cell is based on exactly the same code that moves the player's ship into new cells.

And there you have a great new technique for making a wandering monster that you can use in all sorts of different games.

Swallowing the ship

If the ship and monster collide, the monster swallows the ship and the game ends. Here's how this works.

The game checks whether the ship is in the same array position as the monster. The code in bold directly after the moveMonster function call checks for this:

```
//Move the monster
moveMonster();


//Find out if the ship is touching the monster
if(gameObjects[shipRow][shipColumn] === MONSTER)
{
  endGame();
}
```

This works because moveMonster is called after the ship is moved.

If the ship is in the monster's cell, the endGame function is called. It adds a new check for a sea monster collision. Here's an abridged version of the endGame function with the new code highlighted in bold.

```
function endGame()
{
  if(map[shipRow][shipColumn] === HOME)
  {
   //... Figure out the score
  }
  else if(gameObjects[shipRow][shipColumn] === MONSTER)
  {
    gameMessage
      = "Your ship has been swallowed by a sea monster!";
  }
  else
  {

     //... You run out of food or gold
  }
```

```
//Remove the keyboard listener to end the game
window.removeEventListener("keydown", keydownHandler, false);
}
```

And there the game ends! Do you see now what kind of power a 2D array can give you? It means that game objects can intelligently analyze their environment and make decisions based on where they are. This is an extremely sophisticated skill, but, as you can see, the logic that's built into a 2D array makes it easy to implement.

Summary

The 2D array lets you position and move objects around a game world. With this array, because you can easily find out where an object is and what's surrounding it, your game logic and artificial intelligence are greatly simplified. If you want to make a board game, strategy game, or role-playing game, start here. Now that you understand how 2D arrays work, you can apply these same techniques to the adventure game described in the previous chapter. And as you'll see in later chapters, 2D arrays are going to be at the heart of the action in video games as well.

You have learned most of the core game-programming techniques you need to know. There's one more that you need to know about: **objects**. That will be the subject of our next chapter, and I'll show you how you can use objects along with the canvas technology to create animated characters.

Chapter 6

Game Objects and Animation

All the games we've made so far in this book have been turn-based. That means the player makes a move and then waits for the computer to make its move. Board games, card games, strategy games, and many simulations are turn-based. Starting with this chapter, and continuing in Chapters 7 and 8, you're going to learn all the skills you need to make fast-paced action games.

This is an important chapter, because you're going to learn some fundamental JavaScript programming techniques and a brand-new way of displaying images for games. These are the things you'll learn:

- How to display images using canvas technology.

- What objects are and how to use them for games.

- How to control object states and use states to change the way a game character appears.

- How to make things happen over time, and how to make a timer.

- What a tilesheet is, and how to use it to display images.

And you'll also learn one of the most important game-design skills there is:

- Animation, so that you can display a series of individual images to make game characters that appear to move.

And all of these skills will come together in a fun little action game called Monster Smash, which is shown in Figure 6-1. How many jumping monsters can you smash in 30 seconds?

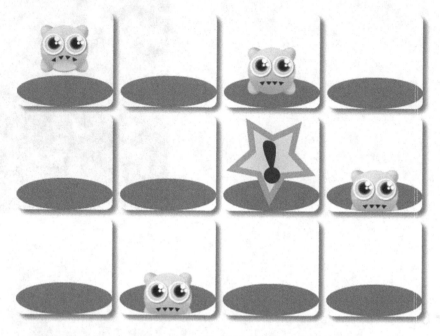

Figure 6-1. Monster Smash

Displaying images with canvas

You already know two ways to display images. You can use an <img> tag and set its src property to the image file you want to use. Or you can use a <div> tag and set its background-image property. But there's a third way, which is possibly best for games: canvas.

Canvas is a sophisticated graphics display technology. It's basically just an HTML tag, <canvas>, which represents a bitmap image that you can control with JavaScript. (Bitmap images are images that are made up of pixels.) You can use canvas to display images and video, make shapes, and render text. The canvas technology is a whole area of specialization in itself, but in this book we're going to use it for what it's best for: a fast and efficient way to render graphics and animation for games.

> Note: Although you can achieve many of these same effects using <div> or even <img> tags, canvas is specialized for displaying quickly changing game graphics. We'll be using it as our preferred display system for the rest of the book. The only time you may still want to consider using <div> or <img> tags to display game graphics is when you have to make a game for an older browser that doesn't support the newer <canvas> tag.

Canvas displays images in something called a context. The context is just the drawing surface that the images are rendered on, as well as the special JavaScript code you use to control it with. The context can be 2D or 3D. The 3D context is called WebGL (for Web Graphics Library), which is a specialized technology in its own right. In this book we're going to use the 2D context.

Here's some code that displays a 64-by-64-pixel image of a video-game monster using canvas. When it runs, you'll see something that looks like Figure 6-2 displayed in the browser window. There are lots of new techniques here, but don't worry: I'll explain them all ahead.

Figure 6-2. Use canvas to display an image

```
<!doctype html>
<title>Displaying an image with canvas</title>

<canvas width="64" height="64"></canvas>

<script>

//1. Get a reference to the canvas
var canvas = document.querySelector("canvas");

//2. Get a reference to the canvas's drawing surface
var drawingSurface = canvas.getContext("2d");

//3. Create a monsterImage variable to hold the new image
var monsterImage = new Image();

//4. Add a listener to the image to call the
//render function when the image has loaded
monsterImage.addEventListener("load", loadHandler, false);

//5. Assign the image's src property to the image you want to load
monsterImage.src = "monster.png";
```

```
function imageLoadHandler()
{
  //6. Draw the monsterImage onto the drawingSurface
  drawingSurface.drawImage(monsterImage, 0, 0);
}

</script>
```

To use canvas you first need to create a <canvas> HTML element. In this example it has a width and height of 65, which matches the dimensions of the image.

```
<canvas width="64" height="64"></canvas>
```

> Note: Of course, you can change these dimensions to any size you like. A <canvas> tag is an HTML element just like any other, so you can change any of its style properties with CSS. You can have as many <canvas> tags as you need in your game, and give them different ids or classes. In these examples, I've added a dashed border to the canvas element with CSS so that you can easily see its edges.

Canvas elements have a hidden drawing surface called a "2D context." Before you can display anything in the canvas, you have to access this drawing surface with JavaScript. Here's how:

```
//Get a reference to the canvas HTML tag
var canvas = document.querySelector("canvas");
```

```
//Access the canvas's drawing surface
var drawingSurface = canvas.getContext("2d");
```

You now have a variable called drawingSurface that references the 2D context. You can use it to load an image. You can think of the drawing surface as a blank piece of paper. It's the same size as the <canvas> tag.

The next step is to create a new image object:

```
var monsterImage = new Image();
```

This creates a blank image object using JavaScript's new Image() statement. new Image() is a built-in feature of JavaScript that creates a blank, invisible <img> tag directly in your program. You can now load and access any image using the monsterImage variable.

The next line adds a load event listener to the image. When the image has finished loading, it will call the loadHandler.

```
monsterImage.addEventListener("load", loadHandler, false);
```

This is needed to solve a technical issue. The image won't load instantly; it takes a few milliseconds for the program to load it from your computer's hard drive. And while the image is loading, the rest of your program will continue to run. That's a problem, because if the image hasn't finished loading before the program tries to display it, it won't be visible. Adding a load event listener solves this problem.

The code then sets the image's `src` attribute to the image file you want to load.

```
monsterImage.src = "monster.png";
```

When the image has finished loading, it will call the `loadHandler` to display the image.

```
function loadHandler()
{
  drawingSurface.drawImage(monsterImage, 0, 0);
}
```

It's the `drawingSurface`'s `drawImage` method that displays the loaded PNG image on the canvas. The `drawImage` method is at the heart of displaying images with canvas, so let's take a close look at how it works.

Using the canvas's drawImage method

`drawImage` is a method that belongs to the canvas's drawing surface (the 2D context). In its simplest form, it takes three arguments:

- The image you want to display.
- The image's x position on the canvas.
- The image's y position on the canvas.

Here's a simple template for using it:

```
drawingSurface.drawImage.(theImage, xPosition, yPosition);
```

The X position is measured from the canvas's left side. The Y position is measured from the top side. This is the same system that we use to position images using CSS. To make the `monsterImage` fill the entire canvas, starting at the top left corner, use X and Y positions of zero, like this:

```
drawingSurface.drawImage(monsterImage, 0, 0);
```

If you want to offset the image from the top and left side by 20 pixels, you could use this code:

```
drawingSurface.drawImage(monsterImage, 20, 20);
```

Figure 6-3 illustrates how this works.

drawingSurface.drawImage(monsterImage, 0, 0);

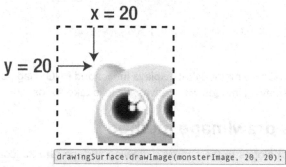

drawingSurface.drawImage(monsterImage, 20, 20);

Figure 6-3. Using the canvas's drawImage method

This shows how you can use drawImage to plot the original PNG image at any position on the drawing surface. But you can also tell drawImage to draw only a specific section of the image. For example, what if you want to draw only the monster's left eye? Use some code that looks like this:

```
drawingSurface.drawImage
(
  monsterImage,
  3, 12, 28, 28,
  0, 0, 28, 28
);
```

Figure 6-4 shows the result.

Figure 6-4. Draw only part of an image onto the canvas

The code that does this is much easier to understand than it at first looks. drawImage is just describing which part of the original source image should be copied onto which part of the canvas. Here's a template you can use to help you make sense of this ("source" is the original image and "destination" is the canvas).

```
drawingSurface.drawImage
(
  /*Image*/        imageName,
  /*Source*/       x, y, height, width,
  /*Destination*/  x, y, height, width
);
```

To copy the monster's eye onto the drawing surface, drawImage first creates an invisible box around the eye in the source PNG image. The box's top left corner has an X position of 3 pixels and a Y position of 12 pixels. It has a height and width of 28 pixels. The highlighted code in the source section describes this box.

```
drawingSurface.drawImage
(
  /*Image*/        monsterImage,
  /*Source*/       3, 12, 28, 28,
  /*Destination*/  0, 0, 28, 28
);
```

drawImage then copies this box into a position on the canvas's drawing surface. It has an X and Y position of 0 and a height and width of 28. The highlighted code in the destination section describes this.

```
drawingSurface.drawImage
(
  /*Image*/        monsterImage,
  /*Source*/       3, 12, 28, 28,
  /*Destination*/  0, 0, 28, 28
);
```

Figure 6-5 illustrates how this all fits together.

monster.png

canvas
drawingSurface

```
drawingSurface.drawImage
(
    monsterImage,
    3, 12, 28, 28,
    0, 0, 28, 28
);
```

```
drawingSurface.drawImage
(
    monsterImage,
    3, 12, 28, 28,
    0, 0, 28, 28
);
```

Figure 6-5. Draw only part of an image onto the canvas

You can draw the copied box anywhere onto the drawing surface. If you want to center it, give it an X and Y position of 18 in the destination section, like this:

```
drawingSurface.drawImage
(
    monsterImage,
    3, 12, 28, 28,
    18, 18, 28, 28
);
```

The source is the same, but the eye has been centered, as you can see in Figure 6-6. The number 18 centers the eye because the eye's total width and height is 28. The canvas's width and height is 64. If you subtract 28 from 64, you get 36. Half of 36 is 18.

Figure 6-6. You can position any part of the original image at any other position on the canvas's drawing surface

You can also change the destination image's height and width to make it bigger or smaller than the original. Change its height and width to 64 pixels in the destination section to make the monster's eye fill the entire canvas, as shown in Figure 6-7.

```
drawingSurface.drawImage
(
    monsterImage,
    3, 12, 28, 28,
    0, 0, 64, 64
);
```

Figure 6-7. Change the destination image's height and width to fill the canvas with a small part of the original image

You can also go the other way. You can make the destination image a quarter of the size and position it at the bottom left corner, as shown in Figure 6-8. Here's the code that does this:

```
drawingSurface.drawImage
(
    monsterImage,
    0, 0, 64, 64,
    32, 32, 32, 32
);
```

Figure 6-8. Shrink and reposition the original image

Before you go any further in this chapter, experiment with canvas. Load some of your own images of different sizes and change some of these values. You'll need to fully understand these basics before you move into animation. You'll find all these working examples in the `displayingWithCanvas.html` file in the chapter's source files.

Note: I've used my own style for formatting the drawImage method so that it's easier to read, but you can format it as a single long line of code if you want to, like this:

```
drawImage(imageName, X, Y, height, width, X, Y, height, width);
```

In this example we've just looked, at the imageName would be replaced with "monsterImage."

Canvas also lets you load video files onto the drawing surface by using these same techniques.

But before we learn more about canvas, let's take a brief interlude and look at another important topic: objects. You'll soon see how combining objects and canvas is at the heart of making animated game characters.

How to make objects

JavaScript lets you create things called objects. An object is a self-contained model for something useful in your game. It's extremely easy to create and use them, and the best way to learn is with a living example. We'll create an object called `robot`, give it some properties, and make it perform an action by using a method.

Object properties

I'm a bit lazy, so I'm going to create a robot to help me do things around the house. I'm going to create a robot object. It will have two properties: the material that it's made from, and a happiness switch. Here's what my robot looks like.

```
var robot = {material: "titanium", happy: true};
```

The object's name is `robot`. You create it with the `var` keyword. You can see that it has two properties: `material` and `happy`. Its material is `"titanium"` and `happy` is set to `true`. The properties are separated by commas and surrounded by curly braces. Figure 6-9 illustrates this.

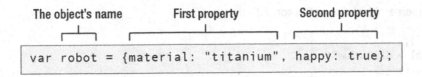

Figure 6-9. An object with two properties

Properties are just variables that belong to objects. You can give them any name you like, and any values: numbers, strings, Booleans, arrays, or even other objects. But unlike variables, a value is assigned with a colon, not an equal sign.

After you've created an object, you can access its properties in the main part of your program like this:

```
robot.material
robot.happy
```

Use the object name, then a dot, and then the property you want to access. Use them like any other variable. For example, if you want to display the robot's properties, just use them with console.log, like this:

```
console.log(robot.material);
console.log(robot.happy);
```

Here's what this displays:

```
titanium
true
```

You can change an object's properties like this:

```
robot.material = "plastic";
robot.happy = false;
```

They're just like ordinary variables.

Objects will often contain many properties, so you can make them easier to read by formatting the code like this:

```
var robot =
{
  material: "titanium",
  happy: true
};
```

(Just remember that the last property isn't followed by a comma, and the final brace is followed by a semicolon.)

You can also create objects using this format:

```
var robot = {};
robot.material = "titanium";
robot.happy = true;
```

Use whichever format you prefer.

Object methods

I want my robot to obey my commands, as any good robot should. I can do this by adding a method. A method is just another name for a function that's inside an object. I'm going to teach my robot to make me breakfast. Here's how:

```
var robot =
{
  material: "titanium",
  happy: true,

  makeBreakfast: function()
  {
    console.log("Here are your waffles and milk, master.");
  }
};
```

I can now command my robot to make me breakfast like this:

```
robot.makeBreakfast();
```

As you might expect, this is what it displays:

```
Here are your waffles and milk, master.
```

It works just like any other ordinary function. The only difference is that it's inside our robot object. That means the makeBreakfast method can't be used directly in the main program unless it's prefaced by the object name and a dot, like this: robot.makeBreakfast();

Here's the format for creating a method inside an object:

```
methodName: function()
{
  ... Any code that the method should run
}
```

You can then call the method like this:

```
objectName.methodName();
```

Easy stuff!

Using object properties inside methods

You can use any of your object's properties to help the method do its work. But to use them, you need to precede the property's name with the word "this" and a dot. Here's how you can refer to our robot's two properties:

```
this.material
this.happy
```

It's easy to see how this works in a real example. Sometimes my robot isn't happy, and so it doesn't always do such a good job with breakfast. Here's my updated robot object with a more complex breakfast-making method.

```
var robot =
{
  material: "titanium",
  happy: true,

  makeBreakfast: function()
  {
    if(this.happy)
    {
      console.log("Here are your waffles and milk, master.");
    }
    else
    {
      console.log("Here's your burnt toast and lukewarm water, master.");
    }
  }
};
```

You can see that the if statement is checking to see whether this.happy is true. Let's now see what happens if my robot tries to make breakfast when it's not happy.

```
robot.happy = false;
robot.makeBreakfast();
```

Here's what will be displayed:

```
Here's your burnt toast and lukewarm water, master.
```

My robot now skulks off, mumbling something about a "robocalypse," and spends the rest of the day very suspiciously uploading thousands and thousands of cat videos onto the Internet. Argh, robots!

Making copies of objects

A neat feature of objects is that you can make more copies of them, and then you can customize each one. A special method called `Object.create` lets you do this. If you want to make a new robot from the one you've already got, you can do it using `Object.create` like this (note that the "O" in Object has to be capitalized):

```
var newRobot = Object.create(robot);
```

The new object is called `newRobot`. It's been created from the original robot, which is in `Object.create`'s parentheses. The `newRobot` contains all the properties and methods of the original robot, and you can access and use them in the same way. Figure 6-10 illustrates how `Object.create` works to make a new object from an old one.

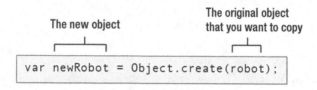

Figure 6-10. Make a copy of an object with Object.create

You can test this new object by asking `newRobot` to make breakfast for you.

```
newRobot.makeBreakfast();
```

It will work just as you'd expect. You can also customize any of the `newRobot`'s properties, like this:

```
newRobot.material = "transparent aluminum";
```

It also has the same properties and methods as the original robot object.

You now have two robots: the original made from titanium, and a new one made from the latest transparent aluminum. You could create and customize an army of waffle-making robots like this if you wanted to. I hope you're hungry.

> *Note: Why can't you just make a new robot using code that looks like this?*
>
> `var newRobot = robot;`
>
> *This will just mean that newRobot is the same object as the original robot. It's a reference to the first robot object, not a new object on its own. That's not what you want. You want to make a new copy of the original robot object so that newRobot is an independent object that you can control and customize. That's what object.Create does for you.*

Adding new properties and methods

You can add properties and methods to an object whenever you like. You can add a `color` property to your robot like this.

```
robot.color = "blue";
```

This new `color` property will be automatically added to the object. This is called adding a property dynamically.

You can also add a new method to an object at any time like this:

```
robot.enslaveHumanity = function()
{
  console.log("The robot starts uploading lots of cat videos in a suspicious manner.");
}
```

Then just call the object's method when you want to use it, like this.

```
robot.enslaveHumanity();
```

An important thing to know is that if you add new properties and methods to an object, all the other objects that you make from it will inherit them. That means that if you add the `enslaveHumanity` method to the original robot, your `newRobot` will automatically be able to use the same method. If you only want your `newRobot` to enslaveHumanity, add the method directly to it.

```
newRobot.enslaveHumanity = function()
{...
```

Now only `newRobot` will be able to upload cat videos. Your original `robot` is still just stuck making breakfast. You'll find a working program with all these examples in the `robotObject.html` file.

> *Note: You can remove properties and methods from objects using the delete keyword:*
>
> *delete robot.material;*

Looping through objects

If you think about it, an object is a lot like an array. Let's get back to basics and take a look at this simple robot object.

```
var robot =
{
  material: "titanium",
  happy: true,
```

```
makeBreakfast: function()
{
    console.log("Here are your waffles and milk, master.");
}
};
```

Imagine that this is an array with three elements. The elements are "titanium," "true," and a function. Each element has a name: "material," "happy," and "makeBreakfast." Do you see it?

No, it's not just your imagination, or mine. It really is an array that uses names instead of index numbers for each element. This means that you can use objects to store information, just as you can with ordinary arrays. The difference is that you can find that information by using a name, instead of just an index number. The technical name for this is an associative array.

> Note: There's an alternative syntax for accessing and changing object properties that makes it clear that objects are really just arrays. You can access any object's property like this:
>
> robot["happy"]
>
> Just surround the property name by square brackets and quotes. You can change a property using this same syntax like this:
>
> robot["happy"] = false;

In the previous chapters you learned how to use a for loop to display all the elements of an array. You can use a for ... in loop to do the same thing with objects. Here's a for...in loop that displays the name and values of the robot's properties and methods:

```
for(var i in robot)
{
    console.log(i + ": " + robot[i]);
}
```

Here's what is displayed in the console:

```
material: titanium
happy: true
makeBreakfast: function(){...
```

The loop repeats three times—once for each property and method. You can see that "i" refers to the property/method name: material, happy, and makeBreakfast. robot[i] in the loop gives you the values titanium, true, and function.

You can also easily find out whether an object contains a specific property. Here's how to find out what material the robot is made from:

```
if("material" in robot)
{
    console.log("The robot is made from: " + robot.material);
}
```

This will display:

```
The robot is made from titanium
```

Pretty nifty! But how does this work if you make another object from an existing one, and you then add new properties and methods to that new object? Let's find out.

Imagine that you make a new robot from the original using `Object.create`.

```
var newRobot = Object.create(robot);
```

Then add a new method or property to newRobot, like this:

```
newRobot.newProperty = "This belongs to the newRobot";
```

Now use a `for...in` loop to find out what properties and methods this new robot has.

```
for(var i in newRobot)
{
    console.log(i + ": " + newRobot[i]);
}
```

Here's what it displays:

```
newProperty: This belongs to the newRobot
material: titanium
happy: true
makeBreakfast: function(){...
```

Those are all the properties and methods of the original robot, plus the `newProperty` that only belongs to newRobot. The original robot will still only have three.

But what if you want to find the property that only belongs to the newRobot? You can use the special hasOwnProperty method. Use it in an if statement inside the loop like this:

```
for(var i in newRobot)
{
    if(newRobot.hasOwnProperty(i))
    {
        console.log(i + ": " + newRobot[i]);
    }
}
```

This will display only the properties and methods that belong to `newRobot`:

`newProperty: This belongs to the newRobot`

`hasOwnProperty` checks to see whether the property in its parentheses (represented by "i") matches a property or method that only belongs to `newRobot`. The `if` statement won't let any of the original `robot`'s properties be displayed. You'll find the working code for all these examples in the `loopingThroughObjects.html` file.

This is really all you need to know about objects. The harder part is recognizing when to use them in your games. That's not always as obvious as you might think, and it takes a bit of practice. We'll be using objects in most of the rest of the projects in this book, so you'll see many good examples of when to use them and when not to.

Object states

A useful feature of objects is that you can give them different states, and you can change their states based on what's happening in the game. For example, you might have a sword object with two states: "sharp" and "dull." The game could start with the sword in its "dull" state. If the player finds a way to sharpen the sword later in the game, you could set the sword's state to "sharp." The sword would behave differently depending on its state. Because these states are contained inside the object, you don't have to worry about maintaining lots of different variables for all the objects in your games. Object states aren't something special built into JavaScript; they're just a style of programming that uses object properties to simplify some tricky problems.

Let's find out how to create and control object states. We'll do this with the help of our video-game monster, who has graciously volunteered to be our dutiful subject of unceasing torment for this chapter. The monster has two states: NORMAL and SCARED. Figure 6-11 shows what these 2 states look like.

Figure 6-11. The monster's two states

I'm going to show you how to create an object that can display these two states. But before I do, let's look at a very basic example.

Here's an object called `monster`. It has two states, which are defined as number constants: NORMAL is "0" and SCARED is "1".

```
var monster =
{
  //Define the monster's states
  NORMAL: 0,
  SCARED: 1,

  //Set its initial state
  state: 0
};
```

It also has a property called state that defines its initial state. The state property is set to "0," which means that the monster's state will be NORMAL when it first loads. You can display the initial monster's state in the console like this:

```
console.log("The monster's initial state: " + monster.state);
```

Some kind of event has to happen in the game to change the monster's state. You can simulate this by creating a keyboard listener that will change the monster's state.

```
//Change the monster's state by pressing a key
window.addEventListener("keydown", keydownHandler, false);

function keydownHandler(event)
{
  //Change the monster's state
  monster.state = monster.SCARED;

  //Display the new state
  console.log("The monster's new state: " + monster.state);
}
```

When you press a key, the monster's state changes to SCARED, which equals 1.

```
monster.state = monster.SCARED;

console.log("The monster's new state: " + monster.state);
```

If this all seems alarmingly obvious and underwhelming, well done! We're off to a very good start.

The next step is to use this state to actually display the monster's correct image.

Displaying the states with canvas

In this next example I'll show you how to combine what you know about objects with what you know about canvas. Run the renderingStates.html program, and you'll see an image of the monster with its NORMAL state displayed. Press any key on the keyboard and its SCARED state will appear. Release the key and it will change back to normal again. You might think that this is done by changing the monster's PNG image when the key is pressed, but it isn't. Instead, there's only one PNG image that contains both of the monster's image states. It's called monsterStates.png and is shown in Figure 6-12. Let's look at how this works before taking a closer look at the program.

Figure 6-12. A single image file contains both monster states

The `monsterStates.png` image is 128 pixels wide and 64 pixels high. It's wide enough to contain two versions of the monster, each of which are 64 pixels wide. The program uses `drawImage` to selectively display the correct section of the image depending on the monster's state. If The monster is NORMAL, the canvas will display only the first section of the source image. It's 64 pixels wide, and its top left corner has an X and Y position of 0.

```
drawingSurface.drawImage
(
  monsterImage,
  0, 0, 64, 64,
  0, 0, 64, 64
);
```

If the monster is SCARED, it only displays the second section. The second section of the image is the same width as the first, but its X position is 64 pixels to the right of the first.

```
drawingSurface.drawImage
(
  monsterImage,
  64, 0, 64, 64,
  0, 0, 64, 64
);
```

Figure 6-13 illustrates this.

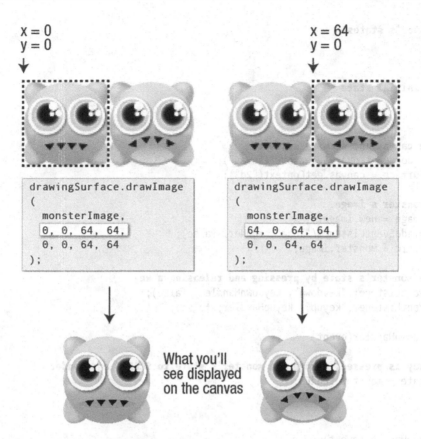

Figure 6-13. Display the part of the image that matches the monster's state

It's like you're using a camera to take a square snapshot of the section of the image that you want to use.

The renderingStates.html file combines this technique with what you've just learned about object states. Here's the complete code listing.

```
<!doctype html>
<title>Rendering states</title>

<canvas width="64" height="64"></canvas>

<script>

var monster =
{
  //The monster's image
  image: "monsterStates.png",
```

```
  //The monster's states
  NORMAL: 0,
  SCARED: 1,

  //Set its initial state
  state: 0
};

//Set up the canvas and drawing surface
var canvas = document.querySelector("canvas");
var drawingSurface = canvas.getContext("2d");

//Load the monster's image
var monsterImage = new Image();
monsterImage.addEventListener("load", render, false);
monsterImage.src = monster.image;

//Change the monster's state by pressing and releasing a key
window.addEventListener("keydown", keydownHandler, false);
window.addEventListener("keyup", keyupHandler, false);

function keydownHandler(event)
{
  //When a key is pressed, change the monster's state to SCARED and render it
  monster.state = monster.SCARED;
  render();
}

function keyupHandler(event)
{
  //When a key is released, change the monster's state to NORMAL and render it
  monster.state = monster.NORMAL;
  render();
}

function render()
{
  //Render the correct state
  switch(monster.state)
  {
    case monster.NORMAL:
      drawingSurface.drawImage
      (
        monsterImage,
        0, 0, 64, 64,
        0, 0, 64, 64
      );
      break;
```

```
      case monster.SCARED:
        drawingSurface.drawImage
        (
          monsterImage,
          64, 0, 64, 64,
          0, 0, 64, 64
        );
  }
  //Shortcut
  /*
  drawingSurface.drawImage
  (
    monsterImage,
    64 * monster.state, 0, 64, 64,
    0, 0, 64, 64
  );
  */
}

</script>
```

You can see that the first part of the program sets up the monster object and then sets up the canvas. When a key is pressed, the monster's state is changed to SCARED and the render function is called.

```
function keydownHandler(event)
{
  monster.state = monster.SCARED;
  render();
}
```

When a key is released, the monster's state is changed back to NORMAL and the render function is called again.

```
function keyupHandler(event)
{
  monster.state = monster.NORMAL;
  render();
}
```

The render function just uses a simple switch statement to figure out which section of the PNG image it should display.

```
function render()
{
  switch(monster.state)
  {
    case monster.NORMAL:
      drawingSurface.drawImage
```

```
    (
      monsterImage,
      0, 0, 64, 64,
      0, 0, 64, 64
    );
    break;

  case monster.SCARED:
    drawingSurface.drawImage
    (
      monsterImage,
      64, 0, 64, 64,
      0, 0, 64, 64
    );
}
```

`drawImage` draws on top of any existing images on the canvas. That means when the monster's SCARED image is displayed, it's drawn on top of the existing NORMAL image.

Rather than using a `switch` statement, there's actually an easier way to change the monster's state. We can use a bit of easy math to make `drawImage` automatically display the correct state. Replace the entire `switch` statement with this bit of code (I've highlighted the bit of math that works the magic):

```
drawingSurface.drawImage
(
  monsterImage,
  64 * monster.state, 0, 64, 64,
  0, 0, 64, 64
);
```

Save the program and run it again, and you'll see that the correct state is automatically displayed. How does it work?

Remember that our monster object's states are just numbers: 0 is NORMAL and 1 is SCARED. There's a reason for this. If you multiply 0 by 64 (the monster's width), you get 0. (Anything times zero is zero, remember?) Why is this important? Because 0 happens to be the X position of the monster's NORMAL state in the image. You can see that in Figure 6-14.

NORMAL = 0

x = NORMAL * 64
x = 0

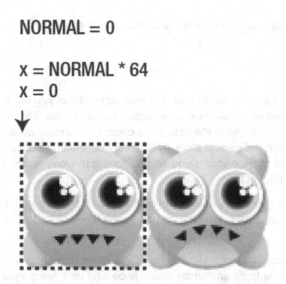

Figure 6-14. Multiply the monster's state by its width to find out which part of the image to display

I think the technical name for this is a "no-brainer." What's a lot more interesting is that if you apply exactly the same formula to the SCARED state, it will also tell you exactly what the X position is of the monster's SCARED image. If you multiply the SCARED state, 1, by 64, you end up with 64 (1 times 64 is 64). That matches the monster's SCARED state in the image, as you can see in Figure 6-15.

SCARED = 1

y = SCARED * 64
y = 64

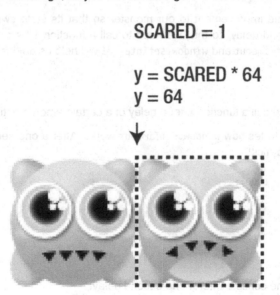

Figure 6-15. Multiply the SCARED state by the monster's width to find the correct section of the image to display

That's a little cooler! The `drawImage` code is doing this in our program by replacing the source image's X position with this formula:

```
64 * monster.state
```

And what's cooler still is that this will work no matter how many states you have. If the monster had 10 states, you can create a single image with a 64-pixel-wide section for each state. Then number your states from 0 to 9. You won't have to make any changes to the `drawImage` code. The formula will automatically display the correct section of the image to match the current state. This is very convenient because it means you can freely add and remove states to test or change your game without having to worry about updating the rendering code to match it. Thank you, mathematics!

Um, yes, but I have a dumb question! Couldn't we just have used two separate image files, used an `<img>` tag, and then changed the `src` attribute to load the correct image for each state, like we did for the adventure and strategy games?

Of course, and the code would be much simpler. But if you understand how this system works, it's at the very root of what you need to know to do animation, which is coming up a few pages from now. It's also at the root of a very efficient system we'll be using for loading and managing game graphics, which you'll learn in later chapters. And, if that's not enough, it's also training your brain to understand how canvas's `drawImage` method works so that you'll be ready to use it to make action games.

Timed state changes

We're going to make a little improvement to our monster so that its state switches back from SCARED to NORMAL after a one-second delay. To this, we need to call a function after a fixed period of time. Two new methods called `window.setTimeout` and `window.setInterval` will help us do this.

Using setTimeout

`window.setTimeout` lets you call a function after a delay of a certain amount of time.

Here's a program that illustrates how `window.setTimeout` works. After a one-second delay, the `timer` function runs and displays the word "tick!"

```
window.setTimeout(timer, 1000);

function timer()
{
  console.log("tick!");
}
```

Here's what you'll see in the console after a one-second delay:

```
tick!
```

window.setTimeout takes two arguments:

- The function you want to call.

- The amount of time, in milliseconds, that you want to wait before the function is called. There are 1,000 milliseconds in one second. That means if you want a delay of one second, use 1,000. If you want a delay of five seconds, use 5,000. If you want a delay of half a second, use 500.

Here's the format for using setTimeout:

```
window.setTimeout(anyFunction, timeInMilliseconds)
```

Using setInterval

If you want to call a function continuously every second, you can use window.setInterval. Here's a program that shows how:

```
window.setInterval(timer, 1000);

function timer()
{
  console.log("tick!");
}
```

It displays "tick!" in the console once each second:

```
tick!
tick!
tick!
tick!
```

... endlessly!

It's often convenient to use setInterval for this task, but you can duplicate this by using setTimeout, as you'll see in later examples.

Quitting a timer with window.clearInterval

If you want to stop setInterval from running, you can use window.clearInterval to quit the timer. Here's a simple program that demonstrates how window.clearInterval works. The timer runs for five seconds, and then window.clearInterval stops it.

```
var interval = window.setInterval(timer, 1000);
var counter = 0;

function timer()
{
  if(counter < 5)
  {
    console.log("tick! " + counter);
  }
```

```
  else
  {
    window.clearInterval(interval);
  }

  counter++;
}
```

It displays "tick!" and the value of the counter each second. It only runs for five seconds. Here's what you'll see when it runs.

```
tick! 0
tick! 1
tick! 2
tick! 3
tick! 4
```

. . . and then it stops.

There's an important relationship between setInterval and clearInterval. setInterval isn't called directly. Instead, it's copied into a variable called interval.

```
var interval = window.setInterval(timer, 1000);
```

This sets the timer running, but it also copies a reference to setInterval into a variable called interval. This is something you haven't seen before: a variable that holds a reference to a function. But it's important, because clearInterval needs this reference to quit the timer. You'll see how soon.

Next, we need a counter variable to keep track of how many times the counter has run. It's initialized to 0.

```
var counter = 0;
```

The timer function is called each second. It adds one to the counter variable and displays "tick!" if the counter is less than five. It will display "tick" once every second for five seconds:

```
function timer()
{
  if(counter < 5)
  {
    console.log("tick! " + counter);
  }
  else
  {
    window.clearInterval(interval);
  }
}
```

When the counter reaches five, `clearInterval` quits the timer like this:

```
window.clearInterval(interval);
```

Its argument is the `interval` variable that contains the reference to the timer. `window.clearInterval` tells it to stop.

> Note: Adding "window" to `setTimeout`, `setInterval`, and `clearInterval` is usually optional.

Creating a timer object

There's one more thing you should learn before you can add a timed state change to the monster. You need to know how to make a timer object. It's a useful technique to learn, and it also illustrates an important JavaScript technical feature called binding that will be easy to understand in this simple example.

Here's an object that contains two methods: `start` and `tick`. The `start` method creates a timer with `setInterval`. When it runs, it will call the object's `tick` method once each second. The `tick` method displays "tick!" in the console.

```
var timer =
{
  start: function()
  {
    var self = this;
    window.setInterval(function(){self.tick();}, 1000);
  },
  tick: function()
  {
    console.log("tick!");
  }
};
```

Remember, this is just an object. It won't start working until the main program kicks it off by calling its `start` method.

```
timer.start();
```

When the timer's `start` method runs, it calls its own internal `tick` method, which displays this in the console:

```
tick!
tick!
tick!
```

... once each second, endlessly.

Here's the timer's `start` method that uses `window.setInterval` to call the `tick` method.

```
start: function()
{
  var self = this;
  window.setInterval(function(){self.tick();}, 1000);
},
```

What's all that confusing stuff? Shouldn't it just look like this?

```
start: function()
{
  window.setInterval(this.tick, 1000);
},
```

In a perfect world, yes, it would. But there's a problem.

"tick" is a method that belongs to this timer object that we've just created. "setInterval" belongs to the "window" object (the "window" object refers to the browser window that the program is running in). They're two different objects. That means that if you use the keyword "this" to refer to properties of "this timer object," the code will really think you mean "this window object." The result is that you'll get a error message, like "can't find variable … ", "undefined … ," or "NaN" (Not a Number).

To fix this, you have to force window.setInterval to remember that the keyword "this" refers to the timer, not the window. Let's find out how to do this.

Remember that you can use the keyword "this" to refer to any property or method that's inside an object. For example, if you had a sword object, it could refer to its own "sharp" and "dull" properties like this:

```
this.sharp
this.dull
```

The keyword "this" refers to "this object."

The problem is that any reference to "this" gets lost if you try and send a property from one object, to another object, as we're doing in our example. To get around this you have to copy the value of "this" into a completely different new variable called "self." Here's how:

```
var self = this;
```

"self" is now locked to "this object," which is the timer object in our example. The timer can now refer to its tick method like this:

```
self.tick();
```

(Using "self" is just a common convention: you can use any variable name you want to.)

But there's one more thing you have to do before you can use `window.setInterval`. You have to wrap "self.tick()" in a function, like this:

```
function()
{
  self.tick();
}
```

You can think of this as sealing the timer object in an airtight space capsule so that it won't be obliterated when it's sent through the `window.setInterval` wormhole. What you finally end up with is these two lines of code:

```
var self = this;
window.setInterval(function(){self.tick();}, 1000);
```

I've highlighted how the function is directly embedded into the `setInterval`'s first argument. Can you see it?

I know, it looks like a rat's nest! But don't worry: it's foolproof, it works perfectly, and you'll get used to it. It means that `window.setInterval` knows exactly which method to call in the timer object. It won't get lost. Use this format whenever you need to send an object's property to a completely different object.

This is an important JavaScript technical issue called binding. It's something you'll have to deal with sooner or later, so it's better that you deal with it now. It's usually best to try and avoid binding issues like this, but sometimes it's unavoidable. And now you know how to do it—binding solved! Fortunately, JavaScript has very few of these technical issues like this to deal with in comparison to most other programming languages.

Making a monster state-change timer

Let's combine what we know about timers with what we know about monsters. Here's a program that displays the monster in its NORMAL state. Press any key, and the monster will switch to its SCARED state. After a one-second delay it will switch back to NORMAL.

```
<!doctype html>
<title>Rendering timed state changes</title>

<canvas width="64" height="64"></canvas>

<script>

var monster =
{
  //The monster's image
  image: "monsterStates.png",

  //The monster's states
  NORMAL: 0,
  SCARED: 1,
```

```
  //Set its initial state
  state: 0
};

//Set up the canvas and drawing surface
var canvas = document.querySelector("canvas");
var drawingSurface = canvas.getContext("2d");

//Load the monster's image
var monsterImage = new Image();
monsterImage.addEventListener("load", render, false);
monsterImage.src = monster.image;

//Change the monster's state by pressing a key
window.addEventListener("keydown", keydownHandler, false);

function keydownHandler(event)
{
  //When a key is pressed, change the monster's state
  becomeScared();
}

function becomeScared()
{
  monster.state = monster.SCARED;
  setTimeout(becomeNormal, 1000);
  render();
}

function becomeNormal()
{
  monster.state = monster.NORMAL;
  render();
}

function render()
{

  drawingSurface.drawImage
  (
    monsterImage,
    64 * monster.state, 0, 64, 64,
    0, 0, 64, 64
  );

}

</script>
```

The monster object is unchanged from previous examples. What happens now is that when a key is pressed, the program calls the becomeScared function.

```
function keydownHandler(event)
{
  becomeScared();
}
```

becomeScared changes the monster's state to SCARED (1) and renders it. It also uses setTimeout to call becomeNormal after a one-second delay.

```
function becomeScared()
{
  monster.state = monster.SCARED;
  setTimeout(becomeNormal, 1000);
  render();
}
```

becomeNormal sets the monster's state back to NORMAL (0).

```
function becomeNormal()
{
  monster.state = monster.NORMAL;
  render();
}
```

With canvas, objects, and timers, you now know enough to start doing animation!

Animation

The first half of this chapter was all about getting you set up with the skills you need to know to start doing animation. So let's put all these bits of the puzzle together and see what we can come up with.

Animation is an optical illusion. First, start with a series of images. Each image has to be slightly different from the next. Then display those images in rapid succession. If the differences between the images are small, and they're displayed quickly enough, your brain is tricked into thinking that those still images are really one moving image. This illusion is called persistence of vision, and it's what all film and video is based on.

In this chapter I'm going to show you how to animate our monster by making it jump up out of a hole in the ground. It's just about the simplest animation that you can create. But even when you create much more sophisticated animations you'll use these identical techniques in the same way. The only differences will be the number of images you'll use and the amount of time between which they're displayed.

Frames and tilesheets

Each image that's used to make an animation is called a frame. All the frames for an animation are usually kept in a single image called a tilesheet. Figure 6-16 shows the tilesheet that we're going to use for our first animation. It's a PNG image that's 128 pixels high and 768 pixels wide. It includes all the frames we're going to use in our animation.

Figure 6-16. All animation frames are in a single PNG image file called a tilesheet

---

Note: A tilesheet is a single image file. It contains all the different images you want to use in your game or animation. All those images are organized as square "tiles." Tilesheets are sometimes called "spritesheets," "tilesets," or "framesets." I'll just call them tilesheets in this book to avoid confusion.

You can make tilesheets by individually drawing each frame of your animation using graphic design software like Illustrator or Photoshop. If your animation isn't too complicated and doesn't use many frames, this will be manageable. But for more complex animations, consider using specialized animation software like Adobe Flash Professional. The latest versions of Flash Professional have an option to generate a spritesheet from an SWF animation file. If you're using a version of Flash Professional earlier than CS6, You can use free software called Zoë (www.createjs.com) or SWFSheet (www.bit-101.com) to quickly convert SWF animations into tilesheets.

To animate these frames, we need to display each individual frame in rapid succession. The technique for doing this is the same as the technique we used for changing the monster's state. The only difference is that we're now dealing with six images instead of just two. You'll find a working example of this in the `animationObject.html` file. Run the program and you'll see that the monster jumps out of the hole over a period of about two seconds. Here's the entire program that makes this work, and I'll explain all the details ahead.

```
<!doctype html>
<title>Animation object</title>

<canvas width="128" height="128"></canvas>

<script>
```

```
//Create the monster object
var monster =
{
  //The monster's image file and the size of each frame cell
  IMAGE: "frames.png",
  SIZE: 128,

  //The numbers of the animation frames and the starting frame
  numberOfFrames: 5,
  currentFrame: 0,

  //Properties of the animation cell's X and Y positions on the tile sheet.
  //They're 0 when this object first loads
  sourceX: 0,
  sourceY: 0,

  //The monster's updateAnimation method
  updateAnimation: function()
  {
    //Use currentFrame to find the correct section of the tilesheet to display
    this.sourceX = this.currentFrame * this.SIZE;
    this.sourceY = 0;

    //Increase currentFrame by 1 if it's no greater than the total number of frames
    if(this.currentFrame < this.numberOfFrames)
    {
      this.currentFrame++;
    }
  }
};

//Set up the canvas and drawing surface
var canvas = document.querySelector("canvas");
var drawingSurface = canvas.getContext("2d");

//Load the animation tilesheet
var image = new Image();
image.addEventListener("load", loadHandler, false);
image.src = monster.IMAGE;

function loadHandler()
{
  //Start the animation
  updateAnimation();
}
```

```
function updateAnimation()
{
  //Set a timer to call updateAnimation every 300 milliseconds
  setTimeout(updateAnimation, 300);

  //Update the monster's animation frames
  monster.updateAnimation();

  //Render the animation
  render();
}

function render()
{
  //Clear the canvas of any previous frames
  drawingSurface.clearRect(0, 0, canvas.width, canvas.height);

  //Draw the monster's current animation frame
  drawingSurface.drawImage
  (
    image,
    monster.sourceX, monster.sourceY, monster.SIZE, monster.SIZE,
    0, 0, monster.SIZE, monster.SIZE
  );
}

</script>
```

An object for animation

The monster object in this example has properties and methods that are specialized for animation.

```
var monster =
{
  //The monster's image file and the size of each frame cell
  IMAGE: "frames.png",
  SIZE: 128,

  //The numbers of the animation frames and the starting frame
  numberOfFrames: 5,
  currentFrame: 0,

  //Properties of the animation cell's X and Y positions on the tilesheet.
  //They're 0 when this object first loads
  sourceX: 0,
  sourceY: 0,
```

```
//The monster's updateAnimation method
updateAnimation: function()
{
  //Use currentFrame to find the correct section of the tilesheet to display
  this.sourceX = this.currentFrame * this.SIZE;
  this.sourceY = 0;

  //Increase currentFrame by 1 if it's no greater than the total number of frames
  if(this.currentFrame < this.numberOfFrames)
  {
    this.currentFrame++;
  }
}
};
```

The object stores the name of the tilesheet PNG file to use for animation. In this example it's an image called frames.png. It also has a property that stores the size of each tile on the sheet (128 pixels).

```
IMAGE: "frames.png",
SIZE: 128,
```

The monster needs a property called numberOfFrames that tells you how many frames are in its animation. There are six frames, so the array represents these frames with the numbers 0 to 5. (Just like array elements, the first frame will be frame number zero.) The object also has a property called currentFrame that we'll use to find out which frame to display.

```
numberOfFrames: 5,
currentFrame: 0,
```

currentFrame is set to 0 so that the animation starts with the first frame.

The object also needs properties called sourceX and sourceY that will tell the program which part of the tilesheet to display. They're initialized to zero when the object first loads. That's because the first frame of the animation has an X position of zero and a Y position of zero on the tilesheet.

```
sourceX: 0,
sourceY: 0,
```

The object has a method called updateAnimation that figures out which frame of the tilesheet to display.

```
updateAnimation: function()
{
  //Use currentFrame to find the correct section of the tilesheet to display
  this.sourceX = this.currentFrame * this.SIZE;
  this.sourceY = 0;
```

```
//Increase currentFrame by 1 if it's no greater than the total number of frames
if(this.currentFrame < this.numberOfFrames)
{
    this.currentFrame++;
}
}
```

It figures out which frame to display along the horizontal axis by multiplying the value of currentFrame by the SIZE.

```
this.sourceX = this.currentFrame * this.SIZE;
```

This is a variation of the same formula we looked at earlier. For example, let's imagine we want to display the third frame. If currentFrame is 2, then 2 multiplied by SIZE (128) is 256. Because the frames start counting at zero, that correctly matches the third frame. Figure 6-17 illustrates how this works.

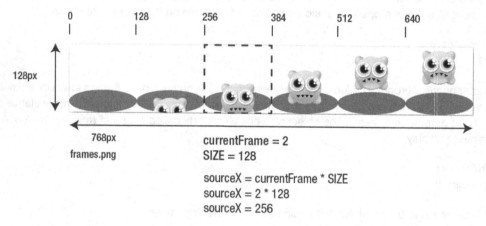

Figure 6-17. How the formula finds the correct X position in the tilesheet for the third frame

The result of this is copied into the object's sourceX property that the program will need to display the frame on the canvas.

In this example we only have frames along the horizontal axis, so the sourceY position will always be zero.

```
this.sourceY = 0;
```

The animation updates only if currentFrame is less than numberOfFrames. That gives us a range from 0 to 5, which matches the six frame numbers: 0, 1, 2, 3, 4, and 5.

```
if(this.currentFrame < this.numberOfFrames)
{
    this.currentFrame++;
}
```

Adding 1 to currentFrame advances the animation by one frame.

Running and rendering the animation

We've just looked at how the monster object works, but it's the job of the main program to actually make it animate. The program loads the monster's tilesheet and calls the loadHandler when the tilesheet is finished loading.

```
var image = new Image();
image.addEventListener("load", loadHandler, false);
image.src = monster.IMAGE;
```

The loadHandler calls the updateAnimation function.

```
function loadHandler()
{
  updateAnimation();
}
```

updateAnimation is an animation loop. Each line of code that's inside it runs once every 300 milliseconds.

```
function updateAnimation()
{
  //Loop all the code in this function by calling updateAnimation every 300 milliseconds
  setTimeout(updateAnimation, 300);

  //Update the monster's animation frames
  monster.updateAnimation();

  //Render the animation
  render();
}
```

How does this code loop? setTimeout is used to call updateAnimation every 300 milliseconds (0.3 seconds).

```
function updateAnimation()
{
  setTimeout(updateAnimation, 300);
```

Can you see what's happening? After 0.3 seconds, setTimeout calls updateAnimation again. Then updateAnimation runs setTimeout again, which again calls updateAnimation after 0.3 seconds. Then updateAnimation runs setTimeout again, which again calls updateAnimation after 0.3 seconds. Then updateAnimation runs. . . . Um, just like that, forever! It's this loop that updates the monster's animation frames at regular intervals. Figure 6-18 illustrates how this loop works.

```
function updateAnimation()
{
    setTimeout(updateAnimation, 300);
    monster.updateAnimation();
    render();
}
```

Figure 6-18. The function calls itself at regular intervals to create the animation loop

Note: A function that calls itself is a programming technique called recursion.

The loop calls these two lines of code every 300 milliseconds:

```
monster.updateAnimation();
render();
```

We looked at how `monster.updateAnimation` works in the previous section. That's the code that advances the monster's next animation frame. The loop then calls the `render` function to display the new frame on the canvas.

The `render` function first clears the canvas of any previous frames. It then uses all the properties from the `monster` object to display the correct frame.

```
function render()
{
    //Clear the canvas of any previous frames
    drawingSurface.clearRect(0, 0, canvas.width, canvas.height);

    //Draw the monster's current animation frame
    drawingSurface.drawImage
    (
        image,
        monster.sourceX, monster.sourceY, monster.SIZE, monster.SIZE,
        0, 0, monster.SIZE, monster.SIZE
    );
}
```

`updateAnimation` calls the `render` function every 300 milliseconds, and each time it runs it displays a new frame. This is what creates the animation effect.

One new thing here is the canvas's `clearRect` method. Its job is to clear the canvas so that it's blank. This code clears the entire canvas:

```
drawingSurface.clearRect(0, 0, canvas.width, canvas.height);
```

The top and left X and Y positions of the canvas are 0 and 0. `canvas.width` and `canvas.height` determine how much of the canvas to clear from those two coordinates. (`canvas.width` and `canvas.height` both equal 128.)

It's always important to clear the canvas first when you're doing animation so that any images from previous frames aren't displayed.

Figure 6-19 shows how `setInterval` calls `updateAnimation` every 300 milliseconds. `updateAnimation` then calls the monster's own `updateAnimation` method, which figures out which frame to display. The `render` method then uses the monster's updated properties to display the correct frame. This is a very stable and flexible system for creating animation that you can use for any kind of game or interactive software.

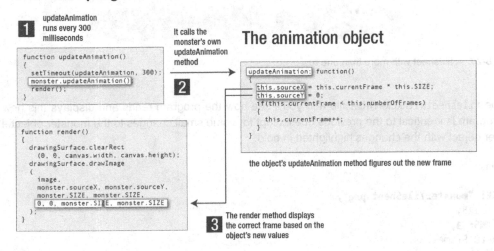

Figure 6-19. The main program updates the animation object, and the `render` function uses the object's updated properties to display the correct frame

> *Note: To keep these examples as clear as possible, I've updated the animation only once every 300 milliseconds, which is about three times per second. For really smooth animation, you'll want to update each frame between 12 to 30 times per second. Twelve frames per second is 83 milliseconds. Thirty frames per second is 33 milliseconds.*

Using a tilesheet with more than one row

The long horizontal tilesheet we used in the previous example is fine for a short animation with only a few frames. But what if you had an animation that used 100 frames? If each frame were 128 pixels wide, you'd have a PNG image with a width of 12,800 pixels! That's just not manageable. It would be better if you could keep all your frames in a rectangular grid shape. If your animation had 100 frames, you could organize those frames into a grid with 10 rows and 10 columns. That way you'd be dealing with an image that was only 1,280 by 1,280 pixels, and that's much easier to work with.

Thanks to a clever math trick that I'll show you in a moment, you can use a tilesheet with more than one row. This next example displays the same animation as in the previous one, but it uses a tilesheet that organizes the frames into two rows, as shown in Figure 6-20.

Figure 6-20. A tilesheet with more than one row

Run the `tilesheetWithRows.html` file and you'll see how the program reads and displays this new tilesheet. The program is identical to the previous one except for some small changes to the monster object. Here's the monster object with the changes highlighted in bold.

```
var monster =
{
  IMAGE: "monsterTileSheet.png",
  SIZE: 128,
  COLUMNS: 3,
  numberOfFrames: 5,
  currentFrame: 0,
  sourceX: 0,
  sourceY: 0,

  updateAnimation: function()
  {
    //Find the frame's correct column and row on the tilesheet
    this.sourceX = Math.floor(this.currentFrame % this.COLUMNS) * this.SIZE;
    this.sourceY = Math.floor(this.currentFrame / this.COLUMNS) * this.SIZE;

    if(this.currentFrame < this.numberOfFrames)
    {
      this.currentFrame++;
    }
  }
};
```

The first new thing is a property called COLUMNS that describes how many columns the tilesheet has.

```
COLUMNS: 3,
```

You can see in Figure 6-20 that the tilesheet has three columns. We don't need to specify the number of rows.

The next change is the formula in the updateAnimation method that finds the sourceX and sourceY values for the correct frame.

```
this.sourceX = Math.floor(this.currentFrame % this.COLUMNS) * this.SIZE;
this.sourceY = Math.floor(this.currentFrame / this.COLUMNS) * this.SIZE;
```

Let's first see how it figures out the sourceX value, which represents the column that the frame is on. It's using a sneaky math trick with the help of the modulus operator:

```
%
```

The modulus operator tells you what the remainder of a division operation is. For example 10 % 3 will give you 1. (That's because 10 divided by 3 is 3, with 1 remainder.) The modulus operator gives you that remainder.

Here's the formula that figures out which column the frame is on:

```
Math.floor(this.currentFrame % this.COLUMNS) * this.SIZE
```

It will always give you 0, 128, and 256 in that order, and it then restarts again at 0. It cycles through the X positions of the tilesheet's three columns. Those numbers will exactly match the X positions of the frame we want to display.

Here's the formula that figures out sourceY, which is the tilesheet row. It's the same, except that it uses a division operator instead of a modulus operator.

```
Math.floor(this.currentFrame / this.COLUMNS) * this.SIZE
```

This will give you three zeros, for the first three frames. Then it will give you three 128s for the next three frames. That also exactly matches the Y positions of the frames we need. If we had a third row of frames, this formula would keep running and give us three 256s for the third row.

The great thing about this system is that once it's in place, it will work for any tilesheet of any size with any number of rows or columns. Also, you don't need an even number of frames. If you had a 10-by-10 sheet with only 93 frames, this system will work. You don't need to make any changes to these formulas. All you need to do is change the COLUMN property on the animation object to match the number of columns that the tilesheet has.

Looping animations

We're going to make an improvement to our animation so that the monster jumps out of the hole and then falls back in again. We'll then loop that animation so that the monster jumps up and down endlessly. We don't have to make any changes to the tilesheet. We just have to use some simple logic to figure out if the animation should currently be running forward or backward. We then just need to add or subtract 1 to currentFrame to display the correct frame. You can see this effect in the animationLoop.html file.

We just need to make a change to the monster animation object to make this happen. Here's the updated monster object, with all the new code highlighted.

```
var monster =
{

    IMAGE: "monsterTileSheet.png",
    SIZE: 128,
    COLUMNS: 3,
    numberOfFrames: 5,
    currentFrame: 0,
    sourceX: 0,
    sourceY: 0,

    //A variable to control the direction of the loop
    forward: true,

    updateAnimation: function()
    {
      this.sourceX
        = Math.floor(this.currentFrame % this.COLUMNS) * this.SIZE;
      this.sourceY
        = Math.floor(this.currentFrame / this.COLUMNS) * this.SIZE;

       //If the last frame has been reached, set forward to false
      if(this.currentFrame === this.numberOfFrames)
      {
        this.forward = false;
      }

      //If the first frame has been reached, set forward to true
      if(this.currentFrame === 0)
      {
        this.forward = true;
      }

      //Add 1 to currentFrame if forward is true, subtract 1 if it's false
      if(this.forward)
      {
        this.currentFrame++;
      }
      else
      {
        this.currentFrame--;
      }
    }
};
```

The monster object has a new property called forward. It determines whether or not the animation will be running forward. It's set to true when the object first loads.

forward: true

The updateAnimation method uses two if statements to figure out if the animation should be running forward or backward. The first checks whether the animation has reached the last frame. If this is the case, the if statement will set forward to false.

```
if(this.currentFrame === this.numberOfFrames)
{
  this.forward = false;
}
```

The second if statement checks whether the animation has reached the first frame. If this is the case, the next if statement sets forward to true.

```
if(this.currentFrame === 0)
{
  this.forward = true;
}
```

The code adds 1 to currentFrame if forward is true, or it subtracts 1 if forward is false. This is what makes the animation move forward or backward.

```
if(this.forward)
{
  this.currentFrame++;
}
else
{
  this.currentFrame--;
}
```

Randomly starting animations

A feature that we're going to want to use in the upcoming Monster Smash game is that the monster should jump out of the hole at a random, unpredictable time. We can create this with a timer that chooses a random time.

To simplify the logic, it's useful to think about the monster having two states: HIDING and JUMPING. When the monster is HIDING, only the empty hole of the first frame should be displayed. When it's JUMPING, the whole animation loop should run. Figure 6-21 illustrates these two states.

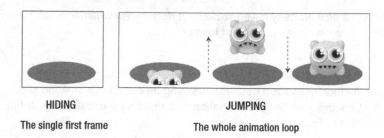

HIDING

The single first frame

JUMPING

The whole animation loop

Figure 6-21. *Two states to help us control when the animation runs*

There are no rules to figuring these states out. When you're planning object states, just make them up as you go along, depending on what you think might be a useful way of describing how your objects should behave. These two states seemed to make sense for the effect I was trying to achieve, and you'll see how I've implemented them next.

You'll find a working example of this in the `randomAnimation.html` file. The animation starts with an empty hole, and the monster will jump out of it at random intervals. Here's the new monster object that does this, with all the new changes highlighted in bold.

```
var monster =
{
  IMAGE: "monsterTileSheet.png",
  SIZE: 128,
  COLUMNS: 3,
  numberOfFrames: 5,
  currentFrame: 0,
  sourceX: 0,
  sourceY: 0,
  forward: true,

  //States
  HIDING: 0,
  JUMPING: 1,
  state: this.HIDING,

  //A property to store the random time
  waitTime: undefined,

  //A method to find a random animation time
  findWaitTime: function()
  {
    this.waitTime = Math.ceil(Math.random() * 60);
  },
```

```
//The monster's updateAnimation method
updateAnimation: function()
{
  //Figure out the monster's state
  if(this.waitTime > 0  || this.waitTime === undefined)
  {
    this.state = this.HIDING;
  }
  else
  {
    this.state = this.JUMPING;
  }

  //Switch the monster's action based on its state
  switch(this.state)
  {
    case this.HIDING:
      this.currentFrame = 0;
      this.waitTime--;
      break;

    case this.JUMPING:
      //If the last frame has been reached, set forward to false
      if(this.currentFrame === this.numberOfFrames)
      {
        this.forward = false;
      }

      //If the first frame has been reached, set forward to true
      if(this.currentFrame === 0 && this.forward === false)
      {
        //Set forward to true, find a new waitTime,
        //set the state to HIDING and break the switch statement
        this.forward = true;
        this.findWaitTime();
        this.state = this.HIDING;
        break;
      }

      //Add 1 to currentFrame if forward is true, subtract 1 if it's false
      if(this.forward)
      {
        this.currentFrame++;
      }
      else
      {
        this.currentFrame--;
      }
  }
```

```
    this.sourceX
      = Math.floor(this.currentFrame % this.COLUMNS) * this.SIZE;
    this.sourceY
      = Math.floor(this.currentFrame / this.COLUMNS) * this.SIZE;
  }
};
```

The two new states are added to the monster object like this:

```
HIDING: 0,
JUMPING: 1,
state: this.HIDING,
```

The initial state is set to HIDING so that the monster won't be visible when the animation first loads.

The monster has a property called waitTime that will be used to store the random time that the monster should jump out of the hole. It also has a method called findWaitTime that figures out what this time should be.

```
waitTime: undefined,

findWaitTime: function()
{
  this.waitTime = Math.ceil(Math.random() * 60);
},
```

waitTime is initialized to undefined. The findWaitTime method chooses a random number between 1 and 60 and assigns it to waitTime. The main program calls monster.findWaitTime when the tilesheet image has loaded.

```
function loadHandler()
{
  //Find a random wait time
  monster.findWaitTime();

  //Start the animation
  updateAnimation();
}
```

This is what gives the monster its first random waitTime. The monster object uses this to figure out what its state should be. If the waitTime is higher than 0, or it hasn't yet been set (if it's undefined), the monster's state will be HIDING. Otherwise, its state will be JUMPING. An if statement in the monster's updateAnimation method figures this out.

```
if(this.waitTime > 0  || this.waitTime === undefined)
{
  this.state = this.HIDING;
}
```

```
else
{
  this.state = this.JUMPING;
}
```

Let's imagine that the `waitTime` is 22. How will it count down to zero? Remember that the monster's `updateAnimation` method is being called every 300 milliseconds. All we need to do is subtract 1 from that number somewhere in the `updateAnimation` method. If we do that, `waitTime` will reach zero in 6.6 seconds.

We can do that with a `switch` statement. If the monster's `state` is `HIDING`, just subtract 1 from `waitTime`, like this.

```
switch(this.state)
{
  case this.HIDING:
  this.currentFrame = 0;
  this.waitTime--;
  break;
```

The `HIDING` case also sets the `currentFrame` to 0, which is the first frame.

When `waitTime` reaches 0, the monster's `state` switches to `JUMPING`, which is the second `case` in the `switch` statement. You can imagine the monster hiding away in the hole, counting each passing second, and then jumping out when it gets to zero.

```
case this.JUMPING:
    //If the last frame has been reached, set forward to false
    if(this.currentFrame === this.numberOfFrames)
    {
      this.forward = false;
    }

    //If the first frame has been reached, set forward to true
    if(this.currentFrame === 0 && this.forward === false)
    {
      this.forward = true;
      this.findWaitTime();
      this.state = this.HIDING;
      break;
    }
```

This is a version of the same code we used for the animation loop in the previous section. The `switch` statement first checks to see if the animation has reached the last frame. If it has, it sets `forward` to `false`, which will reverse the animation.

```
if(this.currentFrame === this.numberOfFrames)
{
  this.forward = false;
}
```

The next `if` statement checks whether the animation has reached the first frame after the animation has reversed. This will be `true` if both `currentFrame` is 0 and `forward` is `false`. If this is the case, it has a lot of work to do: it sets `forward` back to `true`, finds a new random wait time, changes the monster's state to `HIDING`, and breaks the `switch` statement.

```
if(this.currentFrame === 0 && this.forward === false)
{
    this.forward = true;
    this.findWaitTime();
    this.state = this.HIDING;
    break;
}
```

This resets the animation so that the monster can jump out of the hole again.

I don't want to say that this is all you need to know about frame-based animation for games but, really, it almost is! You'll rarely find that you need to do object animation for games that isn't based on one of these techniques. If you create "animation objects" like our monster object, which contain all the properties and methods that your animations need to run, you'll find it easy to manage dozens of animated objects like this in your games if you need to. Give the main program the job of running the objects' `updateAnimation` methods and rendering them with canvas.

So now that we know how to make an animated object, how can we use it in a game?

> Note: This style of animation that uses a series of frames to create the illusion of motion is called frame-based animation. In later chapters you'll learn how to do scripted animation, which is done by changing the X and Y positions of game objects.

Monster Smash!

What can we do with all the skills we've got so far? You learned a lot about grids and maps in the last chapter and a lot about animation objects in this chapter. Let's devise a game that combines these techniques. The game that I've come up with is called Monster Smash, and it's based on the classic carnival game of Whack-A-Mole. You can play `monsterSmashFinished.html` to get a sense of how it works. How many monsters can you smash before the time runs out?

We're going to build this game in few phases. But unlike the previous chapters, I'm not going to linger over the many small details that you should already know by now. Instead, I'll show you how all the major pieces have been put together. And I'll also highlight some important new techniques that you'll need to know to make your own game like this.

So, try it yourself! Work through the rest of this chapter, and see if you can make your own version of the game with your own graphics.

> Note: There are no new techniques here that you need to know to continue with the rest of the book. So if you're suffering from jumping-monster fatigue, you can always skip to the next chapter and come back here later when you need to know how to make a game like this. This is also a slightly more advanced project, so if you're new to programming you may want to return to it after you've had a bit more practice.

Making a smashable monster

We're going to add a HIT state to the monster object that we've got so far. Figure 6-22 illustrates what the HIT state looks like.

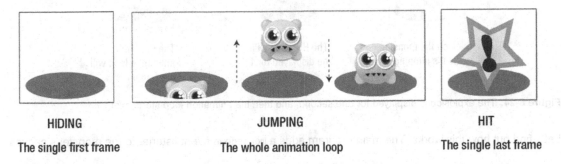

HIDING

The single first frame

JUMPING

The whole animation loop

HIT

The single last frame

Figure 6-22. Add a HIT state

We'll need a new tilesheet to display the HIT state, and you can see it in Figure 6-23.

Figure 6-23. A new tilesheet that adds the HIT state

The new tilesheet adds an extra sixth frame to display the HIT state. The system we've been using to display frames will automatically adjust for this, so we don't have to make any changes to the animation code.

We need to make the monster change to its HIT state when the player presses the left mouse button. We'll add a mousedown event listener that will do this. It will change the monster's state to HIT if the monster is jumping.

Run the monsterSmash1.html file to find a working example that implements all these features. Click on the monster while it's jumping, and you'll see that it changes to its HIT state. The HIT state remains on the screen for one second, and then the random animation loop starts over again. Figure 6-24 illustrates this.

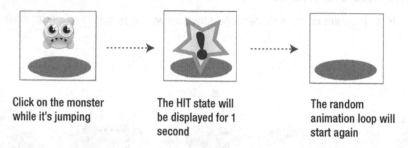

Click on the monster while it's jumping   The HIT state will be displayed for 1 second   The random animation loop will start again

Figure 6-24. The explosion is displayed for one second, and then the animation loop starts over

Let's find out how this works. The main program adds a mousedown event listener to the monster's canvas.

```
canvas.addEventListener("mousedown", mousedownHandler, false);
```

I've also changed the animation loop time to 120 milliseconds so that the animation updates more quickly.

```
function updateAnimation()
{
    //Set a timer to call updateAnimation every 120 milliseconds
    setTimeout(updateAnimation, 120);

    //Update the monster's animation frames
    monster.updateAnimation();

    //Render the animation
    render();
}
```

We want to be able to hit the monster only when it's jumping, not when it's hiding. So the mousedownHandler checks to make sure that the monster's current state is JUMPING. If it is, it switches the monster's state to HIT.

```
function mousedownHandler(event)
{
  if(monster.state === monster.JUMPING)
  {
    monster.state = monster.HIT;
  } .
}
```

The monster object has a new HIT state that displays the new sixth frame in the tilesheet for one second. Here's the entire updated monster object with the new code highlighted. I'll explain how it all works.

```
var monster =
{
  IMAGE: "monsterTileSheet.png",
  SIZE: 128,
  COLUMNS: 3,
  numberOfFrames: 5,
  currentFrame: 0,
  sourceX: 0,
  sourceY: 0,
  forward: true,

  //States
  HIDING: 0,
  JUMPING: 1,
  HIT: 2,
  state: this.HIDING,

  //Properties needed to help reset the animation
  timeToReset: 9,
  resetCounter: 0,

  waitTime: undefined,
  findWaitTime: function()
  {
    this.waitTime = Math.ceil(Math.random() * 60);
  },

  updateAnimation: function()
  {
    this.sourceX
      = Math.floor(this.currentFrame % this.COLUMNS) * this.SIZE;
    this.sourceY
      = Math.floor(this.currentFrame / this.COLUMNS) * this.SIZE;
```

```
//Figure out the monster's state
if(this.state !== this.HIT)
{
  if(this.waitTime > 0  || this.waitTime === undefined)
  {
    this.state = this.HIDING;
  }
  else
  {
    this.state = this.JUMPING;
  }
}

//Change the behavior of the animation based on the state
switch(this.state)
{
  case this.HIDING:
    this.currentFrame = 0;
    this.waitTime--;
    break;

  case this.JUMPING:
    //If the last frame has been reached, set forward to false
    if(this.currentFrame === this.numberOfFrames)
    {
      this.forward = false;
    }

    //If the first frame has been reached, set forward to true
    if(this.currentFrame === 0 && this.forward === false)
    {
      //Set forward to true, find a new waitTime,
      //set the state to HIDING and break the switch statement
      this.forward = true;
      this.findWaitTime();
      this.state = this.HIDING;
      break;
    }

    //Add 1 to currentFrame if forward is true, subtract 1 if it's false
    if(this.forward)
    {
      this.currentFrame++;
    }
    else
    {
      this.currentFrame--;
    }
    break;
```

```
    case this.HIT:
      //Set the current frame to the last one on the tilesheet to display the explosion image
      this.currentFrame = 6;

      //Update the resetCounter by 1
      this.resetCounter++;

      //Reset the animation if the resetCounter equals the timeToReset
      if(this.resetCounter === this.timeToReset)
      {
        this.state = this.HIDING;
        this.forward = true;
        this.currentFrame = 0;
        this.resetCounter = 0;
        this.findWaitTime();
      }
      break;
    }
  }
}
```

This new monster object adds a new HIT state:

```
HIT: 2,
```

Remember that the monster's state is set to HIT by the main program when the mouse clicks on it. This displays the explosion image for a second and then resets the animation. To keep the image displayed for a second, the monster needs two properties to help count the elapsed time since the start of the explosion.

```
timeToReset: 9,
resetCounter: 0,
```

Let's find out how these work.

If the monster's state is HIT, updateAnimation will set the currentFrame to 6, which is the frame that shows the explosion image. It then updates the resetCounter by 1. When the resetCounter equals the timeToReset, the animation is reset. Here's the code that does this.

```
case this.HIT:
  //Set the current frame to the last one on the tilesheet to display the explosion image
  this.currentFrame = 6;

  //Update the resetCounter by 1
  this.resetCounter++;
```

```
//Reset the animation if the resetCounter equals the timeToReset
if(this.resetCounter === this.timeToReset)
{
  this.state = this.HIDING;
  this.forward = true;
  this.currentFrame = 0;
  this.resetCounter = 0;
  this.findWaitTime();
}
break;
```

This code is updated once every 120 milliseconds. With every update it will increase the resetCounter by 1.

```
this.resetCounter++;
```

After approximately one second, the resetCounter will be 9. That equals the timeToReset.

```
if(this.resetCounter === this.timeToReset)
{...
```

When that happens the animation is reset, using the same code from the previous example. The only new addition is that resetCounter is set back to 0, so that we can reuse it to help display the next explosion.

```
this.state = this.HIDING;
this.forward = true;
this.currentFrame = 0;
this.resetCounter = 0;
this.findWaitTime();
```

Because we've carefully set up our display system with canvas, and we're using the same sneaky math trick to find the correct frame on the tilesheet, we don't have to make any other changes to the program.

Making lots of monsters

Now that you know how to make one smashable monster, it's easy to make all the monsters you need for Monster Smash. Just make copies of the original object with Object.create and plot them on a grid. The hard part is now over. And, thanks to the previous chapter, you're already an expert in plotting things on grids. Let's find out how to combine what you've learned about objects with what you know about grids.

Run the monsterSmash2.html file and you'll see a grid of randomly jumping monsters. Click on any of them while they're jumping to make their HIT states appear, as shown in Figure 6-25. It's almost a complete game.

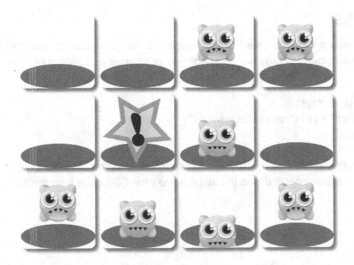

Figure 6-25. Click on any randomly jumping monster to make it explode

Let's first take a very general look at how it works. The program makes 12 copies of the monster object. It then makes 12 canvas elements, as well as 12 canvas drawing surfaces to match. The monster, canvases, and drawing surfaces are all copied into these three arrays.

```
var monsterObjects = [];
var monsterCanvases = [];
var monsterDrawingSurfaces = [];
```

Each monster object will share an array index number with a matching canvas and drawing surface. For example, that means if you wanted to access the ninth monster, you could find its object, canvas, and drawing surface like this.

```
monsterObjects[8]
monsterCanvases[8]
monsterDrawingSurfaces[8]
```

You can reference any monster's canvas and drawing surface by just using the same index number for all of them. This isn't new for you. It's exactly the same technique we used in the adventure game in Chapter 4. In the adventure game we used the consistent mapLocation number to help us find the matching descriptions, images, and help messages for each location.

With this in mind, working with 12 monsters is the same as working with 1 monster. The only difference is you need to loop through each of the 12 monsters to call their updateAnimation methods and display them on the canvas drawing surfaces.

We don't need to make any changes to the monster object all: all this work is being done by the main program. Let's find out how.

The HTML and CSS

The HTML code creates a `<div>` element with a "stage" id. As you'll see, the program is going to create 12 `<canvas>` tags. All those `<canvas>` tags will be absolutely positioned as children of the stage tag.

```html
<!doctype html>
<title>Monster Smash 2</title>
<link rel="stylesheet" href="monsterSmash.css">
<div id="stage"></div>
```

The linked CSS file gives the `<div>` and `<canvas>` tags some basic styling. It also sets up the `<canvas>` tags so that they can be positioned absolutely relative to the stage. Here's the CSS code from the linked `monsterSmash.css` file that does this.

```css
#stage
{
  position: relative;
  width: 552px;
  height: 414px;
}
canvas
{
  display: block;
  position: absolute;
  width: 128px;
  height: 128px;
  box-shadow: 5px 5px 5px rgba(0, 0, 0, 0.5);
  border-radius: 10px;
  cursor: pointer;
}
```

The CSS code also gives the `<canvas>` element a shadow and rounded corners, and it changes the mouse arrow to a pointer.

Building the map

To make the grid of monsters, we need to define the grid's rows and columns, as well as the spacing between each cell. We also need to create empty arrays to store the monster objects, their canvas elements, and their drawing surfaces. Here are the variables that we'll use.

```js
//The number of rows and columns and the size of each cell
var ROWS = 3;
var COLUMNS = 4;
var SIZE = monster.SIZE;
var SPACE = 10;
```

```
//Arrays for the monsters, their canvases and their drawing surfaces
var monsterObjects = [];
var monsterCanvases = [];
var monsterDrawingSurfaces = [];
```

The code loads the tilesheet as usual, with the same code from previous examples.

```
var image = new Image();
image.addEventListener("load", loadHandler, false);
image.src = "../images/" + monster.IMAGE;
```

When the tilesheet has loaded, the loadHandler runs.

```
function loadHandler()
{
  //Plot the grid of monsters
  buildMap();

  //Start the animation loop
  updateAnimation();
}
```

It has two jobs. First, it calls the buildMap function, which plots the monsters on the canvas. It then calls updateAnimation to start the animation loop.

The buildMap function loops through all the rows and columns. It creates a monster object, a canvas element, and a drawing surface for each cell in the grid. It gives them their initial settings and pushes them into the empty arrays we created earlier. It also sets updateAnimation to run every 120 milliseconds, which starts the animation.

```
function buildMap()
{
  for(var row = 0; row < ROWS; row++)
  {
    for(var column = 0; column < COLUMNS; column++)
    {

      //Create a single new monster object,
      //Give it a random time, display its
      //first frame and push it into an array
      var newMonsterObject = Object.create(monster);
      newMonsterObject.findWaitTime();
      monsterObjects.push(newMonsterObject);

      //Create a canvas tag for each monster
      //and add it to the <div id="stage"> tag,
      //position it, add a mousedown listener
      //and push it into an array
```

```
var canvas = document.createElement("canvas");
canvas.setAttribute("width", SIZE);
canvas.setAttribute("height", SIZE);
stage.appendChild(canvas);
canvas.style.top = row * (SIZE + SPACE) + "px";
canvas.style.left = column * (SIZE + SPACE) + "px";
canvas.addEventListener("mousedown", mousedownHandler, false);
monsterCanvases.push(canvas);

//Create a drawing surface and push
//it into the drawingSurfaces array
var drawingSurface = canvas.getContext("2d");
monsterDrawingSurfaces.push(drawingSurface);
    }
  }
}
```

There's a lot going on in the buildMap function. The loop uses Object.create to make 12 new monster objects, 1 for each cell.

```
var newMonsterObject = Object.create(monster);
```

The temporary variable newMonsterObject refers to the current copy of the monster that the loop is making. The loop will run this same code 12 times, and each time it will overwrite newMonsterObject with the next monster it wants to make.

After it creates a new monster, it sets its random wait time.

```
newMonsterObject.findWaitTime();
```

It then pushes the monster into the monsterObjects array.

```
monsterObjects.push(newMonsterObject);
```

The loop then makes a new canvas element. It sets its width and height attributes and appends it to the stage.

```
var canvas = document.createElement("canvas");
canvas.setAttribute("width", SIZE);
canvas.setAttribute("height", SIZE);
stage.appendChild(canvas);
```

It then positions and spaces the canvas element in its correct grid position, using the same formula we looked at in Chapter 5.

```
canvas.style.top = row * (SIZE + SPACE) + "px";
canvas.style.left = column * (SIZE + SPACE) + "px";
```

Next, the loop adds a mousedown event listener to the canvas so that we can click on it.

```
canvas.addEventListener("mousedown", mousedownHandler, false);
```

Finally, the new canvas element is added to the monsterCanvases array.

```
monsterCanvases.push(canvas);
```

The loop then creates the canvas's matching drawing surface (the 2D context) and pushes it into the monsterDrawingSurfaces array.

```
var drawingSurface = canvas.getContext("2d");
monsterDrawingSurfaces.push(drawingSurface);
```

When this loop finishes, we'll have 12 monster objects, 12 canvas elements, and 12 drawing surfaces, all neatly stored in arrays that we can access at any time.

Updating the monster animations

We now need to animate 12 monsters. updateAnimation loops through all the monsters in the monsterObjects array and calls their updateAnimation methods. It then calls the render method to display the result.

```
function updateAnimation()
{
  //Set a timer to call updateAnimation every 120 milliseconds
  setTimeout(updateAnimation, 120);

  //Loop through all the monsters in the monsters array and call their updateAnimation methods
  for(var i = 0; i < monsterObjects.length; i++)
  {
    monsterObjects[i].updateAnimation();
  }

  //Render the animation
  render();
}
```

Notice how each object's own updateAnimation method is being called:

```
monsterObjects[i].updateAnimation();
```

The current monster object is being accessed directly in the array using the loop index variable, i:

```
monsterObjects[i]
```

You then add a dot and the method you want to access:

```
monsterObjects[i].updateAnimation();
```

You can access a method or property of any object that's stored in an array by using this format.

Rendering the animations

To render the animation, you have to be able to access the monster object and its matching drawing surface. Because the monsters and their drawing surfaces were pushed into their arrays at the same time, they'll both share the same array index numbers. So here's the trick to making this work.

1. Loop through all the monster objects. There will be 12 of them.

2. For each loop, create temporary variables that reference the current monster and its matching drawing surface.

3. Use those temporary variables with `drawImage` to make the correct monster object display its current frame on the correct canvas drawing surface.

Here's the code that does this.

```
function render()
{
  for(var i = 0; i < monsterObjects.length; i++)
  {
    //Get reference to the current monster and drawing surface
    var monster = monsterObjects[i];
    var drawingSurface = monsterDrawingSurfaces[i];

    //Clear the current monster's canvas
    drawingSurface.clearRect(0, 0, SIZE, SIZE);

    //Draw the monster's current animation frame
    drawingSurface.drawImage
    (
      image,
      monster.sourceX, monster.sourceY, SIZE, SIZE,
      0, 0, SIZE, SIZE
    );
  }
}
```

You can see that, except for being inside the loop, the `clearRect` and `drawImage` code that displays the monster's animation on the canvas is identical to all the other examples in this chapter.

The important thing to note here is how the code captures temporary references to the current monster and drawing surface in the loop:

```
var monster = monsterObjects[i];
var drawingSurface = monsterDrawingSurfaces[i];
```

It then uses these temporary variables to render the animation. The next time the loop repeats, these variables will be overwritten with the next monster and drawing surface in the arrays. That means each time the render method is called, once every 120 milliseconds, all 12 monster animations will be rendered.

Clicking on the monsters

How does the program know which monster we're clicking on? The monster object itself has no way of detecting mouse clicks. But HTML tags, like <div> or <canvas>, can have mouse event listeners attached to them. The program needs to know that when we click on a <canvas> tag, it should make changes to the matching monster object that it's displaying. This is an easy problem to solve because the array index numbers of the monster objects and the canvas tags are synchronized.

First, recall that the buildMap method attached a mousedown event listener to each of the 12 canvas tags it made in the loop.

```
canvas.addEventListener("mousedown", mousedownHandler, false);
```

That means whenever the left mouse button is pressed down over a canvas tag, it calls the mousedownHandler. This same function is shared by all 12 canvas tags. Here is the whole function, and I'll explain how it works.

```
function mousedownHandler(event)
{
  //Find out which canvas was clicked
  var theCanvasThatWasClicked = event.target;

  //Search the monsterCanvases array for a
  //canvas that matches the one that's been clicked
  for(var i = 0; i < monsterCanvases.length; i++)
  {
    if(monsterCanvases[i] === theCanvasThatWasClicked)
    {
      var monster = monsterObjects[i];
      if(monster.state === monster.JUMPING)
      {
        monster.state = monster.HIT;
      }
    }
  }
}
```

The first thing it does is figure out which of the 12 canvas elements is calling this function. Event listeners have a special parameter called event, which I've highlighted here:

```
function mousedownHandler(event)
{...
```

You can find out which HTML element is calling this event by using the event's target property, like this:

```
event.target
```

So to get a reference to the current <canvas> tag that's being clicked, the function first creates a temporary variable that stores this information.

```
var theCanvasThatWasClicked = event.target;
```

We now have a variable called theCanvasThatWasClicked that's linked to the very same <canvas> tag that called this function.

That's a good first step, but how do we know which monster object this canvas is connected to? We have to search all the <canvas> tags in the monsterCanvases array to find the one that matches it.

```
for(var i = 0; i < monsterCanvases.length; i++)
{
  if(monsterCanvases[i] === theCanvasThatWasClicked)
  {...
```

When it's found a match, the loop gets a reference to the matching monster from the monsterObjects array.

```
var monster = monsterObjects[i]
```

Remember, this works because the index numbers in the canvas and monster arrays are synchronized. monsterCanvases[i] will always refer to the correct monster in monsterObjects[i].

Now that we know which object is connected to that canvas, we check to see if it's JUMPING. If it is, set its state to HIT.

```
if(monster.state === monster.JUMPING)
{
  monster.state = monster.HIT;
}
```

This is the identical bit of code we used in the previous example.

All the mechanics of the game are now in place. The last step is to add some game rules so that it's fun to play.

Finishing the game

How many monsters can you smash in 30 seconds? Let's add a timer and score to find out. The finished version of the game counts the number of monsters smashed, and it tells you how much time is remaining, as you can see in Figure 6-26.

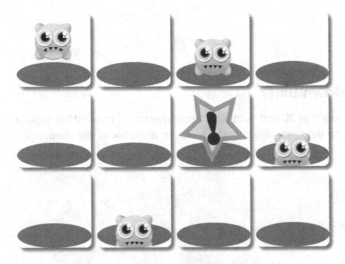

Monsters Smashed: 13 Time left: 11

Figure 6-26. Count the number of monsters smashed and add a countdown timer

The finished game also stops the timer and the animations when the timer reaches zero. Let's see how all these features were added.

Counting the monsters that have been hit

The finished game adds a variable called monstersHit in the main program.

```
var monstersHit = 0;
```

It updates monstersHit by 1 each time the player clicks a jumping monster. You can see this in the highlighted code from the mousedownHandler below.

```
function mousedownHandler(event)
{
  var theCanvasThatWasClicked = event.target;

  for(var i = 0; i < monsterCanvases.length; i++)
  {
    if(monsterCanvases[i] === theCanvasThatWasClicked)
```

```
    {
      var monster = monsterObjects[i]
      if(monster.state === monster.JUMPING)
      {
        monster.state = monster.HIT;
        monstersHit++;
      }
    }
  }
}
```

Making the countdown timer

The countdown timer starts at 30 and subtracts 1 each second. I created the timer as a separate object called gameTimer. It's based on the timer object that we looked at earlier in the chapter. It has a property called time that's initialized to 0.

```
var gameTimer =
{
  time: 0,
  interval: undefined,

  start: function()
  {
    var self = this;
    this.interval = setInterval(function(){self.tick();}, 1000);
  },
  tick: function()
  {
    this.time--;
  },
  stop: function()
  {
    clearInterval(this.interval);
  },
  reset: function()
  {
    this.time = 0;
  }
};
```

The loadHandler in the main program starts the timer after the grid of monsters has been plotted. It sets the gameTimer's time to 30 and calls its start method.

```
function loadHandler()
{
  //Plot the grid of monsters
  buildMap();

  //Start the game timer
  gameTimer.time = 30;
  gameTimer.start();

  //Start the animation loop
  updateAnimation();
}
```

The gameTimer object then calls its own tick method once each second and subtracts 1 from the time.

```
tick: function()
{
  this.time--;
},
```

This runs continuously for the duration of the game.

Ending the game

As you know, the updateAnimation function in the main program is called every 120 milliseconds to update the monster animations. I've added some new code that stops the monster animations if the timer reaches zero, and it also calls the endGame function to end the game. The new code is highlighted below:

```
function updateAnimation()
{
  //Call updateAnimation every 120 milliseconds while the timer is greater than zero.
  if(gameTimer.time > 0)
  {
    setTimeout(updateAnimation, 120);
  }

  //Loop through all the monsters in the monsters array and call their updateAnimation methods
  for(var i = 0; i < monsterObjects.length; i++)
  {
    monsterObjects[i].updateAnimation();
  }

  //check for the end of the game
  if(gameTimer.time === 0)
  {
    endGame();
  }
```

```
//Render the animation
render();
}
```

The animations freeze if the player runs out of time. This is thanks to a new if statement that only runs the animation loop if the timer is greater than zero.

```
if(gameTimer.time > 0)
{
  setTimeout(updateAnimation, 120);
}
```

As soon as gameTimer.time becomes 0, the updateAnimation loop quits, and all the monsters will freeze in place.

The game should also end if the timer equals zero. Another new if statement in the updateAnimation function checks for this. If the timer is zero, it calls the endGame function.

```
if(gameTimer.time === 0)
{
  endGame();
}
```

The endGame function stops the gameTimer object by calling its stop method. It also loops through all the canvas tags and removes their mousedown event listeners. This prevents you from clicking on any more monsters.

```
function endGame()
{
  //Stop the gameTimer
  gameTimer.stop();

  //Remove the mousedown event listeners from the canvas tags so that they can't be clicked
  for(var i = 0; i < monsterCanvases.length; i++)
  {
    var canvas = monsterCanvases[i];
    canvas.removeEventListener("mousedown", mousedownHandler, false);
  }
}
```

Displaying the game information

The finished game tells the player how many monsters have been hit and how much time is remaining. This was easily done using the same techniques you learned in previous chapters. First, the game adds an output HTML tag.

```
<p id="output">Text</p>
```

The main program then creates a reference to it.

```
var output = document.querySelector("#output");
```

And finally the render method, which is called every 120 milliseconds, displays the information. Here's an abridged version of the render method with the code that does this.

```
function render()
{
  //... display the animations...

  //Display the output
  output.innerHTML
    = "Monsters smashed: " + monstersHit
    + ", Time left: " + gameTimer.time;
}
```

The linked monsterSmash.css file adds some very basic styling to the text.

And there's the finished game!

The final code

Here's the final code for monsterSmashFinished.html. You can use it as a reference to help you understand how everything fits together in its proper context. The JavaScript code uses two objects: gameTimer and monster. They've been added first. I've then highlighted where the main program begins.

```
<!doctype html>
<title>Monster Smash Finished</title>
<link rel="stylesheet" href="monsterSmash.css">

<div id="stage"></div>
<p id="output"></p>

<script>

//--- The gameTimer object

var gameTimer =
{
  time: 0,
  interval: undefined,

  start: function()
  {
    var self = this;
    this.interval = setInterval(function(){self.tick();}, 1000);
  },
  tick: function()
```

```
  {
    this.time--;
  },
  stop: function()
  {
    clearInterval(this.interval);
  },
  reset: function()
  {
    this.time = 0;
  }
};

//--- The monster object
var monster =
{
  //The size of each frame on the tilesheet and the tilesheet's number of columns
  IMAGE: "monsterTileSheet.png",
  SIZE: 128,
  COLUMNS: 3,

  //The numbers of the animation frames and the starting frame
  numberOfFrames: 5,
  currentFrame: 0,

  //Properties of the animation frames's X and Y positions on the tilesheet.
  //They're 0 when this object first loads
  sourceX: 0,
  sourceY: 0,

  //A property to control the loop
  forward: true,

  //States
  HIDING: 0,
  JUMPING: 1,
  HIT: 2,
  state: this.HIDING,

  //Properties needed to help reset the animation
  timeToReset: 9,
  resetCounter: 0,

  //A property to store the random time
  waitTime: undefined,
```

```
//A method to find a random animation time
findWaitTime: function()
{
  this.waitTime = Math.ceil(Math.random() * 60);
},

//The monster's updateAnimation method
updateAnimation: function()
{
  this.sourceX
    = Math.floor(this.currentFrame % this.COLUMNS) * this.SIZE;
  this.sourceY
    = Math.floor(this.currentFrame / this.COLUMNS) * this.SIZE;

  //Figure out the monster's state
  if(this.state !== this.HIT)
  {
    if(this.waitTime > 0  || this.waitTime === undefined)
    {
      this.state = this.HIDING;
    }
    else
    {
      this.state = this.JUMPING;
    }
  }

  //Change the behavior of the animation based on the state
  switch(this.state)
  {
    case this.HIDING:
      this.currentFrame = 0;
      this.waitTime--;
      break;

    case this.JUMPING:
      //If the last frame has been reached, set forward to false
      if(this.currentFrame === this.numberOfFrames)
      {
        this.forward = false;
      }

      //If the first frame has been reached, set forward to true
      if(this.currentFrame === 0 && this.forward === false)
      {
        //Set forward to true, find a new waitTime,
        //set the state to HIDING and break the switch statement
        this.forward = true;
        this.findWaitTime();
```

```
                    this.state = this.HIDING;
                    break;
                }

                //Add 1 to currentFrame if forward is true, subtract 1 if it's false
                if(this.forward)
                {
                    this.currentFrame++;
                }
                else
                {
                    this.currentFrame--;
                }
                break;

            case this.HIT:
                //Set the current frame to the last one on the tilesheet to display the explosion image
                this.currentFrame = 6;

                //Update the resetCounter by 1
                this.resetCounter++;

                //Reset the animation if the resetCounter equals the timeToReset
                if(this.resetCounter === this.timeToReset)
                {
                    this.state = this.HIDING;
                    this.forward = true;
                    this.currentFrame = 0;
                    this.resetCounter = 0;
                    this.findWaitTime();
                }
                break;
        }
    }
};

//--- The main program

//Load the animation tilesheet
var image = new Image();
image.addEventListener("load", loadHandler, false);
image.src = "../images/" + monster.IMAGE;

//The number of rows and columns and the size of each cell
var ROWS = 3;
var COLUMNS = 4;
var SIZE = monster.SIZE;
var SPACE = 10;
```

```
//Arrays for the monsters, their canvases, and their drawing surfaces
var monsterObjects = [];
var monsterCanvases = [];
var monsterDrawingSurfaces = [];

//Game variables
var monstersHit = 0;

//Get a referene to the output
var output = document.querySelector("#output");

function loadHandler()
{
  //Plot the grid of monsters
  buildMap();

  //Start the game timer
  gameTimer.time = 30;
  gameTimer.start();

  //Start the animation loop
  updateAnimation();
}

function buildMap()
{
  for(var row = 0; row < ROWS; row++)
  {
    for(var column = 0; column < COLUMNS; column++)
    {

      //Create a single new monster object, give it a random time, display its
      //first frame and push it into an array
      var newMonsterObject = Object.create(monster);
      newMonsterObject.findWaitTime();
      monsterObjects.push(newMonsterObject);

      //Create a canvas tag for each monster and add it to the <div id="stage"> tag,
      //position it, add a mousedown listener and push it into an array
      var canvas = document.createElement("canvas");
      canvas.setAttribute("width", SIZE);
      canvas.setAttribute("height", SIZE);
      stage.appendChild(canvas);
      canvas.style.top = row * (SIZE + SPACE) + "px";
      canvas.style.left = column * (SIZE + SPACE) + "px";
      canvas.addEventListener("mousedown", mousedownHandler, false);
      monsterCanvases.push(canvas);
```

```
        //Create a drawing surface and push it into the drawingSurfaces array
        var drawingSurface = canvas.getContext("2d");
        monsterDrawingSurfaces.push(drawingSurface);
    }
  }
}

function updateAnimation()
{
  //Set a timer to call updateAnimation every 120 milliseconds
  //while the timer is greater than zero.
  if(gameTimer.time > 0)
  {
    setTimeout(updateAnimation, 120);
  }

  //Loop through all the monsters in the monsters array and call
  //their own updateAnimation methods
  for(var i = 0; i < monsterObjects.length; i++)
  {
    monsterObjects[i].updateAnimation();
  }

  //check for the end of the game
  if(gameTimer.time === 0)
  {
    endGame();
  }

  //Render the animation
  render();
}

function endGame()
{
  //Stop the gameTimer
  gameTimer.stop();

  //Remove the mousedown event listeners from the canvas tags so that they can't be clicked
  for(var i = 0; i < monsterCanvases.length; i++)
  {
    var canvas = monsterCanvases[i];
    canvas.removeEventListener("mousedown", mousedownHandler, false);
  }
}
function mousedownHandler(event)
{
  //Find out which canvas was clicked
  var theCanvasThatWasClicked = event.target;
```

```
    //Search the monsterCanvases array for a canvas that matches the one that's been clicked
    for(var i = 0; i < monsterCanvases.length; i++)
    {
        if(monsterCanvases[i] === theCanvasThatWasClicked)
        {
            var monster = monsterObjects[i]
            if(monster.state === monster.JUMPING)
            {
                monster.state = monster.HIT;
                monstersHit++;
            }
        }
    }
}

function render()
{
    for(var i = 0; i < monsterObjects.length; i++)
    {
        //Get reference to the current monster and drawing surface
        var monster = monsterObjects[i];
        var drawingSurface = monsterDrawingSurfaces[i];

        //Clear the current monster's canvas
        drawingSurface.clearRect(0, 0, SIZE, SIZE);

        //Draw the monster's current animation frame
        drawingSurface.drawImage
        (
            image,
            monster.sourceX, monster.sourceY, SIZE, SIZE,
            0, 0, SIZE, SIZE
        );
    }

    //Display the output
    output.innerHTML
        = "Monsters smashed: " + monstersHit
        + ", Time left: " + gameTimer.time;
}

</script>
```

Summary

You now know all about how to display images using canvas, how to make and use objects, how to animate, and how to make timers. You learned how to create a complex game out of lots of simple parts, and this will open the door to making point-and-click games of all sorts. Monster Smash is a perfect game to use with a touch interface, and in Chapter 12 you'll see how easy it will be to adapt this game for touch-based devices.

In the next chapter we're going to extend what we've learned about objects and the canvas to create a system for making interactive game characters.

Chapter 7

Game Sprites

This chapter is one of the most important in the book. It's where we transition from making games to making *video games*. You're going to learn how to make a versatile display system with canvas that you can use to move game objects around the screen using a mouse, keyboard, or touch interface. This system will form the basis for the rest of the games and projects in this book.

Here's what you'll learn about in this chapter:

- Sprites: Things that move around the screen.

- Displaying sprites using canvas.

- Changing a sprite's properties: Its position, size, rotation, visibility, and transparency.

- Creating an animation loop to update a sprite on the screen at 60 frames per second.

- Screen boundaries: Blocking a sprite at the screen edges and screen wrapping.

- Scrolling: Moving a sprite though a large environment.

- Parallax scrolling: Moving a sprite though a shallow 3D environment.

But, first, what is a game sprite, and how can we make one?

Sprites

Sprites are animated game objects that move around the screen. They can be game characters, items that players can collect, projectiles like bullets, particles in an explosion, walls that block a player's movement, or even large backgrounds. Pretty much any individual element that you want to control in a video game is a sprite. Here's what you need to do to make and display sprites in a game.

1. Create a sprite object. This is just an ordinary JavaScript object that contains special properties that can help you move an object around the screen. These properties are the sprite's X and Y positions, its height and width, and its velocity. They can also include its rotation and visibility.

2. Create an animation loop that updates the sprite's properties depending on what's happening in the game. The animation loop should run 30 to 60 times per second so that the sprite appears to move smoothly.

3. Render the sprite. This means that the game should read the sprite's updated properties and use them to display the sprite's image on the screen. We'll use canvas technology for rendering sprites.

In this chapter you'll learn how to do all these things. We'll build a system for making, moving, and displaying sprites for video games that will become the model for the rest of the games in this book. It's a very easy system to learn and use, and it is the basis for all kinds of action games, big or small.

Creating a basic animated sprite

Run the `basicSprite.html` program to see the simplest way that sprites can be made and used for interactive game animation. The program loads an image of a cat, and it uses a sprite to move it from the left side of the screen to the right. The image of the cat is displayed and animated inside a single 550-by-400-pixel canvas element. Figure 7-1 shows what you'll see.

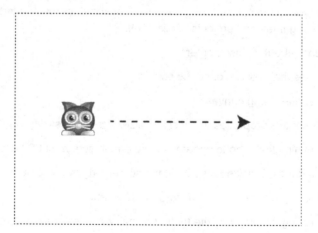

Figure 7-1. The cat sprite slowly moves from the left side of the canvas to the right

Here's the entire program that makes this work. I'll explain it all in detail ahead.

```
<!doctype html>
<title>Basic sprite</title>

<canvas width="550" height="400" style="border: 1px dashed black">

<script>

//--- The sprite object

var spriteObject =
{
  //The X and Y source position of the sprite's image and its height and width
  sourceX: 0,
  sourceY: 0,
  sourceWidth: 64,
  sourceHeight: 64,

  //The X and Y position of the sprite on the canvas as well as its height
  x: 0,
  y: 0,
  width: 64,
  height: 64
};

//--- The main program

//the canvas and its drawing surface
var canvas = document.querySelector("canvas");
var drawingSurface = canvas.getContext("2d");

//An array to store the game sprites
var sprites = [];

//Create the cat sprite.
//Center it on the canvas and push it into the sprites array
var cat = Object.create(spriteObject);
cat.x = 0;
cat.y = 168;
sprites.push(cat);

//Load the cat's image
var image = new Image();
image.addEventListener("load", loadHandler, false);
image.src = "cat.png";

function loadHandler()
{
  //Update the sprite as soon as the image has been loaded
  update();
}
```

```
function update()
{

  //Create the animation loop
  window.requestAnimationFrame(update, canvas);

  //Change the sprite's X position to make it move to the right across the canvas
  cat.x++;

  //Render the animation
  render();
}

function render()
{
  //Clear the previous animation frame
  drawingSurface.clearRect(0, 0, canvas.width, canvas.height);

  //Loop through all the sprites in the "sprites" array and use their properties to display them
  if(sprites.length !== 0)
  {
    for(var i = 0; i < sprites.length; i++)
    {
      var sprite = sprites[i];
      drawingSurface.drawImage
      (
        image,
        sprite.sourceX, sprite.sourceY,
        sprite.sourceWidth, sprite.sourceHeight,
        Math.floor(sprite.x), Math.floor(sprite.y),
        sprite.width, sprite.height
      );
    }
  }
}
```

```
</script>
```

Making sprites

The first step to making sprites is to create a JavaScript object called spriteObject. Here's a blank sprite object without any properties:

```
var spriteObject = {};
```

This will be used as a template to make more sprite objects. In this book, I decided to add the word "Object" to any objects that are just used as templates to make other objects with. This reminds me that I'm not going to use this object directly but that I will only make other objects from it by using Object.create. This is purely my own convention, so don't feel that you need to use it in your own games.

We need to add some properties to it. First, we need some information that will help us display the sprite on the screen using canvas. To render an image with canvas, you have to know the source image's width and height, as well as its X and Y positions. (Review the section on displaying images with canvas from Chapter 6 if you're unsure about this.) Here's what these sprite properties could look like:

```
sourceX: 0,
sourceY: 0,
sourceWidth: 64,
sourceHeight: 64,
```

Most of the sprites for the games in this book will be 64 by 64 pixels, so I've set the dimensions as the source-Width and sourceHeight. If your sprites are of a different size, you can easily overwrite these values, as you'll soon see.

Next, the sprite needs properties that tell it where it should appear on the screen. These are its X and Y positions. We'll give them initial values of zero in this template object, but we'll soon change these when we start making and adding sprites to the game.

```
x: 0,
y: 0,
```

Our sprite also needs width and height properties that tell it how big it should be when it's displayed. Usually these will be the same as the image's original sourceWidth and sourceHeight values.

```
width: 64,
height: 64
```

The only reason you might want to use different width and height values from sourceWidth and sourceHeight is if you want the sprite to be a different size than the original image from the tilesheet.

Here's what our final sprite object looks like when it's done:

```
var spriteObject =
{
  sourceX: 0,
  sourceY: 0,
  sourceWidth: 64,
  sourceHeight: 64,
  x: 0,
  y: 0,
  width: 64,
  height: 64
};
```

We can now use this spriteObject to make other game sprites. Let's use it to make a game character called cat.

```
var cat = Object.create(spriteObject);
```

Our cat object has inherited all of the spriteObject's properties. We can make as many different game sprites from the original spriteObject that we need, give them unique names, and customize all their properties.

We're going to display the cat sprite on a canvas that's 550 by 400 pixels. We can set it to the left center side of the canvas with the following X and Y values.

```
cat.x = 0;
cat.y = 168;
```

Giving the cat a Y position of 168 centers the cat vertically on the canvas. This number is half the canvas height, minus half the cat's height.

> Note: You can use this simple formula to center a sprite in the canvas automatically:
>
> sprite.y = canvas.height / 2 - sprite.height / 2;
>
> sprite.x = canvas.width / 2 - sprite.width / 2;
>
> You'll see this formula used in examples later in this chapter.

In this example we only have one game sprite. But in most games you'll have many. You'll need to store them all in an array. Create an array called sprites and push the new cat sprite into it.

```
var sprites = [];
sprites.push(cat);
```

Adding an "s" to arrays that store lots of certain types of objects, like "sprites," "bullets," or "aliens" is a helpful way to remember that they're used to store those objects.

Now that the cat game sprite is defined and stored in the sprites array, let's see how it's displayed.

Setting up the canvas and sprite images

In the previous chapter we used 12 separate canvas elements to display each animated monster in the Monster Smash game. That was really convenient because it made it easy to attach mouse listeners to the canvas elements so we could figure out which monster was being clicked. But in this example, we're taking a different approach, which you'll soon see is much more typical of most video games. We're creating one big canvas element that will be our "game screen." The big canvas element in this example is 550 by 400 pixels, which defines the edges of the game-playing area. (You can make the canvas any size you like; I've just used 550 by 400 because it's a convenient size for test projects.) We're then positioning the sprite inside that canvas element. That means our HTML code consists of only one <canvas> tag that defines the screen.

```
<canvas width="550" height="400" style="border: 1px dashed black"></canvas>
```

I've added some inline CSS to give the canvas a black dashed border, which lets you see the canvas's boundaries while you're creating and testing your game.

The main program then needs a reference to the canvas and its 2D context drawing surface.

```
var canvas = document.querySelector("canvas");
var drawingSurface = canvas.getContext("2d");
```

The main program also has the job of loading the sprite's image, which is a 64-by-64-pixel PNG file called cat.png.

```
var image = new Image();
image.addEventListener("load", loadHandler, false);
image.src = "cat.png";
```

When the image has loaded, it calls the loadHandler, which starts the animation.

```
function loadHandler()
{
  update();
}
```

Let's find out how the animation works.

Animating and displaying a sprite

The loadHandler calls the update function. The update function runs as a loop, approximately 60 times per second. Every time it runs, it adds 1 to the cat's X position. It also calls the render function to display the cat's new position.

```
function update()
{
  //The animation loop
  window.requestAnimationFrame(update, canvas);

  //Change the sprite's X position to make it move to the right across the canvas
  cat.x++;

  //Render the animation
  render();
}
```

The first thing update does is use requestAnimationFrame to create an animation loop.

```
window.requestAnimationFrame(update, canvas);
```

This calls the update function in a loop, at approximately 60 times per second. This is the same technique we used in the previous chapter with setTimeout to animate the jumping monsters. The advantage to using requestAnimationFrame is that it's synchronized with your computer display's refresh rate, so it produces very smooth animation and uses very little CPU power. Most displays refresh at a rate of about 60 frames per second, which is perfect for game animation. We'll be using requestAnimationFrame for the rest of the games and examples in the book.

requestAnimationFrame requires two arguments: the function you want to call each frame, and the canvas.

```
window.requestAnimationFrame(theFunctionToLoop, theCanvas);
```

requestAnimationFrame is a method of the window object, but adding window is purely optional. (See the next section ahead for more detailed information about how requestAnimationFrame works.)

So now we have a game animation loop that's calling the update method at about 60 frames per second. Here's the next line of the code in the update method.

```
cat.x++;
```

Because this is inside the loop, it means that update is adding 1 to the cat's X position 60 times each second. This is what makes the cat appear to move gradually across the canvas.

The update function also calls the render function 60 times per second.

```
render();
```

The render function loops through all the objects in the sprites array. (There's only one, the cat, in this example, but usually you'll have lots of sprites in a game.) It then uses the sprite's updated properties to display its image on the correct position on the canvas.

```
function render()
{
  //Clear the previous animation frame
  drawingSurface.clearRect(0, 0, canvas.width, canvas.height);

  //1. Make sure that the sprites array contains at least 1 sprite
  if(sprites.length !== 0)
  {
    //2 Loop through all the sprites and use their properties to display them
    for(var i = 0; i < sprites.length; i++)
    {
      var sprite = sprites[i];
      drawingSurface.drawImage
      (
        image,
        sprite.sourceX, sprite.sourceY,
        sprite.sourceWidth, sprite.sourceHeight,
        Math.floor(sprite.x), Math.floor(sprite.y),
        sprite.width, sprite.height
      );
    }
  }
}
```

This render function will work, unchanged, for any number of sprites. You'll see that we'll use this exact same function, with only tiny modifications, for the rest of our games and projects from now on.

This code uses the same canvas rendering system using drawImage that I introduced in Chapter 6. One small modification is that the sprite's X and Y positions are rounded down by using Math.floor.

```
Math.floor(sprite.x), Math.floor(sprite.y),
```

`Math.floor` truncates any fractional values that the sprite's X and Y values might have. This is important because the sprites should only be displayed at whole X and Y position numbers on the canvas, like 135, or 467 (these numbers have no decimal places). In some cases however, sprites might have X and Y values that are fractional, like 135.98 or 467.15. If you try and display fractional X and Y values on the canvas, you might see small but noticeable glitches in the way the sprite's image is rendered. This is especially important when you start using physics formulas, which you'll learn in Chapter 11. Truncating the decimals by using `Math.floor` solves this problem.

requestAnimationFrame

In this book I create the game animation loops in this way:

```
function update()
{
  requestAnimationFrame(update, canvas);
  //...move the sprites
}
```

`requestAnimationFrame` runs very efficiently because it offloads the work of updating the canvas to your computer's display system. It synchronizes the frame rate with the refresh rate of your computer's screen. It takes two arguments: the function that should loop, and the canvas element that will be updated. That second argument, `canvas`, is optional but you should always include it. Adding this second argument prevents the browser from running the animation if the window it's playing in isn't visible. That's important for games on websites, where a user might have multiple browser tabs open. You don't want your game to run in a hidden tab in the background because it will drain power unnecessarily. That's especially important for mobile devices that run on limited battery power.

At the time of writing, `requestAnimationFrame` was a very new method, so it still needed a vendor prefix to work. This might not be a problem by the time you're reading this book, but, just in case it is, here are the vendor prefixes for the three most popular browsers.

- Webkit-based browsers (Chrome and Safari): `webkitRequestAnimationFrame`

- Firefox: `mozRequestAnimationFrame`

- Internet Explorer: `msRequestAnimationFrame`

Until `requestAnimationFrame` without a prefix becomes standard, consider using some extra code to make it work reliably no matter what browser it's running in. You can add this extra code, called a **polyfill**, at the very beginning of your JavaScript program code. In the chapter's source file you'll find a JavaScript file called `requestAnimationFramePolyfill.js`. It was written by Erik Möller, Paul Irish, and Tino Zijdel, and it is used with permission in this book. It has an MIT license, so you're free to use it in your own work. Link it to your program with a `<script>` tag, like this:

```
<script src="requestAnimationFramePolyfill.js"></script>
```

Add it to your HTML code just before the <script> tag that starts your program, like this:

```
<!doctype html>
<title>Game</title>

<canvas width="550" height="400" style="border: 1px dashed black"></canvas>

<script src="requestAnimationFramePolyfill.js"></script>

<script>
//... your JavaScript game program...
```

Now you can use requestAnimationFrame in your program without a vendor prefix and it will work for all browsers. It will also make requestAnimationFrame work in older browsers that don't support it. The code does all this by first checking to see if the requestAnimationFrame capability exists in the browser. If it will work, but not without a vendor prefix, it adds the correct prefix. If the browser can't use requestAnimationFrame at all, even with a prefix, it creates the animation loop using setTimeout. It also provides cross-platform support for the rarely used cancelAnimationFrame method. The code is densely packed, and you probably won't ever need to look at it or change it, but here it is just for your reference.

```
(function() {

var lastTime = 0;
var vendors = ['ms', 'moz', 'webkit', 'o'];

for(var x = 0; x < vendors.length && !window.requestAnimationFrame; ++x)
{
  window.requestAnimationFrame = window[vendors[x]+'RequestAnimationFrame'];
  window.cancelAnimationFrame = window[vendors[x]+'CancelAnimationFrame']
  window[vendors[x]+'CancelRequestAnimationFrame'];
}

if (!window.requestAnimationFrame)
  window.requestAnimationFrame = function(callback, element) {
  var currTime = new Date().getTime();
  var timeToCall = Math.max(0, 16 - (currTime - lastTime));
  var id = window.setTimeout(function() {callback(currTime + timeToCall); }, timeToCall);
  lastTime = currTime + timeToCall;
  return id;
};

if (!window.cancelAnimationFrame)
{
  window.cancelAnimationFrame = function(id)
  {
    clearTimeout(id);
  };
}

}());
```

To keep things as simple as possible, I'm using the plain version of `requestAnimationFrame`, without any prefixes, for all the examples in this book. If the source code doesn't work when you test it on your system, just link the polyfill code as I've described.

Making many sprites

Use object.Create to make as many sprites as you need for your game. Just push them into the sprites array, and the rendering will take care of itself. You can save yourself a lot of trouble by keeping all the sprite images in one tilesheet. Not only does that save you the hassle of having to load lots of individual images, but, as you'll see in later chapters, using tilesheets lets you use some shortcuts to quickly create game levels. You can use one tilesheet for all your game characters, as well as for bigger images like backgrounds.

Run the `manySprites.html` file for an example of a program that uses three sprites. You'll see a cat moving right and a tiger moving up, over a background image. The cat, the tiger, and the background are each individual sprites. Figure 7-2 shows what you'll see.

Figure 7-2. A program with three sprites. The cat moves right and the tiger moves up over a background

This program uses one image called `tileSheetWithBackground.png`. Figure 7-3 shows what it looks like. The cat and tiger are both 64 pixels high and wide. They're on the tilesheet in the long 64-pixel-high row at the top. They both have `sourceY` positions of zero because they're aligned to the top of the image. The large background image is just below them, which means it has a `sourceY` position of 64.

Figure 7-3. A single tilesheet image contains all the images used by the sprites

The code from the `manySprites.html` file that loads this image is identical to the code from the first example, except for the new image name.

It doesn't matter what the sizes of the sprite images are or where they are located on the tilesheet. All that matters is that you know where they are so that you can assign the correct source image locations and dimensions when you create the sprites.

Look at the `manySprites.html` file and you'll see that the first sprite that's created is the `background`.

```
var background = Object.create(spriteObject);
background.sourceY = 64;
background.sourceWidth = 550;
background.sourceHeight = 400;
background.width = 550;
background.height = 400;
background.x = 0;
background.y = 0;
sprites.push(background);
```

You can see that its source values match its position and dimensions on the tilesheet. The background is 550 by 400 pixels, which exactly matches the canvas size. Its X and Y positions are 0, which places it at the canvas's top left corner.

But here's something important to remember about backgrounds: *add them to the sprites array before any other foreground sprites.* That's because the `render` function will render the sprites in the order that you've added them to the array. Sprites that you add later will appear above the sprites that you add first. If you add a background last, it will cover all the smaller sprites below it.

> *Note: The order in which sprites are displayed is called the **stacking order**. You can make sprites appear above or below other sprites by changing their positions in the sprites array.*

After the background is complete, you'll create the cat and tiger sprites next.

```
var cat = Object.create(spriteObject);
cat.x = 0;
cat.y = 168;
sprites.push(cat);

var tiger = Object.create(spriteObject);
tiger.sourceX = 64;
tiger.x = 300;
tiger.y = 336;
sprites.push(tiger);
```

You can see that the tiger's sourceX matches its X position on the tilesheet. We don't have to set its sourceY to 0 because the original spriteObject already has its sourceY value set to 0.

The update animation loop adds a new line of code to move the tiger up to the top of the canvas, which I've highlighted below.

```
function update()
{
  //Create the animation loop
  requestAnimationFrame(update, canvas);

  //Make the cat move right
  cat.x++;

  //Make the tiger move up
  tiger.y--;

  //Render the game
  render();
}
```

It subtracts 1 from the tiger's Y position 60 times per second. This makes the tiger move up.

The rest of the code from this example is unchanged from the first example. To add more sprites, just use another tilesheet with more images and create the sprites using this same model.

Using individual image files for each sprite

While you're designing the game graphics, there are lots of advantages to using one big tilesheet for your game images as opposed to many separate image files. Your images will be quick to load and run, because your program only needs to make one call to the hard drive or server to load the images. That's a big performance boost for games, especially if your game is running on the web. Another advantage is that you can completely change the look of your game just by switching the one tilesheet image, without having to change any other game code. You'll also have far less code to deal with because you'll only have one image file to load. And, if that's not enough, using a tilesheet lets you build your game world quickly and easily with a tile map editor, which you'll learn how to use in Chapter 10.

However, there will be instances where you'll need to load more than one image. For example, if your game uses lots of complex animations, it would make sense to load each animation as a separate tilesheet image just to keep things organized. But if your game is loading more than one image, there's one extra technical issue you have to deal with. The update function, which is your game animation loop, shouldn't run until all the images have completely loaded. That means you have to count the images as they load, and then run the update loop only when the number of loaded images matches the total number of images in your game. Each sprite also needs an extra property to store the name of its image so that drawImage renders the correct image. If you need or want to do this, you'll find a working example in the manyImageFiles.html file. You'll find a complete explanation of how this system works in Chapter 9.

An interactive sprite

Sprites are general-purpose game objects that you should use whenever you want to display or move anything around the game screen. They're extremely versatile. Open the interactiveSprite.html program for a working example of what you can do with them. Figure 7-4 shows what you'll see. Click the up, down, left, and right buttons to move the sprite. Click hide to make the sprite disappear. Click show to make it visible again. Click the bigger and smaller buttons to change the sprite's size.

Figure 7-4. Click the buttons to interactively change the sprite's properties

Each of the buttons changes one of the sprite's properties.

Moving the sprite

The up, down, left, and right buttons change the sprite's X and Y positions on the canvas. Here are the button event listeners that do this.

```
//Up
function upHandler(event)
{
    cat.y -= 10;
}

//Down
function downHandler(event)
{
    cat.y += 10;
}

//Right
function rightHandler(event)
{
    cat.x += 10;
}

//Left
function leftHandler(event)
{
    cat.x -= 10;
}
```

The buttons add 10 to the cat's X position to move it 10 pixels to the right. They subtract 10 to move it 10 pixels to the left. The up and down buttons work the same way by adding 10 to move the cat down and by subtracting 10 to move it up.

Making it bigger and smaller

When you click the bigger and smaller buttons, the cat grows and shrinks by 10 pixels, respectively.

```
//Bigger
function biggerHandler(event)
{
    cat.height += 10;
    cat.width += 10;
    cat.x -= 5;
    cat.y -= 5;
}
```

```
//Smaller
function smallerHandler(event)
{
  cat.height -= 10;
  cat.width -= 10;
  cat.x += 5;
  cat.y += 5;
}
```

The code does this by adding or subtracting 10 to the sprite's height and width. The sprite stays centered because 5 is added or subtracted from its X and Y positions. This makes the cat appear to expand outward.

Hiding and showing the sprite

Making the cat disappear or reappear is accomplished with the help of a new spriteObject property called visible.

```
visible: true
```

It's set to true so that the sprite will be visible when it first loads. Here's the new spriteObject with the visible property.

```
var spriteObject =
{
  sourceX: 0,
  sourceY: 0,
  sourceWidth: 64,
  sourceHeight: 64,
  x: 0,
  y: 0,
  width: 64,
  height: 64,
  visible: true
};
```

The visible property is used by the render function. If it's set to true, drawImage will display the sprite: otherwise it won't. Here are the event handlers for the hide and show buttons that change the cat's visible property.

```
//Hide
function hideHandler(event)
{
  cat.visible = false;
}
```

```
//Show
function showHandler(event)
{
  cat.visible = true;
}
```

Here's the new **render** function that displays this. An extra if statement checks whether the sprite's visible property is true or false.

```
function render(event)
{
  //Clear the previous animation frame
  drawingSurface.clearRect(0, 0, canvas.width, canvas.height);

  //Display the sprites
  if(sprites.length !== 0)
  {
    for(var i = 0; i < sprites.length; i++)
    {
      var sprite = sprites[i];

      //Draw the sprite onto the canvas if its visible property is true
      if(sprite.visible)
      {
        drawingSurface.drawImage
        (
          image,
          sprite.sourceX, sprite.sourceY,
          sprite.sourceWidth, sprite.sourceHeight,
          Math.floor(sprite.x), Math.floor(sprite.y),
          sprite.width, sprite.height
        );
      }
    }
  }
}
```

These are the most basic sprite properties that you'll need. But there are two more properties, rotation and alpha (transparency), that we need to look at in more detail. I'll also show you how to add shadows to sprites.

An interactive sprite with rotation

Many of your game sprites will need to rotate. To see an example, run the file called interactiveSprite WithRotation.html. Click the new rotate left and rotate right buttons to rotate the cat. The cat rotates around its center. You can use the rotation buttons in combination with all the other buttons. Figure 7-5 illustrates what you'll see.

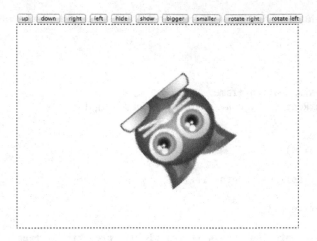

Figure 7-5. Make the sprite rotate

First, a new `rotation` property is added to the sprite object.

```
rotation: 0
```

The `rotation` property's value should be a number from 0 to 360, which represents the degrees of a circle. It's set to 0 so that the sprite won't be rotated when it first loads. Here's the `spriteObject` with the new `rotation` property.

```
var spriteObject =
{
  sourceX: 0,
  sourceY: 0,
  sourceWidth: 64,
  sourceHeight: 64,
  x: 0,
  y: 0,
  width: 64,
  height: 64,
  visible: true,
  rotation: 0
};
```

Here are the rotate left and rotate right button event handlers that change this property.

```
//Rotate right
function rotateRightHandler(event)
{
  cat.rotation += 10;
}
```

```
//Rotate left
function rotateLeftHandler(event)
{
  cat.rotation -= 10;
}
```

Each time a button is clicked, these event handlers will either add or subtract 10 degrees.

But these are only the first steps. We need to add some code to the render function so that it knows how to rotate a sprite. Here's what the new render function looks like. You won't understand it yet, but I'll explain it all ahead.

```
function render(event)
{
  //Clear the previous animation frame
  drawingSurface.clearRect(0, 0, canvas.width, canvas.height);

  //Display the sprites
  if(sprites.length !== 0)
  {
    for(var i = 0; i < sprites.length; i++)
    {
      var sprite = sprites[i];

      if(sprite.visible)
      {
        //Save the current state of the drawing surface before it's rotated
        drawingSurface.save();

        //Rotate the canvas
        drawingSurface.translate
        (
          Math.floor(sprite.x + (sprite.width / 2)),
          Math.floor(sprite.y + (sprite.width / 2))
        );

        drawingSurface.rotate(sprite.rotation * Math.PI / 180);

        drawingSurface.drawImage
        (
          image,
          sprite.sourceX, sprite.sourceY,
          sprite.sourceWidth, sprite.sourceHeight,
          Math.floor(-sprite.width / 2), Math.floor(-sprite.height / 2),
          sprite.width, sprite.height
        );
```

```
      //Restore the drawing surface to its state before it was rotated
      drawingSurface.restore();
    }
   }
  }
}
```

The new code works by rotating the entire canvas drawing surface. It then stamps the image of the cat onto the rotated drawing surface. It then rotates it back to normal. This process is so fast that you can't see it happening. All you'll see is the final rotated cat.

The code that does this uses some very technical features of canvas that you don't need to worry about. They're not important to know in detail for general-purpose game design. All you need to know is that this is the code that you should use if you want to rotate a sprite. I'll explain in general how this code works, and, if you're interested in the individual features of canvas that do all this, you can research this further on your own.

> Note: For a detailed and thorough explanation of all these features of the canvas technology, see Foundation HTML5 Canvas by Rob Hawkes.

First, the code saves the state of the canvas in its pre-rotation state. This is done with the drawingSurface's save method:

```
drawingSurface.save();
```

This is important because in the next steps we'll rotate the entire canvas drawing surface. When we're finished adding the image of the cat, we'll be able to rotate the drawing surface back to normal with the drawingSurface's restore method.

Next, use the translate method to move the drawing surface to the sprite's center point. The center of the sprite is its X position plus half its width and its Y position plus half its height.

```
drawingSurface.translate
(
  Math.floor(sprite.x + (sprite.width / 2)),
  Math.floor(sprite.y + (sprite.width / 2))
);
```

In the next step, use the rotate method to rotate the drawing surface.

```
drawingSurface.rotate(sprite.rotation * Math.PI / 180);
```

This method rotates the entire canvas to match the value of the sprite's rotation property. The sprite's rotation property is a number in degrees. Degrees are convenient to work with because it's easy to visualize how a sprite's rotation can be described by 1 of 360 possible angles. However, canvas uses rotation values called **radians**, which describe rotation in a very different way. When you take a circle's radius and wrap it around the edge of the circle, 1 radian is what you get. This is equal to about 57.2 degrees. A half rotation is 3.14 radians (Pi), and a full rotation is about 6.2 radians, which equals 360 degrees. Radians are used in advanced mathematics because working with them can produce very elegant results. But for everyday use, degrees are more under-standable, which is why we will use them with our game sprites.

This means that if the sprite is using degrees and canvas is using radians, we have to convert the sprite's `rotation` value to radians so that canvas can interpret it properly. There's a standard formula to help us do this.

```
sprite.rotation * Math.PI / 180
```

Multiply the sprite's `rotation` in degrees by the value of Pi (3.14). JavaScript's built-in constant `Math.PI` stores the value of Pi. Then divide the result by 180. The sprite's degrees have now been converted to radians, which the `rotate` method will use to rotate the drawing surface.

Now that the drawing surface is rotated, use `drawImage` to draw the sprite's image onto it.

```
drawingSurface.drawImage
(
  image,
  sprite.sourceX, sprite.sourceY,
  sprite.sourceWidth, sprite.sourceHeight,
  Math.floor(-sprite.width / 2), Math.floor(-sprite.height / 2),
  sprite.width, sprite.height
);
```

After the `translate` method moves the drawing surface to the sprite's center point, that point will become the drawing surface's new 0,0 position. That means if you want the sprite to be centered on that point, you have to move it half its height upward and half its height to the left. This is the code in the `drawImage` method that correctly positions the sprite at that point.

```
Math.floor(-sprite.width / 2), Math.floor(-sprite.height / 2),
```

The result is that the sprite appears exactly where it should and rotates around its center when you click the rotation buttons.

The last thing the code does is use the `restore` method to reset the drawing surface to its original state before the rotation.

```
drawingSurface.restore();
```

The drawing surface is now reset and ready to handle any more rotating sprites.

There's a lot more you can learn about how canvas positions and rotates images, but that's another area of specialization you may want to look into at some point. For most games you'll want to make, however, you don't need to worry about the technical details of this code. Just remember that this is what your `render` function should look like if you want your sprites to rotate.

Adding transparency

Let's add a property to our sprite to control its transparency. Run `interactiveSpriteWithTransparency.html` to see the effect. Click the more transparent and less transparent buttons to gradually make the cat invisible (see Figure 7-6).

Figure 7-6. Add transparency to make the sprite gradually disappear

The new `spriteObject` property that helps us do this is called **alpha**. The word alpha is the fancy graphic design term for transparency. It's initialized to 1.

```
alpha: 1
```

The `alpha` property will be 1 if the sprite is completely opaque. (The word opaque means that the image is solid and not see-through at all.) If the `alpha` is 0, the sprite will be completely transparent. Any values between 0 and 1 will make the sprite semitransparent by varying amounts. For example, to make the sprite halfway visible, set its `alpha` to 0.5. The sprite's `alpha` property is initialized to 1 so that it will be completely opaque when it first loads.

Here's the new `spriteObject` with the added `alpha` property:

```
var spriteObject =
{
  sourceX: 0,
  sourceY: 0,
  sourceWidth: 64,
  sourceHeight: 64,
  x: 0,
  y: 0,
  width: 64,
  height: 64,
  visible: true,
  rotation: 0,
  alpha: 1
};
```

To render the sprite's alpha, we have to use the `drawingSurface`'s `globalAlpha` property. Set `globalAlpha` to the sprite's `alpha` property like this:

```
drawingSurface.globalAlpha = sprite.alpha;
```

This bit of code will need to appear somewhere between the drawingSurface's save and restore methods, like this:

```
drawingSurface.save();
drawingSurface.globalAlpha = sprite.alpha;
drawingSurface.restore();
```

In the example file, I've added the globalAlpha property in the render function, just after the code that handles the sprite's rotation. Here's an abridged version of the new render function that shows where this new line of code has been added.

```
function render()
{
  //...
  //Rotate the canvas

  drawingSurface.translate
  (
    Math.floor(sprite.x + (sprite.width / 2)),
    Math.floor(sprite.y + (sprite.width / 2))
  );

  drawingSurface.rotate(sprite.rotation * Math.PI / 180);

  //Render the sprite's transparency
  drawingSurface.globalAlpha = sprite.alpha;

  //...
}
```

That's the only new line of code you need to add.

Here are the button event handlers that control the sprite's transparency. They increase and decrease the alpha value in increments of 0.1. This gives the sprite a range of 10 different transparency settings, from completely opaque to completely invisible.

```
//More transparent
function moreTransparentHandler(event)
{
  if(cat.alpha > 0.1)
  {
    cat.alpha -= 0.1;
  }
}
```

```
//Less transparent
function lessTransparentHandler(event)
{
  if(cat.alpha < 1)
  {
    cat.alpha += 0.1;
  }
}
```

The **if** statements make sure that the alpha values are never greater than 1 or less than 0. (It doesn't really matter if the values are greater or less than these numbers: they just won't have any visible effect.)

Adding shadows

The last modification we'll add to the sprite is a shadow. Open the `interactiveSpriteWithShadow.html` file for a working example. Click the shadow on and shadow off buttons to make a drop shadow appear under the cat, as shown in Figure 7-7.

Figure 7-7. Add a drop shadow

To make this work, the `spriteObject` first adds a new property called `shadow`. It's set to `true`.

```
shadow: true
```

The `render` function adds an extra if statement to check whether this `shadow` property is true. If it is, it uses four canvas properties that are specialized for displaying shadows. These properties need to be set somewhere between the canvas's `save` and `restore` methods. Here's the new code in the render function that adds the shadow.

```
if(sprite.shadow)
{
  drawingSurface.shadowColor = "rgba(100, 100, 100, 0.5)";
  drawingSurface.shadowOffsetX = 3;
  drawingSurface.shadowOffsetY = 3;
  drawingSurface.shadowBlur = 3;
}
```

(In the example file, I've added this new code just after the line that sets the sprite's alpha.)

The shadowColor property determines the shadow's color. In this example, I've chosen a light gray color and have set its alpha value to 0.5 (semitransparent).

```
drawingSurface.shadowColor = "rgba(100, 100, 100, 0.5)";
```

The next two properties, shadowOffsetX and shadowOffsetY, determine by how many pixels the shadow is offset from the sprite. This example sets these properties to 3, which displays the shadow three pixels below and to the right of the sprite.

```
drawingSurface.shadowOffsetX = 3;
drawingSurface.shadowOffsetY = 3;
```

The last property is the optional shadowBlur, which determines how blurry the shadow is. Giving it a bit of blurriness makes the shadow diffuse and very natural looking. You can experiment with different values, but usually if you give the shadowBlur the same values as the X and Y offsets, it produces a natural looking shadow.

```
drawingSurface.shadowBlur = 3;
```

It you leave out this shadowBlur property, the sprite's shadow will have a hard edge.

The button event handlers that turn the shadow on and off just switches the sprite's shadow property to true or false, depending on which button you click.

```
//Shadow on
function shadowOnHandler(event)
{
  cat.shadow = true;
}
```

```
//Shadow off
function shadowOffHandler(event)
{
  cat.shadow = false;
}
```

And now you've got an easy way to add shadows to your sprites.

Using the final render function

These are most of the sprite properties you'll need for games. As you'll see, we'll use various combinations of these properties for the rest of the games in this book. Just for your reference, here's the final render function that includes the code for all the sprite effects we've created. You can use as much or as little of this code as you need to for your own games.

```
function render(event)

{
    //Clear the previous animation frame
    drawingSurface.clearRect(0, 0, canvas.width, canvas.height);

    //Display the sprites
    if(sprites.length !== 0)
    {
      for(var i = 0; i < sprites.length; i++)
      {
        var sprite = sprites[i];

        if(sprite.visible)
        {
          //Save the current state of the drawing surface before it's rotated
          drawingSurface.save();

          //Rotate the canvas
          drawingSurface.translate
          (
            Math.floor(sprite.x + (sprite.width / 2)),
            Math.floor(sprite.y + (sprite.width / 2))
          );

          drawingSurface.rotate(sprite.rotation * Math.PI / 180);

          //Render the sprite's transparency
          drawingSurface.globalAlpha = sprite.alpha;

          //Add a shadow
          if(sprite.shadow)
          {
            drawingSurface.shadowColor = "rgba(100, 100, 100, 0.5)";
            drawingSurface.shadowOffsetX = 3;
            drawingSurface.shadowOffsetY = 3;
            drawingSurface.shadowBlur = 3;
          }

          //Draw the sprite image from the image file onto the canvas
          drawingSurface.drawImage
          (
            image,
            sprite.sourceX, sprite.sourceY,
            sprite.sourceWidth, sprite.sourceHeight,
            Math.floor(-sprite.width / 2), Math.floor(-sprite.height / 2),
            sprite.width, sprite.height
          );
```

```
    //Restore the drawing surface to its state before it was rotated
    drawingSurface.restore();
    }
   }
  }
}
```

Make sure you check the full code for these examples in the source files so that you can see how everything fits together in its proper context.

Using HTML sprites

Although canvas is generally better for displaying precise, fast-moving game graphics, it's possible to create game sprites just as easily by using HTML and CSS. And, for the most part, it works just as well. In fact, all the action games in this book could use an HTML rendering system, and you probably wouldn't notice any difference in the way they play. If you prefer not to use canvas for some reason, take a look at the interactiveSpriteHTML.html file. This shows a working model of an HTML/CSS sprite-rendering system that duplicates the functionality of the examples we've just looked at, but without using canvas. You can adapt this system to replace canvas rendering for any of the games in this book if you want to.

What reasons could you have for not using canvas? It's easy to attach mouse and touch event listeners to HTML elements. If you're making a complex point-and-click or drag-and-drop game, you might find HTML sprites to be more convenient. You can also use CSS transitions with HTML elements, which is a quick and easy way to add animation effects. Modern browsers display HTML very efficiently so you probably won't notice any performance difference whether you're rendering with HTML or canvas. HTML and canvas work together seamlessly, so you can mix and match them in a game as much as you like.

Moving a sprite with the keyboard

In the previous example you moved the sprite around the canvas by clicking buttons. Moving it around with the keyboard arrow keys is the next step you need to learn to start making games. Run the keyboardControl.html file to see this in action. Use the up, down, left, and right keys on the keyboard to move the cat around the canvas. Figure 7-8 illustrates what you'll see.

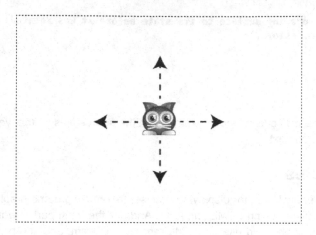

Figure 7-8. Move the sprite with the keyboard

The theory behind how this works is very easy to understand. Find out which direction arrow keys are being pressed, and change the direction that the cat moves to match that direction. However, there are a few extra details we need to solve that aren't obvious right away. The code will need to account for the fact that more than one key might be pressed at the same time. And if, for example, the left and right arrow keys are pressed at the same time, which should take precedence? We'll use a very simple solution to deal with these issues.

Here's the entire program that makes this work. You'll recognize most of the code from the previous examples, but there are a few new things here. You'll notice that the spriteObject has two new properties called vx and vy. They're used to control the sprite's speed, and I'll explain how they work to move the sprite.

```
<!doctype html>
<title>Keyboard control</title>

<canvas width="550" height="400" style="border: 1px dashed black"></canvas>

<script>

//--- The sprite object

var spriteObject =
{
  sourceX: 0,
  sourceY: 0,
  sourceWidth: 64,
  sourceHeight: 64,
  x: 0,
  y: 0,
  width: 64,
  height: 64,
  vx: 0,
  vy: 0
};
```

```
//--- The main program

//The canvas and its drawing surface
var canvas = document.querySelector("canvas");
var drawingSurface = canvas.getContext("2d");

//An array to store the sprites
var sprites = [];

//Create the cat sprite and center it
var cat = Object.create(spriteObject);
cat.x = 243;
cat.y = 168;
sprites.push(cat);

//Load the image
var image = new Image();
image.addEventListener("load", loadHandler, false);
image.src = "cat.png";

//Arrow key codes
var UP = 38;
var DOWN = 40;
var RIGHT = 39;
var LEFT = 37;

//Directions
var moveUp = false;
var moveDown = false;
var moveRight = false;
var moveLeft = false;

//Add keyboard listeners
window.addEventListener("keydown", function(event)
{
  switch(event.keyCode)
  {
    case UP:
      moveUp = true;
      break;

    case DOWN:
      moveDown = true;
      break;

    case LEFT:
      moveLeft = true;
      break;
```

```
      case RIGHT:
        moveRight = true;
        break;
    }
}, false);

window.addEventListener("keyup", function(event)
{
  switch(event.keyCode)
  {
    case UP:
      moveUp = false;
      break;

    case DOWN:
      moveDown = false;
      break;

    case LEFT:
      moveLeft = false;
      break;

    case RIGHT:
      moveRight = false;
      break;
  }
}, false);

function loadHandler()
{
  update();
}

function update()
{
  //The animation loop
  requestAnimationFrame(update, canvas);

  //Up
  if(moveUp && !moveDown)
  {
    cat.vy = -5;
  }
  //Down
  if(moveDown && !moveUp)
  {
    cat.vy = 5;
  }
```

```
//Left
if(moveLeft && !moveRight)
{
  cat.vx = -5;
}
//Right
if(moveRight && !moveLeft)
{
  cat.vx = 5;
}

//Set the cat's velocity to zero if none of the keys are being pressed
if(!moveUp && !moveDown)
{
  cat.vy = 0;
}
if(!moveLeft && !moveRight)
{
  cat.vx = 0;
}

//Move the cat
cat.x += cat.vx;
cat.y += cat.vy;

//Render the sprite
render();
}

function render()
{
  //Clear the previous animation frame
  drawingSurface.clearRect(0, 0, canvas.width, canvas.height);

  //Loop through all the sprites and use their properties to display them
  if(sprites.length !== 0)
  {
    for(var i = 0; i < sprites.length; i++)
    {
      var sprite = sprites[i];
      drawingSurface.drawImage
      (
        image,
        sprite.sourceX, sprite.sourceY,
        sprite.sourceWidth, sprite.sourceHeight,
```

```
        Math.floor(sprite.x), Math.floor(sprite.y),
        sprite.width, sprite.height
      );
    }
  }
}

</script>
```

Moving with velocity

The first new things you should notice are the two new spriteObject properties: vx and vy.

```
vx: 0,
vy: 0
```

They store the sprite's speed and how fast it's going. Actually, it's not really the *speed* of the object that you're storing, but the **velocity**. That's what the *v* stands for in the variable names: *velocity x* and *velocity y*.

Velocity is speed, but it's also a direction. This can be a confusing concept to grasp, so let's look at it in more detail. Have a look at this directive:

```
cat.vx = -5;
```

vx refers to the cat's velocity on the X (horizontal) axis. This actually tells you two things. First, 5 is the number of pixels that you want the sprite to move each frame. The frame rate of our animation loop is 60 frames per second, which means that the object will move 5 pixels each frame, or 300 pixels each second. So that's the first thing: its speed.

Notice the negative sign.

```
cat.vx = -5;
```

What does it tell you? Remember that the very left edge of the canvas has an X value of 0. As you move to the right, the X value increases. If you move to the left, it decreases. That means that those vx values that are negative are actually *pointing to the left*. Positive values *point to the right*. This directive tells you the sprite's speed and direction, also known as velocity. That means this directive says the following:

```
5 pixels to the left.
```

Here's another example:

```
cat.vy = +5;
```

vy refers to the velocity of the object on the Y (vertical) axis. The very top of the canvas has a Y value of 0. As you move down, the Y value increases. That means this directive says the following:

```
5 pixels down.
```

That's its velocity. Not so hard at all, is it? Figure 7-9 is a diagram of how positive and negative values can show direction.

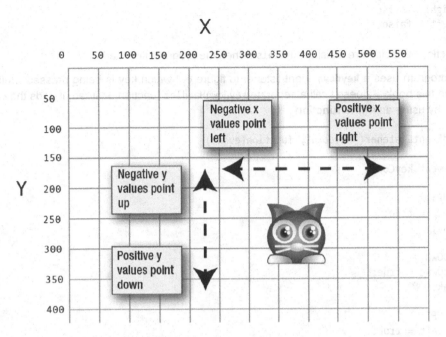

Figure 7-9. You can find the direction of movement by determining whether the X or Y values are positive or negative

If all this seems spectacularly underwhelming and blindingly obvious, good for you! It should be! Now let's see how all this talk of velocity fits in to what's going on in the program.

Using the keyboard's arrow keys

In Chapter 5 you learned how to change the position of the ship in Island Adventure. In that game you used the arrow keys to change the ship's position in an array. In this example, you use the arrow keys to change the values of the cat's vx and vy properties. Later we'll use those properties to move the sprite around the screen.

The main program creates four constants that store the arrow key codes. It also creates four variables that will help us determine in which direction the cat should move.

```
//Arrow key codes
var UP = 38;
var DOWN = 40;
var RIGHT = 39;
var LEFT = 37;
```

```
//Directions
var moveUp = false;
var moveDown = false;
var moveRight = false;
var moveLeft = false;
```

All the direction variables are initialized to false when the program first loads.

The main program uses a **keydown** event listener to figure out which key is being pressed. Unlike most other examples in this book, it doesn't call a separate keydownHandler function. Instead, it adds the code directly to the listener by using an **inline function**.

```
window.addEventListener("keydown", function(event)
{
  switch(event.keyCode)
  {
    case UP:
      moveUp = true;
      break;

    case DOWN:
      moveDown = true;
      break;

    case LEFT:
      moveLeft = true;
      break;

    case RIGHT:
      moveRight = true;
      break;
  }
}, false);
```

An inline function works by replacing the call to the event handler with a function that contains all the code you want to run when the event happens. Here's a simple example, with the function highlighted:

```
window.addEventListener("keydown", function(event){console.log("Hello World!");}, false},
```

This will display "Hello World!" if a key is pressed. If the function contains a lot of code, it's more readable to format it like this:

```
window.addEventListener("keydown", function(event)
{

  console.log("Hello World!");

}, false},
```

An inline function is a convenient way to add code for an event listener if that function won't need to be reused by any other part of your program. (They can't be reused, because they don't have a name and are embedded directly into the line of code that adds the event listener. Inline functions are also called **anonymous functions**.)

In our keyboard example, the function runs when a keydown event happens. It uses a switch statement to set the direction variables to true, depending on which key has been pressed.

```
switch(event.keyCode)
{
  case UP:
    moveUp = true;
    break;

  case DOWN:
    moveDown = true;
    break;

  case LEFT:
    moveLeft = true;
    break;

  case RIGHT:
    moveRight = true;
    break;
}
```

The update function is going to use these values to change the sprite's X and Y positions on the canvas. More on that in a moment, but first let's take a quick look at a new event: keyup.

Figuring out if a key is not being pressed

Knowing that a key is up is just as important for games as knowing that it's down. JavaScript lets you listen for any keys that are being released with the keyup event listener. The main program adds the keyup listener using an inline function like this:

```
window.addEventListener("keyup", function(event)
{
  switch(event.keyCode)
  {
    case UP:
      moveUp = false;
      break;

    case DOWN:
      moveDown = false;
      break;
```

```
        case LEFT:
          moveLeft = false;
          break;

        case RIGHT:
          moveRight = false;
          break;
    }
}, false);
```

It listens for keys that are being *released*. If any of the arrow keys have been released, it sets any of the matching direction variables to `false`. You'll soon see how we use these direction variables to make the cat move and stop.

Making the sprite move

We now have four direction variables that will be either true or false: `moveUp`, `moveDown`, `moveLeft`, and `moveRight`. The next step is to use them to change the cat's velocity so that it will move in the correct direction. If no keys are being pressed, the cat's velocity should be set to zero so that it doesn't move. Here's the entire update animation loop that does this.

```
function update()
{
  //The animation loop
  requestAnimationFrame(update, canvas);

  //Up
  if(moveUp && !moveDown)
  {
    cat.vy = -5;
  }
  //Down
  if(moveDown && !moveUp)
  {
    cat.vy = 5;
  }
  //Left
  if(moveLeft && !moveRight)
  {
    cat.vx = -5;
  }
  //Right
  if(moveRight && !moveLeft)
  {
    cat.vx = 5;
  }
```

```
//Set the cat's velocity to zero if none of the keys are being pressed
if(!moveUp && !moveDown)
{
  cat.vy = 0;
}
if(!moveLeft && !moveRight)
{
  cat.vx = 0;
}

//Move the cat
cat.x += cat.vx;
cat.y += cat.vy;

//Render the sprite
render();
}
```

The first four if statements change the cat's velocity depending on which direction variables are true or false. The code lets one of the up and down directions work at the same time as one of the left and right directions. This lets the cat move diagonally (for example, up and to the left at the same time.) However, the code prevents both up and down or both left and right directions to be active at the same time. For example, if the player presses the left arrow key, and then holds down the right arrow key at the same time, only the first key pressed, the left key, will work. Here's the code that does this.

```
//Left
if(moveLeft && !moveRight)
{
  cat.vx = -5;
}
//Right
if(moveRight && !moveLeft)
{
  cat.vx = 5;
}
```

moveLeft will make the cat move left if moveRight isn't already true.

```
if(moveLeft && !moveRight)
{
  cat.vx = -5;
}
```

moveRight will only make the cat move to the right if moveLeft isn't already true.

```
if(moveRight && !moveLeft)
{
  cat.vx = 5;
}
```

The up and down directions perform the same check.

The last two if statements set the cat's velocity to zero if neither the up or down nor left or right directions are true.

```
if(!moveUp && !moveDown)
{
  cat.vy = 0;
}
if(!moveLeft && !moveRight)
{
  cat.vx = 0;
}
```

This is what stops the cat if the user does not press any arrow keys.

These if statements have set the cat's velocity, but the code hasn't made the cat move yet. To move the cat, assign its vx and vy values to its X and Y properties, like this:

```
cat.x += cat.vx;
cat.y += cat.vy;
```

Because the cat's X and Y values are being updated 60 times per second, it will move. Yay!

> Note: There's another solution to the problem of capturing multiple simultaneous key presses. You can push all the current keys being pressed into an array. Then loop through this array in the update function to figure out which keys are being pressed, and run the code that should match those pressed keys. When a key is released, remove the reference to the key from the array. This might be overkill for simple games like the ones in this book, but if you're making a game that relies on multiple simultaneous inputs, this is a solution you should consider. You'll find a working example of this system, with fully commented code, in the file called keyboardControl_KeyArray.html.

Setting screen boundaries

Now that you can move the cat around the canvas, notice that you can also drive it completely off the edge and keep it going on forever and ever if you want to. Interesting, but not fun! There are three main strategies that game designers use to prevent this from happening.

- Blocking movement at the edge of the screen.

- Screen wrapping, which is what happens when the player leaves the left side of the screen and emerges from the right.

- Scrolling, which happens when the character is in a very big environment and the background moves to reveal unexplored areas.

We'll look at each of these techniques one at a time.

Blocking movement at the screen edges

Like most programming problems, if you understand the logic behind what you're trying to accomplish, all you need to do is figure out a way of representing that logic with programming code. So let's think for a moment about the problem we have to solve.

Let's imagine that you've got a ball that you roll along the floor toward a wall. Here's what happens in real life:

Roll the ball along the floor. When it hits the wall, it will stop.

Easy, right? Well, unfortunately, this is not at all what happens in video games. So get this out of your head right away!

In video games, the "wall" is just an invisible boundary described by numbers. It doesn't really exist. There's no solid object for the ball to hit. So here's what happens in a video game:

Roll the ball along the floor. If it crosses an invisible boundary that we think of as a "wall," push the ball back so that it appears to stop at the wall's boundary.

With this in mind, let's think about what we have to do to stop a sprite at the edge of the screen. First, we have to define is the size of the screen. We then need to check whether the sprite has moved beyond the dimensions of the screen. If it has, we have to push it back into the screen, so that it will have appeared to stop at the edge.

So here's the logic behind what this code has to accomplish:

If the sprite crosses the edge of the screen, push it back into the screen.

Hmm. Easier said than done? Let's see.

We don't have any way of representing "the edge of the screen" as a whole, but you can access the `height` and `width` properties of the canvas to find its dimensions. We can use those properties to figure out the top, bottom, left, and right boundaries. You can then stop the sprite from moving if you discover that its X or Y positions go beyond those boundaries. To see this in action, run the `screenBoundaries.html` program. Move the cat with the arrow keys, and you'll see that you can't move it beyond any of the canvas edges, as shown in Figure 7-10.

Figure 7-10. The cat stops moving when it reaches the edge of the canvas

The code in this example is identical to the previous one, except for a new if/else statement that's been added to the `update` function. Here's an abridged version of the `update` function with the new code.

```
function update()
{
  //... code that moves the cat...

  //Stop the cat at the canvas edges
  if (cat.x < 0)
  {
    cat.x = 0;
  }
  if (cat.y < 0)
  {
    cat.y = 0;
  }
  if (cat.x + cat.width > canvas.width)
  {
    cat.x = canvas.width - cat.width;
  }
  if (cat.y + cat.height > canvas.height)
  {
    cat.y = canvas.height - cat.height;
  }

  //Render the sprite
  render();
}
```

How does this work to stop the cat from crossing the left, top, right, and bottom edges of the screen?

The very left side of the canvas has an X position value of 0. And remember that the sprite's X and Y positions are at the top left corner (the cat's top left ear). That means you can use the following logic to prevent the sprite from crossing the left side of the canvas:

> *If the sprite's X position is less than zero, then set it to exactly zero.*

In code, this same logic looks like this:

```
if (cat.x < 0)
{
  cat.x = 0;
}
```

Remember, *we're pushing the sprite back into the screen* if it crosses the screen boundaries. Let's find out why this works.

If the cat is moving from right to left, its X position value will gradually decrease. If it goes far enough, its X value will eventually reach zero or even become negative. When this happens, the code pushes the cat back so that it's exactly at position zero–the very left edge of the canvas. Figure 7-11 illustrates how this works.

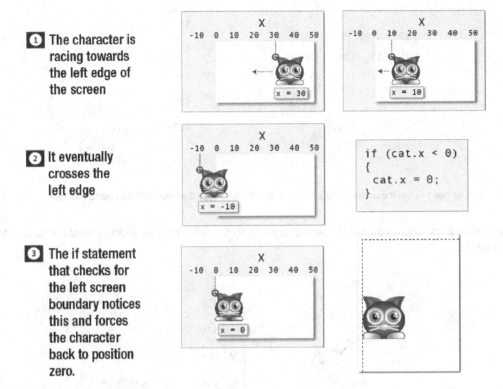

1 The character is racing towards the left edge of the screen

2 It eventually crosses the left edge

```
if (cat.x < 0)
{
    cat.x = 0;
}
```

3 The if statement that checks for the left screen boundary notices this and forces the character back to position zero.

Figure 7-11. How to stop a sprite at the edge of the screen

Even though the sprite does actually move slightly beyond the screen boundaries, you don't ever see it do that; you only see it at the point at which it's been forced back.

This logic works exactly the same for code that checks the top boundary.

If the sprite's Y position is less than zero, then set it to exactly zero.

If the sprite crosses the top of the canvas, it's forced back to a Y position of zero.

```
if (cat.y < 0)
{
    cat.y = 0;
}
```

Things get a little more complicated when the right and bottom stage boundaries are checked. This is because the sprite's X and Y positions are measured from its top left corner. You need to stop the sprite *before* its top left corner reaches the right and bottom boundaries. If you stopped the sprite when its top left corner reached the right or bottom of the canvas, its body would already have disappeared off the edge. Figure 7-12 illustrates this problem.

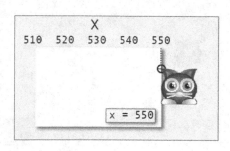 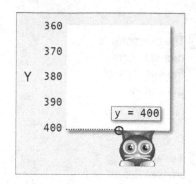

Figure 7-12. You can't directly use the sprite's X and Y positions to stop it at the right and bottom edges

How far should it go before you need to stop it? By exactly the amount of its width or height. Figure 7-13 shows why this works.

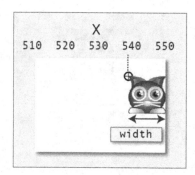 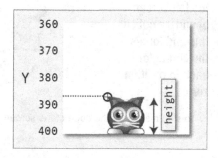

Figure 7-13. Add the sprite's width and height to accurately stop it at the right and bottom edges

Here's what you need to do to accurately stop the sprite at the right and bottom edges:

1. First, *add the sprite's width or height to its X or Y positions.* This will give you the position of the sprite's leading edge.

   ```
   cat.x + cat.width
   ```

2. If that leading edge has a value that is greater than the right or bottom edge of the canvas, move the sprite back to an X or Y position that equals the canvas dimensions, minus the sprite's height or width.

   ```
   cat.x = canvas.width - cat.width
   ```

Here's the code in the `if` statement that checks whether the sprite's X and Y positions have crossed the right and bottom canvas boundaries:

```
if (cat.x + cat.width > canvas.width)
{
```

```
    cat.x = canvas.width - cat.width;
}
if (cat.y + cat.height > canvas.height)
{
    cat.y = canvas.height - cat.height;
}
```

It compensates for the sprite's height and width, and it stops it exactly at the edges of the screen. Figure 7-14 illustrates this.

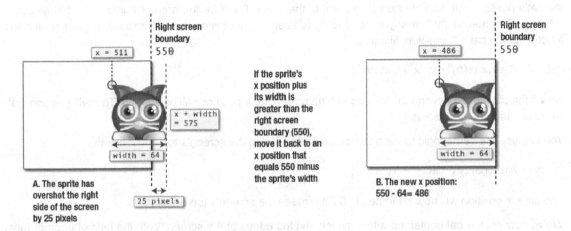

Figure 7-14. Precise screen boundaries that use the sprite's width

Because you're using the height and width properties of the sprite and canvas, you don't have to know how big either of those things is. This code will work, unchanged, no matter what the dimensions of the game sprite or canvas are.

You can find the completed version of this code in the screenBoundaries.html file in this chapter's source files.

Condensing the code

You can condense all this code with the help of two built-in JavaScript functions: Math.max and Math.min.

Math.max is a function that will tell you what the largest number is from any set of numbers that you give it. For example, imagine you want to find out which is the largest number: 2, 6, or 10. You can find it out like this:

```
Math.max(6, 10, 2)
```

This will return 10.

You can assign the result to a variable, like this:

```
var largestNumber = Math.max(6, 10, 20);
```

largestNumber will now have the value 10.

How can this help us to keep a sprite contained within the screen boundaries? Because you can use it to check whether the sprite's position is greater than zero, which represents the left and top edges of the screen.

Here's how to check which is greater, the cat's X position, or the 0, which represents the left side of the screen:

```
Math.max(0, cat.x + cat.vx)
```

If the cat is moving around the screen to the right of zero, the function will return the cat's updated position. That's because the cat's position will be greater than zero. But as soon as the cat crosses the left boundary (0), the cat's position will become *less than zero*. In that case, 0 will be the greater number. So the function will return 0. This means that what you need to do to keep the cat inside the screen's left edge is to assign this function to the cat's X position, like this:

```
cat.x = Math.max(0, cat.x + cat.vx);
```

Now if the cat moves beyond the left edge of the screen, its X position will be set to 0. This will position it at the exact left edge of the screen.

You can use the same logic to keep the cat contained inside the screen's top edge, like this:

```
cat.y = Math.max(0, cat.y + cat.vy);
```

The cat's Y position will now be forced to 0 if it crosses the screen's top edge.

We've now got the cat contained within the left and top edges of the screen. With the help of another function called `Math.min`, we can contain it inside the bottom and right edges as well.

`Math.min` returns whatever the smallest number is in any set of numbers that you give it, like this:

```
Math.min(6, 10, 2)
```

This will return 2.

We can use this to figure out if the cat has crossed the screen's right boundary like this:

```
cat.x = Math.min(cat.x + cat.vx, canvas.width - cat.width);
```

As soon as the cat's X position becomes greater than the width of the canvas minus the cat's width, the cat is set to that position. The result is that the cat will stop at the right edge of the screen.

You can use the same technique to stop the cat at the bottom of the screen, like this:

```
 cat.y = Math.min(cat.y + cat.vy, canvas.height - cat.height);
```

Now all you need to do is combine all these techniques into two lines of code that will move the cat and stop it at all four screen edges. Here's what you end up with:

```
cat.x = Math.max(0, Math.min(cat.x + cat.vx, canvas.width - cat.width));
cat.y = Math.max(0, Math.min(cat.y + cat.vy, canvas.height - cat.height));
```

These two lines of code replace both the four if statements that check the screen boundaries and the code that moves the cat. Here's the new update function that shows you how this code fits in its proper context.

```
function update()
{
  //The animation loop
  requestAnimationFrame(update, canvas);

  //Up
  if(moveUp && !moveDown)
  {
    cat.vy = -5;
  }
  //Down
  if(moveDown && !moveUp)
  {
    cat.vy = 5;
  }
  //Left
  if(moveLeft && !moveRight)
  {
    cat.vx = -5;
  }
  //Right
  if(moveRight && !moveLeft)
  {
    cat.vx = 5;
  }

  //Set the cat's velocity to zero if none of the keys are being pressed
  if(!moveUp && !moveDown)
  {
    cat.vy = 0;
  }
  if(!moveLeft && !moveRight)
  {
    cat.vx = 0;
  }

  //Move the cat and keep it inside the screen boundaries
  cat.x = Math.max(0, Math.min(cat.x + cat.vx, canvas.width - cat.width));
  cat.y = Math.max(0, Math.min(cat.y + cat.vy, canvas.height - cat.height));

  //Render the sprite
  render();
}
```

Now let's look at another way of dealing with a sprite that reaches the edge of the screen.

Screen wrapping

Screen wrapping happens when a sprite disappears from one side of the screen and then reemerges from the opposite side. This is quite a fun effect and very easy to implement. In fact, the logic that's used to accomplish it is almost exactly the *inverse* of the logic we used to block movement at the screen's edges. You can see an example of this in the screenWrapping.html file. Use the arrow keys to move the cat to the edges of the screen. It will reemerge from the other side, as you can see in Figure 7-15.

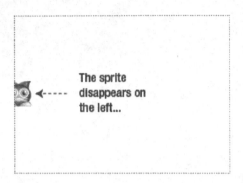
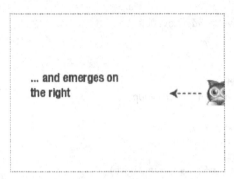

Figure 7-15. Screen wrapping

An if statement in the update function makes this possible.

```
if(cat.x + cat.width < 0)
{
    cat.x = 550;
}
if(cat.y + cat.height < 0)
{
    cat.y = 400;
}
if(cat.x > canvas.width)
{
    cat.x = 0 - cat.width;
}
if(cat.y > canvas.height)
{
    cat.y = 0 - cat.height;
}
```

The if statement uses the sprite's width and height to figure out whether it has completely disappeared off the edge of the canvas. As soon as it detects that this is the case, it positions the sprite on the opposite side of the screen, just beyond the visible boundary. This creates the illusion that the sprite is trapped on the surface of some kind of cylindrical, never-ending plane. Screen wrapping is, of course, a staple of many old-school games like Pac-Man and Asteroids, and now you know how to do it if you ever need to.

Scrolling

Scrolling is an effect that allows a player to move about in an environment that is much bigger than the confines of the game screen. I decided to give my hard-working little cat character a holiday in space: a journey to one of Mars's moons, Phobos. Run the `basicScrolling.html` program and use the keyboard arrow keys to fly the cat in its space capsule around Phobos. Figure 7-16 shows what you'll see.

Figure 7-16. Fly the cat over the surface of Phobos

What's new here in this example is that the program uses two special objects called `camera` and `gameWorld`. We're going to use them to help us figure out which part of the background should be visible and where in the game world the cat should be allowed to move.

The first thing you need to implement scrolling is some kind of huge background image that is much bigger than the canvas. For this example, I found a big, high-resolution picture of Phobos at `photojournal.jpl.nasa.gov`. It's 2,561 by 1,922 pixels. I used the image to make a tilesheet that you can see in Figure 7-17. The tiny 64-by-64-pixel image of the space cat is in the thin strip at the top of the tilesheet, but most of it is dominated by the image of Phobos. Except for this crazy-big image size, you use the tilesheet to make sprites in exactly the same way that you learned from earlier examples.

Yes, space cat
really is at the
top left corner of
the tilesheet

Figure 7-17. A tilesheet that includes the cat and a really big image of Phobos

Creating the game objects

The first thing the code does is create the background sprite.

```
var background = Object.create(spriteObject);
background.sourceY = 64;
background.sourceWidth = 2561;
background.sourceHeight = 1922;
background.width = 2561;
background.height = 1922;
background.x = 0;
background.y = 0;
sprites.push(background);
```

Remember that the background sprite needs to be added to the sprites array first so that it doesn't cover the cat.

The next thing that's created is a new object called gameWorld. Its job is to describe how big the area is that our cat can explore. It has four properties: X, Y, width, and height. Its width and height are set to the background's width and height.

```
var gameWorld =
{
  x: 0,
  y: 0,
  width: background.width,
  height: background.height
};
```

The gameWorld object doesn't display any images. It just defines the size of the world so that we can position the other objects inside it.

The next new object is the camera. Its job is to define the area of the gameWorld that should be displayed on the canvas. The camera is going to follow the cat around while it explores the gameWorld. You can think of the camera object as the frame of a real camera; whatever is within its boundaries will be displayed on the canvas.

The camera also has four properties: X, Y, width, and height. Its width and height are set to the same size as the canvas.

```
var camera =
{
  x: 0,
  y: 0,
  width: canvas.width,
  height: canvas.height
};
```

The camera is also just a model that will simplify a lot of the position calculations for us.

Next, the camera's position is set so that it's exactly centered over the gameWorld.

```
camera.x = (gameWorld.x + gameWorld.width / 2) - camera.width / 2;
camera.y = (gameWorld.y + gameWorld.height / 2) - camera.height / 2;
```

This uses the same automatic centering formula that you learned at the beginning of the chapter.

That last thing to create is the cat sprite. It's also centered in the gameWorld with the same formula.

```
var cat = Object.create(spriteObject);
cat.x = (gameWorld.x + gameWorld.width / 2) - cat.width / 2;
cat.y = (gameWorld.y + gameWorld.height / 2) - cat.height / 2;
sprites.push(cat);
```

With these objects created, we're now all set to start moving them around in our scrolling game world.

Moving the cat and the camera

In the real world, when you want to capture an action on video, you need to follow that action around with your camera. Our scrolling system works in the same way. If the cat moves, the camera moves to follow it.

All the code that does this is in the update animation loop. When you press the arrow keys, the cat moves. The cat's position is constrained to the gameWorld boundaries so that it can't move beyond them. The camera's position is constantly updated so that it remains centered over the cat. However, you don't want the camera to move beyond the edge of the gameWorld. That means you also need to check that it doesn't move beyond the gameWorld's top, bottom, left, and right edges. Here's all the code in the update function that does this. (I've abridged the code that sets the cat's velocity; it's the same as in the previous example.)

```
function update()
{
  //The animation loop
  requestAnimationFrame(update, canvas);

  //...Figure out the cat's velocity based on the direction variables...

  //Move the cat and keep it inside the gameWorld boundaries
  cat.x = Math.max(0, Math.min(cat.x + cat.vx, gameWorld.width - cat.width));
  cat.y = Math.max(0, Math.min(cat.y + cat.vy, gameWorld.height - cat.height));

  //Center the camera to follow the cat
  camera.x = Math.floor(cat.x + (cat.width / 2) - (camera.width / 2));
  camera.y = Math.floor(cat.y + (cat.height / 2) - (camera.height / 2));

  //Keep the camera inside the gameWorld boundaries
  if(camera.x < gameWorld.x)
  {
    camera.x = gameWorld.x;
  }
```

```
    if(camera.y < gameWorld.y)
    {
      camera.y = gameWorld.y;
    }
    if(camera.x + camera.width > gameWorld.x + gameWorld.width)
    {
      camera.x = gameWorld.x + gameWorld.width - camera.width;
    }
    if(camera.y + camera.height > gameWorld.height)
    {
      camera.y = gameWorld.height - camera.height;
    }

    render();
}
```

You can see that the code that moves the cat and keeps it within the gameWorld boundaries is the same as the code that we used in the previous example to keep it contained within the canvas. The only difference is that the canvas dimensions have been replaced by the gameWorld's dimensions.

```
cat.x = Math.max(0, Math.min(cat.x + cat.vx, gameWorld.width - cat.width));
cat.y = Math.max(0, Math.min(cat.y + cat.vy, gameWorld.height - cat.height));
```

The code then keeps the camera's X and Y positions directly centered over the cat.

```
camera.x = Math.floor(cat.x + (cat.width / 2) - (camera.width / 2));
camera.y = Math.floor(cat.y + (cat.height / 2) - (camera.height / 2));
```

This means that when the cat moves, the camera's position will change to remain centered over it. (The X and Y positions need to be rounded down by using Math.floor to truncate any possible decimal values.)

But the camera also needs to be contained inside the game world: it shouldn't display anything outside its edges. Four if statements check for this.

```
if(camera.x < gameWorld.x)
{
  camera.x = gameWorld.x;
}
if(camera.y < gameWorld.y)
{
  camera.y = gameWorld.y;
}
if(camera.x + camera.width > gameWorld.x + gameWorld.width)
{
  camera.x = gameWorld.x + gameWorld.width - camera.width;
}
if(camera.y + camera.height > gameWorld.height)
{
  camera.y = gameWorld.height - camera.height;
}
```

You can alternatively use `Math.max` and `Math.min` to move the `camera` and keep it inside the `gameWorld`. Here's the code you could use:

```
camera.x = Math.max(0, Math.min
(
  Math.floor(cat.x + (cat.width / 2) - (camera.width / 2)),
  gameWorld.width - camera.width
));

camera.y = Math.max(0, Math.min
(
  Math.floor(cat.y + (cat.height / 2) - (camera.height / 2)),
  gameWorld.height - camera.height
));
```

Our scrolling system is now almost ready to go. But there's one important missing component. All of these numbers are just abstract. We've only created a mathematical model for how our scrolling game world should behave. The next step is to use this model to render the game world accurately.

Rendering the scrolling game world

The only part of the game world that should be visible in the canvas is the section that's within the camera's frame. To make this work, the position of the canvas `drawingSurface` needs to be offset so that it's relative to the camera's position.

We can use the canvas `drawingSurface`'s `translate` method to help us do this. `translate` offsets the `drawingSurface` by whatever X and Y pixel numbers you supply for its two arguments. For example, to move the drawing surface 100 pixels to the right and 50 pixels down, you could use this code:

```
drawingSurface.translate(100, 50);
```

(The first number refers to the number of pixels on the X axis, and the second refers to the number of pixels on the Y axis.)

To offset the `drawingSurface` relative to the camera's position, just supply the `translate` method with the camera's negative X and Y positions. Here's how:

```
drawingSurface.translate(-camera.x, -camera.y);
```

This is the only new line of code you need to add to the `render` function to make the scrolling system work. It just needs to appear somewhere between the `save` and `restore` methods. Here's the new `render` function that adds this. I've highlighted the new code.

```
function render(event)
{
  drawingSurface.clearRect(0, 0, canvas.width, canvas.height);
```

```
drawingSurface.save();

//Move the drawing surface so that it's positioned relative to the camera
drawingSurface.translate(-camera.x, -camera.y);

//Loop through all the sprites and use their properties to display them
if(sprites.length !== 0)
{
  for(var i = 0; i < sprites.length; i++)
  {
    var sprite = sprites[i];
    drawingSurface.drawImage
    (
      image,
      sprite.sourceX, sprite.sourceY,
      sprite.sourceWidth, sprite.sourceHeight,
      Math.floor(sprite.x), Math.floor(sprite.y),
      sprite.width, sprite.height
    );
  }
}

drawingSurface.restore();
}
```

All the sprites have X and Y position values that are relative to the gameWorld object's dimensions. But of course the canvas is much smaller than gameWorld. By offsetting the canvas by the camera's position, the sprites will be repositioned inside the canvas so that they'll be visible if they're within the camera's frame.

Remember that games are just information. What's important about this example is that it illustrates how you can create an abstract model of your game world that is completely independent from the rendering system. Because we first created a model of the world using the camera and gameWorld objects, the actual rendering of it is trivial.

Better scrolling

This simple scrolling system can take you quite far, but there's a small problem with it. The camera always stays centered over the cat. The only time it stops moving is when it reaches the game world boundaries. This works, but it would appear much more natural if the camera started following the cat only when the cat moved close to the edges of the screen. This would let the cat freely explore the area inside the screen without making the camera move.

To solve this problem, set up an imaginary **inner boundary**, which is a rectangular area inside the camera's frame. The inner boundary should be exactly half the camera's height and width. The cat will be free to move around within the inner boundary. When the cat reaches the edge, the camera will start to move.

This can be confusing to visualize until you see it actually working. Run the betterScrolling.html file to see an example of this theory in action. Figure 7-18 illustrates how this works.

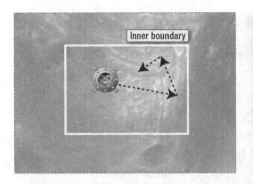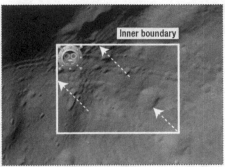

Figure 7-18. The cat is free to move within the inner boundary. When it reaches one of the edges, the camera starts to follow it

This inner boundary is defined by four values that describe the position of its top, bottom, left, and right edges. They're part of the camera object. Here's the new camera object that adds these boundaries.

```
var camera =
{
  x: 0,
  y: 0,
  width: canvas.width,
  height: canvas.height,

  //The camera's inner boundaries
  rightInnerBoundary: function()
  {
    return this.x + (this.width * 0.75);
  },
  leftInnerBoundary: function()
  {
    return this.x + (this.width * 0.25);
  },
  topInnerBoundary: function()
  {
    return this.y + (this.height * 0.25);
  },
  bottomInnerBoundary: function()
  {
    return this.y + (this.height * 0.75);
  }
};
```

You can see that all four boundaries are defined as methods. The job of each method is to return the result of a calculation. Each calculation describes the position of one of the four edges of the inner boundary. The boundaries they define are an area that's half the size of the camera. This is the inner area where the cat can move about freely. Figure 7-19 shows how these calculations define this area.

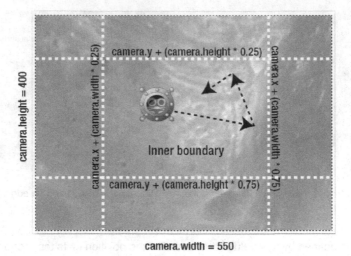

Figure 7-19. Define the camera's inner boundary

Each of these methods uses the `return` keyword to automatically return the result of the method when it's called. Here's the `rightInnerBoundary` method that figures out where the right edge should be.

```
rightInnerBoundary: function()
{
  return this.x + (this.width * 0.75);
},
```

It calculates the right edge by taking the camera's X position and adding 75% of its width. To use this value anywhere in the program, you call this method like this:

```
camera.rightInnerBoundary()
```

Methods like these that just calculate a value and return the result are called **getters**. You'll learn more about getters in Chapter 8.

Here's the new `update` function that uses these variables to make the scrolling work. (I've abridged the code that sets the cat's velocity; it's the same as in the previous examples.)

```
function update()

{
  //The animation loop
  requestAnimationFrame(update, canvas);

  //...Figure out the cat's velocity based on the direction variables...
```

```
//Move the cat and keep it inside the gameWorld boundaries
cat.x = Math.max(0, Math.min(cat.x + cat.vx, gameWorld.width - cat.width));
cat.y = Math.max(0, Math.min(cat.y + cat.vy, gameWorld.height - cat.height));

//Scroll the camera
if(cat.x < camera.leftInnerBoundary())
{
  camera.x = Math.floor(cat.x - (camera.width * 0.25));
}
if(cat.y < camera.topInnerBoundary())
{
  camera.y = Math.floor(cat.y - (camera.height * 0.25));
}
if(cat.x + cat.width > camera.rightInnerBoundary())
{
  camera.x = Math.floor(cat.x + cat.width - (camera.width * 0.75));
}
if(cat.y + cat.height > camera.bottomInnerBoundary())
{
  camera.y = Math.floor(cat.y + cat.height - (camera.height * 0.75));
}


//The camera's world boundaries
if(camera.x < gameWorld.x)
{
  camera.x = gameWorld.x;
}
if(camera.y < gameWorld.y)
{
  camera.y = gameWorld.y;
}
if(camera.x + camera.width > gameWorld.x + gameWorld.width)
{
  camera.x = gameWorld.x + gameWorld.width - camera.width;
}
if(camera.y + camera.height > gameWorld.height)
{
  camera.y = gameWorld.height - camera.height;
}

//Render the game
render();
}
```

Let's have a look at how the first **if** statement works.

```
if(cat.x < camera.leftInnerBoundary())
{
  camera.x = Math.floor(cat.x - (camera.width * 0.25));
}
```

It checks to see whether the cat has crossed the left inner boundary. If it has, the camera begins to follow the cat. The code does this by setting the camera's X position to the cat's X position and subtracting a quarter of the camera's width.

The other three if statements apply this same logic to the top, bottom, and right boundaries. They only make the camera move when the cat has crossed those boundaries. That lets the cat freely explore the inside area of the screen, and the camera will start following it only when it reaches the screen edges.

The next four if statements check the camera's game world boundaries with the same code we used in the previous examples. If you prefer to use the `Math.max` and `Math.min` trick, you can replace all eight if statements with the following four `if` statements:

```
if(cat.x < camera.leftInnerBoundary())
{
  camera.x = Math.max(0, Math.min
  (
    Math.floor(cat.x - (camera.width * 0.25)),
    gameWorld.width - camera.width
  ));
}
if(cat.y < camera.topInnerBoundary())
{
  camera.y = Math.max(0, Math.min
  (
    Math.floor(cat.y - (camera.height * 0.25)),
    gameWorld.height - camera.height
  ));
}
if(cat.x + cat.width > camera.rightInnerBoundary())
{
  camera.x = Math.max(0, Math.min
  (
    Math.floor(cat.x + cat.width - (camera.width * 0.75)),
    gameWorld.width - camera.width
  ));
}
if(cat.y + cat.height > camera.bottomInnerBoundary())
{
  camera.y = Math.max(0, Math.min
  (
    Math.floor(cat.y + cat.height - (camera.height * 0.75)),
    gameWorld.height - camera.height
  ));
}
```

I'm not sure that this is less code, and it's certainly more difficult to read, but I'll leave it up to you to decide which style you prefer to use. There's no technical reason for choosing one over the other.

Parallax scrolling

There's another scrolling technique that we should look at briefly because it's very widely used and extremely effective: **parallax scrolling**.

Parallax is a visual effect in which the position of an object appears to change depending on the point of view from which it's being observed. The effect of parallax scrolling in games is used to create the illusion of shallow depth. It's a simple 3D effect in which distant background objects move at a slower rate than any closer foreground objects. This creates the illusion that the slower-moving objects are farther away. Parallax scrolling can give even simple 2D games a very strong visual impact.

To see how, run the parallaxScrolling.html file, shown in Figure 7-20. Move the cat left and right with the arrow keys. The distant clouds will move at half the speed of the foreground trees and rocks, for a very pleasing illusion of depth.

Figure 7-20. Parallax scrolling is a shallow 3D effect in which the distant background and the foreground move at different speeds

First, you need to split your background scene into two or more separate images. The first will be for things that are far away, like mountains or clouds. Perhaps you could call this distantBackground. Make its height the same as the canvas (238 pixels in this example). But make it really long, with a width of perhaps more than 2,000 pixels. Figure 7-21 illustrates what this could look like.

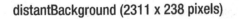

distantBackground (2311 x 238 pixels)

Figure 7-21. A distant background object for things that are far away

Next, you need an image for things that are closer. Perhaps you could call it the foreground. Make it exactly the same size as the distant background. Figure 7-22 shows what this might look like.

foreground (2311 x 238 pixels)

Figure 7-22. A foreground object for things that are closer

Then put them together in a single tilesheet and add an image for a game character. Figure 7-23 shows the parallaxScrollingTileSheet.png file that this example uses.

Figure 7-23. Add the images to a single tilesheet

Create the sprites, and center them. Then, in the update function, move the distantBackground object at half the camera's speed. The directives you use might look like this:

```
distantBackground.x += camera.vx / 2;
```

Try it! It's a mesmerizing effect. And there's also nothing stopping you from adding a third element as an extremely distant background object moving at an even slower rate.

To get you started on your own parallax scrolling experiments, here's the entire code for the parallax Scrolling.html program in the chapter's source files. I'll explain the details ahead.

```
<!doctype html>
<title>Parallax scrolling</title>

<canvas width="550" height="238" style="border: 1px dashed black"></canvas>
```

```
<script>

//--- The sprite object

var spriteObject =
{
  sourceX: 0,
  sourceY: 0,
  sourceWidth: 64,
  sourceHeight: 64,
  x: 0,
  y: 0,
  width: 64,
  height: 64,
  vx: 0,
  vy: 0
};

//--- The main program

//The canvas and its drawing surface
var canvas = document.querySelector("canvas");
var drawingSurface = canvas.getContext("2d");

//An array to store the sprites
var sprites = [];

//Create the distantBackground sprite
var distantBackground = Object.create(spriteObject);
distantBackground.sourceY = 64;
distantBackground.sourceWidth = 1190;
distantBackground.sourceHeight = 238;
distantBackground.width = 1190;
distantBackground.height = 238;
distantBackground.x = 0;
distantBackground.y = 0;
sprites.push(distantBackground);

//Create the foreground sprite
var foreground = Object.create(spriteObject);
foreground.sourceY = 302;
foreground.sourceWidth = 1190;
foreground.sourceHeight = 238;
foreground.width = 1190;
foreground.height = 238;
foreground.x = 0;
foreground.y = 0;
sprites.push(foreground);
```

```
//Create the gameWorld and camera objects
var gameWorld =
{
  x: 0,
  y: 0,
  width: foreground.width,
  height: foreground.height
};

//The camera has 2 new properties: "vx" and "previousX"
var camera =
{
  x: 0,
  y: 0,
  width: canvas.width,
  height: canvas.height,
  vx: 0,
  previousX: 0,

  //The camera's inner scroll boundaries
  rightInnerBoundary: function()
  {
    return this.x + (this.width * 0.75);
  },
  leftInnerBoundary: function()
  {
    return this.x + (this.width * 0.25);
  }
};

//Center the camera over the gameWorld
camera.x = (gameWorld.x + gameWorld.width / 2) - camera.width / 2;
camera.y = (gameWorld.y + gameWorld.height / 2) - camera.height / 2;

//Create the cat sprite and center it
var cat = Object.create(spriteObject);
cat.x = (gameWorld.x + gameWorld.width / 2) - cat.width / 2;
cat.y = 174;
sprites.push(cat);

//Load the image
var image = new Image();
image.addEventListener("load", loadHandler, false);
image.src = "parallaxScrollingTileSheet.png";

//Arrow key codes
var RIGHT = 39;
var LEFT = 37;
```

```
//Directions
var moveRight = false;
var moveLeft = false;

//Add keyboard listeners
window.addEventListener("keydown", function(event)
{
  switch(event.keyCode)
  {
    case LEFT:
      moveLeft = true;
      break;

    case RIGHT:
      moveRight = true;
      break;
  }
}, false);

window.addEventListener("keyup", function(event)
{
  switch(event.keyCode)
  {
    case LEFT:
      moveLeft = false;
      break;

    case RIGHT:
      moveRight = false;
      break;
  }
}, false);

function loadHandler()
{
  update();
}

function update()
{
  //The animation loop
  requestAnimationFrame(update, canvas);

  //Left
  if(moveLeft && !moveRight)
  {
    cat.vx = -5;
  }
```

```
//Right
if(moveRight && !moveLeft)
{
  cat.vx = 5;
}

//Set the cat's velocity to zero if none of the keys are being pressed
if(!moveLeft && !moveRight)
{
  cat.vx = 0;
}

//Move the cat and keep it inside the gameWorld boundaries
cat.x = Math.max(0, Math.min(cat.x + cat.vx, gameWorld.width - cat.width));

//Scroll the camera
if(cat.x < camera.leftInnerBoundary())
{
  camera.x = Math.floor(cat.x - (camera.width * 0.25));
}
if(cat.x + cat.width > camera.rightInnerBoundary())
{
  camera.x = Math.floor(cat.x + cat.width - (camera.width * 0.75));
}

//The camera's world boundaries
if(camera.x < gameWorld.x)
{
  camera.x = gameWorld.x;
}
if(camera.x + camera.width > gameWorld.x + gameWorld.width)
{
  camera.x = gameWorld.x + gameWorld.width - camera.width;
}

//Figure out the camera's velocity by subtracting its position in the
//previous frame from its position in this frame
camera.vx = camera.x - camera.previousX;

//Move the distantBackground at half the speed of the camera
distantBackground.x += camera.vx / 2;

//Capture the camera's current X position so we can use it as the
//previousX value in the next frame
camera.previousX = camera.x;

  render();
}
```

```
function render(event)
{
  drawingSurface.clearRect(0, 0, canvas.width, canvas.height);

  drawingSurface.save();

  //Move the drawing surface so that it's positioned relative to the camera
  drawingSurface.translate(-camera.x, -camera.y);

  //Loop through all the sprites and use their properties to display them
  if(sprites.length !== 0)
  {
    for(var i = 0; i < sprites.length; i++)
    {
      var sprite = sprites[i];
      drawingSurface.drawImage
      (
        image,
        sprite.sourceX, sprite.sourceY,
        sprite.sourceWidth, sprite.sourceHeight,
        Math.floor(sprite.x), Math.floor(sprite.y),
        sprite.width, sprite.height
      );
    }
  }

  drawingSurface.restore();
}

</script>
```

This code uses all the techniques we've learned in this chapter. But it also uses a new technique to calculate the camera's velocity. Let's find out how that works.

Finding the camera's velocity

The camera object has two new properties: vx and previousX.

```
var camera =
{
  x: 0,
  y: 0,
  width: canvas.width,
  height: canvas.height,
  vx: 0,
  previousX: 0,
```

```
  //The camera's inner scroll boundaries
  rightInnerBoundary: function()
  {
    return this.x + (this.width * 0.75);
  },
  leftInnerBoundary: function()
  {
    return this.x + (this.width * 0.25);
  }
};
```

How do these new properties help to figure out the camera's velocity?

There's a simple formula for calculating how fast an object is moving. Subtract the position it had in the previous frame from its current position:

```
velocity = currentPosition - previousPosition
```

This is the general formula that can be used to find out how fast any object is moving. Here's the actual line of code in the update function that uses this formula to calculate the camera's velocity:

```
camera.vx = camera.x - camera.previousX;
```

Imagine that the camera's current X position is 50 and that its position in the previous frame was 45. That means we can interpret the above line of code like this:

```
camera.vx = 50-45;
```

The result is that the camera's vx will be 5:

```
camera.vx = 5;
```

We can now use the camera.vx value to move the distantBackground at half the camera's speed in the update function, like this:

```
distantBackground.x += camera.vx / 2;
```

This is what makes the distantBackground move.

But there's something missing: how do we know what the camera's position was in the previous frame? That value is stored in the camera's previousX property. There's a trick to finding it. At the very end of the update function, just before the render function is called, is this line of code:

```
camera.previousX = camera.x;
```

This captures the camera's current X position and stores it in the previousX property. It does this just before the animation loop ends. Because the camera's position isn't changed again after that point, previousX will still store this value *in the next loop cycle*. It keeps a constant record of what the camera's X position was one frame previously.

Take a look at the complete code listing to see how this code fits in its proper context. You can use this technique for calculating the velocity for any object in a game.

Moving a sprite with the mouse and touch

It's easy to move sprites with the mouse and touch instead of the keyboard. You'll find a detailed explanation of how to use the mouse and touch to control game characters in Chapter 12, but here's a quick introduction to get you started.

Chasing the mouse

Open the `mouseControl.html` file for a basic example of how you could use the mouse to move a game character. Click the mouse to make the cat move, and release it to make the cat stop moving. Figure 7-24 shows what you'll see. Like all proper cats should, it moves in the direction of the mouse.

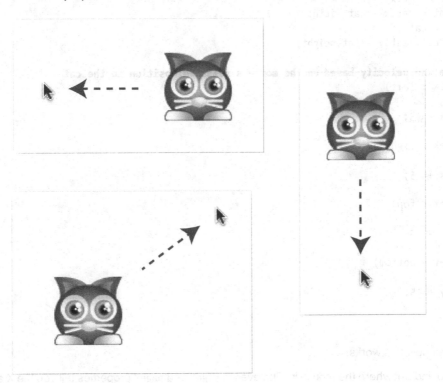

Figure 7-24. The cat chases the mouse

You need two mouse listeners to make this work. You need a **mousedown** listener to set the cat's velocity.

You then need a **mouseup** listener to stop the cat by setting the velocity to zero.

```
canvas.addEventListener("mousedown", mousedownHandler, false);
window.addEventListener("mouseup", mouseupHandler, false);
```

The mousedown listener is added to the canvas. It will activate when the mouse is clicked inside the canvas HTML element. But the mouseup listener is added to the window object, which represents the whole browser area. This is important, because it means that if you release the mouse outside the area of the canvas, it will still work.

Here's the mousedownHandler. It first figures out the mouse's X and Y positions inside the canvas. It then sets the cat's vx and vy properties based on where the mouse is relative to the cat's top, left, bottom, and right edges.

```
function mousedownHandler(event)
{
  //Find the mouse's X and Y positions
  var mouseX = event.pageX - canvas.offsetLeft;
  var mouseY = event.pageY - canvas.offsetTop;

  //Define the cat's four sides
  var left = cat.x;
  var right = cat.x + cat.width;
  var top = cat.y;
  var bottom = cat.y + cat.height;

  //Change the velocity based on the mouse's relative position to the cat
  if(mouseX < left)
  {
    cat.vx -= 5;
  }
  if(mouseX > right)
  {
    cat.vx += 5;
  }
  if(mouseY < top)
  {
    cat.vy -= 5;
  }
  if(mouseY > bottom)
  {
    cat.vy += 5;
  }
}
```

Let's find out how this works.

You need to find out where the mouse is. The event's pageX and pageY properties tell you the X and Y positions of the mouse in the browser window.

```
event.pageX
event.pageY
```

However, you don't want to know the position of the mouse in the browser window. You want to know the exact position of the mouse *inside the canvas element*. If the canvas element is offset from the edge of the browser window with margins, or positioned with the top and left CSS properties, you won't get accurate mouse positions. Fortunately, HTML elements have properties called offsetXLeft and offsetTop that tell you how far they are from the top and left edges of the browser window. You can figure out the canvas's possible offset like this.

```
canvas.offsetLeft;
canvas.offsetTop;
```

That means you can find the exact position of the mouse in the canvas by subtracting this offset from the mouse's position in the browser. The code in this example does this, and it assigns the result to two variables called mouseX and mouseY.

```
var mouseX = event.pageX - canvas.offsetLeft;
var mouseY = event.pageY - canvas.offsetTop;
```

We now have the X and Y positions for the mouse in the canvas.

We now need to figure out where the mouse is relative to the cat's top, left, right, and bottom edges. Our code defines these as variables, so that the logic is a little easier to understand. (Remember the cat's top left corner is its X and Y position.)

```
var left = cat.x;
var right = cat.x + cat.width;
var top = cat.y;
var bottom = cat.y + cat.height;
```

An if statement then finds out where the mouse is relative to these points. It changes the cat's vx and vy properties, which will then move the cat in the correct direction.

```
if(mouseX < left)
{
  cat.vx -= 5;
}
if(mouseX > right)
{
  cat.vx += 5;
}
if(mouseY < top)
{
  cat.vy -= 5;
}
if(mouseY > bottom)
{
  cat.vy += 5;
}
```

The same update function that we've been using all throughout this chapter then uses this very familiar code to move the cat. Here's the abridged update function from this example.

```
function update()
{
  //...
  cat.x += cat.vx;
  cat.y += cat.vy;
  //...
```

When the mouse button is released, the cat's vx and vy properties are set back to zero, which stops the cat from moving.

```
function mouseupHandler(event)
{
  vx = 0;
  vy = 0;
}
```

You can use this system as an alternative to moving a sprite with a keyboard for any of the games and projects in this book. Look at the entire mouseControl.html file in the chapter's source files to see all this code in its proper context.

Moving a sprite by touch

You'll probably make and test most of your games on a computer with a mouse and keyboard. But it's very likely that the finished versions of your games will use a touch interface, so that they can be played on mobile devices and tablets like the iPhone and iPad.

There are three events you can use to capture touch input: touchstart, touchend, and touchmove. These are the touch equivalents to mousedown, mouseup, and mousemove. touchstart is fired when you touch the screen with a finger. touchend is fired when you lift your finger from the screen. touchmove is fired when you move your finger while keeping contact with the screen.

> Note: These events store the positions of up to 11 simultaneous touch points on the screen in an array. You can use this information to create complex multitouch gestures for your games. If you're developing a multitouch game only for iOS devices, you can also use events called **gesturestart**, **gestureend,** and **gesturechange**. These built-in gestures let you easily implement multitouch rotation, pinch, and zoom.
>
> It's beyond the scope of this book to explain how multitouch gesture events work, but you'll find detailed examples in Beginning iPhone and iPad Web Apps by Chris Apers and Daniel Paterson.

You'll find a basic example of how to move a game character with a touch in the touchControl.html file. You'll need to open it in a touch-enabled device to test how it works. Touch anywhere inside the canvas, and the cat will move in that direction.

The code that does this is very similar to the code we used to move the cat with the mouse. The biggest difference is that the mousedown and mouseup events have been replaced with touchstart and touchend.

```
canvas.addEventListener("touchstart", touchstartHandler, false);
window.addEventListener("touchend", touchendHandler, false);
```

Here's the touchstartHandler that moves the cat.

```
function touchstartHandler(event)
{
    //Find the touch point's X and Y positions
    var touchX = event.pageX - canvas.offsetLeft;
    var touchY = event.pageY - canvas.offsetTop;

    //Define the cat's four sides
    var left = cat.x;
    var right = cat.x + cat.width;
    var top = cat.y;
    var bottom = cat.y + cat.height;

    //Change the velocity based on the touch point's relative position to the cat
    if(touchX < left)
    {
        cat.vx -= 5;
    }
    if(touchX > right)
    {
        cat.vx += 5;
    }
    if(touchY < top)
    {
        cat.vy -= 5;
    }
    if(touchY > bottom)
    {
        cat.vy += 5;
    }

    //Prevent the canvas from being selected
    event.preventDefault();
}
```

The touchX and touchY points are captured by using the event's pageX and pageY properties. pageX and pageY tell you the position of the mouse relative to the browser window's top left corner. The amount by which the canvas might be offset from the browser is calculated by using the canvas's offsetLeft and offsetRight properties.

```
var touchX = event.pageX - canvas.offsetLeft;
var touchY = event.pageY - canvas.offsetTop;
```

The other new addition is this bit of code, right at the end of the event handler:

```
event.preventDefault();
```

This prevents the `touchstart` event from selecting the canvas HTML element when you touch it. You don't want to select the canvas, because the browser will highlight the entire canvas element and possibly display options to let you copy or move it. This will override your `touchstart` event code and be very confusing for the player. The reason this happens is that the default action that most browsers have for `touchstart` events is that the touched elements should be selected. Using `event.preventDefault` turns this default action off and lets your own code run.

When you remove your finger from the screen, the `touchend` event is fired. It calls the `touchendHandler`:

```
function touchendHandler(event)
{
  cat.vx = 0;
  cat.vy = 0;

  event.preventDefault();
}
```

This sets the cat's velocity to zero, and it also disables any possible default browser actions that might override this code.

This will get you started thinking about using mouse and touch events in your games, and you'll find many detailed and practical examples in Chapter 12.

Summary

This chapter is the first that takes us into the realm of making video games. You've learned how to make, display, and move sprites by using canvas. We're going to use this same system for the rest of the examples and projects in this book, and you'll soon see how versatile and useful it will be.

You also learned how to set up a player control system by using a keyboard, mouse, and touch interface. Later in this book, you'll learn how to make a sprite move with friction and gravity, as well as some more advanced mouse and touch control systems.

In this chapter, you solved some extremely important problems central to game design that you'll see popping up again and again in different contexts in the chapters that follow. Experiment a bit with some of these techniques on your own, and I'll meet you in Chapter 8 when you're ready. I'll show you how to create an environment in which your game sprites can interact by using collision detection.

Chapter 8

Bumping into Things

What makes most computer games fun to play is that they are, in their essence, stylized simulations of the real world. Like the real world, they contain objects that you can interact with in some way. These objects might be walls that block your movement, friends who help you, or enemies who harm you.

To create these sorts of interactive objects, you first need a way of finding out whether one object is touching another object. In computer programming, this is called **collision detection**. Collision detection is a term for what happens when things bump into one another

In this chapter you're going to learn how to figure out whether two sprites are touching and, if they are, what should happen when they touch. Should the sprites move apart, change states, update a score, or cause another sprite to change in some way? You'll learn all these things.

Most collisions in games fall into two types: collisions between circles and collisions between rectangles. Even if the game sprites are not exactly circular or not exactly rectangular, game designers pretend that they are. That's because the collision detection code for circles and rectangles runs quickly and efficiently. And, in a fast-moving action game, players can never tell that a circle or square is being used for collision instead of the sprite's actual shape.

Figure 8-1 shows a typical example. You can see that a circle and rectangle can be used to roughly represent the shape of the hedgehog. These shapes are called **bounding circles** and **bounding boxes**. Instead of using the actual shape of the hedgehog to check for a collision, your sprites will use one of these bounding shapes. You'll never see these bounding shapes displayed on the canvas. They just exist invisibly as numbers that are used in the collision detection code.

bounding circle   bounding box

Figure 8-1. Use bounding shapes to figure out if two sprites are touching

Does it matter that the bounding circle is a little smaller than the hedgehog's body or that the bounding box doesn't quite match its spikey hairdo? Nope. Sprites move around the screen so quickly that no one notices. Just choose the bounding shape that best matches your sprite. Which shape do you think best matches the hedgehog in Figure 8-2? You would want to use the circle, because the square shape includes empty areas in the top and left and right corners.

In this chapter we'll look at all the classic techniques for doing collision detection with bounding shapes. This is the most math-heavy chapter in the book, but don't let that deter you. I'll explain the math in general terms, but you won't necessarily have to completely understand it to use it. I'll show you some formulas and functions that you can use as is for countless projects. Blindly drop them into your game programs whenever you need to use them, and let them work their magic for you.

Most of this chapter will be about how to handle collisions between two sprites. But before we look at that, let's start with the basics. Let's figure out whether a single point is touching a rectangle. This is the simplest and also one of the most useful kinds of collision detection.

> Note: This chapter uses the same model for creating, displaying, animating, and rendering sprites that we used in Chapter 7. I've kept the code structure and function names in the example programs identical to the examples in that chapter. Refer back to Chapter 7 if you're uncertain of any of the specifics.

Point collisions

It's useful to be able to find out if a point is intersecting within a rectangular area. By a point, I mean a single X and Y position, like the position of the mouse cursor. The rectangular area could be a square-shaped sprite. Run the **pointCollision.html** file for an example of this in action. Move the mouse over the square, and the text changes from "No collision…" to "Collision!" as you can see in Figure 8-2.

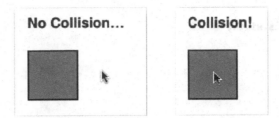

Figure 8-2. Figure out if the mouse cursor is touching a sprite

This is a useful technique to learn because you can use it to find out whether the mouse cursor is over any particular sprite. With a bit more programming you could use this basic system to change a sprite's state when you click on it. Or, you could use the mouse to drag the sprite around the canvas, which you'll learn to do in Chapter 12. Point collisions demonstrate the basic concepts of collision detection in one of its simplest forms. A new feature that I've introduced in this example is that the text is rendered using canvas, not HTML. I'll explain how it works ahead.

To find out if a point is intersecting with a rectangle, you first have to define the left, right, top, and bottom sides of the rectangle. In the previous chapter we created variables to define these four sides of a sprite like this:

```
var left = sprite.x;
var right = sprite.x + sprite.width;
var top = sprite.y;
var bottom = sprite.y + sprite.height;
```

Because we may want to know this information for every sprite in a game, it's better to add these as properties directly in the spriteObject that will be used as the template to make all the game sprites. Here's the new spriteObject that contains these properties.

```
var spriteObject =
{
  sourceX: 0,
  sourceY: 0,
  sourceWidth: 64,
  sourceHeight: 64,
  x: 0,
  y: 0,
  width: 64,
  height: 64,

  //Getters to define the left, right, top and bottom sides
  left: function()
  {
    return this.x;
  },
  right: function()
```

```
{
  return this.x + this.width;
},
top: function()
{
  return this.y;
},
bottom: function()
{
  return this.y + this.height;
}
};
```

The four new properties are actually methods. You can see that they calculate the position of the sprite's sides and then return the result. Use them just like you would any other object method. For example, to find out the position of the sprite's bottom side, just call the bottom method, like this.

```
sprite.bottom();
```

It will return the result of the calculation (this.y + this.height).

> Note: Methods like this that just return properties are called **getters**. Use getters whenever you need to access a sprite property that requires a bit of calculation.

How can we figure out if a point is intersecting with the sprite?

The hitTestPoint function

A function called hitTestPoint helps us do this. It will return true if the point and sprite are touching and false if they aren't. Here's the hitTestPoint function.

```
function hitTestPoint(pointX, pointY, sprite)
{
  var hit = false;

  if(pointX > sprite.left()
  && pointX < sprite.right()
  && pointY > sprite.top()
  && pointY < sprite.bottom())
  {
    hit = true;
  }

  return hit;
}
```

You can see that it takes three arguments. The first is the point's X position, the second is the point's Y position, and the third is any sprite object.

```
functionhitTestPoint(pointX, pointY, sprite)
{...
```

The function has a Boolean variable that tracks whether or not the point and sprite are touching. It's initialized to false.

```
var hit = false;
```

An if statement figures out if the point's X and Y positions are inside the boundaries defined by the sprite's four sides. If they are, hit is set to true.

```
if(pointX > sprite.left()
&& pointX < sprite.right()
&& pointY > sprite.top()
&& pointY < sprite.bottom())
{
   hit = true;
}
```

If the point doesn't intersect the sprite, hit remains false. The function returns the value of whatever hit happens to be.

```
return hit;
```

The job of the hitTestPoint function is to return either true or false, depending on whether or not the point and sprite are touching. That means you can use it with an if statement, like this.

```
if(hitTestPoint(anyXPosition, anyYPosition, anySpriteObject))
{
    //If hitTestPoint is true, run this code
}
```

If the point intersects the sprite, the code in the if statement will run.

Condensing the code

There's an alternative, simplified way to write this function. You can assign the conditional statement that checks for a collision to a variable called hit, like this:

```
var hit
  = pointX > sprite.left() && pointX < sprite.right()
  && pointY > sprite.top() && pointY < sprite.bottom();
```

Then just return the value of hit, which will be either true or false.

```
return hit;
```

Here's the new hitTestPoint function that uses this style.

```
function hitTestPoint(pointX, pointY, sprite)
{
  var hit
    = pointX > sprite.left() && pointX < sprite.right()
    && pointY > sprite.top() && pointY < sprite.bottom();

  return hit;
}
```

You can use whichever style you find more understandable; there's no technical reason for using one over the other.

Using hitTestPoint to detect a collision

Let's find out how the **pointCollision.html** program uses this function to find out whether the mouse and sprite are intersecting.

The square is a sprite, which is centered in the canvas.

```
var square = Object.create(spriteObject);
square.x = canvas.width / 2 - square.width / 2;
square.y = canvas.height / 2 - square.height / 2;;
sprites.push(square);
```

The main program uses mouseX and mouseY variables to store the position of the mouse cursor. The canvas has a mousemove listener that runs whenever you move the mouse over the canvas. The mousemoveHandler finds the X and Y positions of the mouse and copies those values into the mouseX and mouseY variables.

```
//Variables to store the mouse's X and Y positions
var mouseX = 0;
var mouseY = 0;

//Add a mousemove event listener
canvas.addEventListener("mousemove", function(event)
{

  //Find the mouse's X and Y positions on the canvas
  mouseX = event.pageX - canvas.offsetLeft;
  mouseY = event.pageY - canvas.offsetTop;

}, false);
```

The main program also has a variable called message that tells you whether the mouse is touching the sprite. It's set to "No collision..." when the program first loads.

```
var message = "No collision...";
```

The program's update method uses an if statement with hitTestPoint to figure out if the mouse and sprite are touching. If hitTestPoint returns true, the message is set to "Collision!"

```
function update()
{
  //The animation loop
  requestAnimationFrame(update, canvas);

  //Use hitTestPoint to check for a collision and
  //return the result (true or false) to the collision variable
  if(hitTestPoint(mouseX, mouseY, square))
  {
    message = "Collision!";
  }
  else
  {
    message = "No Collision...";
  }

  //Render the sprite
  render();
}
```

The last step is to display the collision message. It's displayed directly on the canvas by using the canvas's text-rendering feature.

Rendering canvas text

Unlike all the other projects in the book so far, the text in this example is displayed with canvas, not HTML. Canvas has its own built-in text-rendering system that's convenient for displaying dynamic text, like scores that are constantly updated, game timers, or brief game messages. It's nice to use because it lets you integrate text seamlessly into the rest of your canvas rendering system, so that you don't have to switch gears into thinking about HTML and CSS if you don't want to. We'll look at the basics of how canvas text rendering works in this chapter, and in Chapter 9 you'll learn how to use it to build a simple message display system for your games.

The main program initializes the canvas text's three most important properties: font, fillStyle, and textBaseline.

```
drawingSurface.font = "normal bold 18px Helvetica";
drawingSurface.fillStyle = "#000";
drawingSurface.textBaseline = "top";
```

As you can see, they're properties of drawingSurface (the canvas's "2D context").

The font property sets the style, weight, size, and font family of the text.

```
drawingSurface.font = "normal bold 24px Helvetica";
```

The four values inside the quotes should match any values you would normally use for these four CSS proper-ties: font-style, font-weight, font-size, and font-family. (font-style and font-weight are optional, so you can leave them out if you want to.)

The fillStyle determines the text color. In this example it's set to #000, which is the shorthand hexadecimal code for black.

```
drawingSurface.fillStyle = "#000";
```

The next property is the textBaseline. This determines how the Y position of the text should be aligned. Setting this to "top" means that the text will be aligned based on the position of its top left corner.

```
drawingSurface.textBaseline = "top";
```

This is a good setting for us because our sprites are also positioned from their top left corners. It means we can apply the same positioning principles to text as we do with sprites.

When you have these three properties set, you're ready to display the text. The fillText method lets you do this. Here's the format for using it.

```
drawingSurface.fillText("Any text", xPosition, yPosition);
```

This will display the words "Any text" at any X and Y position on the canvas.

In the **pointCollision.html** example program, the fillText method is in the render function. It displays the collision message variable 45 pixels above the square.

```
render()
{
  //...Code to display the sprite...

  //Display the message text above the square
  drawingSurface.fillText(message, square.x, square.y - 45);
}
```

Because the render method is called 60 times per second, the text changes instantly as soon as the value of the collision variable changes.

Canvas gives you very fine control over how text is displayed, and you can find out how by doing further research into the Canvas Text API. However, you'll probably find that what I've covered here is about as much as you'll need to know for using canvas text rendering with games. What it's really useful for is short, dynamic bits of text, like a changing score or a brief status message. If your game uses a lot of text, HTML is still the best option. HTML and CSS are specialized for text, and you'll find them much easier to work with for creating game instructions, displaying credits, or performing complex text formatting. To combine canvas with HTML text, use CSS to position and display HTML text elements over the canvas and you've got the best of both worlds.

You can use the **canvasText.html** file in the chapter's source files to experiment with canvas text rendering. It's the simplest program you can make to display text using canvas.

```
<!doctype html>
<title>Canvas text</title>
<meta charset="UTF-8">

<canvas width="550" height="400" style="border: 1px dashed black"></canvas>

<script>

//The canvas and its drawing surface
var canvas = document.querySelector("canvas");
vardrawingSurface = canvas.getContext("2d");

//Canvas text properties
drawingSurface.font = "normal bold 24px Helvetica";
drawingSurface.fillStyle = "#000";
drawingSurface.textBaseline = "top";

//Display the text
drawingSurface.fillText("Any text to display", 100, 180);

</script>
```

This displays the words "Any text to display" in the canvas when it runs.

Circle collisions

Now that you know the basics of collision detection with points, we can start moving on to shapes. Circles are a good place to start, because they embody all of the important things you need to know about collision detection between shapes in the simplest possible way. Circle collision detection is also one of the most widely used kinds of collision detection. When you understand the basics of shape collision detection with circles, you'll find that checking for collisions with more complex shapes, like rectangles, will be much easier to understand.

You can break any collision detection system down into two parts.

1. Figuring out if two shapes are touching.

2. Figuring out what to do when those two shapes touch.

In this section you'll learn how to do both of these things with circles. You'll first learn to figure out whether two circles are touching. You'll then learn how to separate them, so that they appear to be completely solid objects.

Detecting collisions between circles

Here's what you need to do to figure out if two circles are touching.

1. Measure the distance between the circles.

2. If the distance between the circles is less than their combined half-widths, then they must be touching. A circle's half-width is called its **radius**.

Let's first look at the theory behind how to do this, and then we'll see a working example.

First, we have to draw an imaginary line between the center of two circles. This imaginary line is called a **vector**. Figure 8-3 shows a vector between the center points of two circles called c1 and c2.

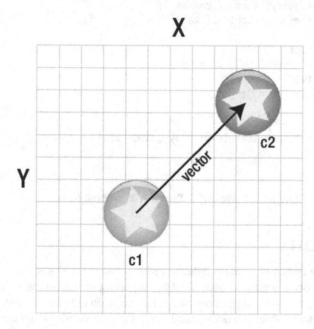

Figure 8-3. A vector that runs between the center points of two circles can help us find out how far apart they are

By "imaginary," I mean this line just exists as numbers. You can describe this vector using two variables called vx and vy.

- **vx**: This tells you how wide the vector is along the X axis. "vx" stands for "vector along the x axis."

- **vy**: This tells you how high the vector is along the Y axis. "vy" stands for "vector along the y axis."

If you have these vx and vy variables that store this information, then you've created a vector that you can use in your game. This can be confusing to visualize, so look carefully at Figure 8-4. It shows how to use the vx and vy variables to describe the vector.

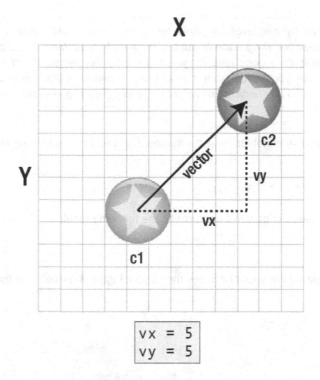

$$vx = 5$$
$$vy = 5$$

Figure 8-4. The vx variable describes how long the vector is. The vy variable describes how high it is

You can easily see in Figure 8-4 that the circles are 5 units apart on the X axis and 5 units apart on the Y axis. That's all that the vx and vy variables are telling you. Here's how you would define these variables:

```
vx = 5
vy = 5
```

The vector that these two variables describe is the diagonal line that you could draw between the start point of vx and the end point of vy.

However, we don't yet know how long the actual diagonal vector line is. But we can figure that out by using the vx and vy values with a special formula called the **Pythagorean theorem**. The Pythagorean theorem is a very common, well-worn formula. Here's how to use it with the vx and vy variables to calculate the exact distance between the circles:

```
magnitude = Math.sqrt(vx * vx + vy * vy);
```

`Math.sqrt` is a built-in JavaScript method that tells you the square root of whatever value is in its argument. I've stored the result in a variable called `magnitude`. Magnitude just means "the length of the vector." It represents the exact distance between the centers of the circles.

> *Note: I usually try and avoid jargon-y terms like "magnitude" when I could just use "distance." However, magnitude is such a commonly used term to describe the length of a vector that it's a good idea for you to become familiar with it. If you see it used somewhere else, you'll know what it means. Just remember that whenever you see the word magnitude in this book, it just refers to the distance between two sprites.*

In Figure 8-4, the vx and vy variables have the values 5 and 5. If you substitute these in the formula above, it will look like this:

```
magnitude = Math.sqrt(5 * 5 + 5 * 5);
```

If you run this code in JavaScript, you'll end up with the following result:

```
magnitude = 5.9
```

That's exactly the length of the vector between the circles. Figure 8-5 illustrates this.

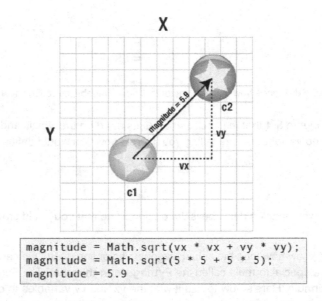

```
magnitude = Math.sqrt(vx * vx + vy * vy);
magnitude = Math.sqrt(5 * 5 + 5 * 5);
magnitude = 5.9
```

Figure 8-5. The vector's magnitude tells you the exact distance between the centers of the circles

You now know exactly how far apart the circles are. The next step is to figure out the circles' combined total radii. What do I mean by "combined total radii"?

Take a look at Figure 8-6 and you'll notice that both the circles are 3 units wide. Half that width is 1.5, which is their radius. If you combine 1.5 and 1.5, the circles' total radii are 3. You can calculate that like this:

```
totalRadii = (c1.width / 2) + (c2.width / 2)
```

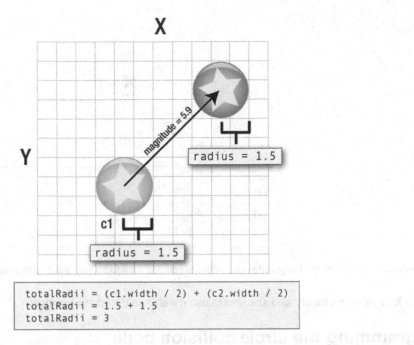

```
totalRadii = (c1.width / 2) + (c2.width / 2)
totalRadii = 1.5 + 1.5
totalRadii = 3
```

Figure 8-6. Calculate the circles' total radii

Why is knowing the total radii important? Because if the vector's magnitude is less than the total radii, then you know the two circles are touching. You can represent this logic in JavaScript like this:

```
if(magnitude < totalRadii)
{
  //The circles are touching!
}
```

In Figure 8-6 the vector's magnitude is 5.9, which is much more than the total radii. That means there's no collision between the circles. But if the magnitude is less than the total radii, the two circles must be touching. Figure 8-7 shows two circles that are clearly touching. The vector's magnitude is 1.14, which is much less than the total radii.

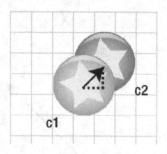

```
vx = 1
vy = 1
magnitude = Math.sqrt(vx * vx + vy * vy);
magnitude = Math.sqrt(1 * 1 + 1 * 1);
magnitude = 1.14
```

Figure 8-7. If the vector's magnitude is less than the circles' total radii, then the circles must be touching

Now let's take this theory and see how to use it with a real working example.

Programming the circle collision code

Run the **circleCollision.html** file. You'll see a small blue circle and a big red circle on the canvas. Use the arrow keys to move the blue circle into the red circle. The text above the red circle displays "Collision!" when the circles touch, and "No collision..." when they aren't touching. Figure 8-8 shows what you'll see. Let's find out how this program was made.

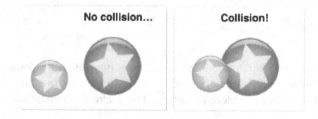

Figure 8-8. Accurate collision detection between circles

Remember that you have to measure the distance between the center points of the circles to figure out if the circles are touching. You also need to know the sprites' radii.

A new sprite object

To help us figure these things out, we're going to add some new getter methods to our spriteObject. We're also going to add vx and vy properties that will help us move the sprite. Here's the updated spriteObject with these new properties and methods.

```
var spriteObject =
{
  sourceX: 0,
  sourceY: 0,
  sourceWidth: 64,
  sourceHeight: 64,
  width: 64,
  height: 64,
  x: 0,
  y: 0,
  vx: 0,
  vy: 0,

  //Getters
  centerX: function()
  {
    return this.x + (this.width / 2);
  },
  centerY: function()
  {
    return this.y + (this.height / 2);
  },
  halfWidth: function()
  {
    return this.width / 2;
  },
  halfHeight: function()
  {
    return this.height / 2;
  }
};
```

The centerX and centerY getters tell you what the sprite's center X and Y positions are. To find the centerX point, add half of the sprite's width to its X position.

```
centerX: function()
{
  return this.x + (this.width / 2);
},
```

The sprite's centerY point is found by adding half the sprite's height to its Y position.

```
centerY: function()
{
  return this.y + (this.height / 2);
},
```

A circle's radius is half its width. However, not all of your sprites will be circles, so to keep this code general I've used the name halfWidth. It returns a number that tells you what half of the sprite's width is.

```
halfWidth: function()
{
  return this.width / 2;
},
```

I've also added a getter called halfHeight. It's not used in this example, but we will use it in later examples in this chapter. It tells you what half the sprite's height is.

```
halfHeight: function()
{
  return this.height / 2;
}
```

The spriteObject also has vx and vy properties, which you learned about in the previous chapter. We're going to use these to help us move the blue circle with the keyboard.

```
vx: 0,
vy: 0,
```

Let's find out how these new sprite properties are used to figure out if the two circles are touching.

Figuring out if there's a collision

The program uses a function called hitTestCircle to find out if two circles are touching. The function takes two sprites as arguments. These sprites are represented by the variable names c1 and c2 (circle 1 and circle 2). The function uses all the formulas we looked at in the previous section to figure out if the circles are touching. Here's the hitTestCircle function.

```
function hitTestCircle(c1, c2)
{
  //Calculate the vector between the circles' center points
  var vx = c1.centerX() - c2.centerX();
  var vy = c1.centerY() - c2.centerY();

  //Find the distance between the circles by calculating
  //the vector's magnitude (how long the vector is)
  var magnitude = Math.sqrt(vx * vx + vy * vy);

  //Add together the circles' total radii
  var totalRadii = c1.halfWidth() + c2.halfWidth();

  //Set hit to true if the distance between the circles is
  //less than their totalRadii
  var hit = magnitude < totalRadii;

  return hit;
}
```

The function will return `true` if there's a collision and `false` if there isn't.

You can use `hitTestCircle` inside an `if` statement to figure out if there's a collision. Here's how to use it.

```
if(hitTestCircle(anySprite, anyOtherSprite))
{
  //If hitTestCircle is true, run this code
}
```

The example program uses this bit of code inside the `update` function. It checks whether the two sprites, `blueCircle` and `redCircle`, are touching. If they are, it changes the message from "No collision…" to "Collision!"

```
if(hitTestCircle(blueCircle, redCircle))
{
  message = "Collision!";
}
else
{
  message = "No collision...";
}
```

And that's really all there is to it. You can use sprites of any size, and this will work just as well without any changes.

Preventing the circles from overlapping

We now have a way to figure out if the circles are touching. But what can we use it for? Let's use it to make the circles completely solid, so they can't intersect. To see the result, run **blockingCircles.html**. Use the arrow keys to move the small blue circle into the big red circle. No matter how hard you try, the circles will never overlap. They seem to be real, solid objects. Figure 8-9 illustrates this.

Figure 8-9. The circles appear to be completely solid

Of course, the circles aren't solid objects at all; this is just an amazing illusion performed with the help of some clever math. Let's find out how this trick was done.

Here's what you have to do to make this work.

1.   When the circles collide, find out by how much they're overlapping.

2.   Push the circles apart by the amount of overlap.

When the circles collide, they'll overlap a certain amount. You can figure this out by subtracting the vector's magnitude by the circles' total radii. Here's the formula for figuring this out.

```
overlap = totalRadii- magnitude;
```

The next step is to figure out the direction that the collision occurred in. We can do this by dividing the vector's vx and vy values by its magnitude. We'll store the result in two new variables called dx and dy.

Here's how to calculate the magnitude, which you learned in the previous section:

```
magnitude = Math.sqrt(vx * vx + vy * vy);
```

Now divide the vx and vx values by the magnitude.

```
dx = vx / magnitude;
dy = vy / magnitude;
```

dx and dy now represent the direction that the collision occurred in (dx and dy are together known as the **unit vector**). If we multiply them by the amount of overlap, we can find the exact position that the first circle should be in so that its edge touches the edge of the second circle. Add this to the moving circle's position to precisely move it out of the collision.

```
circle.x += overlap * dx;
circle.y += overlap * dy;
```

The result is that the two circles will be touching exactly at their edges.

Don't agonize too much over these formulas. It would be really hard to figure them out for yourself and they're difficult to visualize. The standard formulas for doing these sorts of things come from a branch of mathematics called **vector math**. Just use them with gleeful abandon whenever you want to achieve this effect. And, as I like to say, "Thank you, Mathematics!"

> Note: Even if you don't think that you're good at math, vector math is extremely interesting and easy to learn. If you understand it, it will give you almost limitless control over the position of sprites in your games.

The **blockingCircles.html** file uses these formulas in a new function called blockCircle. The first part of the function is identical to the code that we used in hitTestCircle. The new lines of code are in the if statement that runs if the two circles touch. Here's the blockCircle function.

```
function blockCircle(c1, c2)
{
  //Calculate the vector between the circles' center points
  var vx = c1.centerX() - c2.centerX();
  var vy = c1.centerY() - c2.centerY();

  //Find the distance between the circles by calculating
  //the vector's magnitude (how long the vector is)
  var magnitude = Math.sqrt(vx * vx + vy * vy);

  //Add together the circles' total radii
  var totalRadii = c1.halfWidth() + c2.halfWidth();

  //Figure out if there's a collision
  if(magnitude < totalRadii)
  {
    //Yes, a collision is happening.
    //Find the amount of overlap between the circles
    var overlap = totalRadii - magnitude;

    //Normalize the vector.
    //These numbers tell us the direction of the collision
    dx = vx / magnitude;
    dy = vy / magnitude;

    //Move circle 1 out of the collision by multiplying
    //the overlap with the normalized vector and add it to circle 1's position
    c1.x += overlap * dx;
    c1.y += overlap * dy;
  }
}
```

Use blockCircle inside the update function like this.

```
blockCircle(firstSprite, secondSprite);
```

That's all you need to do to prevent two circles from overlapping. In Chapter 11 you'll learn how to make these circles bounce apart.

Rectangle collisions

Figuring out whether two rectangles are touching is probably the most useful and widely used collision detection technique for games. The basic system is the same as checking for collisions with circles. First, you need to figure out if two rectangles are touching. Next, you have to make your game do something interesting when that happens. But there's one important technical difference. A circle only has a radius, but a rectangle has a width and a height. Unless it's a square, the height and width might be different. The collision code for rectangles has to account for this. Also, it's often useful to know on which side of the rectangle the collision is occurring. All this makes the collision code for rectangles a little more complex than the collision code for circles. But, as you'll see, it's not difficult once you grasp the basic concepts.

Detecting collisions between rectangles

Here's how to find a collision between two rectangles:

1. Find out how far apart the rectangles are. Use a vector between the rectangles' center points to figure this out, just as you did with circles.

2. Check to see if the distance between the rectangles is less than their combined half-widths. If it is, a collision might be occurring on the X axis. But you don't know this yet. You also have to check the Y axis.

3. Check to see if the distance between the rectangles on the Y axis is less than their combined half-heights. If it is, then you know that a collision is definitely happening.

Before we look at the code that does this, let's take a closer look at why this works.

The first step is to draw a vector between the rectangles. In Figure 8-10, the rectangular sprites are 5 units apart on the X axis and 5 units apart on the Y axis. That means you can describe the vector between them like this:

vx = 5
vy = 5

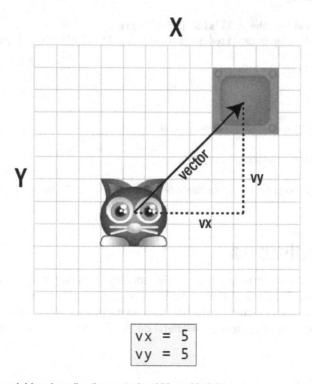

Figure 8-10. The vx and vy variables describe the vector's width and height

Next, we have to calculate the rectangles' combined half-widths and half-heights. If the rectangular sprites are called r1 and r2, this is what the code might look like.

```
combinedHalfWidths = (r1.width / 2) + (r2.width / 2);
combinedHalfHeights = (r1.height / 2) + (r2.height / 2);
```

Figure 8-11 shows what these numbers look like.

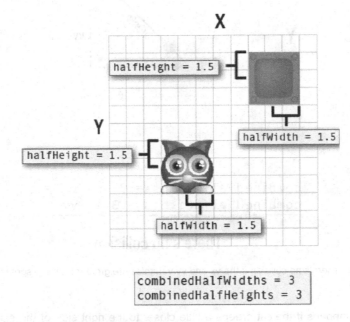

Figure 8-11. Find the combined half-heights and half-widths

You can see that it's really simple math. But it also might seem like a lot of useless information! It's not: here's why it's important:

If the combined half-widths and half-heights are less than the vx and vy variables, then the sprites are touching.

Let's go on a practical tour of why this works:

1. Imagine that a cat is moving around on the game screen. You want to know whether or not it's touching a box. Check the vx and vy variables against the combined half-height and half-widths of the cat and box. If the vx and vy variables have a greater value than the half-widths and half-heights, then there's no collision. Figure 8-12 illustrates this.

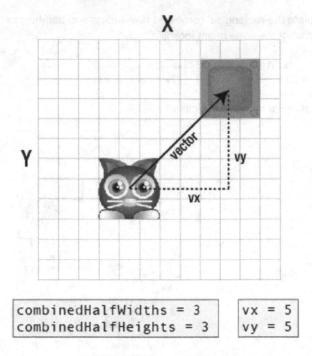

| combinedHalfWidths = 3 | vx = 5 |
| combinedHalfHeights = 3 | vy = 5 |

There's no collision

Figure 8-12. There's no collision if the vx and vy variables are greater than the sprites' combined half-widths and half-heights

2. But what happens if the cat creeps a little closer to the right side of the screen? As soon as its vx value becomes less than the combined half-widths, a possible collision might be on its way. But it's not happening yet, because the vy value is still greater than the combined half-heights. You can see this in Figure 8-13.

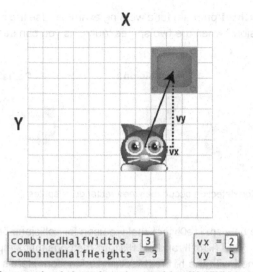

combinedHalfWidths = 3	vx = 2
combinedHalfHeights = 3	vy = 5

The vx value is less than the combinedHalfWidths.
A collision might be approaching!

Figure 8-13. There's the potential of a collision occurring if the vx value becomes less than the combined half-widths

3. If both the vx and vy values are less than the combined half-widths and half-heights, you know that the sprites are colliding. You can see this in Figure 8-14.

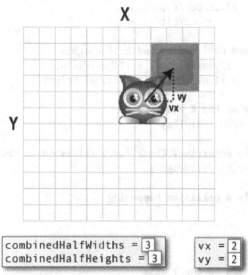

combinedHalfWidths = 3	vx = 2
combinedHalfHeights = 3	vy = 2

The vx and vy values are less than the
combinedHalfWidths and combinedHalfHeights.
A collision is definitely occuring!

Figure 8-14. A collision is definitely occurring if both the vx and vy values are less than the half-widths and half-heights

465

Run the **rectangleCollision.html** program for a working example. Use the arrow keys to move the cat into the box. The text displays "Collision!" when the two sprites touch, as you can see in Figure 8-15.

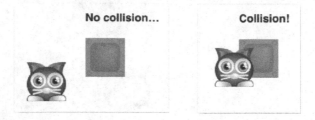

Figure 8-15. An accurate collision detection occurs between rectangular sprites

This program uses the same new spriteObject that we used for collisions between circles. The spriteObject contains the centerX, centerY, halfWidth, and halfHeight methods that simplify the collision calculations. The collision detection is performed with the hitTestRectangle function. Here's the entire function. Can you see how it works based on the previous explanation?

```
function hitTestRectangle(r1, r2)
{
  //A variable to determine whether there's a collision
  var hit = false;

  //Calculate the distance vector
  var vx = r1.centerX() - r2.centerX();
  var vy = r1.centerY() - r2.centerY();

  //Figure out the combined half-widths and half-heights
  var combinedHalfWidths = r1.halfWidth() + r2.halfWidth();
  var combinedHalfHeights = r1.halfHeight() + r2.halfHeight();

  //Check for a collision on the X axis
  if(Math.abs(vx) < combinedHalfWidths)
  {
    //A collision might be occurring. Check for a collision on the Y axis
    if(Math.abs(vy) < combinedHalfHeights)
    {
      //There's definitely a collision happening
      hit = true;
    }
    else
    {
      //There's no collision on the Y axis
      hit = false;
    }
  }
}
```

```
  else
  {
    //There's no collision on the X axis
    hit = false;
  }

  return hit;
}
```

The function returns true if there's a collision and false if there isn't.

One new thing is that it uses JavaScript's Math.abs method to check whether the vx and vy variables are less than the half-widths, like this:

Math.abs(vx) < combinedHalfWidths

What does Math.abs do? It makes negative numbers positive. That simplifies the code quite a bit because it means we don't have to do an extra check for negative vx and vy values.

Use hitTestRectangle inside an if statement to check for collisions between sprites, like this:

```
if(hitTestRectangle(anySprite, anyOtherSprite))
{
    //Any code you want to run if the sprites are colliding
}
```

The example program uses this bit of code inside the update function. It checks whether the two sprites, cat and box, are touching. If they are, it changes the message from "No collision…" to "Collision!"

```
if(hitTestRectangle(cat, box))
{
  message = "Collision!";
}
else
{
  message = "No collision...";
}
```

The rectangle collision system in this chapter is based on the Separating Axis Theorem (SAT) developed by the legendary computer scientist Stefan Gottschalk. It capitalizes on the fact that, in any game, the chance that two objects are not colliding is far more likely than that they are colliding. It's very efficient because you can find out immediately whether two objects might be colliding just by testing one axis. This means the collision function can skip most of the collision code most of the time. That's great for games because it saves a lot of processing power. You can also use this same system for 3D collision detection. Just add an additional if statement to check for any overlaps on the third (Z) axis.

Here's a more condensed version of hitTestRectangle. It saves a lot of code by testing for a collision on both X and Y axes and returning the result with just one line. If you're not going to be checking for collisions between thousands of sprites at 60 frames per second you'll certainly find that this works plenty fast enough for most games.

```
function hitTestRectangle(r1, r2)
{
  //This will return true if there's a collision on both the X and Y axes

  return Math.abs(r1.centerX() - r2.centerX())
  < r1.halfWidth() + r2.halfWidth()
  && Math.abs(r1.centerY() - r2.centerY())
  < r1.halfHeight() + r2.halfHeight();
}
```

So now that we know how to detect collisions between rectangular sprites, what's it useful for? In the next few sections we'll build an interactive playground of little techniques that will show you all sorts of fun you can have with colliding sprites. Here's what you'll do.

- Learn to make a sprite change its state.

- Reduce a game character's health meter.

- Update a game score when two sprites touch.

- Make solid walls and boxes that sprites can't move through.

- Make sprites that you can push around the screen.

It's everything you need to start making some innovative and imaginative video games.

Changing a sprite's state

As if our poor little monster didn't get enough punishment in Chapter 6! Run the **changingStates.html** program and use the arrow keys to move the cat into the monster. The monster opens its mouth while the cat is touching it. When the cat moves away, it closes its mouth again.

Figure 8-16. The monster opens its mouth when the cat touches it

As you may have guessed, the collision code is making the monster change its state from NORMAL to SCARED. It's a very easy effect to achieve, but you need to set up the monster's states properly. The monster also needs a method that will change its states and choose the correct image to display from a tilesheet.

Let's first look at the new properties in the monster object and then at how the main program makes it change its state. Here's the monster object with its new properties highlighted.

```
var monster = Object.create(spriteObject);
monster.sourceX = 64;
monster.x = 350;
monster.y = 100;
monster.NORMAL = [1, 0];
monster.SCARED = [0, 1];
monster.state = monster.NORMAL;
monster.update = function()
{
  this.sourceX = this.state[0] * this.sourceWidth;
  this.sourceY = this.state[1] * this.sourceHeight;
}
sprites.push(monster);
```

You can see that the monster's states, NORMAL and SCARED, are arrays.

```
monster.NORMAL = [1, 0];
monster.SCARED = [0, 1];
```

The first number in the array is the column of the state's image on the tilesheet. The second number is the row. Figure 8-17 shows the **collisionTileSheet.png** file that we're using in this example. (The tilesheet also includes an image for a health meter that we'll use later. It's not used in this example.)

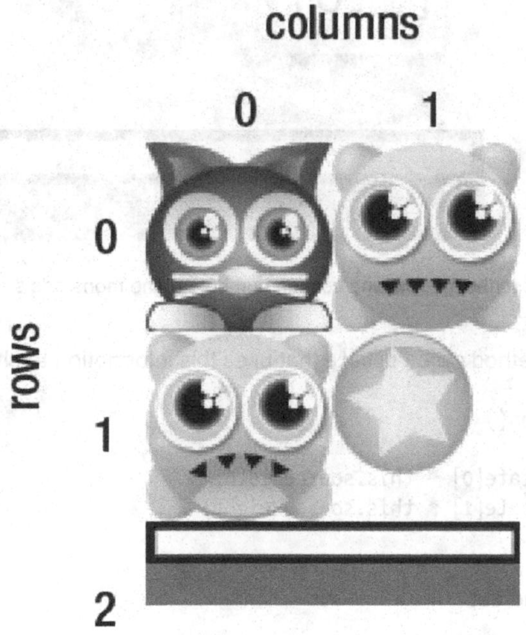

Figure 8-17. The monster's states are on the tilesheet

You can see that the monster's NORMAL state is in column 1 and row 0.

```
monster.NORMAL = [1, 0];
```

Its SCARED state is in column 0 and row 1.

```
monster.SCARED = [0, 1];
```

Figure 8-18 illustrates this.

Figure 8-18. Use arrays to describe the row and column numbers of the monster's states on the tilesheet

The monster also has a method called update that uses this information to change its state.

```
monster.update = function()
{
  this.sourceX = this.state[0] * this.sourceWidth;
  this.sourceY = this.state[1] * this.sourceHeight;
}
```

How does it work? Let's find out.

The update function in the main program checks for a collision between the cat and the monster. If it detects one, it sets the monster's state to SCARED. If there's no collision, it sets the monster's state to NORMAL. It then calls the monster's own update method so that the change will be visible.

```
if(hitTestRectangle(cat, monster))
{
  monster.state = monster.SCARED;
}
else
{
  monster.state = monster.NORMAL;
}

monster.update();
```

The monster's update method changes the monster's sourceX and sourceY properties to match the state's new image described by the array.

```
monster.update = function()
{
  this.sourceX = this.state[0] * this.sourceWidth;
  this.sourceY = this.state[1] * this.sourceHeight;
}
```

If the state is SCARED, you could interpret these lines of code like this.

```
this.sourceX = 0 * 64;
this.sourceY = 1 * 64;
```

That accurately changes the monster's source image. Because the main program's render function is using sourceX and sourceY to display the sprite's image, the monster's state changes instantly.

> Note: You can use this same technique with hitTestPoint to make an interactive button for a game user interface with canvas. Use three button images that show the button's three different states: up, hover, and active. Create a sprite that represents this button. Then use hitTestPoint to find out if the mouse is over the button and change the button's state to display a different button image.

Changing a character's health meter

Many action games use a health meter to let you know how well a game character is doing. If the character bumps into something that's bad for it, like an enemy or a bullet, its health meter goes down. When it reaches zero, the poor character dies, and the game ends. ("Bhwahahaha!" The Evil Game Designer laughs wickedly!)

You can see a working example of this in the **healthMeter.html** program. Use the arrow keys to move the cat into the monster. The monster's health meter decreases while they're touching. When the meter is completely down to zero, "Game Over!" is displayed above it. Figure 8-19 shows what you'll see.

Figure 8-19. The health meter is reduced when the sprites collide

The health meter is actually two different sprites called innerMeter and outerMeter. innerMeter is a red line. outerMeter is a black border. You can see these in the **collisionTileSheet.png** file that this example is using.

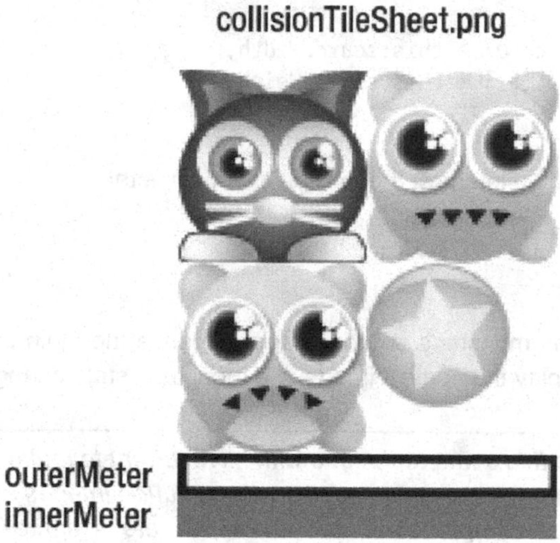

collisionTileSheet.png

outerMeter
innerMeter

Figure 8-20. The health meter is made from two sprites, each with separate images in the tilesheet

Each sprite is 128 pixels wide and 14 pixels high. (Yes, your sprites can be any size or shape, and you can place their images anywhere on the tilesheet.) You make these two sprites just like you would any other sprites.

```
//Create the innerMeter and center it above the monster
var innerMeter = Object.create(spriteObject);
innerMeter.sourceY = 142;
innerMeter.sourceWidth = 128;
innerMeter.sourceHeight = 14;
innerMeter.width = 128;
innerMeter.height = 14;
innerMeter.x = monster.x - 32;
innerMeter.y = monster.y - 32;
sprites.push(innerMeter);
```

```
//Create the outerMeter and position it over the inner meter
var outerMeter = Object.create(spriteObject);
outerMeter.sourceY = 128;
outerMeter.sourceWidth = 128;
outerMeter.sourceHeight = 14;
outerMeter.width = 128;
outerMeter.height = 14;
outerMeter.x = innerMeter.x;
outerMeter.y = innerMeter.y;
sprites.push(outerMeter);
```

The innerMeter is centered above the monster.

```
innerMeter.x = monster.x - 32;
innerMeter.y = monster.y - 32;
```

The outerMeter's X and Y positions are *exactly the same as those for the* innerMeter.

```
outerMeter.x = innerMeter.x;
outerMeter.y = innerMeter.y;
```

Because the outerMeter is added to the sprites array second, it's displayed above the innerMeter. And because the outerMeter's center is transparent, the innerMeter shows through from underneath. This makes these two separate sprites look like one single sprite.

The update function in the main program uses hitTestRectangle to check for a collision between the cat and the monster. If there's a collision, it reduces the innerMeter's width and sourceWidth by 1.

```
if(innerMeter.width > 0)
{
  innerMeter.width--;
  innerMeter.sourceWidth--;
}
```

It will reduce the width only if the innerMeter's width is greater than zero. This makes the health meter stop when it runs out.

It's important to reduce both the width and sourceWidth at the same time. That prevents the image of the innerMeter from distorting (appearing to become squashed) when its width is reduced. Keeping the width and sourceWidth synchronized means that the meter's image becomes cropped, rather than resized. You won't notice the difference in this example because the innerMeter is just a uniform solid color. But if your meter had a gradient fill or some sort of fill pattern, like a row of hearts, you'd definitely want to make sure to synchronize the width and sourceWidth to avoid distortion.

Another if statement in the update function checks to see if the innerMeter's width is less than 1. If it is, it displays the game over message.

```
if(innerMeter.width < 1)
{
  message = "Game Over!";
}
```

This message is displayed with the same canvas text-rendering system you learned at the beginning of the chapter.

Updating a score

Most games keep track of whether a player has won or lost by updating a score based on how well the player is doing. In this next example you'll learn how to update a score and end the game when a certain score has been reached. Run the **updateScore.html** program and try it out. Each time the cat bumps into the monster, the score is increased by 1. When the score reaches 5, "Game Over!" is displayed. Figure 8-21 shows what you'll see.

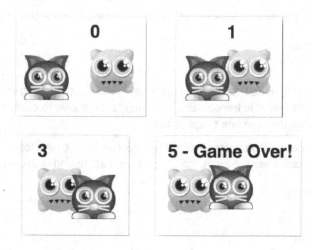

Figure 8-21. Use collision detection to increase a score

An important feature of this system is that the score only updates once each time the sprites touch. The score doesn't increase again until the sprites separate and then collide on a different occasion. This means the code has to disable the collision detection after the first frame in which it detects a collision. As you'll see, this is very easy to implement.

The program uses a score variable to count the score. It has another variable called collisionHasOccured that it uses to prevent further collisions after the first hit. A message variable will display the "Game Over!" text at the end of the game. The main program initializes these variables like this.

```
var score = 0;
var collisionHasOccured = false;
var message = "";
```

The update function checks for a collision using hitTestRectangle. When it detects a collision, it updates the score. It also sets collisionHasOccurred to true. This prevents the score from updating again during the current collision. When the sprites separate, collisionHasOccurred is set to false. That allows the score to be updated again in the next collision.

```
if(hitTestRectangle(cat, monster) && score < 5)
{
  if(!collisionHasOccurred)
  {
    score++;
    collisionHasOccurred = true;
  }
}
else
{
  collisionHasOccurred = false;
}
```

The code first checks to see if there's a collision and if the score is less than 5.

```
if(hitTestRectangle(cat, monster) && score < 5)
{
```

The next if statement then checks if collisionHasOccurred is false.

```
if(!collisionHasOccurred)
{
```

If all these tests pass, the score is updated by 1, and collisionHasOccurred is set to true.

```
score++;
collisionHasOccurred = true;
```

Because collisionHasOccurred is now true, the score won't be updated again, while the sprites are still touching.

If the sprites aren't touching, collisionHasOccurred is set to false.

```
else
{
  collisionHasOccurred = false;
}
```

This lets the score be updated again the next time the sprites collide.

Another if statement in the update function sets the "Game Over!" message if the score is 5:

```
if(score === 5)
{
  message = " - Game Over!";
}
```

The render function displays the score and the message above the monster.

```
drawingSurface.fillText(score + message, monster.x, monster.y - 40);
```

Any scoring system you'll need to use in your games will just be a variation of this basic system.

Preventing rectangles from overlapping

Now you know how to figure out if two rectangular sprites are touching. The next step is to prevent them from overlapping. This lets you make solid boundaries in your games, like walls or boxes. In this next section you'll learn how to do this.

How can you prevent two rectangles from overlapping? You can only do this if you know by how much they are overlapping when they collide. If you can figure this out, you can push the rectangles apart by the same amount. hitTestRectangle can't help you because it doesn't give you any information about the amount of overlap between the rectangles in a collision. Figure 8-22 illustrates this problem.

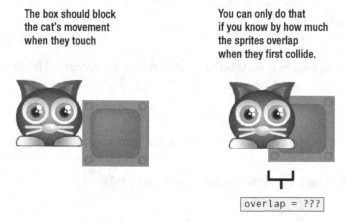

Figure 8-22. You can separate rectangular sprites in a collision if you know by how much they're overlapping. But how can you figure that out?

Let's look at a situation where these two sprites are overlapping. You know that a collision occurs between rectangles when the distance between them is less than their combined half-widths and half-heights. Figure 8-23 illustrates a typical example.

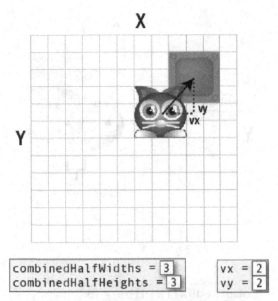

combinedHalfWidths = 3   vx = 2
combinedHalfHeights = 3   vy = 2

**The vx and vy values are less than the
combinedHalfWidths and combinedHalfHeights so
a collision is definitely occuring.**

Figure 8-23. The two sprites have collided

So how can we figure out by how much they're overlapping? You can do this with a very simple calculation. Just subtract the vector's vx and vy values from the sprites' half-widths and half-heights. Store the amounts in variables called overlapX and overlapY. Figure 8-24 illustrates why this works.

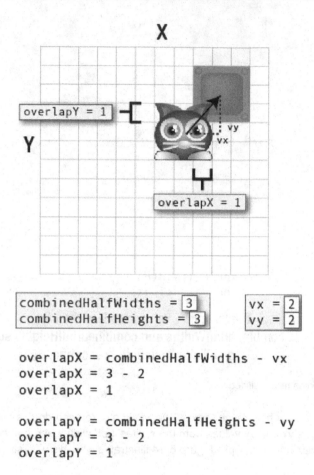

overlapX = combinedHalfWidths - vx
overlapX = 3 - 2
overlapX = 1

overlapY = combinedHalfHeights - vy
overlapY = 3 - 2
overlapY = 1

Figure 8-24. Figure out the amount of overlap

The last step is to separate the sprites so that they're not touching. Now that you know by how much they're overlapping, this is easy to do. Just subtract the amount of overlap from the sprite's X and Y positions, like this:

```
sprite.x = sprite.x - overlapX;
sprite.y = sprite.y - overlapY;
```

This is the same as saying that *the sprite's new position will be the same as its old position, minus the amount of overlap.*

This will move the sprite out of the collision. Figure 8-25 illustrates this.

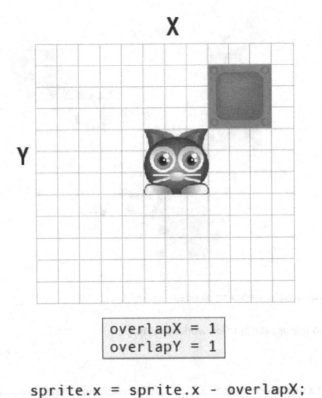

```
overlapX = 1
overlapY = 1
```

$$sprite.x = sprite.x - overlapX;$$
$$sprite.y = sprite.y - overlapY;$$

Figure 8-25. Subtract the amount of overlap from the sprite's current position to move it out of the collision

This system we've just looked at moves the sprite out of the collision on both the X and Y axes. However in most cases there will be slightly more overlap on the X axis or the Y axis. In that case, you want to move the sprite out of the collision on the axis that has the least amount of overlap. The axis with the least amount of overlap is the side on which the collision is occurring. We'll find out how to do this next.

Using the blockRectangle function

All you need to do next is convert this logic into programming code. You'll find a working example in the **blockingRectangles.html** file. Use the arrow keys to try and move the cat through the box. You can't, however, because the cat's movement is blocked in all directions. No matter how hard you try, the box and cat won't overlap. Figure 8-26 shows what you'll see.

Figure 8-26. The cat is blocked by the box on all sides

A single line of code in the update function works this magic.

```
blockRectangle(cat, box);
```

In some of your games it might be important to know on which side the collision is occurring on. The blockRectangle method has a very useful feature that tells you this. It returns a string back to the main program that tells you which side of the cat is touching the box. To find the collision side, change the above line in the example program so that it looks like this.

```
message = blockRectangle(cat, box);
```

Save and run the program again. The program now tells you which side of the cat is touching the box. It will display "left," "right," "top," or "bottom". (It will tell you the side of the sprite that you provided first in the function's arguments, the cat in this case.) If there's no collision, it displays "none." Figure 8-27 shows what you'll see. The render function displays the message text by using the same canvas text-rendering system we used in earlier examples.

Figure 8-27. Find out on which side the collision is occurring

You'll see how we'll use this information in the platform game that we'll make in Chapter 11.

The blockRectangle method has one more trick up its sleeve. Switch the order of the sprite arguments, so that they look like this.

```
blockRectangle(box, cat);
```

Save and run the program. The cat can now push the box all over the canvas, in any direction. Figure 8-28 illustrates this.

Figure 8-28. Let the cat push the box

How is this possible? By changing the order of the arguments, the effect of the code is on the box, not the cat. The only difference is that because the cat is moving, the box has to continuously reposition itself in front of the direction the cat is traveling in to prevent the two objects from overlapping.

Here's the entire blockRectangle function that does this. You'll notice that its first part checks for a collision between the sprites by using the same code from hitTestRectangle. What's new is the code that runs after the collision is detected. It figures out which direction the collision is occurring in. It then uses that information to calculate the amount of overlap between the rectangles, and it then separates them by that same amount. blockRectangle also has a variable called collisionSide that stores which side the collision occurs on. It returns the collisionSide variable to the main program so that can you use that information in the game if you need to. The function uses the names r1 and r2 (rectangle 1 and rectangle 2) to represent the sprites.

```
function blockRectangle(r1, r2)
{
  //A variable to tell us which side the collision is occurring on
  var collisionSide = "";

  //Calculate the distance vector
  var vx = r1.centerX() - r2.centerX();
  var vy = r1.centerY() - r2.centerY();

  //Figure out the combined half-widths and half-heights
  var combinedHalfWidths = r1.halfWidth() + r2.halfWidth();
  var combinedHalfHeights = r1.halfHeight() + r2.halfHeight();

  //Check whether vx is less than the combined half-widths
  if(Math.abs(vx) < combinedHalfWidths)
  {
    //A collision might be occurring!
    //Check whether vy is less than the combined half-heights
    if(Math.abs(vy) < combinedHalfHeights)
    {
      //A collision has occurred! This is good!
      //Find out the size of the overlap on both the X and Y axes
      var overlapX = combinedHalfWidths - Math.abs(vx);
      var overlapY = combinedHalfHeights - Math.abs(vy);

      //The collision has occurred on the axis with the
      //*smallest* amount of overlap. Let's figure out which
      //axis that is

      if(overlapX >= overlapY)
      {
        //The collision is happening on the X axis
        //But on which side? vy can tell us
        if(vy > 0)
        {
          collisionSide = "top";

          //Move the rectangle out of the collision
          r1.y = r1.y + overlapY;
        }
```

```
        else
        {
            collisionSide = "bottom";
            //Move the rectangle out of the collision
            r1.y = r1.y - overlapY;
        }
    }
    else
    {
        //The collision is happening on the Y axis
        //But on which side? vx can tell us
        if(vx > 0)
        {
            collisionSide = "left";

            //Move the rectangle out of the collision
            r1.x = r1.x + overlapX;
        }
        else
        {
            collisionSide = "right";

            //Move the rectangle out of the collision
            r1.x = r1.x - overlapX;
        }
    }
}
else
{
    //No collision
    collisionSide = "none";
}
}
else
{
    //No collision
    collisionSide = "none";
}

return collisionSide;
}
```

The first part of the function checks for a collision between the sprites by using the same code from hitTestRectangle. When it finds a collision, it first works out the amount of overlap on both the X and Y axes.

```
var overlapX = combinedHalfWidths - Math.abs(vx);
var overlapY = combinedHalfHeights - Math.abs(vy);
```

The code then compares these overlap values against the vx and vy values to find out on which side of the first object the collision is occurring. When the code knows that, it can use the correct overlap value to reposition the first sprite so that it's no longer touching the second sprite.

```
if(overlapX >= overlapY)
{
  //The collision is happening on the X axis
  //But on which side? vy can tell us
  if(vy > 0)
  {
    collisionSide = "top";

    //Move the rectangle out of the collision
    r1.y = r1.y + overlapY;
  }
  else
  {
    collisionSide = "bottom";

    //Move the rectangle out of the collision
    r1.y = r1.y - overlapY;
  }
}
else
{
  //The collision is happening on the Y axis
  //But on which side? vx can tell us
  if(vx > 0)
  {
    collisionSide = "left";

    //Move the rectangle out of the collision
    r1.x = r1.x + overlapX;
  }
  else
  {
    collisionSide = "right";

    //Move the rectangle out of the collision
    r1.x = r1.x - overlapX;
  }
}
```

The last thing it does is set collisionSide to "none" if there's no collision on either axis. It then returns the values of collisionSide ("top," ""bottom," "left," "right," or "none") to the main program.

```
    else
    {
      //No collision
      collisionSide = "none";
    }
  }
  else
  {
    //No collision
    collisionSide = "none";
  }

  return collisionSide;
}
```

And that's really all there is to it. You can see that the logic is slightly intricate, but if you spend a few minutes carefully stepping through the code in your own mind, you'll also see that it's pretty straightforward.

Because the `collisionSide` variable tells you the side of a collision, you could possibly use it in a game scenario like this:

```
var catsCollisionSide = blockRectangle(cat, box);
if(catsCollisionSide === "bottom")
{
  //The cat is standing on the box, so release the swarm of killer bees!
}
```

I'll leave it up to your skill and imagination to actually program this game. (I can't wait to play it!). In Chapter 11 you'll see how we can use collisionSide to help us make a platform game.

Using collision functions in your games

You learned how to make five very important collision functions in this chapter: hitTestPoint, hitTestCircle, blockCircle, hitTestRectangle, and blockRectangle. You'll be able to use them for countless game projects, over and over again. They're your bread and butter of collision detection.

But now that you know how they work, do you really want to bother typing them out or looking at them again? No way! You just want to make games. So to help you out, the chapter's source files contains a file called **collision.js**. It's a pure JavaScript file that just contains these five collision functions. If you ever need to use any of them in a game, just link the **collision.js** file to your main HTML file with a <script> tag like this.

```
<!doctype html>
<title>Any game</title>
<meta charset="utf-8">
<script src="collision.js"></script>
```

You can call these functions in exactly the same way as you would normally; they just won't be visible in your main program. This way you'll never have to think about these functions again or have them clutter up your game code. Have fun!

Summary

In this chapter you learned all the classic collision detection techniques for video games. You'll find that almost every 2D action game you'll make will use at least one of these techniques in some way.

But before you jump ahead to the next chapter, take a short break and make a game. Hey, don't be scared; you can do it! And that's what this book is all about, after all—making your own games. If you combine the collision detection techniques from this chapter with the player control techniques from Chapter 7, you have all the tools you need to make some pretty sophisticated games.

And that's what you're going to do in the next chapter. You're going to take all the skills you've learned so far and put them together to make your first real video game.

Chapter 9

Making Video Games

How can you take what you know about canvas, sprites, and collision detection and put them together to make a real game? This chapter will show you how. You're going to learn how to make a game called Alien Armada, shown in Figure 9-1. In this game, you will try to shoot down the invading aliens before they reach the bottom of the screen. It's just about the simplest video game you can make that contains all the elements for making most kinds of action arcade games. I'll walk you through each step of the development process, and at the end of the chapter you'll have a solid model for building video games of all kinds. If you know how to make this game, making a more complex game is just a matter of adding more detail.

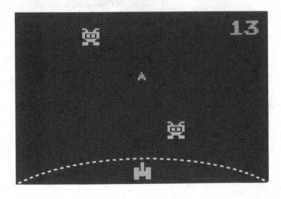

Figure 9-1. Shoot down 60 invading aliens to save the Earth

A unique feature of the game is that it uses sound effects and music. You'll find out how to add sounds to games at the end of this chapter.

The file and folder structure

Figure 9-2 illustrates how the game's folders and files are structured. It follows the same format as the other project in this book. The main JavaScript program code is in the **alienArmada.js** files, numbered from 1 to 6. Each new number represents a new phase of the game with more features. **alienArmadaFinished.js** is the final version of the game.

Figure 9-2. The game's files and folders

objects.js is a file that just contains the custom objects the game uses. It includes the spriteObject, alienObject, and messageObject. I'll introduce you to these objects as we work through the projects. I've kept all these objects in their own files so that they don't clutter up the game's main program code.

collision.js contains all the collision functions that you learned to use in Chapter 8.

The only code in the CSS file is the embedded font, which is used to display the score and game messages.

The **sound** folder contains the MP3 and OGG files, which are the sound effects and music. I'll show you how to add those to the game at the end of the chapter.

The tilesheet

In the **images** folder you'll find the tilesheet used in this game, shown in Figure 9-3. You can see that it includes the images for the cannon, alien, missile, explosion, and the game background.

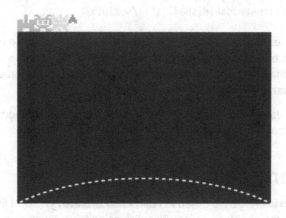

Figure 9-3. The **alienArmada.png** tilesheet

The HTML file

alienArmada.html loads the CSS and JS files, and it also sets up the canvas.

```
<!doctype html>
<meta charset="utf-8">
<title>Alien Armada!</title>

<!-- The stylesheet -->
<link rel="stylesheet" href="alienAttack.css">

<!-- The sounds -->
<audio id="music">
  <source src="../sounds/music.mp3" type="audio/mpeg" loop>
  <source src="../sounds/music.ogg" type="audio/ogg" loop>
</audio>
```

```
<audio id="shootSound">
  <source src="../sounds/shoot.mp3" type="audio/mpeg">
  <source src="../sounds/shoot.ogg" type="audio/ogg">
</audio>
<audio id="explosionSound">
  <source src="../sounds/explosion.mp3" type="audio/mpeg">
  <source src="../sounds/explosion.ogg" type="audio/ogg">
</audio>

<!-- The canvas -->
<canvas width="480" height="320"></canvas>

<!-- The game code -->
<script src="../src/objects.js"></script>
<script src="../src/collision.js"></script>
<script src="../src/alienArmadaFinished.js"></script>
```

The HTML files link three MP3 and OGG files by using the `<audio>` and `<source>` tags. You learned how to do this in Chapter 1. At the end of this chapter I'll show you how to play these sounds in your game. I've included these two file types so that the game will currently work with both Webkit-based browsers (Chrome and Safari) and Gecko-based browsers (Firefox).

This project loads the JavaScript code with the `<script>` tag's `src` property. This is the same system you learned at the end of Chapter 2 for linking a JavaScript file to an HTML file.

Starting the project

The final game program is in a JS file called **alienArmadaFinished.js**. You'll find it in the **src** folder of the **Alien Armada** project folder in the chapter's source files. I'm going to walk you through the design and development processes of each phase of this game. I've organized each phase into its own JS file, numbered **alienArmada1.js** to **alienArmada6.js**. To load and run each phase of the game, open the **alienArmada.html** file and change the src property of the `<script>` tag to load the correct JS file. For example, when you first open the HTML file, you'll see this `<script>` tag, which links to the finished game program.

```
<script src="../src/alienArmadaFinished.js"></script>
```

To load the first phase of the game, change the src property to **alienArmada1.js**, like this:

```
<script src="../src/alienArmada1.js"></script>
```

This first phase of the game creates the background and cannon sprite. It also sets up the cannon's keyboard control system and screen boundaries. You'll find that much of that code is very similar to the code we've used in previous chapters.

However, I've introduced two important new features:

■ A flexible system for loading lots of sounds and images. In previous chapters we only needed to load one image: the tilesheet. This game uses sounds as well as images, and before the game runs, all those sounds and images should be loaded and ready to use. You'll learn how to count the number of sounds and images you need to load, and then you can start the game only when they've finished loading.

■ A game state manager. A new way to change the game's state depending on whether the player is playing the game, has won, or has lost.

You're going to need to use these two features for almost every game you make from now on, and I'll explain exactly how they work in the pages ahead.

The alienArmada1.js file

As you learned in Chapter 2, if you want a linked JS file to run right away, you should insert it into an *immediate function*. The entire **alienArmada1.js** program is enclosed within the braces of an immediate function, like this:

```
(function(){

   //All the game's program code goes here

}());
```

alienArmada1.js does all the usual work of setting up the sprites and canvas and of loading the images. It sets up the game animation loop in the update function. It also lets the player control the cannon with the keyboard arrow keys and gives the cannon some screen boundaries. This is an important starting point for many games, so I'm going to list the entire file here for your reference.

The **game state manager** and the new system I've used to load the tilesheet are new components here. I'll explain how both features work in the pages ahead.

```
(function(){

//The canvas
var canvas = document.querySelector("canvas");

//Create the drawing surface
var drawingSurface = canvas.getContext("2d");

//Arrays to store the game objects and assets to load
var sprites = [];
var assetsToLoad = [];
```

```
//Create the background
var background = Object.create(spriteObject);
background.x = 0;
background.y = 0;
background.sourceY = 32;
background.sourceWidth = 480;
background.sourceHeight = 320;
background.width = 480;
background.height = 320;
sprites.push(background);

//Create the cannon and center it
var cannon = Object.create(spriteObject);
cannon.x = canvas.width / 2 - cannon.width / 2;
cannon.y = 280;
sprites.push(cannon);

//Load the tilesheet image
var image = new Image();
image.addEventListener("load", loadHandler, false);
image.src = "../images/alienArmada.png";
assetsToLoad.push(image);

//Variable to count the number of assets the game needs to load
var assetsLoaded = 0;

//Game states
var LOADING = 0
var PLAYING = 1;
var OVER = 2;
var gameState = LOADING;

//Arrow key codes
var RIGHT = 39;
var LEFT = 37;

//Directions
var moveRight = false;
var moveLeft = false;

//Add keyboard listeners
window.addEventListener("keydown", function(event)
{
  switch(event.keyCode)
  {
    case LEFT:
      moveLeft = true;
      break;
```

```
      case RIGHT:
        moveRight = true;
    }
}, false);

window.addEventListener("keyup", function(event)
{
    switch(event.keyCode)
    {
      case LEFT:
        moveLeft = false;
        break;

      case RIGHT:
        moveRight = false;
    }
}, false);
```

//Start the game animation loop
```
update();

function update()
{
```
    //The animation loop
```
    requestAnimationFrame(update, canvas);
```

    //Change what the game is doing based on the game state
```
    switch(gameState)
    {
    case LOADING:
        console.log("loading...");
        break;

      case PLAYING:
        playGame();
        break;

      case OVER:
        endGame();
        break;
    }
```

    //Render the game
```
    render();
}
```

```
function loadHandler()
{
  assetsLoaded++;
  if(assetsLoaded === assetsToLoad.length)
  {
      //Remove the load event listener
      image.removeEventListener("load", loadHandler, false);

      //Start the game
      gameState = PLAYING;
  }
}

function playGame()
{
    //Left
    if(moveLeft && !moveRight)
    {
      cannon.vx = -8;
    }
    //Right
    if(moveRight && !moveLeft)
    {
      cannon.vx = 8;
    }

    //Set the cannon's velocity to zero if none of the keys are being pressed
    if(!moveLeft && !moveRight)
    {
      cannon.vx = 0;
    }

    //Move the cannon and keep it within the screen boundaries
    cannon.x = Math.max(0, Math.min(cannon.x + cannon.vx, canvas.width - cannon.width));
}

function endGame()
{
 //Empty for now
}

function render()
{
 drawingSurface.clearRect(0, 0, canvas.width, canvas.height);

    //Display the sprites
    if(sprites.length !== 0)
```

```
{
  for(var i = 0; i < sprites.length; i++)
  {
    var sprite = sprites[i];
    drawingSurface.drawImage
    (
      image,
      sprite.sourceX, sprite.sourceY,
      sprite.sourceWidth, sprite.sourceHeight,
      Math.floor(sprite.x), Math.floor(sprite.y),
      sprite.width, sprite.height
    );
  }
}
}());
```

Loading multiple assets

Assets are what game designers call the images, sounds, videos, or other extra files that you want to use in your game. They could also be data files, like XML or JSON, that store game-level maps. In 3D games assets might be models and textures. In the previous two chapters our games have only needed to load one asset: a single PNG tilesheet image. In complex game projects you may need to load more than one tilesheet, and you'll certainly want to load numerous sounds.

All of these assets need to be loaded before the main part of your program runs. The reason for this is that if the program tries to access an asset that hasn't fully loaded, you'll either get an error message, or, more likely, the game will simply just not work and you won't know why.

If your game is being played over the Web and the sounds and images have to be loaded from a web server, it can take several seconds, or even minutes, for the game's assets to load. But even if you're just playing your game locally on your computer, it can take two or three milliseconds to load an image or sound. Your JavaScript programs run much faster than that, so you need to prevent your programs from continuing until all their assets have finished loading.

You know that when you want to load an image, you have to attach a load event listener to it. When the image has loaded, the loadHandler starts the game. If you want to load more than one image, your program has to count the number of images that have loaded and will run the rest of the program only when all images have finished loading. This is not difficult to do, and the system I'll show you next works as well for images as it does for sounds and videos.

Here's how I've used this system to load the Alien Armada tilesheet. First, you need an array to store the assets your game will load.

```
var assetsToLoad = [];
```

Next, create a reference to the asset you want to load, and then attach an event listener to it. Then push it into the assetsToLoad array.

```
var image = new Image();
image.addEventListener("load", loadHandler, false);
image.src = "../images/alienArmada.png";
assetsToLoad.push(image);
```

Create any more assets that you need (sounds, images, or videos) and push them into the assetsToLoad array if you need them. Make sure they all call the same loadHandler.

Next, create a variable called assetsLoaded that we'll use to count the assets when they load. Initialize it to zero.

```
var assetsLoaded = 0;
```

The next step is to add 1 to assetsLoaded each time the loadHandler runs. When assetsLoaded equals the number of elements in the assetsToLoad array, you know that everything has loaded. You can then start the game.

```
function loadHandler()
{
  assetsLoaded++;
  if(assetsLoaded === assetsToLoad.length)
  {
    //Remove the load event listener
    image.removeEventListener("load", loadHandler, false);

    //Start the game
    gameState = PLAYING;
  }
}
```

The event listener is no longer needed when everything has loaded. removeEventListener removes it.

```
image.removeEventListener("load", loadHandler, false);
```

The game then starts playing using this bit of code:

```
gameState = PLAYING;
```

What does that do? We'll find out next.

As long as you remember to push new assets that you want to load into the assetsToLoad array, this system will work for any number of things you want your game to load. You'll see how we use it at the end of the chapter to load the game's sound effects and music.

> *Note: This will all work if everything loads as you expect it to do. But what if an image or sound doesn't load? In a big game project, you should work out a system for dealing with this so that it's easier for you to debug the game if things go wrong. You could possibly do this by having a game state called ERROR that will display a compatibility page if something fails to load. You'll learn all about game states next.*

Using a game state manager

In previous chapters you learned how to use states to control the behavior of game objects. Using states is just as convenient for controlling the behavior of your entire game. Using game states can simplify a lot of your game logic because it means you won't have to set and check multiple Boolean variables to change how your game is behaving.

To use game states you first need to think about what the important states of your game are. For simple games, you'll have three: LOADING, PLAYING, and OVER. Those are the three states I've used in Alien Armada, although in more complex games you might have dozens of different states. I've defined the three states in the beginning of the program like this.

```
var LOADING = 0
var PLAYING = 1;
var OVER = 2;
var gameState = LOADING;
```

The game's initial state is set to LOADING. This is stored in the gameState variable.

After the game creates the sprites and initializes the game variables, the main program calls the update function.

```
update();
```

You know from previous chapters that the job of the update function is to run the game animation loop using setTimeout and call the render function. That's what it does in this game too, except it also has a new job. It uses a switch statement to call different functions based on the game's current state.

```
function update()
{
    //The animation loop
    requestAnimationFrame(update, canvas);

    //Change what the game is doing based on the game state
    switch(gameState)
    {
      case LOADING:
        console.log("loading...");
        break;
```

```
    case PLAYING:
      playGame();
      break;

    case OVER:
      endGame();
      break;
  }

    //Render the game
    render();
}
```

The functions it calls will change based on what the current game state is. This update function checks gameState 60 times per second, which means that if you change gameState from PLAYING to OVER anywhere in your code, it will change the game's behavior instantly.

When the game first loads, gameState is set to LOADING. When all the assets have finished loading, the loadHandler sets the gameState to PLAYING, as you saw in the previous section.

```
gameState = PLAYING;
```

As soon as this gameState is changed, the switch statement in the update function runs the PLAYING case.

```
case PLAYING:
  playGame();
  break;
```

It calls the playGame function. The playGame function is where all the game's core logic will be. In this version of the game, it sets the cannon's velocity and prevents it from crossing the right and left screen boundaries.

```
function playGame()
{
    //Left
    if(moveLeft && !moveRight)
    {
      cannon.vx = -8;
    }
    //Right
    if(moveRight && !moveLeft)
    {
      cannon.vx = 8;
    }

    //Set the cannon's velocity to zero if none of the keys are being pressed
    if(!moveLeft && !moveRight)
    {
      cannon.vx = 0;
    }
```

```
    //Move the cannon and keep it within the screen boundaries
    cannon.x = Math.max(0, Math.min(cannon.x + cannon.vx, canvas.width - cannon.width));
}
```

As you will soon see, the playGame function will become the heart of all our game code.

The switch statement in the update function also has an OVER state.

```
case OVER:
  endGame();
  break;
```

You can use this to end the game at anytime by setting the gameState to OVER, like this:

```
gameState = OVER;
```

You'll want to do this if the player wins or loses the game. If this happens, the endGame function will run.

```
function endGame()
{
    //Code that should run to end the game
}
```

endGame doesn't do anything in this first version of the game, but you'll see in later steps how we'll use it to end the game if the player wins or loses.

Now that we've got this basic game template set up and running, let's give the cannon some missiles to file.

Firing missiles

alienArmada2.js is the next version of the game, which lets the cannon fire missiles. Press the spacebar and the cannon will fire missiles toward the top of the screen, as shown in Figure 9-4.

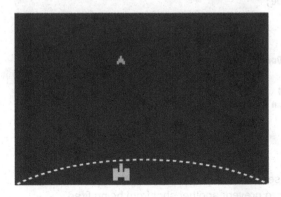

Figure 9-4. Press the spacebar to fire missiles

When the spacebar is pressed, a new missile sprite is created. It's added to a missiles array that contains all the missiles that are presently in the game. If the missile crosses the top of the screen, the game removes it from both the missiles array and the sprites array. Let's find out how this works.

The main program initializes an empty array called missiles that will store all the missiles that the player fires.

```
var missiles = [];
```

It then adds a constant to represent the SPACE key code.

```
var RIGHT = 39;
var LEFT = 37;
var SPACE = 32;
```

We also need two new variables to help us manage when missiles should be fired.

```
var shoot = false;
var spaceKeyIsDown = false;
```

We only want a missile to be fired when the spacebar is pressed once and released but not if the spacebar is held down continuously. The spaceKeyIsDown variable will tell us whether or not the spacebar is currently being held down. If it is, we want to prevent more than one missile being fired for each tap of the spacebar. Here's how these variables are handled with the keydown listener.

```
window.addEventListener("keydown", function(event)
{
  switch(event.keyCode)
  {
    case LEFT:
      moveLeft = true;
      break;

    case RIGHT:
      moveRight = true;
      break;

    case SPACE:
      if(!spaceKeyIsDown)
      {
        shoot = true;
        spaceKeyIsDown = true;
      }
  }
}, false);
```

If the spacebar is pressed, and it's not already down, the code sets the shoot variable to true. It also sets spaceKeyIsDown to true to prevent another shot from being fired.

```
case SPACE:
  if(!spaceKeyIsDown)
  {
    shoot = true;
    spaceKeyIsDown = true;
  }
```

spaceKeyIsDown will be true until the keyup event sets it back to false again.

```
window.addEventListener("keyup", function(event)
{
  switch(event.keyCode)
  {
    case LEFT:
      moveLeft = false;
      break;

    case RIGHT:
      moveRight = false;
      break;

    case SPACE:
      spaceKeyIsDown = false;
  }
}, false);
```

This will allow another shot to be fired after the spacebar is released.

The playGame function checks to see if shoot is true and, if it is, it calls the fireMissile function. It also sets shoot back to false to prevent more than one shot from being fired. Here's the if statement that does this: it's placed inside an abridged version of the playGame function so that you can see where it fits.

```
function playGame()
{
  //... code that sets the cannon's velocity...

  if(shoot)
  {
    fireMissile();
    shoot = false;
  }

  //... code that moves the cannon...
}
```

Here's the fireMissile function that does the work of creating a missile sprite. It sets its height and width, its speed (−8), centers it over the cannon, and pushes it into the sprites array. It also pushes it into the new missiles array.

```
function fireMissile()
{
    //Create a missile sprite
    var missile = Object.create(spriteObject);
    missile.sourceX = 96;
    missile.sourceWidth = 16;
    missile.sourceHeight = 16;
    missile.width = 16;
    missile.height = 16;

    //Center it over the cannon
    missile.x = cannon.centerX() - missile.halfWidth();
    missile.y = cannon.y - missile.height;

    //Set its speed
    missile.vy = -8;

    //Push the missile into both the sprites and missiles arrays
    sprites.push(missile);
    missiles.push(missile);
}
```

An important detail is that the missile is pushed into *two* arrays: the sprites array *and* the missiles array. The sprites array includes all the game sprites. It's used by the render function to draw the sprites with canvas. The missiles array only includes the missiles. It's used to move the missiles and check them for collisions with other sprites. You'll see how soon.

> *Note: It's actually possible to use only one array, the sprites array, although your code will end up being more complex. That's because you'll have to account for the different types of sprites that are in your game, because each of them needs to be handled in different ways. If you'd like to try this, create a new spriteObject property called type. When you create a new sprite, set its type to whatever kind of thing the game object is, like "missile" or "alien". Then to specifically deal with these objects, loop through the sprites array and check the type of each sprite. Only make changes to the type of sprite you're interested in. This isn't necessarily a better solution, and it's certainly more complex, so you'll need to decide for yourself which style you feel more comfortable working with.*

If you test the code at this point, you'll see that every time you press the spacebar a missile appears just above the cannon. The next step is to make the missile move. You do this in the playGame function. Here's the entire new playGame function with the code that makes the missiles move to the top of the screen. When they cross the top screen boundaries, they're removed.

```
function playGame()
{
    //Left
    if(moveLeft && !moveRight)
```

```
  {
    cannon.vx = -8;
  }
  //Right
  if(moveRight && !moveLeft)
  {
    cannon.vx = 8;
  }

  //Set the cannon's velocity to zero if none of the keys are being pressed
  if(!moveLeft && !moveRight)
  {
    cannon.vx = 0;
  }

  //Fire a missile if shoot is true
  if(shoot)
  {
    fireMissile();
    shoot = false;
  }

  //Move the cannon and keep it within the screen boundaries
  cannon.x = Math.max(0, Math.min(cannon.x + cannon.vx, canvas.width - cannon.width));

  //Move the missiles
  for(var i = 0; i < missiles.length; i++)
  {
    var missile = missiles[i];

    //Move it up the screen
    missile.y += missile.vy;

    //Remove the missile if it crosses the top of the screen
    if(missile.y < 0 - missile.height)
    {
      //Remove the missile from the missiles array
      removeObject(missile, missiles);

      //Remove the missile from the sprites array
      removeObject(missile, sprites);

      //Reduce the loop counter by 1 to compensate for the removed element
      i--;
    }
  }
}
```

The code loops through all the `missile` sprites in the `missiles` array. It first gets a reference to the current missile in the loop.

```
var missile = missiles[i];
```

It then applies the missile's vy value to its Y position. This is what makes it move up the screen.

```
missile.y += missile.vy;
```

The missiles were created with vy values of −8, which make them move up at 8 pixels per frame.

An `if` statement checks whether the missile has moved beyond the top of the screen. If it has, the new `removeObject` function removes it from both the `missile` array and the `sprites` array.

```
removeObject(missile, missiles);
removeObject(missile, sprites);
```

I'll show you how this custom function works in a moment.

The last thing the loop does is reduce the loop index variable by 1.

```
i--;
```

This compensates the loop counter for the object we've just removed.

Here's the `removeObject` function that removes the missile from the `missiles` and `sprites` arrays. It needs two parameters: the object you want to remove, and the array you want to remove it from. It uses `indexOf` to check whether the object is in the array and then, if it finds it, it splices it out of its current array index position.

```
function removeObject(objectToRemove, array)
{
  var i = array.indexOf(objectToRemove);
  if (i !== -1)
  {
    array.splice(i, 1);
  }
}
```

Your video games are often going to need to remove lots of objects, so keeping this work contained in a specialized function like this will save you from having to re-write lots of repetitive code.

Making aliens

The next phase of the game makes aliens appear at random positions above the top of the screen. A new alien appears once every 1.6 seconds, but gradually they start appearing with greater frequency. When the first alien reaches the bottom of the screen, "Game Over!" is displayed in the console. Open the **alienArmada3.js** file to find out how all this works. Figure 9-5 shows what you'll see when you run the program.

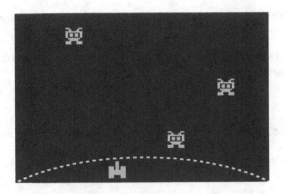

Figure 9-5. It's raining aliens!

The alienObject

In the **objects.js** file you'll find the alienObject. It's made using Object.create from the same spriteObject that we used in the previous chapter. It's got two states, NORMAL and EXPLODED, and an update method that changes its displayed state.

```
var alienObject = Object.create(spriteObject);
alienObject.NORMAL = 1;
alienObject.EXPLODED = 2;
alienObject.state = alienObject.NORMAL;
alienObject.update = function()
{
  this.sourceX = this.state * this.width;
};
```

We're going to make new aliens in the game by using this alienObject as the standard template. It contains all the properties of the original spriteObject, plus these new ones. We're not going to change the alien's state in this current phase of the project, but we will at a later phase.

The game also needs an array in which to store all the aliens. An empty aliens array is initialized by the main program when it creates all the other game object arrays.

```
var aliens = [];
```

The alien timer

The game needs to know how frequently it should create aliens. It uses a variable called alienFrequency that determines the number of milliseconds that should elapse before a new alien is made. The main program initializes alienFrequency to 100 when the game first starts.

```
var alienFrequency = 100;
```

The number 100 refers to the number of times that the game's playGame function will run before a new alien is made.

The game also needs a variable called alienTimer that will count the number of times the playGame function runs. It's initialized to zero.

```
var alienTimer = 0;
```

Here's the code from the abridged playGame function that figures out if the time is right to make a new alien.

```
Function playGame()
{

    //... the code that moves the cannon and missiles...

    //Add one to the alienTimer
    alienTimer++;

    //Make a new alien if alienTimer equals the alienFrequency
    if(alienTimer === alienFrequency)
    {
      makeAlien();
      alienTimer = 0;

      //Reduce alienFrequency by one to gradually increase the frequency that aliens are created
      if(alienFrequency > 2)
      {
        alienFrequency--;
      }
    }
}
```

Remember that playGame is being called by the update function 60 times per second. Each time it runs, it adds 1 to the alienTimer.

```
alienTimer++;
```

When alienTimer equals the alienFrequency, the makeAlien function is called.

```
if(alienTimer === alienFrequency)
{
  makeAlien();
}
```

If alienFrequency equals 100, it means that the playGame function will have run 100 times before it calls makeAlien. (That's about 1.6 seconds, because playGame runs at 60 frames per second.) You'll see how the makeAlien function adds a new alien to the game in the steps ahead.

The alienTimer is also reset back to zero so that it can start counting toward making the next new alien.

```
alienTimer = 0;
```

A feature of this game is that as you continue playing you'll notice that the aliens start to appear with greater frequency. That's because each time a new alien is created, `alienFrequency` is reduced by 1.

```
if(alienFrequency > 2)
{
  alienFrequency--;
}
```

This means that after the first alien is created, `alienFrequency` will equal 99. After the second alien, `alienFrequency` will equal 98. The longer you play, the more quickly aliens will appear and the harder the game gets.

The makeAlien function

The job of actually adding the alien to the game is done by the `makeAlien` function. It's very similar to the `fireMissile` function. It creates an `alien` sprite, gives it a random X position, assigns its velocity, and adds it to the `sprites` and `aliens` arrays.

```
function makeAlien()
{
    //Create the alien
    var alien = Object.create(alienObject);
    alien.sourceX = 32;

    //Set its Y position above the top screen boundary
    alien.y = 0 - alien.height;

    //Assign the alien a random X position
    var randomPosition = Math.floor(Math.random() * 15);
    alien.x = randomPosition * alien.width;

    //Set its speed
    alien.vy = 1;

    //Push the alien into both the sprites and aliens arrays
    sprites.push(alien);
    aliens.push(alien);
}
```

The aliens are added to the game just beyond the top of the screen. Here's their starting Y position.

```
alien.y = 0 - alien.height;
```

The aliens are each 32 pixels high, so the start Y position will be −32. (The top of the screen is a Y position of 0, which means that −32 will place the aliens 32 pixels *above* that.) When they start moving it means they emerge gradually from the top of the screen, as though they're arriving from a long journey through deep space.

The aliens are each given a random X position. Each alien is 32 pixels wide, and the canvas is 480 pixels wide. That means that there are 15 possible start X positions that the aliens can evenly occupy without overlapping (480 / 32 = 15). The code does this by choosing a random number between 0 and 14 and then multiplying it by the alien's width.

```
var randomPosition = Math.floor(Math.random() * 15);
alien.x = randomPosition * alien.width;
```

The result is that the aliens appear to emerge from 1 of 15 fixed positions along the top of the screen.

> *Note: You can modify this line of code so that the number of fixed positions are worked out automatically. Just replace 15 with (canvas.width / alien.width).*
>
> *var randomPosition = Math.floor(Math.random() * (canvas.width / alien.width));*

Very importantly, the new alien is pushed into both the sprites and aliens arrays.

```
sprites.push(alien);
aliens.push(alien);
```

Now let's find out how the aliens move from the top to the bottom of the screen.

Moving the aliens

The playGame function has the job of moving the aliens. It does this in a loop just below the alien timer code. Here's an abridged version of the playGame function with the code that does this.

```
function playGame()
{
    //... The cannon, missiles, and alien timer...

    //Loop through the aliens
    for(var i = 0; i < aliens.length; i++)
    {
        var alien = aliens[i];

        if(alien.state === alien.NORMAL)
        {
            //Move the current alien if its state is NORMAL
            alien.y += alien.vy;
        }

        //Check if the alien has crossed the bottom of the screen
        if(alien.y > canvas.height + alien.height)
```

```
    {
        //End the game if an alien has reached Earth
        gameState = OVER;
    }
}

}
```

The code loops through all the `alien` objects in the `aliens` array. If the alien's state is `NORMAL`, it moves the alien.

```
if(alien.state === alien.NORMAL)
{
    alien.y += alien.vy;
}
```

The aliens all have an initial state of `NORMAL` when they're created, and there's no code in this phase of the game that changes their state. (However, they'll stop moving when their state is set to `EXPLODED`, which you'll see later.)

The code then checks to see if the alien has crossed the bottom boundary of the screen:

```
if(alien.y > canvas.height + alien.height)
{
    //End the game if an alien has reached Earth
    gameState = OVER;
}
```

If it has, the `gameState` is set to `OVER`. This is a good example of a game state change. As soon as this happens, the `switch` statement in the `update` function runs the `OVER` case, highlighted below.

```
function update()
{
    requestAnimationFrame(update, canvas);

    switch(gameState)
    {
        case LOADING:
            console.log("loading...");
            break;

        case PLAYING:
            playGame();
            break;

        case OVER:
            endGame();
            break;
    }
```

```
//Render the game
render();
}
```

You can see that it calls the endGame function. In this phase of the game the endGame function's only job is to display "Game Over!" in the console.

```
function endGame()
{
  console.log("Game Over!");
}
```

You'll also notice that when the game state changes to OVER, it has a very useful side effect: all the action stops on the screen. The aliens, cannon, and missiles stop moving. That's because the playGame function that was doing the job of moving them isn't being called anymore. The game's action is completely frozen, which is great, because that's usually what you want to have happen when a game ends. This is all thanks to our simple little game state manager.

We've got aliens and we've got missiles—now let's make them collide!

Shooting down aliens

alienArmada4.js is the next version of the game that lets you shoot down the aliens. When a missile hits an alien, the missile disappears and the alien image is replaced with an image of an explosion. After one second, the explosion image also disappears. Figure 9-6 show what you'll see when you run the game.

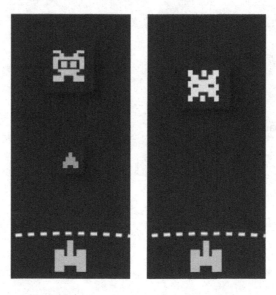

Figure 9-6. Fire missiles to shoot down the aliens

Each time an alien is hit, 1 is added to the game's score. The main program initializes a score variable to zero when the game first loads. It creates another variable called scoreNeededToWin, which determines the number of aliens the player needs to shoot down to win the game.

```
var score = 0;
var scoreNeededToWin = 60;
```

The code loops through all the aliens and uses hitTestRectangle to find out if any of them are colliding with any of the missiles. If there is a collision, the missile is removed and the alien is destroyed with the custom destroyAlien function. This loop happens inside the playGame function just after the previous code that moves the aliens.

```
for(var i = 0; i < aliens.length; i++)
{
  var alien = aliens[i];

  for(var j = 0; j < missiles.length; j++)
  {
    var missile = missiles[j];

    if(hitTestRectangle(missile, alien)
    && alien.state === alien.NORMAL)
    {
      //Destroy the alien
      destroyAlien(alien);

      //Update the score
      score++;

      //Remove the missile
      removeObject(missile, missiles);
      removeObject(missile, sprites);

      //Subtract 1 from the loop counter to compensate for the removed missile
      j--;
    }
  }
}
```

This code needs to check for a collision between all the aliens and all the missiles. It first loops through all the aliens. The current alien in the loop is assigned to a temporary variable called alien. Another loop then runs to check that alien against all the missiles. The current missile that's being checked in this second loop is assigned to a temporary variable called missile.

```
for(var i = 0; i < aliens.length; i++)
{
  var alien = aliens[i];
```

```
for(var j = 0; j < missiles.length; j++)
{
  var missile = missiles[j];
  ...
```

Two loops working together like this is called a **nested for loop**. It's just a loop inside a loop. It guarantees that all the aliens will be checked for collisions against all the missiles.

> Note: In a nested for loop, the second loop uses a counter variable called "j".

An `if` statement then uses `hitTestRectangle` to find out if the missile and alien are touching and if the alien's state is `NORMAL`.

```
if(hitTestRectangle(missile, alien) && alien.state === alien.NORMAL)
{...
```

The alien's state needs to be `NORMAL` because we don't want to check for a collision if it's already been hit and had its state changed to `EXPLODED`. You'll see why soon.

If there's a collision, the alien is sent to the `destroyAlien` function, which I'll explain ahead.

```
destroyAlien(alien);
```

The code then adds 1 to the player's score, removes the missile using the `removeObject` function, and reduces the loop counter by 1.

```
score++;
removeObject(missile, missiles);
removeObject(missile, sprites);
j--;
```

The loop counter needs to be reduced by 1 to compensate for the removed element.

The `destroyAlien` function changes the alien's state to `EXPLODED`. It also removes the alien from the game after one second.

```
function destroyAlien(alien)
{

  //Change the alien's state and update the object
  alien.state = alien.EXPLODED;
  alien.update();

  //Remove the alien after one second
  setTimeout(removeAlien, 1000);
```

```
  function removeAlien()
  {
    removeObject(alien, aliens);
    removeObject(alien, sprites);
  }
}
```

When the alien is hit by a missile, its EXPLODED state displays the explosion image from the tilesheet. It uses the same system for changing an object's state that you learned in Chapter 8.

```
alien.state = alien.EXPLODED;
alien.update();
```

While the alien's state is EXPLODED, it stops moving down the screen and can't be hit by more missiles.

The explosion is visible on the screen for one second before it disappears. I created this delay by using setTimeout and calling a function called removeAlien after 1,000 milliseconds.

```
setTimeout(removeAlien, 1000);

function removeAlien()
{
  removeObject(alien, aliens);
  removeObject(alien, sprites);
}
```

A new feature of this code is that the removeAlien function is actually inside the destroyAlien function.

These are all the basic techniques you need to know for collision detection in these kinds of action video games.

Now let's find out how the game displays the score and game over messages.

Displaying game messages

Run the **alienArmada5.js** to see the next version of the game that displays the messages. It displays these three things:

- A score that shows you the number of aliens hit.
- A message that says "EARTH SAVED!" if you shoot 60 aliens.
- A message that says "EARTH DESTROYED!" if one of the aliens makes it to the bottom of the screen.

Figure 9-7 illustrates these. Let's find out how they work.

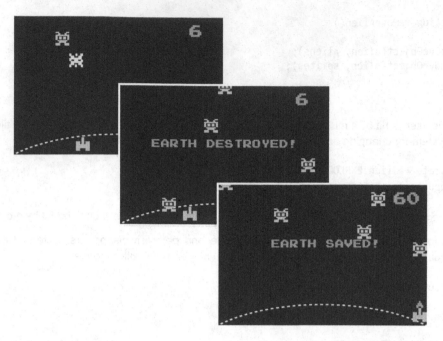

Figure 9-7. The game's messages

Setting up the game messages

The messages are displayed in the emulogic font. You'll find it in the **fonts** folder and it's embedded by the CSS file.

```css
@font-face
{
  font-family: emulogic;
  src: url("../fonts/emulogic.ttf");
}
```

> Note: If you're making a commercial game, make sure that you have the rights to the fonts you're using. Many fonts, just like images, need to be purchased and licensed. You can find a selection of excellent and completely free fonts at these websites: www.fontsquirrel.com, www.google.com/webfonts, and www.edgefonts.com.

The message text is displayed with canvas by using the same simple system we used in Chapter 8. In the **objects.js** file you'll find a messageObject that the game uses to create messages.

```
var messageObject =
{
  x: 0,
  y: 0,
  visible: true,
  text: "Message",
  font: "normal bold 20px Helvetica",
  fillStyle: "red",
  textBaseline: "top"
};
```

It includes these default settings so that you can test to make sure your game messages are working. You'll customize all these properties when you create new messages from this messageObject template.

All the game messages are stored in an array called messages. It's initialized as empty by the main program when the game first loads.

```
var messages = [];
```

The render function then needs to know how to display a message. Here's the code in the render function that does this.

```
function render()
{

  //... the code that renders the sprites...

  //Display game messages
  if(messages.length !== 0)
  {
    for(var i = 0; i < messages.length; i++)
    {
      var message = messages[i];
      if(message.visible)
      {
        drawingSurface.font = message.font;
        drawingSurface.fillStyle = message.fillStyle;
        drawingSurface.textBaseline = message.textBaseline;
        drawingSurface.fillText(message.text, message.x, message.y);
      }
    }
  }
}
```

The main program creates two message objects: scoreDisplay and gameOverMessage. scoreDisplay's job is to display the score variable in the top right corner of the screen. It's assigned an X and Y position and a font, and it is then pushed into the messages array.

```
var scoreDisplay = Object.create(messageObject);
scoreDisplay.font = "normal bold 30px emulogic";
scoreDisplay.fillStyle = "00FF00";
scoreDisplay.x = 400;
scoreDisplay.y = 10;
messages.push(scoreDisplay);
```

The gameOverMessage displays the message the player sees at the end of the game. It's set up in the same way, but there's one important difference. Its visible property is set to false. You can see this in the highlighted code below.

```
var gameOverMessage = Object.create(messageObject);
gameOverMessage.font = "normal bold 20px emulogic";
gameOverMessage.fillStyle = "00FF00";
gameOverMessage.x = 70;
gameOverMessage.y = 120;
gameOverMessage.visible = false;
messages.push(gameOverMessage);
```

visible is false so that the gameOverMessage isn't displayed when the game first starts. The game will set visible to true only after the game has finished and it's time to display the game over message.

Displaying the score and ending the game

Whenever the player shoots down an alien, 1 is added to the score. The new score is displayed immediately with this line of code:

```
scoreDisplay.text = score;
```

That's all that's needed to display the updated score throughout the entire game.

The next new line of code checks whether the score equals scoreNeededToWin. If it does, the gameState is set to OVER.

```
if(score === scoreNeededToWin)
{
    gameState = OVER;
}
```

As you know, when the gameState becomes OVER the endGame function is run. It's the endGame function that displays the game over messages, so let's see what it does.

Displaying the game over messages

Here's the endGame function that displays the game over messages. The first thing it does is set the gameOverMessage's visible property to true. It then checks whether the player achieved the scoreNeededToWin. A different message is displayed depending on the outcome.

```
function endGame()
{
  gameOverMessage.visible = true;

  if(score < scoreNeededToWin)
  {
    gameOverMessage.text = "EARTH DESTROYED!";
  }
  else
  {
    gameOverMessage.x = 120;
    gameOverMessage.text = "EARTH SAVED!";
  }
}
```

(The gameOverMessage's X position is changed to 120 if it displays "EARTH SAVED!" so that the text is centered in the screen.)

We now have a complete working game. The last step is to add some sound effects and music.

Adding sound

Open and run **alienArmada6.js** for the next version of the game that includes sound. You'll hear music playing in the background and sound effects when you shoot missiles and the aliens explode.

The first step to using sound is to link the sound files to the HTML file. Open **alienArmada.html** and you'll see that the <audio> tags link the three sounds that we're going to use in the game.

```
<audio id="music">
  <source src="../sounds/music.mp3" type="audio/mpeg" loop>
  <source src="../sounds/music.ogg" type="audio/ogg" loop>
</audio>
<audio id="shootSound">
  <source src="../sounds/shoot.mp3" type="audio/mpeg">
  <source src="../sounds/shoot.ogg" type="audio/ogg">
</audio>
<audio id="explosionSound">
  <source src="../sounds/explosion.mp3" type="audio/mpeg">
  <source src="../sounds/explosion.ogg" type="audio/ogg">
</audio>
```

The sounds are in both MP3 and OGG formats in order to maintain broad current compatibility across different browsers.

Note: You can use open source software called Audacity to help you convert sounds to different file types.

The first file, music, contains some game music. Notice that it includes the loop attribute. This will make the music loop continuously throughout the game. shootSound is the sound the cannon makes when it fires missiles, and explosionSound is the sound that the aliens make when they explode.

The HTML file links these sounds, but the JavaScript program has to load them before they can be used in the game. Let's find out how.

> *Note: At the time of writing, only Safari, Chrome, and the latest version of Internet Explorer support MP3 audio files. OGG sound files are supported by Firefox. Sound-file compatibility across browsers changes frequently, so make sure you're aware of which formats are currently supported by the browsers you're targeting.*
>
> *If you're looking for music for your games, software like GarageBand or ACID Pro can help you make soundtracks easily with precomposed loops. You can also purchase royalty-free music for use in your game from many websites. If you're feeling adventurous, let a computer compose your soundtrack for you at* tones.wolfram.com.

Loading sounds

Here's the code at the beginning of the program that loads the sounds. This code appears just under the code that loads the tilesheet image. Each sound is loaded in the same way, using a few new methods and events you haven't seen before. I'll explain how this works next.

```
var music = document.querySelector("#music");
music.addEventListener("canplaythrough", loadHandler, false);
music.load();
assetsToLoad.push(music);

var shootSound = document.querySelector("#shootSound");
shootSound.addEventListener("canplaythrough", loadHandler, false);
shootSound.load();
assetsToLoad.push(shootSound);

var explosionSound = document.querySelector("#explosionSound");
explosionSound.addEventListener("canplaythrough", loadHandler, false);
explosionSound.load();
assetsToLoad.push(explosionSound);
```

The code first needs to create a reference to the sound by assigning it to a variable.

```
var music = document.querySelector("#music");
```

Next, it adds an event listener to the sound.

```
music.addEventListener("canplaythrough", loadHandler, false);
```

The event is called `canplaythrough`. This event is triggered when the program determines that it "can play through" the entire sound from beginning to end. If it can, it means the sound has been completely loaded. You can see that the listener will call the `loadHandler` when the sound is loaded. The `loadHandler` is the same one that's called when the tilesheet image is loaded. You'll see how the `loadHandler` loads the sounds and images in the steps ahead.

The program then uses the `load` method to load the sound.

```
music.load()
```

It then pushes it into the `assetsToLoad` array.

```
assetsToLoad.push(music);
```

All three sounds and the tilesheet image call the `loadHandler` when they've finished loading.

```
function loadHandler()
{
  assetsLoaded++;
  if(assetsLoaded === assetsToLoad.length)
  {
    //Remove the load event listener from the image and sounds
    image.removeEventListener("load", loadHandler, false);
    music.removeEventListener("canplaythrough", loadHandler, false);
    shootSound.removeEventListener("canplaythrough", loadHandler, false);
    explosionSound.removeEventListener("canplaythrough", loadHandler, false);

    //Play the music
    music.play();
    music.volume = 0.3;

    //Start the game
    gameState = PLAYING;
  }
}
```

All the sounds and the image have been added to the `assetsToLoad` array, which means that `assetsToLoad` will equal four when everything has loaded. The `if` statement then removes all the event listeners.

```
image.removeEventListener("load", loadHandler, false);
music.removeEventListener("canplaythrough", loadHandler, false);
shootSound.removeEventListener("canplaythrough", loadHandler, false);
explosionSound.removeEventListener("canplaythrough", loadHandler, false);
```

The music will start playing as soon as the game starts. You can make any sound play with the `play` method.

```
music.play();
```

I also want the music to play more quietly than the other game sounds. You can control how loud or quiet a sound is with the volume property. It accepts any values between 0 (inaudible) to 1 (full volume) I've set the music's volume to 0.3, which is about one-third of its maximum level.

```
music.volume = 0.3;
```

Finally, the if statement changes the gameState to PLAYING to start the game.

```
gameState = PLAYING;
```

Now that the sounds are loaded and the music is playing, let's find out how to play the sound effects.

> Note: You may also want the game to work if no sounds are loaded. In that case, push your sounds into a soundsToLoad array and use a soundLoadHandler to check whether sounds have loaded. Use a variable called soundsLoaded to count the sounds that have loaded successfully. Then you'll need to decide how your program should behave if the sounds don't load or if they don't load after a certain amount of time.

Playing sound effects

You can make any sound effect play by using the play method when you want it to be heard. When the player fires missiles, the shootSound should play. Here's the new code that's been added to the fireMissile function that plays the sound.

```
function fireMissile()
{
    //... the code that creates the missile...

    //Play the firing sound
    shootSound.currentTime = 0;
    shootSound.play();
}
```

The first thing the code does is set the shootSound's currentTime property to 0.

```
shootSound.currentTime = 0;
```

This resets the sound to its start position. It's like pushing the play button to get right to the beginning of the track. currentTime is a number in milliseconds. The very beginning of the sound is 0. If you want to make a sound play from a start position other than the beginning, give currentTime any other number in milliseconds. For example, if you wanted a sound to start playing from the five-second mark, set currentTime to 5,000.

All you need to do next is call the sound's play method.

```
    shootSound.play();
```

You'll now hear the shootSound whenever you fire a missile. The explosion sound works in exactly the same way.

explosionSound should play whenever an alien explodes. These two new lines of code in the destroyAlien function make it play.

```
function destroyAlien(alien)
{

    //...change the alien's state and remove it...

    //Play the explosion sound
    explosionSound.currentTime = 0;
    explosionSound.play();
}
```

You can see that it uses exactly the same code that we used to make the shootSound play.

More about sound for games

These are most of the techniques you need to know to add sound effects and music to most games. However, sounds have many more properties and events that can give you much finer control. Do a web search for "HTML5 sound properties and events" to bring up a complete list.

At the time of writing, web browser support for sound is a little bit quirky. That means sounds don't always play the way they should. Some web browsers seem to struggle most when they try to play multiple instances of the same sound in rapid succession, which, unfortunately, is a common requirement in games. It's likely that these problems will have been solved by the latest versions of browsers by the time you're reading this.

> Note: You may also want to consider using the Web Audio API. This is a newer set of JavaScript methods and events for loading and playing sound that are designed to be very precise and should handle playing multiple instances of the same sound well. The Web Audio API is still experimental at the time of writing, but most of the current browsers support it with the use of vendor prefixes like "moz" or "webkit." Do a web search for "Web Audio API" for details.

The final game code

Here's the complete game code from the **alienArmadaFinished.js** file that you can use as a reference.

```
(function(){

//The canvas
var canvas = document.querySelector("canvas");
```

```
//Create the drawing surface
var drawingSurface = canvas.getContext("2d");

//Arrays to store the game objects and assets to load
var sprites = [];
var assetsToLoad = [];
var missiles = [];
var aliens = [];
var messages = [];

//Create the background
var background = Object.create(spriteObject);
background.x = 0;
background.y = 0;
background.sourceY = 32;
background.sourceWidth = 480;
background.sourceHeight = 320;
background.width = 480;
background.height = 320;
sprites.push(background);

//Create the cannon and center it
var cannon = Object.create(spriteObject);
cannon.x = canvas.width / 2 - cannon.width / 2;
cannon.y = 280;
sprites.push(cannon);

//Create the score message
var scoreDisplay = Object.create(messageObject);
scoreDisplay.font = "normal bold 30px emulogic";
scoreDisplay.fillStyle = "#00FF00";
scoreDisplay.x = 400;
scoreDisplay.y = 10;
messages.push(scoreDisplay);

//The game over message
var gameOverMessage = Object.create(messageObject);
gameOverMessage.font = "normal bold 20px emulogic";
gameOverMessage.fillStyle = "#00FF00";
gameOverMessage.x = 70;
gameOverMessage.y = 120;
gameOverMessage.visible = false;
messages.push(gameOverMessage);

//Load the tilesheet image
var image = new Image();
image.addEventListener("load", loadHandler, false);
image.src = "../images/alienArmada.png";
assetsToLoad.push(image);
```

```
//Load the sounds
var music = document.querySelector("#music");
music.addEventListener("canplaythrough", loadHandler, false);
music.load();
assetsToLoad.push(music);

var shootSound = document.querySelector("#shootSound");
shootSound.addEventListener("canplaythrough", loadHandler, false);
shootSound.load();
assetsToLoad.push(shootSound);

var explosionSound = document.querySelector("#explosionSound");
explosionSound.addEventListener("canplaythrough", loadHandler, false);
explosionSound.load();
assetsToLoad.push(explosionSound);

//Variable to count the number of assets the game needs to load
var assetsLoaded = 0;

//Game states
var LOADING = 0
var PLAYING = 1;
var OVER = 2;
var gameState = LOADING;

//Arrow key codes
var RIGHT = 39;
var LEFT = 37;
var SPACE = 32;

//Directions
var moveRight = false;
var moveLeft = false;

//Variables to help fire missiles
var shoot = false;
var spaceKeyIsDown = false;

//Game variables
var score = 0;
var scoreNeededToWin = 60;
var alienFrequency = 100;
var alienTimer = 0;
```

```
//Add keyboard listeners
window.addEventListener("keydown", function(event)
{
  switch(event.keyCode)
  {
    case LEFT:
      moveLeft = true;
      break;

    case RIGHT:
      moveRight = true;
      break;

    case SPACE:
      if(!spaceKeyIsDown)
      {
        shoot = true;
        spaceKeyIsDown = true;
      }
  }

}, false);

window.addEventListener("keyup", function(event)
{
  switch(event.keyCode)
  {
    case LEFT:
      moveLeft = false;
      break;

    case RIGHT:
      moveRight = false;
      break;

    case SPACE:
      spaceKeyIsDown = false;
  }
}, false);

//Start the game animation loop
update();

function update()
{
    //The animation loop
    requestAnimationFrame(update, canvas);
```

```
  //Change what the game is doing based on the game state
  switch(gameState)
  {
    case LOADING:
      console.log("loading...");
      break;

    case PLAYING:
      playGame();
      break;

    case OVER:
      endGame();
      break;
  }

  //Render the game
  render();
}

function loadHandler()
{
  assetsLoaded++;
  if(assetsLoaded === assetsToLoad.length)
  {
    //Remove the load event listener from the image and sounds
    image.removeEventListener("load", loadHandler, false);
    music.removeEventListener("canplaythrough", loadHandler, false);
    shootSound.removeEventListener("canplaythrough", loadHandler, false);
    explosionSound.removeEventListener("canplaythrough", loadHandler, false);

    //Play the music
    music.play();
    music.volume = 0.3;

    //Start the game
    gameState = PLAYING;
  }
}

function playGame()
{
  //Left
  if(moveLeft && !moveRight)
  {
    cannon.vx = -8;
  }
```

```
//Right
if(moveRight && !moveLeft)
{
  cannon.vx = 8;
}

//Set the cannon's velocity to zero if none of the keys are being pressed
if(!moveLeft && !moveRight)
{
  cannon.vx = 0;
}

//Fire a missile if shoot is true
if(shoot)
{
  fireMissile();
  shoot = false;
}

//Move the cannon and keep it within the screen boundaries
cannon.x = Math.max(0, Math.min(cannon.x + cannon.vx, canvas.width - cannon.width));

//Move the missiles
for(var i = 0; i < missiles.length; i++)
{
  var missile = missiles[i];

  //Move it up the screen
  missile.y += missile.vy;

  //Remove the missile if it crosses the top of the screen
  if(missile.y < 0 - missile.height)
  {
    //Remove the missile from the missiles array
    removeObject(missile, missiles);

    //Remove the missile from the sprites array
    removeObject(missile, sprites);

    //Reduce the loop counter by 1 to compensate for the removed element
    i--;
  }
}

//Make the aliens

//Add one to the alienTimer
alienTimer++;
```

```
//Make a new alien if alienTimer equals the alienFrequency
if(alienTimer === alienFrequency)
{
  makeAlien();
  alienTimer = 0;

  //Reduce alienFrequency by one to gradually increase the frequency that aliens are created
  if(alienFrequency > 2)
  {
    alienFrequency--;
  }
}

//Loop through the aliens
for(var i = 0; i < aliens.length; i++)
{
  var alien = aliens[i];

  if(alien.state === alien.NORMAL)
  {
      //Move the current alien if its state is NORMAL
      alien.y += alien.vy;
  }

  //Check if the alien has crossed the bottom of the screen
  if(alien.y > canvas.height + alien.height)
  {
      //End the game if an alien has reached Earth
      gameState = OVER;
  }
}

//--- The collisions

//Check for a collision between the aliens and missiles
for(var i = 0; i < aliens.length; i++)
{
  var alien = aliens[i];

  for(var j = 0; j < missiles.length; j++)
  {
    var missile = missiles[j];

    if(hitTestRectangle(missile, alien)
    && alien.state === alien.NORMAL)
    {
        //Destroy the alien
        destroyAlien(alien);
```

```
                //Update the score
                score++;

                //Remove the missile
                removeObject(missile, missiles);
                removeObject(missile, sprites);

                //Subtract 1 from the loop counter to compensate for the removed missile
                j--;
            }
        }
    }

    //--- The score

    //Display the score
    scoreDisplay.text = score;

    //Check for the end of the game
    if(score === scoreNeededToWin)
    {
        gameState = OVER;
    }
}

function destroyAlien(alien)
{
    //Change the alien's state and update the object
    alien.state = alien.EXPLODED;
    alien.update();

    //Remove the alien after one second
    setTimeout(removeAlien, 1000);

    //Play the explosion sound
    explosionSound.currentTime = 0;
    explosionSound.play();

    function removeAlien()
    {
        removeObject(alien, aliens);
        removeObject(alien, sprites);
    }
}
```

```
function endGame()
{
  gameOverMessage.visible = true;
  if(score < scoreNeededToWin)
  {
    gameOverMessage.text = "EARTH DESTROYED!";
  }
  else
  {
    gameOverMessage.x = 120;
    gameOverMessage.text = "EARTH SAVED!";
  }
}

function makeAlien()
{
    //Create the alien
    var alien = Object.create(alienObject);
    alien.sourceX = 32;

    //Set its Y position above the screen boundary
    alien.y = 0 - alien.height;

    //Assign the alien a random X position
    var randomPosition = Math.floor(Math.random() * 15);
    alien.x = randomPosition * alien.width;

    //Set its speed
    alien.vy = 1;

    //Push the alien into both the sprites and aliens arrays
    sprites.push(alien);
    aliens.push(alien);
}

function fireMissile()
{
    //Create a missile sprite
    var missile = Object.create(spriteObject);
    missile.sourceX = 96;
    missile.sourceWidth = 16;
    missile.sourceHeight = 16;
    missile.width = 16;
    missile.height = 16;

    //Center it over the cannon
    missile.x = cannon.centerX() - missile.halfWidth();
    missile.y = cannon.y - missile.height;
```

```
    //Set its speed
    missile.vy = -8;

    //Push the missile into both the sprites and missiles arrays
    sprites.push(missile);
    missiles.push(missile);

    //Play the firing sound
    shootSound.currentTime = 0;
    shootSound.play();
}

function removeObject(objectToRemove, array)
{
  var i = array.indexOf(objectToRemove);
  if (i !== -1)
  {
    array.splice(i, 1);
  }
}

function endGame()
{
  gameOverMessage.visible = true;
  if(score < scoreNeededToWin)
  {
    gameOverMessage.text = "EARTH DESTROYED!";
  }
  else
  {
    gameOverMessage.x = 120;
    gameOverMessage.text = "EARTH SAVED!";
  }
}

function render()
{
  drawingSurface.clearRect(0, 0, canvas.width, canvas.height);

    //Display the sprites
    if(sprites.length !== 0)
    {
      for(var i = 0; i < sprites.length; i++)
      {
        var sprite = sprites[i];
        drawingSurface.drawImage
```

```
    (
      image,
      sprite.sourceX, sprite.sourceY,
      sprite.sourceWidth, sprite.sourceHeight,
      Math.floor(sprite.x), Math.floor(sprite.y),
      sprite.width, sprite.height
    );
  }
}

//Display game messages
if(messages.length !== 0)
{
  for(var i = 0; i < messages.length; i++)
  {
    var message = messages[i];
    if(message.visible)
    {
      drawingSurface.font = message.font;
      drawingSurface.fillStyle = message.fillStyle;
      drawingSurface.textBaseline = message.textBaseline;
      drawingSurface.fillText(message.text, message.x, message.y);
    }
  }
}
}

}());
```

Summary

You now know how to make video games! Alien Armada is a very basic model for dozens of similar games you could make using this format. All the important features of video-game design are right here in this chapter: loading multiple assets, changing game states, using collision detection, adding and removing sprites, displaying game messages, and playing sounds. You'll be able to use this game as a template for many of the game projects you make from now on.

Why not try it? Before you move on to the next chapter, make your own action arcade game using the code from this chapter as a starting point. Just gradually replace my code, sounds, and images with your own, and you'll have your own original arcade game working in no time.

In the next chapter we're going to take a detailed look at one of the most interesting video-game genres: maze games.

Chapter 10

Maze Games

Many kinds of video games that you'll want to make are maze games. These are games where a player has to navigate an environment with walls and obstacles to find useful items and evade enemies. In this chapter I'm going to show you all the basics you need to know to start making maze games of your own. You'll learn all the classic design techniques, and we'll look at two complete demo games: Time Bomb Panic and Monster Mayhem. Figure 10-1 shows what those finished games look like. You'll find them in the chapter's source files.

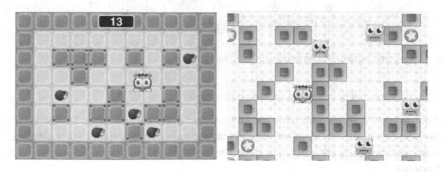

Figure 10-1. Time Bomb Panic and Monster Mayhem

In Time Bomb Panic you need to collect all the bombs before the time runs out. Monster Mayhem is a two-level scrolling maze game where you need to collect all the stars and avoid the wandering monsters.

You'll learn how to make and change game levels quickly using 2D arrays, and how to implement special techniques like scrolling. You'll soon see that once you understand the basic principles behind maze game design that it's very quick and easy to make a complex game with relatively little code.

> *Note: The games in this chapter use the **tile-based** system of game design. Tile-based game design is very powerful and efficient because it lets you create complex game worlds, game logic, and enemy Artificial Intelligence (AI) with very little code. The name "tile-based" comes from the fact that the game world is described as a grid, using 2D arrays. Each cell in the grid is a "tile." You had a gentle introduction to tile-based game design in Chapter 5. It's easy to understand how tile-based games work in the context of maze games, but when you become comfortable using this system you'll find that games in most other genres will benefit from originating with a tile-based approach.*

Planning maze games

The most important decision you need to make when making a new maze game is how big each cell of the maze grid will be. Figure 10-2 illustrates a screenshot from Time Bomb Panic. You can see that the whole game is based on a grid of squares. Each square is 64 pixels wide and high. The entire game screen is 704 pixels wide and 512 pixels high.

Figure 10-2. Maze games are based on grids with fixed cell sizes

The size of each maze cell is important for these reasons:

- The maze cell size will determine the size of most of the sprite images in your tilesheet. As you'll soon see, you can make sprites of any size in maze games. But fixing them to a size that's the same as, or no larger than, each cell leads to a clean design and lets you use some very convenient programming shortcuts.

- Your moving game characters need X and Y positions that let them align neatly with nonmoving objects in the game. If you give your moving objects a velocity that's divisible by the maze cell size, they'll move smoothly around the corners of maze walls without getting stuck on the edges. You'll see how and why this works in the pages ahead.

- You can use 2D arrays to design and build your levels. If you use fixed cell sizes you can build large game worlds with very little code. You can also use a tile map editor to help you easily build complex game levels.

The maze games in this chapter use a constant called SIZE that determines the size of each maze cell. In all these examples, it's set to 64.

```
var SIZE = 64;
```

The first game we'll look at in this chapter is Time Bomb Panic, which you'll find in the chapter's source files. The structure for its folder, file, and code is identical to what was used for Alien Armada in Chapter 9. It uses the same spriteObject and messageObject in the **objects.js** file to make the game objects. All the collision functions are in the **collision.js** file. You'll find its tilesheet, shown in Figure 10-3, in the **images** folder.

Figure 10-3. The Time Bomb Panic tilesheet

The sprite images that are used for the walls, floor, boxes, and the game character are all each 64 by 64 pixels. However, the bomb is a little smaller. The black rectangle that displays the score and the game over image are much bigger.

Your game program will need to know the number of columns in your tilesheet. The tilesheet in Figure 10-3 has five columns. The games in this chapter use a variable called `tilesheetColumns` to store this information.

```
var tilesheetColumns = 5;
```

Your program will need to use this number to accurately map the tilesheet images to the 2D array, as you'll see. (It is not important to know the number of rows. As you'll see, the formula that we use to plot the images onto the game screen will calculate the number of tilesheet rows automatically.)

Building the maze

I have something surprising to tell you: you already know how to make maze games! Remember Island Adventure from Chapter 5? That was really just a turn-based maze game. If you understand how that game was made, you'll find the next few sections of this chapter very familiar.

Mazes are built using 2D arrays that describe the game world. To construct the maze, you loop through the arrays to plot images on the screen that correspond to the array contents. This is just what we did in Island Adventure, so, relax, there's nothing really new to learn there. What is new in these next examples is how the maze is constructed by using sprites and canvas. I'm also going to show you a nifty little trick you can use to automatically load the correct sprite images from the tilesheet into the correct maze locations.

You'll find all the working code for these examples in the **timeBombPanic.js** file in the chapter's source files.

Designing the maze with 2D arrays

It's a good idea to build your maze with two different 2D arrays. The first array, called `map`, should contain all the nonmoving things in the game, like the floors and walls. The second, called `gameObjects`, should contain all the things that move or change in your game. These could include the game characters and any objects that need to be collected.

Here are the `map` and `gameObjects` arrays used in Time Bomb Panic.

```
//The game map
var map =
[
  [3,3,3,3,3,3,3,3,3,3,3,3],
  [3,1,1,1,1,1,1,1,1,1,1,3],
  [3,1,2,2,2,1,2,1,2,1,3],
  [3,1,1,2,1,1,1,1,1,1,3],
  [3,1,1,1,1,2,1,1,2,1,3],
  [3,1,2,1,2,2,1,2,2,1,3],
  [3,1,1,1,1,1,2,1,1,1,3],
  [3,3,3,3,3,3,3,3,3,3,3,3]
];
```

```
//The game objects map
var gameObjects =
[
  [0,0,0,0,0,0,0,0,0,0,0,0],
  [0,0,0,0,0,0,0,0,0,0,0,0],
  [0,0,0,0,0,0,0,0,0,0,5,0],
  [0,0,0,0,0,4,0,0,0,0,0,0],
  [0,0,5,0,0,0,0,0,0,0,0,0],
  [0,0,0,0,0,0,5,0,0,0,0,0],
  [0,0,0,0,5,0,0,5,0,0,0,0],
  [0,0,0,0,0,0,0,0,0,0,0,0]
];

//Map code
var EMPTY = 0;
var FLOOR = 1;
var BOX = 2;
var WALL = 3;
var ALIEN = 4;
var BOMB = 5;

//The size of each tile cell
var SIZE = 64;

//The number of rows and columns
var ROWS = map.length;
var COLUMNS = map[0].length;

//The number of columns on the tilesheet
var tilesheetColumns = 5;
```

Figure 10-4 shows how each array describes each layer of the map. It also shows the tilesheet images that correspond to the map code. (Refer back to Chapter 5 if you're unsure of these details.)

```
var map =
[
  [3,3,3,3,3,3,3,3,3,3,3],
  [3,1,1,1,1,1,1,1,1,1,3],
  [3,1,2,2,2,1,2,1,2,1,3],
  [3,1,1,2,1,1,1,1,1,1,3],
  [3,1,1,1,1,2,1,1,2,1,3],
  [3,1,2,1,2,2,1,2,2,1,3],
  [3,1,1,1,1,1,2,1,1,1,3],
  [3,3,3,3,3,3,3,3,3,3,3]
];

var gameObjects =
[
  [0,0,0,0,0,0,0,0,0,0,0],
  [0,0,0,0,0,0,0,0,0,0,0],
  [0,0,0,0,0,0,0,0,0,5,0],
  [0,0,0,0,0,4,0,0,0,0,0],
  [0,0,5,0,0,0,0,0,0,0,0],
  [0,0,0,0,0,0,5,0,0,0,0],
  [0,0,0,0,5,0,0,5,0,0,0],
  [0,0,0,0,0,0,0,0,0,0,0]
];
```

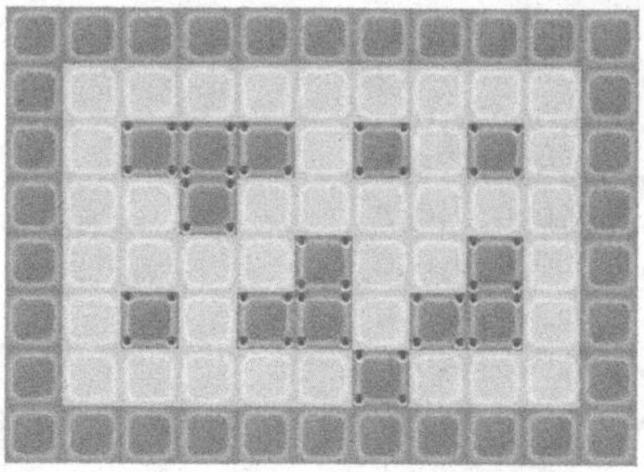

Figure 10-4. The game level is made by using two map layers

The map code

Here's the game's map code.

```
var EMPTY = 0;
var FLOOR = 1;
var BOX = 2;
var WALL = 3;
var ALIEN = 4;
var BOMB = 5;
```

Each number represents a sprite image on the tilesheet. The first sprite, FLOOR, is number 1, and the rest of the numbers follow sequentially. Figure 10-5 illustrates this. If your tilesheet has more than one row, just continue the numbering on that row. This is the same system you used to number frames for animation in Chapter 6.

```
var EMPTY = 0;
var FLOOR = 1;
var BOX = 2;
var WALL = 3;
var ALIEN = 4;
var BOMB = 5;
```

```
var map =                          var gameObjects =
[                                  [
[3,3,3,3,3,3,3,3,3,3,3,3],           [0,0,0,0,0,0,0,0,0,0,0,0],
[3,1,1,1,1,1,1,1,1,1,1,3],           [0,0,0,0,0,0,0,0,0,0,0,0],
[3,1,2,2,2,1,2,1,2,1,1,3],           [0,0,0,0,0,0,0,0,0,0,0,0],
[3,1,1,2,1,1,1,1,1,1,1,3],           [0,0,0,0,0,0,0,0,0,0,0,0],
[3,1,1,1,1,2,1,1,2,1,1,3],           [0,0,0,0,0,0,0,0,0,0,0,0],
[3,1,2,1,2,2,1,2,2,1,1,3],           [0,0,0,0,0,0,0,0,0,0,0,0],
[3,1,1,1,1,1,2,1,1,1,1,3],           [0,0,0,0,0,0,0,0,0,0,0,0],
[3,3,3,3,3,3,3,3,3,3,3,3]            [0,0,0,0,0,0,0,0,0,0,0,0]
];                                 ];
```

Figure 10-5. The map code refers to the position numbers of the sprite images on the tilesheet

Empty cells have the code *0*. You'll soon see how we use that to prevent plotting an image in that location. The larger sprite images on the tilesheet aren't used for creating the game level so we can ignore them for now.

Note: This map code system is entirely optional, so feel free to use any other system that you find useful. This system I've used, which starts numbering sprite images at "1," matches the output of popular tile map editors like Tiled, which you'll learn to use at the end of this chapter.

The BUILD_MAP game state

In Chapter 9 you learned how to use game states to change how the game is behaving. Alien Armada used three game states: LOADING, PLAYING, and OVER. Time Bomb Panic uses these same states but includes one more: BUILD_MAP.

```
var LOADING = 0;
var BUILD_MAP = 1;
var PLAYING = 2;
var OVER = 3;
var gameState = LOADING;
```

After the loadHandler loads the tilesheet image, it changes the gameState to BUILD_MAP, as you can see in the highlighted code below.

```
function loadHandler()
{
  assetsLoaded++;
  if(assetsLoaded === assetsToLoad.length)
  {
    //Remove the load handler
    image.removeEventListener("load", loadHandler, false);

    //Build the map
    gameState = BUILD_MAP;
  }
}
```

The switch statement in the update function has a new case that checks for this.

```
function update()
{
  //The animation loop
  requestAnimationFrame(update, canvas);

  //Change what the game is doing based on the game state
  switch(gameState)
  {
    case LOADING:
      console.log("loading...");
      break;

    case BUILD_MAP:
      buildMap(map);
      buildMap(gameObjects);
      createOtherObjects();
      gameState = PLAYING;
      break;

    case PLAYING:
      playGame();
      break;

    case OVER:
      endGame();
      break;
  }

  //Render the game
  render();
}
```

You can see that the BUILD_MAP case calls a function called buildMap twice. The argument in the buildMap function is each of the 2D arrays that describe the game level: map and gameObjects.

```
buildMap(map);
buildMap(gameObjects);
```

This custom `buildMap` function takes the 2D arrays and uses them to plot the game sprites on the canvas by using the map code. We'll look at that in detail next.

The `BUILD_MAP` case also calls another function called `createOtherObjects`.

```
createOtherObjects();
```

This function creates the sprites in the game that are larger than 64 by 64 pixels. This includes the "game over" image and the rectangular time board display at the top of the screen. We'll see how this works after we look at the `buildMap` function.

When those three functions have finished running, all the game sprites will have been created and plotted in their correct positions. The `BUILD_MAP` case then sets the `gameState` to `PLAYING`, and the game action starts.

```
gameState = PLAYING;
```

Let's find out how that `buildMap` function takes the 2D array data and creates and positions the game sprites.

Building the level map

The `buildMap` function runs twice: once for the `map` array and again for the `gameObjects` array.

```
buildMap(map);
buildMap(gameObjects);
```

As you'll see, the `buildMap` function loops through each array and creates a sprite for each matching map code. It gives those sprites X and Y positions that match their column and row positions in the arrays. All the sprites it creates will be added to an array called `sprites`, which is what canvas uses to render them. (This is the same system for rendering sprites with canvas that we used in previous chapters.) Also, the bombs and boxes need to be added to their own arrays so we can use them for collision detection. Before the `buildMap` function runs, the main program needs to make empty arrays to store all these objects.

```
var sprites = [];
var boxes = [];
var bombs = [];
```

The alien game character also needs to be referenced by other functions in the program. That means it has to be defined in the main program along with all the other game variables.

```
var alien = null;
```

It's given an initial value of `null` because it won't be created until the `buildMap` function runs.

Here's the complete `buildMap` function, and I'll explain how it works ahead.

```
function buildMap(levelMap)
{
  for(var row = 0; row < ROWS; row++)
  {
    for(var column = 0; column < COLUMNS; column++)
    {
      var currentTile = levelMap[row][column];

      if(currentTile !== EMPTY)
      {
        //Find the tile's X and Y positions on the tilesheet
        var tileSheetX = Math.floor((currentTile-1) % tilesheetColumns) * SIZE;
        var tileSheetY = Math.floor((currentTile-1) / tilesheetColumns) * SIZE;

        switch (currentTile)
        {
          case FLOOR:
            var floor = Object.create(spriteObject);
            floor.sourceX = tileSheetX;
            floor.sourceY = tileSheetY;
            floor.x = column * SIZE;
            floor.y = row * SIZE;
            sprites.push(floor);
            break;

          case BOX:
            var box = Object.create(spriteObject);
            box.sourceX = tileSheetX;
            box.sourceY = tileSheetY;
            box.x = column * SIZE;
            box.y = row * SIZE;
            sprites.push(box);
            boxes.push(box);
            break;

          case WALL:
            var wall = Object.create(spriteObject);
            wall.sourceX = tileSheetX;
            wall.sourceY = tileSheetY;
            wall.x = column * SIZE;
            wall.y = row * SIZE;
            sprites.push(wall);
            break;

          case BOMB:
            var bomb = Object.create(spriteObject);
            bomb.sourceX = tileSheetX;
            bomb.sourceY = tileSheetY;
            bomb.sourceWidth = 48;
```

```
        bomb.sourceHeight = 36;
        bomb.width = 48;
        bomb.height = 36;
        bomb.x = column * SIZE + 10;
        bomb.y = row * SIZE + 16;
        bombs.push(bomb);
        sprites.push(bomb);
        break;

      case ALIEN:
        //Note: "alien" has already been defined in the main
        //program so you don't need to precede it with "var"
        alien = Object.create(spriteObject);
        alien.sourceX = tileSheetX;
        alien.sourceY = tileSheetY;
        alien.x = column * SIZE;
        alien.y = row * SIZE;
        sprites.push(alien);
        break;
      }
    }
  }
 }
}
```

The buildMap function has one parameter: levelMap. That's the 2D array that you want to use, which will be the map or gameObjects arrays.

```
function buildMap(levelMap)
{...
```

The code then loops through the array's rows and columns in the familiar format you learned in Chapter 5.

```
for(var row = 0; row < ROWS; row++)
{
  for(var column = 0; column < COLUMNS; column++)
  {
```

Each time the loop repeats, the current element that's being checked is assigned to a temporary variable called currentTile.

```
var currentTile = levelMap[row][column];
```

It will have one of six values: EMPTY, FLOOR, BOX, WALL, BOMB, or ALIEN. We don't want to create any sprites if the value is EMPTY, so an if statement first checks for this.

```
if(currentTile !== EMPTY)
{...
```

If it's *not* EMPTY, the rest of the code is allowed to run. Its first job is to find out where the sprite's image is on the tilesheet. It figures out the sprite's tilesheet column and tilesheet row with the help of these two lines of code:

```
var tilesheetX = Math.floor((currentTile–1) % tilesheetColumns) * SIZE;
var tilesheetY = Math.floor((currentTile–1) / tilesheetColumns) * SIZE;
```

This is the same system we used to find the X and Y positions of frames for animation in Chapter 6.

> Note: The only difference in this system from Chapter 6 is that 1 is subtracted from the value of currentTile, like this:
>
> currentTile–1
>
> Why is that? It's because our map code system starts numbering the sprite images at "1." FLOOR is 1, BOX is 2, WALL is 3, and so on. But for this loop to load the correct image, the first image should actually be number "0." In our map code, 0 is reserved for empty cells. Subtracting 1 to all the currentTile numbers compensates for this. I've used this system because the map code matches the output of many map tile editors, and it's convenient to use 0 to indicate empty cells.

The switch statement uses tileSheetX and tileSheetY to create a box sprite.

```
case BOX:
  var box = Object.create(spriteObject);
  box.sourceX = tileSheetX;
  box.sourceY = tileSheetY;
  box.x = column * SIZE;
  box.y = row * SIZE;
  sprites.push(box);
  boxes.push(box);
  break;
```

This is the same basic code we used to create sprites in previous chapters. The code gives the box sprite X and Y position numbers on the canvas by multiplying its column and row numbers in the array by SIZE (64).

```
box.x = column * SIZE;
box.y = row * SIZE;
```

For example, if the box is at column 3 and row 2 in the array, it will have an X position of 192 and a Y position of 128 on the canvas.

Finally, the box sprite is pushed into both the sprites and boxes arrays.

```
sprites.push(box);
boxes.push(box);
```

It needs to be in the sprites array so that the render function can render it to the canvas. It needs to be in the boxes array so that the game can loop through the boxes to check them for collisions with the alien, as you'll see in the pages ahead.

The rest of the cases in the switch statement apply the same logic in creating the rest of the sprites in the maze. One exception is the BOMB case. The bombs in the game are each 48 pixels wide and 36 pixels high. That makes them smaller than the standard 64-by-64-pixel width and height that all the other map sprites have. That's not a problem, however; all the code needs to do is specify the size of the bombs when it creates them.

```
bomb.sourceWidth = 48;
bomb.sourceHeight = 36;
bomb.width = 48;
bomb.height = 36;
```

The bombs also need to be centered inside each 64-by-64-pixel map cell. To do this, just add 10 to the bomb's X position and 16 to its Y position.

```
bomb.x = column * SIZE + 10;
bomb.y = row * SIZE + 16;
```

If you customize the size and position of sprites like this, you can use sprites of any size in your level maps.

> Note: Alternatively, you could just center the image of the bomb in its 64-by-64-pixel cell in the tilesheet. That way you don't need to change its width or height, and it will appear centered when it's rendered on the game screen.

Each bomb sprite also needs to be pushed into the bombs array so that we can check the bombs for collisions with the alien.

```
bombs.push(bomb);
```

Layering the map level arrays

Remember that the buildMap function is called twice: once for each of the arrays.

```
buildMap(map);
buildMap(gameObjects);
```

This builds the game level in two layers. The sprites in the map layer will be added to the sprites array first. That means canvas will render them first as well. The sprites in the gameObjects array are added to the sprites array next, and that means they'll be rendered above the first layer. This very naturally makes the gameObject sprites, like the alien and bombs, appear above the environment sprites, like the floor.

Now you know how the game level is built, but there are other sprites in the game that aren't part of the game level that we need to create as well.

Making bigger sprites and game messages

There are two more sprites that the game needs to make: timeDisplay and gameOverDisplay. The timeDisplay is the rounded black rectangle with the yellow border that acts as the background for the countdown timer. The gameOverDisplay is the large graphic of a big explosion that appears at the end of the game. Figure 10-6 shows where these sprites are on the tilesheet and how they appear in the game.

Figure 10-6. Big sprites and message objects

The game also needs two message objects to display text: gameOverMessage and timerMessage. gameOverMessage displays the words "You Lost!" in Figure 10-6, and timerMessage is the countdown timer that starts at 20 and ends at 00.

These sprites and message objects aren't referenced in the 2D arrays, so we have to create them manually. Fortunately, that's exactly how you've been creating sprites in the previous chapters up till now, so you'll see that it's very routine to do this.

The variables that store these objects are all defined by the main program when it first loads.

```
var timeDisplay = null;
var gameOverDisplay = null;
var gameOverMessage = null;
var timerMessage = null;
```

They're initialized as null to show that they don't contain any objects yet. The game also needs an array called messages to store the message objects.

```
var messages = [];
```

The render function will display all the message objects that are in the messages array.

The createOtherObjects function that makes these objects is called after the buildMap creates the game level.

```
case BUILD_MAP:
  buildMap(map);
  buildMap(gameObjects);
  createOtherObjects();
  gameState = PLAYING;
  break;
```

createOtherObjects makes the timeDisplay and gameOverDisplay sprites using the tilesheet images and manually assigns them X and Y positions. It also creates two message objects: timerMessage and gameOverMessage.

```
function createOtherObjects()
{
  timeDisplay = Object.create(spriteObject);
  timeDisplay.sourceX = 0;
  timeDisplay.sourceY = 64;
  timeDisplay.sourceWidth = 128;
  timeDisplay.sourceHeight = 48;
  timeDisplay.width = 128;
  timeDisplay.height = 48;
  timeDisplay.x = canvas.width / 2-timeDisplay.width / 2;
  timeDisplay.y = 8;
  sprites.push(timeDisplay);

  gameOverDisplay = Object.create(spriteObject);
  gameOverDisplay.sourceX = 0;
  gameOverDisplay.sourceY = 129;
  gameOverDisplay.sourceWidth = 316;
  gameOverDisplay.sourceHeight = 290;
  gameOverDisplay.width = 316;
  gameOverDisplay.height = 290;
  gameOverDisplay.x = canvas.width / 2-gameOverDisplay.width / 2;
  gameOverDisplay.y = canvas.height / 2-gameOverDisplay.height / 2;
  gameOverDisplay.visible = false;
  sprites.push(gameOverDisplay);

  gameOverMessage = Object.create(messageObject);
  gameOverMessage.x = 275;
  gameOverMessage.y = 270;
  gameOverMessage.font = "bold 30px Helvetica";
  gameOverMessage.fillStyle = "black";
  gameOverMessage.text = "";
  gameOverMessage.visible = false;
  messages.push(gameOverMessage);

  timerMessage = Object.create(messageObject);
  timerMessage.x = 330;
  timerMessage.y = 10;
  timerMessage.font = "bold 40px Helvetica";
```

```
    timerMessage.fillStyle = "white";
    timerMessage.text = "";
    messages.push(timerMessage);
}
```

You can see that the two sprites are pushed into the sprites array, and the two message objects are pushed into the messages array.

The gameOverDisplay will become visible only when the game ends. That's why its visible property is set to false.

```
gameOverDisplay.visible = false;
```

Now with all the game sprites and messages created, the game is ready to start playing. The last thing the BUILD_MAP case does is change the gameState to PLAYING.

```
case BUILD_MAP:
    buildMap(map);
    buildMap(gameObjects);
    createOtherObjects();
    gameState = PLAYING;
    break;
```

Now let's find out how the game mechanics of Time Bomb Panic work.

Playing Time Bomb Panic

Like most of the other game projects in this book, the playGame function is where all the fun takes place. It moves the objects, handles collision detection, and figures out how well the player is doing. Most of the code in the playGame function will be very familiar to you by now, but let's take a quick tour of how it all fits together as well as some of the specific issues you need to deal with for maze games.

Moving the player character

The alien player character's vx and vy velocity is set to 4 or −4, depending on the direction it's moving in. Each map cell size is 64 by 64 pixels. At the beginning of this chapter I suggested that moving objects in maze games should use velocities that divide evenly into maze cell dimensions. This is so that they align neatly with the corners of boundaries, like walls and boxes. It means they can navigate smoothly around the maze without getting their edges caught on walls. The alien's velocity, 4 or −4, divides evenly into 64, so it fits the bill.

Figure 10-7 illustrates why this works. You can see that if the alien moves up through the maze in even steps of 4 pixels per frame, it will eventually reach a position that is aligned exactly with the top of the box.

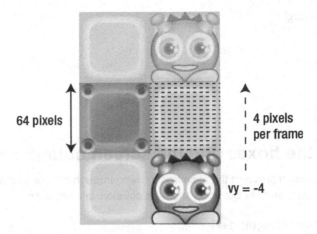

Figure 10-7. Move sprites with velocities that divide evenly into the map cell sizes

The keyboard arrow keys determine the direction that the alien should move in, just as they did in previous chapters. The code in the playGame function uses this information to set the alien's velocity. The velocity is then added to the alien's X and Y properties to make it move. Here's the code from the playGame function that does this.

```
//Up
if(moveUp && !moveDown)
{
  alien.vy = -4;
}
//Down
if(moveDown && !moveUp)
{
  alien.vy = 4;
}
//Left
if(moveLeft && !moveRight)
{
  alien.vx = -4;
}
//Right
if(moveRight && !moveLeft)
{
  alien.vx = 4;
}

//Set the alien's velocity to zero if none of the keys are being pressed
if(!moveUp && !moveDown)
{
  alien.vy = 0;
}
```

```
if(!moveLeft && !moveRight)
{
  alien.vx = 0;
}

//Move the alien
alien.x += alien.vx;
alien.y += alien.vy;
```

Collisions with the boxes and the screen boundaries

The blockRectangle function prevents the alien from moving through the boxes that define the maze. The code loops through all the boxes and checks each one for a collision with the alien.

```
for(var i = 0; i < boxes.length; i++)
{
  blockRectangle(alien, boxes[i]);
}
```

If there's a collision, blockRectangle separates the objects. (You'll find the blockRectangle function, along with all the other collision functions, in the collision.js file.)

There's a 64-pixel-wide border around the maze that defines its area. This border is filled with WALL objects. Rather than checking for collisions with each of these wall objects, the game just adds or subtracts 64 from the code that defines the alien's screen boundaries.

```
if(alien.x < 64)
{
  alien.x = 64;
}
if(alien.y < 64)
{
  alien.y = 64;
}
if(alien.x + alien.width > canvas.width-64)
{
  alien.x = canvas.width-alien.width-64;
}
if(alien.y + alien.height > canvas.height-64)
{
  alien.y = canvas.height-alien.height-64;
}
```

This keeps the alien neatly inside the maze.

You can replace all the code that moves the alien and sets its screen boundaries with these two lines of code if you prefer:

```
alien.x = Math.max(64, Math.min(alien.x + alien.vx, canvas.width-alien.width-64));
alien.y = Math.max(64, Math.min(alien.y + alien.vy, canvas.height-alien.height-64));
```

Defusing the bombs

The main program creates and initializes a variable called bombsDefused when the game first loads.

```
var bombsDefused = 0;
```

Each time the player touches a bomb, bombsDefused is increased by 1. The bomb then disappears from the screen by setting its visible property to false. When bombsDefused equals the number of elements in the bombs array (5), the gameState is set to OVER and the game ends.

This happens in the playGame function. The code loops through all the bombs in the bombs array.

```
for(var i = 0; i < bombs.length; i++)
{
  var bomb = bombs[i];

  if(hitTestCircle(alien, bomb) && bomb.visible)
  {
    bomb.visible = false;
    bombsDefused++;
    if(bombsDefused === bombs.length)
    {
      gameState = OVER;
    }
  }
}
```

An if statement uses hitTestCircle to check for a collision between the current bomb in the loop and the alien. It also checks to see if the bomb is visible.

```
if(hitTestCircle(alien, bomb) && bomb.visible)
{...
```

I used hitTestCircle in this example because the bombs and alien are roughly circular. Also, we only want to check for a collision if the bomb is visible, because that means it hasn't yet been defused.

If those two things are true, the bomb is made invisible. That removes it from the game:

```
bomb.visible = false;
```

> *Note: In Alien Armada from Chapter 9, objects were removed from the game by splicing them out of the object arrays. Making objects invisible is an alternative way to remove them from a game. If you have only a limited number of objects to remove, such as the five bombs in this game, it's probably the best way. That's because it uses very little code and, if you need to reuse the bomb objects in this level for some reason, you can bring them back into the game just by setting their* visible *properties to* true *again. When you have an unknown or limitless group of objects to remove, like the missiles and aliens from Alien Armada, it's usually best to splice them out of the object arrays completely. That's because you don't want your game code to process potentially hundreds of different objects that aren't being used.*

The next thing the code does is increase bombsDefused by 1:

```
bombsDefused++;
```

It then checks whether all the bombs have been defused (if bombsDefused equals bombs.length).

```
if(bombsDefused === bombs.length)
{
  gameState = OVER;
}
```

If all bombs are defused, it sets the gameState to OVER to end the game.

The game can end if the player defuses all the bombs, but it can also end if the time runs out. Let's find out how Time Bomb Panic uses a special gameTimer object to count the seconds down to zero.

The game timer

When the game starts, the player has 20 seconds to defuse all the bombs. If the player doesn't defuse them all before the time reaches 0, the player loses. The remaining time is displayed at the top center of the screen.

Time Bomb Panic uses a custom object called gameTimer that you'll find in the **objects.js** file. It's based on the timer that I showed you how to make in Chapter 6. It has four methods: start, tick, stop, and reset. Its job is to start at a specific time and to then count down the seconds.

```
var gameTimer =
{
  time: 0,
  interval: undefined,

  start: function()
  {
    var self = this;
    this.interval = setInterval(function(){self.tick();}, 1000);
  },
```

```
  tick: function()
  {
    this.time--;
  },
  stop: function()
  {
    clearInterval(this.interval);
  },
  reset: function()
  {
    this.time = 0;
  }
```

To use it, assign a start time, in seconds like this:

```
gameTimer.time = 20;
```

Then call its start method:

```
gameTimer.start();
```

The gameTimer's start method uses setInterval to call the tick method every second.

```
start: function()
{
  var self = this;
  this.interval = setInterval(function(){self.tick();}, 1000);
},
```

The tick method's only job is to reduce the time by 1, like this:

```
tick: function()
{
  this.time--;
},
```

You can stop the timer at any time by calling its stop method.

```
gameTimer.stop();
```

And you can reset its time property back to 0 by calling its reset method.

```
gameTimer.reset();
```

This is a very simple but useful timer that you can use in any games where you need to count seconds. Let's find out how it's used in Time Bomb Panic.

The main program sets the gameTimer's time property to 20 and then starts the timer.

```
gameTimer.time = 20;
gameTimer.start();
```

The playGame function displays the time by using the timerMessage object. Remember that the timerMessage is the message object that's visible in the black rectangle at the top of the screen, shown in Figure 10-8. Only one line of code is needed to display the remaining time:

```
timerMessage.text = gameTimer.time;
```

Figure 10-8. The timerMessage object displays the remaining time

This will update automatically whenever the time changes.

There's an interesting feature about the way the time is displayed. When the time drops into single digits, like 9, 8, and 7, the program adds an extra leading 0 to the display. That means those numbers will display like this: 09, 08, 07, as you can see in Figure 10-9.

Figure 10-9. An extra leading 0 is added to single digits

This is just to make the numbers look nicely centered in the rectangle. Here's the bit of code in the playGame function that does this:

```
if(gameTimer.time < 10)
{
  timerMessage.text = "0" + gameTimer.time;
}
```

An if statement checks to see if the time is less than 10. If it is, it adds an extra 0 to the string that's copied into the timerMessage's text property.

If the time equals 0, it means the player has run out of time and the game should end.

```
if(gameTimer.time === 0)
{
  gameState = OVER;
}
```

This sets the gameState to OVER. It means the endGame function will be called, so let's find out what that does.

Ending the game

endGame stops the gameTimer. It also sets the gameOverDisplay's visible property to true. It then figures out whether the player has won or lost, depending on whether all the bombs were defused.

```
function endGame()
{
  gameTimer.stop();
  gameOverDisplay.visible = true;
  gameOverMessage.visible = true;

  if(bombsDefused === bombs.length)
  {
    gameOverMessage.text = "You Won!";
  }
  else
  {
    gameOverMessage.text = "You Lost!";
  }
}
```

The if statement uses the gameOverMessage to display "You Won!" or "You Lost," depending on the outcome, as you can see in Figure 10-10.

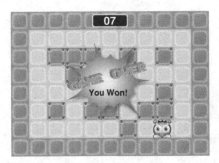

Figure 10-10. The game displays a different "game over" message depending on whether the game has been won or lost

You can see that the actual game mechanics of Time Bomb Panic are really straightforward. The only really new things in this game were the game timer and the use of 2D arrays to build the level map. And now that you know how that's done, you can create new maze levels for this game just by creating new arrays. The basic game logic will remain the same.

In the next section I'll show you how you can expand this concept to make a big, scrolling game world. But, before I do, here's the complete code listing for the **timeBombPanic.js** file that you can use as a reference for your own games. Make sure you check out the HTML, **objects.js**, and **collision.js** files in the chapter's source files as well.

The complete code for Time Bomb Panic

```
(function(){

//The canvas
var canvas = document.querySelector("canvas");
var drawingSurface = canvas.getContext("2d");

//The game map
var map =
[
  [3,3,3,3,3,3,3,3,3,3,3],
  [3,1,1,1,1,1,1,1,1,1,3],
  [3,1,2,2,2,1,2,1,2,1,3],
  [3,1,1,2,1,1,1,1,1,1,3],
  [3,1,1,1,1,2,1,1,2,1,3],
  [3,1,2,1,2,2,1,2,2,1,3],
  [3,1,1,1,1,1,2,1,1,1,3],
  [3,3,3,3,3,3,3,3,3,3,3]
];

//The game objects map
var gameObjects =
[
  [0,0,0,0,0,0,0,0,0,0,0,0],
  [0,0,0,0,0,0,0,0,0,0,0,0],
  [0,0,0,0,0,0,0,0,0,0,5,0],
  [0,0,0,0,0,4,0,0,0,0,0,0],
  [0,0,5,0,0,0,0,0,0,0,0,0],
  [0,0,0,0,0,0,5,0,0,0,0,0],
  [0,0,0,0,5,0,0,5,0,0,0,0],
  [0,0,0,0,0,0,0,0,0,0,0,0]
];

//Map code
var EMPTY = 0;
var FLOOR = 1;
var BOX = 2;
var WALL = 3;
var ALIEN = 4;
var BOMB = 5;

//The size of each tile cell
var SIZE = 64;

//The number of rows and columns
var ROWS = map.length;
var COLUMNS = map[0].length;
```

```
//The number of columns on the tilesheet
var tilesheetColumns = 5;

//Sprites we need to access by name
var alien = null;
var timeDisplay = null;
var gameOverDisplay = null;
var gameOverMessage = null;
var timerMessage = null;

//Arrays to store the game objects
var sprites = [];
var messages = [];
var boxes = [];
var bombs = [];

var assetsToLoad = [];
var assetsLoaded = 0;

//Load the tilesheet image
var image = new Image();
image.addEventListener("load", loadHandler, false);
image.src = "../images/timeBombPanic.png";
assetsToLoad.push(image);

//Game variables
var bombsDefused = 0;

//The game timer
gameTimer.time = 20;
gameTimer.start();

//Game states
var LOADING = 0;
var BUILD_MAP = 1;
var PLAYING = 2;
var OVER = 3;
var gameState = LOADING;

//Arrow key codes
var UP = 38;
var DOWN = 40;
var RIGHT = 39;
var LEFT = 37;

//Directions
var moveUp = false;
var moveDown = false;
var moveRight = false;
var moveLeft = false;
```

```
//Add keyboard listeners
window.addEventListener("keydown", function(event)
{
  switch(event.keyCode)
  {
    case UP:
      moveUp = true;
      break;

    case DOWN:
      moveDown = true;
      break;

    case LEFT:
      moveLeft = true;
      break;

    case RIGHT:
      moveRight = true;
      break;
  }
}, false);

window.addEventListener("keyup", function(event)
{
  switch(event.keyCode)
  {
    case UP:
      moveUp = false;
      break;

    case DOWN:
      moveDown = false;
      break;

    case LEFT:
      moveLeft = false;
      break;

    case RIGHT:
      moveRight = false;
      break;
  }
}, false);

//Start the game animation loop
update();
```

```
function update()
{
  //The animation loop
  requestAnimationFrame(update, canvas);

  //Change what the game is doing based on the game state
  switch(gameState)
  {
    case LOADING:
      console.log("loading...");
      break;

    case BUILD_MAP:
      buildMap(map);
      buildMap(gameObjects);
      createOtherObjects();
      gameState = PLAYING;
      break;

    case PLAYING:
      playGame();
      break;

    case OVER:
      endGame();
      break;
  }

  //Render the game
  render();
}

function loadHandler()
{
  assetsLoaded++;
  if(assetsLoaded === assetsToLoad.length)
  {
    //Remove the load handler
    image.removeEventListener("load", loadHandler, false);

    //Build the level
    gameState = BUILD_MAP;
  }
}

function buildMap(levelMap)
{
  for(var row = 0; row < ROWS; row++)
```

```
{
  for(var column = 0; column < COLUMNS; column++)
  {
    var currentTile = levelMap[row][column];

    if(currentTile !== EMPTY)
    {
      //Find the tile's X and Y positions on the tilesheet
      var tilesheetX = Math.floor((currentTile-1) % tilesheetColumns) * SIZE;
      var tilesheetY = Math.floor((currentTile-1) / tilesheetColumns) * SIZE;

      switch (currentTile)
      {
        case FLOOR:
          var floor = Object.create(spriteObject);
          floor.sourceX = tilesheetX;
          floor.sourceY = tilesheetY;
          floor.x = column * SIZE;
          floor.y = row * SIZE;
          sprites.push(floor);
          break;

        case BOX:
          var box = Object.create(spriteObject);
          box.sourceX = tilesheetX;
          box.sourceY = tilesheetY;
          box.x = column * SIZE;
          box.y = row * SIZE;
          sprites.push(box);
          boxes.push(box);
          break;

        case WALL:
          var wall = Object.create(spriteObject);
          wall.sourceX = tilesheetX;
          wall.sourceY = tilesheetY;
          wall.x = column * SIZE;
          wall.y = row * SIZE;
          sprites.push(wall);
          break;

        case BOMB:
          var bomb = Object.create(spriteObject);
          bomb.sourceX = tilesheetX;
          bomb.sourceY = tilesheetY;
          bomb.sourceWidth = 48;
          bomb.sourceHeight = 36;
          bomb.width = 48;
          bomb.height = 36;
          bomb.x = column * SIZE + 10;
```

```
            bomb.y = row * SIZE + 16;
            bombs.push(bomb);
            sprites.push(bomb);
            break;

        case ALIEN:
            //Note: "alien" has already been defined in the main
            //program so you don't need to precede it with "var"
            alien = Object.create(spriteObject);
            alien.sourceX = tilesheetX;
            alien.sourceY = tilesheetY;
            alien.x = column * SIZE;
            alien.y = row * SIZE;
            sprites.push(alien);
            break;
        }
      }
    }
  }
}

function createOtherObjects()
{
  timeDisplay = Object.create(spriteObject);
  timeDisplay.sourceX = 0;
  timeDisplay.sourceY = 64;
  timeDisplay.sourceWidth = 128;
  timeDisplay.sourceHeight = 48;
  timeDisplay.width = 128;
  timeDisplay.height = 48;
  timeDisplay.x = canvas.width / 2-timeDisplay.width / 2;
  timeDisplay.y = 8;
  sprites.push(timeDisplay);

  gameOverDisplay = Object.create(spriteObject);
  gameOverDisplay.sourceX = 0;
  gameOverDisplay.sourceY = 129;
  gameOverDisplay.sourceWidth = 316;
  gameOverDisplay.sourceHeight = 290;
  gameOverDisplay.width = 316;
  gameOverDisplay.height = 290;
  gameOverDisplay.x = canvas.width / 2-gameOverDisplay.width / 2;
  gameOverDisplay.y = canvas.height / 2-gameOverDisplay.height / 2;
  gameOverDisplay.visible = false;
  sprites.push(gameOverDisplay);

  gameOverMessage = Object.create(messageObject);
  gameOverMessage.x = 275;
  gameOverMessage.y = 270;
```

```
gameOverMessage.font = "bold 30px Helvetica";
gameOverMessage.fillStyle = "black";
gameOverMessage.text = "";
gameOverMessage.visible = false;
messages.push(gameOverMessage);

timerMessage = Object.create(messageObject);
timerMessage.x = 330;
timerMessage.y = 10;
timerMessage.font = "bold 40px Helvetica";
timerMessage.fillStyle = "white";
timerMessage.text = "";
messages.push(timerMessage);
}

function playGame()
{
  //Up
  if(moveUp && !moveDown)
  {
    alien.vy = -4;
  }
  //Down
  if(moveDown && !moveUp)
  {
    alien.vy = 4;
  }
  //Left
  if(moveLeft && !moveRight)
  {
    alien.vx = -4;
  }
  //Right
  if(moveRight && !moveLeft)
  {
    alien.vx = 4;
  }

  //Set the alien's velocity to zero if none of the keys are being pressed
  if(!moveUp && !moveDown)
  {
    alien.vy = 0;
  }
  if(!moveLeft && !moveRight)
  {
    alien.vx = 0;
  }

  alien.x += alien.vx;
  alien.y += alien.vy;
```

```
//Alien's screen boundaries with 64-pixel padding
//to compensate for the screen border
if(alien.x < 64)
{
  alien.x = 64;
}
if(alien.y < 64)
{
  alien.y = 64;
}
if(alien.x + alien.width > canvas.width–64)
{
  alien.x = canvas.width–alien.width–64;
}
if(alien.y + alien.height > canvas.height–64)
{
  alien.y = canvas.height–alien.height–64;
}

//Alternatively, move the alien and set its screen boundaries at the same time with this code:
//alien.x = Math.max(64, Math.min(alien.x + alien.vx, canvas.width–alien.width – 64));
//alien.y = Math.max(64, Math.min(alien.y + alien.vy, canvas.height–alien.height – 64));

//Collisions with boxes
for(var i = 0; i < boxes.length; i++)
{
  blockRectangle(alien, boxes[i]);
}

//Collisions with bombs
for(var i = 0; i < bombs.length; i++)
{
  var bomb = bombs[i];

  //If there's a collision, make the bombs invisible,
  //reduce bombsDefused by 1, and check whether the player has won the game
  if(hitTestCircle(alien, bomb) && bomb.visible)
  {
    bomb.visible = false;
    bombsDefused++;
    if(bombsDefused === bombs.length)
    {
      //Change the game state to OVER if the player has defused all the bombs
      gameState = OVER;
    }
  }
}
```

```
      //Display the gameTimer
      timerMessage.text = gameTimer.time;

      //This modification adds an extra 0 to the time if the time is less than 10
      if(gameTimer.time < 10)
      {
        timerMessage.text = "0" + gameTimer.time;
      }

      //Check whether the time is over
      if(gameTimer.time === 0)
      {
        gameState = OVER;
      }
    }

    function endGame()
    {
      gameTimer.stop();
      gameOverDisplay.visible = true;
      gameOverMessage.visible = true;

      if(bombsDefused === bombs.length)
      {
        gameOverMessage.text = "You Won!";
      }
      else
      {
        gameOverMessage.text = "You Lost!";
      }
    }

    function render()
    {
      drawingSurface.clearRect(0, 0, canvas.width, canvas.height);

      //Display the sprites
      if(sprites.length !== 0)
      {
        for(var i = 0; i < sprites.length; i++)
        {
          var sprite = sprites[i];
          if(sprite.visible)
          {
            drawingSurface.drawImage
            (
                image,
                sprite.sourceX, sprite.sourceY,
                sprite.sourceWidth, sprite.sourceHeight,
```

```
            Math.floor(sprite.x), Math.floor(sprite.y),
            sprite.width, sprite.height
        );
      }
    }
  }

  //Display the game messages
  if(messages.length !== 0)
  {
    for(var i = 0; i < messages.length; i++)
    {
      var message = messages[i];
      if(message.visible)
      {
        drawingSurface.font = message.font;
        drawingSurface.fillStyle = message.fillStyle;
        drawingSurface.textBaseline = message.textBaseline;
        drawingSurface.fillText(message.text, message.x, message.y);
      }
    }
  }
}

}());
```

Scrolling Time Bomb Panic

You can make mazes or game worlds of any size by using 2D arrays. All you need to do is apply the scrolling techniques you learned in Chapter 7. You can add these to the game without having to change any of the game's logic or mechanics. For an example, take a look at the scrolling version of Time Bomb Panic that you'll find in the **timeBombScroll** folder in the chapter's source files. The game plays in the same way, but now you have a much bigger maze to explore and a little more time to explore it in. Figure 10-11 shows what the new game looks like.

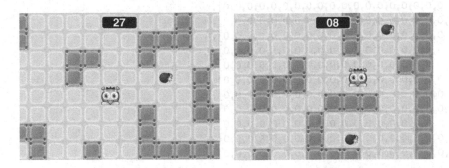

Figure 10-11. Create a big scrolling game world for players to explore

The new scrolling code was just dropped in around the existing code, and it works as you see it. Let's find out how this was done.

Making big level maps

To make a big level map, just use really big arrays. Open the **timeBombScroll.js** fie and you'll find the new map and gameObjects arrays. They use exactly the same format as the first version of the game, but they're just much bigger. They have 22 columns and 16 rows.

```
var map =
[
  [3,3,3,3,3,3,3,3,3,3,3,3,3,3,3,3,3,3,3,3,3,3],
  [3,1,1,1,1,1,1,1,1,1,1,1,1,1,1,1,1,2,1,1,1,3],
  [3,1,2,1,1,2,1,1,1,1,1,1,1,1,1,1,1,2,1,1,1,3],
  [3,1,1,1,1,2,1,1,1,2,2,2,1,1,1,1,1,2,1,1,1,3],
  [3,1,1,1,1,2,1,1,1,1,1,1,1,1,2,1,1,1,1,1,2,3],
  [3,1,1,2,2,2,1,1,1,1,1,2,2,2,1,1,1,1,1,1,1,3],
  [3,1,1,1,1,1,1,1,2,2,1,1,2,1,1,1,2,2,2,1,1,3],
  [3,1,1,1,1,1,1,1,2,1,1,1,1,1,1,2,1,1,1,1,1,3],
  [3,1,1,1,1,1,1,1,1,1,1,1,1,1,1,2,1,1,1,1,1,3],
  [3,1,1,1,1,1,1,1,1,1,1,1,1,2,1,1,2,2,2,1,1,3],
  [3,1,1,2,2,2,2,1,1,1,1,1,2,1,1,1,1,1,1,1,1,3],
  [3,1,1,1,1,1,2,1,1,2,1,1,2,2,2,2,2,1,1,1,1,3],
  [3,1,1,1,1,1,1,1,1,2,1,1,1,1,1,1,2,2,2,2,1,3],
  [3,1,1,2,1,1,1,1,1,2,2,1,1,2,2,1,2,1,1,1,1,3],
  [3,1,1,2,1,1,2,1,1,1,1,1,1,1,2,1,1,1,1,1,1,3],
  [3,3,3,3,3,3,3,3,3,3,3,3,3,3,3,3,3,3,3,3,3,3]
];

var gameObjects =
[
  [0,0,0,0,0,0,0,0,0,0,0,0,0,0,0,0,0,0,0,0,0,0],
  [0,0,0,0,0,0,0,0,0,0,0,0,0,0,0,0,0,0,0,0,0,0],
  [0,0,0,0,0,0,0,0,0,0,0,0,0,0,0,0,0,0,0,5,0,0],
  [0,0,0,5,0,0,0,0,0,0,0,0,0,0,0,0,0,0,0,0,0,0],
  [0,0,0,0,0,0,0,0,0,0,0,0,0,0,0,0,0,0,0,0,0,0],
  [0,0,0,0,0,0,0,0,0,0,0,0,0,0,0,0,0,0,0,0,0,0],
  [0,0,0,0,0,0,0,0,0,0,0,0,0,0,0,0,0,0,0,0,0,0],
  [0,0,0,0,0,0,0,0,0,0,0,0,0,5,0,0,0,0,0,0,0,0],
  [0,0,0,0,0,0,0,0,0,0,0,4,0,0,0,0,0,0,5,0,0,0],
  [0,0,0,0,0,0,0,0,0,0,0,0,0,0,0,0,0,0,0,0,0,0],
  [0,0,0,0,0,0,0,0,0,0,0,0,0,0,0,0,0,0,0,0,0,0],
  [0,0,0,0,0,0,0,0,0,0,0,0,0,0,0,0,0,0,0,0,0,0],
  [0,0,0,0,5,0,0,0,0,0,0,0,0,0,0,0,0,0,0,0,0,0],
  [0,0,0,0,0,0,0,0,0,0,0,0,0,0,0,0,0,0,0,0,0,0],
  [0,0,0,0,0,0,0,0,0,0,0,0,0,0,0,0,0,0,0,5,0,0],
  [0,0,0,0,0,0,0,0,0,0,0,0,0,0,0,0,0,0,0,0,0,0]
];
```

These arrays can be as big as you like, even thousands of rows or columns if you wanted to make a continent-sized game world.

> Note: You could also generate your map arrays by using for loops to create your game world randomly, or according to certain rules. Generated game maps are a vast and fascinating area of specialization that a web search will turn up lots of information about.

Adding gameWorld and camera objects

As you learned in Chapter 7, you need to define two new objects to help you implement scrolling: a gameWorld object and a camera object. The gameWorld object defines the size of the map that you want to use. The camera object defines the area of that map that will be visible on the screen. The camera also defines the inner boundaries in which the player character can move freely without any scrolling.

Here's the new code in the **timeBombScroll.js** file that defines the gameWorld and camera Objects and that gives them their initial values.

```
var gameWorld =
{
  x: 0,
  y: 0,
  width: map[0].length * SIZE,
  height: map.length * SIZE,
};

var camera =
{
  x: 0,
  y: 0,
  width: canvas.width,
  height: canvas.height,

  //The camera's inner scroll boundaries
  rightInnerBoundary: function()
  {
    return this.x + (this.width / 2) + (this.width / 4);
  },
  leftInnerBoundary: function()
  {
    return this.x + (this.width / 2)-(this.width / 4);
  },
  topInnerBoundary: function()
  {
    return this.y + (this.height / 2)-(this.height / 4);
  },
```

```
  bottomInnerBoundary: function()
  {
    return this.y + (this.height / 2) + (this.height / 4);
  }
};
```

The camera is then centered over the gameWorld like this:

```
camera.x = (gameWorld.x + gameWorld.width / 2)—camera.width / 2;
camera.y = (gameWorld.y + gameWorld.height / 2)—camera.height / 2;
```

The next step is to the move the camera to follow the alien character.

Scrolling the camera

The alien is moved within the gameWorld boundaries by using these two lines of code in the playGame function.

```
alien.x = Math.max(64, Math.min(alien.x + alien.vx, gameWorld.width—alien.width - 64));
alien.y = Math.max(64, Math.min(alien.y + alien.vy, gameWorld.height—alien.height - 64));
```

This lets the alien explore anywhere inside the map, within its 64-pixel-wide border.

The camera follows the alien. Its position is moved in the playGame function. Here's the new code that does this. It's been added to the playGame function, just after the existing game code. It moves the camera if the alien moves beyond the camera's inner boundaries. It also prevents the camera from crossing the game world's boundaries. This is the same basic code we used in Chapter 7.

```
//Scroll the camera
if(alien.x < camera.leftInnerBoundary())
{
  camera.x = Math.floor(alien.x—(camera.width / 4));
}
if(alien.y < camera.topInnerBoundary())
{
  camera.y = Math.floor(alien.y—(camera.height / 4));
}
if(alien.x + alien.width > camera.rightInnerBoundary())
{
  camera.x = Math.floor(alien.x + alien.width—(camera.width / 4 * 3));
}
if(alien.y + alien.height > camera.bottomInnerBoundary())
{
  camera.y = Math.floor(alien.y + alien.height—(camera.height / 4 * 3));
}

//The camera's gameWorld boundaries
if(camera.x < gameWorld.x)
```

```
{
  camera.x = gameWorld.x;
}
if(camera.y < gameWorld.y)
{
  camera.y = gameWorld.y;
}
if(camera.x + camera.width > gameWorld.x + gameWorld.width)
{
  camera.x = gameWorld.x + gameWorld.width—camera.width;
}
if(camera.y + camera.height > gameWorld.height)
{
  camera.y = gameWorld.height—camera.height;
}
```

Preventing the UI sprites from scrolling

Not all the sprites in the game should scroll—only those that are part of the game level should. We don't want any of the user interface (UI) elements to scroll. That includes the game messages as well as the timeDisplay and gameOverDisplay sprites. They should remain on fixed positions on the screen so that they appear to float above the game world.

To prevent certain sprites from scrolling, add a new property to the spriteObject that's the template for all the sprites in the game. In the **objects.js** file you'll see that the spriteObject we're using in this game has a new property called scrollable. It's set to true. Here's an abridged version of the spriteObject that shows this.

```
var spriteObject =
{
  //... the sprite's size and position...

  scrollable: true,
  //... the sprite's getters...
};
```

This will let all sprites be scrollable by default. To prevent any particular sprites from scrolling, set this to false.

Here's the code in the createOtherObjects function that prevents the timeDisplay and gameOverDisplay from being scrollable.

```
timeDisplay.scrollable = false;
gameOverDisplay.scrollable = false;
```

None of the messages need to be scrolled, so we don't have to set up this same system for the message objects.

Rendering the scrolling game world

The final step is to render this scrolling system with canvas. This is the same technique we used in Chapter 7. The only difference in this game is that not all the sprites are scrollable. The code checks for this and will scroll only the scrollable sprites. The nonscrolling sprites are given X and Y positions relative to the camera's position, like this:

```
camera.x + sprite.x, camera.y + sprite.y,
```

That keeps them fixed in the same place on the screen.

None of the messages are scrolled. Here's the entire render function so that you can see all the code in its proper context.

```
function render()
{
  //Clear the drawing surface
  drawingSurface.clearRect(0, 0, canvas.width, canvas.height);

  //Position the gameWorld relative to the camera
  drawingSurface.save();
  drawingSurface.translate(-camera.x, -camera.y);

  //Display the sprites in the gameWorld
  if(sprites.length !== 0)
  {
    for(var i = 0; i < sprites.length; i++)
    {
      var sprite = sprites[i];

      //display the scrolling sprites
      if(sprite.visible && sprite.scrollable)
      {
        drawingSurface.drawImage
        (
          image,
          sprite.sourceX, sprite.sourceY,
          sprite.sourceWidth, sprite.sourceHeight,
          Math.floor(sprite.x), Math.floor(sprite.y),
          sprite.width, sprite.height
        );
      }

      //display the nonscrolling sprites
      if(sprite.visible && !sprite.scrollable)
      {
        drawingSurface.drawImage
        (
          image,
```

```
        sprite.sourceX, sprite.sourceY,
        sprite.sourceWidth, sprite.sourceHeight,
        Math.floor(camera.x + sprite.x), Math.floor(camera.y + sprite.y),
        sprite.width, sprite.height
      );
    }
  }
}

drawingSurface.restore();

//Display the game messages
if(messages.length !== 0)
{
  for(var i = 0; i < messages.length; i++)
  {
   var message = messages[i];
   if(message.visible)
   {
     drawingSurface.font = message.font;
     drawingSurface.fillStyle = message.fillStyle;
     drawingSurface.textBaseline = message.textBaseline;
     drawingSurface.fillText(message.text, message.x, message.y);
   }
  }
 }
}
```

And this is really all you need to know about scrolling. The size and complexity of the game world you make is entirely up to you, so let your imagination run wild.

Our maze world is a very lonely place at the moment, so let's find out how to fill it with creatures to give the player some company. In the next few sections we'll look at a few examples of programs that will lead up to the next big game in this chapter: Monster Mayhem!

Wandering maze monsters

Every good maze should have a monster, and in the next few sections I'll show you how to add one. Maze monsters need to have a little bit of intelligence to find their way around a maze, but, fortunately, not too much. Here's what our monsters will need to be able to do:

- Choose a direction: up, down, left, or right

- Know when to change direction. They should only change direction when they're precisely aligned with maze corridors.

- Know how far they should move before deciding to choose another direction.

- Avoid walls.

- Look for the player.

Our maze monsters will do all these things. But let's first start with something simple so that you can see the basic principles at work.

A moving monster

In the chapter's source files you'll find a file called **movingMonster.html**. Run the program and you'll see a monster moving around a 64-pixel grid of squares. The monster changes direction only when it's aligned to the grid. Figure 10-12 illustrates what you'll see.

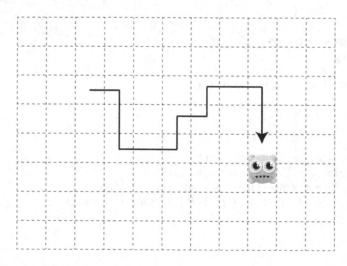

Figure 10-12. The monster moves around a grid of squares

The background grid is just a big image, so the monster isn't aware of any of the grid lines. What the monster *does* know is that each cell is 64 by 64 pixels. That's the key to making it move and change direction.

The monsterObject

A monsterObject is used to store some of the information that we'll need to move the monster. It's based on the same spriteObject that we've been using in previous examples, but it adds a new property: speed.

```
monsterObject = Object.create(spriteObject);
monsterObject.speed = 1;
```

speed is how many pixels per frame the monster should move. This should be a number that divides evenly into 64 (1, 2, 4, 8, 16, or 32). You'll see why soon.

The monster sprite in this example is made by using this new monsterObject. It's given an initial position and velocity, and it is pushed into the sprites array.

```
var monster = Object.create(monsterObject);
monster.x = 320;
monster.y = 256;
```

```
monster.vx = monster.speed;
monster.vy = 0;
sprites.push(monster);
```

Making the monster move

The playGame function moves this monster sprite. It checks whether the monster is aligned with the corner of a grid cell and then decides whether it should change the monster's direction. It also changes the monster's direction if the monster reaches the edge of the screen. Here's the entire playGame function, and I'll walk you through the details of how it works.

```
function playGame()
{
  monster.x += monster.vx;
  monster.y += monster.vy;

  //Check whether the monster is at a grid cell corner
  if(Math.floor(monster.x) % 64 === 0
  && Math.floor(monster.y) % 64 === 0)
  {
    //If it is at a corner, change its direction
    changeDirection(monster);
  }

  //Check the monster's screen boundaries
  if(monster.x < 0)
  {
    monster.x = 0;
    changeDirection(monster);
  }
  if(monster.y < 0)
  {
    monster.y = 0;
    changeDirection(monster);
  }
  if(monster.x + monster.width > canvas.width)
  {
    monster.x = canvas.width-monster.width;
    changeDirection(monster);
  }
  if(monster.y + monster.height > canvas.height)
  {
    monster.y = canvas.height-monster.height;
    changeDirection(monster);
  }
}
```

The code moves the monster using these familiar lines of code:

```
monster.x += monster.vx;
monster.y += monster.vy;
```

It then checks whether the monster's position is aligned with a grid cell corner.

```
if(Math.floor(monster.x) % 64 === 0 && Math.floor(monster.y) % 64 === 0)
{ ...
```

This works by checking to see if the monster's X and Y positions are evenly divisible by 64. If they are, and the modulus operator returns no remainders, then we know that the monster must be at a corner. Figure 10-13 illustrates these cell corner positions.

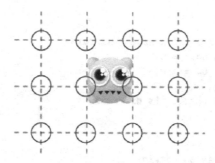

Figure 10-13. If the monster's position divides evenly into the size of the grid cell, then you know the monster is at a cell corner

> Note: This is why it's important that the monster's speed divides evenly into 64. If it doesn't, then this if statement will never be true, and the monster's direction will never change. Math.floor is applied to the monster's position to rule out the possibility of any decimal values in the monster's X and Y position numbers.

Changing the direction

The changeDirection function chooses a random number between 1 and 7. If the number is less than 5, the monster chooses a new random direction. Each number between 1 and 4 correlates to a direction: RIGHT, LEFT, UP, or DOWN. The monster is then given a new velocity that matches this direction.

```
function changeDirection(monster)
{
  var UP = 1;
  var DOWN = 2;
  var LEFT = 3;
  var RIGHT = 4;

  var direction = Math.ceil(Math.random() * 7);
```

```
if(direction < 5)
{
  switch(direction)
  {
    case RIGHT:
      monster.vx = monster.speed;
      monster.vy = 0;
      break;

    case LEFT:
      monster.vx = -monster.speed;
      monster.vy = 0;
      break;

    case UP:
      monster.vx = 0;
      monster.vy = -monster.speed;
      break;

    case DOWN:
      monster.vx = 0;
      monster.vy = monster.speed;
  }
}
}
```

If the random number is 5, 6, or 7, the monster won't choose a new direction. This gives the monster a roughly 40% chance of continuing in the same direction each time it reaches a cell corner. You can play around with these probabilities to customize how often, and in which directions, the monster prefers to move.

These basic concepts all apply to moving a monster around a real maze as well. But in a real maze, there are a few more things the monster has to think about. It should avoid walls, and, possibly, it should try and find the player's character. In our next example we'll find out how to do these things.

Navigating maze walls

In the chapter's source files you'll find an example program called **monsterMaze.html**. Three monsters chase the player around a small maze. The monsters change direction only when they're at a passage intersection, and they usually choose a direction that will take them closer to the player's character. The monsters also open their mouths when then come within range of the alien. Figure 10-14 illustrates the game.

Figure 10-14. Monsters chase the player around a maze

The basic game code is very similar to Time Bomb Panic. What's new is an important function called changeDirection that figures out when and where the monster should move. Before we look at the changeDirection function, let's take a quick tour of how the game is put together to review some maze game basics.

Setting up the game

All the game-programming code is in the **monsterMaze.js** file. The level is built using two arrays: one for the environment map and one for the game objects. Notice that the three monsters are in the gameObjects array.

```
//The game map
var map =
[
  [5,5,5,5,5,5,5,5,5,5,5],
  [5,1,1,1,1,1,1,1,1,1,5],
  [5,1,2,2,2,1,2,1,2,1,5],
  [5,1,1,2,1,1,1,1,1,1,5],
  [5,1,1,1,1,2,1,1,2,1,5],
  [5,1,2,1,2,2,1,2,2,1,5],
  [5,1,1,1,1,1,2,1,1,1,5],
  [5,5,5,5,5,5,5,5,5,5,5]
];
```

```
//The game objects map
var gameObjects =
[
  [0,0,0,0,0,0,0,0,0,0,0,0],
  [0,0,0,0,0,0,0,0,0,0,3,0],
  [0,0,0,0,0,0,0,0,0,0,0,0],
  [0,0,0,0,0,4,0,0,0,0,0,0],
  [0,0,3,0,0,0,0,0,0,0,0,0],
  [0,0,0,0,0,0,0,0,0,0,0,0],
```

```
    [0,0,0,0,0,0,0,0,3,0,0,0],
    [0,0,0,0,0,0,0,0,0,0,0,0]
];
```

```
//Map code
var EMPTY = 0;
var FLOOR = 1;
var BOX = 2;
var MONSTER = 3;
var ALIEN = 4;
var WALL = 5;
```

> *Note: Importantly for this example, the monsters need to be placed in a position on the map that puts them at a maze passage intersection. Intersections are the places in the maze where a passage changes direction or joins with another passage. The monsters need to start at these intersections so that they can properly choose their initial direction, as you will see ahead.*

The buildMap function builds the level in the same way as in Time Bomb Panic. An important detail is that when it creates the monster sprites, it runs a function called changeDirection that will give the monsters their initial starting positions.

```
case MONSTER:
  var monster = Object.create(monsterObject);
  monster.sourceX = tilesheetX;
  monster.sourceY = tilesheetY;
  monster.x = column * SIZE;
  monster.y = row * SIZE;

  //Make the monster choose a random start direction
  changeDirection(monster)
  monsters.push(monster);
  sprites.push(monster);
  break;
```

The monsterObject has also been upgraded from the previous example. You'll find it in the **objects.js** file. It adds some properties to help change the monster's state.

```
monsterObject = Object.create(spriteObject);
monsterObject.sourceX = 128;
```

```
//The monster's states
monsterObject.NORMAL = [2,0];
monsterObject.SCARED = [2,1];
monsterObject.state = monsterObject.NORMAL;
monsterObject.update = function()
```

```
{
  this.sourceX = this.state[0] * this.width;
  this.sourceY = this.state[1] * this.height;
};
```

```
//The monster's allowed speed
monsterObject.speed = 1;
```

```
//Properties to help the monster change direction
monsterObject.NONE = 0;
monsterObject.UP = 1;
monsterObject.DOWN = 2;
monsterObject.LEFT = 3;
monsterObject.RIGHT = 4;
monsterObject.validDirections = [];
monsterObject.direction = monsterObject.NONE;
monster.hunt = true;
```

You can see that the monster has five constants that define the possible directions in which it can move. An array called validDirections will be used to store the directions that the monster could be allowed to move in. The monster's initial direction is set to NONE. You'll soon see how all these properties are used in the game's changeDirection function.

The monster also has a property called hunt that will determine whether the monster will hunt for the player. It's set to true.

```
monster.hunt = true;
```

The playGame function loops through all the monster sprites in the monsters array. It moves each monster, and it also checks whether each monster is at a maze cell corner. If it is, the changeDirection function is called.

```
for(var i = 0; i < monsters.length; i++)
{
  var monster = monsters[i];

  //Move the monsters
  monster.x += monster.vx;
  monster.y += monster.vy;

  //Check whether the monster is at a tile corner
  if(Math.floor(monster.x) % SIZE === 0 && Math.floor(monster.y) % SIZE === 0)
  {
    //Change the monster's direction
    changeDirection(monster);
  }

  //... additional code that changes the monster's state...
}
```

(This for loop contains some additional code that opens the monster's mouth if the alien is nearby. We'll take a look at how that works in later sections.)

If the monster is at a cell corner, it's sent to the changeDirection function to figure out which direction it should move in.

```
changeDirection(monster);
```

Let's find out how that works next.

Changing the monster's direction

The code that changes the monster's direction is based very closely on the code that moves the sea monster in Island Adventure from Chapter 5. In fact, before you continue reading, take a few minutes to review how that code works. The basic principle is identical, as is the first part of the code.

The code works by figuring out what kinds of objects are on the map surrounding the monster. The monster can only move on FLOOR cells. The code tests each of the four possible directions that the monster can move in: up, down, left, and right. Whichever direction contains a FLOOR cell will be pushed into the monster's validDirections array. At the end of the four direction tests, the validDirections array will only contain those directions that will lead the monster to FLOOR cells.

But the code needs to do a little more work. The monster should only change its direction if it's at a maze passage intersection or if it's in a cul-de-sac (dead end). And it should choose a direction that will take it closer to the player's character. How will it figure these things out? One small step at a time, of course.

First, here's the entire changeDirection function that you can use as a reference. I'll explain it all in detail ahead.

```
function changeDirection(monster)
{
  //Clear any previous direction the monster has chosen
  monster.validDirections = [];
  monster.direction = monster.NONE;

  //Find the monster's column and row in the array
  var monsterColumn = Math.floor(monster.x / SIZE);
  var monsterRow = Math.floor(monster.y / SIZE);

  //Find out what kinds of things are in the map cells
  //that surround the monster. If the cells contain a FLOOR cell,
  //push the corresponding direction into the validDirections array
  if(monsterRow > 0)
  {
    var thingAbove = map[monsterRow-1][monsterColumn];
    if(thingAbove === FLOOR)
    {
      monster.validDirections.push(monster.UP);
    }
  }
}
```

```
    if(monsterRow < ROWS-1)
    {
      var thingBelow = map[monsterRow + 1][monsterColumn];
      if(thingBelow === FLOOR)
      {
        monster.validDirections.push(monster.DOWN);
      }
    }
    if(monsterColumn > 0)
    {
      var thingToTheLeft = map[monsterRow][monsterColumn-1];
      if(thingToTheLeft === FLOOR)
      {
        monster.validDirections.push(monster.LEFT);
      }
    }
    if(monsterColumn < COLUMNS-1)
    {
      var thingToTheRight = map[monsterRow][monsterColumn + 1];
      if(thingToTheRight === FLOOR)
      {
        monster.validDirections.push(monster.RIGHT);
      }
    }

    //The monster's validDirections array now contains 0 to 4 directions that
    //contain FLOOR cells. Which of those directions will the monster
    //choose to move in?

    //If a valid direction was found, figure out if the monster is at a
    //maze passage intersection.
    if(monster.validDirections.length !== 0)
    {
      //Find out if the monster is at an intersection
      var upOrDownPassage
        = (monster.validDirections.indexOf(monster.UP) !== -1
        || monster.validDirections.indexOf(monster.DOWN) !== -1);

      var leftOrRightPassage
        = (monster.validDirections.indexOf(monster.LEFT) !== -1
        || monster.validDirections.indexOf(monster.RIGHT) !== -1);

      //Change the monster's direction if it's at an intersection or
      //in a cul-de-sac (dead end)
      if(upOrDownPassage && leftOrRightPassage
      || monster.validDirections.length === 1)
      {
        //Optionally find the closest distance to the alien
```

```
        if(alien !== null && monster.hunt === true)
        {
          findClosestDirection(monster);
        }

        //Assign a random validDirection if the alien object doesn't exist in the game
        //or a validDirection wasn't found that brings the monster closer to the alien
        if(alien === null || monster.direction === monster.NONE)
        {
          var randomNumber = Math.floor(Math.random() * monster.validDirections.length);
          monster.direction = monster.validDirections[randomNumber];
        }

        //Choose the monster's final direction
        switch(monster.direction)
        {
          case monster.RIGHT:
            monster.vx = monster.speed;
            monster.vy = 0;
            break;

          case monster.LEFT:
            monster.vx = -monster.speed;
            monster.vy = 0;
            break;

          case monster.UP:
            monster.vx = 0;
            monster.vy = -monster.speed;
            break;

          case monster.DOWN:
            monster.vx = 0;
            monster.vy = monster.speed;
        }
      }
    }
  }
```

Analyzing the level map

The first thing the changeDirection function does is clear the monster's direction and validDirections properties so that they don't contain any values that may have been assigned previously.

```
monster.validDirections = [];
monster.direction = monster.NONE;
```

We now have to figure out which directions the monster can move in that are valid. The monster can't pass through boxes or walls. That means the valid directions should only contain floor objects.

There are actually two ways we could do this. The first way would be to use hitTestRectangle. We could loop through all the monsters and check whether they're colliding with any boxes or walls. If there's a collision, we could make the monster choose a new direction. This would actually work just fine up to a point.

But there's a better way. We can use what we know about 2D arrays to find out where in the map array the monster is and what kinds of things are surrounding it. This is a technique called **tile-based collision**. The advantage of this approach is that we can get specific information about the surrounding objects and use that information to make an intelligent decision about what to do. It also means we only need to do four collision checks, one for each direction, rather than a collision check for every box and wall in the game, of which there are dozens.

First, we need to locate the monster inside the map array. Here's what the map array looks like. It tells us where all the environment objects are: floors, walls, and boxes.

```
var map =
[
  [5,5,5,5,5,5,5,5,5,5,5],
  [5,1,1,1,1,1,1,1,1,1,5],
  [5,1,2,2,2,1,2,1,2,1,5],
  [5,1,1,2,1,1,1,1,1,1,5],
  [5,1,1,1,1,2,1,1,2,1,5],
  [5,1,2,1,2,2,1,2,2,1,5],
  [5,1,1,1,1,1,2,1,1,1,5],
  [5,5,5,5,5,5,5,5,5,5,5]
];
```

But you can also see that there are no monsters in this array. The monster positions are being described by X and Y positions on the canvas. The objects in the map array are being described by column and row numbers. Our first job then is to convert the monster's X and Y canvas positions to the array's column and row numbers. If we can do that, we'll know where in the map array the monster will be. And, once we know that, we can figure out what objects are surrounding it.

Luckily, it's very easy to convert the monster's X and Y positions into array column and row numbers. All you need to do is divide the X and Y positions by the game's cell SIZE, (64).

```
var monsterColumn = Math.floor(monster.x / SIZE);
var monsterRow = Math.floor(monster.y / SIZE);
```

Math.floor is used to truncate any possible decimal values. monsterColumn and monsterRow now tell us exactly where in the map array the monster is.

The code then uses the same if statement from Island Adventure to find out which things surrounding the monster are FLOOR cells. If it finds a FLOOR cell, it pushes it into the monster's validDirections array.

```
if(monsterRow > 0)
{
  var thingAbove = map[monsterRow-1][monsterColumn];
  if(thingAbove === FLOOR)
```

```
    {
      monster.validDirections.push(monster.UP);
    }
  }
  if(monsterRow < ROWS-1)
  {
    var thingBelow = map[monsterRow + 1][monsterColumn];
    if(thingBelow === FLOOR)
    {
      monster.validDirections.push(monster.DOWN);
    }
  }
  if(monsterColumn > 0)
  {
    var thingToTheLeft = map[monsterRow][monsterColumn-1];
    if(thingToTheLeft === FLOOR)
    {
      monster.validDirections.push(monster.LEFT);
    }
  }
  if(monsterColumn < COLUMNS-1)
  {
    var thingToTheRight = map[monsterRow][monsterColumn + 1];
    if(thingToTheRight === FLOOR)
    {
      monster.validDirections.push(monster.RIGHT);
    }
  }
}
```

validDirections now contains 0 to 4 possible directions that the monster can move in: UP, DOWN, LEFT, or RIGHT. If the monsters were just moving around the maze totally at random, we could just leave things like this and simply choose any random valid direction. But our maze monsters are a little smarter than that. They only want to change directions when they're at a maze passage intersection. Let's find out how they do this.

Finding the passageways

Maze passage intersections are any points where vertical and horizontal passages meet. Figure 10-15 illustrates most of the major passage intersections within the map. These are all points where the monsters should decide whether they want to continue in the same direction or choose a new direction.

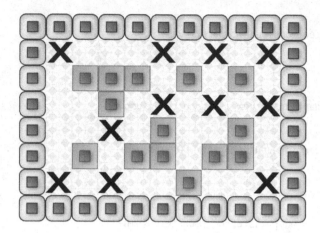

Figure 10-15. Maze passage intersections

All the passage intersections share one thing in common. They contain at least one valid direction that goes either UP or DOWN and at least one valid direction that goes LEFT or RIGHT. That means they all have at least one vertical direction and one horizontal direction that contains floor cells. Figure 10-16 illustrates this.

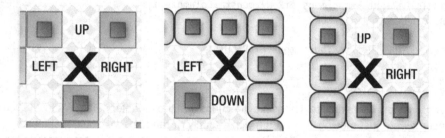

Figure 10-16. All passage intersections have at least one valid vertical direction and one valid horizontal direction

Now that we know this interesting fact, we can test whether any of the monster's valid directions meet these criteria. The next bit of code does just that. It uses indexOf to check whether the monster's valid directions contain at least one UP and DOWN direction and one LEFT or RIGHT direction. If it finds an UP or DOWN direction, the code flags this by setting a variable called upOrDownPassage to true. If it finds a LEFT or RIGHT direction, it then sets a variable called leftOrRightPassage to true.

```
var upOrDownPassage
  = (monster.validDirections.indexOf(monster.UP) !== -1
  || monster.validDirections.indexOf(monster.DOWN) !== -1);

var leftOrRightPassage
  = (monster.validDirections.indexOf(monster.LEFT) !== -1
  || monster.validDirections.indexOf(monster.RIGHT) !== -1);
```

If both upOrDownPassage *and* leftOrRightPassage are true, then the monster is definitely at a passage intersection.

Escaping from cul-de-sacs

But there's one more problem the monster needs to solve. What if it runs into a cul-de-sac (a dead end)? Figure 10-17 illustrates the cul-de-sacs in the maze. If the monster finds itself in one of those, it should also change its direction. But how will we know if the monster is in one?

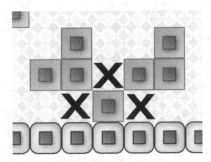

Figure 10-17. A cul-de-sac has only one valid exit route

Take a good look at Figure 10-17: in each cul-de-sac, *there's only one way out*.

That means that if the monster's validDirections array has found only one valid direction, then the monster must be in a cul-de-sac. Here's how you can test for this:

```
if(monster.validDirections.length === 1)
{
  //The monster must be in a cul-de-sac
}
```

Our code has now figured out whether the monster is at a passage intersection or if it's in a cul-de-sac. We can now use this information to make the monster move in one of the valid directions.

Choosing the right direction

Here's the if statement that chooses the monster's final direction.

```
if(upOrDownPassage && leftOrRightPassage || monster.validDirections.length === 1)
{
    //Optionally find the closest distance to the alien
    if(alien !== null && monster.hunt === true)
    {
      findClosestDirection(monster);
    }

    //Assign a random validDirection if the alien object doesn't exist in the game
    //or a validDirection wasn't found that brings the monster closer to the alien
    if(alien === null || monster.direction === monster.NONE)
    {
```

```
      var randomNumber = Math.floor(Math.random() * monster.validDirections.length);
      monster.direction = monster.validDirections[randomNumber];
  }

  //Choose the monster's final direction
  switch(monster.direction)
  {
    case monster.RIGHT:
      monster.vx = monster.speed;
      monster.vy = 0;
      break;

    case monster.LEFT:
      monster.vx = -monster.speed;
      monster.vy = 0;
      break;

    case monster.UP:
      monster.vx = 0;
      monster.vy = -monster.speed;
      break;

    case monster.DOWN:
      monster.vx = 0;
      monster.vy = monster.speed;
  }
}
```

The code first checks to see whether the monster is at a passage intersection or in a cul-de-sac. If either of those things is true, we know the monster is in a location in the maze where it should change direction.

```
if(upOrDownPassage && leftOrRightPassage || monster.validDirections.length === 1)
{...
```

The code then determines whether the monster should try and find the direction closest to the player. It will do this if the monster's hunt property is true and the alien object exists in the game. If both those things are true, it calls the findClosestDirection function.

```
if(alien !== null && monster.hunt === true)
{
  findClosestDirection(monster);
}
```

I'll explain how findClosestDirection works in detail in the next section. However, if the findClosestDirection function isn't called, any random valid direction will be chosen by the next if statement. It runs if the alien doesn't exist in the game or if the monster hasn't been assigned a new direction yet.

```
if(alien === null || monster.direction === monster.NONE)
{
  var randomNumber = Math.floor(Math.random() * monster.validDirections.length);
  monster.direction = monster.validDirections[randomNumber];
}
```

The monster's direction property now contains one of the randomly chosen directions from its validDirections array. The final switch statement then changes the monster's velocity to match the chosen direction.

```
switch(monster.direction)
{
  case monster.RIGHT:
    monster.vx = monster.speed;
    monster.vy = 0;
    break;

  case monster.LEFT:
    monster.vx = -monster.speed;
    monster.vy = 0;
    break;

  case monster.UP:
    monster.vx = 0;
    monster.vy = -monster.speed;
    break;

  case monster.DOWN:
    monster.vx = 0;
    monster.vy = monster.speed;
}
```

The monster will now move in a direction that lets it explore the maze in an intelligent way.

If you prefer, you can replace this last switch statement with this next bit of alternative code. It does the same thing, but it's a bit more advanced conceptually.

```
var moveByDirection =
[
  [0, -1],
  [0, 1],
  [-1, 0],
  [1, 0]
];

monster.vx = monster.speed * moveByDirection[monster.direction - 1][0];
monster.vy = monster.speed * moveByDirection[monster.direction - 1][1];
```

The four possible directions are represented by the numbers in a 2D array called moveByDirection. They represent UP, DOWN, LEFT, and RIGHT, in that order. The two elements in each subarray are multiplied by the monster's speed and assigned to its vx and vy properties. This makes the monster move in the correct direction. Using [monster.direction − 1] as the array index selector means that the correct pair of numbers is chosen in the 2D array. There's no technical reason for using this code over the easier-to-understand switch statement, but it's an interesting solution.

Now let's find out how to make the monsters hunt the player.

Hunting the player

As you saw in the last section, if the monster's hunt property is true and the alien object exists in the game, the findClosestDirection function will run.

```
if(alien !== null && monster.hunt === true)
{
  findClosestDirection(monster);
}
```

Its job is to figure out which of the monster's valid directions will take it closest to the alien. It does this by measuring the distance between the monster and the alien; it then figures out which of the four directions is the closest one. Here's the complete findClosestDirection function.

```
function findClosestDirection(monster)
{
  var closestDirection = undefined;

  //Find the distance between the monster and the alien
  var vx = alien.centerX()−monster.centerX();
  var vy = alien.centerY()−monster.centerY();

  //If the distance is greater on the X axis...
  if(Math.abs(vx) >= Math.abs(vy))
  {
    //Try left and right
    if(vx <= 0)
    {
      closestDirection = monsterObject.LEFT;
    }
    else
    {
      closestDirection = monsterObject.RIGHT;
    }
  }
  //If the distance is greater on the Y axis...
  else
  {
    //Try up and down
    if(vy <= 0)
    {
      closestDirection = monsterObject.UP;
    }
```

```
  else
  {
    closestDirection = monsterObject.DOWN;
  }
}

//Find out if the closestDirection is one of the validDirections
for(var i = 0; i < monster.validDirections.length; i++)
{
  if(closestDirection === monster.validDirections[i])
  {
    //If it is, assign the closestDirection to the monster's direction
    monster.direction = closestDirection;
  }
}
}
```

The function first creates a local variable called closestDirection that it will use to store the closest direction that it finds.

```
var closestDirection = undefined;
```

The code then plots a vector between the center of the alien and the monster.

```
var vx = alien.centerX() - monster.centerX();
var vy = alien.centerY() - monster.centerY();
```

vx tells us the distance between the objects on the X axis. vy tells us the distance between the objects on the Y axis. The vx and vy variables together describe a vector between the objects. (Do a quick review of Chapter 8 if you are unsure about vectors and how they work.)

We want to move the monster in the horizontal or vertical direction with the *greatest amount of distance* between it and the alien. Why is that? Take a look at Figure 10-18.

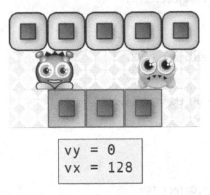

```
vy = 0
vx = 128
```

Figure 10-18. Move the monster along the axis with the greatest distance between the objects

It's obvious that the monster should choose the left direction along the X axis if it wants to get closer to the player. However, the X axis is also the one with the greatest distance between the objects.

Still confused? Let's untangle this.

The alien and the monster are at the same height on the screen. That means they have exactly the same Y positions. Let's imagine they both have a Y position of 64. When we calculate the vy value between them, it will be 0. Here's what the vy calculation will look like using real numbers:

```
vy = alien.centerY()–monster.centerY();
vy = 64–64;
vy = 0;
```

However, there are about 128 pixels between them on the X axis. That means the vx calculation will evaluate like this:

```
vx = 128;
```

So the vx value is greater than the vy value.

We can see from Figure 10-18 that the monster should move along the X axis, and it's now clear that this is also the axis with the greatest distance between the objects. This tells us that if we find the axis with the greatest distance between the objects, we also know that the monster's final direction choice will be on that axis.

That's what the next bit of code does. It checks whether the distance is greater on the X or Y axis. It then narrows down the search between the LEFT and RIGHT or UP and DOWN directions. If the vx value is less than 0, it will be LEFT. If the vy value is less than 0, it will be UP.

```
//If the distance is greater on the X axis...
if(Math.abs(vx) >= Math.abs(vy))
{
  //Try left and right
  if(vx <= 0)
  {
    closestDirection = monsterObject.LEFT;
  }
  else
  {
    closestDirection = monsterObject.RIGHT;
  }
}
//If the distance is greater on the Y axis...
else
{
  //Try up and down
  if(vy <= 0)
  {
    closestDirection = monsterObject.UP;
  }
```

```
  else
  {
    closestDirection = monsterObject.DOWN;
  }
}
```

At the end of this, `closestDirection` will be the direction that moves the monster closer to the alien.

However, we don't know yet if that direction is actually one of the monster's valid directions. It will only help the monster if the closest direction is also a `FLOOR` cell. So the code then needs to loop through all the monster's valid directions and see if there's a match with the `closestDirection`.

```
for(var i = 0; i < monster.validDirections.length; i++)
{
  if(closestDirection === monster.validDirections[i])
  {
    monster.direction = closestDirection;
  }
}
```

If the `closestDirection` matches a valid direction, then it's assigned to the monster's `direction` property.

```
monster.direction = closestDirection;
```

If it doesn't find a match, then the monster's `direction` property will remain at its initial value of `NONE` and the rest of the code in the `changeDirection` function will later assign any valid random direction.

Changing the monster's state

The game example has a cute feature: when the monsters are near the alien, their mouths open. This is an easy thing to implement. It happens in the `playGame` function, within the same loop that moves the monster and checks whether it should change direction.

```
for(var i = 0; i < monsters.length; i++)
{
  var monster = monsters[i];

  //...the code that moves the monster and checks whether it should change direction...

  //Plot a vector between the monster and alien
  var vx = alien.centerX()-monster.centerX();
  var vy = alien.centerY()-monster.centerY();

  //Find the distance between the circles by calculating
  //the vector's magnitude (how long the vector is)
  var magnitude = Math.sqrt(vx * vx + vy * vy);
```

```
  if(magnitude < 192)
  {
    monster.state = monster.SCARED;
  }
  else
  {
    monster.state = monster.NORMAL;
  }

  //Update the monster to reflect state changes
  monster.update();
}
```

The code plots a vector between the monster and the alien. It then calculates the vector's magnitude, using the same formula you learned in Chapter 8 (the Pythagorean theorem).

```
var vx = alien.centerX() – monster.centerX();
var vy = alien.centerY() – monster.centerY();
var magnitude = Math.sqrt(vx * vx + vy * vy);
```

A simple if statement then checks whether the magnitude is less than 192. If it is, the monster's state is set to SCARED. If it's greater than 192, the monster's state is set to NORMAL. It's a simple and fun little effect that adds a nice touch of melodrama to the game.

More about pathfinding

Our maze monsters now have a little bit of intelligence, but they're definitely not budding Einsteins. Okay, let's be frank: they're pretty much dumb as mud. They try, but, despite their enthusiasm, the monsters can't really navigate around corners too well, so it's easy to throw them off the trail. Still, they'll eventually find their quarry and this will provide a comfortable challenge in a simple maze game.

This has been an introduction to very big topic of game design called **pathfinding**. It's how game characters find their way around game worlds. We've covered all the basic principles that you need to know to start your own pathfinding experiments. Can you make the monsters smarter? Carefully think about how you want your monsters to behave and also the problems they'll need to solve to navigate their environment. You'll be able to use all the basic techniques in this chapter to fine-tune many variations of this basic pathfinding example to make much more complex, and smarter, maze monsters.

> Note: To find the shortest path between any points in a maze, you'll need to use the classic A* (A-Star) algorithm. A web search will bring up many resources to help you implement it if you need to.

Switching game levels

Now it's your turn! Take everything you learned in this chapter and make a game with it. Use maze maps, collect objects, and use scrolling and pathfinding monsters. With a bit of time, creativity, and imagination you'll be able to come up with a great game. But, if you're anything like me, your ambitions will get away with you, and, before you know it, you'll end up with a much bigger game than you expected. Suddenly the simple little maze game becomes a multilevel dungeon crawler with dozens of areas to explore and countless quests and puzzles to solve.

You'll need some way of managing that complexity. The first step is to try and break your game down into manageable levels. When a player completes one level, load the next one. To do this, keep all of your level information in arrays. Work out a system to load the level information into your game when a player completes a level. There are many ways that you could do this, and you'll learn more by working out your own system rather than blindly following mine. You have all the skills to do it.

To help you get started, take a look at the game Monster Mayhem in the chapter's source files. It's a two-level scrolling maze game that uses all the techniques from this chapter. Collect all the stars and avoid the monsters. There's nothing new there, and I'll leave it up to you to go through the source files if you're curious about any of the specifics. But what we should take a close look at is how the game stores the game levels and how it switches them when the player completes a level.

Figure 10-19 illustrates how the game plays. When you've collected all the stars in the level, the game displays "Level Complete" for one second before the next level loads. When you've collected all the stars on that second level, the game displays "Game Over." If you touch any of the monsters during the game, the game ends and displays "You Lost."

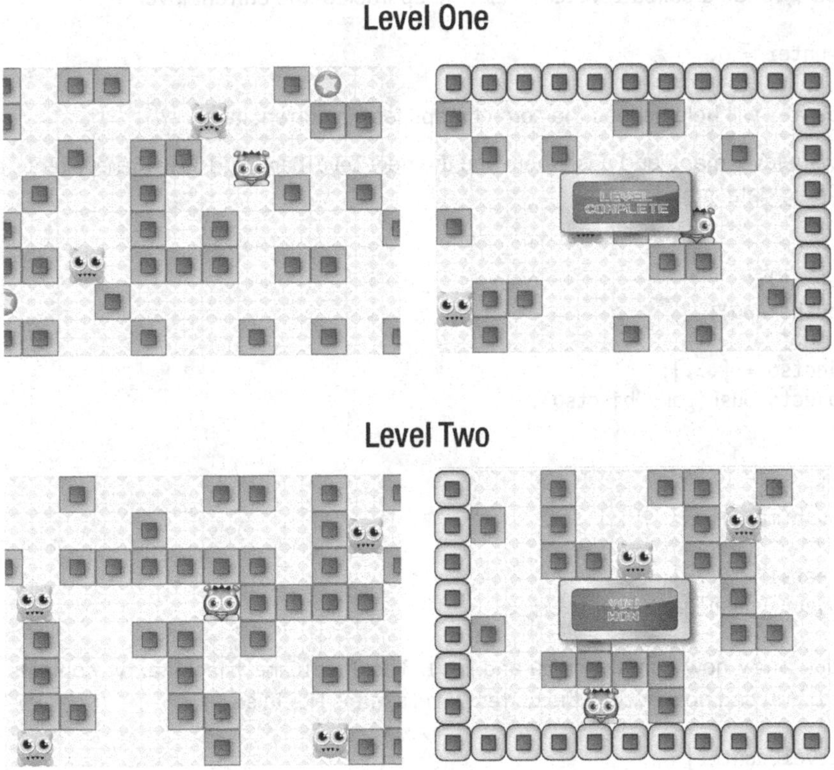

Level One

Level Two

Figure 10-19. Collect all the stars and avoid the monsters in Monster Mayhem

> Note: To make Monster Mayhem easier to play, the monsters' hunt properties have been set to false. Set this to true for a greater challenge. For greater variety, set it to true only if a monster is close to the player.

This is a basic model for a multilevel game, so let's walk through how the levels are made, stored, and loaded.

Keep level maps in arrays

The first thing you need to do is store all of your level maps in arrays. Yes, each level map already is an array, but you have to put it into yet another array to store and load it when needed. Let's find out how this is done in Monster Mayhem.

Each level uses two maps: the environment map and the game objects map. First, create arrays to store each of these map types.

```
var levelMaps = [];
var levelGameObjects = [];
```

We also need a variable called levelCounter to keep track of the current level.

```
var levelCounter = 0;
```

The levelCounter will help us load the correct maps for the current level.

Next, create the level maps and push them into the new levelMaps and levelGameObjects arrays like this (the actual array map data is abridged):

```
//Level 0
var map0 = [...];
levelMaps.push(map0);

var gameObjects0 = [...];
levelGameObjects.push(gameObjects0);

//Level 1
var map1 = [...];
levelMaps.push(map1);

var gameObjects1 = [...];
levelGameObjects.push(gameObjects1);
```

The levelMaps array now contains map0 and map1. The levelGameObjects array contains gameObjects0 and gameObjects1. You can now access the current level's maps like this:

```
levelMaps[levelCounter]
levelGameObjects[levelCounter]
```

This will reference the correct maps for the correct level, depending on the value of levelCounter. Here's how the BUILD_MAP state uses this to create the current game level.

```
case BUILD_MAP:
  buildMap(levelMaps[levelCounter]);
  buildMap(levelGameObjects[levelCounter]);
  createOtherSprites();
  gameState = PLAYING;
  break;
```

When the game first starts, levelCounter has a value of 0, and so the first level maps will be loaded.

Use a LEVEL_COMPLETE state

To switch levels, use a new LEVEL_COMPLETE game state.

```
var LOADING = 0;
var BUILD_MAP = 1;
var PLAYING = 2;
var OVER = 3;
var LEVEL_COMPLETE = 4;
var gameState = LOADING;
```

Here's how the LEVEL_COMPLETE state is selected by the update function. When this state is set, it calls the levelComplete function. The levelComplete function will reset the game data and advance the levelCounter so that the next level loads.

```
function update()
{
  //The animation loop
  requestAnimationFrame(update, canvas);

  //Change what the game is doing based on the game state
  switch(gameState)
  {
    case LOADING:
      console.log("loading...");
      break;

    case BUILD_MAP:
      buildMap(levelMaps[levelCounter]);
      buildMap(levelGameObjects[levelCounter]);
      createOtherSprites();
      gameState = PLAYING;
      break;

    case PLAYING:
      playGame();
      break;
```

```
      case LEVEL_COMPLETE:
       levelComplete();
       break;

        case OVER:
          endGame();
          break;
    }

    //Render the game
    render();
}
```

The gameState changes to LEVEL_COMPLETE in the playGame function. This happens when the player has picked up all the stars in the stars array.

```
if(starsCollected === stars.length)
{
  gameState = LEVEL_COMPLETE;
}
```

The levelComplete function will now be called, which does the job of displaying a message and loading the next level.

Loading the next level

Here's the entire levelComplete function. I'll explain how it works after the code listing.

```
function levelComplete()
{
  //Make the levelCompleteDisplay visible
  levelCompleteDisplay.visible = true;

  //Update the timer that changes the level by 1
  levelChangeTimer++;

  //Load the next level after one second
  if(levelChangeTimer === 60)
  {
    loadNextLevel();
  }

  function loadNextLevel()
  {
    //Reset the timer that changes the level
    levelChangeTimer = 0;

    //Update the levelCounter by 1
    levelCounter++;
```

```
//Load the next level if there is one or end the game if there isn't
if(levelCounter < levelMaps.length)
{
    //Clear the arrays of objects
    sprites = [];
    monsters = [];
    boxes = [];
    stars = [];

    //Reset any gameVariables
    starsCollected = 0;

    //Re-center the camera
    camera.x = (gameWorld.x + gameWorld.width / 2)-camera.width / 2;
    camera.y = (gameWorld.y + gameWorld.height / 2)-camera.height / 2;

    //Make sure the gameWorld size matches the size of the next level
    gameWorld.width = levelMaps[levelCounter][0].length * SIZE,
    gameWorld.height = levelMaps[levelCounter].length * SIZE,

    //Build the maps for the next level
    gameState = BUILD_MAP;
}
else
{
    gameState = OVER;
}
}
}
```

The first thing that happens when a level finishes is that the game gives the player a message that says "Level Complete." This is a sprite called `levelCompleteDisplay`. It's displayed by setting its `visible` property to `true`.

```
levelCompleteDisplay.visible = true;
```

It should remain visible for about one second before the next level loads. The main program has initialized a variable called `levelChangeTimer` to 0. The `levelComplete` function adds 1 to it.

```
levelChangeTimer++;
```

Because this code is being run 60 times per second by the game's `update` function, the `levelChangeTimer` will equal 60 after 1 second. When that happens, we can load the next level.

```
if(levelChangeTimer === 60)
{
    loadNextLevel();
}
```

The if statement calls the loadNextLevel function. The first thing loadNextLevel does is to reset the levelChangeTimer to 0. It then updates the levelCounter by 1.

```
function loadNextLevel()
{
    //Reset the timer that changes the level
    levelChangeTimer = 0;

    //Update the levelCounter by 1
    levelCounter++;
```

The function should load the next level only if there actually is a new level to load. If the game is on the last level already, there won't be another level to load. The code checks for this by comparing the value of levelCounter to the length of the levelMaps array. If levelCounter is less than levelMaps.length, then there will still be new levels to load. Otherwise, the game should end.

```
if(levelCounter < levelMaps.length)
{
    //... load the next level...
}
else
{
    gameState = OVER;
}
```

If there is a new level to load, the code clears all the arrays that contain the game objects.

```
sprites = [];
monsters = [];
boxes = [];
stars = [];
```

They need to be cleared so that they can be filled up with the objects for the next new level. The code also needs to reset any game variables that the level might need to use. In Monster Mayhem this means that the starsCollected variable has to be reset to 0.

```
starsCollected = 0;
```

It's possible that the next level map won't be the same size at the previous one. To make sure, set the gameWorld object's width and height to the current map's size.

```
gameWorld.width = levelMaps[levelCounter][0].length * SIZE,
gameWorld.height = levelMaps[levelCounter].length * SIZE,
```

You'll also need to re-center the camera over the gameWorld.

```
camera.x = (gameWorld.x + gameWorld.width / 2) - camera.width / 2;
camera.y = (gameWorld.y + gameWorld.height / 2) - camera.height / 2;
```

The last job is to change the gameState to BUILD_MAP to create the new level.

```
gameState = BUILD_MAP;
```

Because we've increased the levelCounter by 1, the buildMap function will use the next set of level maps to create the level.

All of these details will, of course, vary depending on the specific game you're making, but you can use this basic structure to help you plan how you're going to handle loading new levels in your own games.

Using a tile map editor

In this chapter you learned how to design game levels by using 2D arrays. It's fun, quick, and easy to do. At least, it's fun for the first few times. If you're designing a game with 100 levels, or you've decided to make a continent-sized game map with 10,000 columns and rows, staring at all those little numbers crammed into the arrays will drive you to despair in about half an hour. Trust me, you don't want to be designing and editing a 10,000-column 2D array by hand! That's when you need a **tile map editor**.

A tile map editor is software that lets you load your tilesheet and that uses the sprite images to compose your game level. It will then generate an array based on that level that you can use in your game. This means that you can visually design your level, and then just drop the finished array into your program.

Tiled is a free open source tile map editor for Windows, Mac OS X, and Linux. You can download it at www.mapeditor.org. Figure 10-20 is a screenshot of how I used it to help me design the second level in Monster Mayhem.

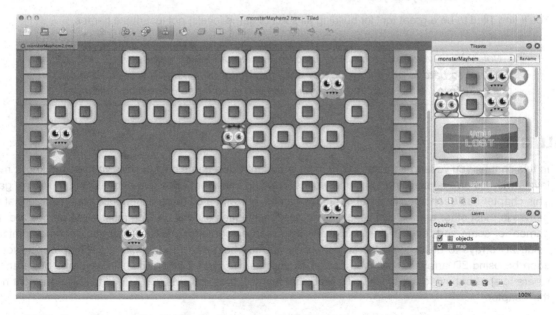

Figure 10-20. Use a tile map editor like Tiled to help you generate 2D arrays using a visual layout

Here's a quick-start guide to using Tiled to help you quickly design your own level maps.

1. First, set Tiled up so that it will save your game level as 2D array data. In the **Preferences** menu, set **store tile layer data** to **CSV**.

2. Select **File ➤ New** to start creating a new level. Select **orthogonal** for the orientation. Set the **tile size** to the size of your tilesheet sprites. For the games in this chapter I used a tile of 64 by 64 pixels. Set the **map size** to the number of columns and rows you want your map to occupy. Click **OK** to start building the new level.

3. Next you need to load your tilesheet image file. Select **Map ➤ New Tileset**. Give the tilesheet a name and browse to your game's tilesheet image file. Click **OK**, and your tilesheet will be loaded into the right side of the editor.

4. You can now click on individual tiles and use them with the stamp tool to compose your level. Tiled lets you create different map layers, so you could have one layer for your environment and another for your game objects. When you're finished designing the level, each map layer will be a separate 2D array. That's perfect for creating separate map and gameObject arrays, as I've suggested you do in this chapter.

5. Save your work. Tiled saves it with a ".tmx" file extension.

6. Open the TMX file in a text editor. You'll see some XML data, and then the level arrays that Tiled generated. The arrays are 1D arrays, but they're formatted into columns and rows so that you can easily turn them into 2D arrays. Just add square brackets around the array data by using the same format in this chapter. You can just ignore all the extra XML data.

7. Add the 2D arrays to your game.

You'll find Tiled to be a great tool for building all sorts of game levels, not just maze games.

> Note: When you have a bit more practice making tile-based games, you'll realize that it's not so hard to program your very own map editor from scratch with JavaScript. You already have all the skills to do it. Try it when you're up for an interesting challenge!

Summary

In this chapter you've learned some of the most important video-game design skills you need to know: making levels with 2D arrays, scrolling big game worlds, creating intelligent enemies, and building multilevel games. This chapter has been specifically about maze games, but with a bit more experience you'll realize that video games in most other genres can benefit from these techniques as well. In fact, most video games are "maze games" of some sort, even if they're cleverly disguised as something else. When you become comfortable using 2D arrays to build game levels, especially with the help of a fun tool like a tile map editor, you may soon be using 2D arrays to help you design all your games. And if you're planning a game but aren't sure where to start or how to approach it, it's likely that many of the problems you'll need to solve are right here in this chapter.

So what happens if you take a maze game and add some gravity and a bit of bounce? You get a platform game—and that's what the next chapter is all about.

Chapter 11

Platform Games and Physics

One of the most popular video-game genres is the **platform game**. It's the type of game where you run and jump around a game world to solve puzzles, collect objects, or vanquish enemies. The "platforms" refer to the ledges and boxes the game characters can jump on to explore the world. Platform games are fun to make and also pose some very interesting programming and design challenges. From a programming point of view, if you can program a platform game, you've reached a benchmark in your development as a game designer.

In this chapter, I'm going to show you all the skills you need to know to make your own platform game. We'll take a detailed look at some core video-game design techniques:

- Natural motion using physics simulations

- Complex player character behavior

- Collisions with accurate bounce effects

- Enemy Artificial Intelligence behaviors for platform games

We'll look at all these techniques within a practical, real-world context in a complete demo game, Hedgehog Apocalypse, shown in Figure 11-1. You'll be able to use this game as the starting point for building your own original platform games.

Figure 11-1. Can you squash all the hedgehogs and reach the exit?

First, let's take a detailed look at the techniques in physics you need to know to make objects move naturally.

Natural motion using physics

When something bumps into a wall, what happens? A bouncy rubber ball traveling at high speed bounces back at an angle. Something heavier, such as a rock, falls with a thud. Here's another example: when you step on a car's accelerator, the car gradually increases in speed and takes a bit of time to slow down after you hit the brakes. These sorts of physical reactions are part of what makes real-world games such as tennis and car racing so much fun.

Over the next few pages, you'll see how we can create a moving game character that moves in the way that you would expect it to in the real world. We'll look at the following characteristics:

- Acceleration: Gradually speeding up.

- Friction: Gradually slowing down.

- Bouncing: Changing the direction of motion when the object hits the edge of the screen.

- Gravity: Adding a force that pulls the object to the bottom of the screen.

- Jumping: Using one of the most required movements for video-game characters.

All these techniques apply physics to the object's motion. Most of them boil down to a simple formula that's applied to the object's vx and vy properties. Although the formulas are simple, it's sometimes far from obvious how they can be used in a practical way. It's exactly this practical application for games that you'll learn in this chapter.

> *Note: In this book, most of the physics calculations that we'll apply are based on a system called Euler integration (its popular name is "easy video game physics"). Video-game physics appear to be absolutely precise in the context of a video game but are actually only approximations of the real thing. Games use approximated physics because the amount of CPU power that is required to process them is far, far less than if you used calculations from a physics textbook. If you need to do textbook-level physical simulations of the real world, do a bit of research into Verlet Integration and Runge Kutte (RK) integration.*

To start experimenting with physics, we first need to create a sprite object with properties that we can use to apply some physics formulas.

A new spriteObject for physics and platform games

Here's the new spriteObject that we'll be using as a template to make sprites for all the games in this chapter. I've highlighted the new properties, which have been given some initial values.

```
var spriteObject =
{
    sourceX: 0,
    sourceY: 0,
    sourceWidth: 64,
    sourceHeight: 64,
    width: 64,
    height: 64,
    x: 0,
    y: 0,
    vx: 0,
    vy: 0,
    visible: true,

    //Physics properties
    accelerationX: 0,
    accelerationY: 0,
    speedLimit: 5,
    friction: 0.96,
    bounce: -0.7,
    gravity: 0.3,

    //Platform game properties
    isOnGround: undefined,
    jumpForce: -10,
```

```
    //Getters
    centerX: function()
    {
      return this.x + (this.width / 2);
    },
    centerY: function()
    {
      return this.y + (this.height / 2);
    },
    halfWidth: function()
    {
      return this.width / 2;
    },
    halfHeight: function()
    {
      return this.height / 2;
    }
};
```

You'll see how each of these new properties is used in the examples ahead.

The simplest type of physics motion is acceleration, so let's see how to make it work with our new spriteObject.

Acceleration

Acceleration means to gradually increase velocity, just as your bicycle does when you start pedaling faster. To speed up game objects gradually, you need to add a value to your object's vx or vy properties in the game animation loop. Remember that vx refers to "velocity on the X axis" and vy refers to "velocity on the Y axis." In a nutshell, these properties represent an object's speed, traveling either horizontally or vertically.

To gradually increase an object's velocity on the X axis, you need to use an addition assignment operator (+=) to add the value of the acceleration to the vx property. Your code might look something like this:

```
vx += 0.2;
```

On the Y axis, your code might look like this:

```
vy += 0.2;
```

Where does 0.2 come from? That's the value of acceleration. Exactly what the number is depends entirely on you and how quickly or slowly you want the object to speed up. A larger number such as 0.6 makes the object accelerate faster, and a lower number such as 0.1 makes it accelerate much more slowly. Choosing the right number is just a matter of trial and error and observing the effect it has on the object.

Run the **acceleration.html** file in the chapter's source files. Move the cat character around the screen with the arrow keys. When you press any arrow key, the cat gradually speeds up before reaching its maximum speed of five pixels per frame, as illustrated in Figure 11-2.

gradually speeds up
- - - - - - - - - - ➤

Figure 11-2. Gradually increase an object's speed with acceleration

The acceleration.html program

Here's the entire **acceleration.html** application class. I've highlighted all the code that's involved in applying acceleration and moving the character.

```
<!doctype html>
<meta charset="utf-8">
<title>Acceleration</title>

<canvas width="550" height="400" style="border: 1px dashed black">

<script type="text/javascript">

//--- The sprite object

var spriteObject =
{
  sourceX: 0,
  sourceY: 0,
  sourceWidth: 64,
  sourceHeight: 64,
  width: 64,
  height: 64,
  x: 0,
  y: 0,
  vx: 0,
  vy: 0,
  visible: true,

  //Physics properties
  accelerationX: 0,
  accelerationY: 0,
  speedLimit: 5,
  friction: 0.96,
  bounce: -0.7,
  gravity: 0.3,
```

```
//Platform game properties
isOnGround: undefined,
jumpForce: -10,

//Getters
centerX: function()
{
  return this.x + (this.width / 2);
},
centerY: function()
{
  return this.y + (this.height / 2);
},
halfWidth: function()
{
  return this.width / 2;
},
halfHeight: function()
{
  return this.height / 2;
}
};
```

//--- The main program

//The canvas
```
var canvas = document.querySelector("canvas");
var drawingSurface = canvas.getContext("2d");
```

//Object arrays
```
var sprites = [];
var assetsToLoad = [];
var assetsLoaded = 0;
```

//The cat
```
var cat = Object.create(spriteObject);
cat.x = canvas.width / 2 - cat.halfWidth();
cat.y = canvas.height / 2 - cat.halfHeight();
sprites.push(cat);
```

//Load the tilesheet image
```
var image = new Image();
image.addEventListener("load", loadHandler, false);
image.src = "cat.png";
assetsToLoad.push(image);
```

```
//Game states
var LOADING = 0;
var PLAYING = 1;
var gameState = LOADING;

//Arrow key codes
var UP = 38;
var DOWN = 40;
var RIGHT = 39;
var LEFT = 37;

//Directions
var moveUp = false;
var moveDown = false;
var moveRight = false;
var moveLeft = false;

//Add keyboard listeners
window.addEventListener("keydown", function(event)
{
  switch(event.keyCode)
  {
    case UP:
      moveUp = true;
      break;

    case DOWN:
      moveDown = true;
      break;

    case LEFT:
      moveLeft = true;
      break;

    case RIGHT:
      moveRight = true;
      break;
  }
}, false);

window.addEventListener("keyup", function(event)
{
  switch(event.keyCode)
  {
    case UP:
      moveUp = false;
      break;
```

```
        case DOWN:
          moveDown = false;
          break;

        case LEFT:
          moveLeft = false;
          break;

        case RIGHT:
          moveRight = false;
          break;
      }
}, false);

update();

function update()
{
    //The animation loop
    requestAnimationFrame(update, canvas);

    //Change what the game is doing based on the game state
    switch(gameState)
    {
      case LOADING:
        console.log("loading...");
        break;

      case PLAYING:
        playGame();
        break;
    }

    //Render the game
    render();
}

function loadHandler()
{
  assetsLoaded++;
  if(assetsLoaded === assetsToLoad.length)
  {
    gameState = PLAYING;
  }
}
```

```
function playGame()
{
  //Set the cat's acceleration if the keys are being pressed
  //Up
  if(moveUp && !moveDown)
  {
    cat.accelerationY = -0.2;
  }
  //Down
  if(moveDown && !moveUp)
  {
    cat.accelerationY = 0.2;
  }
  //Left
  if(moveLeft && !moveRight)
  {
    cat.accelerationX = -0.2;
  }
  //Right
  if(moveRight && !moveLeft)
  {
    cat.accelerationX = 0.2;
  }

  //Set the cat's velocity and acceleration to zero if none of the keys are being pressed
  if(!moveUp && !moveDown)
  {
    cat.accelerationY = 0;
    cat.vy = 0;
  }
  if(!moveLeft && !moveRight)
  {
    cat.accelerationX = 0;
    cat.vx = 0;
  }

  //Apply the acceleration
  cat.vx += cat.accelerationX;
  cat.vy += cat.accelerationY;

  //Limit the speed
  if (cat.vx > cat.speedLimit)
  {
    cat.vx = cat.speedLimit;
  }
  if (cat.vx < -cat.speedLimit)
  {
    cat.vx = -cat.speedLimit;
  }
```

```
    if (cat.vy > cat.speedLimit)
    {
      cat.vy = cat.speedLimit;
    }
    if (cat.vy < -cat.speedLimit)
    {
      cat.vy = -cat.speedLimit;
    }

    //Move the cat
    cat.x += cat.vx;
    cat.y += cat.vy;

    //Display the result
    console.log("cat.vx:   " + cat.vx);
    console.log("cat.x:   " + cat.x);
    console.log("----------");

    //Screen boundaries
    if (cat.x < 0)
    {
      cat.x = 0;
    }
    if (cat.y < 0)
    {
      cat.y = 0;
    }
    if (cat.x + cat.width > canvas.width)
    {
      cat.x = canvas.width - cat.width;
    }
    if (cat.y + cat.height > canvas.height)
    {
      cat.y = canvas.height - cat.height;
    }
}

function render()
{
  drawingSurface.clearRect(0, 0, canvas.width, canvas.height);

  //Display the sprites
  if(sprites.length !== 0)
  {
    for(var i = 0; i < sprites.length; i++)
    {
      var sprite = sprites[i];
      if(sprite.visible)
      {
        drawingSurface.drawImage
```

```
    (
      image,
      sprite.sourceX, sprite.sourceY,
      sprite.sourceWidth, sprite.sourceHeight,
      Math.floor(sprite.x), Math.floor(sprite.y),
      sprite.width, sprite.height
    );
  }
 }
 }
}
```

```
</script>
```

Despite the length of the code, it's nothing more than a slight modification of the run-of-the mill code you've been using in the last few chapters. I'm sure that you recognize most of it. Let's look at what's new and see how acceleration works.

The cat has three properties that store the new acceleration data. They're given their initial values in the `spriteObject`:

```
accelerationX: 0,
accelerationY: 0,
speedLimit: 5,
```

The `accelerationX` and `accelerationY` properties store the values that determine by how much the object accelerates. Because you don't want the object to move when it first appears on the screen, `accelerationX` and `accelerationY` are initialized to zero. `speedLimit` is the maximum speed that you want the object to travel. A value of 5 means that the object will travel a maximum of no more than five pixels per frame.

The work of assigning a value to the character's `accelerationX` and `accelerationY` properties is done by the `playGame` function when any of the keyboard arrow keys are pressed.

```
//Up
if(moveUp && !moveDown)
{
  cat.accelerationY = -0.2;
}
//Down
if(moveDown && !moveUp)
{
  cat.accelerationY = 0.2;
}
//Left
if(moveLeft && !moveRight)
{
  cat.accelerationX = -0.2;
}
```

```
//Right
if(moveRight && !moveLeft)
{
  cat.accelerationX = 0.2;
}
```

If accelerationX has a positive value, the object moves to the right. A negative value makes it move left. A positive accelerationY value makes the object move down, and a negative value makes it move up.

When any of the arrow keys are pressed, these new values are assigned. All you need to do to make the cat move is to assign these values to its vx and vy properties. You can do this easily enough with two lines of code in the playGame function:

```
cat.vx += cat.accelerationX;
cat.vy += cat.accelerationY;
```

However, if you leave this as is, the acceleration values are added to the object's velocity on every frame, without any limit to how fast the object can go. This means that the object eventually moves so fast that it will be nothing more than a blur on the screen. This won't be of much use in most games, so it's usually a good idea to assign a speed limit. The spriteObject has a speedLimit property that's initialized to 5.

```
speedLimit: 5,
```

The section of code in the playGame function prevents the cat from moving faster than this speed limit:

```
if (cat.vx > cat.speedLimit)
{
  cat.vx = cat.speedLimit;
}
if (cat.vx < -cat.speedLimit)
{
  cat.vx = -cat.speedLimit;
}
if (cat.vy > cat.speedLimit)
{
  cat.vy = cat.speedLimit;
}
if (cat.vy < -cat.speedLimit)
{
  cat.vy = -cat.speedLimit;
}
```

The acceleration values are added to the cat's velocity only if the vx and vx properties are within its speed limit, which is 5 in this case. This means that the cat will accelerate up to five pixels per frame and then travel at a constant rate. The logic behind this is exactly the same logic that is used to set screen boundaries.

If you prefer, you can use Math.min and Math.max to condense these four if statements into these two lines of code:

```
cat.vx = Math.min(cat.speedLimit, Math.max(cat.vx, -cat.speedLimit));
cat.vy = Math.min(cat.speedLimit, Math.max(cat.vy, -cat.speedLimit));
```

The next step is to add these new velocity values to the cat's X and Y positions. That's done with some venerable old friends—essentially the same directives you've been using since Chapter 7:

```
cat.x += cat.vx;
cat.y += cat.vy;
```

In fact, these two directives are all you will *ever* need to move the object, even though the physics involved in making them move can become quite complex. All the physics calculations are applied to the vx and vy properties; they are then simply assigned to the object's X and Y properties to make it move.

So how does this actually work to accelerate the object? The acceleration is added incrementally to the cat's vx and vy properties in each frame until it reaches the speed limit. The effect is just as you see it on the screen.

The last thing that the code does is stop the cat from moving if none of the arrow keys are being pressed:

```
if(!moveUp && !moveDown)
{
  cat.accelerationY = 0;
  cat.vy = 0;
}
if(!moveLeft && !moveRight)
{
  cat.accelerationX = 0;
  cat.vx = 0;
}
```

This sets the object's acceleration and velocity to zero when the correct keys are released.

Friction

Friction is the exact opposite of acceleration: it causes an object to gradually slow down. Figure 11-3 illustrates this.

Figure 11-3. Friction makes an object gradually slow down

Let's see how friction works with our cat character. Run the **friction.html** program and move the cat around the screen with the arrow keys. You'll notice that the cat gradually speeds up and then gradually slows down when you release the keys. It looks like it's floating around the screen.

The **friction.html** program is almost identical to the code we just looked at, except for a few small additions. The biggest change is in the playGame function. Two new lines of code multiply the cat's vx and vy properties by its friction value. This happens just below the lines that add acceleration, and I've highlighted them below:

```
//Apply the acceleration
cat.vx += cat.accelerationX;
cat.vy += cat.accelerationY;

//Apply friction
cat.vx *= cat.friction;
cat.vy *= cat.friction;
```

The spriteObject initializes the friction property to 0.96.

```
friction: 0.96,
```

A friction value of 1 amounts to "no friction." (The reason for this is because any value multiplied by 1 remains the same.) So anything less than 1 gradually slows the object down. Values from 0.94 to 0.98 apply friction very gradually, for very fluid movement. Values such as 0.7 or 0.6 slow the object very quickly.

There are a few more changes to the code that improve the fluency of the cat's movement. When the arrow keys are pressed to accelerate the cat, friction is set to 1 (no friction). This lets the cat accelerate smoothly without any drag.

```
//Up
if(moveUp && !moveDown)
{
  cat.accelerationY = -0.2;
  cat.friction = 1;
}
//Down
if(moveDown && !moveUp)
{
  cat.accelerationY = 0.2;
  cat.friction = 1;
}
//Left
if(moveLeft && !moveRight)
{
  cat.accelerationX = -0.2;
  cat.friction = 1;
}
//Right
if(moveRight && !moveLeft)
{
  cat.accelerationX = 0.2;
  cat.friction = 1;
}
```

When all four arrow keys are released, friction is set back to 0.96 to slow the cat down.

```
if(!moveUp && !moveDown)
{
  cat.accelerationY = 0;
}
if(!moveLeft && !moveRight)
{
  cat.accelerationX = 0;
}
if(!moveUp && !moveDown && !moveLeft && !moveRight)
{
  cat.friction = 0.96;
}
```

Why does this work? Because when you multiply a number by another number that's less than 1, like 0.96, the result is a number that's proportionately smaller than the first number. (Multiplying a number by 0.96 gives you a result that's 96% of the original value.) For example, let's imagine that the cat's velocity is 5. If you multiply 5 by 0.96, you'll get 4.8. If you multiply 4.8 by 0.96 you'll get 4.6. By doing this continuously inside the game loop the velocity is gradually reduced by 4% in each frame until it eventually reaches zero. That's why the cat slows down.

And that's it for friction!

Bouncing

Now that you've got acceleration and friction working, you can make objects bounce. To make an object bounce, just reverse its velocity based on the angle at which it strikes the other object. This is very easy to do if you want to make an object bounce off the screen edges. It gets more complicated if you want to make an object bounce off another object. In this next section I'll show you three techniques you can use to add bounce to your games.

Bouncing off the screen edges

Run the **bounce.html** program and move the cat around the screen with the arrow keys. Now you can bounce the cat off the screen edges, as shown in Figure 11-4.

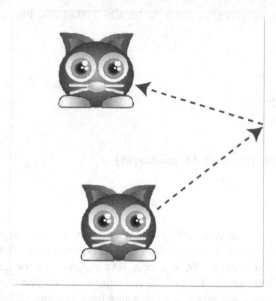

Figure 11-4. Bounce the cat off the edges of the screen

This works with the help of the spriteObject's bounce property.

```
bounce: -0.7,
```

The bounce value has to be negative because bouncing works by *reversing* the object's velocity. A value of −0.7 creates the effect of a moderate bounce. A value of −1 makes the object super bouncy. A value of 1 makes the object completely bounceless. Any value less than −1 makes the object look like it's hitting an extremely springy surface, such as a trampoline. This is important to keep in mind if you want to make a springing platform in a game.

The bounce property is used in the section of code that checks for screen boundaries. I've highlighted the relevant code below:

```
//Left
if(cat.x < 0)
{
  cat.vx *= cat.bounce;
  cat.x = 0;
}
//Up
if(cat.y < 0)
{
  cat.vy *= cat.bounce;
  cat.y = 0;
}
```

```
//Right
if(cat.x + cat.width > canvas.width)
{
  cat.vx *= cat.bounce;
  cat.x = canvas.width - cat.width;
}
//Down
if(cat.y + cat.height > canvas.height)
{
  cat.vy *= cat.bounce;
  cat.y = canvas.height - cat.height;
}
```

All that's happening is that the cat's velocity is being multiplied by the bounce value, which is negative. If you reverse an object's velocity, it looks as if it is bouncing. No, I'm not hiding anything from you here—this remarkable effect is achieved with only four lines of dead-simple code. Who said physics was difficult?

Bouncing off rectangles

Run the **rectangleBounce.html** program to see how to use this same system to make two rectangular objects bounce apart. Move the cat into the box and it bounces away at the correct angle, shown in Figure 11-5.

Figure 11-5. Bounce a rectangular object off another rectangular object

This is done with the help of a new version of the blockRectangle method. It checks for a collision between two rectangles. It separates them if there is a collision and then bounces the first rectangle off the second rectangle. The playGame function uses the new blockRectangle function like this:

```
blockRectangle(cat, box, true);
```

It has a new third argument. If the third argument is true, the cat will bounce off the box. If it's false, the objects will separate without any bounce effect. This third argument is optional, so if you leave it out there won't be any bounce.

The blockRectangle function definition declares this new third argument as the bounce parameter. If this third argument is left out, it sets bounce to a default value of false, which means there won't be any bounce effect. Here's the first part of the blockRectangle function that does this.

```
function blockRectangle(r1, r2, bounce)
{
  //Set bounce to a default value of false if it's not specified
  if(typeof bounce === "undefined")
  {
    bounce = false;
  }

  //...
```

The function first checks to see whether bounce has been given a value with the help of the typeof operator. typeof tells you what "type of" variable bounce is.

```
typeof bounce
```

If bounce hasn't been given a true or false value, it will be an "undefined" variable. If that's the case, it should be assigned a default value of false, to prevent the bounce effect from working.

```
if(typeof bounce === "undefined")
{
  bounce = false;
}
```

This if statement will kick in if you leave out the third argument when you call blockRectangle, like this:

```
blockRectangle(cat, box);
```

In this case the third argument is omitted, and so bounce will be set to false by default.

> Note: You can use typeof to check whether a variable is of any of these types: "number," "string," "boolean," "object," "undefined," or null. Surround each of these types, except for null, by quotation marks.
>
> This is actually optional for Boolean parameters. They'll automatically be interpreted as false if they're not defined.

The rest of the new blockRectangle function then does its usual work of checking for a collision and then separating the objects. If bounce is set to true, it reverses the first object's velocity. If the collision happens on the Y axis (the top or bottom), the object's vy value is reversed like this:

```
if(bounce)
{
  r1.vy *= -1;
}
```

If the collision happens on the X axis (the left or right), the vx value is reversed.

```
if(bounce)
{
  r1.vx *= -1;
}
```

This is the same trick we used to reverse the object's velocity when it hit the edges of the screen.

These are the only new additions to the blockRectangle function that are needed to create the bounce effect. The rest of the code is unchanged from Chapter 8. Here's the entire new blockRectangle function with the new code highlighted so that you can see it all in its proper context.

```
function blockRectangle(r1, r2, bounce)
{
  //Set bounce to a default value of false if it's not specified
  if(typeof bounce === "undefined")
  {
    bounce = false;
  }

  //Create an optional collision vector object to represent the bounce surface
  var s = {};

  //A variable to tell us which side the collision is occurring on
  var collisionSide = "";

  //Calculate the distance vector
  var vx = r1.centerX() - r2.centerX();
  var vy = r1.centerY() - r2.centerY();

  //Figure out the combined half-widths and half-heights
  var combinedHalfWidths = r1.halfWidth() + r2.halfWidth();
  var combinedHalfHeights = r1.halfHeight() + r2.halfHeight();

  //Check whether vx is less than the combined half widths
  if(Math.abs(vx) < combinedHalfWidths)
  {
    //A collision might be occurring!
    //Check whether vy is less than the combined half heights
    if(Math.abs(vy) < combinedHalfHeights)
    {
      //A collision has occurred! This is good!
      //Find out the size of the overlap on both the X and Y axes
      var overlapX = combinedHalfWidths - Math.abs(vx);
      var overlapY = combinedHalfHeights - Math.abs(vy);
```

```
//The collision has occurred on the axis with the
//*smallest* amount of overlap. Let's figure out which
//axis that is

if(overlapX >=  overlapY)
{
  //The collision is happening on the X axis, but on which side? vy can tell us
  if(vy > 0)
  {
    collisionSide = "top";

    //Move the rectangle out of the collision
    r1.y = r1.y + overlapY;
  }
  else
  {
    collisionSide = "bottom";

    //Move the rectangle out of the collision
    r1.y = r1.y - overlapY;
  }

  //Bounce
  if(bounce)
  {
    r1.vy *= -1;
  }
}
else
{
  //The collision is happening on the Y axis, but on which side? vx can tell us
  if(vx > 0)
  {
    collisionSide = "left";

    //Move the rectangle out of the collision
    r1.x = r1.x + overlapX;
  }
  else
  {
    collisionSide = "right";

    //Move the rectangle out of the collision
    r1.x = r1.x - overlapX;
  }
```

```
    //Bounce
    if(bounce)
    {
      r1.vx *= -1;
    }
  }
}
else
{
  //No collision
  collisionSide = "none";
}
}
else
{
  //No collision
  collisionSide = "none";
}

return collisionSide;
}
```

> Note: Remember that you can dampen the bounce effect by multiplying the object's vx and vy values with a number less than 1. For example, for a more moderate bounce, use a number like −0.5, like this:
>
> r1.vy *= −0.5;
>
> r1.vx *= −0.5;

Now let's find out how to apply this same technique to bouncing against circles.

Bouncing off circles

Run the **circleBounce.html** file and use the arrow keys to bounce the small circle off the big circle. The small circle bounces away at the correct angle, no matter from which direction it hits the big circle, as shown in Figure 11-6.

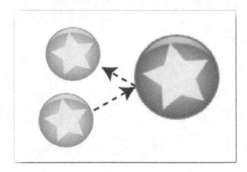

Figure 11-6. Bounce the small circle off the big circle

This is done with the help of a new version of the blockCircle function. It adds a new optional third argument, which should be true if you want the bounce effect to work.

```
blockCircle(blueCircle, redCircle, true);
```

This new version of blockCircle also requires another function called bounceOffSurface that does the math needed to figure out the correct bounce angle. You'll find both blockCircle and bounceOffSurface in the circleBounce.html file.

The circle is bounced by reversing its velocity, which is the same technique we used in the previous two examples. But there's one crucial difference. To bounce an object off the screen edges or the sides of a box, you're just dealing with two surfaces. The object can either bounce off the flat horizontal surface of the X axis or the 90-degree vertical surface of the Y axis. But because circles are round, they don't have any flat surfaces to bounce off. Instead, they have continuously curving surfaces. That means that anything that hits them will bounce away at a slightly different angle depending on where it strikes the circle's surface. Instead of just two bounce surfaces, circles have an almost infinite number. And that means that things that hit it can be deflected at an almost infinite number of angles.

How can we figure out the correct angle for deflecting the colliding object? We need to use a bit of vector math to help us. Luckily, however, you don't need to do any of this math yourself. The blockCircle and bounceOffSurface functions do it all for you. You never need to know how they work, just how to use them in your games. If that's good enough for you, you can happily skip the next section of the chapter and jump to the section on gravity later in the chapter. You won't have missed anything you need to know.

However, if you're curious about the theory and math behind how it works, read on!

Finding the collision angle

To bounce two circles apart, you first have to figure out the angle of the surface on which the collision is happening. You then have to figure out what the bouncing circle's new velocity will be when it strikes this surface. Let's first take a look at how to calculate the collision surface.

As you know, to figure out how far apart two circles are you have to plot a distance vector between them. The distance vectors are just vx and vy values that, together, calculate the distance between the circles on the X and Y axes. If the two circles are called c1 and c2, you can figure out their distance vector like this:

```
vx = c1.centerX() - c2.centerX();
vy = c1.centerY() - c2.centerY();
```

All vectors have a property called a **normal**. The vector's normal is another vector that is exactly perpendicular (at right angles) to the main vector. Vectors actually have two normals: a **left normal** and a **right normal.** You can describe the left normal with two variables called lx and ly. Here's how you calculate the left normal.

```
lx = vy;
ly = -vx;
```

You can describe the right normal with two variables called rx and ly.

```
rx = -vy;
ly = vx;
```

Here's a simple way to understand normals. Stand up with your back against the wall. Think of your body as the main vector, which is described by vx and vy. Hold up your left arm straight out against the wall at a 90-degree angle to your body. That's the left normal (lx and ly). Hold up your right arm straight out against the wall at a 90-degree angle to your body. That's the right normal (rx and ry).

Figure 11-7 shows the main vector and its left and right normals for two colliding circles.

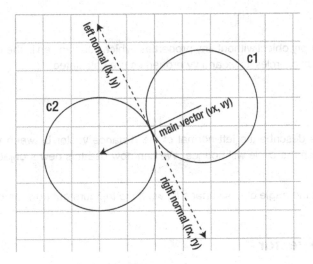

Figure 11-7. The main vector and its left and right normals

Why is this important? The circle needs a flat surface to bounce against. *The normals describe that flat surface.* Instead of thinking about a circle hitting another circle, think about a circle hitting a sloping line. The sloping line described by the normals is the collision surface we need to bounce the circle on. Figure 11-8 illustrates this.

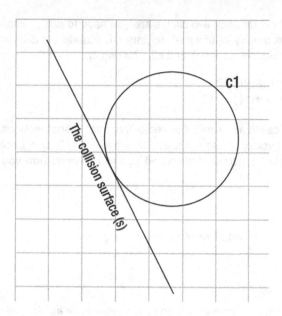

Figure 11-8. The vector's normals become the collision surface

In the code that we'll look at here, this collision surface is represented by an object called s. ("s" stands for "surface.")

```
var s = {};
```

It's first created as an empty object without any properties, which you can see in the line of code. At the moment of collision between the two circles its vx and vy properties are calculated:

```
s.vx = vy;
s.vy = -vx;
```

Its vx and vy properties describe the left normal of the distance vector between the circles. It's the angled collision surface on which the circle will bounce. We can now use this new s object to help us calculate that bounce.

Now that we know what the angle of this surface is, we have to figure out how the circle's velocity will change when it hits this surface.

Finding the bounce vector

In the example code, the bouncing circle is called c1. Its X velocity is c1.vx. Its Y velocity is c1.vy. As you know, this velocity is the circle's speed. But it's also a vector that describes the direction in which the circle is moving. To make the circle bounce at the correct angle, we need to figure out how this velocity should change when it hits the sloping collision surface. What we need to do is figure out its bounce vector. Figure 11-9 illustrates this. The dotted arrow is the bounce vector that we need to find.

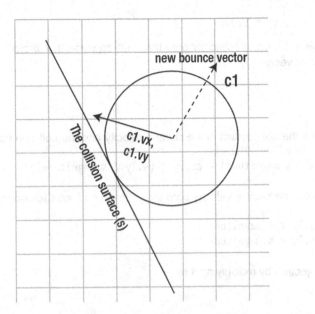

Figure 11-9. You need to use the collision surface and the circle's velocity to figure out the bounce vector

Luckily for us, mathematics has some standard formulas and procedures for doing this. I'll walk you through these formulas and explain in general what they do. To fully understand them requires a deeper understanding of vector math, which I'll leave you to research further on your own if you need to. You can use these steps as a starting point to learn more about these vector math concepts.

First, the collision surface, the object called s, needs some new properties that will help simplify the formulas. We need to know its magnitude (how long the vector is). We'll give the s object a property called **magnitude** and apply the Pythagorean theorem to figure out its value.

```
s.magnitude = Math.sqrt(s.vx * s.vx + s.vy * s.vy);
```

We also need to know what the s object's **unit vector** is. A unit vector is the smallest size the vector can be. It describes the direction that the vector is pointing in. The unit vector is described by properties called dx and dy.

```
s.dx = s.vx / s.magnitude;
s.dy = s.vy / s.magnitude;
```

dx and dy will be really small numbers that are less than zero. If you multiply them with any other numbers, you can create new vectors that point in the same direction as the original vector but with different magnitudes. (Unit vectors are sometimes called **normalized** vectors.) Unit vectors are the building blocks for creating new vectors.

We now have enough information to start calculating the circle's bounce vector. We first need to create a value called a **dot product** between the circle's velocity and the collision surface. The dot product's job is to find out if the vectors are pointing in the same direction or in a different direction.

625

```
dp1 = c1.vx * s.dx + c1.vy * s.dy;
```

We then need to project the circle's velocity onto the collision surface. A projection is like casting a shadow of one vector onto another vector.

```
p1Vx = dp1 * s.dx;
p1Vy = dp1 * s.dy;
```

The next step is to find the dot product of the circle's velocity and the collision surface's left normal.

```
dp2 = c1.vx * (s.lx / s.magnitude) + c1.vy * (s.ly / s.magnitude);
```

Then we need to project the circle's velocity onto the collision surface's left normal.

```
var p2Vx = dp2 * (s.lx / s.magnitude);
var p2Vy = dp2 * (s.ly / s.magnitude);
```

Next, reverse this projection by multiplying it by −1.

```
p2Vx *= -1;
p2Vy *= -1;
```

Then add the projections together to create the bounce vector (bounceVx and bounceVy).

```
bounceVx = p1Vx + p2Vx;
bounceVy = p1Vy + p2Vy;
```

The last step is to apply the bounce vector to the circle's velocity.

```
c1.vx = bounceVx;
c1.vy = bounceVy;
```

This will make the circle bounce at the correct angle.

These are the basic formulas and procedures you need to use to calculate an object's bounce. Let's find out how they're used in the code.

Looking at the bounce code

To make a circle bounce off another circle, call the blockCircle function. The first two arguments are the two circles, and the third Boolean value determines whether to enable the bounce effect.

```
blockCircle(blueCircle, redCircle, true);
```

In the circleBounce.html example file, this happens in the playGame function.

Here's the entire new blockCircle function. Most of it is identical to the original version of this function from Chapter 8. I've highlighted the new code in bold.

```
function blockCircle(c1, c2, bounce)
```

```
{
  //Set bounce to a default value of false if it's not specified
  if(typeof bounce === "undefined")
  {
    bounce = false;
  }
  //Calculate the vector between the circles' center points
  var vx = c1.centerX() - c2.centerX();
  var vy = c1.centerY() - c2.centerY();

  //Find the distance between the circles by calculating
  //the vector's magnitude (how long the vector is)
  var magnitude = Math.sqrt(vx * vx + vy * vy);

  //Add together the circles' combined half-widths
  var combinedHalfWidths = c1.halfWidth() + c2.halfWidth();

  //Figure out if there's a collision
  if(magnitude < combinedHalfWidths)
  {
    //Yes, a collision is happening.
    //Find the amount of overlap between the circles
    var overlap = combinedHalfWidths - magnitude;

    //Normalize the vector.
    //These numbers tell us the direction of the collision
    dx = vx / magnitude;
    dy = vy / magnitude;

    //Move circle 1 out of the collision by multiplying
    //the overlap with the normalized vector and add it to circle 1's position
    c1.x += overlap * dx;
    c1.y += overlap * dy;

    //The new bounce code
    if(bounce)
    {
      //Create a collision vector object to represent the bounce surface
      var s = {};

      //Find the bounce surface's vx and vy properties
      //(This represents the left normal of the vector between the circles)
      s.vx = vy;
      s.vy = -vx;

      //Bounce c1 off the surface
      bounceOffSurface(c1, s);
    }
  }
}
```

The last if statement contains the important new code. If the bounce parameter is true, the code creates a new object called s that represents the collision surface. It then calls the bounceOffSurface function that uses the circle (c1) and the surface (s) as arguments.

```
bounceOffSurface(c1, s);
```

The bounceOffSurface function does all the math that I explained in the previous section. You can use this function to bounce any object off any angled surface, not just circles. In this example, the object called o represents the circle.

```
function bounceOffSurface(o, s)
{
  //1. Calculate the collision surface's properties

  //Find the surface vector's left normal
  s.lx = s.vy;
  s.ly = -s.vx;

  //Find its magnitude
  s.magnitude = Math.sqrt(s.vx * s.vx + s.vy * s.vy);

  //Find its unit vector
  s.dx = s.vx / s.magnitude;
  s.dy = s.vy / s.magnitude;

  //2. Bounce the object (o) off the surface (s)

  //Find the dot product between the object and the surface
  var dp1 = o.vx * s.dx + o.vy * s.dy;

  //Project the object's velocity onto the collision surface
  var p1Vx = dp1 * s.dx;
  var p1Vy = dp1 * s.dy;

  //Find the dot product of the object and the surface's left normal (s.lx and s.ly)
  var dp2 = o.vx * (s.lx / s.magnitude) + o.vy * (s.ly / s.magnitude);

  //Project the object's velocity onto the surface's left normal
  var p2Vx = dp2 * (s.lx / s.magnitude);
  var p2Vy = dp2 * (s.ly / s.magnitude);

  //Reverse the projection on the surface's left normal
  p2Vx *= -1;
  p2Vy *= -1;

  //Add up the projections to create a new bounce vector
  var bounceVx = p1Vx + p2Vx;
  var bounceVy = p1Vy + p2Vy;
```

```
//Assign the bounce vector to the object's velocity
o.vx = bounceVx;
o.vy = bounceVy;
}
```

When all this is done, the bounce vector is assigned to the circle's velocity and the effect is as you see it in the example.

You'll find these new versions of the collision function, blockCircle and blockRectangle, along with bounceOffSurface in the updated **collision.js** file in the chapter's source files. I'll be using them from now on for the rest of the games and examples in this book.

Gravity

Gravity is just as easy to implement as the other physical forces. All you need to do is create one more value and add it to the object's vy property.

> Note: Since we've been talking so much about vectors, you can think of gravity as a vertical vector pointing down. The game character's vy property is also a vector that's pointing down. So when you add gravity to the vy property, you're actually increasing the magnitude of the vy vector.

To see gravity at work, run the **gravity.html** program. The cat will drop to the bottom of the screen and sit there. If you press the up arrow key, the cat moves up. When the up arrow is released again, the cat falls downward until you press the up arrow key again. If it hits the ground, it bounces. Figure 11-10 illustrates what you'll see.

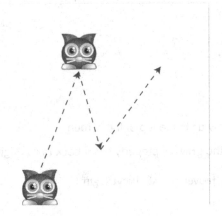

Figure 11-10. Use the arrow keys to make the cat fly

Even though the code is very simple, the result is a very convincing simulation of the real world. In fact, it's almost scarily realistic! Let's see how it works.

The spriteObject has a property called gravity, which is initialized to 0.3:

```
gravity: 0.3,
```

Like the other values, 0.3 is just one that came about through trial and error, and it produces a natural-looking effect in this context. A higher number increases gravity, and a lower number decreases it.

Applying gravity to the cat is simply a matter of adding it to the cat's vy property in the playGame function:

```
cat.vy += cat.gravity;
```

That's it! That's all you need to do to implement gravity. Here's how this line of code fits into the other code in the playGame function:

```
//Apply acceleration
cat.vx += cat.accelerationX;
cat.vy += cat.accelerationY;

//Apply friction
cat.vx *= cat.friction;

//Apply gravity
cat.vy += cat.gravity;
```

(The other small change to this code from the previous examples is that friction isn't added to the vy property. It doesn't need to be, because gravity takes care of that.)

That's how gravity makes the cat fall to the bottom of the screen, but how do you make it appear to fly when you press the up arrow? The playGame animation loop sets the cat's gravity to 0 if the up key is pressed, highlighted in the code below.

```
if(moveUp && !moveDown)
{
  cat.accelerationY = -0.2;
  cat.gravity = 0;
  cat.friction = 1;
}
```

This allows the cat to float freely up to the top of the screen.

When the keys are released, the gravity property is set back to its original value of 0.3.

```
if(!moveUp && !moveDown && !moveLeft && !moveRight)
{
  cat.friction = 0.96;
  cat.gravity = 0.3;
}
```

> *Note: In this example, gravity is a property of the cat sprite. But often in games gravity will be a global property that affects all objects. In a gravity-based game, you may want to consider initializing a gravity variable in the main program and applying it universally to all sprites.*

There's one more bit of fine-tuning that the code does. The cat should fall to the ground at a faster rate than it ascends. I modified the speed limit in the `if` statement that checks to see how fast the cat is moving down the screen. It lets the cat to fall at a maximum speed that's up to twice the value of `speedLimit`. If it reaches that speed, the console displays "Terminal velocity!"

```
if (cat.vx > cat.speedLimit)
{
  cat.vx = cat.speedLimit;
}
if (cat.vx < -cat.speedLimit)
{
  cat.vx = -cat.speedLimit;
}
if (cat.vy > cat.speedLimit * 2)
{
  cat.vy = cat.speedLimit * 2;
  console.log("Terminal velocity!");
}
if (cat.vy < -cat.speedLimit)
{
  cat.vy = -cat.speedLimit;
}
```

Multiplying the `speedLimit` by 2 allows the cat to fall twice as fast as it climbs. You could use this check for terminal velocity in a Lunar Lander–type game to figure out whether the spacecraft is going too fast when it hits the planet surface.

Jumping

Probably half of all video games ever made use jumping as a primary character action. All it boils down to is a temporary increase in the object's Y velocity. Once you understand how acceleration, friction, and gravity work, jumping is not at all difficult to implement. However, there's an additional thing to keep in mind that makes it a little more complex:

- You want your object to be able to jump when it's on the ground and only on the ground. But how will your object know that it's on the ground? And what is the "ground," anyway? The code has to be able to figure these things out.

Let's look at an example of jumping in action and how to solve these problems. Run the **jumping.html** program to see a practical example. Use the left and right arrow keys to move the cat horizontally and then press the spacebar to make it jump. Figure 11-11 illustrates this.

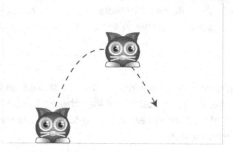

Figure 11-11. Press the spacebar to make the cat jump

The spriteObject has two properties that are needed for jumping:

```
isOnGround: undefined,
jumpForce: -10,
```

isOnGround is a Boolean value that tells the game whether the object is on the ground. It's initialized as undefined because you might not always know whether the object will be on the ground when the game starts.

jumpForce is the force with which the cat will jump. It needs to jump up, so jumpForce has a negative value (−10). The actual value that you give it is again a matter of trial and error. You'll need to make sure that its value is enough to counteract gravity and any other forces that might be acting on the object.

The program uses the left and right arrow keys to make the cat move horizontally, and the spacebar makes the cat jump. A variable called jump is used to tell the game that the spacebar has been pressed. It's set to true when the spacebar is pressed and to false when it's released. Here's the code in the main program that sets up this keyboard interface.

```
//Key codes
var RIGHT = 39;
var LEFT = 37;
var SPACE = 32;

//Directions
var moveRight = false;
var moveLeft = false;
var jump = false;

//Key listeners
window.addEventListener("keydown", function(event)
{
  switch(event.keyCode)
  {
    case LEFT:
      moveLeft = true;
      break;
```

```
      case RIGHT:
        moveRight = true;
        break;

      case SPACE:
        jump = true;
        break;
    }
  }, false);

window.addEventListener("keyup", function(event)
{
  switch(event.keyCode)
  {
      case LEFT:
        moveLeft = false;
        break;

      case RIGHT:
        moveRight = false;
        break;

      case SPACE:
        jump = false;
        break;
    }
  }, false);
```

How does the object know whether it's on the ground? This is something that could become quite complex, depending on the game you're designing, so you'll need to think about this carefully when you start any project that uses jumping. In this simple example, the cat is "on the ground" when it's at the bottom of the screen. So all you need to do is set isOnGround to true in the same section of code that checks for the bottom screen boundary.

```
//Left
if(cat.x < 0)
{
  cat.vx *= cat.bounce;
  cat.x = 0;
}
//Top
if(cat.y < 0)
{
  cat.vy *= cat.bounce;
  cat.y = 0;
}
//Right
if(cat.x + cat.width > canvas.width)
```

```
{
  cat.vx *= cat.bounce;
  cat.x = canvas.width - cat.width;
}
//Bottom
if(cat.y + cat.height > canvas.height)
{
  cat.y = canvas.height - cat.height;
  cat.isOnGround = true;
  cat.vy = -cat.gravity;
}
```

In this example, the cat will bounce when it hits the top, left, or right edges of the screen but not when it hits the ground.

The other important thing that happens in this code is that the cat's vy is set to *negative gravity* when the cat hits the ground. The highlighted bit of code illustrates this.

```
if(cat.y + cat.height > canvas.height)
{
  cat.y = canvas.height - cat.height;
  cat.isOnGround = true;
  cat.vy = -cat.gravity;
}
```

This is important because it neutralizes the force of gravity acting on the cat.

In most games with jumping, game characters also need to know when they're standing on platforms. That makes detecting the ground a little more complex, but we'll be looking at a solution to that in the next section.

The playGame animation loop makes the cat jump when the spacebar is pressed.

```
if(jump && cat.isOnGround)
{
  cat.vy += cat.jumpForce;
  cat.isOnGround = false;
  cat.friction = 1;
}
```

If the spacebar is pressed, the code checks to see whether the cat is on the ground. If it is, it adds the jumpForce value to the vertical velocity. It also sets isOnGround to false.

The last thing to do is make sure there's no speed-limit check if the cat is moving upward. Limiting the speed when the cat is jumping will put an unnatural choke on the jump effect. The jumping.html program uses these three speed-limit checks for all directions except up.

```
if(cat.vx > cat.speedLimit)
{
  cat.vx = cat.speedLimit;
}
```

```
if(cat.vx < -cat.speedLimit)
{
  cat.vx = -cat.speedLimit;
}
if(cat.vy > cat.speedLimit * 2)
{
  cat.vy = cat.speedLimit * 2;
}
```

A final refinement is that friction is applied only when the cat is on the ground. This lets the cat move freely and fluidly when it's in the air.

```
if(cat.isOnGround)
{
  cat.vx *= cat.friction;
}
```

And that's really all there is to it. Figure 11-12 illustrates how this whole system works.

```
if(jump && cat.isOnGround)
{
  cat.vy += cat.jumpForce;
  cat.isOnGround = false;
  cat.friction = 1;
}
```

```
cat.isOnGround = true;
cat.vy = -cat.gravity;
```

1 When the cat is at the bottom of the screen, its isOnGround property is set to true and gravity is neutralized.

2 If the player presses the space key and the cat is on the ground, the code applies the jumpForce to the cat's vy value. It also sets isOnGround to false, because the cat will be now be in the air.

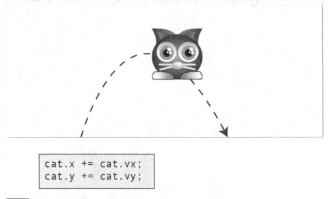

```
cat.x += cat.vx;
cat.y += cat.vy;
```

3 The playGame function makes the cat jump when it applies the new vy value to the cat's y position. Gravity is responsible for bringing it down to earth again. When it hits the bottom of the screen, isOnGround is again set to true, which allows the cat to jump again.

Figure 11-12. How to make an object jump

Jumping on platforms

You know how to make a game character jump, and you also know how to make solid objects by using blockRectangle. If you put these two skills together, you can make a box that a game character can jump on. You'll find an example of this in the **platforms.html** program. The cat can jump onto the box, as you can see in Figure 11-13.

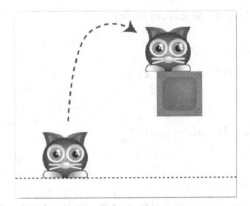

Figure 11-13. Jump onto platforms

The program creates a box sprite and positions it on the screen.

```
var box = Object.create(spriteObject);
box.x = 350;
box.y = 250;
sprites.push(box);
```

The playGame function then uses blockRectangle to prevent the cat and box from intersecting. You'll recall from Chapter 8 that blockRectangle returns a value called collisionSide. collisionSide is a string that tells you which side of the cat is touching the box. It can have any of these values: "left," "right," "top," "bottom," or "none." You assign this return value to a variable when you call blockRectangle if you want to use this information.

That's just what the playGame function does. It calls blockRectangle and assigns the return value to a variable called collisionSide.

```
var collisionSide = blockRectangle(cat, box, false);
```

This line of code prevents the cat and box from intersecting, but it also tells us on which side the collision is happening. Here's the if statement that changes the cat's velocity, depending on which side of the box the cat is touching.

```
if(collisionSide === "bottom" && cat.vy >= 0)
{
  //Tell the game that the cat is on the ground if it's standing on top of a platform
  cat.isOnGround = true;

  //Neutralize gravity by applying its exact opposite force to the character's vy
  cat.vy = -cat.gravity;
}
else if(collisionSide === "top" && cat.vy <= 0)
{
  cat.vy = 0;
}
```

```
else if(collisionSide === "right" && cat.vx >= 0)
{
  cat.vx = 0;
}
else if(collisionSide === "left" && cat.vx <= 0)
{
  cat.vx = 0;
}
if(collisionSide !== "bottom" && cat.vy > 0)
{
  cat.isOnGround = false;
}
```

If the collision is happening on the cat's bottom side, and the cat is moving down, it means that the cat is standing on top of the box. If that's the case, we have to set the cat's isOnGround property to true. This will reset the cat's jump ability so that it can jump off the platform. The code also needs to neutralize the effect of gravity so that the cat can move smoothly to the left and right on top of the platform. It does this by assigning negative gravity to the cat's vy property.

```
if(collisionSide === "bottom" && cat.vy >= 0)
{
  cat.isOnGround = true;
  cat.vy = -cat.gravity;
}
```

> Note: You can see that this if statement checks for two conditions: whether the bottom of the cat is touching the platform and whether the cat is moving down. Here's the code that checks if the cat is moving down toward the bottom of the screen:
>
> cat.vy >= 0
>
> If the cat's vy is less than zero, then it must be traveling downward. This extra check is important to prevent the cat from getting hooked on the corners of boxes in game environments with lots of platforms that are stacked closely together.

If the cat hits the bottom or sides of the platform, its vx or vy values are set to zero. This makes it appear as if the box is absorbing the force of the collision, which is a very natural-looking effect. (This code also checks the direction that the cat is moving in to prevent it from getting caught on corners in a game with lots of platforms.)

```
else if(collisionSide === "top" && cat.vy <= 0)
{
  cat.vy = 0;
}
else if(collisionSide === "right" && cat.vx >= 0)
{
  cat.vx = 0;
}
```

```
else if(collisionSide === "left" && cat.vx <= 0)
{
  cat.vx = 0;
}
```

> Note: If you want the cat to bounce off the sides of the box, include true as the third argument when you call blockRectangle. Then make sure you don't set that cat's vx and vy properties to 0 or neutralize gravity when it collides with the box.

The last thing the code does is set isOnGround to false if the cat isn't standing on a platform but is moving downward. This is to prevent the player from being able to make the cat jump if it slides off a platform.

```
if(collisionSide !== "bottom" && cat.vy > 0)
{
  cat.isOnGround = false;
}
```

And this is the only new code you need to know! You now have a fun little toy to play with: how will you use it to make a game? Think about the skills you learned in Chapters 9 and 10, and you'll realize that you already know how. But just in case you have any doubts, we'll take a detailed look at how to make a basic platform game in the next section.

Hedgehog Apocalypse!

Continuing with this book's tradition of terrible video-game titles, I present you with Hedgehog Apocalypse! In this gripping adventure, the enchanted meadowlands have been overrun with cute and friendly little hedgehogs. But, fear not, our flat-footed cat is on the scene to restore order by jumping on their heads. Can you squash all three hedgehogs and escape to the exit at the top of the screen without being bitten? Run **hedgehogApocalypse.html** in the chapter's source files to find out. Figure 11-14 illustrates how the game plays.

Figure 11-14. Jump and squash your way to the exit in Hedgehog Apocalypse!

While you're still learning how to make games, it can be daunting to even contemplate how to begin making a platform game like Hedgehog Apocalypse! Where do you start, and how do you put all the pieces together to make a finished game like this?

First, the most important thing to know about platform games is that they're just maze games with gravity added in. You know all about maze games from Chapter 10, so all you need to do is fuse those skills with what you have learned about gravity and platform games. The code structure and basic techniques used to build Hedgehog Apocalypse! are identical to those we used to build Time Bomb Panic and Monster Mayhem. However, the new context can be a little disorienting, so in this second half of the chapter I'm going to take you on a tour of how Hedgehog Apocalypse! was made, from start to finish. You'll be able to use this as the starting point for building your own platform game, which, I dearly hope, will be much better than this one!

Designing the level

I started with a tilesheet containing all the characters, the environment, and UI elements, which you can see in Figure 11-15. I drew them all with Adobe Illustrator, and I then laid them out as a single image in a 64-by-64-pixel grid. Along with the usual game sprites are some tiles that will just be used for background detail. The blue sky is represented by an empty blue tile. All the grass at the bottom of the game screen will be made by repeating the single grass image tile. I also wanted to include some clouds in the background that were wider than 64 pixels, so I split the cloud image across two tiles.

Figure 11-15. Start with a tilesheet

I loaded up the tilesheet into Tiled, and I then began to lay out the level. (Refer back to Chapter 10 for steps on how to get started using Tiled.) The game screen is 16 tiles wide and 12 high. Each tile is 64 by 64 pixels, so the final game-screen size will be 1,024 by 768 pixels. I created a layer in Tiled called map that will contain all the environment and background sprites. This includes the box platforms, empty blue sky tile, grass at the bottom of the screen, and also the clouds.

As you can see from the tilesheet, a single cloud image is split across two tiles. To add a cloud, I selected both image sections together and dragged them onto the workspace, as you can see in Figure 11-16. You can add any images to a level map that are bigger that the standard tile size by using this technique. For example, maybe you want to include an image of a really big tree. Draw the tree to be any size you want. If it occupies the space of six tiles, just drag all six tiles onto the game level.

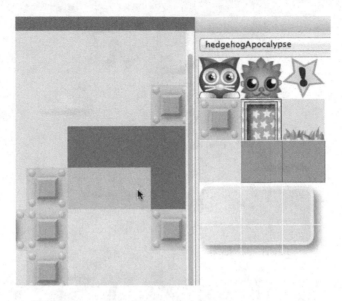

Figure 11-16. Add tilesheet images that are larger than the standard tile size by selecting multiple tiles together

When the map environment was finished, I ended up with the level layout you can see in Figure 11-17. You can see that the grass at the bottom of the level was made by just repeating the single grass image tile 16 times.

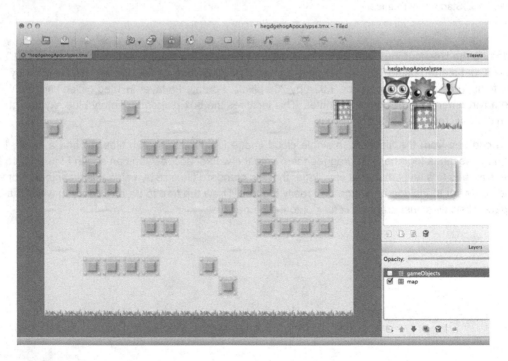

Figure 11-17. The finished map layer

The next step was to add all the game objects. I created a layer in Tiled called **gameObjects** and dragged the cat and hedgehog tiles onto the workspace. The cat and hedgehog sprites will move, so these positions represent where they will be when the game starts. Figure 11-18 shows the finished level design.

Figure 11-18. Add sprites to the gameObjects layer

There are two images from the tilesheet that I didn't use in this map. The star image with the exclamation mark in the center will be displayed when the hedgehog gets squashed. It represents the hedgehog's SQUASHED state, and you'll see how it's used ahead. There's also a large green rectangle with a pink border on the tilesheet that will be used to display game messages. It's a sprite that's created separately from the rest of the level sprites in the game program's createOtherSprites function. Again, you'll see how this works ahead.

The level map arrays

When I finished designing the level I then saved it and opened the resulting TMX file within a text editor. Tiled creates a separate array for each map layer. I formatted them as 2D arrays and added them to the game program. Here's the result, with the matching map code.

```
//The game map
var map =
[
  [7,7,8,9,7,7,7,8,9,7,7,7,8,9,7,7],
  [8,9,7,7,4,9,7,7,7,8,9,7,7,7,8,5],
```

```
  [4,7,7,7,7,7,8,9,7,7,7,8,9,7,4,4],
  [7,7,4,7,7,4,4,4,4,7,7,7,7,7,7,7],
  [8,9,4,7,7,7,7,8,9,7,7,4,8,9,7,7],
  [7,4,4,4,7,8,9,7,7,7,4,4,7,7,4,8],
  [9,7,8,9,7,7,7,8,9,4,7,4,9,7,7,7],
  [7,7,7,7,7,4,4,7,7,7,7,4,4,4,4,7],
  [8,9,7,7,7,7,7,7,7,8,9,7,7,8,9,7],
  [7,7,4,4,4,4,7,7,4,7,7,7,7,7,7,7],
  [7,7,7,7,7,7,7,7,7,4,7,7,7,7,7,7],
  [6,6,6,6,6,6,6,6,6,6,6,6,6,6,6,6]
]
```

//The game objects map

```
var gameObjects =
[
  [0,0,0,0,0,0,0,0,0,0,0,0,0,0,0,0],
  [0,0,0,0,0,0,0,0,0,0,0,0,0,0,0,0],
  [0,0,0,0,0,0,2,0,0,0,0,0,0,0,0,0],
  [0,0,0,0,0,0,0,0,0,0,0,0,0,0,0,0],
  [0,0,0,0,0,0,0,0,0,0,0,0,0,0,0,0],
  [0,0,0,0,0,0,0,0,0,0,0,0,0,0,0,0],
  [0,0,0,0,0,0,0,0,0,0,0,0,2,0,0,0],
  [0,0,0,0,0,0,0,0,0,0,0,0,0,0,0,0],
  [0,0,2,0,0,0,0,0,0,0,0,0,0,0,0,0],
  [0,0,0,0,0,0,0,0,0,0,0,0,0,0,0,0],
  [0,0,0,0,0,0,0,0,0,0,0,0,0,0,0,0],
  [0,0,0,0,0,0,0,1,0,0,0,0,0,0,0,0]
];
```

//Map code
```
var EMPTY = 0;
var CAT = 1;
var HEDGEHOG = 2;
var BOX = 4;
var DOOR = 5;
```

//The size of each tile cell
```
var SIZE = 64;
```

Notice that there's no map code for the sky, clouds, and grass. That's because the game doesn't need to reference them specifically. When the sky, clouds, and grass are created, they'll just be pushed into the sprites arrays without any special treatment.

> *Note: This game uses an identical file, folder, and code structure to the games that were shown in Chapter 10, so refer back to those games if you have any questions about the game program code that isn't covered in this chapter.*

Initializing the game objects and object arrays

The cat and door objects will need to be specifically referenced in the game. The game also needs to make a gameOverDisplay object and gameOverMessage object to display game messages. The main program initializes the variables that will store these objects.

```
var cat = null;
var door = null;
var gameOverDisplay = null;
var gameOverMessage = null;
```

The game also needs arrays in which to store all the boxes, hedgehogs, game messages, and sprites. The main program initializes these as well.

```
var sprites = [];
var hedgehogs = [];
var boxes = [];
var messages = [];
```

The game also needs a variable that keeps track of the number of hedgehogs that have been squashed.

```
var hedgehogsSquashed = 0;
```

We're now ready to build the map.

Building the level map

When the tilesheet image has loaded, the buildMap function runs. As with the games from Chapter 10, it runs twice: once for each array.

```
function buildMap(levelMap)
{
  for(var row = 0; row < ROWS; row++)
  {
    for(var column = 0; column < COLUMNS; column++)
    {
      var currentTile = levelMap[row][column];

      if(currentTile != EMPTY)
      {
        //Find the tile's X and Y positions on the tilesheet
        var tilesheetX = Math.floor((currentTile - 1) % tilesheetColumns) * SIZE;
        var tilesheetY = Math.floor((currentTile - 1) / tilesheetColumns) * SIZE;

        switch (currentTile)
        {
          case CAT:
            cat = Object.create(spriteObject);
            cat.sourceX = tilesheetX;
```

```
            cat.sourceY = tilesheetY;
            cat.x = column * SIZE;
            cat.y = row * SIZE;
            sprites.push(cat);
            break;

         case HEDGEHOG:
            var hedgehog = Object.create(hedgehogObject);
            hedgehog.sourceX = tilesheetX;
            hedgehog.sourceY = tilesheetY;
            hedgehog.x = column * SIZE;
            hedgehog.y = row * SIZE;
            hedgehog.vx = hedgehog.speed;
            sprites.push(hedgehog);
            hedgehogs.push(hedgehog);
            break;

         case BOX:
            var box = Object.create(spriteObject);
            box.sourceX = tilesheetX;
            box.sourceY = tilesheetY;
            box.x = column * SIZE;
            box.y = row * SIZE;
            sprites.push(box);
            boxes.push(box);
            break;

         case DOOR:
            door = Object.create(spriteObject);
            door.sourceX = tilesheetX;
            door.sourceY = tilesheetY;
            door.x = column * SIZE;
            door.y = row * SIZE;
            sprites.push(door);
            break;

         default:
            var sprite = Object.create(spriteObject);
            sprite.sourceX = tilesheetX;
            sprite.sourceY = tilesheetY;
            sprite.x = column * SIZE;
            sprite.y = row * SIZE;
            sprites.push(sprite);
      }
    }
   }
  }
 }
```

You can see here that the background sky, clouds, and grass sprites *don't* have any specific reference. They're all created by the last default case, which just creates them as general sprite objects and pushes them into the sprites array. As long as they're in the sprites array, they'll be displayed by canvas, but the game doesn't need them for anything else. They're just used for level decoration. The important game objects, however, (the cat, door, boxes, and hedgehogs) are all important to the game logic so they're given special treatment by each of the switch statement's cases.

Creating the user interface

When the player wins or loses the game, a message is displayed in a rounded rectangle, shown in Figure 11-19.

Figure 11-19. The user interface objects

The rounded rectangle is a sprite called gameOverDisplay. The text is a message object called gameOverMessage. Both of these objects are created by the createOtherObjects function. createOtherObjects runs when the buildMap function has finished building the level.

```
function createOtherObjects()
{
  gameOverDisplay = Object.create(spriteObject);
  gameOverDisplay.sourceX = 0;
  gameOverDisplay.sourceY = 192;
  gameOverDisplay.sourceWidth = 192;
  gameOverDisplay.sourceHeight = 128;
  gameOverDisplay.width = 192;
  gameOverDisplay.height = 128;
  gameOverDisplay.x = canvas.width / 2 - gameOverDisplay.width / 2;
  gameOverDisplay.y = canvas.height / 2 - gameOverDisplay.height / 2;
  gameOverDisplay.visible = false;
  sprites.push(gameOverDisplay);

  gameOverMessage = Object.create(messageObject);
  gameOverMessage.x = gameOverDisplay.x + 20;
  gameOverMessage.y = gameOverDisplay.y + 34;
  gameOverMessage.font = "bold 30px Helvetica";
  gameOverMessage.fillStyle = "black";
  gameOverMessage.text = "";
  gameOverMessage.visible = false;
  messages.push(gameOverMessage);
}
```

Both of these objects have their `visible` properties set to `false` when they're first created. When the game finishes, `visible` will be set to `true` so that they can be displayed.

Jumping on boxes

The code that makes the cat jump and move is identical to the code we looked at earlier in this chapter. But instead of there being only one box to jump on, the cat now has about a dozen. All the box objects are in the boxes array. The `playGame` function loops through all of them to check for collisions with the cat.

```
for(var i = 0; i < boxes.length; i++)
{
  var collisionSide = blockRectangle(cat, boxes[i], false);

  if(collisionSide === "bottom" && cat.vy >= 0)
  {
    cat.isOnGround = true;
    cat.vy = -cat.gravity;
  }
  else if(collisionSide === "top" && cat.vy <= 0)
  {
    cat.vy = 0;
  }
  else if(collisionSide === "right" && cat.vx >= 0)
  {
    cat.vx = 0;
  }
  else if(collisionSide === "left" && cat.vx <= 0)
  {
    cat.vx = 0;
  }
  if(collisionSide !== "bottom" && cat.vy > 0)
  {
    cat.isOnGround = false;
  }
}
```

Moving the hedgehogs

When the hedgehogs are created their vx properties are assigned the value of `hedgehog.speed`, which is 1.

`hedgehog.vx = hedgehog.speed;`

This means that each hedgehog will move to the left at 1 pixel per frame when the game first starts. Like the maze games in Chapter 10, the hedgehogs' speed should divide evenly into 64.

The hedgehogs move back and forth along the platforms. When they reach the end of a platform, they reverse direction, as shown in Figure 11-20.

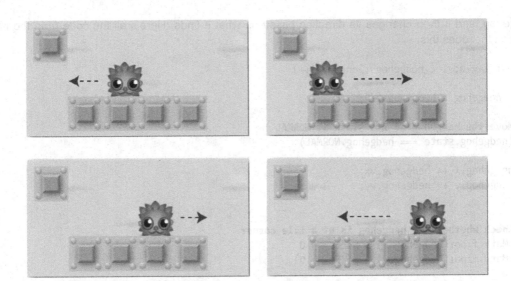

Figure 11-20. The hedgehogs move back and forth along the platforms

The hedgehogs will also reverse direction if they bump into a box, as shown in Figure 11-21.

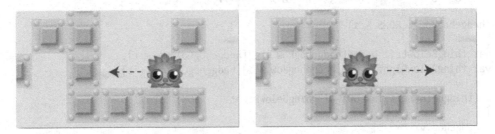

Figure 11-21. The hedgehogs reverse direction if they bump into a box

The hedgehogs will behave like this no matter how long the platforms are or where they are placed on the map. They do this by checking where on the level map they are, and they will change their direction if they don't like where they're going. The code that does this is similar to the code that the maze monsters used to move around in the mazes, only much simpler. Let's find out how it works.

The hedgehogs' movements are based on these two rules:

- A hedgehog will move only if there's a BOX cell under it. If there isn't, it reverses direction.

- A hedgehog will move only if there are no BOX cells to the left or right of it. If there are, it reverses direction.

The game program figures this out by using a familiar technique from Chapter 10. It finds out where on the map the hedgehog is by converting the hedgehog's X and Y screen positions into array column and row positions. It then compares this array position to the map array. It checks to see what kinds of things are surrounding the hedgehog, and it then changes its direction based on what it finds. Here's all the code from the playGame function that does this.

```
for(var i = 0; i < hedgehogs.length; i++)
{
  var hedgehog = hedgehogs[i];

  //Move the hedgehog if its state is NORMAL
  if(hedgehog.state === hedgehog.NORMAL)
  {
    hedgehog.x += hedgehog.vx;
    hedgehog.y += hedgehog.vy;
  }

  //Check whether the hedgehog is at a tile corner
  if(Math.floor(hedgehog.x) % SIZE === 0
  && Math.floor(hedgehog.y) % SIZE === 0)
  {
    //Change the hedgehog's direction if there's no BOX under it
    //or if there's a BOX to the left or right of it
    //Find the hedgehog's column and row in the array
    var hedgehogColumn = Math.floor(hedgehog.x / SIZE);
    var hedgehogRow = Math.floor(hedgehog.y / SIZE);

    if(hedgehogRow < ROWS - 1)
    {
      var thingBelowLeft = map[hedgehogRow + 1][hedgehogColumn - 1];
      var thingBelowRight = map[hedgehogRow + 1][hedgehogColumn + 1];

      if(thingBelowLeft !== BOX || thingBelowRight !== BOX)
      {
        hedgehog.vx *= -1;
      }
    }

    if(hedgehogColumn > 0)
    {
      var thingToTheLeft = map[hedgehogRow][hedgehogColumn - 1];
      if(thingToTheLeft === BOX)
      {
        hedgehog.vx *= -1;
      }
    }

    if(hedgehogColumn < COLUMNS - 1)
```

```
    {
      var thingToTheRight = map[hedgehogRow][hedgehogColumn + 1];
      if(thingToTheRight === BOX)
      {
        hedgehog.vx *= -1;
      }
    }
  }
}
```

Let's find out how all this works. The code loops through all the hedgehogs and moves them if their states are NORMAL.

```
for(var i = 0; i < hedgehogs.length; i++)
{
  var hedgehog = hedgehogs[i];

  //Move the hedgehog if its state is NORMAL
  if(hedgehog.state === hedgehog.NORMAL)
  {
    hedgehog.x += hedgehog.vx;
    hedgehog.y += hedgehog.vy;
  }
```

(Hedgehogs can also have SQUASHED states, and we don't want to move them if they've been squashed, as you'll soon see.)

The code then checks to see if the hedgehog's screen position is a cell corner. If it is, it converts its X and Y positions into an array column and row number.

```
if(Math.floor(hedgehog.x) % SIZE === 0
&& Math.floor(hedgehog.y) % SIZE === 0)
{
  var hedgehogColumn = Math.floor(hedgehog.x / SIZE);
  var hedgehogRow = Math.floor(hedgehog.y / SIZE);
```

It then finds out what is to the bottom left and right of the hedgehog, as shown in Figure 11-22.

Figure 11-22. Check to make sure the hedgehog is on a box

If any of those things aren't BOX cells, the hedgehog reverses direction.

```
if(hedgehogRow < ROWS - 1)
{
  var thingBelowLeft = map[hedgehogRow + 1][hedgehogColumn - 1];
  var thingBelowRight = map[hedgehogRow + 1][hedgehogColumn + 1];

  if(thingBelowLeft !== BOX || thingBelowRight !== BOX)
  {
    hedgehog.vx *= -1;
  }
}
```

The hedgehog's direction is reversed by multiplying its vx property by −1.

The code then checks to see what's directly to the right and left of the hedgehog. If finds a BOX cell, it will also reverse the hedgehog's direction, as shown in Figure 11-23.

Figure 11-23. Check to see if there are boxes next to the hedgehog

```
if(hedgehogColumn > 0)
{
  var thingToTheLeft = map[hedgehogRow][hedgehogColumn - 1];
  if(thingToTheLeft === BOX)
  {
    hedgehog.vx *= -1;
  }
}

if(hedgehogColumn < COLUMNS - 1)
{
  var thingToTheRight = map[hedgehogRow][hedgehogColumn + 1];
  if(thingToTheRight === BOX)
  {
    hedgehog.vx *= -1;
  }
}
```

And that's all there is to it! You can place the hedgehogs on any platform on the map, no matter where the platform is or how long it is, and the hedgehogs will behave just as you expect them to. This gives you a lot of flexibility for experimenting with different level design layouts without having to change any of the game code.

Of course, you can give your hedgehogs much more intelligence, like we did with the maze monsters in Chapter 10, but I'll leave those improvements up to you.

Squashing the hedgehogs

The funnest part of the game is squashing the hedgehogs. When the cat jumps on the hedgehog's head, a cartoon explosion appears and the cat bounces away. The explosion image stays on the screen for one second before vanishing. Figure 11-24 illustrates the effect.

Figure 11-24. The cat bounces off the hedgehog when it squashes it from above

When the cat hits the hedgehog from above, the cat bounces away using the new blockCircle function that I introduced earlier in this chapter. The hedgehogs have two states: NORMAL and SQUASHED. When the hedgehog is SQUASHED the game displays the explosion image for one second by using the same technique we used to explode aliens in Alien Armada in Chapter 9.

Here's the hedgehogObject that you'll find in the **objects.js** file.

```
hedgehogObject = Object.create(spriteObject);
```

```
//The hedgehog's states
hedgehogObject.NORMAL = [1,0];
hedgehogObject.SQUASHED = [2,0];
hedgehogObject.state = hedgehogObject.NORMAL;

hedgehogObject.update = function()
{
  this.sourceX = this.state[0] * this.sourceWidth;
  this.sourceY = this.state[1] * this.sourceHeight;
};
```

```
//The hedgehog's allowed speed
hedgehogObject.speed = 1;
```

You can see that the hedgehog's SQUASHED state references the explosion image in the tilesheet. It uses the same technique for changing states that you learned in Chapter 8.

The playGame function loops through all the hedgehogs and checks whether any of them are touching the cat. If they are, the code checks whether the cat is dropping on the hedgehog from above. If it is, it means that the hedgehog is being squashed. If the cat isn't dropping from above, then, bad luck, the game ends. Here's all the code that does this.

```
for(var i = 0; i < hedgehogs.length; i++)
{
  var hedgehog = hedgehogs[i];

  if(hedgehog.visible && hitTestCircle(cat, hedgehog)
  && hedgehog.state === hedgehog.NORMAL)
  {
    if(cat.vy > 0)
    {
      blockCircle(cat, hedgehog, true);
      hedgehogsSquashed++;
      squashHedgehog(hedgehog);
    }
    else
    {
      gameState = OVER;
    }
  }
}
```

The collision test checks for three things: is the hedgehog visible, are the objects touching, and is the hedgehog's state NORMAL? If all those three things are true, a collision is registered.

```
if(hedgehog.visible && hitTestCircle(cat, hedgehog)
&& hedgehog.state === hedgehog.NORMAL)
```

The code uses hitTestCircle to test for a collision because both the cat and hedgehog are roughly circular.

The code then checks to see if the cat is dropping down from above. If the cat's vy property is greater than zero, then this must be the case.

```
if(cat.vy > 0)
{...
```

If this isn't true, then the cat must be below or to the left or right of the hedgehog. That's bad, because these hedgehogs bite! In that case, the game ends.

```
gameState = OVER;
```

Figure 11-25. If the cat hits the hedgehog from the sides or from below, the player loses

Figure 11-25 illustrates what happens. But if the cat is dropping on the hedgehog from above, three things happen. The blockCircle function is used to bounce the cat away, hedgehogsSquashed is increased by one, and the squashHedgehog function is called.

```
blockCircle(cat, hedgehog, true);
hedgehogsSquashed++;
squashHedgehog(hedgehog);
```

squashHedgehog removes the hedgehog from the game.

```
function squashHedgehog(hedgehog)
{
  //Change the hedgehog's state and update it
  hedgehog.state = hedgehog.SQUASHED;
  hedgehog.update();

  //Remove the hedgehog after one second
  setTimeout(removeHedgehog, 1000);

  function removeHedgehog()
  {
    hedgehog.visible = false;
  }
}
```

It changes the hedgehog's state to SQUASHED and calls its update function.

```
hedgehog.state = hedgehog.SQUASHED;
hedgehog.update();
```

This makes the hedgehog display the explosion image. The hedgehog also won't move while its state is SQUASHED, so the explosion remains frozen in place at the hedgehog's last position.

setTimout is then used to make the hedgehog invisible after one second.

```
setTimeout(removeHedgehog, 1000);
function removeHedgehog()
{
  hedgehog.visible = false;
}
```

This is what removes it from the game.

Ending the game

The game will end if the cat is bitten by a hedgehog. But the player can win the game if the cat reaches the door and if all the hedgehogs have been squashed. This bit of code in the playGame function checks for this.

```
if(hitTestRectangle(cat, door))
{
  //Check if all the hedgehogs have been squashed
  if(hedgehogsSquashed === 3)
  {
    gameState = OVER;
  }
}
```

When the gameState is OVER, the endGame function runs. It makes the gameOverDisplay and gameOverMessage visible and tells players whether they've won or lost.

```
function endGame()
{
  gameOverDisplay.visible = true;
  gameOverMessage.visible = true;

  if(hedgehogsSquashed === 3)
  {
    gameOverMessage.text = "You Won!";
  }
  else
  {
    gameOverMessage.text = "You Lost!";
  }
}
```

And so ends Hedgehog Apocalypse!

> *Note: To keep this game code as simple as possible, the game animation stops immediately when the cat has squashed all the hedgehogs and reaches the door. But in a real game, you'll want to switch to a new game level at this point. In that case, it would make more sense to let the game run on for a second or so. The cat could maybe disappear into the door and you could display a game message. You can accomplish this by adding a LEVEL_COMPLETE game state, the same way we did for Monster Mayhem in Chapter 10. Add all the game actions you want to have happen when the level changes to the function that runs when the game state is set to LEVEL_COMPLETE.*

Preventing the arrow keys from scrolling the browser window

There's a minor technical problem that needs to be fixed. If the game canvas is bigger than the browser window, the browser window will scroll if you press the arrow keys or spacebar. These are the default behaviors that these keys have in web browsers. But, of course, it conflicts with our use for those keys, which is to move the cat around the game world. Fortunately, JavaScript has a method called `event.preventDefault` that stops the browser from assigning these default behaviors to keys.

To use it, just add `event.preventDefault()` to the event that you want to override. So in Hedgehog Apocalypse! you could use:

```
window.addEventListener("keydown", function(event)
{
  switch(event.keyCode)
  {
    case LEFT:
      moveLeft = true;
      break;

    case RIGHT:
      moveRight = true;
      break;

    case SPACE:
      jump = true;
      break;
  }
  event.preventDefault();

}, false);
```

This works for keyboard keys and other forms of input, like the mouse and touch. You'll learn more about `event.preventDefault` in the next chapter.

The complete code listing

Here's the complete code listing that you can use as a reference. The `hedgehogApocalypse.html` file sets up the canvas and loads the JavaScript files.

```
<!doctype html>
<meta charset="utf-8">
<title>Hedgehog Apocalypse</title>

<!-- The canvas -->
<canvas width="1024" height="768"></canvas>

<!-- The game code -->
<script src="../src/objects.js"></script>
<script src="../src/collision.js"></script>
<script src="../src/hedgehogApocalypse.js"></script>
```

object.js contains the new spriteObject we're using in this chapter, as well as the same messageObject we used in Chapters 9 and 10. It also includes the hedgehogObject, which we looked at earlier. **collision.js** contains all the new collision functions that we've used in this chapter. The main game code is **hedgehogApocalypse.js**, and here's its entire code listing.

```
(function(){

//The canvas
var canvas = document.querySelector("canvas");
var drawingSurface = canvas.getContext("2d");

//The game map
var map =
[
  [7,7,8,9,7,7,7,8,9,7,7,7,8,9,7,7],
  [8,9,7,7,4,9,7,7,7,8,9,7,7,7,8,5],
  [4,7,7,7,7,7,8,9,7,7,7,8,9,7,4,4],
  [7,7,4,7,7,4,4,4,4,7,7,7,7,7,7,7],
  [8,9,4,7,7,7,7,8,9,7,7,4,8,9,7,7],
  [7,4,4,4,7,8,9,7,7,7,4,4,7,7,4,8],
  [9,7,8,9,7,7,7,8,9,4,7,4,9,7,7,7],
  [7,7,7,7,7,4,4,7,7,7,7,4,4,4,4,7],
  [8,9,7,7,7,7,7,7,7,8,9,7,7,8,9,7],
  [7,7,4,4,4,4,7,7,4,7,7,7,7,7,7,7],
  [7,7,7,7,7,7,7,7,7,4,7,7,7,7,7,7],
  [6,6,6,6,6,6,6,6,6,6,6,6,6,6,6,6]
]

//The game objects map

var gameObjects =
[
  [0,0,0,0,0,0,0,0,0,0,0,0,0,0,0,0],
  [0,0,0,0,0,0,0,0,0,0,0,0,0,0,0,0],
  [0,0,0,0,0,0,0,2,0,0,0,0,0,0,0,0],
  [0,0,0,0,0,0,0,0,0,0,0,0,0,0,0,0],
  [0,0,0,0,0,0,0,0,0,0,0,0,0,0,0,0],
```

```
    [0,0,0,0,0,0,0,0,0,0,0,0,0,0,0,0,0,0],
    [0,0,0,0,0,0,0,0,0,0,0,0,0,0,2,0,0,0],
    [0,0,0,0,0,0,0,0,0,0,0,0,0,0,0,0,0,0],
    [0,0,2,0,0,0,0,0,0,0,0,0,0,0,0,0,0,0],
    [0,0,0,0,0,0,0,0,0,0,0,0,0,0,0,0,0,0],
    [0,0,0,0,0,0,0,0,0,0,0,0,0,0,0,0,0,0],
    [0,0,0,0,0,0,0,1,0,0,0,0,0,0,0,0,0,0]
];
```

```
//Map code
var EMPTY = 0;
var CAT = 1;
var HEDGEHOG = 2;
var BOX = 4;
var DOOR = 5;
```

```
//The size of each tile cell
var SIZE = 64;
```

```
//Sprites we need to access by name
var cat = null;
var door = null;
var gameOverDisplay = null;
var gameOverMessage = null;
```

```
//The number of rows and columns
var ROWS = map.length;
var COLUMNS = map[0].length;
```

```
//The number of columns on the tilesheet
var tilesheetColumns = 3;
```

```
//Arrays to store the game objects
var sprites = [];
var hedgehogs = [];
var boxes = [];
var messages = [];
```

```
var assetsToLoad = [];
var assetsLoaded = 0;
```

```
//Load the tilesheet image
var image = new Image();
image.addEventListener("load", loadHandler, false);
image.src = "../images/hedgehogApocalypse.png";
assetsToLoad.push(image);
```

```
//Game variables
var hedgehogsSquashed = 0;
```

```
//Game states
var LOADING = 0;
var BUILD_MAP = 1;
var PLAYING = 2;
var OVER = 3;
var gameState = LOADING;

//Key codes
var RIGHT = 39;
var LEFT = 37;
var SPACE = 32;

//Directions
var moveRight = false;
var moveLeft = false;
var jump = false;

//Add keyboard listeners
window.addEventListener("keydown", function(event)
{
  switch(event.keyCode)
  {
    case LEFT:
      moveLeft = true;
      break;

    case RIGHT:
      moveRight = true;
      break;

    case SPACE:
      jump = true;
      break;
  }
  event.preventDefault();
}, false);

window.addEventListener("keyup", function(event)
{
  switch(event.keyCode)
  {
    case LEFT:
      moveLeft = false;
      break;

    case RIGHT:
      moveRight = false;
      break;
```

```
        case SPACE:
          jump = false;
          break;
    }
}, false);

//Start the game animation loop
update();

function update()
{
  //Start the animation loop
  setTimeout(update, 16);

  //Change what the game is doing based on the game state
  switch(gameState)
  {
    case LOADING:
      console.log("loading...");
      break;

    case BUILD_MAP:
      buildMap(map);
      buildMap(gameObjects);
      createOtherObjects();
      gameState = PLAYING;
      break;

    case PLAYING:
      playGame();
      break;

    case OVER:
      endGame();
  }

  //Render the game
  render();
}

function loadHandler()
{
  assetsLoaded++;
  if(assetsLoaded === assetsToLoad.length)
  {
    //Remove the load handlers
    image.removeEventListener("load", loadHandler, false);
```

```
    //Build the map
    gameState = BUILD_MAP;
  }
}

function buildMap(levelMap)
{
  for(var row = 0; row < ROWS; row++)
  {
    for(var column = 0; column < COLUMNS; column++)
    {
      var currentTile = levelMap[row][column];

      if(currentTile != EMPTY)
      {
        //Find the tile's X and Y positions on the tilesheet
        var tilesheetX = Math.floor((currentTile - 1) % tilesheetColumns) * SIZE;
        var tilesheetY = Math.floor((currentTile - 1) / tilesheetColumns) * SIZE;

        switch (currentTile)
        {
          case CAT:
            cat = Object.create(spriteObject);
            cat.sourceX = tilesheetX;
            cat.sourceY = tilesheetY;
            cat.x = column * SIZE;
            cat.y = row * SIZE;
            sprites.push(cat);
            break;

          case HEDGEHOG:
            var hedgehog = Object.create(hedgehogObject);
            hedgehog.sourceX = tilesheetX;
            hedgehog.sourceY = tilesheetY;
            hedgehog.x = column * SIZE;
            hedgehog.y = row * SIZE;
            hedgehog.vx = hedgehog.speed;
            sprites.push(hedgehog);
            hedgehogs.push(hedgehog);
            break;

          case BOX:
            var box = Object.create(spriteObject);
            box.sourceX = tilesheetX;
            box.sourceY = tilesheetY;
            box.x = column * SIZE;
            box.y = row * SIZE;
            sprites.push(box);
```

```
                boxes.push(box);
                break;

            case DOOR:
                door = Object.create(spriteObject);
                door.sourceX = tilesheetX;
                door.sourceY = tilesheetY;
                door.x = column * SIZE;
                door.y = row * SIZE;
                sprites.push(door);
                break;

            default:
                var sprite = Object.create(spriteObject);
                sprite.sourceX = tilesheetX;
                sprite.sourceY = tilesheetY;
                sprite.x = column * SIZE;
                sprite.y = row * SIZE;
                sprites.push(sprite);
            }
        }
      }
    }
  }
}

function createOtherObjects()
{
  gameOverDisplay = Object.create(spriteObject);
  gameOverDisplay.sourceX = 0;
  gameOverDisplay.sourceY = 192;
  gameOverDisplay.sourceWidth = 192;
  gameOverDisplay.sourceHeight = 128;
  gameOverDisplay.width = 192;
  gameOverDisplay.height = 128;
  gameOverDisplay.x = canvas.width / 2 - gameOverDisplay.width / 2;
  gameOverDisplay.y = canvas.height / 2 - gameOverDisplay.height / 2;
  gameOverDisplay.visible = false;
  sprites.push(gameOverDisplay);

  gameOverMessage = Object.create(messageObject);
  gameOverMessage.x = gameOverDisplay.x + 20;
  gameOverMessage.y = gameOverDisplay.y + 34;
  gameOverMessage.font = "bold 30px Helvetica";
  gameOverMessage.fillStyle = "black";
  gameOverMessage.text = "";
  gameOverMessage.visible = false;
  messages.push(gameOverMessage);
}
```

```
function playGame()
{
  //--- The cat

  //Left
  if(moveLeft && !moveRight)
  {
    cat.accelerationX = -0.2;
    cat.friction = 1;
  }
  //Right
  if(moveRight && !moveLeft)
  {
    cat.accelerationX = 0.2;
    cat.friction = 1;
  }
  //Space
  if(jump && cat.isOnGround)
  {
    cat.vy += cat.jumpForce;
    cat.isOnGround = false;
    cat.friction = 1;
  }

  //Set the cat's acceleration, friction, and gravity
  //to zero if none of the arrow keys are being pressed
  if(!moveLeft && !moveRight)
  {
    cat.accelerationX = 0;
    cat.friction = 0.96;
    cat.gravity = 0.3;
  }

  //Apply the acceleration
  cat.vx += cat.accelerationX;
  cat.vy += cat.accelerationY;

  //Apply friction
  if(cat.isOnGround)
  {
    cat.vx *= cat.friction;
  }

  //Apply gravity
  cat.vy += cat.gravity;

  //Limit the speed
  //Don't limit the upward speed because it will choke the jump effect
```

```
if (cat.vx > cat.speedLimit)
{
  cat.vx = cat.speedLimit;
}
if (cat.vx < -cat.speedLimit)
{
  cat.vx = -cat.speedLimit;
}
if (cat.vy > cat.speedLimit * 2)
{
  cat.vy = cat.speedLimit * 2;
}

//Move the cat
cat.x += cat.vx;
cat.y += cat.vy;

//Check for a collision between the cat and the boxes
for(var i = 0; i < boxes.length; i++)
{
  var collisionSide = blockRectangle(cat, boxes[i], false);

  if(collisionSide === "bottom" && cat.vy >= 0)
  {
    //Tell the game that the cat is on the ground if it's standing on top of a platform
    cat.isOnGround = true;

    //Neutralize gravity by applying its exact opposite force to the character's vy
    cat.vy = -cat.gravity;
  }
  else if(collisionSide === "top" && cat.vy <= 0)
  {
    cat.vy = 0;
  }
  else if(collisionSide === "right" && cat.vx >= 0)
  {
    cat.vx = 0;
  }
  else if(collisionSide === "left" && cat.vx <= 0)
  {
    cat.vx = 0;
  }
  if(collisionSide !== "bottom" && cat.vy > 0)
  {
    cat.isOnGround = false;
  }
}
```

```
//-- The hedgehogs

for(var i = 0; i < hedgehogs.length; i++)
{
  var hedgehog = hedgehogs[i];

  //Move the hedgehog if its state is NORMAL
  if(hedgehog.state === hedgehog.NORMAL)
  {
    hedgehog.x += hedgehog.vx;
    hedgehog.y += hedgehog.vy;
  }

  //Check whether the hedgehog is at a cell corner
  if(Math.floor(hedgehog.x) % SIZE === 0
  && Math.floor(hedgehog.y) % SIZE === 0)
  {
    //Change the hedgehog's direction if there's no BOX under it.
    //Find the hedgehog's column and row in the array
    var hedgehogColumn = Math.floor(hedgehog.x / SIZE);
    var hedgehogRow = Math.floor(hedgehog.y / SIZE);

    if(hedgehogRow < ROWS - 1)
    {
      var thingBelowLeft = map[hedgehogRow + 1][hedgehogColumn - 1];
      var thingBelowRight = map[hedgehogRow + 1][hedgehogColumn + 1];

      if(thingBelowLeft !== BOX || thingBelowRight !== BOX)
      {
        hedgehog.vx *= -1;
      }
    }

    if(hedgehogColumn > 0)
    {
      var thingToTheLeft = map[hedgehogRow][hedgehogColumn - 1];
      if(thingToTheLeft === BOX)
      {
        hedgehog.vx *= -1;
      }
    }

    if(hedgehogColumn < COLUMNS - 1)
    {
      var thingToTheRight = map[hedgehogRow][hedgehogColumn + 1];
      if(thingToTheRight === BOX)
      {
        hedgehog.vx *= -1;
      }
```

```
      }
    }
  }

  //Collision between the cat and the hedgehogs
  for(var i = 0; i < hedgehogs.length; i++)
  {
    var hedgehog = hedgehogs[i];

    if(hedgehog.visible && hitTestCircle(cat, hedgehog)
    && hedgehog.state === hedgehog.NORMAL)
    {
      if(cat.vy > 0)
      {
        blockCircle(cat, hedgehog, true);
        hedgehogsSquashed++;
        squashHedgehog(hedgehog);
      }
      else
      {
        gameState = OVER;
      }
    }
  }

  //Collision between the cat and the door
  if(hitTestRectangle(cat, door))
  {
    //Check if all the hedgehogs have been squashed
    if(hedgehogsSquashed === 3)
    {
      gameState = OVER;
    }
  }

  //Screen boundaries
  //Left
  if (cat.x < 0)
  {
    cat.vx = 0;
    cat.x = 0;
  }
  //Up
  if (cat.y < 0)
  {
    cat.vy = 0;
    cat.y = 0;
  }
```

```
    //Right
    if (cat.x + cat.width > canvas.width)
    {
      cat.vx = 0;
      cat.x = canvas.width - cat.width;
    }
    //Down
    if (cat.y + cat.height > canvas.height)
    {
      cat.vy = 0;
      cat.y = canvas.height - cat.height;
      cat.isOnGround = true;
      cat.vy = -cat.gravity;
    }
}

function squashHedgehog(hedgehog)
{
  //Change the hedgehog's state and update the object
  hedgehog.state = hedgehog.SQUASHED;
  hedgehog.update();

  //Remove the hedgehog after one second
  setTimeout(removeHedgehog, 1000);

  function removeHedgehog()
  {
    hedgehog.visible = false;
  }
}

function endGame()
{
  gameOverDisplay.visible = true;
  gameOverMessage.visible = true;

  if(hedgehogsSquashed === 3)
  {
    gameOverMessage.text = "You Won!";
  }
  else
  {
    gameOverMessage.text = "You Lost!";
  }
}
```

```
function render()
{
  drawingSurface.clearRect(0, 0, canvas.width, canvas.height);

  //Display the sprites
  if(sprites.length !== 0)
  {
    for(var i = 0; i < sprites.length; i++)
    {
      var sprite = sprites[i];
      if(sprite.visible)
      {
        drawingSurface.drawImage
        (
          image,
          sprite.sourceX, sprite.sourceY,
          sprite.sourceWidth, sprite.sourceHeight,
          Math.floor(sprite.x), Math.floor(sprite.y),
          sprite.width, sprite.height
        );
      }
    }
  }

  //Display the game messages
  if(messages.length !== 0)
  {
    for(var i = 0; i < messages.length; i++)
    {
      var message = messages[i];
      if(message.visible)
      {
        drawingSurface.font = message.font;
        drawingSurface.fillStyle = message.fillStyle;
        drawingSurface.textBaseline = message.textBaseline;
        drawingSurface.fillText(message.text, message.x, message.y);
      }
    }
  }
}

}());
```

Summary

This has been a basic introduction to platform games and physics, but you'll find all the building blocks here to help you build a game that could become quite complex. Add a bit of puzzle solving and task completion, and maybe a few more enemies, and you'll be well on your way to making a really fun game. You could also add a weapon and even a scrolling game world so the player could explore a large area. The techniques we used to make scrolling maze games in Chapter 10 will work perfectly with this platform game system. What about items that give the player some special abilities, or maybe some vehicles to drive? And what about moving platforms? It could be interesting!

In the next chapter, we'll take a closer look at enemy artificial intelligence, scripted motion, and how to move objects and fire bullets in 360 degrees. We'll also take a detailed look at how to program games that use a mouse or touch interface.

Chapter 12

Touch and the Mouse

Most of the games you'll make will be created and tested on a computer with a mouse and keyboard. But your finished games will almost certainly be played on touch-based interfaces, like tablets and mobile devices. In this chapter you'll learn how to create game user interfaces that use both a mouse and touch interface to control the action.

In this chapter I'm going to show you a wide range of practical ways to control different kinds of game characters that you'll be able to use for various kinds of projects. You'll learn how to use rotation to control classic video-game objects like spaceships and cars, as well as how to use rotation with interactive enemies. In the chapter's source files you'll find versions of each control system for the keyboard, mouse, and touch interface that you'll be able to mix and match to use in your own games. We'll also use all the techniques in this chapter to create a drag-and-drop user interface for canvas-based sprites.

And in this last chapter, I'm also going to give you some suggestions about where to take your learning further, and I'll introduce you to a few exciting new technologies that you'll definitely want to use with your games.

Finding the mouse and touch X and Y positions

It's almost certain that your finished games will be played on touch-based devices. However, it's also very likely that you'll design your game on a computer that uses a mouse and keyboard. Luckily, if you can design your game so that it works well using a mouse-based control system, there are only a few small changes you need to make to get it working with a touch-based interface.

In this first part of the chapter I'll show you some classic mouse-based control systems, and I'll then show you how you need to change them to work with a touch system.

Using the mouse

When you make game interfaces that use the mouse, two variables will tell you the X and Y positions of the mouse on the game screen. You could call them mouseX and mouseY, and they are defined at the start of your game program, like this:

```
var mouseX = 0;
var mouseY = 0;
```

It's possible that you might need to hide the mouse when it's over the canvas. You can do it with this bit of code:

```
canvas.style.cursor = "none";
```

You might want to do this if you're creating a custom mouse cursor that stays fixed to the mouse's position, as you'll see in the example ahead.

You'll also need to capture the mouse's position when it moves around the canvas. First, attach a mousemove event listener to the canvas, like this:

```
canvas.addEventListener("mousemove", mousemoveHandler, false);
```

The mousemove listener is fired whenever the mouse "moves" over the canvas. When this happens, it calls the mousemoveHandler, which captures the mouse's X and Y positions.

```
function mousemoveHandler(event)
{
  mouseX = event.pageX - canvas.offsetLeft;
  mouseY = event.pageY - canvas.offsetTop;
}
```

event.pageX and event.pageY are the mouse's X and Y positions. However, they show the mouse's position *relative to the browser window*. That means that if the canvas has a 30-pixel left margin, the very left side of the canvas will have a mouseX value of 30. Usually you'll want the very left side of the canvas to have a mouseX value of 0 and for the very top to have a mouseY value of 0, no matter where the canvas is in the browser window. Luckily you can use the canvas.offsetLeft and canvas.offsetTop properties to compensate for this. Subtract them from event.pageX and event.pageY, like in the example code above. mouseX and mouseY will then contain the X and Y positions of the mouse relative to the canvas's top left corner, no matter where the canvas happens to be.

You can now use mouseX and mouseY to help you move your game sprites. Open the **followMouse.html** program in the chapter's source files. Move the mouse, and Button Fairy, the new up-and-coming star of this chapter, moves around to follow it. Figure 12-1 shows what you'll see.

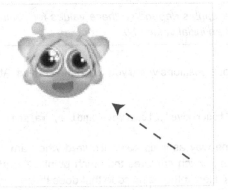

Figure 12-1. Move the mouse to make Button Fairy fly around the screen

The game program moves the sprite in the playGame animation loop. It centers the fairy sprite directly over the mouse's position.

```
function playGame()
{
  fairy.x = mouseX - (fairy.halfWidth());
  fairy.y = mouseY - (fairy.halfHeight());
}
```

This is the most basic technique for moving a sprite with the mouse, and you can use it to make a custom mouse pointer for any of your games.

Now let's find out how to make this work with a touch-based interface.

Using touch

The first thing you need to do when making a touch-based game is to disable the touch device's automatic touch actions. Most touch devices let you zoom and scroll the screen by pinching, dragging, or double-tapping. These actions will almost certainly conflict with the touch actions that you've programmed into your game. To disable these default behaviors on touch-based devices, add this <meta> tag to your HTML code.

```
<meta name="viewport" content="width = device-width, initial-scale = 1.0, user-scalable = no">
```

Add it just below the <!doctype html> tag. It will set the HTML page's width to the width of the device and will disable scrolling.

Just like with the mouse, you need two variables that store the touch point's X and Y positions.

```
var touchX = 0;
var touchY = 0;
```

> Note: If any of your sprites depend on these values for setting their initial speeds, give touchX and touchY an initial value of 0.

You then need to capture those positions when you touch the canvas. Attach a touchmove listener to the canvas to do this.

```
canvas.addEventListener("touchmove", touchmoveHandler, false);
```

touchmove behaves the same way as mousemove. It's fired when any touch point moves across the canvas. It calls the touchmoveHandler, which captures the touch point's X and Y positions and copies them into the touchX and touchY variables. Here's the basic code that does this:

```
function touchmoveHandler(event)
{
  //Find the touch point's x and y position
  touchX = event.targetTouches[0].pageX - canvas.offsetLeft;
  touchY = event.targetTouches[0].pageY - canvas.offsetTop;

  //Prevent the canvas from being selected
  event.preventDefault();
}
```

There are some new things in this code that illustrate an important difference between mouse points and touch points. When you play a game with the mouse, there will only ever be one mouse point on the screen. But with a touch interface, you may have up to 10 fingers touching the screen at the same time. When a touch event is fired, all the touch points on the screen are copied into an array called touches. You can access this array in any touch event handler like this:

```
event.touches
```

For example, if there are three fingers on the screen the touches array will have three elements: 0, 1, 2. Each of these is a touch point with properties you can access, like their pageX and pageY values that give you their screen positions. That means that, if needed, you could access the first touch point's X position like this:

```
event.touches[0].pageX
```

touches is just an ordinary array, so you can manipulate it like you would any other array.

The touches array contains all the touch points on the entire screen, but that might not be what you want for your game. It's very likely that you'll only be interested in the touch points that are actually on the canvas. In that case, you can use another array called targetTouches. It only includes the touch points that are actually on the HTML element that fired the event, like the canvas. You can access this array in the touch event handler like this:

```
event.targetTouches
```

For example, let's say you've got two fingers on the screen. One is on a <button> element, and the other is controlling a game character on the <canvas> element. If the touch event is attached to the canvas, targetTouches will contain just the one touch point that's on the canvas. It's that point you're interested in if you want to control a game sprite. You can find that point like this:

```
touchX = event.targetTouches[0].pageX - canvas.offsetLeft;
touchY = event.targetTouches[0].pageY - canvas.offsetTop;
```

The examples in this chapter use this method for finding the touch point on the canvas.

> Note: Touch events also have a third array called changedTouches. This array stores the touch points that are actively involved in triggering the event. For example, if you removed a finger from a touch screen, changedTouches will tell you the finger that was removed. You could use this to access the position of the removed finger with changedTouches in a touchend event. You might find uses for changedTouches if you're creating a game with complex multitouch events.

There's one additional technical detail you have to deal with for touch events. A lot of devices will start scrolling the browser window automatically when you use a touchmove event. You can disable this with the event's preventDefault method.

```
event.preventDefault();
```

The three touch events you can use are touchmove, touchstart, and touchend. Here are the touch actions they respond to, along with their corresponding mouse events.

Touch event	When is it fired?	Related mouse event
touchmove	When a finger is dragged over the screen.	mousemove
touchstart	When a finger touches the screen.	mousedown
touchend	When a finger is removed from the screen.	mouseup

Open the **followTouch.html** program on a touch-based device to see all this at work. You can drag Button Fairy around the screen with a finger. Here's the code in the playGame animation loop that makes this work.

```
function playGame()
{
  fairy.x = touchX - (fairy.halfWidth());
  fairy.y = touchY - (fairy.halfHeight());
}
```

You can see that this basic code that moves the sprite is exactly the same as the example using the mouse. The `mouseX` and `mouseY` variables have just been replaced with the new `touchX` and `touchY` variables.

Just set up your touch events like I've shown you, and any game that works with the mouse will work with a touch interface as well. For convenience I've used mouse-based examples for most of the code in this chapter but you'll find the corresponding touch-based code for all these examples in the chapter's source files.

> Note: Of course, you'll need to test your touch-based games on a touch-based device. If you're not designing and testing a game directly on a touch-screen computer, you can use a touch simulator. Some current browsers, like Chrome, let you select the "user agent" in the JavaScript console settings to simulate a touch device like a tablet or mobile phone. Chrome's console also lets you emulate touch events, so that you can test whether your touch events are working even if you're developing your game on a computer with a keyboard and mouse. If you're developing a game for Apple devices you can use the iOS simulator, which is part of Apple's free Xcode development software.

Now that you know the basics of controlling a sprite with the mouse and touch, let's look at some more sophisticated techniques for moving game characters.

Moving a sprite with easing

It's likely that in a game scenario you will want your character to move with a little more grace than simply staying fixed exactly to the mouse position. You can use a simple technique called **easing** that gradually slows an object to a stop. You can use easing to create some very elegant systems to move objects.

Run the **easingMouse.html** program to see the effect. Move the mouse, and Button Fairy will chase it around the screen. When the mouse stops moving, she'll gracefully ease into position under it, as you can see in Figure 12-2. This is a really easy effect to implement.

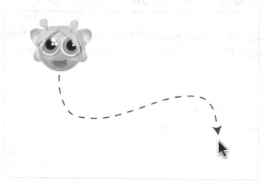

Figure 12-2. Button Fairy follows the mouse with a bit of a delay

The program first defines EASING as a constant.

```
EASING = 0.1;
```

This determines how pronounced the effect will be. A smaller number will make the movement slower, and a larger number will make it faster. A good number to begin with is 0.1. (Your easing value doesn't need to be a constant, but in these examples the values are not changed.)

Here's the code in the playGame function that uses the EASING constant to produce the effect.

```
function playGame()
{
  //Figure out the distance between the mouse and the center of the fairy
  var vx = mouseX - (fairy.x + fairy.halfWidth());
  var vy = mouseY - (fairy.y + fairy.halfHeight());
  distance = Math.sqrt(vx * vx + vy * vy);

  //Move the fairy if it's more than 1 pixel away from the mouse
  if (distance >= 1)
  {
    fairy.x += vx * EASING;
    fairy.y += vy * EASING;
  }
}
```

The code first calculates a distance between the fairy and the mouse by using some familiar code.

```
var vx = mouseX - (fairy.x + fairy.halfWidth());
var vy = mouseY - (fairy.y + fairy.halfHeight());
distance = Math.sqrt(vx * vx + vy * vy);
```

Now that the program knows what the distance is between the two points, the code uses an if statement to move the object if the distance between the mouse and the fairy is greater than 1 pixel:

```
if(distance >= 1)
{
  fairy.x += vx * EASING;
  fairy.y += vy * EASING;
}
```

If the distance is less than or equal to 1 pixel, then the mouse and fairy will be at the same position, so obviously you won't need to change the fairy's position.

These two lines inside the if statement create the easing effect:

```
fairy.x += vx * EASING;
fairy.y += vy * EASING;
```

This multiplies the distance between the fairy and the mouse by 0.1, and it adds the result to the fairy's current position. Keep in mind that 0.1 represents 10% of the total distance between the mouse and fairy. Because this happens inside the animation loop, it means that with each frame the fairy will move closer to the mouse by 10%. And so the distance between the mouse and fairy gradually decreases. But because the easing value remains unchanged at 10% the difference in the fairy's position between frames also becomes proportionally less and less over time. That's why the fairy gradually slows down and finally stops as it gets closer to the mouse.

You can implement easing using this simple formula inside a game animation loop:

```
(origin - destination) * easingValue;
```

You can make the animation happen faster or slower by changing the easing value. You can also use this easing formula with `height`, `width`, `rotation`, and `alpha` properties, to make the sprite gradually change its size, rotation, or transparency.

And that's it! Easing is one of the most useful and easiest motion techniques, and you'll find countless uses for it in your games.

Optimizing easing

Easing uses the Pythagorean theorem to calculate the distance between two points.

```
distance = Math.sqrt(vx * vx + vy * vy);
```

It needs to use the `Math.sqrt` function to do this. One pitfall of `Math.sqrt` is that it's one of the most CPU-intensive math functions you can use. If you can avoid using it, you'll save a great deal of processing power.

How can you avoid it? By exchanging CPU power for brainpower: use a hand-held calculator and precalculate the value yourself! Here's how.

Let's say you want to run some code if an object comes within 75 pixels of another object. First, calculate the distance squared, like this:

```
var distanceSquared:Number = (vx * vx + vy * vy);
```

Then run some code if that distance is less than 75 pixels.

```
if (distanceSquared < 75 * 75)
{
  //Directives to run if the object is within range...
}
```

This gives you the same result that `Math.sqrt` would have given you (5,625). By calculating the value yourself, you can drop `Math.sqrt`, and the effect will be exactly the same, except that you'll probably notice that your object moves a little more smoothly across the screen. Current JavaScript compilers are very optimized, so you may not need to do this in your game. But if you're making a complex game with hundreds of calculations happening in each frame, you may want to consider optimizing any code that uses `Math.sqrt` like this.

Click to move an object

With a small modification, you can make Button Fairy fly to any point on the screen that you click on. Run the **clickToMoveMouse.html** program to see the effect. Click anywhere on the canvas and Button Fairy serenely flutters to that spot, as illustrated in Figure 12-3.

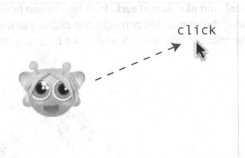

click

Figure 12-3. Click the canvas to make Button Fairy fly to that spot

The code first initializes the mouseX and mouseY values to the fairy's center point when the program first loads. This is so that both the mouse and fairy will have the same initial start point. It prevents the fairy from easing to the top left corner of the screen (position 0, 0) when the program loads.

```
var mouseX = fairy.x + fairy.halfWidth();
var mouseY = fairy.y + fairy.halfHeight();
```

The code then uses a mousedown event to capture the mouse's position when the mouse button is pressed down over the canvas.

```
canvas.addEventListener("mousedown", mousedownHandler, false);

function mousedownHandler(event)
{
  mouseX = event.pageX - canvas.offsetLeft;
  mouseY = event.pageY - canvas.offsetTop;
}
```

The mouse's X and Y positions are stored in the mouseX and mouseY variables. Those two numbers are then used as points to move the fairy to. That position is changed only when the player clicks the mouse. The rest of the code is identical to the previous example.

Easy easing!

679

A mouse-based and touch-based platform game

Now that you know the basics of using the mouse and touch points to control game characters, you can start using these techniques in real games. One thing you'll definitely want to do is create a mouse-based or touch-based platform game. It turns out that this is really easy to implement, and the code needed to do it is actually a little simpler than the code we used to make a keyboard-controlled platform game character in Chapter 11. Run the **platformsMouse.html** and **platformsTouch.html** files to see how it plays. In the mouse-based version, make the cat move by moving the mouse left and right and clicking to make it jump. In the touch-based game, use your finger to move the mouse right and left and make it jump with the jump button. Figure 12-4 shows what you'll see.

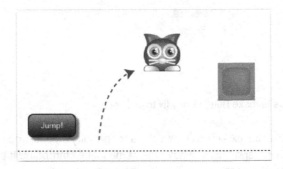

Figure 12-4. A touch-based platform game character

Mouse-based platforms

Open the **platformsMouse.html** file and you'll see that the code is almost identical to the platform code from Chapter 11. However, all the keyboard events are gone. Instead, a mousemove event is used to capture the mouse's position.

```
canvas.addEventListener("mousemove", mousemoveHandler, false);

function mousemoveHandler(event)
{
  mouseX = event.pageX - canvas.offsetLeft;
  mouseY = event.pageY - canvas.offsetTop;
}
```

A mousedown event is used to make the cat jump.

```
canvas.addEventListener("mousedown", mousedownHandler, false);

function mousedownHandler(event)
{
  if(cat.isOnGround)
```

```
  {
    cat.vy += cat.jumpForce;
    cat.isOnGround = false;
  }
}
```

The `playGame` function moves the mouse by using the easing formula we just looked at.

```
 cat.vx = (mouseX - (cat.x + cat.halfWidth())) * 0.2;
```

And those are the only changes you need to make. The rest of the code is identical to the **platforms.html** program from Chapter 11.

Touch-based platforms

The touch version of this system uses a button to make the cat jump.

```
jumpButton.addEventListener("touchstart", touchstartHandler, false);
```

The `jumpButton`'s `touchstartHandler` runs the jump code.

```
function touchstartHandler(event)
{
  if(cat.isOnGround)
  {
    cat.vy += cat.jumpForce;
    cat.isOnGround = false;
  }

  event.preventDefault();
}
```

To see how to integrate all this into a real working game, check out the mouse-based version of Hedgehog Apocalypse! in this chapter's source files.

Rotation

Along with easing, rotation is one of the most useful motion techniques for games. You can see rotation put to good use in the **rocketMouse.html** example file. Use the mouse to change the rocket's rotation and to click to fire bullets. Use the spacebar to make the rocket fly in the direction in which it's pointing. Figure 12-5 shows what you'll see.

Figure 12-5. Use the mouse to fly the rocket around the screen and fire bullets

Rotating sprites with canvas

In Chapter 7 you learned how to make sprites that you can rotate on the screen using canvas. Before we look at the mechanics of making an object rotate, let's first briefly review how to render sprites that you can rotate.

First, your spriteObject has to have a rotation property.

```
rotation: 0,
```

This will be a number in degrees that will represent the sprite's angle of rotation.

Next, you need to use a render method that can rotate sprites on the canvas. Here's the render method from Chapter 7 that we used to do this.

```
function render()
{
  drawingSurface.clearRect(0, 0, canvas.width, canvas.height);

  //Display the sprites
  if(sprites.length !== 0)
  {
    for(var i = 0; i < sprites.length; i++)
    {
      var sprite = sprites[i];

      //Save the current state of the drawing surface before it's rotated
      drawingSurface.save();

      //Rotate the canvas
      drawingSurface.translate
      (
        Math.floor(sprite.x + sprite.halfWidth()),
        Math.floor(sprite.y + sprite.halfHeight())
      );
      drawingSurface.rotate(sprite.rotation * Math.PI / 180);
```

```
if(sprite.visible)
{
  drawingSurface.drawImage
  (
    image,
    sprite.sourceX, sprite.sourceY,
    sprite.sourceWidth, sprite.sourceHeight,
    Math.floor(-sprite.halfWidth()), Math.floor(-sprite.halfHeight()),
    sprite.width, sprite.height
  );
}

//Restore the drawing surface to its state before it was rotated
drawingSurface.restore();
    }
  }
}
```

This is the `render` function that's used for all the examples involving rotation in this chapter.

You can use this code to display a rotated sprite, but only if you know that angle of rotation. How can you make a sprite rotate toward the mouse? We'll find out how to calculate that next.

Calculating rotation

The rotation effect is achieved with the help of a bit of simple trigonometry. If you're a mathophobe, rest assured that you don't need to necessarily *understand* the trigonometry we'll look at to be able to use it. In other words, feel free to skip this section! JavaScript does the math for you—just use these formulas with the correct numbers and your objects will rotate. And once you see it in use, you'll see how easy it is to apply it whenever you need to rotate an object toward another object. If you're really interested in the theory behind the math, read on; otherwise, see you at the next section.

JavaScript has a built-in method called `Math.atan2` that will give you the correct angle of rotation between two points. However, one little technical detail you need to deal with is that `Matn.atan2` returns the value of the angle in *radians*. The sprite objects that we're using in this book don't use radians for their rotation values; they use *degrees*. So once you've got the value in radians, you need to apply a very simple calculation to convert it into degrees. When you have that value, you can rotate the object.

Let me show you just how easy this all is. Figure 12-6 is a grid showing the positions of a rocket and the mouse on the screen.

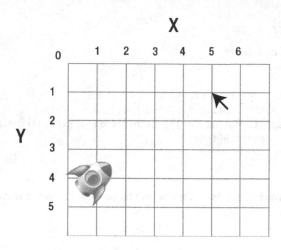

Figure 12-6. Find the angle of rotation between the rocket and the mouse

Here's how to find out the rocket's angle of rotation.

1. Find the positions of the rocket and the mouse:

   ```
   mouseX = 5
   mouseY = 1
   rocket.x = 1
   rocket.y = 4
   ```

2. Subtract the X and Y positions of the mouse from the X and Y positions of the rocket.

   ```
   rocket.x - mouseX = -4
   rocket.y - mouseY = 3
   ```

3. Plug these numbers into the `Math.atan2` function. It is very important that the y value come first:

   ```
   Math.atan2(3, -4)
   ```

This returns a number in radians. Unfortunately, this is not useful for rotating our sprite. We need to convert this number to degrees, which is the type of value expected by the rocket's `rotation` property.

To convert radians to degrees, you can use a simple calculation: multiply the value in radians by 180 divided by Pi (3.14). Just to make things easier for you, JavaScript has a built-in function called `Math.PI` that returns the value of Pi automatically. Here's what the final line of code might look like:

```
Math.atan2(3, -4) * (180 / Math.PI)
```

This gives you a value in degrees:

```
143
```

Figure 12-7 shows how you can visualize this.

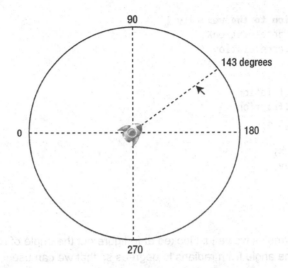

Figure 12-7. Use JavaScript's built- in `Math.atan2` function to find the angle of rotation

Great! You now have a number that you can use to rotate the rocket. You can use it in a directive like this:

```
rocket.rotation = Math.atan2(3, -4) * (180 / Math.PI);
```

Whenever you need to rotate an object toward another object, this is the formula you need to use. It's probably about 50% of the trigonometry you'll ever need to know for your games, and you didn't actually have to do the math yourself! The other 50% you'll need to know is coming up next.

Using rotation in a game

Let's apply this theory and find out how to make the rocket rotate in the **rocketMouse.html** example.

Here's the code in the `playGame` animation loop that moves and rotates the rocket.

```
function playGame()
{
    //Find the angle between the center of the rocket and the mouse
    angle = Math.atan2(mouseY - rocket.centerY(), mouseX - rocket.centerX());

    //Convert the angle's radians into rotation degrees
    rocket.rotation = angle * (180 / Math.PI);

    //Figure out the acceleration based on the angle
    rocket.accelerationX = Math.cos(angle) * rocket.speed;
    rocket.accelerationY = Math.sin(angle) * rocket.speed;
```

```
//Add the acceleration to the velocity
rocket.vx += rocket.accelerationX;
rocket.vy += rocket.accelerationY;

//Add friction
rocket.vx *= rocket.friction;
rocket.vy *= rocket.friction;

//Move the rocket
rocket.x += rocket.vx;
rocket.y += rocket.vy;

//...
}
```

The code uses all the formulas we've just looked at to figure out the angle of rotation between the rocket and the mouse. It converts the angle from radians to degrees so that we can use it with the rocket's rotation property. It then multiplies the angle with the rocket's speed and adds it to the rocket's acceleration. When that acceleration is applied to the rocket's velocity, the velocity will move the rocket at the correct angle. Let's find out how all these individual lines of code do all this.

Rotating the rocket

A mousemove event captures the mouse's X and Y positions and stores them in the mouseX and mouseY variables. The code in the playGame function then uses these numbers to calculate the angle between the rocket and the mouse.

```
angle = Math.atan2(mouseY - rocket.centerY(), mouseX - rocket.centerX());
```

This gives us the rocket's angle in radians. The next step is to covert that number to degrees and assign it to the rocket's rotation property.

```
rocket.rotation = angle * (180 / Math.PI);
```

This is the line of code that actually makes the rocket rotate.

Moving the rocket

But the rocket does more than just rotate. If you press the spacebar, the rocket moves in the direction of its rotation. The spriteObject that the rocket is made from has a property called speed. It's initialized to 0.

```
speed: 0,
```

When the spacebar is pressed, the keydownHandler sets the rocket's speed to 0.2:

```
function keydownHandler(event)
{
  switch(event.keyCode)
  {
    case SPACE:
      rocket.speed = 0.2;
      rocket.friction = 1;
  }
}
```

To make the rocket move in the direction in which it's pointing, you need to multiply its speed by the rotation angle. This is done with the help of two more specialized trigonometry functions: Math.cos and Math.sin. Both functions take one argument, which is the angle value in radians. Their job is to return the ratio of two sides of the triangle formed by the measurement of the angle. Multiply the values they produce by the rocket's speed. Then apply their final result to the rocket's vx and vy values. That will make the rocket move in its direction of rotation.

Here's the code from the example that does this:

```
//Figure out the acceleration based on the angle
rocket.accelerationX = Math.cos(angle) * rocket.speed;
rocket.accelerationY = Math.sin(angle) * rocket.speed;

//Add the acceleration to the velocity
rocket.vx += rocket.accelerationX;
rocket.vy += rocket.accelerationY;
```

This is what makes the rocket move at the correct angle.

> Note: For a thorough explanation of how to use trigonometry for games and interactive animation, see "Foundation HTML5 Animation with JavaScript" by Billy Lamberta and Keith Peters (Apress, 2011).

The rocket stops moving when the spacebar is released. The keyupHandler does this by setting the rocket's speed to 0.

```
function keyupHandler(event)
{
  switch(event.keyCode)
  {
    case SPACE:
      rocket.speed = 0;
```

```
        rocket.friction = 0.96;
        break;
    }
}
```

This is the code that makes the rocket rotate and move, but it can also fire bullets in any direction. Let's find out how.

Firing bullets in all directions

If you press the left mouse button, the rocket will fire bullets in whatever direction it's pointing. The code for firing bullets is essentially the same as what we used in Alien Armada from Chapter 9. What's new is that when a bullet is created, it's added to the screen at the tip of the rocket. Then to make the bullets move, they're given velocities that are determined by the rocket's angle.

Creating and positioning the bullet sprites

Let's first take a look at the code that creates the bullet sprites, adds them to the screen, and gives them their initial velocities.

```
canvas.addEventListener("mousedown", mousedownHandler, false);

function mousedownHandler(event)
{
    //Create a bullet sprite
    var bullet = Object.create(spriteObject);
    bullet.sourceX = 256;
    bullet.sourceWidth = 10;
    bullet.sourceHeight = 10;
    bullet.width = 10;
    bullet.height = 10;

    //Center it over the rocket
    var radius = 32;
    bullet.x
      = rocket.centerX() - bullet.halfWidth()
      + (radius * Math.cos(angle));

    bullet.y
      = rocket.centerY() - bullet.halfHeight()
      + (radius * Math.sin(angle));

    //Set its speed
    bullet.vx = Math.cos(angle) * 7;
    bullet.vy = Math.sin(angle) * 7;
```

```
//Push the bullet into both the sprites and bullets arrays
sprites.push(bullet);
bullets.push(bullet);
}
```

A variable called `radius` tells us how far from the rocket's center the bullets should be placed. The rocket is 64 pixels wide. So if you think of the rocket as tracing a circle when it rotates, its radius will be half that, which is 32 pixels.

```
var radius = 32;
```

The code then assigns the bullets' X and Y positions with these two lines of code:

```
bullet.x
  = rocket.centerX() - bullet.halfWidth()
  + (radius * Math.cos(angle));

bullet.y
  = rocket.centerY() - bullet.halfHeight()
  + (radius * Math.sin(angle));
```

It's a lot of code to look at, so I've broken each important phase of the calculation onto its own line so that it's easier to read. The code first places the bullet at the very center of the rocket, like this:

```
rocket.centerX() - bullet.halfWidth()
```

Figure 12-8 shows where this center point is.

Figure 12-8. Position the bullet in the center of the rocket

The next step is to find the point on the edge of the rocket that matches the rocket's rotation. To do this, feed the angle value to the `Math.cos` function and multiply the result by the `radius` (highlighted below).

```
bullet.x
  = rocket.centerX() - bullet.halfWidth()
  + (radius * Math.cos(angle));
```

This is added to the center point calculation in the previous step.

The same thing is done to find the Y position, but the only difference is that the `radius` is multiplied by the return value of `Math.sin`.

```
bullet.y
  = rocket.centerY() - bullet.halfHeight()
  + (radius * Math.sin(angle));
```

The result is that the bullet is placed 32 pixels from the center of the rocket at a point that matches the angle of the rocket. Figure 12-9 illustrates where this point is.

Figure 12-9. The point on the edge of the rocket that matches the angle of rotation

Setting the bullet's speed

The last step to creating the bullet is to set its initial speed. To do this, multiply its speed by the return value of `Math.cos` and `Math.sin`. In this example, the bullet's speed is 7, which means it will move at 7 pixels per frame.

```
bullet.vx = Math.cos(angle) * 7;
bullet.vy = Math.sin(angle) * 7;
```

The newly created bullet is then pushed into the `bullets` and `sprites` arrays so that it can be moved and displayed.

There's another way to set the bullet's speed that's better for most games like this. Add the rocket's velocity to the calculation. Here's how:

```
bullet.vx = Math.cos(angle) * 7 + rocket.vx;
bullet.vy = Math.sin(angle) * 7 + rocket.vy;
```

This makes the bullet's speed relative to the rocket's speed. That means that if the rocket is moving at 5 pixels per frame, the bullet's speed will be 12 (7 plus 5). This is important for game objects that fire bullets and that can move and rotate at the same time. It prevents the bullets from bunching up in front of the rocket if the rocket is moving in the same direction as the bullets.

Moving the bullets

The hard work is now done! To move the bullets, just loop through the `bullets` array and apply the bullet's velocity to its X and Y positions. Check whether it crosses the screen boundaries and remove it if it does. Here's the code in the `playGame` function that does this.

```
for(var i = 0; i < bullets.length; i++)
{
  var bullet = bullets[i];

  //Move it
  bullet.x += bullet.vx;
  bullet.y += bullet.vy;

  //Remove the bullet if it crosses the top of the screen
  if (bullet.centerY() < 0
  || bullet.centerX() < 0
  || bullet.centerX() > canvas.width
  || bullet.centerY() > canvas.height)
  {
    //Remove the bullet from the bullets array
    removeObject(bullet, bullets);

    //Remove the bullet from the sprites array
    removeObject(bullet, sprites);

    //Reduce the loop counter by 1 to compensate for the removed element
    i--;
  }
}

function removeObject(objectToRemove, array)
{
  var i = array.indexOf(objectToRemove);
  if (i !== -1)
  {
    array.splice(i, 1);
  }
}
```

This rocket is a classic video-game object that you can use and adapt for many different games. In the chapter's source files you'll find the touch-based version of this code, called **rocketTouch.html**, which is shown in Figure 12-10. Use your finger to rotate the rocket, press the Go! button to make it move, and press the Shoot! button to fire bullets.

Figure 12-10. A touch-based space rocket

In the chapter's source files you'll also find a file called **rocketKeyboard.html**, which is a version of this space-ship code that uses the keyboard exclusively.

Driving a car

With a little twist to the rocket code you can make a car that you can drive around the screen, as you can see in Figure 12-11. Run the **carMouse.html** file to try it out. The car follows the mouse, and the car rolls to a stop if it reaches the mouse's position.

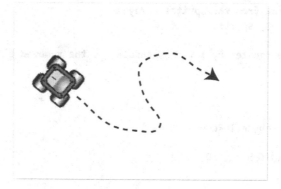

Figure 12-11. Drive a car around the screen

The spriteObject that the car is made from has speed and speedLimit properties that the code will use to figure out how fast the car should go.

```
speed: 0,
speedLimit: 5,
```

The biggest difference between the spaceship and the car is that you can change the car's direction even if it's not accelerating. This is done with the help of a Boolean variable called accelerate. It's also a property of the spriteObject.

```
accelerate: false,
```

It's set to true when the left mouse button is pressed and false when it's released. This works like stepping on and releasing a car's accelerator pedal.

Here are the mousedown and mouseup listeners that do this.

```
canvas.addEventListener("mousedown", mousedownHandler, false);
canvas.addEventListener("mouseup", mouseupHandler, false);

function mousedownHandler(event)
{
  car.accelerate = true;
}

function mouseupHandler(event)
{
  car.accelerate = false;
}
```

The playGame function uses the car's accelerate property to decide whether or not to move the car. The car will accelerate only if the mouse is at a distance that's greater than half the car's width (its radius). Here's the code from the playGame function that does this.

```
function playGame()
{
  if(car.accelerate)
  {
    //Increase the car's speed if it's under the speed limit
    if(car.speed < car.speedLimit)
    {
      car.speed += 0.1;
    }
  }
  else
  {
    //Add friction to the speed if the car is not accelerating
    car.speed *= car.friction;
  }

  //Figure out the distance between the mouse and the center of the car
  var vx = mouseX - (car.x + car.halfWidth());
  var vy = mouseY - (car.y + car.halfHeight());
  distance = Math.sqrt(vx * vx + vy * vy);

  //Calculate the acceleration based on the angle of rotation if the
  //mouse is outside the car's radius
  if(distance > car.halfWidth())
```

```
  {
    angle = Math.atan2(mouseY - car.centerY(), mouseX - car.centerX());
    car.accelerationX = car.speed * Math.cos(angle);
    car.accelerationY = car.speed * Math.sin(angle);
  }
  else
  {
    //Slow the car to a stop if it's near the mouse
    car.accelerationX *= 0.8;
    car.accelerationY *= 0.8;
  }

  car.vx = car.accelerationX;
  car.vy = car.accelerationY;

  //Move and rotate the car
  car.x += car.vx;
  car.y += car.vy;
  car.rotation = angle * (180 / Math.PI);
}
```

The code first checks whether accelerate is true. If it is, it increases the car's speed, within the speed limit. If accelerate is false, the code applies some friction to slow the car down.

```
if(car.accelerate)
{
  //Increase the car's speed if it's under the speed limit
  if(car.speed < car.speedLimit)
  {
    car.speed += 0.1;
  }
}
else
{
  //Add friction to the speed if the car is not accelerating
  car.speed *= car.friction;
}
```

A feature of this car control system is that the car will rotate and accelerate only if the mouse is far enough away from the car's center. If the mouse's distance is greater than 32 (the car's half-width), then the car will accelerate and rotate as you would expect. But if the mouse is inside this radius, the car won't rotate and will slow to a stop. Figure 12-12 illustrates this. Without this check the car will rapidly flip directions if the mouse gets too close, which looks like a glitch. That's because it will try to constantly align its rotation toward the mouse, even if the mouse gets within a few pixels of its center. It would look as chaotic as if you were driving a car and you were violently changing the direction of the car as quickly and haphazardly as a fly buzzing around your head.

The car moves
and rotates

The car doesn't rotate
and slows to a stop

Figure 12-12. Accelerate and rotate the car only if the mouse is outside its radius

To implement this, the code first figures out the distance between the mouse and the center of the car.

```
var vx = mouseX - (car.x + car.halfWidth());
var vy = mouseY - (car.y + car.halfHeight());
distance = Math.sqrt(vx * vx + vy * vy);
```

It checks whether this distance is greater than the car's radius (its half-width). If it is, it figures out the acceleration based on the angle. If the mouse is inside the radius, the car is slowed to stop very quickly by applying friction of 0.8.

```
if(distance > car.halfWidth())
{
  //Accelerate the car based on the angle
  angle = Math.atan2(mouseY - car.centerY(), mouseX - car.centerX());
  car.accelerationX = car.speed * Math.cos(angle);
  car.accelerationY = car.speed * Math.sin(angle);
}
else
{
  //Slow the car to a stop if it's near the mouse
  car.accelerationX *= 0.8;
  car.accelerationY *= 0.8;
}
```

The rest of the code then uses these numbers to move and rotate the car.

```
car.vx = car.accelerationX;
car.vy = car.accelerationY;

car.x += car.vx;
car.y += car.vy;
car.rotation = angle * (180 / Math.PI);
```

You'll find keyboard- and touch-based versions of this car control system called **carKeyboard.html** and **carTouch.html** in the chapter's source files.

Creating a tank with a rotating turret

What would happen if you fused the code for the rocket with the code for the car? You might end up with a tank that has a turret that rotates and fires bullets, as shown in Figure 12-13. Run the **tank.html** program to see this everything-plus-the-kitchen-sink example in action. Use the keyboard to move the tank and the mouse to rotate the turret and fire bullets. Take a look at the source code for details if you ever need to make something like this.

Figure 12-13. A tank with a rotating gun turret

Killer Bee Pandemonium

We've made a lot of fun little toys in this chapter, and it doesn't take much work to turn them into a real game. I let my imagination wander for a dangerous few moments and came up with an action-shooter called Killer Bee Pandemonium. Open the **killerBeePandemonium.html** file and play the game. Button Fairy can fly around the screen and shoot the bee. The Killer Bee flies toward her and fires bullets if she's within range. The scoreboards at the top of the screen keep track of the number of hits each has achieved.

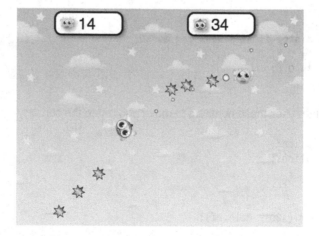

Figure 12-14. Can Button Fairy save the woodland creatures from the grumpy Killer Bee?

The game doesn't use any new techniques, but it mixes and matches many of the techniques we've looked at in this chapter in new ways. In the next few sections we'll take a step-by-step look at how Button Fairy and Killer Bee were made, as well as how they're used in the final game.

Making Button Fairy

The **buttonFairy.html** program contains all the important code that makes Button Fairy work but without the clutter of the rest of the game code. Open it in a browser and you'll see that you can fly Button Fairy around the screen by moving the mouse, much like you could in the easing examples we looked at earlier in the chapter. An orange circle, the fairy's "wand," rotates around the fairy and angles itself toward the mouse. Click the mouse button and you can fire stars in all directions. The stars are removed when they hit the screen boundaries. Figure 12-15 shows what you'll see.

Figure 12-15. Button Fairy flies in the direction her wand is pointing in and she can fire stars in all directions

Button Fairy is essentially a fusion of the easing motion code, with the rocket's bullet-firing code. The code that moves Button Fairy is identical to the easing code. The code that fires stars is also identical to the code that fires bullets in the rocket example. The only slightly new thing is her wand. That's the yellow dot that fires stars in all directions. It rotates around the center of the fairy and always points toward the mouse, which is useful for aiming. The wand is positioned in a 64-pixel radius distance from the center of the fairy. The code that positions it is very similar to the code that positions the bullets in the rocket example.

```
//Find the angle between the center of the fairy and the mouse
angle = Math.atan2(mouseY - fairy.centerY(), mouseX - fairy.centerX());
```

```
//Move the wand around the fairy
var radius = 64;
wand.x = fairy.centerX() + (radius * Math.cos(angle)) - wand.halfWidth();
wand.y = fairy.centerY() + (radius * Math.sin(angle)) - wand.halfHeight();
```

This code runs in the playGame function, so the wand's position is updated in each frame.

New stars are created when the left mouse button is pressed. When new stars are created, they're added to the screen at the wand's X and Y positions.

```
star.x = wand.centerX() - star.halfWidth();
star.y = wand.centerY() - star.halfHeight();
```

Their velocities are calculated by using the same angle value that positions the wand.

```
star.vx = Math.cos(angle) * 7;
star.vy = Math.sin(angle) * 7;
```

You'll find a touch-based version of this code in the chapter's source file called **buttonFairyTouch.html**, which uses a button to fire stars, as shown in Figure 12-16.

Figure 12-16. A touch-based Button Fairy

Now let's find out how to make Button Fairy's arch nemesis, Killer Bee.

Making Killer Bee chase the mouse

Run the **beeFollowMouse.html** file for a focused example of how Killer Bee follows a target, shown in Figure 12-17. It rotates toward the mouse if it's within a 300-pixel range. When it reaches the mouse it circles around it with very bee-like persistence.

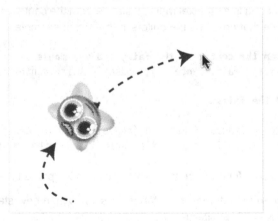

Figure 12-17. The bee rotates toward the mouse and follows it around the screen

This effect is achieved through a combination of easing and rotation. The spriteObject that the bee is made from moves by using two new properties called speed and rotationSpeed.

```
speed: 3,
rotationSpeed: 0.3,
```

speed is how fast the bee should move when it's going toward the target. rotationSpeed is the amount in degrees that it should rotate in each frame when it's turning. Here's the entire playGame function that uses these properties to make the bee move:

```
function playGame()
{

  //Calculate the vector between the mouse and the bee
  var vx = mouseX - bee.centerX();
  var vy = mouseY - bee.centerY();

  //The distance between the mouse and the bee
  var distance = Math.sqrt(vx * vx + vy * vy);

  //The range, in pixels, to which the bee should be sensitive
  var range = 200;

  if (distance <= range)
  {
    //Find out how much to move
    var moveX = bee.rotationSpeed * vx / distance;
    var moveY = bee.rotationSpeed * vy / distance;

    //Increase the bee's velocity
    bee.vx += moveX;
    bee.vy += moveY;

    //Find the total distance to move
    var moveDistance = Math.sqrt(bee.vx * bee.vx + bee.vy * bee.vy);

    //Apply easing
    bee.vx = bee.speed * bee.vx / moveDistance;
    bee.vy = bee.speed * bee.vy / moveDistance;

    //Find the angle in radians
    angle = Math.atan2(bee.vy, bee.vx);

    //Convert the radians to degrees to rotate the bee correctly
    bee.rotation = angle * 180 / Math.PI + 90;
  }
```

```
//Apply friction
bee.vx *= bee.friction;
bee.vy *= bee.friction;

//Move the bee
bee.x += bee.vx;
bee.y += bee.vy;
}
```

The code calculates the distance between the bee and the mouse. If the distance is less than the range value (200), the bee moves.

The bee moves by using a variation of the easing formula we looked at earlier. It's a little more complex, however, because you want to limit the bee's speed and the rate at which it turns. Here are the steps the code takes and the formulas it uses to accomplish each task:

1. After the code finds out how far the bee is from the mouse, it figures out by how much the bee should move. It multiplies the bee's rotationSpeed by its velocity and then divides that by the distance. It assigns the result to moveX and moveY variables:

    ```
    var moveX = bee.rotationSpeed * vx / distance;
    var moveY = bee.rotationSpeed * vy / distance;
    ```

2. The values of these new variables are used to modify the velocity:

    ```
    bee.vx += moveX;
    bee.vy += moveY;
    ```

3. The bee's new vx and vy properties are used to find the total distance required to move it:

    ```
    var moveDistance = Math.sqrt(bee.vx * bee.vx + bee.vy * bee.vy);
    ```

4. The code then uses this new moveDistance value along with the bee's speed property to find the correct velocity:

    ```
    bee.vx =  bee.speed * bee.vx / moveDistance;
    bee.vy =  bee.speed * bee.vy / moveDistance;
    ```

This is a variation of our easing formula, with the speed property representing the easing value.

5. Finally, the code rotates the bee toward the mouse. This is the same formula we've been using for rotation throughout the book. The addition of +90 is there to offset the rotation of the bee object by 90 degrees. Without that, the leading edge of the bee would be its right side. (That's because of the way the object was drawn, with its "front" being the stinger on the bee's head.) Any objects you use with this code might be oriented differently, so you'll probably want to adjust 90 to another number that you can figure out by trial and error when you see the direction toward which your object rotates.

    ```
    bee.rotation = angle * 180 / Math.PI + 90;
    ```

If the mouse is *not* within the bee's range, the following code kicks in, which gradually slows the bee down with friction:

```
//Apply friction
bee.vx *= bee.friction;
bee.vy *= bee.friction;

//Move the bee
bee.x += bee.vx;
bee.y += bee.vy;
```

With a bit of simple logic and a few careful adjustments to the easing formula, you will have a very effective following behavior. In this example, the bee chases the mouse, but you can make it chase any other object by just changing the target object in the code that calculates the distance vector, like this:

```
var vx = thingToChaseX - bee.centerX();
var vy = thingToChaseY - bee.centerY();
```

Making the bee fly away from the mouse

You can make the bee fly away from the mouse with two small changes. First, give the bee a *negative rotation* so that it points in the opposite direction:

```
bee.rotation = angle * 180 / Math.PI + -90;
```

The "+90" has just been changed to "-90."

Next, give the bee a negative velocity:

```
bee.x += -bee.vx;
bee.y += -bee.vy;
```

And that's it! The bee will now flee from the mouse in frenetic terror, as illustrated in Figure 12-18. You'll find the touch-based version of this code in the **beeFollowTouch.html** file.

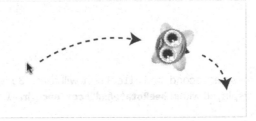

Figure 12-18. Get too close and the bee flies away

Using a timer to fire bullets

In the final game, Killer Bee not only chases Button Fairy but also fires bullets at set intervals. This is done with a simple counter that calls a `fireBullet` function every half-second. You'll find a focused example of this at work in the **beeRotateAndShootMouse.html** file, shown in Figure 12-19.

Figure 12-19. The bee flies toward the mouse and fires bullets at it

The program uses two variables to make this work:

```
var bulletTimer = 0;
var timeToFire = 30;
```

The `playGame` function updates the `bulletTimer` by 1. If `bulletTimer` reaches the value of `timeToFire`, the `fireBullet` function is called. The `fireBullet` function creates bullets with the same code we've looked at elsewhere. `bulletTimer` is also reset back to 0 so that it can start counting toward the next interval to fire bullets.

```
bulletTimer++;

if(bulletTimer === timeToFire)
{
  fireBullet();
  bulletTimer = 0;
}
```

This code is updated 60 times per second, so `bulletTimer` will reach 30 twice each second. The touch-based version of this program is displayed within **beeRotateAndShootTouch.html**.

Putting together the finished game

Killer Bee Pandemonium was not difficult to make. The hard part was figuring out the control systems for the bee and the fairy. That includes all the code that we've looked at in the last few sections. After that was done, I dropped the bee and fairy code as is into a game program and added some simple collision detection.

The game level isn't complex, so I didn't think it made sense to create it with a 2D array. Instead, the bee, fairy, background, and game messages are created as individual sprites in the same section of code that initializes all the other game variables. In Figure 12-20 you can see that the background is just one big image that even includes the scoreboards.

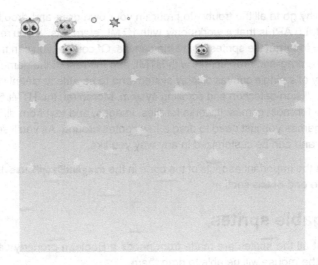

Figure 12-20. The game's tilesheet image

Take a look at the full code in the chapter's source code if you're curious about how any of the details work, but you won't find any surprises. The mouse-based version is called **killerBeeMouse.html** and the touch-based version is called **killerBeeTouch.html**.

Using drag and drop for canvas

The last game interface we're going to look at implements a drag-and-drop capability for canvas. Open the **dragAndDropMouse.html** file and use the mouse to move the three animals around the screen. If you move the mouse over an animal, the arrow changes to a hand icon. When you press the mouse button down, you can move the animal to a new location. Release the mouse to drop it in place at that new spot. If you drop an animal over another one, it will stack above it. If you select an animal from the bottom or middle of the stack, it will jump to the top. Figure 12-21 illustrates this.

drag   **drop**   **re-order**

Figure 12-21. Using drag-and-drop with canvas

Before we reinvent the wheel, you should know that HTML5 contains a complete drag-and-drop application programming interface (API) for HTML elements. The API has properties and events that let you easily make a drag-and-drop interface. That might be all you need. A web search will turn up lots of information on how to implement it.

So if that's the case, why go to all the trouble to program your own drag-and-drop interface from scratch? The limitation with the HTML5 API is that it works only with HTML elements. If you're using canvas as a display system, there's no way to target the sprites inside the canvas. Of course, you can freely mix HTML and canvas, so you could render the drag-and-drop sprites with HTML and the rest of the game with canvas. However, you might like the simplicity of a single canvas display system and to be able to cleanly integrate the drag-and-drop functionality with the collision detection and scrolling system. Moreover, the HTML5 drag-and-drop API is more generic than you need for most games: it works for files, images, and text from different sources and between applications. In most games you just need to drag a few sprites around. As you'll see, a drag-and-drop system is not difficult to make and can be customized in any way you like.

Let's first walk through the important aspects of the code in the **dragAndDropMouse.html** file. You'll find the complete code listing at the end of this section.

Selecting draggable sprites

The spriteObject that all the sprites are made from needs a Boolean property called draggable. This determines whether or not the mouse will be able to drag them.

```
draggable: true,
```

If you set this to false for any of your sprites, the code will prevent them from being dragged.

The program uses a variable called dragSprite that will store a reference to the current sprite that's being dragged around the screen. dragSprite is initialized to null when the program loads.

```
var dragSprite = null;
```

When the mouse button is pressed, the mousedownHandler checks to see if there are any sprites under the mouse. It loops through all the sprites and uses hitTestPoint to check whether the point of the mouse is over any of them. (Check back to Chapter 8 for a review of how hitTestPoint works.) If it finds a hit, it assigns the sprite to the dragSprite variable. It then moves this new dragSprite to the end of the sprites array so that the canvas will display it above all the other sprites. This is what makes the selected sprite appear above all the other sprites, at the top of the stack.

```
function mousedownHandler(event)
{
  //Loop through all the sprites in reverse and find out if the mouse is over any of them
  for(var i = sprites.length - 1; i > -1; i--)
  {
    sprite = sprites[i];

    if(hitTestPoint(mouseX, mouseY, sprite)
    && sprite.draggable)
```

```
    {
        //Assign the sprite to the dragSprite variable
        dragSprite = sprite;

        //Push the dragSprite to the end of the sprites array so that it's
        //displayed last, above all the other sprites
        sprites.push(dragSprite);

        //Splice the dragSprite from its previous position in the sprites array
        sprites.splice(i, 1);
        break;
    }
  }
}
```

There's an interesting aspect of the for loop that you haven't seen before. It loops through all the sprites *in reverse*.

```
for(var i = sprites.length - 1; i > -1; i--)
{...
```

The first sprite that it checks will be the last one in the array. This is important because sprites that are last in the array are displayed above the other sprites. This means that when you click on a group of sprites that are stacked on top of each other, this code will select the one at the top of the stack as the dragSprite. It's like choosing the top card from a deck of cards. If this loop wasn't reversed like this, the sprite at the bottom of the stack would be chosen as the dragSprite, and that wouldn't look right.

Calculating the mouse's velocity

When the mouse moves, the selected dragSprite moves with it. This requires a bit of sleight of hand to implement. We can't tell the sprite to exactly match the mouse's X and Y positions; otherwise, the sprite's corner will snap to the mouse, which won't look natural. Instead, we want the selected sprite to move along with the mouse relative to the point on the sprite where the mouse was when the button was pressed. This makes it look as if the sprite is stuck to the bottom of the mouse while it's being dragged, which looks right. Most drag-and-drop systems use this effect.

To make this work, we have to figure out the difference between the mouse's position between the current frame and the previous frame. This is essentially the mouse's velocity. We then have to move the sprite by this amount.

When the program loads, it initializes these four variables:

```
var mouseX = 0;
var mouseY = 0;
var oldMouseX = 0;
var oldMouseY = 0;
```

The mouseX and mouseY variables will store the mouse's position for the current frame. The oldMouseX and oldMouseY variables will store the mouse's position from the *previous* frame. By subtracting the old position from the new position, you can find out exactly by how much you need to move the sprite.

Here's the mousemoveHandler that uses these variables to move the sprite.

```
function mousemoveHandler()
{
  //Find the mouse's X and Y positions on the canvas
  mouseX = event.pageX - canvas.offsetLeft;
  mouseY = event.pageY - canvas.offsetTop;

  //Turn the cursor into a hand pointer if it is over a sprite
  for(var i = 0; i < sprites.length; i++)
  {
    sprite = sprites[i];

    if(hitTestPoint(mouseX, mouseY, sprite)
    && sprite.draggable)
    {
      canvas.style.cursor = "pointer";
      break;
    }
    else
    {
      canvas.style.cursor = "auto";
    }
  }

  //Move the dragSprite if it's not null
  if(dragSprite !== null)
  {
    dragSprite.x = mouseX - (oldMouseX - dragSprite.x);
    dragSprite.y = mouseY - (oldMouseY - dragSprite.y);
  }

  //Capture the current mouse position to use in the next frame
  oldMouseX = mouseX;
  oldMouseY = mouseY;
}
```

The code first finds the mouse's X and Y positions. It then loops through all the sprites and changes the mouse pointer into a hand icon if it's over any draggable sprites.

```
for(var i = 0; i < sprites.length; i++)
{
  sprite = sprites[i];

  if(hitTestPoint(mouseX, mouseY, sprite)
  && sprite.draggable)
```

```
  {
    canvas.style.cursor = "pointer";
    break;
  }
  else
  {
    canvas.style.cursor = "auto";
  }
}
```

The next bit of code actually makes the sprite move. If the `dragSprite` isn't `null`, the code moves it by the amount of offset between the mouse's current and previous positions.

```
if(dragSprite !== null)
{
  dragSprite.x = mouseX - (oldMouseX - dragSprite.x);
  dragSprite.y = mouseY - (oldMouseY - dragSprite.y);
}
```

> Note: If you want the sprite to be dragged from its center point, replace the two lines of code above with these two lines:
>
> dragSprite.x = mouseX - (dragSprite.width / 2);
>
> dragSprite.y = mouseY - (dragSprite.height / 2);

But wait a moment! How do we know what the `oldMouseX` and `oldMouseY` values are? That's in fact the very last thing the `mousemoveHandler` does. It assigns the mouse's current X and Y positions to the `oldMouseX` and `oldMouseY` variables.

```
oldMouseX = mouseX;
oldMouseY = mouseY;
```

This saves the mouse's current position so that we can access it in the next frame. In the next frame, this current position will have become the *old position*. The difference between the two positions will be the mouse's velocity. It's a clever trick.

When the mouse button is released, the `mouseupHandler` sets the `dragSprite` back to `null` so that a new sprite can be selected.

```
function mouseupHandler()
{
  //Release the dragSprite by setting it to null
  dragSprite = null;
}
```

These are all the important mechanics of this drag-and-drop system.

The drag-and-drop code listing

Here's the entire **dragAndDropMouse.html** file from the chapter's source files so that you can see how everything fits together in its proper context. To use this in a game, add the game logic in the playGame function.

```html
<!doctype html>
<meta charset="utf-8">
<title>Canvas drag and drop</title>

<style>
*
{
  -webkit-user-select: none;
  -moz-user-select: none;
  user-select: none;
}
</style>

<canvas width="550" height="400" style="border: 1px dashed black"></canvas>

<script>

//--- The sprite object

var spriteObject =
{
  sourceX: 0,
  sourceY: 0,
  sourceWidth: 64,
  sourceHeight: 64,
  width: 64,
  height: 64,
  x: 0,
  y: 0,
  visible: true,

  //A draggable property
  draggable: true,

  //Getters
  left: function()
  {
    return this.x;
  },
  right: function()
  {
    return this.x + this.width;
  },
```

```
  top: function()
  {
    return this.y;
  },
  bottom: function()
  {
    return this.y + this.height;
  },
  centerX: function()
  {
    return this.x + (this.width / 2);
  },
  centerY: function()
  {
    return this.y + (this.height / 2);
  },
  halfWidth: function()
  {
    return this.width / 2;
  },
  halfHeight: function()
  {
    return this.height / 2;
  }
};
```

```
//--- The main program

//The canvas and its drawing surface
var canvas = document.querySelector("canvas");
var drawingSurface = canvas.getContext("2d");

//Object arrays
var sprites = [];
var assetsToLoad = [];
var assetsLoaded = 0;

//Create the sprites
var cat = Object.create(spriteObject);
cat.x = canvas.width / 2 - cat.halfWidth();
cat.y = canvas.height / 2 - cat.halfHeight();
sprites.push(cat);

var tiger = Object.create(spriteObject);
tiger.sourceX = 64;
tiger.x = 100;
tiger.y = 100;
sprites.push(tiger);
```

```
var hedgehog = Object.create(spriteObject);
hedgehog.sourceX = 128;
hedgehog.x = 375;
hedgehog.y = 250;
sprites.push(hedgehog);

//Load the image
var image = new Image();
image.addEventListener("load", loadHandler, false);
image.src = "dragAndDrop.png";
assetsToLoad.push(image);

//Variables to store the mouse's position and velocity
var mouseX = 0;
var mouseY = 0;
var oldMouseX = 0;
var oldMouseY = 0;

//A variable to store the current sprite being dragged
var dragSprite = null;

//Event listeners
canvas.addEventListener("mousemove", mousemoveHandler, false);
canvas.addEventListener("mousedown", mousedownHandler, false);
window.addEventListener("mouseup", mouseupHandler, false);

//Game states
var LOADING = 0;
var PLAYING = 1;
var gameState = LOADING;

update();

function update()
{
  //The animation loop
  requestAnimationFrame(update, canvas);

  //Change what the game is doing based on the game state
  switch(gameState)
  {
    case LOADING:
      console.log("loading...");
      break;

    case PLAYING:
      playGame();
      break;
  }
```

```
  //Render the game
  render();
}

function playGame()
{
  //Add game logic here
}

function mousedownHandler(event)
{
  //Loop through all the sprites and find out if the mouse is over any of them
  for(var i = sprites.length - 1; i > -1; i--)
  {
    sprite = sprites[i];

    if(hitTestPoint(mouseX, mouseY, sprite)
    && sprite.draggable)
    {
      //Assign the sprite to the dragSprite variable
      dragSprite = sprite;

      //push the dragSprite to the end of the sprites array so that it's displayed last
      sprites.push(dragSprite);

      //Splice the dragSprite from its previous position in the sprites array
      sprites.splice(i, 1);
      break;
    }
  }
}

function mousemoveHandler(event)
{
  //Find the mouse's X and Y positions on the canvas
  mouseX = event.pageX - canvas.offsetLeft;
  mouseY = event.pageY - canvas.offsetTop;

  //Turn the cursor into a hand pointer if it is over a sprite
  for(var i = 0; i < sprites.length; i++)
  {
    sprite = sprites[i];

    if(hitTestPoint(mouseX, mouseY, sprite)
    && sprite.draggable)
    {
      canvas.style.cursor = "pointer";
      break;
    }
  }
```

```
    else
    {
      canvas.style.cursor = "auto";
    }
  }

  //Move the dragSprite if it's not null
  if(dragSprite !== null)
  {

    dragSprite.x = mouseX - (oldMouseX - dragSprite.x);
    dragSprite.y = mouseY - (oldMouseY - dragSprite.y);

    /*
    //Use this to drag the sprite from the center
    dragSprite.x = mouseX - (dragSprite.width / 2);
    dragSprite.y = mouseY - (dragSprite.height / 2);
    */
  }

  //Capture the current mouse position to use in the next frame
  oldMouseX = mouseX;
  oldMouseY = mouseY;
}

function mouseupHandler(event)
{
  //Release the dragSprite by setting it to null
  dragSprite = null;
}

function loadHandler()
{
  assetsLoaded++;
  if(assetsLoaded === assetsToLoad.length)
  {
    gameState = PLAYING;
  }
}

function hitTestPoint(pointX, pointY, sprite)
{
  return pointX > sprite.left() && pointX < sprite.right()
  && pointY > sprite.top() && pointY < sprite.bottom();
}
```

```
function render()
{
  drawingSurface.clearRect(0, 0, canvas.width, canvas.height);

  //Display the sprites
  if(sprites.length !== 0)
  {
    for(var i = 0; i < sprites.length; i++)
    {
      var sprite = sprites[i];
      if(sprite.visible)
      {
        drawingSurface.drawImage
        (
          image,
          sprite.sourceX, sprite.sourceY,
          sprite.sourceWidth, sprite.sourceHeight,
          Math.floor(sprite.x), Math.floor(sprite.y),
          sprite.width, sprite.height
        );
      }
    }
  }
}

</script>
```

The source files contain a touch-based version of this system called **dragAndDropTouch.html**.

Combining a touch interface and the mouse in one program

For all these examples there have been two versions of each program: a touch version and mouse version. Isn't it possible just to create just one game that contains both interfaces and then let the program decide which to use, based on the capabilities of the device it's being played on? It definitely is. The best current way to do this is to use an excellent open source JavaScript library called Modernizr. It runs a series of comprehensive tests that will tell you what features a device supports, and it then lets you load the correct section of your program that enables certain features.

To use Modernizr, visit its website at www.modernizr.com and follow the instructions for installing the code library. Then use it in this if statement to check for touch capability and selectively enable mouse or touch events:

```
if (Modernizr.touch)
{
    //Add the touch event listeners and enable any extra buttons or CSS styles
}
else
```

```
{
    //Add the mouse event listeners
}
```

You can also use Modernizr to help you test for other HTML5 device capabilities like geolocation, local storage, or web sockets.

> Note: If you need to test for different device-screen sizes, consider using a CSS **media query**. A great introduction to this is Ethan Marcotte's article "Responsive Web Design" at www.alistapart.com. **Responsive design** is a big topic in application development about strategies for accommodating for a wide range of different screen sizes and device capabilities.

Where do you go next?

Believe it or not, you're now a game designer! If you've made it through to these last few pages in the book and have made some of your own games based on what you learned along the way, you've now got all the skills you need to start making games professionally. Or just for serious fun, which is cool too! Of course, there's always more you can learn, but it's now mostly just a matter of detail and practice.

To get you started on the next phase of this journey, let's take a look at some of the things you'll need to know, and I'll offer a few suggestions about where you can take your learning next.

What you should know about JavaScript and HTML5

You've learned a lot about JavaScript, but you haven't learned everything there is to know about it. That's not necessarily a bad thing, because there's lots of extra stuff in JavaScript that you won't need for game design. The JavaScript language includes many alternate ways of doing things, to give programmers as much choice as possible. One of JavaScript's weaknesses is that it's almost *too flexible* and gives you *too much* choice. If you can achieve the same effect five different ways, which is the best way? Don't worry: this book has shown you what I think are those best ways. I've stuck to the simplest, easiest-to-understand, and most modern coding practices. In all, this book has covered about 50% of JavaScript's features. But it's doubtful whether you'll ever need to use much of the remaining 50%, so relax! JavaScript isn't hard, and you can consider yourself an experienced developer at this point.

However, there are a few features of JavaScript that I've omitted that you really should be aware of. That's because they're widely used and you'll need to understand them to make sense of code you read in other books or on the Web.

You'll also discover that when you start making games that need to run on a wide variety of web browsers or computing platforms, not everything will work as you expect. That's because older browsers and mobile devices don't support some of JavaScript's and HTML5's newest features, and they can be a little buggy. There's a vast amount of information on the Internet documenting browser bugs and incompatibilities, and you should always research the platforms you're designing a game for to be aware of what the likely pitfalls may be. This information is constantly changing, but in this last section of the book, I'll show you some of the most useful techniques you need to know to maximize your game's cross-platform compatibility.

Constructor functions

In this book I showed you how to make new objects from existing objects by using `Object.create`:

```
var newObject = Object.create(existingObject);
```

`Object.create` is a relatively new JavaScript method that's been widely supported only very recently. I've used it as the preferred way of making new objects in this book—but it's not the only way.

There's another way to make new objects using something called a **constructor function**. A constructor function is a style of creating objects that many programmers prefer because it mimics the syntax of programming languages like C++ and Java.

> Note: C++, Java, and Objective-C are **class-based languages**. They use a programming structure called a **class**, which is a template that's used to make new objects. In class-based languages, you can't use an object until you've created it from a class template first. JavaScript is a **prototype-based** language. It doesn't use classes. In prototype-based languages you work with objects directly, without having to make copies of them first.

Here's how to create new objects using a constructor function. First create an object that you want to use to make new objects from. But this is no ordinary object. It's is actually a *function* that behaves like an object. Here's a Robot object that's made using a function.

```
function Robot()
{
  this.mood = "happy";
}
```

Yes, it's just an ordinary function. But, as you'll soon see, you can use it like an object. The Robot object has one property, mood, which is set to "happy". Notice that the "R" in "Robot" is capitalized. This is optional, but it's an important naming convention that's always used when you make an object with a function.

> Note: How can a function work like an ordinary object? That's because, in JavaScript, everything, including functions, is really an object. You can access and change the properties of functions just like you can access and change the properties of any ordinary object. I haven't mentioned this until now, because it's a slightly confusing concept. But keep this in mind because it will be important for you to remember as you continue learning more about JavaScript.

Here's how you make a new object from the `Robot` object:

```
var newRobot = new Robot();
```

The `new` keyword is used to *construct* the `newRobot` object. That's why this is called a **constructor function**.

You can access and change the `newRobot` 's properties just like you would any other object. Here's how to access its `mood` property.

```
newRobot.mood
```

It will have the value `"happy"`, which it inherited from the original `Robot` object.

The original `Robot` object can also include methods. Here's a method called `displayMood` that will display the robot's mood in the console.

```
function Robot()
{
  this.mood = "happy";
}
Robot.prototype.displayMood = function()
{
  console.log("I am feeling " + this.mood);
};
```

You can see that the method is added to the Robot's built-in `prototype` property.

```
Robot.prototype.displayMood = function() {//...method's code here...};
```

All object methods need to be added to this `prototype` property if you want to use this style of creating objects.

Any new object made from the original `Robot` can now use this method, like this:

```
newRobot.displayMood();
```

This will display "I am feeling happy" in the console.

These are the only new things you need to know if you want to make objects like this using a constructor function. Take a look at the **constructorFunction.html** program in the chapter's source files for a working example.

A fallback for Object.create

One potential disadvantage of making new objects by using `Object.create` is that, at the time of writing, only the most modern browsers support it. This might not be a problem for you, but if your game needs to work on much older browsers, you'll either need to create new objects by using a constructor function or by using a **fallback**. A fallback is a bit of extra code that will run if a browser doesn't support `Object.create`. If `Object.create` isn't in the browser's JavaScript library, the fallback code will add it, by coding it from scratch. (Fallback code like this is sometimes called a **polyfill**.)

Here's the standard `Object.create` fallback code that's widely used:

```
if(typeof Object.create !== "function")
{
  Object.create = function(o)
  {
    function F() {}
    F.prototype = o;
    return new F();
  };
}
```

Add this bit of code to the very beginning of your program and you can use `Object.create` to make new objects, even if your game is running on an old browser.

An upgrade message for canvas

If you think your game might be played on a browser that doesn't support canvas, you should provide a message to tell users that their browsers won't support it. Here's a simple way to do that.

```
<canvas width="300" height="300">
    Your browser doesn't support canvas. Please upgrade it.
</canvas>
```

If the browser doesn't support canvas, the user will see the message asking him or her to upgrade the browser. If the browser supports canvas, the game will play as normal and the message won't be shown. You can include any HTML code inside the `<canvas>` tags to use as a fallback. You could optionally include a download link or an image, or you can possibly redirect the user to another web page.

JavaScript frameworks and APIs

A **framework** is a library of prebuilt, reusable JavaScript code that you can load into your program to help you quickly implement complex or difficult tasks. This can be really useful because you can add sophisticated features in your games like interactive 3D animations and complex physics simulations without having to write them or understand how the underlying code works. Just load the framework into your game, learn the methods and properties you need to know to make them work, and you're good to go.

Some very popular JavaScript frameworks are jQuery, Dojo, Prototype, and script.aculo.us, but there are thousands of them. Here are a few that are particularly useful for games.

- **Box2dweb:** This can create complex physics-based games, like Angry Birds. It's compatible with all the techniques in this book. It's a JavaScript port of the popular Box2d library that was originally written in C++ and available for many other programming languages.

- **3D Engines:** There are a number of frameworks specialized for creating 3D graphics and games. Some of the best include Three.js and CopperLicht.

- WebGL: This is a 3D display technology that's part of the HTML5 standard. It lets you directly program your computer's GPU (graphics processing unit) so that you can create very fast, highly optimized 3D graphics. It uses its own programming language called Open GL ES to do this. GL ES is not hard to learn and it is a useful skill to have. However, if you're not concerned about the fine minutiae of programming 3D graphics from scratch and just want to make 3D games quickly and easily, consider using one of the 3D engines I listed above. Most 3D engines, like Three.js, use WebGL as their rendering system, so you can avoid having to program your game world directly with Open GL ES.

- CreateJS: This is a collection for frameworks specialized for game development. It includes frameworks for controlling sounds, animating sprites, and preloading images, videos, and other game assets. If the sounds in your game are behaving in especially quirky ways, consider using the SoundJS framework.

- Geolocation API: This framework is part of the HTML5 standard, so most modern browsers support it natively. It lets you find a user's location, so you could incorporate that into a game with real-time map and GPS data.

- Fullscreen API: This can expand any HTML element, like <canvas>, to fill the entire browser window. This is great for immersive action games.

- Mouse Lock API: This allows you to lock the mouse position to the game screen so that you can control game action even if the mouse leaves the game window.

- Gamepad API: This lets you play your games with console gamepad controllers.

- Modernizr: This detects the HTML and CSS capabilities of the browser that your game is being played on. You can use this information to selectively change your code so that it works on older browsers that may not support the most modern HTML5 and CSS3 features. If Modernizr detects a missing feature that your game depends on, you can use a polyfill to replicate that feature in the older browser.

- Keep an eye on the developing HTML5 standards for improving sound handling in games with the Web Audio API.

Most of these frameworks are free, open source, easy to learn, and fun to use.

Saving game data and files

You might need to save some data in your game (such as a score or a game level) so that the player can quit the game and continue later. HTML5 has three complete APIs for saving game data and working with local file storage.

- Web Storage API: This will save game data and create files locally on a user's computer.

- Indexed Database API: This will store data as a structured database. This is useful if you want to store a large amount of information, like a player registry. You could also use it to store level data for a big game world.

- File API: This can help you access files and folders on a user's system.

- Offline API: You can use this if you're making a web-based game that you also want players to be able to play offline. It lets you determine which game files should run locally so that the player doesn't need to be connected to the net to play the game.

These are sophisticated and powerful frameworks that you'll find many uses for in your games.

Multiplayer games

It's always more fun to play games with friends. To make multiplayer games, you need to store game data on a server on the Internet so that other players can access that data to update their own game screens. There are quite a few ways you can do this, but all require some research into additional *server-side technologies*. Your games will need to communicate with these server-side technologies, but to implement most of them you might need to learn new programming languages such as PHP or Java. Do a bit of research into Java socket servers such as SmartFoxServer and ElectroServer, among many others.

You can create a high-score list for your games using PHP, and you can store game data using a MySQL database. You can avoid Java and PHP directly by storing game data in a content management system (CMS) and accessing the data in your game with XML.

A more recent technology that you should consider is node.js. It's a framework that lets you program a server directly by using pure JavaScript. That means you can take all of the programming skills you learned in this book, as is, to program your back-end game code. You won't have to learn a new programming language.

There are also a few HTML5 APIs that you'll need to learn and use to help you work with online data. These are both part of the official W3C HTML5 standard.

- XMLHttpRequest: Update your game with server data **asynchronously** (without having to reload the page).
- WebSockets: Communicate with the server to send and receive data in real time. Use WebSockets to create a real-time multiplayer game or chat system.

Creating multiplayer games is a big topic, but you'll find a good introduction on how to do it with node.js in *HTML5 Games Most Wanted* (Apress, 2012).

Games for mobile devices, tablets, and the desktop

You can use all the skills you've learned in this book to make games for mobile phones and touch-based tablets, like the iPad. You don't need to learn any other programming language, like Objective-C, and you can sell your HTML5 games in app stores. Because HTML5 and JavaScript are open source and cross-platform, you'll find it easy to adapt your game to work on the widest variety of devices without having to change your original game code. There are no other technologies that give you such a wide potential distribution for your games.

This book has been all about the mechanics of how to design and program games. You'll be able to use these techniques for years to come, and you can easily adapt them to other technologies if needed. One thing I've specifically avoided in this book is how to target specific platforms, like iOS or Android apps. The reason for this is that the details about how to do this are different for each platform and are rapidly changing. But, in general, once you have a working game, you'll only need to make a few small modifications to it to package and publish it as an app. So where do you start?

At the time of writing, the most commonly used technology is PhoneGap. It does the work of packaging your game into an application, and the finished files it produces will run on various devices. Visit www.phonegap.com for a list of Getting Started guides on how to do this for each device. CocoonJS is a similar service which as been specifically designed for HTML5 games.

You'll also need to tailor your game to the capabilities and specifications of each device. How big should the screen size be, can the player rotate the orientation, and which device capabilities do you want to allow or disable? You'll need to do a bit of research into each device and platform to help you do this. Here are two excellent books that you can start with.

- *Beginning iPhone and iPad Web Apps Scripting with HTML5, CSS3, and JavaScript,* by Chris Apers and Daniel Paterson (Apress, 2010)

- *Pro Android Web Game Apps: Using HTML5, CSS3, and JavaScript,* by Juriy Bura and Paul Coates (Apress, 2012)

HTML5 and JavaScript are also becoming viable technologies for creating desktop applications. You can use them to create native software applications for Windows 8, or you can package your game by using Adobe AIR to run your game on Windows, Linux, or Mac.

This is a quickly changing field, so keep your eye out for new developments.

Summary

As every game designer knows, making games is much more fun than playing them. Like an artist who's just learned how to mix paints and sketch out a few simple scenes, a bit of practice is all you'll need, and you'll be well on your way to creating that masterpiece. You've now got a solid foundation in game design with HTML5 and JavaScript—go and make some great games!

Index

A

▌I

■ S

■V, W, X, Y, Z